AMERICA'S LAST
VIETNAM BATTLE

AMERICA'S LAST VIETNAM BATTLE

Halting Hanoi's 1972 Easter Offensive

Dale Andradé

University Press of Kansas

Originally published in 1995 by Hippocrene Books, Inc., as *Trial by Fire: The 1972 Easter Offensive, America's Last Vietnam Battle*.

Published by the University Press of Kansas (Lawrence, Kansas 66049), which was organized by the Kansas Board of Regents and is operated and funded by Emporia State University, Fort Hays State University, Kansas State University, Pittsburg State University, the University of Kansas, and Wichita State University.

Library of Congress Cataloging-in-Publication Data

Andradé, Dale.
America's last Vietnam battle : halting Hanoi's 1972
Easter Offensive / Dale Andradé.
p. cm. — (Modern war studies)
Originally published: Trial by fire. New York: Hippocrene Books, 1995.
Includes bibliographical references and index.
ISBN 0-7006-1131-2 (pbk. : alk. paper)
1. Easter Offensive, 1972. 2. Vietnamese Conflict, 1961–1975—United States.
I. Title. II. Series.
DS557.8.E23 A53 2001
959.704'3373—dc21
2001026796

British Library Cataloguing in Publication Data is available.

Printed in the United States of America
10 9 8 7 6 5 4 3 2 1

TO THE ADVISERS

CONTENTS

List of Illustrations   *ix*

List of Abbreviations   *xi*

Acknowledgments   *xiii*

Prologue   *1*

Introduction: On the Eve of Destruction   *5*

PART I. MAIN THRUST: THE BATTLE FOR
QUANG TRI AND HUE

1 The Blazing Front Line   *29*

2 Western Collapse   *39*

3 Piercing the Ring of Steel   *51*

4 The Bridge at Dong Ha   *63*

5 Surrender at Camp Carroll   *78*

6 Firebase Pedro   *91*

7 Consolidation and Counteroffensive   *99*

8 Things Fall Apart   *108*

9 The Citadel   *127*

10 The Imperial City   *149*

11 The Slow March North   *165*

12 Retaking Quang Tri   *176*

PART II. DIVIDE AND CONQUER:
THE BATTLE FOR II CORPS

13 Setting the Stage   *201*

14 Intelligence Picture   *210*

15 Opening Shots   *220*

16 Closing In on the Highlands   *228*

17 Designing a Defense   *252*

18 Crisis at Kontum   *265*

19 Tightening the Noose   276

20 Regrouping   287

21 ARVN on the Offensive   297

22 Mopping Up   320

PART III. BESIEGED: THE BATTLE FOR AN LOC

23 Hell in a Very Insignificant Place   333

24 Loc Ninh   351

25 Tanks in the Wire   360

26 Preparing for the Worst   381

27 The Shelling Game   398

28 Air Resupply   409

29 Second Round   420

30 Relief from the South   436

31 End Siege   444

PART IV. SUFFERING THE CONSEQUENCES

32 War in the Delta   461

33 Taking the War to Hanoi   472

34 Winners and Losers   484

Epilogue: The Last Patrol   495

Notes   501

Bibliographic Essay   537

Index   541

ILLUSTRATIONS

Photos

North Vietnamese soldiers set out along the Ho Chi Minh Trail   *14*

North Vietnamese troops break through at Firebase Sarge   *42*

3d ARVN Division operations bunker   *65*

Captured North Vietnamese T-54 tank south of Dong Ha   *73*

South Vietnamese civilians flee the fighting   *114*

Enemy soldiers find the base at Ai Tu abandoned   *124*

U.S. adviser burns classified documents in Quang Tri   *128*

North Vietnamese soldiers enter Quang Tri City on 29 April   *141*

M113 armored personnel carrier guards the citadel in Hue   *157*

North Vietnamese crewman killed during the battle for Quang Tri   *167*

The slow South Vietnamese push toward Quang Tri City   *174*

A captured North Vietnamese soldier   *180*

South Vietnamese marines hunt enemy armor   *183*

North Vietnamese soldiers prepare to defend Quang Tri citadel   *190*

South Vietnamese marines and adviser near the ruins of citadel   *195*

John Paul Vann's helicopter at SRAG headquarters in Pleiku   *206*

John Paul Vann's personal helicopter, an OH-58 Kiowa   *230*

AT-3 Sagger wire-guided missile   *236*

North Vietnamese tank leads infantry near Tan Canh   *240*

Colonel Ly Tong Ba briefs Saigon officials   *254*

North Vietnamese soldiers before the battle for Kontum   *267*

South Vietnamese artillery fires back at the enemy   *270*

A South Vietnamese soldier and an officer help a woman board an aircraft for evacuation   *275*

The wreck of a C-130 transport plane sits on the Kontum airfield   *290*

William Bricker stands beside his demolished quarters in Kontum   *304*

One of the 23d ARVN Division's ammunition dumps early in the battle   *307*

Major Wade Lovings surveys damage to the command post   *308*

Soldiers from the 44th ARVN Regiment survey their compound   *315*

Rhotenberry and Ba stand beside the wreckage of a
North Vietnamese tank   *318*
Brigadier General Le Van Hung   *352*
North Vietnamese troops fire a recoilless rifle near Loc Ninh   *358*
A-37 Dragonfly from the U.S. Air Force   *365*
Soviet-made T-54 tank burns in the streets of An Loc   *392*
South Vietnamese soldiers stand near a captured
12.7mm antiaircraft gun   *400*
President Thieu awards Brigadier General Hung for bravery   *450*
Thieu poses with soldiers from the 5th ARVN Division
after the siege of An Loc   *457*

Maps

I Corps   *30*
Quang Tri   *33*
Key locations and fire support bases (I Corps)   *37*
NVA attacks across the DMZ, Quang Tri Province, 30 March 1972   *44*
The defense of Quang Tri, 2 April 1972   *61*
The shrinking 3d Infantry Divison AO, Quang Tri Province   *110*
Thua Thien and Hue Municipality   *150*
The defense of Hue, 5 May 1972   *159*
II Corps   *202*
Kontum   *205*
Pleiku   *208*
Western highlands battlefield   *216*
Binh Dinh and Qui Nhon Municipality   *221*
Battle for Kontum   *280*
III Corps and Capital Special Zone   *334*
Binh Long   *337*
Enemy base areas on Cambodian-RVN border   *339*
Tay Ninh   *346*
NVA plan of attacks in III Corps   *361*
Key locations, Binh Long Province, III Corps   *375*
The defense of An Loc, 12 April 1972   *385*
NVA attack on An Loc, 11 May 1972   *429*
IV Corps   *462*
Enemy base areas in IV Corps   *464*
Enemy regimental dispositions in IV Corps, 1 April 1972   *465*
Enemy attacks in IV Corps   *469*
North Vietnam   *473*

ABBREVIATIONS

ANGLICO	Air and Naval Gunfire Liaison Company
ARVN	Army of the Republic of Vietnam
CARP	computer aerial release point
CIA	Central Intelligence Agency
CINCPAC	commander in chief, Pacific
CORDS	Civilian Operations and Revolutionary Development Support
COSVN	Central Office for South Vietnam
DIA	Defense Intelligence Agency
DRAC	Delta Regional Assistance Command
FRAC	First Regional Assistance Command
GRADS	ground radar delivery system
GVN	government of Vietnam
HALO	high-altitude, low-opening
HEAT	high-explosive, antitank
LAW	light antitank weapon
LST	landing ship transport
MACV	Military Assistance Command, Vietnam
MTIs	moving target indicators
NLF	National Liberation Forces
NSA	National Security Agency
NVA	North Vietnamese Army
PLAF	People's Liberation Armed Forces
ROK	Republic of Korea
RVN	Republic of Vietnam
RVNAF	Republic of Vietnam Armed Forces
SAM	surface-to-air missile
SEAL	sea, air, and land
SOG	Studies and Observations Group
SRAC	Second Regional Assistance Command
SRAG	Second Regional Assistance Group
TOW	tube-launched, optically tracked, wire-guided
TRAC	Third Regional Assistance Command

USARV	U.S. Army in the Republic of Vietnam
VC	Viet Cong
VNMC	Vietnamese Marine Corps

ACKNOWLEDGMENTS

Despite the passage of years and the volume of work written about the Vietnam War, the final years of American involvement there remain largely uncharted terrain. And although the Easter Offensive was the Vietnam War's biggest battle, it has been largely ignored by researchers; even participants have been strangely silent on the subject.

Part of this has to do with timing. When North Vietnam launched its offensive in 1972, most of America's combat troops had returned home to a nation that badly wanted to forget the war. Those left in Vietnam were advisers assigned to South Vietnamese units; strictly speaking, they were not supposed to take part in the fighting, though in fact the part played by U.S. advisers during the Easter Offensive was crucial to its outcome. Advisers were the conduit to American airpower and supplies, and in many places their very presence bolstered the morale of scared and tired South Vietnamese soldiers.

Naturally, this book would have been impossible without the help of those advisers. While there are too many to thank personally here, each gave freely of his time and knowledge, and I am grateful to them all. However, special thanks must go to Colonel William Miller, senior adviser to the 5th ARVN Division during the early days of the battle at An Loc and a consummate infantryman. Colonel Miller's razor-sharp memory, tactical acumen, and down-to-earth insights provided valuable material for this book.

On the other side of the research coin are the documents. My way along the paper trail was made easier by the professional research staffs at the National Archives and the U.S. Army Center of Military History in Washington, D.C., as well as those at the Military History Institute at Carlisle Barracks, Pennsylvania. They patiently steered me through the maze of document-finding aids, answered questions, and pointed me toward other sources. At the National Archives in particular, Richard Boylan and his research staff—Jeannine Swift, Cliff Snyder, and Susan Francis-Haughton—know the Vietnam records so well that searching through them became almost effortless. Another archivist, Howard Feng, used his intimate knowledge of the advisory group records to point me toward valuable documents. On several occasions he informed me ahead of time about new records about to be arranged and declassified.

Others generously helped me as well. Fellow military historian Charles D. Melson with the U.S. Marine Corps Historical Center in Washington, D.C., provided his knowledge of marine advisers and endured many lengthy brainstorming sessions about strategy and tactics. Frank Brown, a U.S. Navy corpsman during the early days of the Easter Offensive, gave me access to his photo collection. Douglas Pike placed his vast experience as a Vietnam-watcher at my disposal, helping me understand the intricacies of Hanoi's decision-making process. Darrel D. Whitcomb, a former U.S. Air Force pilot, kept me from becoming too focused on the ground, continually reminding me that those in the air played a crucial role in halting the enemy offensive.

Special thanks goes to Robert Destatte. His unique combination of superlative Vietnamese language skills and a keen knowledge of the North Vietnamese military and its arcane organization and history brought me important insights into our former enemy's war machine. His translations offered me access to the virtually untapped Vietnamese-language sources that are so important to understanding the war as a whole rather than as a purely American experience.

Although others helped with the preparation of this book, the responsibility for its content belongs with the author. Any errors in fact or interpretation are my own.

PROLOGUE

Firebase Delta was doomed. Surrounded by charging enemy troops, the small garrison of South Vietnamese marines was down to its last few bullets as everyone waited for helicopters they knew would never come. The tiny sandbagged hilltop fort sat forlornly on the Co Rac Plateau overlooking the South Vietnam–Laos border, a mere twelve miles from the demilitarized zone. Firebase Delta was the southern anchor of Operation Lam Son 719, the limited South Vietnamese invasion of Laos launched in February 1971 to show the world that Saigon could run its own war without relying on American troops. For the first time in the history of the war, the South Vietnamese launched a large-scale cross-border offensive operation with no support from U.S. ground troops or advisers.

Saigon's objective was to drive westward along Route 9 from the old U.S. Marine base at Khe Sanh, cut the Ho Chi Minh Trail, and seize the town of Tchepone, about twenty-five miles inside Laos. Some 16,000 South Vietnamese troops supported by American helicopters and tactical air strikes easily punched into Laos but met resistance at the halfway point. Reacting to the threat to their supply line, 36,000 North Vietnamese troops backed by armor and heavy artillery halted the attack and pushed the South Vietnamese out of Laos. Saigon's troops sustained 9,000 casualties—more than half of its attacking force—and the Americans lost almost 200 helicopters. An estimated 20,000 North Vietnamese lost their lives.[1]

The final drama was played out on 22 March at Firebase Delta when the desperate marines called for air strikes on their own position, then abandoned the ruined firebase and tried to escape on foot. Forced to leave behind the wounded, one marine described their plight. "They lay there crying, knowing the B-52 bombs would fall on them," he recalled. "They asked buddies to shoot them, but none of us could bring himself to do that. So the wounded cried out for grenades. . . . I could not bear it."[2]

Escaping in small groups, the marines fought through the North Vietnamese noose, some dying in the attempt, others making their way to safety. But at least they had a fighting chance. Those who made it heard the thunder as tons of bombs fell on Firebase Delta just after midnight. The unfortunate wounded became part of the shattered landscape, a terrible burial after a battle gone wrong almost from the onset. "No more bodies," said a marine survivor. "They all became dust."[3]

So ended Lam Son 719. Both sides claimed victory—the South Vietnamese because they reached Tchepone, their original goal, and the North Vietnamese because they badly mauled Saigon's troops as they withdrew from Laos. Losses on both sides were heavy, and in the short term it seems clear that the North Vietnamese capability to launch a spring campaign against the South was disrupted for that year. But over the long term, North Vietnamese base areas and logistical lines remained functional. Saigon had failed to decisively defeat the enemy despite sending its best units into battle—the Airborne Division, the marines, and the crack 1st Division of the Army of the Republic of Viet Nam (ARVN). If the elite could be routed by the North Vietnamese, how far had the American advisory effort come in a decade?

The simple answer was that it had not come very far. Problems that plagued the South Vietnamese military in 1962 stood unremedied in 1971. This was true from the top down. Once again, the weaknesses inherent in Saigon's politicized leadership were showcased, beginning with South Vietnamese president Nguyen Van Thieu. When division commanders proved unwilling to obey orders from the overall commander, Lieutenant General Hoang Xuan Lam, Thieu did not intercede. The reason was political: the elite units involved in the operation were part of the palace guard, traditionally the president's insurance against a coup, and he did not want to upset them. Thieu also personally meddled in the operation, sometimes making military decisions without notifying his field commanders.

Lam Son 719 also highlighted the inherent immobility of the South Vietnamese army, despite seven years of fighting in concert with the U.S. Army—the most mobile in the world. South Vietnamese divisions had become static, rarely operating away from the area where they were stationed. Only the Airborne Division and the marines were capable of fighting anywhere in the country, and they proved themselves inadequate to the task.

Finally, the operation clearly showed that the South Vietnamese army could not operate without U.S. advisers. For years it had relied on the Americans, particularly when it came to coordinating helicopter flights and calling in artillery and air strikes. During Lam Son 719, South Vietnamese officers had to do these jobs alone, and they failed miserably.

But the South Vietnamese were not alone in making mistakes. The Americans also fell short, even when taking into account the severe limitations placed on them by Washington. Restrictive rules of engagement forbade U.S. ground units from entering Laos and also prevented air controllers from coordinating tactical air strikes. Despite all this, however, American military planning was faulty. First, preparations for the offensive were kept so secret that participating South Vietnamese units had little time for their own planning and training. Even the South Vietnamese Joint General Staff, Saigon's equivalent of the U.S. Joint Chiefs of Staff, was not told about Lam Son 719 until the last minute. Combined with South Vietnamese shortcomings, American oversecrecy was disastrous.

In Washington the Nixon administration publicly called Lam Son 719 a success, but privately officials were critical. Nixon himself was furious over what he regarded as insufficient American support for Operation Lam Son 719, though he later softened his tone and charitably observed that "the Communists put up stronger resistance than anticipated and the American military command in Saigon failed to respond to this unexpectedly intense level of combat with the necessary increase in air cover for the invading forces." Nixon sent his military aide, Brigadier General Alexander Haig, to Vietnam on a fact-finding mission. Haig's report was harsh. "When I got there," he said, "it was clear that the operation was not receiving the kind of leadership and management from the American force structure that it should have."[4]

For North Vietnam, Lam Son 719 was also an important watershed. During the initial days of the South Vietnamese invasion, the North Vietnamese had been unable to mount a counteroffensive, instead retreating into the interior as they had in Cambodia during the incursion there in the spring of 1970. Only after the South Vietnamese virtually self-destructed before reaching Tchepone did Hanoi's troops come together, and even then they relied on overwhelming numbers rather than tactics to drive out the South Vietnamese. For the first time during the war, the North Vietnamese used heavy artillery and massed tanks, yet they handled them poorly, with little coordination between armor and infantry. As a result they lost dozens. Yet Lam Son 719 became an epiphany for Hanoi, a leap of faith from the doctrine of irregular warfare to the final stage of Mao Zedong's guerrilla strategy—conventional war.

The lessons were clear. The question in the spring of 1971 was who would best learn them. Saigon needed to alter the deeply entrenched politicization of its military and learn to fight alone. Washington would have to take a serious look at the validity and sincerity of its attempts to shape the South Vietnamese military. Hanoi sought to exploit its growing conventional strength and learn to fight a new kind of war. How well each side absorbed these lessons would be put to the test one year later when North Vietnam launched the biggest and boldest attack of the war—the Easter Offensive.

ON THE EVE
OF DESTRUCTION

The two greatest opponents of armies in Vietnam have always been weather and terrain. Of these, weather is the greatest foe because it cannot be altered. Two monsoons, neither covering the entire country at one time, dominate South Vietnam's weather. The northeast winter monsoon extends from November to April, when moisture-laden air currents from the Gulf of Tonkin cover the coastal lowlands of central and northern South Vietnam with dense clouds and rain. Scraping the rugged peaks of the Annamite Mountains, the air currents drop their remaining moisture, leaving the western highland plateau, the plains north of Saigon, and the Mekong Delta dry. The southwest summer monsoon begins in May and lasts until late October, when hot, humid air sweeps in from the Indian Ocean, lashing the southern highlands and the delta with rain and turning roads into impassable quagmires. While the monsoons dictated the yearly cycle of life for farmers, they also limited the period for sustained military campaigns to the dry season, when the ground dries out enough to permit the movement of men and matériel.

No one was more aware of the weather factor than American intelligence officers who spent their entire Vietnam tours trying to predict North Vietnamese intentions. With almost numbing regularity, Hanoi spent the rainy season planning offensives to be launched as the dry season arrived. Often these offensives began during Tet, the Vietnamese New Year holiday, to take advantage of lingering rain and clouds, which provided cover from American war planes. This pattern created an "intelligence cycle" for analysts, a sort of deadline when estimates of enemy capabilities and intentions were due on the desks of military commanders.

A plethora of intelligence organizations haunted South Vietnam, but sheer numbers did not make the task easier. In fact, they rarely agreed on interpretations of the intelligence evidence before them. The Central Intelligence Agency (CIA) concentrated, for the most part, on human intelligence, recruiting agents inside the communist political and military apparatus. Best evidence indicates they were not particularly successful.

5

The National Security Agency (NSA), a supersecret organization of some 90,000 men and women, worked around the world in search of electronic intelligence. Replete with state-of-the-art equipment, the NSA was capable of listening in on radio and telephone conversations from party officials or military commanders in the field. One of its installations aimed at intercepting electronic intelligence in Vietnam was located in Nakhon Phanom, Thailand. Another was on the island of Okinawa. Aircraft equipped with NSA listening gear flew over Laos near the North Vietnamese border, ingesting thousands of hours of electronic transmissions. Technicians in various stations, or at the main NSA complex outside Baltimore, Maryland, combed through the material for useful tidbits of information. But the NSA suffered from two shortcomings. First, the sheer quantity of material often obscured important intelligence; second, valuable information sometimes reached those who needed it in the field too late to be of any use.[1]

Each branch of the U.S. military also had its own intelligence service, each mostly concerned with narrow parochial tactical matters. By 1972 the most important of these was army military intelligence, whose analysts served up facts and figures concerning the location and movement of enemy troops. At the top of the military intelligence heap was the Defense Intelligence Agency (DIA), a confederation of analysts from all services tasked with providing overall assessments of enemy intentions and capabilities.

The general questions facing all intelligence services at the end of 1971 were basically the same as in past years. Was Hanoi planning an offensive for the spring of 1972, and if so, what was its likely intensity? In searching for answers, analysts turned to several sources. The most important were North Vietnamese logistical trends. Was Hanoi increasing the flow of supplies and manpower down the Ho Chi Minh Trail? Analysts also looked at North Vietnamese infiltration levels. Were new units moving into South Vietnam? Prisoner of war interrogations, analysis of captured documents, and studies of enemy losses also provided pieces for the puzzle. Finally, there were "open" sources: propaganda publications written by communist officials as general policy statements. These were often overlooked because they were thought to be full of communist lies, but a discerning observer could often detect in them subtle changes over time.[2]

But of all the intelligence sources, it was the Ho Chi Minh Trail that always provided answers. While the North Vietnamese could conceal the conclusions of their politburo meetings, disguise manpower and training, and mask battle losses, they could not completely hide their movement down the Trail. As Hanoi became more reliant on North Vietnamese troops to fight the war in place of local Viet Cong guerrillas in the years since the 1968 Tet debacle, it had to move massive quantities of troops and supplies into South Vietnam. The communists were good at disguising their movements, but they could not launch a major offensive without alerting Saigon and Washington.

American technology had also improved intelligence-gathering over the years. For decades the North Vietnamese had relied on darkness and cloud cover to conceal their movement down the Trail, but by 1971 infrared photography and airborne moving target indicators (MTIs) allowed reconnaissance planes flying high over Laos to cut through the weather and locate tanks and vehicles lurking below. In addition, there was a new generation of movement sensors placed along the Trail using aircraft or special long-range reconnaissance teams.

Although the Ho Chi Minh Trail was a complex web of pathways and roads, there were a handful of mountain passes that could not be avoided. These choke points were sprinkled with an assortment of sensors that responded to heat, sound, and vibrations; while these devices were not foolproof, it was impossible for the North Vietnamese to move large numbers of men and equipment through them without alerting the sensors.

In September 1971 the intelligence wheels geared up to produce the annual estimate of enemy capabilities and intentions. Although this was business as usual for the army, there was an air of renewed urgency in Washington. Nixon was running his reelection campaign on a platform of withdrawal from Vietnam.

The "build-down" was rapid. At the end of 1971, a total of 158,120 American soldiers remained in South Vietnam. Despite mounting signs of a coming communist offensive, Washington remained committed to "Vietnamizing" the war, though for most soldiers unlucky enough to remain in Vietnam as America's resolve waned, this was hardly reassuring. Even during the height of the Easter Offensive, the U.S. troop drawdown continued unabated, and by the end of 1972 only 24,000 troops would still be incountry.[3]

The man in charge of "Vietnamization"—as the process of turning the war back over to Saigon came to be known—was General Creighton W. Abrams, the commander of Military Assistance Command, Vietnam (MACV). When MACV was formed in February 1962, its primary function was to control the buildup of advisers sent to Vietnam by President John F. Kennedy. In 1965 it managed the injection of U.S. combat troops and fought the war according to Washington's strategy. Finally, in 1972, MACV had come full circle—supervising a withdrawal in place of the buildup—and was once again only an advisory chain of command. Abrams had played a key role in implementing this policy evolution.

Abrams first saw combat during World War II as an armor officer under General George S. Patton Jr., gaining fame in 1944 when he led the breakout from Normandy that drove the Germans back to the Moselle River. Abrams also commanded the relief force that smashed German units surrounding American airborne troops at Bastogne during the Battle of the Bulge.

In peacetime Abrams climbed the military career ladder, reaching the rank of brigadier general in 1956. Then, in 1962, he was given a job that could potentially end his brilliant career when he was placed in command of a federal force charged with enforcing a court order allowing James Meredith, a black, to enter the University of Mississippi. The following year Abrams was back in the South, this time in Birmingham, Alabama, where racial unrest threatened to erupt into violence. But rather than self-destruct under the high-profile scrutiny surrounding his job, Abrams excelled, and in 1964 he was promoted to lieutenant general. In September of the same year Abrams got a fourth star and was appointed vice chief of staff of the army. In May 1967 he became General William C. Westmoreland's deputy at MACV.[4]

When Abrams took over Westmoreland's job in July 1968, he emphasized a combination of conventional war and pacification, a strategy he called "One War." Indeed, the Vietnam War had changed considerably by the time Abrams became MACV commander. The 1968 Tet Offensive had largely destroyed the Viet Cong and denied Hanoi the military victory it had sought. On the other hand, the Tet battles focused American public opinion on the "unwinnability" of the war and eventually forced a withdrawal from Vietnam. Abrams would preside over that withdrawal while at the same time beating the enemy on the battlefield and preparing the South Vietnamese army to fight on alone.

Washington's dedication to the ongoing troop stand-down placed additional pressure on Abrams and, in particular, the intelligence agencies. Ever mindful of the 1968 Tet Offensive, they could not afford another surprise. General Westmoreland, now the army chief of staff, was often a conduit between the brass in Washington and officers in South Vietnam. He responded to a Joint Chiefs of Staff query about the progress of intelligence estimates for 1972 by saying, "I can assure you that careful attention has been given to preparation of plans to counter any enemy offensive. Both the Vietnamese and the Americans are confident that they can handle the situation."[5]

If Abrams and Westmoreland were outwardly confident about Saigon's ability to counter an enemy offensive, they were reassured by final drafts of intelligence findings that crossed their desks in November 1971. According to the CIA's official estimate of enemy intentions in 1972, "One thing Hanoi cannot do in the remaining months of this dry season; it cannot launch a nationwide military offensive on anything approaching the scale of Tet 1968." Combined estimates of other intelligence agencies concurred, predicting "that the North Vietnamese were making no special effort" for a big offensive in 1972. The State Department predicted that the North Vietnamese would launch "a heavy and sustained set of ground attacks for a period of several weeks," but it speculated that "the enemy's objectives . . . are not military, but political and psychological." Not that Hanoi did not mean to increase the pressure during the year—it always had some sort of dry-season offensive planned—but MACV believed that "the new year was to be one in which North Vietnam was planning no spectaculars."[6]

How did the analysts arrive at this conclusion? The bottom line—as always—was movement of men and matériel down the Ho Chi Minh Trail. This crucial indicator showed that "there was nothing unusual or ominous about the NVA's resupply efforts." Soldiers were moving south, but most intelligence estimates agreed that the majority of these were to replace combat losses of the past year. No new units were identified in the field, and interrogation of North Vietnamese prisoners indicated nothing out of the ordinary, just another slow year as the United States continued to turn the war over to the South Vietnamese. In the words of one DIA analyst, "It was feet on the desk time."[7]

That was in November. One month later everything changed, and an entirely new intelligence estimate was needed. A combination of factors led Major General Richard R. Stewart, a U.S. Air Force officer in charge of DIA's worldwide intelligence production effort, to order a new estimate. One important change was the discovery of an "exceptionally large" tank park near a staging area, called Bat Lake by analysts because of its shape. Air force reconnaissance photos of the lake situated near the point where North Vietnam, South Vietnam, and Laos meet showed a concentration of armor larger and farther south than anything ever before encountered. Analysts also noticed a dramatic increase in the number of North Vietnamese soldiers heading south along the Ho Chi Minh Trail. That in itself might only mean that the logistical pipeline was clogged somewhere along the way, but there was an important difference: this time Hanoi was moving entirely new units toward South Vietnam. This could only mean that the communists meant to increase the stakes in 1972.[8]

Evidence also pointed to a fundamental change of plan within Hanoi's politburo. In December a "usually reliable source" handed U.S. intelligence officials a copy of an unnumbered policy resolution that outlined "guidelines and key missions for the VC/NVA [Viet Cong/North Vietnamese

Army] forces in the future." Although these resolutions did not clearly define military strategy, they did provide glimpses of political trends within the communist politburo. And this particular resolution was important because it indicated that a dramatic shift from continued protracted war to conventional war had occurred sometime during December 1971. The language in the resolution was unambiguous, calling for "tilting the balance of forces through the use of main-force warfare and political initiative." This was the strongest and most precise language to date.[9]

General Abrams concluded that the resolution "signifies a departure from previous indications in VC/NVA strategy for 1972, by suggesting an early return to main force warfare." Intelligence analysts were surprised by the document because it signified a drastic departure from COSVN (Central Office for South Vietnam, the liaison between orders emanating from Hanoi and its soldiers in South Vietnam) Resolution 39 of November 1971, which admitted that a continuation of protracted warfare was in order because of the military defeats that inevitably resulted from face-to-face encounters with U.S. troops. "This new resolution for 1972 . . . would seem to be an indication that the enemy now believes the time [for a return to main-force warfare] is opportune and assesses himself to be prepared for the general offensive and popular uprising in selected areas," read one conclusion. Something had clearly caused Hanoi to change strategy in midstride.[10]

This was interesting news to U.S. military planners. It provided evidence of what they had maintained all along: that the communists were groping for new strategies to replace past failed ones. To Abrams, it also indicated that Hanoi had abandoned "the equilibrium phase of the protracted warfare strategy even though he has been unable to accomplish the rebuilding of his greatly weakened infrastructure and support." It also meant that Hanoi's decision was probably politically motivated, leading Abrams to conclude that any future enemy offensive would stress "possible propaganda advantages and [the] effect on the US public opinion."[11]

Why should the enemy switch so suddenly to main-force warfare, General Abrams asked his intelligence staff? Initial conclusions drawn from the purloined resolution and from other sources led analysts to believe that Hanoi regarded Vietnamization as a failure, but one which needed to be discredited in the eyes of the world. The resolution called for "strong, determined attacks to be launched against ARVN main force units, inflicting heavy losses." Analysts believed that Hanoi expected "this action to lead to a more rapid disintegration of both the ARVN and the government," a goal that Abrams dismissed as "somewhat unrealistic" on the part of North Vietnamese planners.[12]

Still, Abrams was certain enough of the intelligence indicators that he predicted a major offensive. In a report to Washington on 16 January 1972, he warned that recent indicators "all point quite clearly in my view to a major military action by the North in South Vietnam during the weeks ahead. In fact, it is my view that it will evolve into the maximum military effort the North is capable of making in the next few months." Three days later, Abrams's suspicions turned to virtual certainty when he told his immediate superior, Commander in Chief of the Pacific Admiral John S. McCain, that "the enemy is preparing and positioning his forces for a major offensive. Although we cannot be sure at this time of his precise plan of attack it is apparent that he is going to attempt to face us with the most difficult situation of which he is capable." The dire prediction was an unwelcome beginning to the new year, but given the pattern of past North Vietnamese offensives, it came as no surprise. What was different about 1972, Abrams predicted, was that the coming struggle would be fierce and probably decisive.[13]

Most intelligence agencies concurred in this new assessment. CIA estimates declared that "the next major enemy campaign will soon erupt in South Vietnam." DIA also revised its forecast, sending the new report to the Joint Chiefs of Staff in early January 1972. Colonel Peter F. C. Armstrong, a U.S. Marine Corps officer, gave the briefing to a gathering of the military's highest brass as well as Secretary of Defense Melvin Laird. The evidence was clear, Colonel Armstrong argued. The North Vietnamese planned a major offensive during the 1972 dry season, and they would make "widespread use of armor." The best estimates available pointed to an attack anytime after the last week in February, following the Tet holidays.[14]

Secretary Laird was not pleased with the analysis, and Colonel Armstrong later recalled that he "cast a baleful eye on me and seemed annoyed about what I was reporting." Laird interrupted repeatedly and questioned DIA's conclusions, a natural reaction considering his desire to extract America's remaining troops from Vietnam with as few complications as possible. After all, Laird had been in Saigon in early December, returning to Washington armed with MACV's prediction that North Vietnamese activity would be "low to moderate" in 1972.[15]

Despite this clear and ringing warning, many in Washington remained unconvinced. In late January, Laird, apparently ignoring the briefing he had received in Saigon, told Congress that a large communist offensive "was not a serious possibility" because local Viet Cong forces in South Vietnam were too disorganized. Just across the Potomac River, General Westmoreland, the army chief of staff, held a press conference at the Pentagon, where he gave yet another interpretation by telling a gathering of reporters that although some sort of enemy offensive was likely, "the logistics are limited to the point where he will have to reduce the magnitude of his offensive in a matter of days." Clearly, predicting Hanoi's capabilities was one thing; discerning its intentions quite another.[16]

Meanwhile, North Vietnam continued the buildup. Sensors placed along the Ho Chi Minh Trail and in the demilitarized zone went wild as tanks and heavy trucks rumbled along in an unbroken stream. During January 1972 sensors had picked up an average of twenty-five "movers" per day. In February the average ballooned to ninety per day, and according to intelligence trail watchers, "the increase has continued through the first three weeks of March." The surge seemed to confirm that Hanoi had not made the decision to invade until very late in 1971, or at least did not give the orders until after the new year.[17]

By early February North Vietnam's intent was crystal clear, causing many observers to marvel at the boldness of the buildup. "One of the biggest mysteries is why they [the North Vietnamese] are advertising this as much as they have," speculated one army analyst. "They are either very confident of success or in the end they are going to do nothing."[18]

But few analysts really believed Hanoi was doing it all for nothing. Enemy preparations from the demilitarized zone south to Saigon were reaching alarming proportions. Of particular concern to MACV was an increase in North Vietnamese antiaircraft defenses inside South Vietnam. Surface-to-air missiles (SAMs) were the bane of U.S. pilots flying missions over North Vietnam, but pilots had never encountered missiles in South Vietnam.

That luxury seemed about to change. General John D. Lavelle, commander of the 7th Air Force, complained that the missile buildup was a serious problem for warplanes flying interdiction missions. "The current enemy missile deployment is seriously disrupting our efforts to impede this logistics flow," observed Lavelle. "The SAM threat to allied aircraft resulting from this buildup is untenable to the prosecution of the war." Deployment of the SAMs had begun in early February, and within three weeks almost a dozen batteries were identified in or near South Vietnamese territory. The air force did its best to knock them out, but more took their place.[19]

In late February there were few lingering doubts at MACV headquarters about the looming offensive. "During recent weeks the enemy threat has continued to increase," wrote General Abrams to his corps-level senior advisers. "I am convinced he now has sufficient major ground elements in position to launch his offensive." By the middle of February he was even more certain. "In a few more days we should have received enough indications to allow a reasonably precise estimate as to when he will begin his attacks," predicted MACV. "He obviously intends to rely heavily on artillery in the forthcoming campaign."[20]

This is not to say that MACV read all the evidence correctly—military intelligence rarely works so perfectly. At the highest level, U.S. intelligence seemed to possess an accurate picture of both North Vietnamese intentions and timing. Yet down the chain of command there were different interpretations of the evidence. Information is always incomplete, leaving analysts to fill in holes with educated guesses. Under such circumstances it is only natural to look to the past for guidance. Since the North Vietnamese had never before launched an all-out conventional invasion, it was logical to look for other explanations for the buildup.

Which is exactly what happened. In I Corps (pronounced "eye" Corps), the five northernmost provinces in South Vietnam, U.S. intelligence believed that the North Vietnamese possessed the military capability to "temporarily seize objectives such as fire support bases and population centers." On the other hand, the report confidently concluded, "allied surveillance and interdiction will severely hamper the enemy's capability to marshal sufficient forces to conduct major offensive operations." On the eve of the offensive, I Corps continued to believe that "massed enemy formations remain vulnerable to detection and subsequent attack by TAC [tactical] air, B-52 strikes, artillery bombardment and combat air assault." Considering the dismal record of past efforts to stem the tide of North Vietnamese infiltration, this was a bold statement.[21]

Le Tien Kien shifted the heavy rucksack on his back and trudged down the path. These were the first steps in a long journey, a trip down the Ho Chi Minh Trail to South Vietnam. To Kien, his North Vietnamese army (formally known as Quan Doi Nhan Dan Viet Nam, or People's Army of Vietnam) unit was just part of a long line of people's heroes marching to fight a war of liberation against the imperialist Americans and their puppets in Saigon. But to military planners in Hanoi, Kien and thousands of other soldiers like him were part of a massive buildup in preparation for a new offensive.

It was late 1971, and every North Vietnamese soldier sent on the journey down the Ho Chi Minh Trail knew that something big was under way. The draft had previously been increased to take more youths into the military, and units from all over North Vietnam were being moved. Some infiltrated into the South; others moved down into the demilitarized zone, the decimated strip of no-man's-land along the seventeenth parallel.

North Vietnamese soldiers set out along the Ho Chi Minh Trail. Disease and bombing by U.S. aircraft would thin the ranks before their arrival in South Vietnam. (Author's collection)

As Kien marched, his morale rose like the rolling mountains that lay before him. His muscles were lean and strong. Food was plentiful, for the soldiers were still in central Laos near the North Vietnamese border— friendly territory. Fatigue would replace idealism soon enough, but for now the march was invigorating, and Kien was flushed with patriotism as he recalled the events that had led him to become a soldier in the People's Army of Vietnam.

Le Tien Kien had always dreamed of marching into battle. As a high school student he had placed duty as a soldier above scholastic excellence. Kien often daydreamed in class: "I could go and fight the Americans now, and then resume my studies later." The village political cadres had encouraged Kien's obsession with patriotic duty. They told him he could always take his graduation exams later, but his country needed him now. "Do not give up this opportunity to go and fight the American aggressors," they preached. Kien's father agreed. "I am too old now to hold a gun," he told his son. "So on behalf of our family, fulfill your duty to the Fatherland."[22]

When Le Tien Kien donned the khaki uniform and pith helmet of a North Vietnamese soldier, he became even more deeply conscious of the glorious responsibility entrusted to him by his native land. He had trained hard and absorbed the lessons taught by soldiers who had fought in the South. For eight months the instructors stressed physical conditioning so the recruits could "forge iron legs and bronze shoulders" for the arduous journey ahead. They taught Kien standard infantry techniques—marksmanship, how to set booby traps, how to construct a field bunker—and when it was over he was promoted to squad leader. At the barracks where the soldiers were billeted, Kien constructed a small training area and obstacle course so he and his men could remain honed while they awaited the order to go south. The political cadres noticed Kien's zealousness and were impressed.

Now the training was over, and the war was about to begin. To the North Vietnamese soldiers, fighting did not simply mean closing with the enemy in combat; it also included the trek down the Ho Chi Minh Trail. North Vietnam's communist leaders had praised the efforts of those who marched to the South, calling their exploits "a brilliant feat of arms in the history of our people's anti-U.S. resistance war." By this definition Le Tien Kien and his comrades were already at war.[23]

Spirits soared throughout the entire column. The soldiers were off to wage glorious battle against a despised aggressor and its Saigon puppet. One broke out in song: "Be worthy of our province's revolutionary tradition! Fight well!" Other soldiers took up the tune, and soon the entire company joined in: "Uncle Ho is with us in our march forward. Today Uncle Ho calls on us."

But Uncle Ho's call to fight bravely in the South might never have been fulfilled were it not for the efforts of hundreds—perhaps thousands—of workers stationed along the Ho Chi Minh Trail. Their lives were devoted to just one thing: maintaining the trail for the never-ending columns of trucks carrying supplies for the big buildup. They manned way stations, re-supplied the troops moving southward, and repaired roads after American bombing raids. The last job was probably the most important. As soon as the rumbling explosions of a B-52 raid ceased, armies of workers appeared from spider holes along the trail and went to work. These men—and some women—labored day and night, digging out the debris and filling in craters caused by the giant bombs. In the early years they had done their work with shovels and buckets; by 1972 they had tractors to lighten the labor. But the work was still backbreaking, and there was always the danger that they would be caught out in the open by American bombers.

Trail engineers, as they were called, had been seen by Hanoi as an important part of the communist war effort since the early days of the struggle. In May 1959 the Military Commission of the Party Central Committee passed an official resolution creating Group 559, a unit charged with "creating the first foot-travel route connecting the North and South, and organizing the sending of people, weapons, and supplies to the revolution in the South." In the early days Group 559, also called Truong Son troops because they had to cross the rugged Truong Son Mountains on the trip south, numbered only a few hundred. Lacking sophisticated machinery, they used bicycles to move artillery, weapons, and supplies along narrow trails. By 1972 the Trail had become a road—even a highway—and the Truong Son troops smoothed the way for thousands of tons of supplies despite a concerted bombing campaign.[24]

Vu Tien De was one of the Truong Son troops. Like thousands of his comrades, he had come south willing to die in the struggle to unite Vietnam. De was a trail engineer, part of a battalion assigned by Group 559 to keep the Ho Chi Minh Trail open. His battalion's area of responsibility was Base Area 611, a region of rugged mountains just over the Laotian border southwest of the demilitarized zone. For many years he had lived this dangerous life, braving the bombs to keep the road open, but the period leading up to the 1972 offensive was the most difficult he could remember. American planes came more often, and their bombs were more accurate.

Vu Tien De recalled a typical experience. He was on station one day waiting for the next big truck convoy heading south when the bombs struck. Bright flashes illuminated the sky, and the mountain shuddered under the crashing impact. Leaping onto his bulldozer, De waited for a report from a nearby reconnaissance squad. The road was blocked by a B-52 strike, it reported. Columns of smoke still rose into the sky as the bomb disposal crews went to work. They neutralized delayed-fuse bombs and moved loose debris out of the way. Then the trail engineers moved out.[25]

De bulldozed through the night while other men held lanterns. Tiny flames sprang to life on the road as De uncovered bits of phosphorous from the bombs, but they were quickly pushed over the side along with the tons of dirt torn up by the air raid. Fighter planes roared overhead, dropping parachute flares, their flickering flame casting a garish light over the jungle. De worked on, though there was always the danger that more planes would come and bomb the workers.

Along the way lay deep bomb craters. In the uneven light cast by the lanterns, De ran the risk of riding his bulldozer off the side of the steep ravine to his right. Worse, a delayed-fuse bomb might be underfoot, just waiting to blast him into oblivion. Despite the risks, one crater after another was filled.

Suddenly the ground ahead erupted into a geyser of dirt. One of the delayed-fuse bombs he feared went off with a roar, covering the bulldozer in dirt. As his comrades raced to his aid, De managed to crawl out and help uncover the machine. By dawn they were done, and the convoy could again move down the trail.

Later in the day, the bulldozer rested back in its shelter while De drank water from a canteen. Rest periods had to be snatched whenever possible because when the bombs fell, no one stopped work until the damage was cleared.

Near nightfall the big bombers came again. They flew high in the sky, out of sight and sound until the explosions shredded the earth asunder. De again sat atop his bulldozer, moving dirt and filling craters. This time, he had just begun work when a second string of bombs fell nearby. De was thrown to the ground, where he and a comrade clung to the dirt as the explosions roared. When it was over, they checked each other for injuries, then got back to work. This time the other man drove the bulldozer while De lit the way with his lantern. Then it was done. De put down the lantern and fired a flare, signaling that the road was clear.

The constant flow of supplies moved inexorably toward the battlefront.

For almost four years—since the failed 1968 Tet Offensive—Hanoi's dogged strategy of protracted war ground down American resolve to go the distance. North Vietnam's decision makers were well aware of Washington's political and military dilemma, linking the withdrawal as an inevitable consequence of American association with the "illegitimate regime" in Saigon. But despite various disagreements over specific policy within the communist politburo, all agreed that 1972 was to be a crucial year, demanding decisive action. Although Hanoi had retreated from its General Offensive plan of 1967–68, there was never any doubt that when the time was right there would be a return to the third stage of guerrilla warfare—the final offensive. The question was, When should it be launched?

Following the North Vietnamese military defeat during the 1968 Tet Offensive, Hanoi decided that caution was the better part of valor and dropped back into low-level guerrilla war punctuated by sporadic main force engagements. A key document, COSVN Resolution 55, spelled out the strategy: "Never again, and under no circumstances are we going to risk our entire military force for just an offensive." Although those words had been Hanoi's guiding principle for three years, some members of the ruling politburo were ready for a change.[26]

The leading proponents of moving forward rapidly were Vo Nguyen Giap and Le Duan, two of the most powerful men in Hanoi. Giap was well known as the general who had fought two of the Western world's greatest military powers—France and the United States—to a standoff. Giap had humiliated France in 1954 during a battle in an insignificant valley called Dien Bien Phu, a victory that earned him a prominent place in the world press. Yet Giap was quick to point out that his strategic savvy stemmed from revolutionary fervor, not military training: "The only military academy I have been to is that of the bush," he once boasted.[27]

Admirers called Giap "Nui Lua," the "volcano beneath the snow," in reference to a boiling personality thinly concealed by a calm exterior. Giap had a forceful personality, though he was also arrogant, abrasive, and dogmatic. Others described him more kindly. One French acquaintance characterized him as "very orderly, logical, Cartesian." But even detractors credited Giap with an "eloquent bluntness."[28]

Although he is widely credited with improving on Mao Zedong's guerrilla warfare doctrine, General Giap actually added very little to it, cleaving dogmatically to the concept of armed struggle as opposed to political struggle. An admirer of Soviet military technology, which he studied during several visits to Russia, Giap seldom bothered to conceal his dislike of China. Beijing's ideology bored Giap, giving rise to frequent arguments within the politburo over his political correctness. In fact, Giap was a nationalist first and a communist second; he placed what he regarded as North Vietnamese interests before those of international communism. This attitude made Giap many powerful enemies, including Truong Chinh, Hanoi's acknowledged ideologist and a proponent of Chinese communist strategy.

In countless politburo meetings and military writings, Giap argued in favor of conventional war. In the early 1950s he launched three offensives against the French—all disastrous—before succeeding in capitalizing on French strategic stupidity and tactical blunders to win at Dien Bien Phu. Yet in reality Giap had little to do with that battle. The plan was conceived by an obscure Chinese adviser named Wei Guoqing, and field operations fell under the command of General Nguyen Chi Thanh. Giap, as minister of defense, was far from the planning and the action, though he managed to be photographed periodically at the front.[29]

Giap was not a soldier; he was an academic who gained his knowledge of tactics from books. He never fought in battle or shared the hardships of a long campaign, but this did not deter him from sending countless soldiers to their deaths. Giap continued his unimaginative head-on confrontations against the U.S. Army during the mid-1960s. For almost two decades he tried to repeat his spectacular victory at Dien Bien Phu, first battling the 1st Cavalry Division in the Ia Drang Valley in 1965 and then the U.S. Marines at Khe Sanh in 1968. Both engagements ended in failure for Giap. Then there was the 1968 Tet Offensive, which brought the Viet Cong out of their secret hideouts and into South Vietnam's cities in an attempt to spur a "general uprising." That, too, failed. By modern Western standards, Giap's leadership wrought disastrous consequences. During the Tet Offensive alone, his headlong tactics resulted in as many as 40,000 dead; between 1964 and 1971, an estimated 500,000 North Vietnamese soldiers perished. None of these horrendous casualties brought Hanoi any territory in the South, and they resulted in the virtual destruction of the Viet Cong. But unlike most of history's great generals, Giap cared little for the lives of the men he sent into battle. "Every two minutes 300,000 people die on this planet," he once remarked coldly to a journalist. "What are 45,000 for a battle? In war death doesn't count."[30]

Although some historians have characterized Giap as a brilliant general—an "Asian Napoleon"—there is little evidence to support the conclusion. Giap's many defeats exhibited a tendency to accept excessive losses while fighting for dubious military objectives. His few victories were based on meticulous planning and an ability to move men and supplies great distances over seemingly impassable terrain. General Giap was a logistical genius, not a great tactical practitioner. In fact, many in the North Vietnamese politburo questioned Giap's leadership in the wake of the Tet Offensive, but his continued close relationship with Ho Chi Minh kept him in charge of the military.

Upon Ho's death in September 1969, there was no one to protect Giap, and his political fortunes declined. In June 1971 he was removed as vice chairman of the National Defense Council (second only to Ho Chi Minh) and placed fifth in the hierarchy behind four civilians, including his archrival Truong Chinh. In the face of what could only have been considered a humiliation, Giap needed a resounding military victory to restore his reputation.[31]

Giap did have political allies, however. During the debate over the proposed shift from protracted war to an all-out conventional offensive in 1972, his political partner was none other than Le Duan, first secretary of the Lao Dong (Worker's) Party. Western analysts regarded Le Duan as the chief architect of Hanoi's crusade to conquer South Vietnam. In the years before the 1954 partition, Le Duan was the leader of the communist movement in southern Vietnam, where he was instrumental in establishing what became the Viet Cong. "In a real sense," observed one Vietnam expert, "he is the father of the present war."[32]

After Ho Chi Minh's death, Le Duan's waxing influence signaled a shift in communist strategy from the Chinese model of guerrilla war to a more militarily aggressive program as championed by the Soviet Union. This was a profound change for a man who advocated guerrilla war in the early days of the movement. In fact, Le Duan had been so dedicated to the Maoist principles of revolution that Soviet premier Nikita Khrushchev once said that Le Duan "talks, thinks, and acts like a Chinese." Yet by 1971 Le Duan was leaning toward Moscow, a move probably brought about by his conclusion that only Soviet technology could stand up to the sophisticated weapons of the United States. So adroit was Le Duan's maneuvering through the perilous pitfalls of the widening Soviet-Chinese schism that by late 1971 aid to Hanoi from both communist giants came, in the words of veteran Vietnam-watcher Douglas Pike, "with virtually no strings attached."[33]

Giap and Le Duan had had plenty of disagreements before 1972, and they would have them again in the war's final year. Bui Tin, a former North Vietnamese army officer with close ties to high-ranking government officials, recalled that both before and after the 1972 offensive "Le Duan deliberately provoked General Giap," often blaming him for military failures. But for the time being they had a common cause, and in a communist system where political correctness was paramount, strength lay in numbers.[34]

Le Duan was apparently backed by a broad spectrum of Hanoi's elite; indeed, by design, North Vietnamese government was one of collective leadership, causing each politburo member to live and die by consensus. Although first among equals, Le Duan could not impose his decisions roughshod over the wishes of other members. One clue that consensus had been reached became clear in late 1971, when North Vietnam's severely censored military newspaper, *Quan Doi Nhan Dan,* spelled out the objective: "Being held in an unfavorable strategic position, the enemy can only use a small part of his troops. Though numerous, he is outnumbered; though strong he is weak. . . . The main goal of fighting must be the destruction of enemy manpower."[35]

This was quite a change from protracted guerrilla warfare. But was Hanoi ready to undertake the third stage of Mao's three phases of guerrilla warfare—the final military destruction of the enemy? This was a crucial question that had dominated communist politburo meetings since 1968.

Planning for some sort of offensive began during the Nineteenth Plenum of the Central Committee held in late 1970 and early 1971, brought on by dramatic changes in Hanoi's situation. Several factors had converged to create a bleak military, economic, and political picture for North Vietnam in the coming year. The joint U.S.–South Vietnamese invasion of Cambodia in the spring of 1970, though not decisive, had seriously damaged the North Vietnamese logistical system that supported communist troops in the southern section of South Vietnam. Pacification was steadily dismantling Viet Cong control in the countryside, and North Vietnam's economy was in a shambles. Yet there were positive signs as well. The United States was withdrawing from Vietnam, leaving the South Vietnamese army overextended. A serious blow by Hanoi could humiliate President Nixon on the eve of his election campaign and unbalance U.S. negotiations in Paris.[36]

Although there was agreement that 1972 would be a crucial year for both Hanoi and Washington, there was serious disagreement over the correct course of action. One faction argued that 1973 would provide the best opportunity for a conventional invasion of South Vietnam for the simple reason that, by then, the United States would have totally withdrawn from Vietnam. And given the shape of American politics and public opinion at the time, the soldiers were unlikely to return even if Hanoi blatantly violated the 1954 Geneva Accords. Since victory would then be assured, they argued, why not wait until 1973?

Le Duan and his supporters rejected this course of action, stressing that it was too risky to allow the United States to complete its Vietnamization program and pump additional arms into the South Vietnamese logistical pipeline. Besides, if pacification continued unabated, there was a strong possibility that the Viet Cong might not hold on that long. Plus, if the North Vietnamese could win a decisive victory in 1972, before the Americans withdrew completely, it would be regarded as an American military defeat and greatly enhance Hanoi's prestige.

It appears that no firm decision was made during the Nineteenth Plenum, although Le Duan probably consolidated his position and edged the politburo toward an offensive in 1972, contingent upon procuring additional aid from the Soviet Union and China.[37]

Despite the dogged determination of Hanoi's leaders, by 1971 North Vietnam's economy was in ruins. Although President Lyndon B. Johnson had imposed a unilateral bombing halt in November 1968, Hanoi had only partially managed to rebuild its military and industrial base. Then-premier Truong Chinh ceased most major military operations in the South and used the bombing halt to take stock of the situation. North Vietnam's few factories had been decimated, along with the production of coal, which had been North Vietnam's main export in the years before 1965. Electrical capacity had been cut by two-thirds, and major petroleum storage facilities were mostly destroyed. By 1971 Hanoi and the port city of Haiphong had been largely rebuilt, though agricultural production remained sluggish. North Vietnam's rice crop in 1968 was 4 million metric tons. In 1971 it was only up to about 5 million metric tons, a measly gain considering that for three years not a single American bomb had fallen on the North.

Rearmament was Hanoi's primary consideration, however. American bombing of strategic targets in North Vietnam had had little effect on munitions because Hanoi produced almost none of its own, relying instead on its communist allies in Moscow and Beijing for weapons. But despite a common political ideology, relations between the three countries grew rocky during the early 1970s. The timing could not have been worse for Hanoi, and it probably helped convince the politburo that waiting until 1973 to launch an offensive risked a further deterioration of relations.

North Vietnam's dilemma over the nature and timing of an offensive against South Vietnam occurred within a matrix of shifting international politics. While China continued to regard itself as the ideological leader of Third World revolutions, it also strove to enhance its image within the international community. This was not an easy feat given Beijing's radical politics, but the key lay in normalizing relations with the United States. At the same time, the Soviet Union played a game of détente with Washington.

Hanoi naturally viewed all this with trepidation, but with the benefit of hindsight it seems that while the temporary thawing of superpower relations appeared to hurt North Vietnam's standing, it actually may have helped. The superpower game forced Moscow and Beijing to prove their revolutionary credentials by giving increased support to Hanoi without corresponding conditions. Yet this was only a temporary advantage that forced the North Vietnamese to act quickly against South Vietnam or risk being left behind by international events.

The first surprise came in the summer of 1971, when the United States announced that President Richard Nixon would journey to China sometime during the first half of 1972. The announcement caught Hanoi's politburo off guard, since only three months previously Beijing had announced that "the Chinese people are determined to take all necessary measures; not flinching even from the greatest national sacrifices, to give all-out support and assistance to the Vietnamese and other Indochinese peoples for the thorough defeat of the U.S. aggressors."[38]

Hanoi responded to Nixon's surprise move by accusing the United States of attempting to divide the communist world with "perfidious maneuvers" in a "false offensive" for a final peace in Vietnam. China correctly regarded the comments as being subtly aimed at Beijing as well, and it responded by sending Deputy Premier Li Hsien-nien to Hanoi with promises of continued military support. Careful China-watchers noted that despite the seeming rift between the two Asian communist nations brought about by Nixon's coming visit to Beijing, Hanoi found itself in the unique position of having its powerful northern neighbor coming south with firm pledges of aid. Usually Hanoi had to journey north with its hand out.[39]

The Chinese move prompted the Soviet Union to offer North Vietnam increased aid as well. In December 1971, Soviet president Nikolai V. Podgorny went to Hanoi and publicly guaranteed "additional aid without reimbursement." How much aid was not stipulated, but U.S. intelligence later estimated that Soviet and Chinese military and economic aid to North Vietnam between 1970 and 1972 was about $1.5 billion.[40]

The Soviets had always supplied North Vietnam with weapons, but in the spring of 1971 they went further, shipping T-54 tanks and 130mm howitzers, two of the most potent conventional weapons in the Soviet arsenal. The T-54 carried a 100mm main gun, mounted thick armor, and had a driving range of almost 200 miles. Though by definition a heavy tank, it was lighter and more primitive than its Western counterparts and was poorly made. The T-54 reportedly caught fire easily, had a short engine life, and was cramped inside.

The 130mm howitzer, on the other hand, was an example of state-of-the-art engineering, a product of Soviet reliance on artillery in conventional war. It outranged every gun in the U.S. arsenal except for the 175mm howitzer, of which the South Vietnamese had only a few batteries. In addition to these heavy weapons, the Soviet Union sent the AT-3 Sagger antitank missile and the SA-7 Strela shoulder-launched surface-to-air missile. The introduction of each of these weapons would alter the nature of battle in South Vietnam.[41]

Although Soviet tanks and artillery were often of shoddy construction and frequently broke down, their very simplicity was an advantage to the North Vietnamese, who lacked the military sophistication to handle complex weapons systems. Even so, it took skill to effectively employ tanks and artillery in combat, and the North Vietnamese soldier lacked any knowledge of these techniques. To compensate, Moscow offered advanced armor training in the Soviet Union to more than 3,000 select North Vietnamese tank crews. Soviet cadres also taught North Vietnamese officers the basic doctrine of overwhelming the enemy with artillery fire before assaulting with armor.[42]

With the issue of armaments settled, only one question remained: Could North Vietnam's army stand up to Saigon's regulars backed by American airpower on a conventional battlefield? A partial answer had come in February 1971 when the South Vietnamese army attacked North Vietnamese base areas in Laos during the U.S.-supported Operation Lam Son 719. To Giap, the rout of Saigon's withdrawing troops was proof that his army could defeat the South Vietnamese even if they retained the aid of U.S. air support.

In May 1971 Giap saw his opening. When the Party Central Committee met in Hanoi to discuss how the lessons of Lam Son 719 could be utilized in future operations, he and Le Duan argued that the communist defense and counterattack in Laos showed that the North Vietnamese military possessed the skill to exploit the changing situation in South Vietnam. Yet the window of opportunity would be small, and to be victorious the army had to act quickly. Le Duan and Vo Nguyen Giap were a formidable pair, and though there was continued opposition, the politburo eventually agreed to mount a mechanized attack using North Vietnamese troops during 1972.

Giap apparently chose one of his own military disciples, General Van Tien Dung, to command North Vietnamese forces during the offensive. Dung had been a division commander during the war against the French and in 1953 was promoted to chief of staff of the People's Army. During the 1960s Giap and Dung shared military responsibilities: Giap ran the war in the South while Dung built up North Vietnam's air defenses and planned infiltration into South Vietnam along the Ho Chi Minh Trail. In 1971 General Dung was given a field command, the last rung on the chain of command before taking control of all forces during the Easter Offensive.[43]

In December 1971 all political and military decisions must have been finally in place because the ubiquitous *Quan Doi Nhan Dan* suddenly spoke with a single and very firm voice. Though certainly not the final word on North Vietnamese policy, the communist newspaper was authoritative and provided Hanoi-watchers with a window into the minds of the ruling politburo. In mid-December it published a series of seven articles written by an author calling himself Chien Thang—the Victor—a pseudonym used by a number of high-ranking policy makers during past years. This time it was generally believed that the real author was General Vo Nguyen Giap.

The tenor of the articles was optimistic. Underlying them all was the opinion that the United States was beset by problems brought on by its long and unhappy involvement in Vietnam. Much of the content was political diatribe, but the fourth article quickly caught the attention of intelligence analysts. Using rhetoric about "important changes that have taken place on the battlefield," the author emphasized the preeminence of armed struggle in war—the core political philosophy held by Le Duan and General Giap—and stressed the key role of "main-force attacks" within that struggle. Only main-force units can "conduct major enemy-annihilating campaigns, launch big attacks, directly strike at the enemy's strongest forces and, thereby, definitely weaken him," argued Chien Thang. Most important, he continued, conventional warfare created a situation of "upsetting and confusing enemy strategies, rapidly changing the balance of forces and the situation on the battlefield, and creating a radical development in the war."

It was the "rapidly changing" aspect of the argument that was unique, for it indicated that Hanoi was suddenly willing to forsake protracted warfare and force some sort of a decision. Analysts also found the new position interesting because public mention of main-force warfare in North Vietnam's press had been rare since the 1968 Tet Offensive. General Abrams was told by his intelligence staff that the "recurrence of such discussion is considered significant" and that Hanoi was probably "indulging in psychological preparation of the North Vietnamese for anticipated main-force actions, and providing self-justification." The bold statements were probably also aimed at convincing the troops who would do the bloody fighting that their sacrifice would serve an important purpose.[44]

Hanoi probably had four major objectives in mind. First, the communists hoped to influence the 1972 U.S. presidential elections, upset the tempo of Nixon's Vietnamization, and hasten the withdrawal of American troops from South Vietnam, though this was certainly a minor objective. Second, Hanoi intended to demonstrate to the Soviet Union and China that North Vietnam was still a credible fighting machine. In addition, it hoped to skew the mounting cooperation between both communist giants and the United States. Third, North Vietnam wanted to reverse the advances made by Saigon's pacification program, which had been increasingly effective during the years since the 1968 Tet Offensive. Finally—and most important—Hanoi wanted to alter the military balance in South Vietnam. A resounding defeat of Saigon's army would demonstrate the futility of Vietnamization and weaken the American position at the Paris peace talks. Before a settlement was reached, Hanoi wanted to be in possession of as much South Vietnamese territory as possible—preferably at least one provincial capital. As the communists were always quick to point out, military success dictates diplomatic success.

Without credible and detailed histories from Vietnam's communist rulers, it is impossible to fully understand Hanoi's decision making in the months preceding the Easter Offensive. On the one hand, communist officials seemed optimistic about their chances for a decisive victory. As the D-day for the offensive approached, the Party Central Committee issued a directive predicting that "in this decisive test of strength between us and the enemy, our success on the battlefield is strategically decisive. Now more than ever before, the responsibility of the armed forces is very heavy and glorious."[45] On the other hand, it seems that many officials doubted that the offensive would result in complete victory over South Vietnam. Even General Giap saw the struggle as ongoing. "The battle that will decide the future of our people began more than twenty-five years ago," he told an interviewer during the Easter Offensive. "A battle, no matter how important it may be, whether Issus or Hastings, Philippi or Belle-Alliance, can only represent the high point of a developing situation."[46]

PART ONE
Main Thrust:
The Battle for Quang Tri and Hue

ONE

THE BLAZING
FRONT LINE

North Vietnam called its spring 1972 assault on the South the Nguyen Hue Offensive, a name rich in historical significance for all Vietnamese. Nguyen Hue was the birth name of Emperor Quang Trung, the great Vietnamese ruler who in 1789 marched his army through the jungles and mountains of central Vietnam to the outskirts of Hanoi, where he surprised and defeated a Chinese occupation force. With this battle, Vietnam ended more than a thousand years of Chinese rule. Almost two centuries later, Hanoi hoped to again drive a foreign power from Vietnamese soil and unify a divided nation.

Hanoi's primary military objectives lay in I Corps, South Vietnam's five northernmost provinces. Most of the region was covered with jungle-clad mountains ranging from the Laotian border on the west toward the South China Sea. Between the foothills and the sea lay a narrow strip of farmland, home to most of the region's population. The proximity of South Vietnam's two northernmost provinces—Quang Tri and Thua Thien—to North Vietnam's southern border made them favorite haunts of the North Vietnamese army dating back to the days immediately following partition in 1956. In fact, Saigon called I Corps the "blazing front line" because it bore the brunt of constant enemy pressure.[1]

Geography favored the enemy in northern I Corps—the region's close proximity to North Vietnam meant short supply lines running from the home front to the battlefront. In early 1972 North Vietnam had three divisions and eleven independent regiments inside I Corps or poised on its borders. The 308th NVA Division was perched above the demilitarized zone, the 304th NVA Division lurked just over the border in Laos, and the 324B NVA Division prepared to move into the A Shau Valley northwest of Hue, South Vietnam's ancient imperial capital. These were commanded by the B-4 Front, Hanoi's political and military command for northern I Corps, while most of the independent regiments were directly under the control of the B-5 Front, the communist command for the demilitarized zone region and southern North Vietnam.[2]

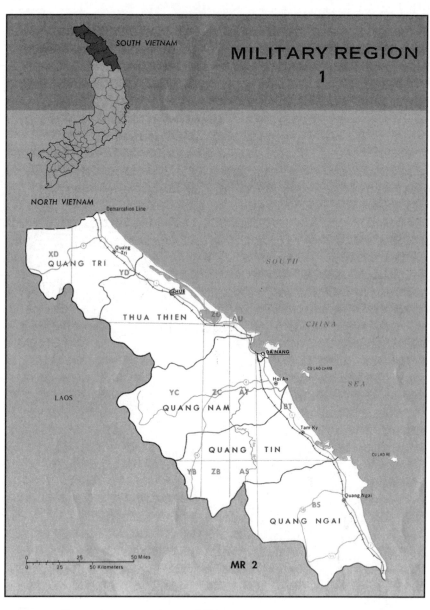

I Corps

On the South Vietnamese side, I Corps had three divisions, the 1st and 3d ARVN Divisions in Quang Tri and Thua Thien Provinces, and the 2d ARVN Division farther south. Supplementing this force was the 51st ARVN Regiment, the 1st Ranger Group (with three mobile and six border ranger battalions), and the 1st Armored Brigade, a total of fewer than 25,000 troops. Several Territorial Force militia units rounded out the defense.

Command of I Corps fell to Lieutenant General Hoang Xuan Lam, an officer who epitomized the ineffectiveness of Saigon's command structure. Lam had the political acumen to excel in Saigon's politics, but he was a poor military commander who had proved his incompetence as commander of the ill-fated Operation Lam Son 719 into Laos during the spring of 1971. A native of Hue, Lam knew the region well, but he consistently underestimated the enemy threat and took few steps to put together a credible defense.

Crucial to any defense Lam might devise was the 3d ARVN Division, a brand-new unit created in October 1971 as part of the Vietnamization program. Military officers frequently pointed out that while U.S. withdrawals had cut the number of troops defending the region almost in half, enemy attacks were not diminishing. "Because these [North Vietnamese] forces are in a sanctuary-like situation," wrote Lieutenant General Melvin Zais, the outgoing commander of American troops in I Corps during the summer of 1970, "they are free to build up and organize their forces, and wait for a U.S. withdrawal or for the right moment to strike. Adequate forces must be available to defeat or deter such a move."[3]

But where would this force come from? The two South Vietnamese divisions stationed in I Corps at that time were not enough to defend the region against the enemy forces poised in Laos and North Vietnam. According to one of the senior American advisers to the South Vietnamese I Corps command, "To compensate for the withdrawal of U.S. forces from the northern two provinces, it is estimated that an additional ARVN standard division of twelve battalions would be required." This force, he argued, would have to come from outside I Corps.[4]

One possibility was to move a division from the less-threatened Mekong Delta in the South, or from the strategic reserve around Saigon, but neither plan was acceptable to the South Vietnamese high command. President Thieu was reluctant to move his elite reserve force—a virtual palace guard—away from the capital, and each of the four regional commanders adamantly opposed relinquishing command of even a single division. These objections highlighted one of the fundamental flaws of the South

Vietnamese military—its paralyzing immobility. Years of static security duty had rooted the divisions firmly to their home bases; soldiers brought their families to live with them, officers became entrenched in local politics, and regional commanders grew accustomed to predictable campaigning. The reality was that by late 1970, despite almost two years of Vietnamization, Saigon's military force of more than a million men— formed into twelve divisions plus several ranger, armored cavalry, and artillery units—was virtually frozen in place. And it remained so despite the continuing drawdown of American combat troops.

Not until after Operation Lam Son 719 were concrete steps taken to remedy the situation. As panicked South Vietnamese troops streamed out of Laos with the enemy close on their heels, Saigon realized that the combination of increasing enemy strength, decreasing American troops, and continued immobility of the South Vietnamese army could only end in disaster. President Thieu resolved to send the 9th ARVN Division north from the Mekong Delta, then suddenly changed his mind. In August 1971 Saigon announced the creation of a brand-new division, designated the 3d ARVN Division, or the "Ben Hai Division," after the river flowing through the demilitarized zone.[5]

MACV was caught completely by surprise. General Abrams tried to persuade the South Vietnamese Joint General Staff to reconsider the plan to move the 9th ARVN Division north, but the South Vietnamese stood their ground. Actually, the Americans should not have been stunned. The move was less of a political liability because it did little to alter the status quo. What it did alter was the precariously balanced American Vietnamization timetable and budget. MACV objected principally to being forced to equip and train a new division while at the same time managing the U.S. withdrawal. But seeing he had little choice, in September Abrams reluctantly agreed to the activation of the new division in I Corps with the understanding that the South Vietnamese must come up with their own equipment.

The 3d ARVN Division was built around the 2d ARVN Regiment of the 1st ARVN Division, one of the strongest and most reliable infantry units in the South Vietnamese army. Rounding out the order of battle were two new regiments—the 56th and 57th—both made up of reluctant transferees from local territorial militia units, draftees, and even prisoners from military jails. By 1971 Saigon was clearly scraping the bottom of the manpower barrel.

On 20 October the division was officially activated, though it was at less than one-third strength, and sent north to the demilitarized zone. Although on paper the 3d ARVN Division was new, in reality it added little to the South Vietnamese defensive posture in the face of the enemy buildup.

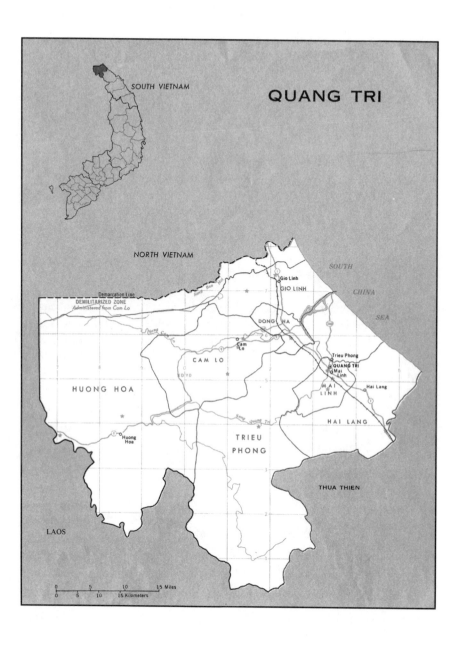

SOUTH VIETNAM

QUANG TRI

NORTH VIETNAM

SOUTH

CHINA

SEA

Demarcation Line
DEMILITARIZED ZONE
Administered from Cam Lo

Gio Linh
GIO LINH

DONG HA

Cam
Lo

CAM LO

Trieu Phong

QUANG TRI
Mai
Linh

HUONG HOA

MAI
LINH

Hai Lang

Huong
Hoa

HAI LANG

TRIEU
PHONG

THUA THIEN

LAOS

0   5   10   15 Miles
0   6   10   15 Kilometers

Ironically, the division was scheduled to become "combat ready" on 30 March, the very day the North Vietnamese launched the Easter Offensive.

Commanded by Brigadier General Vu Van Giai, the former deputy commander of the 1st ARVN Division, the new division was responsible for the defense of northern Quang Tri Province. Giai was considered one of the best of South Vietnam's junior general officers, though he was also known to be rigid and authoritarian. From his headquarters at Ai Tu Combat Base just north of the provincial capital of Quang Tri City, Giai planned his defense. Two of the division's three regiments, the 56th and 57th, were deployed along a handful of firebases dotting the plain just south of the demilitarized zone. The 2d ARVN Regiment occupied Camp Carroll, a large combat base located along Highway 9 about six miles southwest of the district town of Cam Lo. Highway 9 was the main road running east-west from the Laotian border to Highway 1, South Vietnam's principal thoroughfare.

The 3d ARVN Division also had operational control over two marine brigades from Saigon's general reserve, the 147th and 258th Vietnamese Marine Corps (VNMC) Brigades, which were deployed in an arc between Highway 9 to the west and the Thach Han River to the south. The marines faced west toward Laos, the most likely avenue of attack. Along the coast, the least likely point for a North Vietnamese attack, were stationed the Territorial Forces, also under the control of the 3d ARVN Division.

Because the division was brand-new, MACV ordered the First Regional Assistance Command (FRAC), the overall advisory command in I Corps, to assign a new advisory team to help bring it up to speed. Dubbed Advisory Team 155, it was the largest division advisory unit in the history of the war. Team 155 was commanded by Colonel Donald J. Metcalf, a meticulous officer who had seen combat in three wars. An unpopular commander, Metcalf was considered aloof, arrogant, and overly concerned with the little irrelevancies of military life. Despite the team's proximity to the battle-front, Metcalf saw to it that its compound was kept spotless—even down to the neatly trimmed lawns between the rows of corrugated tin barracks.

Advisory Team 155 was headquartered at Ai Tu Combat Base about four miles northwest of Quang Tri City. The command bunker stood beside General Giai's tactical operations center, which was surrounded by a ten-foot-thick ring of sandbags and a six-foot wire fence. A faded sign on the gate bore the eagle crest of the U.S. 101st Airborne Division, a remnant of the huge American presence in years past. The bunker's interior was full of scurrying South Vietnamese officers and radios for calling in everything from air strikes to naval gunfire.

General Giai took his new command seriously. Soon after deploying to northern I Corps in late 1971, the 3d ARVN Division embarked on a heavy training program, supervised directly by Giai. The general helicoptered from base to base, surveying the defenses and noting their strengths and weaknesses. Giai was particularly displeased with the big firebases his division had inherited from the Americans because they concentrated his limited troop strength and made inviting artillery targets. Well aware of the South Vietnamese army's immobility, Giai sought to overcome this weakness by dispersing his division into smaller temporary bases that could be moved if threatened by the enemy's heavy weapons. In the face of a building enemy troop presence just across the demilitarized zone, Giai accelerated his training program to bring the green 56th and 57th ARVN Regiments up to combat readiness.

Giai was not shy about sharing his concerns with General Lam, but the I Corps commander ignored his subordinate's suggestions and requests and made certain that any complaints did not reach Saigon. In this respect, Lam was neglecting his responsibility to act as a conduit within the chain of command stretching from the Joint General Staff in Saigon down to the 3d ARVN Division. But as a good soldier, Giai followed orders and hoped for the best.

Despite command problems at the corps level, the division's training went on unabated. In late March Giai decided to rotate two of his regiments to better familiarize them with northern I Corps' defenses and to keep them from feeling too comfortable in a single firebase. The plan involved exchanging the 56th ARVN Regiment from its positions around Firebase Charlie 2 north of the Cam Lo River with the 2d ARVN Regiment stationed around Camp Carroll. As a training exercise the move was sound, though from a tactical standpoint there was nothing to be gained by shuttling troops laterally between firebases. Usually such a move is used to replace troops at the front with fresh units from the rear, but in this case both regiments were already at the front—and both were fresh. The wisdom of the exercise was placed further in doubt by intelligence from Saigon predicting that the North Vietnamese had set 29 March as D-day for their invasion. Going ahead with the troop move in the face of such information was foolhardy, but neither Lam nor Giai halted the exercise. To make matters worse, Giai and his adviser, Colonel Metcalf, planned to depart the front lines for an extended holiday weekend in Saigon, leaving the division exercise virtually unsupervised.[6]

The troop shuffle went wrong from the beginning. On the morning of 30 March, Giai discovered that despite his best intentions the traditional immobility of the South Vietnamese army was insurmountable. A shortage of trucks slowed the move, low clouds and rain cut visibility and mired the roads, and within hours the two regiments were hopelessly disorganized. The crucial point came at 11:30 A.M. when the two regimental command posts shut down their radios, loaded them onto trucks, and moved to their new positions. For more than an hour both commanders were out of touch with each other as well as with the division headquarters.

The American advisers should have been part of the exercise from the beginning, but many were not. Lieutenant Colonel William C. Camper, senior adviser to the 56th ARVN Regiment, was surprised when General Giai's order came down. "I wasn't sure what to make of the order," recalled Camper, though given the confused state of affairs in northern I Corps, he was not really surprised. "The move was illogical."[7]

Then disaster struck. At almost exactly noon on 30 March, the North Vietnamese opened up with all the artillery they had been so busily moving into place for the past several months. The countryside reeled from the roar of the booming guns as rounds rained down on the disorganized South Vietnamese. Since neither regimental command post had completed the rotation, none of the officers could really exert command. Instead, the South Vietnamese milled about looking for bunkers and foxholes where they could hide from the well-aimed bombardment. The defenders' artillery never had a chance to fire back.[8]

In Camp Carroll with the disorganized 56th ARVN Regimental command post, Lieutenant Colonel Camper took stock of the situation. "They knew exactly where everything was, and they fired from six different positions," he recalled. Clearly the North Vietnamese had meticulously planned their attack.[9]

At the 3d ARVN Division headquarters, Colonel Metcalf watched helplessly while the division command staff milled around. He later recalled that it was several hours "before it finally began to sink in that we were being subjected to an all-out attack by several divisions of the NVA."[10]

Some Americans believed something more sinister than fate lay behind the debacle. "The timing of Giai's relief-in-place operation, the unprofessional manner in which it was executed, and his disregard of the warnings of a major attack, inevitably lead to the hypothesis of treason," wrote the senior U.S. Marine Corps adviser in northern I Corps. "The precise timing of the multitude of events about to unfold could not have happened just by chance."[11]

Whether it was treason or tragedy, the South Vietnamese were in trouble. From the west, all that stood in the path of the enemy advance were

Key locations and fire support bases (I Corps)

four small firebases—Khe Gio, Nui Ba Ho, Sarge, and Holcomb. Khe Gio and Holcomb, the most isolated and vulnerable of the bases, were abandoned within hours of the opening attack. That left three lonely outposts in the path of the communists' western thrust—Sarge, Nui Ba Ho, and Mai Loc. All were manned by South Vietnamese marines and a handful of American advisers.

In the cloud-shrouded mountains crowding the Laotian border, the North Vietnamese massed for the attack on the three firebases. For weeks they had watched the South Vietnamese, mapping out artillery positions and noting infantry concentrations. On the morning of 30 March everything was ready. The order to attack came at 11:00 A.M. "The whole battlefield roared up," noted a North Vietnamese officer. "Barrage after barrage of artillery descended on [the South Vietnamese]. The whole base quaked. Enemy artillery sites were buried in smoke and flames. Clouds of smoke rose like mushrooms."[12]

Another North Vietnamese soldier recorded the opening shots in his diary: "The hour for action has struck. The boom of our artillery shakes jungle and hills. Shells whiz over our heads. After a thirty-minute barrage, all enemy gun emplacements on Highway 9 are paralyzed. Before us, Firebase Dong Toan [Firebase Sarge] is engulfed in flames. Four helicopters turn up: two are immediately shot down and the rest hastily turn tail. B-52s come for saturation bombing all around the base. But our shelling becomes only fiercer."[13]

TWO

WESTERN COLLAPSE

The North Vietnamese had to be up to something, thought Major Walter E. Boomer. After sitting on top of this godforsaken mountain for the past several weeks, he had learned to identify subtle changes in the surrounding countryside. Since early March, signs of increased North Vietnamese activity were everywhere.

Major Boomer was senior adviser to the 4th Battalion, 147th VNMC Brigade. Baby-faced and blond, the picture of a southern gentleman, Boomer got along well with his counterparts and genuinely cared for their plight. He had seen action as a company commander in 1966 and 1967 and had been awarded the Silver Star for valor, making this latest advisory tour more than just a last-minute combat punch in the military career ticket. Unlike many other American advisers of his time, Major Boomer believed in Vietnamization, and, although he saw plenty of incompetence and cowardice in the South Vietnamese military, he believed it was Saigon's best chance for survival. Naturally, Boomer regarded the marines as the cream of the crop.

The Vietnamese marines were a cut above most of the military. Considered an elite unit, they were part of the strategic reserve, parceled out for combat as Saigon saw fit. South Vietnam's Marine Corps was formally established on 1 October 1954 and placed under the control of the navy, but over the next fifteen years it went through several reorganizations. By 1962 the marines still consisted of only a single brigade; in October 1968 a second brigade was added, and the marines were redesignated a division. In June 1970 the marines built a third brigade with a total division strength of around 15,000 men. Then, in February 1971, they moved from Saigon to I Corps to take part in Operation Lam Son 719, the South Vietnamese attack into Laos, and remained there through 1972.

Despite the marines' reputation as fearless warriors, the political nature of their role in the strategic reserve often tainted their use in combat. When they were deployed to a region by decree from Saigon—as they were to I Corps beginning in February 1971—they fell under the operational control of the corps commander. No army general concerned with his political future was willing to risk decimating part of the strategic reserve in battle, so the marines often performed a secondary role. General Lam was caught in this same quandary in Quang Tri Province in the spring of 1972. He had placed the marines along the western edge of the so-called Ring of Steel, the sharp edge of the South Vietnamese defense along the demilitarized zone and the Laotian border.[1]

Crucial to the marines' defensive responsibilities in 1972 was the western approach into northern I Corps. The gateways into the region were two tiny outposts—Sarge and Nui Ba Ho—both defended by the 4th VNMC Battalion. As was customary in the Vietnamese marines, the battalion was divided into two tactical groups and split between the two outposts. Alpha group on Sarge included the battalion headquarters, commanded by Major Tran Xuan Quang. Major Boomer stayed on Sarge with his counterpart. In addition to the headquarters group, there were two rifle companies and the 81mm mortar platoon. On Nui Ba Ho, about two miles to the north, Bravo group, consisting of the remaining two rifle companies, was led by Major Nguyen Dang Hoa, the battalion executive officer.

Captain Ray L. Smith, the battalion deputy senior adviser, was the lone American on Nui Ba Ho. A rawboned country boy from Oklahoma, Smith had a reputation as a fearless fighter and a faultless leader. Best of all, he spoke Vietnamese, which gained him the undying respect of his counterparts. Smith had seen this region before. As a lieutenant in the 1st Battalion, 1st Marines at Khe Sanh during the 1968 Tet Offensive, Captain Smith had displayed uncommon bravery. By any definition he was a marine's marine.

Sarge and Nui Ba Ho were neither comfortable nor particularly strategically placed. The combination often made Major Boomer wonder why they were even part of the 3d ARVN Division's Ring of Steel. In years past, when the U.S. Marines held down northern I Corps, the main outpost had been Vandegrift Combat Base, a brigade-sized compound used as a forward staging point for operations west to the Laotian border. Now the last vestiges of the defensive positions had retreated up onto the tops of steep-sided mountains, little more than watchful eyes set high in the hills. To the south they overlooked the deep valley carved by the Quang Tri River as it flowed gently through the thickly forested Ba Long Valley toward the South China Sea. About three miles to the west was Highway 9, the main east-west axis bisecting the region (although called a *Quoc-lo* or "national highway," it was in reality a narrow road, paved only in places). From just below Sarge the road wound its way to the Laotian border, through the mountain wilderness of central Laos, finally ending at the great Mekong River on the Thai border. To the North Vietnamese, Highway 9 was the path to victory in northern I Corps.

To Major Boomer the road was a harbinger of things to come. The marines saw sporadic movement near Highway 9, often accompanied by the sound of trucks in the forest. On a couple of occasions the advisers saw piles of wooden crates stacked along the road in the distance. Suddenly, they would disappear. Major Boomer reasoned that they were probably supplies left during the night for enemy units building up in the jungle below.

In early March General Giai, the 3d ARVN Division commander, had paid the marines a visit in their isolated outposts. Major Boomer reported the mysterious boxes and voiced his concerns, noting that "something significant was going on to the west." The general agreed but believed the division lacked the strength to aggressively patrol toward the Laotian border. That decision would prove fatal.

Day after day the marines sat in their outposts. They rarely patrolled, and when they did, they stayed out of the valley around Highway 9. It did not take any sophisticated intelligence to know that the enemy was staging for something, and to put a platoon, or even a company, down there meant certain destruction. Major Boomer later recalled that the marines spent their time "looking wistfully to the west hoping that we were secure on the mountain peaks that we occupied."[2]

The waiting came to an end as daylight broke on the morning of 30 March. North Vietnamese gunners greeted the rising sun with an artillery barrage on both outposts, sending the marines running for cover. Major Boomer knew this was no routine attack; it was too heavy and too concentrated—and very accurate. As Boomer and the battalion commander reported the attack to their superiors over the radio in the command bunker, two rounds landed directly on top of them. Miraculously, no one was badly hurt, though other positions on the mountaintop were not so fortunate. South Vietnamese marines in the more exposed trenches began taking casualties immediately, and within minutes the dead and wounded were piling up.

At the east end of the base was a small radio intelligence bunker manned by two American soldiers who spent their time listening in on North Vietnamese transmissions. Late in the morning, after enduring hours of uninterrupted shelling, Major Boomer peered out of his bunker and saw that the listening post had been leveled by a direct hit. During a lull in the firing he crawled over to the rubble to help the radiomen. The bunker's timbers were in flames, and there was no sign of life. The two radiomen were the first American casualties of the Easter Offensive.[3]

Nui Ba Ho had come under attack at the same time as Sarge, though the battle began differently for Captain Ray L. Smith. During the morning, a

North Vietnamese troops break through the wire at Firebase Sarge. (Author's collection)

perimeter patrol ran into a small enemy force about 900 yards northwest of Nui Ba Ho. As the marines fought their way back to the base, the North Vietnamese artillery opened up. At about 11:00 in the morning Smith saw a troubling sight. Three company-sized North Vietnamese units were marching in tight formation across Highway 9 toward Nui Ba Ho.

Captain Smith called frantically over the radio for fire support, but none came. Had the South Vietnamese artillery fired, or had air support been available, the bunched-up enemy would have been badly mauled in the open valley. As it was, neither base received any support from artillery or air. A curtain of thick, low-lying clouds kept the fighter planes grounded, while artillery at nearby firebases kept silent because the South Vietnamese crews had run for cover when the offensive began and refused to come out and man their batteries. Because of the savage intensity of the enemy barrage, the 81mm mortar on Sarge was immobilized, leaving one 60mm mortar, Nui Ba Ho's sole indirect fire weapon, to provide the only counterbattery fire. By midafternoon the entire crew had been killed or wounded. Sarge and Nui Ba could do nothing but endure the pounding.

Because Nui Ba Ho was only a small pinpoint atop its mountain cradle, it was a difficult target for the North Vietnamese gunners to hit. Captain

Smith watched the rounds strike long, then short, then long again; only a few actually hit the base. Fluent in Vietnamese, he listened in on the North Vietnamese spotters as they struggled with the target. By about 3:00 in the afternoon the enemy switched to mortars and began bringing accurate 60mm and 82mm fire onto the northern section of Nui Ba Ho.[4]

A few hours later the firing slowed, and the first infantry attack began. Behind a curtain of rocket-propelled grenades and machine-gun bullets, three human wave assaults washed onto a marine platoon manning a small rocky knoll about 600 yards north of the firebase. The defenders managed to push them all back. Another position outside the main perimeter, this one just east of Nui Ba Ho, was overrun. Seven marines—all wounded—managed to get inside the main base. To the south they were not so lucky. During a mass assault against a squad position, the marines fired a flechette round from a 106mm recoilless rifle into the North Vietnamese. Hundreds of steel darts flashed from the barrel like a giant shotgun round, vaporizing a handful of the attackers. The gunners slammed home a second round, but the gun failed to fire, and the position was overrun. All but a few of the marines were killed; the survivors managed to flee back into the Nui Ba Ho perimeter.

At 7:00 P.M. the North Vietnamese rushed the northern edge of Nui Ba Ho with about 100 men—nearly a company. Captain Smith watched in horror as the mass formation streamed toward the wire. Every available marine raced for the perimeter, firing as they ran. When the sun slowly slipped behind the mountains to the west, the enemy relented, leaving behind some fifty dead comrades scattered over the torn ground.

With night cloaking the mountain, the enemy infantry stopped its assaults. But it did not rest. In the blackness to the north, Captain Smith could hear the North Vietnamese dragging artillery up the steep hill for the final obliteration of Nui Ba Ho. Throughout the night, mortar rounds pounded the base, while small sapper teams crept close enough to the wire to hurl grenades and dynamite at the defenders. There was no sleep in Nui Ba Ho or Sarge that night.

A few hours before midnight the beleaguered marines managed to get their first air support. An AC-119 Stinger gunship came on station, but because of poor visibility the crew was unable to open fire for fear of hitting the marines. Stinger was a twin-engine Fairchild Flying Boxcar converted to mount an awesome array of high-tech target acquisition gear and fast-firing weapons. Volume of fire was Stinger's claim to fame. Two multi-barreled 20mm cannon and four 7.62mm miniguns could pour out thousands of rounds per minute, making Stinger an ideal aerial weapons platform for

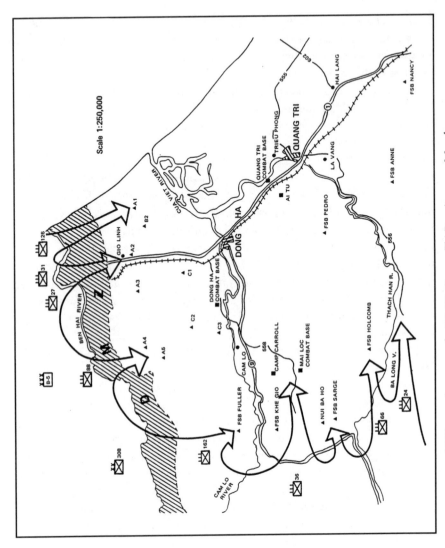

NVA attacks across the DMZ, Quang Tri Province, 30 March 1972

close support of troops on the ground. But none of this technology did the marines at Nui Ba Ho any good, so the gunship lumbered off toward Sarge to see if it could be of help there.[5]

Daybreak brought a barrage of fire from enemy recoilless rifles placed at four or five positions around Nui Ba Ho during the night. Behind the opening rounds streamed another mass infantry attack, but it was broken by the lone 106mm recoilless rifle inside the perimeter. A dozen more broken bodies were added to the pile of enemy dead outside the wire. But the North Vietnamese had anticipated this and soon concentrated their fire on the hapless recoilless rifle crew, killing or wounding all of them.

Then the big guns opened up again. This time Captain Smith noticed they were more accurate; most of the rounds exploded on top of the hill. The handful of rough bunkers inside the base collapsed under the barrage, and the trenches were half buried in loose dirt and debris. Throughout the early afternoon the North Vietnamese concentrated on leveling Nui Ba Ho with artillery.

One bright spot remained for the marines to focus on. The tiny platoon position just outside the base's northern perimeter was still holding out, though it was completely cut off from its fellow marines. The North Vietnamese apparently decided that they had already wasted too many men on the survivors because beginning at about noon on 31 March they totally ignored them, concentrating instead on Nui Ba Ho itself. As more infantry attacks swarmed toward the main base, the marines could see the handful of defenders to the north firing madly into the rear and flanks of the attacking enemy. In a battle with such lopsided odds, the scene was an inspiration to the defenders.

At 3:00 P.M. the marines on Nui Ba Ho got their first artillery support. A battery of 105mm howitzers from Firebase Mai Loc to the east opened up and helped turn back another series of assaults against the northern perimeter. Captain Smith watched a North Vietnamese 75mm recoilless rifle blow apart under the impact of a direct hit from one of the howitzers.

The North Vietnamese had virtually ignored Firebase Sarge throughout the day on 31 March. They poured on just enough artillery fire to keep the marines there from reinforcing Nui Ba Ho. As the battle raged, Major Boomer listened to the fighting over the radio, frustrated by his inability to come to the aid of his compatriot. His hopes sank as the enemy swarmed around Captain Smith's position.

The enemy's unrelenting attacks against the northern face of Nui Ba Ho had taken a deadly toll on the defenders. Although the North Vietnamese had also been moving men around the south side of the base throughout the day, there had been little action on that front. Captain Smith knew an attack from that quarter would inevitably come, but for now the northern perimeter was most pressing. As casualties mounted, the marines shifted troops to the north, thinning the ranks on the south to a dangerous level.

During a lull in the firing, Captain Smith moved off to the southern side of the perimeter for a look around. The sight that greeted him there was not reassuring. A platoon of North Vietnamese soldiers was manhandling some sort of large artillery piece up the steep slope in preparation for a new assault. Reaching for his radio, Smith called for air support. Although the cloud cover was still too thick for accurate air support, he asked for fighters anyway.

Luck smiled on the marines that afternoon. As a flight of F-4 Phantoms winged their way toward Nui Ba Ho, the clouds clinging to the mountaintops parted just enough for the jets to see their target. They swooped down and unleashed their deadly payloads on the North Vietnamese congregating on the south slope. As the Phantoms pulled up for home, the clouds closed in, and Nui Ba Ho was again shrouded in mist.

The enemy scattered as the bombs exploded. When the smoke cleared, the defenders could see only a dozen or so bodies on the ground, but the impending attack had clearly been halted in its tracks. Captain Smith scrambled back to the bunker and the action along the northern perimeter.

Just before nightfall another frontal assault rushed at the wire, and again luck smiled on the marines. A rain of 105mm artillery rounds smashed the attackers just as they reached the wire, mangling dozens and blunting the attack. Mai Loc's intermittent artillery support had come through just in time.

Darkness settled in, bringing with it a low fog that slithered across the mountaintop and sank into the valleys. For two hours the North Vietnamese probed the northern perimeter, never striking hard, but never letting up the pressure either. Stinger came back, but it could not accurately pinpoint targets through the fog. The marines heard the moan of the twin props as the gunship flew a tight circle around Nui Ba Ho. Several times, parachute flares popped overhead, casting a dull glow over the battle but providing little illumination. Then at 9:30 P.M. one flare floated low enough to bathe the area in light.

Captain Smith gasped at the sight before him. Caught in the sputtering white glare like rats in a floodlight beam were dozens of North Vietnamese soldiers, picking their way through the rows of razor wire. Behind them, waiting quietly in ranks, stood the assault group.

"Give me HE [high explosive] right on the northern wire. You know the coordinates!" Smith screamed into the radio. Within minutes the rounds poured in and broke the attack, but the enemy kept up the pressure. One of the marine company commanders broke in on the radio and angrily asked whoever was tossing grenades around to be more careful where they threw them. Smith and his counterpart looked at each other and shrugged; no one was throwing grenades. The only explanation was that the North Vietnamese had managed to make it inside the perimeter. A few minutes later another frantic call on the radio confirmed that the enemy was inside the wire and had surrounded the command bunker.

There was no choice but to evacuate Nui Ba Ho. The defenders had lost control, and no one could tell for sure which areas were held by marines, and which by the enemy. The commander was nowhere to be found, and marines were fleeing in all directions.

Captain Smith peered out of his bunker. The first thing he saw was a group of about five North Vietnamese soldiers crouching just outside the door. Clutching his rifle, Smith raced out the door and past the startled enemy soldiers, who failed to fire a shot. Zigzagging between bunkers and sandbagged trenches, he finally linked up with a group of marine survivors at the southeast corner of the perimeter. The frightened men milled about, unwilling to break out of the wire for fear of tripping the mines they had placed before the battle to keep the enemy away. Now the North Vietnamese were inside, and the marines could not get out.

More marines, including Smith's counterpart, Major Hoa, managed to find the group huddled near the wire. Hoa ordered the marines to move out, but no one budged. An argument erupted. Some men said they feared stepping on mines surrounding the perimeter; others countered that if they stayed, the North Vietnamese would surely kill them all. In no mood for debate, Captain Smith grabbed the nearest marines and threw two of them into the razor wire. No mines exploded. The rest began moving slowly in single file through the perimeter when suddenly a burst of automatic rifle fire chattered over their heads from a mere five yards to the rear. Smith turned and fired from the hip, killing a lone North Vietnamese soldier, then motioned for the marines to speed up. Caution no longer mattered because the firing would certainly bring reinforcements.

Captain Smith took the lead. When the marines again slowed for fear of mines, he decided to set an example. Leaping forward, Smith twisted in the air and landed flat on his back in the tangled razor wire. If I do trip a mine, he recalled foolishly thinking, the radio on my back will protect me from the blast. Again there was no explosion. As Captain Smith lay in the wire, the marines surged forward, climbing over his body as if it were a bridge. When they had passed, the cut and bleeding American tore himself from the coils and, leaving most of his tattered clothes dangling in the wire, joined his men outside the perimeter.

Smith glanced at his watch—it was about 10:30 P.M.—then called for one last artillery strike to cover their retreat. As the rounds whistled overhead, the marines moved off down the slope of Nui Ba Ho and headed for the relative safety of the base at Mai Loc about five miles due east.

Major Boomer listened helplessly as the battle unfolded on Nui Ba Ho. Firebase Sarge was spared the fury of the North Vietnamese attack, but it was clearly next. At about 10:45 on the night of 31 March, Boomer got a call from Captain Smith.

"Our position has been overrun," said the calm voice over the radio. From his vantage point down the hill from Nui Ba Ho, Smith reported that he could see the North Vietnamese swarming over the fortifications at the top of the mountain. Major Boomer felt his heart sink. He and Smith had become good friends during their time as advisers in Vietnam, and now Boomer was certain that his fellow marine was "going to buy the farm." But he was also concerned about his own situation. Nui Ba Ho dominated the northern approach to Sarge, and if it fell to the communists, Boomer's position would become untenable. A few minutes later he heard Smith calling for artillery directly on the mountaintop, the last resort of a soldier in deep trouble. It was the last transmission from Bravo Group, and Boomer did not expect to see Captain Smith ever again.

The situation was becoming critical for the marines on Sarge, and some hard decisions had to be made. The endless artillery barrage had slowly whittled down the garrison, while enemy infantry probes added to the casualties. An hour or so before midnight, just as Nui Ba Ho was confirmed lost to the enemy, Major De, the battalion commander, told Boomer that it was time to go. The officer was torn between remaining and fighting to the last man and pulling off the mountain in an attempt to save what was left of his battalion, but in the end it was best to retreat and fight another day. In the long run, the South Vietnamese were clearly going to lose Sarge and Nui Ba Ho.

Major Boomer called the 3d ARVN Division forward command at Ai Tu at 3:40 on the morning of 1 April. "Uniform, Uniform [3d ARVN Division call sign], this is Mike . . . moving . . ." was all he said. Then the radio went dead, and the war swallowed up the 4th VNMC Battalion. The advisers at Ai Tu assumed the worst and sadly turned their attention to the other hot spots opening all around the Ring of Steel.

But Major Boomer was not lost. The surviving marines on Sarge headed northeast off the mountain toward Mai Loc. Unable to destroy his radio codes, Boomer threw them into a deep ravine. Someone's going to chew me out for this breech of security, thought Boomer, but it was the best he could do considering the circumstances.

The retreating column quickly bogged down under the weight of dozens of wounded marines. The morning sun found them deep in the jungle, still headed east, trying to keep quiet and unseen. By noon they had not encountered any North Vietnamese, and it seemed as if they might make it out unscathed. Major Boomer had been unable to contact Ai Tu since the column left Sarge because he had become separated from his radio operator. When they were reunited later in the day, the marine had lost the radio. Boomer later recalled that if he could have killed the man quietly, he would have done so on the spot.

Just before dark, the marines stopped for a meal of uncooked rice. No one moved around or spoke for fear of alerting any North Vietnamese in the area. Major Boomer felt particularly alone out in the jungle. He had no idea what was going on around him, and although he guessed that the enemy attacks on Sarge and Nui Ba Ho were not isolated incidents, he would have been astonished to find that all of northern I Corps was reeling from the force of North Vietnam's biggest offensive of the war.

The marines moved slowly throughout the night. By the morning of 1 April they had descended from the steep slopes and thick forest of the mountains onto a plain of gently rolling hills covered with tall grass and a sprinkling of trees. Up to this point their luck had held and they had evaded the enemy. But it was too good to continue.

Major Boomer heard low voices ahead in the tall grass. Sinking to one knee, he motioned for the rest of the column to halt. Two separate North Vietnamese units of unknown size stood directly ahead, though they did not seem to be aware of the marines' presence. Waiting might prove disastrous, so the decision was made to sneak between them.

At about 9:00 A.M. the marines moved forward. Almost immediately a few men opened fire—no one could say for sure who shot first—and the South Vietnamese panicked. The stress of moving through terrain swarming with enemy troops proved too much for the frightened marines, who broke and ran. Major Boomer yelled for them to halt; when that did not work, he aimed his rifle and fired over the heads of the fleeing men. But in the midst of the confusion, no one even noticed. As the men streamed by him, Boomer saw the terror in their eyes. He could forgive the marines for their fear after almost two days on the run, but they were leaving behind dozens of wounded men, and that was inexcusable.

The pursuing North Vietnamese recognized Boomer's shouts as the voice of an American and shouted, "*covan, covan*"—the Vietnamese word for adviser. Both enemy columns maneuvered in an attempt to encircle Boomer, who would be a valuable prize. Major Boomer had lost contact with the battalion commander, and with the marines fleeing in all directions he could see that it was futile to try to organize the battalion to return fire. It was every man for himself—including the wounded.

One South Vietnamese officer, an artillery lieutenant, remained behind to help Boomer. The two men picked up what gear they could carry and headed east. Silence was no longer important; speed was crucial. After more than an hour the sounds of pursuit trailed off, and Boomer and the marine lieutenant paused to look at the map. They were only a few miles from the 147th VNMC Brigade headquarters at Mai Loc.

Enemy artillery fire increased, but Boomer noticed that most of it was aimed at Mai Loc. The marines made their way over the hills as rounds whistled far overhead. At about 2:00 in the afternoon they came upon a small village about a mile northeast of Mai Loc. Major Boomer could scarcely believe the sight before him. Dozens of South Vietnamese marines—including the battalion commander—had managed to break out of the encirclement and made it to safety. Remnants of Bravo Group on Nui Ba Ho had also straggled in—including Captain Ray Smith. After the beating suffered by the marines on Nui Ba Ho, Boomer was sure his friend was dead.

Food was the first order of business. Boomer had not eaten in days, and he sat among the South Vietnamese marines and ate as much as his body could hold. In the distance, Mai Loc came under renewed attack as the North Vietnamese concentrated fierce fire on the base. It was like watching a play, thought Boomer. As the men ate in relative comfort, artillery crashed into Mai Loc. There was nothing to be done but just sit and watch.

The 147th VNMC Brigade headquarters in Mai Loc was clearly the next North Vietnamese target. Sarge, Nui Ba Ho, and Fuller, another firebase to the south, had all fallen. Only Mai Loc and Camp Carroll stood between the North Vietnamese and a clear shot toward the provincial capital of Quang Tri City near the coast.

Major Boomer got on the radio to Mai Loc to discuss the situation with the advisers there. Everyone agreed that Mai Loc would soon become untenable and that the best chance of survival lay in linking the tattered 4th VNMC Battalion with the brigade headquarters. Together they could withdraw to the east.

THREE

PIERCING THE RING OF STEEL

As North Vietnamese units were pushing the marines out of their positions along the western rim of the Ring of Steel, other forces were punching straight south over the demilitarized zone. Part of the 308th NVA Division pushed along the sandy coastal plains between the sea and Highway 1, and along the road itself. The rest of the division moved unopposed through the sparsely populated foothills and valleys to the Laotian border.

This part of the enemy offensive was completely unexpected, though U.S. intelligence agencies had squabbled over the possibility for months. Analysts at the DIA had cautiously predicted an invasion through the demilitarized zone, while the CIA downplayed the possibility.[1]

Even the South Vietnamese were surprised. General Lam, the I Corps commander, was well aware of the North Vietnamese troop concentration just north of the demilitarized zone, but he never expected that the communists would so blatantly flout the 1954 Geneva Accords by invading directly south. When asked what he would do if the North Vietnamese did thrust south over the demilitarized zone, Lam replied, "They cannot." His reply was not necessarily an arrogant one; he was simply responding based on past communist performance. He reasoned that Hanoi would repeat its standard tactic of coming around the demilitarized zone through Laos and then attack South Vietnam from the northwest.

American advisers did not disagree with Lam's assessment. The top American adviser in I Corps, Major General Frederick J. Kroesen, did not expect a full-fledged communist assault south over the demilitarized zone. Years later, Kroesen recalled, "I never gave it sufficient credibility to think that preparing for such an attack ought to be given the highest priority for defensive preparations. I did think that Giai and Lam both ought to be aware and alert and concerned at least secondarily about that kind of attack because we knew the North Vietnamese had armor up there."[2]

Division-level advisers also concurred with General Lam's opinion of North Vietnamese intentions. Colonel Raymond R. Battreall, an armor adviser and chief of staff with the U.S. Army Advisory Group at FRAC, studied intelligence papers, talked to advisers on the ground, and saw no reason to doubt the conventional wisdom. "Nobody seriously considered the idea that they might just drive across the demilitarized zone," he later recalled. "Perhaps this is another lesson in the folly of dealing with enemy intentions instead of enemy capabilities."[3]

The North Vietnamese certainly had the capability to push south, and that was precisely what they did. In concert with the traditional attack from across the Laotian border, communist troops smashed into the "Alpha group" of tiny firebases arranged in a loose arc just south of the demilitarized zone. The initial North Vietnamese thrust concentrated on the firebases along the northern perimeter. After the fateful troop rotation, most of the bases were within the 57th ARVN Regiment's new area of responsibility. But one in particular, Alpha 4, was staffed with marine advisers. Known as Con Thien—the so-called Hill of Angels—during the height of the U.S. Marine Corps' tenure in Vietnam, Alpha 4 took a beating from enemy artillery beginning just before noon on 30 March and lasting for more than twenty-four hours.

When the American advisers flew out of the beleaguered base during the bombardment, most of the 600 South Vietnamese defenders fled. Yet retreat was probably the only alternative because Alpha 4 was primarily a base for launching patrols along the demilitarized zone, not a key defensive point. It had no artillery, relying instead on a battery of 105mm howitzers at Charlie 2, about four miles to the south. The North Vietnamese seemed well aware of this because within minutes of the opening salvo their artillery destroyed all of Charlie 2's guns, leaving Alpha 4 virtually defenseless. One of the marine advisers commented after the battle that defense of Alpha 4 was hopeless from the beginning. "There was no way to stand up to what they were throwing at us," he said. "We had nothing firing back at their artillery batteries."[4]

But it was the northernmost base—Alpha 2—that was the main target for North Vietnamese gunners in the area. Sitting astride Highway 1 just north of the district capital of Gio Linh and about five miles south of the demilitarized zone, it was the 3d ARVN Division's most exposed and vulnerable outpost, and one of only two bases in the area containing artillery. The firebase was small, an elongated oval perimeter with its axis running north to south. Pointing defiantly at the demilitarized zone and the buildup of enemy forces, the northern end of Alpha 2 sat on a narrow hill, its steep sides adding a natural barrier to the man-made defenses. Inside rows of razor wire and sandbagged trench lines, the base was divided into four sections dominated by an old French watchtower. From the northern quarter of Alpha 2 sprouted the barrels of six 105mm howitzers positioned in an arc at the oval's top edge.

In the second sector, just behind the artillery, stood the watchtower, a concrete affair thrusting up about twenty-five feet into the air. Just behind it was a small helicopter landing pad. Part of the watchtower was below ground, a perfect place to wait out an artillery bombardment, but the main room was at ground level. Inside, a wooden stairway spiraled up to an exposed platform at the top of the tower that provided an unobstructed view in all directions. From this vantage point an observer could see for miles across an empty rolling plain covered with scruffy brush and grass. Once there had been a few trees, but artillery bombardments had long since reduced them to jagged stumps. To the north was the barren demilitarized zone; to the east in the distance rolled a low fringe of sand dunes along the shore of the Tonkin Gulf. A range of tree-clad mountains rose abruptly about ten miles to the west, and about seven miles to the south flowed the languid Cua Viet River.

A small garrison lived in the third sector. Two rows of about six sand-bagged Quonset huts separated by a narrow dirt road provided austere comfort for the soldiers. In the southernmost quadrant was the supply dump and motor pool. The base entrance was at the southernmost end.

A contingent of five U.S. Marines was stationed in Alpha 2 along with the South Vietnamese soldiers. They were not advisers but a spotter team with an Air and Naval Gunfire Liaison Company (ANGLICO) tasked with coordinating air support and naval gunfire from warships stationed off the coast. The commander of the small detachment, First Lieutenant David C. Bruggeman, had arrived in Alpha 2 with his men more than a week before.

The ANGLICO team was not pleased with its assignment to Alpha 2 because it had a reputation as one of the most poorly maintained firebases in northern I Corps. During a tour of firebases in the region in late January 1972, an evaluation team reported to FRAC that Alpha 2 "is in a pretty bad state of repair and provides inadequate protection to some of its inhabitants." Poor fields of fire made the bunkers all but useless, sandbags had been eroded, and the razor wire had been beaten down and overgrown with weeds. Nevertheless, Alpha 2 and the other northern firebases were integral to the 3d ARVN Division's Ring of Steel, so the advisers had no choice but to go.[5]

Like most of the rest of the northern perimeter, the regimental command at Alpha 2 was not yet settled in after the troop rotation of 30 March when the enemy struck. Chaos reigned, but the defenders of Alpha 2 remained in their positions. As the North Vietnamese bombardment heated up, however, the garrison retreated to the rear of the base, leaving the howitzers unmanned. By doing so, the South Vietnamese became nothing more than rats in a trap waiting for the inevitable North Vietnamese assault. Lieutenant Bruggeman knew it was time to evacuate his men. Under a rain of enemy artillery, he radioed his superiors at Ai Tu combat base and reported blandly that "the ARVNs were not responding favorably to the protracted shelling."[6]

With Alpha 2's artillery out of action without putting up much of a fight, survival remained in the hands of the small marine contingent. Bruggeman was on the radio constantly as he called for air support and naval gunfire. Heavy cloud cover and the demand for limited air assets all over northern I Corps made air strikes around Alpha 2 a rare treat. Bruggeman shifted most of his attention to calling for fire missions from American warships steaming off the coast. In the early hours of the offensive, only one U.S. Navy destroyer, the *Buchanan,* was close enough offshore to aid the beleaguered firebase. The ship quickly maneuvered into position and lent its five-inch guns to the defense of Alpha 2.

Knowing that North Vietnamese tactics were one-dimensional, Lieutenant Bruggeman feared the consequences of the inevitable enemy ground assault. When it came, the South Vietnamese would certainly not rise to the occasion and protect the Americans. They were on their own. By late afternoon the South Vietnamese had abandoned even the foxholes around the northern perimeter, leaving the northern approach to the firebase unguarded. The marines could see enemy soldiers creeping closer on three sides now. On the evening of 31 March, Bruggeman requested that he be allowed to evacuate Alpha 2.

Back at Ai Tu, ANGLICO Sub Unit One commander First Lieutenant Joel Eisenstein told Colonel Metcalf, the 3d ARVN Division senior adviser, that the position at Alpha 2 was untenable and that the time to evacuate was now. Metcalf did not agree with the assessment that Alpha 2 was in danger of being overrun, and he argued that the base was badly needed as eyes and ears for the crumbling division. The marines were to remain in place, ordered Metcalf.

Lieutenant Eisenstein probably would have ignored the order and evacuated the men, but all American helicopters in the area were under Team 155 command; Metcalf had to approve any mission. After a long night spent screaming, begging, and threatening the Team 155 staff, Eisenstein got tentative permission to plan an evacuation mission to Alpha 2 early on the morning of 1 April. But Metcalf ordered that the flight not be launched without his direct approval.

Armed with the order to prepare a rescue, Eisenstein went searching for a helicopter. None was available, so he went out to the airstrip and sat down to wait for the first chopper that appeared. One finally came in from a resupply run, and the pilots, warrant officers Ben Neilsen and Robert Sheridan, agreed to fly into Alpha 2, but only with Cobra gunship support.

While they waited for the gunships, Lieutenant Eisenstein planned the rescue. In a series of radio conversations he told Bruggeman to evacuate to the southern edge of the base when given the signal and wait there. Because all the secure radios had been destroyed, Eisenstein had to talk in the clear, so he did not tell Bruggeman which route the helicopters would take. There was little doubt that the North Vietnamese were diligently listening to everything said on the air.

Eisenstein sat idle, pacing nervously as he waited for the Cobras. They arrived within the hour. All the pilots were briefed on the mission, and although they were not familiar with the area that far north, they agreed to fly in. Their only protection would come from the warships offshore. A second destroyer, the *Joseph P. Strauss,* had joined the *Buchanan,* and all their guns would lay down suppressing fire north of Alpha 2. But they had to go in immediately. Sustained enemy shelling of Quang Tri threatened any helicopter that remained on the ground.

Colonel Metcalf was not in the bunker and could not be reached. He had left that morning with General Giai on a flight to some of the firebases for a damage survey. The advisory team executive officer was also nowhere to be found. Permission would have to come from somewhere else.

Eisenstein called his senior noncommissioned officer, Sergeant Swift, at Ai Tu combat base and told him he need the go-ahead for a rescue mission. "Get Colonel Turley's permission," he said. "We can't wait for Metcalf to return."

Lieutenant Colonel Gerald Turley was the senior marine adviser in northern Quang Tri Province, though his presence there was a fluke. Turley had flown into the area on an inspection tour on the eve of the offensive and found himself stuck there when the attack began. As artillery rained down to the north and west, Turley tried to learn all he could about the situation so he could be a help rather than a hindrance. When Eisenstein's impassioned call came in, Turley was standing right next to Sergeant Swift in the command bunker, though he was reluctant to give his permission. "Please colonel, let them go," pleaded Swift. "Lieutenant Bruggeman says he can see NVA troops all around Alpha 2."

Still, Turley hesitated. The base was under the operational control of the 57th ARVN Regiment and was part of the army's advisory chain of command. Besides, he was not even supposed to be there; an army adviser would be sent in soon to take his place. But marines needed to be rescued, and time was running out. "Tell them to launch," Turley finally said, and Sergeant Swift immediately relayed the order to Eisenstein.[7]

The three helicopters took off from Quang Tri and flew north. Lieutenant Eisenstein planned to approach Alpha 2 from the southeast, taking advantage of the gradually sloping ground. If the helicopters stayed low enough, the enemy would not see them until the last instant. The Cobras remained back a ways, ready to pounce if the lead slick got into trouble. Armed to the teeth with rockets and miniguns, the attack helicopters were a formidable threat to any North Vietnamese caught out in the open. The terrain around Alpha 2 was an ideal killing field for the hungry Cobras.

The plan went off without a hitch. As the rescue helicopter hugged the ground, Lieutenant Eisenstein set up the directional heading for the final run into the besieged base. The Cobras popped higher into the sky and carpeted the area to the north and northwest of Alpha 2 with rocket and minigun fire. Swarming back and forth across the base like menacing wasps, the gunships kept up the suppression fire. Behind the curtain of lead, the slick raced in toward the landing pad inside the base.

The North Vietnamese quickly sized up the situation and responded in force. Opening up with everything they had, the enemy gunners targeted the landing pad, hoping to hit the helicopter. Lieutenant Eisenstein recalled that "it appeared as if the entire base was covered with a tremendous amount of smoke."

The helicopter came on anyway. Flaring at the last second, the chopper slammed down hard on the dirt landing pad. Through the swirling dust and smoke, Eisenstein could see an American standing near the old French watchtower, furiously waving his arms. It turned out to be Sergeant Newton, one of the advisers.

Leaping from the chopper, Eisenstein and one crewman raced across the landing zone toward the tower. All was not well with the advisers. Sergeant Newton was trying to drag the motionless body of Lieutenant Bruggeman toward safety. Apparently, Bruggeman had been hit by a fragment just moments before as he waited for the helicopter to land. The marine lieutenant was obviously badly wounded; in fact, no one could be certain he was still alive. Eisenstein and the helicopter crewman grabbed Bruggeman and hauled him back to the waiting chopper, followed closely by three marines carrying as much gear as they could hold.

The firing mysteriously calmed down to almost nothing. Perhaps the enemy gunners had used up their immediate supply of ammunition, or maybe they were disoriented when the helicopter went out of sight behind the watchtower, but for a few precious minutes the Americans found themselves braving only scattered small-arms fire. Sensing that something was up, South Vietnamese soldiers began to poke their heads out of bunkers and foxholes. Seeing the helicopter, they swarmed toward the landing zone. They walked over the bodies of dead and badly wounded buddies, men left in the open when the attack had begun some twenty-four hours earlier.

The Americans were aboard the helicopter, but one marine was missing. "Where is Worth?" screamed Eisenstein over the roar of the rotors. Corporal James Worth, one of the ANGLICO team members, was nowhere to be found. Running back to the tower, Eisenstein looked quickly around, conscious that the lull in the North Vietnamese bombardment would not last forever. Over on one edge of the landing zone, a handful of South Vietnamese soldiers were suddenly mowed down by machine-gun fire. Eisenstein raced back to the helicopter.

Several soldiers had congregated near the helicopter, trying to get on before it left. Eisenstein threw a few badly wounded men aboard, then ordered the pilot into the sky. One South Vietnamese holding an M79 40mm grenade launcher clung to the skids as the chopper lifted off; Eisenstein slammed his foot into the soldier's chest, knocking him backward into the crowd gathering below. As the helicopter climbed higher, the soldier stared straight into Eisenstein's eyes. A single picture raced through the American's mind. "That son-of-a-bitch is gonna blow us out of the sky with that M79," he thought. "If he can't go, he's not gonna let anyone else go either." But the man did not fire, and the chopper swung out over the perimeter wire.

Artillery rounds again pounded Alpha 2 as the chopper took off. As it banked away from the firebase, Eisenstein saw a group of North Vietnamese soldiers circling around to the south just outside the wire. They must be trying to seal off any further escape, he thought. Inside the base, Eisenstein could still see South Vietnamese soldiers mounting trucks and trying to drive out the south gate. He wondered if any of them would make it. Then the helicopter dipped down over a low rise, and Alpha 2 was no more. Out of danger now, Eisenstein could not shake the image of the frantic soldier clutching his grenade launcher. He would never forget the look in that man's eyes.

Once safely beyond the range of North Vietnamese gunners, the pilot climbed a little higher off the deck. Below them on Highway 1, just north of the town of Dong Ha, the road was clogged with refugees fleeing the communist offensive. But Eisenstein could only be concerned with Lieutenant Bruggeman's condition, not the chaos below. Eisenstein cradled the marine's lifeless form. Blood and gray brain matter oozed down Eisenstein's arm, and he noticed that his hand was all that kept the back of Bruggeman's skull together. Eisenstein screamed to the pilot to radio ahead for a medevac.

They landed at Ai Tu rather than Quang Tri as originally planned, and a waiting navy corpsman helped lay Bruggeman onto a stretcher. But it was all to no avail. Lieutenant Bruggeman died on the medevac to Danang without ever regaining consciousness. Corporal James Worth, the marine left behind at Alpha 2, was never seen again and was listed as missing in action.

Silence hung like death over Alpha 2. For the North Vietnamese the fall of this tiny outpost, along with the other northern bases, was an early milestone, an easy victory to savor as they moved relentlessly south.

Local Viet Cong guerrillas had played a major role in the assault on Alpha 2, or Doc Mieu as the Vietnamese called it. They had harassed the defenders off and on over the past months; one time they had managed to erect a flag of the National Liberation Front (NLF—the Viet Cong) on the outer perimeter. An armored personnel carrier sent out to tear down the flag had struck a mine, and the infantry escort "showed a clean pair of heels" as they fled. The enemy banner remained in place for seventeen days.

Now Alpha 2 was just another graveyard for the men and machines of the South Vietnamese army. A communist soldier stopped to survey the ghostly scene. In the midst of the sandbagged clearing covered with the detritus of battle lay a helmet with a bullet hole pierced cleanly through the crown. "Look how accurately our bullets hit," exclaimed the soldier. "They've surely got eyes!"[8]

The fall of Alpha 2 was a disastrous blow to the northern half of the Ring of Steel. Realizing the seriousness of the situation, General Giai searched for a fallback strategy. His American adviser, Colonel Metcalf, recommended the South Vietnamese withdraw from the remaining firebases north of the Mieu Giang River. Up to this point the 57th ARVN Regiment was still holding out at a handful of other firebases, but it was clearly doomed. The troops had not been settled into their new positions following the rotation of 30 March, but even if they had been, it is unlikely they could have withstood the terrific pounding from North Vietnamese artillery. By the afternoon of 1 April, the northern face of the Ring of Steel was untenable.

General Giai had always regarded reliance on these bases as a futile defense against a concerted enemy attack, but I Corps policy had been fixed on contesting any territorial encroachment by the North Vietnamese. That meant pressing out as close to the borders as possible, even though the South Vietnamese army lacked the resources and manpower to adequately defend such an expanded perimeter. The events of the past two days showed just how unrealistic this strategy was. At 6:00 P.M. on 1 April, General Giai ordered the division to reorganize south of the natural barrier formed by the Cam Lo, Mieu Giang, and Cua Viet Rivers.[9]

The reasons behind the withdrawal were fourfold. First, given that the I Corps command had never anticipated an attack across the demilitarized zone, the northern firebases were not designed to be a main line of defense. Second, the regiment had a better chance of fending off the enemy if it was free to maneuver. Remaining inside the firebases left the South Vietnamese in a barbed wire cage. Third, a strategic withdrawal would give the division commanders more time to "clarify the situation." At this point, no one was quite sure about the enemy's main thrust: Was it from the north or the west? Fourth, General Giai "wanted to create a killing zone by withdrawing all friendly elements from the real estate between the demilitarized zone and the Cua Viet River."[10]

Unfortunately, the withdrawal coincided with the first rumors of North Vietnamese tanks moving south down Highway 1. Already demoralized by a lack of good radio communications, and by the sight of refugees streaming down the highway, the frightened soldiers began to break and run. General Giai correctly saw the situation as critical. Dashing to his helicopter, he flew to the town of Dong Ha. He strode into the middle of the bridge, grabbed one of the fleeing soldiers, and demanded to know why they were running.

"Tanks! Tanks!" stammered the frightened soldier. He was not sure which he should fear more, enemy tanks or his division commander.

Brimming with contempt, Giai let go of the man, straightened into his ramrod soldier's posture, and looked north across the bridge. "Show me a tank and I will go with you," he said, "and we will destroy it together."[11]

There were no tanks, but Giai's personal example of courage still had little effect. By nightfall on 1 April, all South Vietnamese bases north of the river had fallen, and the best that could be said of the "withdrawal" was that the South Vietnamese had temporarily slowed the enemy advance. On the positive side, the evacuation created a vast free-fire zone with nothing in it except for enemy soldiers. Flights of three B-52 bombers—called Arc Lights—were flown continuously, providing a curtain of protection for the South Vietnamese as they reformed south of the river.

As part of the division's reorganization, General Giai decided to move his headquarters out of range of the enemy's 130mm artillery to the city of

Quang Tri, about four miles southeast of the present command center at Ai Tu Combat Base. However, he still needed to maintain Ai Tu as a fire co-ordination center, staffed by American advisers. As the division senior adviser, Colonel Metcalf was responsible for organizing the move.

Metcalf stepped into the cluttered operations center just before 7:00 on the evening of 1 April. The operations adviser, Lieutenant Colonel Turley, was used to seeing the tall army colonel around the bunker—usually accompanying General Giai—but after more than forty-eight hours of fighting, he had spent less than thirty minutes actually talking with him. Turley recalled that Metcalf rarely said much, nor did he ever countermand an order issued from the command post. "Throughout this period he had given no tactical guidance to assist our U.S. advisory effort," recalled Turley. "Since the invasion began, no meetings of the U.S. advisers had been held, nor had any written operational summaries been prepared for higher U.S. headquarters."

Metcalf did not remain silent this time, however. He called Turley away from the hustle and bustle of advisers plotting map coordinates and talking into radios and told him that General Giai was moving the division headquarters back to Quang Tri City. The majority of the division advisory staff would go with him, but as the senior American at Ai Tu, Turley would remain in the tactical operations center and take charge of all supporting arms. This was a major responsibility, and Turley was "dumbfounded" by the magnitude of the order.

"Colonel, you can't split the division's G-3 operations and intelligence sections away from the U.S. supporting arms, air and naval gunfire, and still integrate these assets into the battle effectively," explained the surprised marine. Metcalf agreed that the task would be difficult, but he was adamant.

Turley again protested. "Sir, I can't do what you're asking. This is an ARVN and U.S. Army operation. I'm a marine. Christ, I'm just visiting up here. Until yesterday I thought FRAC was a misspelled word." Turley correctly pointed out that he was still unfamiliar with the division's defensive plans and that he did not even know the names of the army regimental senior advisers. After several more minutes of argument, Metcalf pulled rank, and the issue was settled. As he turned to leave, Metcalf took out a pack of cigarettes and put them in Turley's hand. "Good luck," he said, then walked out of the bunker. Turley didn't smoke.[12]

Making the best of an unusual situation, Turley took command of the forward base, calling in air strikes and naval gunfire against the advancing North Vietnamese. But if Metcalf had been lax in his leadership role before

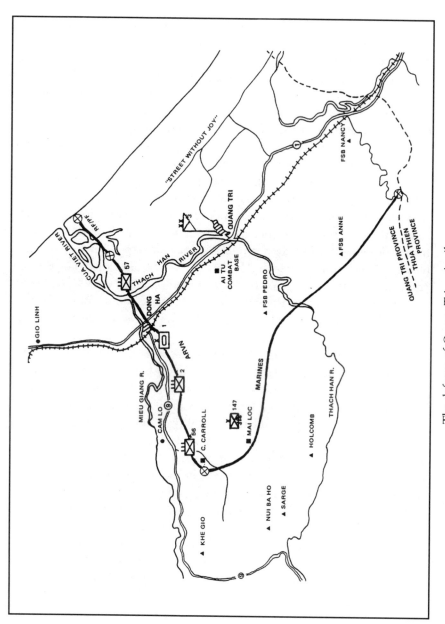

The defense of Quang Tri, 2 April 1972

the move, he was more so afterward. According to the operations log and other U.S. marine advisers, Turley received no "major guidance" from Metcalf and only limited communication from FRAC. Turley was also discouraged to find that when Team 155 went south with the 3d ARVN Division it abandoned twenty-two machine guns, three 81mm mortars, and several radios. Metcalf wrote them off as "combat losses," arguing that "these items could not be evacuated without seriously jeopardizing the lives of the personnel of Team 155." Yet according to Turley, no one at Ai Tu was in serious danger from the enemy during the first two days of the offensive.[13]

General Giai set up his new headquarters inside Quang Tri City's citadel, a fortress built by the French during the nineteenth century. From here, Giai took stock of his forces as the first day of April came to a close. The Regional Forces maintained defensive positions from the coastline to about three miles inland, while the 57th ARVN Regiment stood between the militia's left flank and Dong Ha on Highway 1. West from Dong Ha—the new perimeter's center—was given to the well-disciplined 2d ARVN Regiment.

While the units dug in along the new perimeter could count on the river to help slow the North Vietnamese assault from the north, the western approaches were completely exposed. From the edge of the 2d ARVN Regiment's area of operations, the defensive line curved southward to join the Vietnamese marines clinging to a handful of embattled firebases between the Cam Lo and Quang Tri Rivers. Nui Ba Ho and Sarge had fallen, leaving only Mai Loc, Holcomb, and Camp Carroll to stand against the onslaught. The entire area was the responsibility of the 56th ARVN Regiment and the 147th VNMC Brigade. Although the marines were considered a good unit, the 56th ARVN Regiment was not. General Giai found himself forced to rely on one of the worst units in the South Vietnamese army to hold one of the most crucial bases in northern I Corps, Camp Carroll, a major firebase housing the largest concentration of artillery north of Danang.

By nightfall on 1 April the situation in northern I Corps was critical. General Giai could still not discern whether the main thrust of the North Vietnamese offensive was from the north or the west. At Ai Tu Combat Base, Lieutenant Colonel Turley was convinced that enemy units poised just below the demilitarized zone were the spear point of the invasion. If he was correct, then the North Vietnamese would travel south along Highway 1, the only road capable of moving tanks and infantry at high speed. But any assault from the north would come up short against the Mieu Giang/Cua Viet River system unless the enemy could capture the one major crossing in the vicinity of Highway 1—the bridge at Dong Ha.

FOUR

THE BRIDGE
AT DONG HA

Easter Sunday brought no hope of resurrection for the faltering South Vietnamese. Survivors from the fallen firebases to the north and west converged on Ai Tu Combat Base, bringing with them dire reports of crumbling defenses and seemingly invincible enemy advances. Enemy artillery concentrated on the few remaining South Vietnamese strongholds, pounding them into ineffectiveness. Nor did relief come from the air. The low steel gray clouds and sputtering rains of the waning monsoon kept the fighter planes on the ground, bombs hanging uselessly from fully loaded pylons.

From his bunker at the beleaguered Ai Tu Combat Base, Lieutenant Colonel Turley could only watch as the North Vietnamese closed in, calling in B-52 strikes and coordinating naval gunfire from the ships offshore. But his responsibilities were about to become even more onerous. At 9:15 on Easter morning, Turley got a call from the newly established 3d ARVN Division headquarters at Quang Tri citadel. It was Colonel Metcalf, the division senior adviser, and his orders were succinct: "You are directed to take over as senior American adviser to the 3d ARVN Division, Forward, by order of the Commanding General, FRAC."[1]

The call was unexpected. Turley later remembered thinking that the world seemed to be falling apart. As he had dreaded since the previous day when the division had moved south, Turley was now officially in charge of coordinating all U.S. forces and advisers in northern Quang Tri Province. "How could this have happened to me?" he wondered.[2]

The answer to that question would have to wait because from north of the Mieu Giang River came the first reports of enemy armor on the move. Panicked calls from the battered 57th ARVN Regiment reported twenty T-54 and PT-76 tanks on Highway 1 north of the fallen Alpha 2 firebase. When asked if the regiment could hold the tanks north of the river, an adviser replied that it could not. That single short message suddenly focused all attention on the town of Dong Ha and its bridge, both of which were virtually undefended.

South of Dong Ha was the 3d VNMC Battalion, not much of a match for the reported regiment of North Vietnamese troops headed down Highway 1. But despite the danger, the battalion was not committed to defend the bridge. At Ai Tu Lieutenant Colonel Turley tried to point out the need to defend Dong Ha.

"Sir, you've got to act," Turley told Colonel Ngo Van Dinh, commander of the 258th VNMC Brigade. He pointed to Dong Ha on the map, noting the thickening cluster of grease pencil streaks that marked the approach of enemy units.

Dinh remained silent for several moments. Then he said simply, "I cannot."

Turley was dumbfounded. "Colonel, we're desperate! You've got to move the 3d Battalion around to the south side of the bridge. If you don't, we're going to lose the God-damned war!"[3]

Dinh told Turley what he already knew, which was that he was unwilling to make any move without approval from Saigon. Every adviser understood the politics within the South Vietnamese command structure, but with Dong Ha in danger, Turley had little patience for it. Still, Dinh would not commit his forces to defend Dong Ha without specific orders from the Marine Division commander in Saigon, Lieutenant General Le Nguyen Khang. Although the marines were under the operational control of the 3d ARVN Division, politics demanded that each service answer to its own chain of command despite orders from the division commander. It was this unwieldy command system, with its political overtones, that would ultimately cause the destruction of the South Vietnamese in northern I Corps.

Finally, Colonel Dinh got word to commit the 3d VNMC Battalion to Dong Ha. At around 10:00 in the morning the marines moved north, taking with them four jeep-mounted 106mm recoilless rifles, not much of a defense against enemy tanks. Dinh also sent orders to the battalion commander, Major Le Ba Binh, to hold Dong Ha at all costs.

The battalion took up positions south of the river and waited for the enemy. Sometime during the morning a North Vietnamese flag was raised on the old railroad trestle spanning the river a few hundred yards from the main bridge. Its appearance spooked the South Vietnamese and started a new spate of rumors, including one that the town had fallen. Upon hearing the report, Major Binh told his American adviser, Captain John W. Ripley, that he intended to stop the rumor. Word went out to both South Vietnamese and American radio nets that the town remained in friendly hands. "As long as one marine draws a breath of life," he said, "Dong Ha will belong to us."[4]

Captain Ripley approved of his counterpart's bravado. The credo of elite units demanded courage above and beyond the standard for ordinary sol-

Situated inside the Quang Tri Citadel, the 3d ARVN Division operations bunker was built to withstand heavy shelling. (Frank Brown)

diers, and Ripley's career was part of that tradition. He graduated from the U.S. Naval Academy in 1962 and went to Vietnam as a company commander in October 1966. During a battle in August 1967 he won the Silver Star, then returned to the States and later to duty with the Royal Marines in Great Britain. In July 1971 Ripley was back in Vietnam, this time as an adviser.

From a vantage point near the river, Ripley and Binh wondered how they could stop the North Vietnamese. Across the water they could see the scarlet, blue, and gold Viet Cong flag fluttering in the morning breeze like an omen of things to come.

"Tanks," said Ripley incredulously. "How many do you think? A platoon? A battalion?"

Major Binh had still not gotten over his surprise at hearing that enemy armor was headed his way. "Any more than five, we cannot handle," he replied. "We have only ten light anti-tank weapons. Ten rounds. My marines have never shot at tanks. They do not know how to attack them."[5]

Both men knew there would certainly be more than five tanks, but they would do their best to stop them. Binh ordered two rifle companies to deploy along the south bank and dig in. Another company would cover the main bridge, and the fourth would block a smaller bridge just upriver. This

French-built structure could not support tanks or heavy equipment, but infantry might try to cross there. Watching the men dig in, Ripley felt pride for these *soi bien*—wolves of the sea. They just might hold, he thought.

The defensive preparations were hampered by increasing numbers of refugees fleeing the battle, some of them over the bridge, others along Highway 9 from the west. Mixed in with the horde were soldiers—deserters—many of whom had shed their uniforms to blend in with the civilians, and most were unarmed. They walked silently, all pride and honor stripped away like their uniforms. As the refugee column shuffled south, Major Binh leaped into the road to confront the deserters.

"Linh di dau do?" Binh yelled at one soldier. Where are you going? There was no answer as the deserter kept walking. Binh grabbed him by the shirt, then drew his pistol and shot him in the head. But if the act was meant to deter other deserters from continuing their flight, it did not work. They passed by the angry marine officer standing defiantly over the dead soldier as if nothing had happened.[6]

At 11:00 the marines received some unexpected reinforcement from a unit of South Vietnamese army tanks. The 20th Tank Regiment (called, simply, 20th Tanks) arrived south of Dong Ha with orders from General Giai to hold the town and prepare for a counterattack north of the river. Actually only a battalion by American standards, the 20th Tanks was made up of M48A3 Sheridan medium tanks, some of the most modern in the U.S. armor arsenal. They used new long-range ammunition, sported powerful searchlights, and employed sophisticated ranging and sighting equipment.[7]

The formation of the 20th Tank Regiment was a reaction to the American drawdown. The last U.S. armor unit, the 1st Brigade of the 5th Mechanized Infantry Division, departed from South Vietnam in August 1971, leaving only three South Vietnamese armored cavalry squadrons in all of I Corps. Aware that this was a serious weakness, the Joint General Staff authorized the formation of the 20th Tank Regiment on 31 July 1971. Training was hampered by deficiencies in the armor maintenance program, which were exacerbated by the language barrier and a lack of technical understanding by South Vietnamese tankers.

Gunnery was also a problem. Well acquainted with the older M41 tank and its optical aiming system, South Vietnamese armor crews found it difficult to understand the M48's new range finder and ballistic computer. The best translation for the concept came out to something like "adding machine" in Vietnamese, an imprecise term at best. However, on 1 November a gunnery program straight out of the Fort Knox armor school got under way. By the end of January 1972, forty-one out of fifty-one tank crews qualified on a gunnery test using the same criteria as those used for U.S. units.[8]

Experiences gleaned from the South Vietnamese incursion into Laos in early 1971 were also used to refine the unit's organization. The most unusual aspect of the 20th Tanks was the addition of a 270-man armored rifle company. The South Vietnamese had learned in Laos that armored vehicles were vulnerable to antitank weapons when not protected by infantry. So when 20th Tanks went into combat, it would have ninety riflemen riding with each tank squadron.

From the beginning, U.S. advisers believed that forming the 20th Tanks was a wise decision. "It is becoming increasingly likely that we will meet the enemy's . . . tanks in battle," predicted Colonel Raymond Battreall, I Corps' senior armor adviser. "This is no cause for alarm: only for readiness."[9]

But the new unit was not quite ready. A final training exercise was scheduled for 13 March, but poor weather during the gunnery phase delayed the graduation exercise until 27 March. Three days later the exercise became the real thing, and 20th Tanks found itself facing the ultimate test—survival on the battlefield.

When the North Vietnamese opened the offensive on 30 March, the tankers were engaged in some last-minute training and maintenance. Just before noon, Armor Command headquarters received a frantic message from I Corps ordering the 20th Tanks to drop everything and return to Quang Tri. As Colonel Battreall recalled, "There was no explanation of what was going on here."[10]

The armor commander for I Corps, Major General Nguyen Van Toan, was unwilling to blindly commit his tanks without more information. Along with Colonel Battreall, Toan jumped into his helicopter and flew to Quang Tri for a talk with General Giai. Only then did Toan discover the extent of the enemy offensive and the precariousness of the South Vietnamese defenses. Uncertain of where the main enemy thrust would come from, and thoroughly unskilled in armor tactics, Giai wanted to piecemeal the 20th Tanks to positions scattered around the battlefield. Toan persuaded Giai that such a move would be unwise and premature; it would be better to hold the unit together and keep it as a division reserve, to be committed as a powerful counterattack when enemy intentions were more clear.

Working day and night for the next three days, 20th Tanks launched a new maintenance program, stocked up on spare parts and ammunition, and gave last-minute briefings. Major James E. Smock, the senior adviser to the 20th Tanks, provided the unit with everything it needed, from spare parts to gunnery tips. On the morning of 2 April, however, it was clear that the crash course could not continue. North Vietnamese artillery was shelling Quang Tri City, and the officers worried that their tanks might be destroyed inside the division compound without firing a shot. Colonel Battreall suggested to Giai that 20th Tanks should be sent out into the countryside, where it could rely on its mobility to survive. Giai agreed and ordered the unit north to the high ground south of the Mieu Giang River near Dong Ha at the intersection of Highways 1 and 9. Amid growling engines and twisting treads, Colonel Battreall saluted the tanks as they dashed through the perimeter gate toward Dong Ha. There were forty-four M48A3 tanks in all, ten fewer than the full-strength complement.

The armor column reached Dong Ha and the marine defenders with no opposition, though enemy infantry had already taken up positions on the northern side of the river. Lieutenant Colonel Nguyen Huu Ly, commander of the 20th Tanks, decided to organize his defense along both major roads. The 3d Squadron settled in along Highway 1 just south of the Dong Ha Bridge, with the 2d Squadron as a reserve just to the southwest. The 1st Squadron was sent down Highway 9 to watch for an enemy advance from the west. Although the squadron did not know it, the North Vietnamese had set up an ambush along Highway 9 in anticipation of just such a move. But rather than follow the road to their position, the tanks moved along a ridgeline, skirting the highway and bypassing the enemy. The armored column came in behind the North Vietnamese, and, according to Colonel Battreall, "they eliminated that ambush and got a good body count out of it." There were also prisoners, some of them from the 203d NVA Tank Regiment, who told their captors that they had been sent in dismounted with the mission of capturing South Vietnamese armor and using it as their own.[11]

Sometime before noon the North Vietnamese tried to cross the river. Infantry from the 36th NVA Regiment dashed over the old railroad bridge, and soon the enemy had a foothold on the south side of the river. Captain Ripley called for naval gunfire support to stop the enemy advance, and within minutes rounds from the destroyers *Buchanan, Waddell, Hamner,* and *Anderson* whistled overhead. For over an hour the ships shelled both approaches to the bridge, keeping the North Vietnamese pinned down and destroying several trucks.

But not all the enemy were dying under the canopy of naval gunfire. Ripley spotted four PT-76 tanks skirting the riverbank east of Dong Ha and called in another salvo from the destroyers. All four tanks were destroyed while Ripley and his counterpart watched from a patch of high ground south of the river. "We could see them burning clearly," he later recalled.

"When the tanks were hit and burning [we] both were surprised and elated in seeing the potential of naval gunfire."[12]

Their elation did not last long. A few miles to the north, behind the series of low hills rolling toward the demilitarized zone, were the telltale clouds of dust marking the progress of another armored column. Again, luck was with the South Vietnamese. As the enemy tanks trundled south, the sky cleared enough to allow aircraft to enter the battle. A flight of A-1 Skyraiders, World War II–vintage propeller-driven planes armed with a bewildering array of bombs, bullets, and rockets, appeared overhead. Diving through an opening in the clouds, they pounced on the enemy tanks, strafing and bombing the fast-moving column. The South Vietnamese pilots reported eleven tanks destroyed.

One Skyraider was shot down. As the wounded plane spiraled toward the ground, the pilot bailed out. Firing tapered off as both sides paused to watch the parachute blossom in the sky, then billow with the morning breeze. The marines held their breath and waited to see on which side of the river the unfortunate pilot would land: the fickle winds carried him north to certain capture.

Watching the Skyraiders swooping on their prey in the distance, Lieutenant Colonel Ly knew that many of the enemy would manage to get through to the bridge. He ordered his 1st Squadron—still in position along Highway 9—to move east and intercept those who did escape the aerial attack. The squadron had just taken up position in the scrub-covered hills nearer to Dong Ha when the North Vietnamese came into view on the north side of the river. Roaring along the road in single file, hatches open, the tanks were clearly not expecting any opposition. When 1st Squadron opened fire, the enemy was still between 2,800 and 3,200 yards away—extreme range for the M48A3s' guns. But in the first salvo the South Vietnamese managed to destroy nine PT-76s and two T-54s.[13]

Confusion reigned among the North Vietnamese. Unable to see what was firing at them, the enemy tanks milled, then scattered, retreating back north without firing a shot. While monitoring North Vietnamese radio communications during the one-sided shooting match, an officer from the 20th Tanks reported that the enemy tank commander was dumbfounded by the attack. "He knew he was receiving direct fire from a high-velocity weapon," recalled Colonel Battreall, "but couldn't comprehend where the fire was coming from, because of the long range." Battreall was proud of the 20th Tanks' performance, later noting that "that kind of gunnery is on a par with the Israelis in the Sinai [in 1973] and probably better than all but the very finest of U.S. tank units could accomplish."[14]

Other North Vietnamese tanks were on the way, however. A squadron appeared at the north end of the bridge fifteen minutes past noon, then paused as if waiting for orders. As the South Vietnamese moved to react, the lead tank edged onto the roadway and cautiously began to cross the river.

At the other end of the bridge was a squad of marines led by Sergeant Huynh Van Luom. In each hand he held an M72 light antitank weapon (LAW), a single-shot, disposable rocket launcher designed as an infantryman's best defense against armor. Whether or not it would work against the heavily armored T-54 was still an unanswered question, but Sergeant Luom was betting his life that it would. As the forty-ton tank clanked across the bridge, he lay one LAW beside him, put the other to his shoulder, and aimed over the top of the tube.

The tank stopped. Perhaps the commander suspected a trap, or maybe he simply felt vulnerable on the bridge. In that moment of stillness Luom fired, but the round went high over the tank's chassis. The second rocket did not miss. It slammed into the T-54's frontal armor with a metallic thud, then ricocheted into the turret ring and exploded, jamming the turret with its barrel cocked uselessly to one side. Not a fatal hit, but the tank was clearly wounded. It backed off the bridge while the marines cheered Sergeant Luom's success. Captain Ripley, calling the incident "the bravest single act of heroism I've ever heard of, witnessed, or experienced," credited Luom with stopping the momentum of the entire enemy attack.[15]

Apparently the North Vietnamese decided that Dong Ha was too well defended to risk another attack because what was left of their armored column backed off the road, turned west, and headed along the river toward the town of Cam Lo some eight miles distant. There was another bridge there, one closer to the main axis of the enemy offensive, and it was largely undefended. At the time, it seemed as if the North Vietnamese hoped to rush straight down Highway 1, over the Dong Ha Bridge, and into Quang Tri City.

Certainly many American advisers believed that Highway 1 and the Dong Ha Bridge were the main objectives of the offensive. Colonel Battreall would later argue that the North Vietnamese placed most of their emphasis on Dong Ha. In his opinion, "The enemy was making a high-speed approach with his armor column, with the clear intention of going hi diddle diddle, right down the middle, all the way to Quang Tri." Lieutenant Colonel Turley stated in his account that the events leading up to the morning of 2 April "had the effect of now focusing all the enemy's effort—the entire invasion—on capturing Dong Ha with its strategic bridge."[16]

But the enemy was presumably clever enough to realize that they could not base their entire strategy on successfully capturing the bridge before it was reinforced or destroyed. When they met stiff resistance, the enemy simply broke away and looked for an easier target. Indeed, the North Vietnamese order of battle during the opening days of the offensive showed a preponderance of units—including armor—arrayed from the west, not the north. The reason was simple. After more than a decade of conflict, North Vietnamese infiltration and resupply lines emptied into South Vietnam via the Ho Chi Minh Trail through Laos. Fuel lines for tanks and trucks were in Laos and the Ba Long Valley, not the demilitarized zone, making an all-out attack from the north impractical. Also, ammunition stockpiles were in Laos. Because of this logistical line, it seems likely that the enemy thrust from the north was a secondary front, a left jab to divert attention from the right hook coming from the west.

Not that the North Vietnamese would not have liked to capture Dong Ha. The town itself was unimportant, but the bridge was the key to all movement along Highway 1 from the Mieu Giang River south to Quang Tri City. Unlike most of the other bridges along the river, the one at Dong Ha could easily support even the heaviest tanks. American Navy Seabees had built the bridge in 1967 to handle the influx of heavy weapons and equipment moving north from Saigon to the embattled provinces in I Corps. But now, four days into the Easter Offensive, everything north of the river was in enemy hands, and the bridge had suddenly become a liability.

Demolishing the bridge seemed to be the best solution. The enemy armor would be contained north of the river, giving the South Vietnamese more time to build a defense. But without the bridge the South Vietnamese would lose any chance to launch a counteroffensive. Lieutenant Colonel Ly, the aggressive commander of the 20th Tanks, proposed immediately sending one tank troop and one company from the 3d VNMC Battalion over the bridge to establish a foothold on the north side of the river in preparation for a counterattack. General Giai agreed with the plan in principle but balked at actually ordering the move. Instead, he ordered the 1st Armored Brigade north to assume command of all forces around Dong Ha.[17]

The 1st Armored Brigade was really little more than a headquarters unit equipped with sophisticated communications gear—a mobile armored command post—which was used to coordinate the organic armor units in northern I Corps. In addition, General Giai gave the 1st Armored Brigade operational control over most of the units north of Quang Tri City, including the marines, a conglomeration of ranger units, a 155mm artillery battery, and what was left of the 3d ARVN Division's three infantry regiments.

Although this seemed like an unwieldy command structure, Colonel Nguyen Trong Luat, the armored brigade commander, was glad to have the job. For three days Luat had begged Giai to use his tanks, but the general had insisted on keeping them in reserve until he could better discern the enemy's intentions. Finally, just before noon, Giai called Luat to his headquarters in the Quang Tri City citadel. Colonel Battreall and the brigade senior adviser, Lieutenant Colonel Louis C. Wagner, went along.

Giai paced the floor of the command bunker. Colonel Battreall recalled that the general was "very agitated, frustrated by the lack of control and lack of communications." Colonel Luat pointed out that the armored brigade had precisely the capabilities that the division lacked. After several minutes of deliberation, Giai agreed and ordered Luat to "establish a defensive position south of the Mieu Giang River in the vicinity of Dong Ha." The lead elements of the brigade left the base at La Vang just before 2:30 in the afternoon, but because of the heavy flow of refugees streaming down Highway 1, the main column took almost two hours to cover the eight miles to Dong Ha.

However, at Dong Ha there was still no decision on whether to blow the bridge. While the South Vietnamese dithered, events were taking on a life of their own. Throughout the morning of 2 April, commands flashed back and forth to the advisers—blow the bridge, hold the bridge, prepare the way for the 20th Tanks to cross to the north side. No one seemed to know what to do. The picture was no clearer at FRAC headquarters, where General Kroesen only knew that the Dong Ha Bridge was still standing as of 10:00 in the morning. Although information available to the South Vietnamese I Corps command staff was limited, someone—perhaps General Lam himself—ordered the 3d ARVN Division to at least get ready to blow the bridge. Several hundred pounds of explosives were hauled down to the base by engineers from the 57th ARVN Regiment, but they did not rig the bridge for demolition. Kroesen noted in his daily journal that "friendly elements are preparing to destroy the bridge."[18]

What happened next is to this day unclear. Following the tentative North Vietnamese attempt to push armor over the bridge, the two Americans at Dong Ha, Major Smock and Captain Ripley, looked to Ai Tu for some sort of decision, but their superiors were silent. Both records and the recollections of participants are vague about when and how the decision was made to demolish the bridge, though one thing is apparent. Sometime after noon, Smock radioed Lieutenant Colonel Turley at Ai Tu (some accounts say Ripley made the call, but since Smock was the senior officer, it seems likely that Turley was in touch mostly with him) and asked for permission to blow the bridge.

Captured North Vietnamese T-54 tank on the plains south of Dong Ha. The communists' poor use of armor cost them dozens of tanks during the offensive. (U.S. Army)

"I asked permission to move forward with U.S. advisers and destroy the bridge," reported Smock. According to an after-action report submitted by Smock, Turley replied: "Smock, I can't give you that kind of approval, but the bridge must be destroyed." Smock justified his request by saying, "I was confident that destruction of the bridge and retention of our present positions would probably slow or stop their advance until reinforcements arrived."[19]

After an ill-planned attempt to knock down the bridge by firing the M48 tanks' main guns at the massive struts failed completely, Smock asked for volunteers to set charges under the structure, but none of the South Vietnamese soldiers wanted to go along. Even Lieutenant Colonel Ly, the armor commander, was reluctant to move because he had received no word from his superiors. As Smock sarcastically pointed out, "Once more ARVN was experiencing difficulty acquiring . . . approval." Only Captain Ripley volunteered to go along.[20]

Beneath the bridge were the South Vietnamese engineers and 500 pounds of dynamite and plastic explosives. When the Americans arrived, they found the South Vietnamese scared half to death and totally incapable of setting the charges. Ripley recalled that "no humans . . . ever looked more hopeless or helpless."[21]

Because Ripley had experience with demolitions, he placed the charges and set the detonators while Smock handed up the boxes of explosives. Carrying the boxes one by one, Ripley crawled hand over hand along the underside of the bridge, placing the explosives along the supporting I beams. Smock stayed at the fence, muscling the fifty-pound boxes into position. Occasionally North Vietnamese infantry on the north side of the river would fire at the furtive figures, but the steel I beams and concrete pylons provided effective cover.

After about two hours the explosives were in place. "I could no longer care what happened," said Smock, "so I sat down and had a cigarette amid those demolitions while John Ripley just sighed relief and relaxed in place on the steel girders."[22]

But the explosives failed to detonate, and the bridge remained in place. As Ripley later observed, "For some reason the doggone thing didn't work." Before either Ripley or Smock could do anything about the problem, yet another contradictory order came down the chain of command: the bridge was not to be destroyed. The word came with the arrival of the 1st Armored Brigade, which pulled into Dong Ha sometime around 4:00 in the afternoon. General Giai was again entertaining the idea of establishing a bridgehead north of the river. If the South Vietnamese tanks had actually moved across the bridge at that moment, they would have encountered little resistance from the enemy. When the 1st Armored Brigade arrived, Lieutenant Colonel Wagner, the senior adviser, noted that "the only action at this time was sporadic small arms and mortar fire." Most significantly, there were no North Vietnamese tanks in the area.[23]

The confusion presented Lieutenant Colonel Wagner with a serious problem. Although the bridge had not yet blown, the faulty explosives packed under the bridge made it impossible to send the South Vietnamese tanks over to the north side of the river. Wagner and a small group of American advisers—including Ripley and Colonel Battreall—held an informal conference near the bridge to decide what to do. Jets thundered in the sky above, but Wagner paid little attention.

Suddenly the bridge was torn apart by a huge explosion. Colonel Battreall recalled that "a horrendous damn shrieking, swishing sound came down out of the overcast, and the bridge went sky-high." The blast caught the advisers by surprise, but it soon became clear that the jets screaming unseen in the dense cloud cover had bombed the bridge and set off the explosives placed by Ripley and Smock. Aerial photos taken immediately after the bombing showed a string of smoking craters along the length of the bridge—not enough to collapse the structure, but more than enough to make it impassable to tanks.[24]

The airstrike that blew the bridge was a Combat Skyspot, a high-tech method of delivering bombs using laser beams. Strike aircraft equipped with special radar beacons received vectors from an air control center in Danang to a precomputed release point, then dropped their bombs on command from the radar center. The Skyspot was called in during the early afternoon, though no one could remember by whom. In his report, Lieutenant Colonel Wagner noted, "Aircraft began bombing north of the river. . . . Demolitions on the bridge exploded at this time, dropping a span on the south side of the bridge. The explosion appeared to be a sympathetic detonation, although it could not be verified whether friendly personnel had blown it deliberately or not."[25]

Either way, the Dong Ha Bridge was down, and the threat of North Vietnamese armor streaming south on Highway 1 was no longer a factor. But as Wagner had observed several hours earlier, the enemy had already abandoned its meager effort to cross the bridge, concentrating instead on the western approach. Topography forced the North Vietnamese to bypass the natural barrier created by the Mieu Giang River, an easy task that Hanoi's troops had been doing since the beginning of the war by attacking from the Laotian border to the west. The Easter Offensive was no different. By the afternoon of 2 April there were very few enemy troops to be found anywhere near Dong Ha.[26]

As the drama at the Dong Ha Bridge was coming to a close, two other events were unfolding, both of which added to the mounting confusion. Just north of Cam Lo, an EB-66 radar surveillance plane was shot down by one of the first North Vietnamese SA-2 surface-to-air missiles fired from inside South Vietnam. Only Lieutenant Colonel Iceal Hambleton, the plane's navigator, managed to bail out, and for the next twelve days "Bat-21 Bravo"—Hambleton's radio call sign—was the subject of a massive air and ground rescue effort. During that time the U.S. Air Force lost two rescue helicopters and several observation aircraft before enlisting a special operations team made up of South Vietnamese naval commandos and a U.S. Navy SEAL (an acronym for sea, air, and land, the navy's special operations component).[27]

But from the perspective of the 3d ARVN Division and its losing battle in northern I Corps, the most damaging aspect of the Bat-21 incident was the imposition of a no-bombing zone around the downed airman by the

U.S. Air Force. For most of the twelve-day period of the rescue, B-52s and tactical aircraft were forbidden from flying air support missions against the North Vietnamese, who were concentrating their forces in the area south and west of the Cam Lo River. Even the artillery and naval gunfire missions were called off, a decision that exasperated advisers on the ground. General Kroesen angrily observed that giving the air force absolute fire control "was a peacetime system imposed on a wartime situation for which it was totally anachronistic." Lieutenant Colonel Turley was more sarcastic when he noted that the "unilateral rear area arrangement of giving the USAF control of all TAC air, naval gunfire and artillery fire probably seemed like a rational decision to officers eighty kilometers from the battle lines. However, it was a tragic decision for the 3d ARVN Division."[28]

Initially the no-fly zone covered a seventeen-mile radius, virtually the entire 3d ARVN Division area of operations. It was later reduced to 2,700 yards, but during the first ten days of April the South Vietnamese were unable to fire artillery or request tactical air strikes in the area. Even after Bat-21's rescue on 14 April, the no-fly zone was maintained for a few days because, according to the air force, the North Vietnamese might be lured into concentrating their forces in the exclusion zone, creating a "lucrative" bombing target. But Major David Brookbank, the U.S. Air Force liaison officer on the ground with the 3d ARVN Division forward command post at Ai Tu, reported that "this trap by deception to my knowledge was never exploited by Arc Light bombing."[29]

The U.S. Air Force understandably placed the highest priority on rescuing downed air crews, but in this case the policy was flawed. The bottom line was that the air force placed the life of Bat-21 above the survival of the 3d ARVN Division and the U.S. army and marine advisers on the ground. In the grand scope of the offensive in northern I Corps, it is unlikely that the imposition of an exclusion zone tilted the balance in favor of the enemy—it was already going badly. But, as Major Brookbank pointed out, the exclusion zone gave the North Vietnamese "an opportunity unprecedented in the annals of warfare to advance at will."[30]

It was this steady enemy advance that prompted the second incident following the action at Dong Ha. Lieutenant Colonel Turley, feeling increasingly exposed in the 3d ARVN Division forward base at Ai Tu, sent a message to the navy destroyer squadron sitting offshore apparently requesting a landing by U.S. Marines to tip the balance against the enemy. Copies of the message circulated through the naval chain of command, then up to FRAC, and finally to MACV, where the senior marine representative, Brigadier General William H. Lanagan, saw the message. Clearly this was a politically unwise request during the continuing American withdrawal, despite the seriousness of the situation, and Lanagan thought Turley "had gone crazy." MACV wanted to know "who the hell was Turley," since he was not part of the regular U.S. Marine advisory team, and ordered him to Saigon to explain his actions. Only then did MACV discover that Turley had been placed in charge of the 3d ARVN Division advisers at Ai Tu. After the situation was cleared up, Turley went back to the battlefront and then to Danang, where he became the FRAC operations officer.

Meanwhile, the North Vietnamese pushed on. During the afternoon of 2 April, attention turned toward the major base in northern Quang Tri Province—Camp Carroll. Perched less than a mile south of Highway 9, this potent firebase was in deep trouble. More than any other South Vietnamese position—even the bridge at Dong Ha—Camp Carroll was the strategic keystone for both sides. For the South Vietnamese, its large artillery component was crucial; the biggest guns were capable of firing at ranges up to twenty miles. For the enemy, Camp Carroll was the strongest obstacle standing in the way of its push from the west. With Camp Carroll out of the way, Highway 9 was open for the taking, as was the flat expanse of sparsely populated plain stretching all the way to Highway 1. Camp Carroll was the doorway to Quang Tri City.

FIVE

SURRENDER AT CAMP CARROLL

The North Vietnamese made no secret of the fact that they intended to take Camp Carroll. An entire artillery regiment, along with supporting infantry, had made the initial thrust from the west, easily overrunning Firebase Khe Gio and pressing ahead of the units assigned to capture Nui Ba Ho and Sarge. Some of the earliest shots fired during the opening hours of the Easter Offensive on 30 March were aimed at Camp Carroll.

For the South Vietnamese, the bombardment instilled fear and chaos. Disorganized masses of troops from the 56th ARVN Regiment rushed for the relative safety of Camp Carroll, making a mockery of the troop rotation begun around noon. An hour later about 1,800 soldiers poured into the base; the rest of the regiment fled to parts unknown. In the midst of chaos, Lieutenant Colonel Pham Van Dinh, the regimental commander, tried hard to contact his battalion commanders, but few answered over the radio.

Lieutenant Colonel Dinh had once been a hero in the South Vietnamese army. During the 1968 Tet Offensive he earned the sobriquet "Young Lion" when he personally placed South Vietnam's colors back atop the citadel in Hue after his unit helped wrest the ancient city back from the North Vietnamese. But glowing praise and a hero's reputation seemed to have corroded Dinh's leadership abilities. Once a trim fighter in an immaculate uniform, by 1972 he had become a pudgy man, more politician than soldier, putting his efforts into playing the intricate power games of the I Corps command system rather than attending to the war. Military affairs were left to his executive officer, the xenophobic Lieutenant Colonel Vinh Phong, a man known for his dislike of American advisers.

Lieutenant Colonel William Camper was the senior American (there were only two) assigned to the 56th ARVN Regiment. Camper was not thrilled at being stuck in a tough spot with a unit not known for its bravery and competence. But Camper was probably the most experienced combat adviser on Advisory Team 155. He had first served with the 2d ARVN Regiment in 1964 and 1965. Back in Vietnam in 1972, he was again assigned to his old unit, but the division senior adviser decided that the newly formed 56th ARVN Regiment was more in need of an adviser than the veteran 2d ARVN Regiment. So Camper found himself with a green unit caught flat-footed in the middle of an artillery bombardment, sitting on the most crucial piece of real estate in western Quang Tri Province.

For two days he had sweated it out, enduring a constant bombardment that damaged most of the radio equipment and all the generators. Camper had a backpack radio that allowed him to talk with his superiors at the Team 155 command bunker, but even that was inconsistent because artillery rounds shredded his outside antenna on a regular basis. A low curtain of dense clouds kept most of the fighter planes or helicopter gunships on the ground back in Danang. Air support was limited to B-52s, but there were not enough of the big bombers to go around. To make matters worse, since there were no American advisers at the battalion level, Camper had no clear idea of the 56th ARVN Regiment's overall condition. Could the soldiers stand up to a concerted infantry assault? Would they even try?[1]

Defensively, Camp Carroll was a formidable stronghold. Situated in the low foothills hugging the eastern slopes of the Annamite mountains, the firebase controlled the terrain for fifteen miles in all directions. Behind a ring of heavy timbers, sandbags, and rolls of razor wire squatted a network of reinforced bunkers and one of the most awesome arrays of artillery in all of I Corps. A battery of 175mm howitzers—one of the biggest field artillery pieces in the world—had been left by the last elements of the 101st Airborne Division when it left in early March 1972. In all, Camp Carroll boasted twenty-two artillery pieces, including 155mm and 105mm batteries, plus scores of heavy machine guns and small-arms positions. Camp Carroll was clearly the best hope for a strong stand on Quang Tri Province's northwestern front, so it came as no surprise when General Giai ordered the 56th ARVN Regiment to hold at all costs.

Camper was more concerned about the fate of his deputy adviser than about General Giai's orders. Major Joseph Brown, the only other American assigned to the regiment, had been with the supply column during the opening salvo on 30 March and had not been seen since. Late at night on 1 April, Camper got good news: Major Brown and part of the supply train had managed to evade North Vietnamese units and enter Camp Carroll from the east. The tattered remnants of a battalion that had been overrun at Khe Gio Firebase earlier in the day also wandered in. Khe Gio was one of the first defensive positions to fall in the gathering storm of North Vietnamese divisions to the west. Though there was little to celebrate, the two advisers settled down in their dank bunker lit only by a sputtering candle, opened a pair of warm Cokes—one of the few luxuries left in the camp—and pondered the future.

At dawn the next day—Easter Sunday—the pressure increased. Infantry probes from the north and west suddenly merged into three all-out assaults as the 24th NVA Regiment hurled itself at Camp Carroll. But the enemy found that the base was not as easy to crack as the tiny firebases they had so easily trampled in the preceding two days, and by noon the attacks had died down.

"Happy Easter," said Major Brown dryly during a lull in the fighting. Over cups of warm C ration coffee the two officers toasted the holy day as three 130mm artillery rounds crashed into the compound. Between artillery rounds, the advisers decided to check the perimeter. Camper and Brown shrugged into their flak jackets and stepped outside. A light drizzle cloaked the base, shrouding the silent South Vietnamese artillery positions in a ghostly gray pall. Nothing moved; whatever South Vietnamese soldiers were manning the perimeter had dug in as deep as they could, hoping to escape the artillery and the rain. The advisers scurried from bunker to bunker, pausing to talk with the frightened soldiers and doing what they could to help out.

As they toured the perimeter, a forward air controller came up on the radio saying he had two air force fighters overhead; did Camp Carroll need them? Camper pondered the offer for a moment. The low clouds made tactical air support a rarity, but since the enemy had eased off somewhat, the jets could be put to better use at the battered firebases to the southwest, which were barely clinging to life. Camper thumbed his radio receiver: "Send them to someone who needs them more."

"Roger," replied the pilot, then the radio sputtered and went dead. The silence after a conversation with a forward air controller was always a little depressing, thought Camper. The disembodied voice on the radio seemed like a long-lost friend calling at a time of dire need. Without a doubt, the little planes were a lifeline between the vulnerable advisers on the ground and the awesome cudgel of American aerial firepower.

The advisers turned back to the South Vietnamese, many of whom were wounded, though none seriously. Brown knelt down to dress a dirty shoulder wound on one man as Camper attended to some shrapnel in the leg of another. Looking around, the two advisers noticed that there were no officers to be seen. "Have you seen any ARVN officers lately?" questioned Lieutenant Colonel Camper.

"Not since the last attack began. I wonder what they're up to. They haven't asked us for any help, which is sort of strange," replied Brown.

Turning to the wounded soldier, Camper asked, "Where is your *dai uy*, your captain?" The man only shrugged, then grimaced in pain as Camper tightened the dressing. He replied that he had not seen any of the company officers in two or three hours, not since the last round of fighting began.

Back at their bunker a few hours later, Camper was still perplexed by the mysterious disappearance of the South Vietnamese officers. Whatever the answer, it probably lay with Colonel Dinh over at the regimental command bunker. After a habitual pause at the bunker entrance to listen for incoming rounds, they sprinted across the open ground to the command bunker.

Standing in the covered entrance of the big regimental bunker was Lieutenant Colonel Vinh Phoy, Dinh's executive officer. Camper and Brown saluted, but Phoy ignored them. It was no secret that Camper and Phoy hated each other. Camper characterized their relationship as being "like matches and gasoline."

"We're looking for Colonel Dinh. Is he around?" asked Camper.

Lieutenant Colonel Phoy did not answer for a second, letting his disdain for the foreigners show clearly. When he finally spoke, his words were short and crisp: "The colonel is in a staff meeting."

Camper and Brown glanced at each other. Advisers were supposed to be present at staff meetings. They moved for the door, but Phoy blocked the way. "The colonel does not wish to be disturbed," he said.

The Americans knew further argument was futile, so they turned to go back to their bunker. In an attempt to remain polite, Camper looked back over his shoulder as they left and told the arrogant executive officer, "I'll check back later."

At about noon the desultory bombardment ceased altogether, leaving the South Vietnamese to wonder what was next. At 2:00 P.M. Colonel Dinh emerged from the command bunker and strolled over to see Camper and Brown. The advisers saw him coming and went out to greet him; Camper could see that Dinh looked grave, so the news had to be bad.

The two Americans saluted smartly. Dinh wasted no time getting what was on his mind out in the open. "Everyone refuses to fight," he said softly, gazing down at his feet. "I tried to bolster their spirit, but they want to surrender."

Camper was shocked. Even in his wildest nightmares, he never imagined anything like this. It was a disaster. He tried to reason with the demoralized commander, to tell him that together they could talk the officers into fighting, but Dinh just shook his head. "No one will fight. I shot one man to persuade the others to fight, but they will not. I have been in touch with the National Liberation Front forces and they have promised to treat my men well. This is the only way to prevent more death." Almost as an afterthought Dinh said, "Do you want to surrender with us?"

"No," was all Lieutenant Colonel Camper could say. This explained the sudden halt in the enemy artillery bombardment, he thought. He wanted to kill this coward standing before him. Although Dinh insisted that he had tried to get his men to fight, the American doubted it. Hell, it was probably his idea to surrender, thought Camper.

Dinh offered the Americans another option. "You and Major Brown can hide among the troops as they go out the gate to surrender," he said. "Once outside the gate you can fall into the tall grass and crawl away." Dinh was trying to show his counterpart that he was not panicking, that the decision to surrender had been reached rationally. After all, thought Dinh, General Giai had left him no choice but surrender. He had ordered the decimated regiment to hold at all costs, even though there was no possibility of reinforcement.

Camper shook his head. No, that was not acceptable. He and Brown would find some way out of the camp on their own. Then Colonel Dinh made an even more ridiculous offer. "If it will save face, we can commit suicide together," he offered.

Camper was repelled by the thought. "Americans don't do that," he replied. Quickly changing the subject, Camper pointed out that there were still a few operational light tanks in camp, two of them mounted with fast-firing 40mm guns—called Dusters—that could be used to spearhead a break-out. Perhaps they could link up with the defenders at Mai Loc just to the south. An element of South Vietnamese marines and their American advisers were still there, at this time relatively untouched by the North Vietnamese.

Dinh shook his head. "It will not work," he muttered.

Camper was furious, but he could not show it now. Rage contributed nothing to the situation; all that mattered was getting out of Camp Carroll. He and Major Brown were on their own. "Colonel, we wish you luck," Camper said as he prepared to leave. "Major Brown and I will take care of ourselves from this moment on. We can no longer advise you, and you no longer have any responsibility to us. You must do what you think is best and we will do the same."

Dinh nodded in understanding. He had one request, however. "Please do not tell General Giai that I am surrendering," he implored.

What an infuriating group of people, thought Camper. They were so fatalistic that they would rather surrender than fight, but they still regarded saving face as paramount. He felt the anger welling up again and had to consciously stop himself from bringing his rifle in line with the coward's chest and pulling the trigger. But even if the other South Vietnamese officers did not kill him for such a rash act, he still would have accomplished nothing because Lieutenant Colonel Vinh would carry through with the surrender anyway.

"I'm not concerned about General Giai. All I care about is us." Camper gestured toward Major Brown as he spoke. "I will call my senior officer and notify him of what is happening."

Dinh nodded, then turned on his heel and walked back to the command bunker. The other officers followed. For a moment Camper and Brown watched them, the gray mist an appropriately somber backdrop for the incredible events unfolding at Camp Carroll. The Americans returned to their bunker to come up with a plan of their own.

As Brown destroyed classified documents and gathered up gear and ammunition for the escape, Camper radioed his superiors at the Team 155 headquarters in Ai Tu, the 3d ARVN Division forward headquarters northwest of Quang Tri City. He was vague on the radio, not wanting to give anything away to the enemy, who was certainly monitoring the airwaves. The fact that Colonel Dinh had managed to quietly negotiate a surrender with the North Vietnamese was strong evidence that there was plenty of American radio equipment in enemy hands.

"The American advisers at Camp Carroll are no longer needed with the 56th Regiment. We are leaving the perimeter for Mai Loc at once," he said cryptically, then waited for the reply.

The call came in to Ai Tu just after 3:00 P.M. The radioman at the division bunker asked for clarification. "What's the reason for your departure?" he asked.

"Can't say over the radio," was the reply.[2]

Lieutenant Colonel Gerald Turley, the U.S. Marine officer suddenly left in command of the 3d ARVN Division forward advisory base at Ai Tu, heard the message and was furious. There was enough to worry about without a couple of damned army officers trying to bug out when the situation got hot. He snatched the radio handset and barked his orders.

"Damn it colonel, stay at your post and do your job."

Camper was a bit taken aback, but it was an order from a superior. "Roger. Out." He put down the radio and nodded knowingly to Brown.

Lieutenant Colonel Turley immediately realized he had violated the unwritten "adviser's code" by ordering Camper to remain at his post. Only the man on the ground could accurately judge the combat situation, and since there were so few Americans left in the chain of command, it was imperative that decisions be left to the adviser in the field. Turley was under great pressure in his unwanted position as acting senior adviser, and he had made the wrong call.[3]

Despite the direct order, neither man intended to stay in Camp Carroll. Major Brown continued to dump kerosene on everything that was to be left behind. Gathering up their weapons and gear and putting them just outside the bunker, Camper then ignited several thermite grenades and threw them inside. The white-hot explosion set off the kerosene, and soon the bunker was burning brightly.

Two South Vietnamese radio operators asked to go along with the Americans. They had been assigned to Camper by Dinh, and the men had formed a good relationship. The more men the better, reasoned Camper, especially if they would fight, and he felt certain that these men would.

South Vietnamese officers were slowly moving from bunker to bunker, rousting out the frightened soldiers. They moved toward the center of the perimeter and milled about, waiting for orders. What a tragedy, thought Camper. Camp Carroll was not in bad shape and could probably hold its own against the present North Vietnamese onslaught. Despite the mauling they had taken during the troop shuffle on 30 March, 1,800 soldiers inside the perimeter was a strong force. Then there were the artillery batteries, which could easily batter the enemy if only the South Vietnamese gunners would emerge from their holes and fire them. They seemed willing enough to come out in order to surrender.

The Americans and their two South Vietnamese compatriots were saddled up and ready to go. Each had shed all but the most essential equipment, keeping mainly ammunition and water. At 3:20 P.M. Camper radioed Ai Tu once more. His message was more specific this time, his voice more adamant. There was nothing left to hide. "We're leaving Camp Carroll," said Camper. It was a statement, not a request. "The base commander wants to surrender. The white flag is going up in ten minutes."

Camper had a final word with the regimental operations officer, the only South Vietnamese in the camp who spoke much English. With nothing left to lose, and still insulted at being deceived by Colonel Dinh, Camper spoke his mind freely. "You don't know what you are doing," he explained. "You are a coward and should come with us and we will fight our way out." The man simply bowed his head and said he had to follow orders. They were the last words Camper spoke to any South Vietnamese officer from the disgraced regiment.

The four men walked down the low hill from their bunker toward the southeastern edge of the perimeter, moving through groups of soldiers stacking their weapons in piles as officers stood silently by. Camper tried not to look. Nothing was more repugnant to a professional military man than cowardice. And at Camp Carroll it was especially demoralizing because there was no reason to surrender. It reminded him of a movie he had seen as a youngster about the American surrender to the Japanese at Corregidor in the early days of World War II. Poor leadership was the only explanation for what was happening. Camper tried to stop thinking about it as he and the other three men began cutting a gap through the jagged coils of sharp razor wire.

Fire Support Base Mai Loc lay almost two miles due south of Camp Carroll, but it might as well have been 100 miles away. Just outside the perimeter lay a network of mines, and beyond that, the enemy. As the small group neared the outer ring of concertina wire, the North Vietnamese spotted it. The enemy had refrained from firing on Camp Carroll as the surrender was proceeding, but escape was not to be permitted. Some of the North Vietnamese—Camper estimated about a company—moved to cut off the retreat. As they closed, Major Brown and the two South Vietnamese radiomen opened fire. Camper reached for the radio and called Ai Tu. "We're pinned down just outside the perimeter," yelled Camper over the staccato bursts of his teammates' rifles.

Major "Jimmy" Davis, the Team 155 operations officer, answered the call. By this time, everybody at Ai Tu was aware of the touch-and-go situation up at Camp Carroll, and the safety of the American advisers was paramount.

Fortune smiled on the besieged quartet huddled like insects caught by a rising storm they could not possible hope to stand against. A combination of lucky timing by a resupply helicopter and quick thinking on the part of the radio operators at Ai Tu intervened against fate and snatched the advisers from certain death.

"There's a Chinook lifting ammunition to the marines at Mai Loc in the air. I'll try to get him," said Captain Avery, one of the Team 155 operations watch team manning the radios.

The CH-47 cargo helicopter was approaching Mai Loc with a badly needed load of 105mm howitzer rounds for the desperate defenders, and it was pure chance that the radiomen were able to find the correct frequency.

"We've got two Americans at Camp Carroll who need your help. The ARVN are surrendering and the bad guys are closing in."

"Roger," replied the pilot as he dropped into Mai Loc and released the ammunition pallets slung in a net beneath the helicopter's belly. However, instead of landing and disgorging the rest of its cargo, the Chinook climbed back into the sky, heeled over, and turned north toward Camp Carroll. The marine advisers on the ground called frantically, asking why the chopper was not landing, but the pilot had already switched frequencies and did not hear the call.[4]

Lieutenant Colonel Camper had no idea what was happening. To him, Coachman 005 was just another desperate straw to grasp. As instructed by the radiomen in Ai Tu, he switched his radio frequency and called the big helicopter.

Coachman 005 came on the air immediately. "I read you loud and clear. We're inbound to your position. Give me instructions."

Camper had to think quickly. With the North Vietnamese closing in around them, the Chinook could not land outside the wire. They had to go back the way they had come. "Look for the wind sock next to the helipad inside the perimeter," he radioed. "Land there. We're outside the wire, but will pull back through the wire."

Camper motioned to the other three men, all of whom were still firing coolly and deliberately at the North Vietnamese. "Pull back. There's a chopper coming in to get us."

Without a pause the men stood and ran for the ragged perimeter wire. The North Vietnamese stopped firing at the fleeing men, thinking that they had driven them back into the pen with the others. The deep thump of the CH-47's twin rotors sounded over the treetops, but nobody could see the helicopter.

The North Vietnamese saw it first. Sharp bursts of small-arms fire tore skyward at the racing chopper, but the pilot was oblivious to it.

"Watch out. That's the enemy firing at you," radioed Camper. "Must be the same company that pinned us down."

As the Chinook came into view, both Camper and the North Vietnamese got a surprise. Racing low behind the Chinook was a pair of Cobra gunships. It was their job to protect the big CH-47 against just this sort of threat. They slashed down on the surprised North Vietnamese, peppering them with rockets and scattering them like ants. The Cobras continued to circle, snarling back and forth as the cargo helicopter swooped in low.

The door gunner in the Chinook saw the wind sock first. Leaning out of the chopper's side door over the M60 machine gun, he kept his eyes on the landing pad while calling out directions to the pilot. Then he reached for the D grips of his machine gun and hammered away at the running shapes of North Vietnamese soldiers below.

The South Vietnamese inside Camp Carroll had watched the entire episode. Not one lifted a hand to help, not even to fire a rifle in support of the beleaguered advisers. Now, when they saw the helicopter coming in, they sprang to life. Dozens of soldiers raced for the hovering helicopter, and as the wheels touched down, they swarmed all over it.

Major Brown and the two South Vietnamese radiomen were the first on board. As Camper turned to climb in, he was almost thrown aside by the rush of South Vietnamese soldiers. He stood defiantly on the ramp and allowed only those soldiers still carrying weapons to enter the helicopter. The rest were cowards who did not deserve a ride out of the base. They had decided to surrender; let them live with the decision, Camper reasoned.

One unarmed soldier tried to slip past. Camper grabbed him by the shirt and angrily flung him from the helicopter. Two more skulked up the ramp, hoping they might slip by, but in a frenzy Camper roughly pushed them back.

"Colonel, for God's sake, let's get out of here," yelled Brown from inside the Chinook's cavernous belly. The North Vietnamese had recovered from their initial surprise and were shooting at the helicopter from just outside the wire. The pilot revved the turbines in anticipation of a fast getaway, and the CH-47 bounced from side to side as the rotors pulled it slightly off the ground. With Camper finally aboard, the helicopter roared into the sky and veered hard to the southeast, clinging to the treetops on the way to Quang Tri City. In all, about thirty South Vietnamese soldiers rode out of Camp Carroll with the American advisers. All of them still had their rifles.

Lieutenant Colonel Camper looked down at the base as it shrunk from view. All was quiet down there as the remnants of the 56th ARVN Regiment prepared to surrender. The helicopter pilot reported over the radio that he saw white flags going up all over the place. What a tragedy, thought Camper. What a disgrace.

Yet not all the South Vietnamese inside Camp Carroll chose surrender. One marine artillery battery, placed inside the firebase to augment support to the marine units on the western perimeter, radioed Mai Loc saying it would not give up. As the victorious North Vietnamese marched through the front gates to accept the 56th ARVN Regiment's surrender, Bravo Battery lowered its guns and fired point-blank. It fought to the last man.[5]

Nor did all the infantry units go along with Colonel Pham Van Dinh's decision to give up. An entire battalion of 300 men rallied behind its commander and broke free of the perimeter. Over the next few days the unit exfiltrated east to Dong Ha "intact and under control." Although they were tired and shell-shocked, most of the soldiers still had their weapons. In fact, by mid-April almost 1,000 soldiers from the ill-fated 56th ARVN Regiment had filtered through enemy lines to Dong Ha, Quang Tri, and Ai Tu. They were sent south to Danang for refitting and retraining before being sent back into combat in Quang Nam Province during the summer.[6]

The ordeal of the American advisers was not yet over. Ground fire hit a hydraulic line running the Chinook's rear rotors, and engine pressure began to fall. Instead of flying to Quang Tri City, the helicopter was forced to land at the first level spot the pilot could find, in this case right in the middle of Highway 1 near the coast. Unfortunately, the enemy was already there, and the chopper settled down in the midst of an enemy 122mm rocket barrage.

Camper and Brown dashed to the side of the road and flung themselves face first into a ditch. Bullets whined overhead, punctuated by the occasional whoosh-bang of incoming rockets. Crawling cautiously along the side of the road, the Americans soon ran into a jeep carrying two advisers from a tank unit forging north to reinforce the 3d ARVN Division. Since Camper was the senior officer, they all agreed to set up a defensive perimeter and wait out the North Vietnamese attack. In the meantime, Camper radioed FRAC asking for a B-52 strike on Camp Carroll. He did not care if the surrendering regiment was still there; he wanted the base destroyed before the enemy took over the base artillery and turned it against the South Vietnamese still fighting. As it turned out, the enemy made no attempt to use the big guns captured at Camp Carroll. The North Vietnamese knew they would be bombed into oblivion if they remained at the base; they quickly abandoned it, though not before towing out a few of the artillery pieces. One 175mm gun was later placed on display in Hanoi as a symbol of the North Vietnamese army's battle prowess.[7]

After the short firefight died down, Camper called for another helicopter and flew to Ai Tu. The armor advisers continued their drive north, while Camper and Brown flew up to the division headquarters in Quang Tri City. Colonel Metcalf, the senior adviser to the 3d ARVN Division and Camper's boss, asked what had happened. Although Camp Carroll was a crucial piece in northern I Corp's crumbling puzzle, there were other pressing problems keeping Colonel Metcalf busy. He wanted to know the whole story.

General Giai was also in the command bunker. When Camper recited the story about Dinh's cowardly surrender, Giai was furious. But his anger was directed at Camper, not Dinh. The "Young Lion of Hue" could not possible have surrendered his entire regiment; in Giai's mind it was Camper who was the coward. He believed that the American advisers had run, leaving the South Vietnamese to their fate. But the advisers at Ai Tu knew what had happened, and it soon became obvious that Camp Carroll had surrendered when all communication with the 56th ARVN Regiment suddenly went off the air at about 3:30 P.M. Metcalf was also aware of this, but he did not defend his adviser against Giai's misconception.

Not until the next day, 3 April, did the ignominious fate of the 56th ARVN Regiment become clear to the doubting South Vietnamese general.

In a communist radio broadcast picked up by American monitors, Colonel Pham Van Dinh helped the North Vietnamese exploit their victory. During the broadcast he was fully cooperative with his new masters, telling his former brothers-in-arms, "I think that your continued sacrifice at this time means nothing. . . . [F]ind out how to get in touch with the NLF in order for you to return to the people. Your action will effectively assist in ending the war quickly and also save your life." Dinh also confessed, "My personal feeling is that the NLF is going to win the war. The NLF is ready all the time to welcome you back. The NLF is expecting you to return very soon." An orderly retreat was also out of the question, he maintained, because "most of the troops of my unit in all ranks refused to fight anymore."[8]

Major Ton That Man, an infantry battalion commander at Camp Carroll, also cooperated with his captors. In another radio broadcast he recalled that the base "shook and wavered at the very first shellings by PLAF [People's Liberation Armed Forces]. . . . In such a situation, how could we continue to fight? Our regiment's commander then summoned a briefing . . . a meeting of particular significance for it decided on the fate of 600 officers and men in this base. Within only five minutes, all agreed to offer no more resistance and decided to go over to the Liberation forces' side."[9]

Colonel Metcalf ordered the tired advisers back to FRAC headquarters in Danang for a change of clothes and reassignment. Later in the day General Giai called Camper and asked him to return to Quang Tri to talk. The general sounded more understanding this time. He had heard the radio broadcast and had spoken with some of the soldiers who had come out on the Chinook with Camper, so he knew the real story. Giai apologized for his curt comments of the day before. Colonel Metcalf then reassigned Camper as senior adviser to the 2d ARVN Regiment, his old unit. Major Brown was again his deputy.

To Lieutenant Colonel William Camper the surrender of Camp Carroll was a betrayal of the personal honor between soldiers. He had not been consulted by his counterpart, Colonel Dinh, and from a tactical viewpoint, there was no need to give up. They should have fought on. The I Corps leadership was also aghast at Camp Carroll's surrender. Brigadier General Thomas W. Bowen, the I Corps deputy senior adviser, later recalled that "until Camp Carroll was lost we didn't get too excited." Suddenly, the regiment was gone, and the South Vietnamese command did not understand why. "General Lam was outraged. A whole regiment—gone just like that. He wanted to execute everybody who had anything to do with it."[10]

With Camp Carroll in enemy hands, the Ring of Steel was fatally punctured. The big 175mm guns had provided a security blanket for the network of other bases facing the Laotian border. As of nightfall on 2 April, however, only Mai Loc still stood. But not for long. The loss of Camp Carroll robbed Mai Loc of artillery support and made it vulnerable to ground attack. The North Vietnamese, smelling blood, quickly coiled to strike.

News of Camp Carroll's surrender came as a shock to the marine advisers at Mai Loc, and they knew they were next. Without any friendly bases to the north and west, Mai Loc was in danger of being encircled by North Vietnamese forces. By 4:00 P.M., what had been a sporadic enemy bombardment turned into a continuous and crushing pounding, which the marines correctly identified as the prelude to an all-out infantry assault. The South Vietnamese marines bravely fired back, though their howitzers were no match for the communists' 130mm guns. An hour later the marines fired their last round. Silent in the face of the continuing enemy shelling, Mai Loc was evacuated on the evening of 2 April.

SIX

FIREBASE PEDRO

With Camp Carroll and Mai Loc out of the way, the North Vietnamese advancing east from the Laotian border had almost unrestricted access to Quang Tri Province north of the Thach Han River. Only one lonely outpost stood between the advancing enemy and Quang Tri City—a tiny firebase called Pedro. Squatting forlornly on a flat plain about seven miles southwest of Quang Tri City, Firebase Pedro was not meant to stand in the way of an armor assault, but intelligence indicated that it would have to do just that in the near future.

A few days before the opening of the offensive, South Vietnamese marines patrolling the scrubby ground near Pedro ran into enemy units. On 27 March a squad set up an ambush around a water hole about three miles southwest of the firebase. They had just gotten into position when a group of enemy soldiers appeared. During the sharp firefight five North Vietnamese were killed, but the marines suffered two dead and three wounded. One U.S. Marine adviser recalled that although the ambush was not properly executed, "We came out on the better end of the stick."[1]

The ambush would have been routine except that one of the dead North Vietnamese was carrying a map with all the trails, streams, and—most important—every South Vietnamese firebase in Quang Tri Province, as well as brief descriptions of the units stationed at each firebase. Major Robert Cockell, senior adviser to the 1st VNMC Battalion, was impressed by the find. "This is a pretty good indicator to me that if the reconnaissance elements down to the squad level had information like that, their intelligence was pretty darn good," he later observed.

The next day the marines again made contact with the enemy, killing two North Vietnamese soldiers carrying B-40 rocket-propelled grenades. For the next few days it was quiet around Firebase Pedro. In fact, when the offensive broke at noon on 30 March, it was still quiet. "We were more or less like flies on the wall just watching the world go by for the better part of two days because we just had no contact," recalled Major Cockell.

Then, late on 31 March, two companies of marines tangled with at least two unidentified North Vietnamese units. After nightfall the marines disengaged, leaving their little hilltop for an adjacent knoll. The move was fortuitous because just before dawn the enemy mortared the marines' former position and followed the bombardment with a company-sized assault. The North Vietnamese pulled up at the crest, dismayed at finding their quarry gone. But another surprise was only moments away. The marines called in artillery fire on the hilltop as the North Vietnamese milled about, decimating the attackers. Thirty-two bodies were later found, leading one adviser to note, "We had some real fine kills there."[2]

Firebase Pedro itself was hit with desultory artillery fire beginning late on 31 March, but the real bombardment began during the afternoon of 2 April. Rockets and the dreaded 130mm howitzers pounded the base, shredding bunkers and trench lines with shrapnel. Constructed with very little overhead cover, Pedro was never meant to take punishment from heavy artillery. Even in their sandbagged defenses, the marines began to take casualties from lethal overhead bursts. Well aware of this shortcoming, the 1st VNMC Battalion commander, Major Nguyen Dang Tong, reasoned that the only way to survive was to pull out of Pedro and take up positions nearby.

During a lull in the shelling the marines slipped outside the wire, but North Vietnamese artillery spotters saw them go. As the marines rushed back and forth between various high points in the terrain, artillery rounds followed, though by dark they were able to settle in on a small hill for the night.

At about 8:30 the next morning they were shelled once again, convincing Major Hoa that constant movement was the only way to survive. So for the next four days the 1st VNMC Battalion patrolled west of Pedro, leaving less than a company inside the firebase. The North Vietnamese were quiet, however, mounting only a single sapper attack on Pedro during the night of 4 April.

But fate frowned on the enemy. The sappers sneaked through a shallow draw toward the perimeter wire surrounding the firebase, unaware that marine units were positioned on both sides. By the time the North Vietnamese made it to the wire, they were already badly mauled; the two South Vietnamese marine platoons defending Pedro kept the charge at bay while artillery from Ai Tu Combat Base did the rest. "There were quite a few pieces of NVA down there in the wire," recalled one American adviser after the one-sided firefight.[3]

On the morning of 6 April the 1st VNMC Battalion was relieved by a ranger battalion and moved to Ai Tu to take over perimeter security for the southern half of the combat base. For all practical purposes Firebase Pedro was abandoned by the South Vietnamese in favor of actively patrolling the countryside to the southwest. The move seemed sound; the North Vietnamese had not shown any signs of massing for a serious attack from this angle, and there was no evidence of tanks in the area. But just to be safe, a team of engineers was brought in to lay about 500 antitank mines along the western approaches to the firebase.

Two events brought the limited action around Pedro into sharper relief. The first occurred on 8 April when two companies of the 5th VNMC Battalion moved west out of Firebase Jane (about seven miles south of Quang Tri City along Highway 1) into the Hai Lang Forest in search of enemy patrols. What they found was a company or so of North Vietnamese dug in deep within the trees and well armed with machine guns and mortars. The opening barrage killed the entire battalion command group, leaving the U.S. marine adviser, Captain Marshall N. Wells, to lead the disorganized battalion back to Firebase Jane with the North Vietnamese in hot pursuit.

In a second incident, intelligence indicated that the enemy planned to strike near Ai Tu with infantry and armor. This was the first serious report of large units of North Vietnamese infantry and the only mention of tanks so far south in Quang Tri Province. Firebase Pedro was the only position north of the Thach Han River and west of Highway 1 between the enemy and Quang Tri City. The commander of the 369th VNMC Brigade, Colonel Pham Van Chung, turned his attention from the north, where marines and South Vietnamese army troops still held the ground near Dong Ha, to the mounting threat in the west. Suddenly the defense of Pedro seemed much more important.[4]

A new marine unit was destined to play the pivotal role in the coming battle. During the confusion of the first week in April, the 6th VNMC Battalion, officially part of the 258th VNMC Brigade, had been left at Firebase Barbara as most of the rest of the brigade moved north toward Dong Ha. Rather than try to catch up later, the battalion was ordered to reinforce Ai Tu Combat Base on 1 April, where it remained until 8 April. The increased activity around Pedro convinced the brigade commander to shift the 6th VNMC Battalion from Ai Tu—the marines walked into the little firebase during the afternoon of 8 April.

Major Do Huu Tung, the battalion commander, positioned one company inside Pedro but wisely decided to keep his command group and the remaining troops outside the base. One platoon occupied a low hill that overlooked Pedro, while the remaining troops were placed at other points along the northeast edge of the firebase, where they dominated an uncharted dirt road running between Pedro and Ai Tu. Major Tung suspected that the North Vietnamese would try to sneak tanks along the trail, and he wanted a blocking force between the two bases.[5]

Late that night the North Vietnamese shelled Firebase Pedro with 130mm artillery and mortars. Among the explosions the marines heard the dull thud of direct fire rounds slamming into the base. Although they wanted to believe it was a recoilless rifle, everyone knew it was probably armor warming up for an attack at first light. From a position just a mile from Pedro, Captain William Wischmeyer, assistant adviser to the 6th VNMC Battalion, dryly observed, "The fire was very intense and reduced the position to rubble."[6]

At 6:00 A.M. on 9 April the assault began. Sixteen T-54 tanks backed by a regiment of North Vietnamese infantry rushed along the road from the west. An hour later the first tanks ripped through the wire at Pedro. Captain Wischmeyer watched the action through his binoculars. "He rolled fast across the interior of the firebase and a few minutes later a second tank followed. They stopped . . . fired their cannons into the compound and then moved on. The tanks moved very fast, they rolled through the wire like you couldn't believe."

What Wischmeyer could not see was the carnage inside Firebase Pedro. The T-54s shredded the twin rows of concertina wire around the base and slammed into the network of dilapidated bunkers. Some men of the defending company dropped their weapons and fled into the foothills, but one platoon could not get away. The tanks ran back and forth over the bunkers, grinding their treads until they had smashed the plywood and sandbags into dust. Those marines who were not crushed to death perished in a hail of fire from the tanks' main guns and machine guns.

Seven tanks took up positions around the captured firebase, apparently waiting for the infantry to catch up. When the assault first began, the armor contingent rushed forward at over twenty miles per hour and quickly outdistanced the foot soldiers. Suddenly four or five tanks blundered into the minefield, setting off a row of explosions. With one unexpected blow the North Vietnamese lost one quarter of their armor force.

The rest of the tanks roared onward. The two that had smashed Pedro moved off the base and turned north toward the fleeing marines. Captain Wischmeyer watched in horror as two other tanks turned directly toward his position with the battalion command group. Then, with no warning, the lead tank blew up. Everyone thought a marine had knocked it out with a LAW, but it was later discovered that the tank probably hit a mine. Either way, the T-54 was out of action. But the other tank kept coming. "The damn thing looked about three stories wide and moving about seventy knots," exaggerated Captain Wischmeyer. The South Vietnamese were also frightened—"in a controlled state of panic" was how Wischmeyer characterized them.[7]

The command group moved off the rise as the tank approached. It hoped to evade the monster, but wherever the group turned, it followed. Then, as the tank closed in on the marines, it lost sight of its quarry. "The tank approached us, I'd say within probably 500 meters of us and parked behind a hill," recalled Captain Wischmeyer. "Why they didn't look over the hill I don't know, but I'm very glad they didn't." In all the confusion the enemy tank failed to fire its main gun. The delay was fatal. From a position some 900 yards to the northeast, a handful of South Vietnamese tanks appeared and quickly knocked out the T-54.[8]

The friendly tanks were from 2d Troop, 20th Tank Regiment, part of the same unit that had dueled with North Vietnamese armor near the Dong Ha bridge on 2 April. The battalion had been shifted to the south and was in Quang Tri City refueling and rearming when the North Vietnamese hit Firebase Pedro. The 258th VNMC Brigade commander, Lieutenant Colonel Dinh, patched together a reaction force of eight M48 tanks, twelve M113 armored personnel carriers, and two infantry companies from the 1st VNMC Battalion, which had left Firebase Pedro for Ai Tu on 6 April. Captain Lawrence Livingston, the deputy battalion adviser, was along for the ride.[9]

As South Vietnamese tanks engaged the enemy, 105mm howitzers from Ai Tu Combat Base and naval gunfire from destroyers offshore added their firepower to the battle. The senior U.S. Marine adviser in the area, Major Robert Cockell, estimated that "somewhere around 4,000 rounds of friendly artillery were placed on Pedro" during the day, effectively driving the North Vietnamese infantry out of the area. According to another adviser, "This left the tanks in an untenable position. . . . None escaped."[10]

Actually, some did escape, but not for long. During the afternoon of 9 April, the clouds parted just enough to allow four South Vietnamese air force A-1E Skyraiders to duck below the cloud cover and pinpoint the North Vietnamese attackers. The World War II–era propeller-driven planes dove on the enemy tanks and within minutes had destroyed five as they maneuvered to attack the 6th VNMC Battalion command group. The combination of artillery, naval gunfire, and air support was enough to halt the North Vietnamese in their tracks. In all, thirteen North Vietnamese tanks—out of the original sixteen—were destroyed around Pedro that day.[11]

That left three enemy tanks running rampant, not to mention the North Vietnamese infantry. One tank managed to escape to the west, but the remaining two were captured. A lone South Vietnamese marine private accounted for one of them. As he waited in his foxhole, he heard the clank of tank treads directly to his front. Swallowing the fear rising in his throat, he peered over the earthen rim of his hole and saw that the tank was alone, with its hatches open. Best of all, the slight incline obstructed the driver's view. Brandishing his M16, the marine leaped from the foxhole and demanded that the crew surrender—which it quickly did. The captured tank was decorated with the eagle, globe, and anchor emblem of the South Vietnamese marines and later driven back to Saigon as a war trophy.[12]

By the morning of 10 April the situation around Pedro stabilized enough to allow Bravo Command Group of the 1st VNMC Battalion to return to Ai Tu Combat Base and resume its defensive role. Both companies, along with several machine-gun-mounted armored personnel carriers, set out along the narrow dirt road, keeping a watchful eye out for the enemy. "Everyone smelled a rat," was how Captain Wischmeyer characterized the mood during the cautious advance.

As it turned out, the suspicions were well founded. Two North Vietnamese battalions had straddled the road southwest of Ai Tu, constructing trenches and bunkers with overhead cover against air strikes. Their mission was to knock out the tracked vehicles and prevent the column from getting back to Ai Tu. But the enemy was not yet in place, and the marines spotted movement to their front and stopped short. One company of the 6th VNMC Battalion, which was still near Pedro, moved up, and after a reconnaissance by fire the battalion commander ordered an assault. Bravo Command Group led the charge, and during the fighting the battalion executive officer was cut down by a machine gun. Captain To Ton Te was a respected officer, and his death was mourned. The advisers lauded Captain Te and evoked images of an honorable death in battle when they later observed that "he was killed like a marine, went down like a marine, up there trying to engage the enemy."[13]

With no one in command, Captain Lawrence Livingston rallied the faltering marines and directed four South Vietnamese tanks into action. The tables were turned. For the first time during the offensive in northern I Corps, North Vietnamese infantry got a taste of what it was like to be overrun by armor. "The battle was fought until dark at hand grenade range," read the after-action report. "The enemy died in his holes and the better part of his force was killed." As the marines swept through the North Vietnamese defenses, they counted 211 bodies, a terrible toll that rendered both battalions combat ineffective.[14]

The marines captured antiaircraft and antitank weapons as well as mortars, small arms, and documents. One document taken from a prisoner revealed that the North Vietnamese had tasked one infantry regiment and an armor battalion with overrunning both Pedro and Ai Tu, then striking the southern flank of the Dong Ha defenses. Threatened with encirclement from the south, the South Vietnamese would have had little choice but to retreat, leaving Quang Tri City open to attack from all sides. Instead, the North Vietnamese were stopped short. Faced with the virtual loss of two battalions on the road northeast of Firebase Pedro, the North Vietnamese on the western front were forced to concentrate primarily on survival. For the next seven days they fought small actions as they tried to break away to the north and west, but sweeps by the marines accounted for another 396 North Vietnamese killed.[15]

The action at Firebase Pedro was overshadowed by the deteriorating situation to the north, but in the face of daily advances by North Vietnamese troops even limited successes stood out boldly. With hindsight it seems that the successful defense of Pedro was a crucial—and next to the fall of Camp Carroll, perhaps *the* crucial—event of the first two weeks of the offensive. Had Pedro fallen, previous limited successes by the marines and the 3d ARVN Division would have meant nothing. The consolidation of defenses south of the Mieu Giang and Cua Viet Rivers on 2 April and the stand by South Vietnamese tanks and marines at the Dong Ha Bridge could hinder the enemy advance only if the rear was secure. As it was, the victory at Pedro allowed the South Vietnamese to maintain the shaky status quo. FRAC became aware of this only after the fact:

> Phase II of the current NVA offensive probably began on 9 April with attacks directed against FSB Pedro. . . . The attack was conducted to force the withdrawal of 3d Div[ision] units located to the north and destroy them by further attacks. . . . Attacks from the west on 9 and 10 April . . . continue to indicate attempts to flank defenses on the Mieu Giang River west of Dong Ha and to force their withdrawal southward.[16]

This analysis swung attention from north to west, where it would remain until the fall of Quang Tri, though General Lam sometimes deluded himself into thinking he could turn the tide by simply pushing north on Highway 1. As enemy forces pressed in from the west, there was a danger that the South Vietnamese still in position south of the Mieu Giang River might be cut off from Quang Tri City. That possibility made the stand at Dong Ha much less tactically significant. But for now the assault was blunted.

On 12 April General Giai and Colonel Metcalf flew down to Ai Tu, where they met Colonel Dinh, the 258th VNMC Brigade commander, for an impromptu victory ceremony. Cash rewards were handed out to each marine who had a confirmed tank kill, at the going rate of 20,000 piasters (about fifty dollars) each. But there was some question of who—or what—had killed the tanks. Although stories abounded of marines knocking out T-54s with handheld M72 LAWs, no adviser could confirm them. In fact, aircraft, artillery, and mines may have accounted for all the North Vietnamese armor. Whatever the real story, by issuing the rewards, General Giai raised morale during a time when most news out of Quang Tri Province was depressing.[17]

SEVEN

CONSOLIDATION AND COUNTEROFFENSIVE

In Danang, Major General Frederick Kroesen watched carefully as the situation in northern I Corps stabilized. What had been a full-scale shooting war at the beginning of April simmered down to "moderate activity" by 11 April. But Kroesen held no illusions. "The NVA has had sufficient time to complete resupply operations and positioning of forces to continue the attacks," he reported to General Abrams in Saigon. "Operational reports indicate the enemy has lost considerable infantry and armor, however there is no indication that we have done major damage to his artillery. There are no signs that the enemy has altered plans to seize Quang Tri."[1]

Yet FRAC was willing to give the South Vietnamese defenders the benefit of the doubt. In Quang Tri Province the 3d ARVN Division was badly battered, but it had weathered the storm; in Kroesen's words, "It did not collapse or disappear. It has instead rebounded strongly and can still be counted an effective force." A bold assessment, but there was some evidence to back it up. First, although the 56th ARVN Regiment, part of which surrendered at Camp Carroll on 2 April, was "ineffective" and had been assigned to Danang for retraining, the other two regiments were still in action. Second, many of the soldiers who had scattered before the initial enemy assault rejoined their units by the second week in April. General Lam, his staff, and the American advisers in Danang agreed that "on the whole there is a great confidence for the future tempered with recognition that serious problems can still develop."[2]

FRAC's cautious prediction would be put to the test on two fronts in the coming weeks as both sides maneuvered for advantage in mid-April. The South Vietnamese planned to break out of the tightening enemy offensive, while the North Vietnamese sought to consolidate their early gains and push on to Quang Tri City. Following the attack on Firebase Pedro the enemy paused, perhaps awaiting new orders, perhaps because new supplies needed to be stockpiled. Whatever the case, the lull would not last long.

The most ominous sign of North Vietnamese intentions came on 12 April when U.S. intelligence identified new North Vietnamese armor units near Quang Tri City. "Interrogation of a PW [prisoner of war] indicates elements of the 203 NVA Tank Regiment have infiltrated through the Ba Long Valley and are possibly located in the crescent area west of Quang Tri City," warned one report. It turned out to be three battalions of about seventy-five tanks. This was the culmination of a process that had begun on the first day of the invasion, though it was overshadowed by the much-acclaimed North Vietnamese drive through the demilitarized zone and down Highway 1. Enemy forces had succeeded in moving through the Ba Long Valley virtually unnoticed. After Nui Ba Ho, Sarge, and Holcomb fell on 1 April, the South Vietnamese lost their eyes along Highway 9 from the Laotian border. Only the successful South Vietnamese stand at Pedro hindered the enemy's envelopment of Quang Tri City, and even that was only an inconvenience.³

Remote sensors along Highway 9 also picked up heightened activity from the west, which intelligence believed "indicates continuous logistical resupply and infiltration." General Kroesen began to realize that the western front may have been the most important axis of the North Vietnamese offensive all along, though he characterized the actions there as "repositioning and resupply of troops prior to launching further attacks." But the North Vietnamese were not "repositioning"; they had been there all along. At least four regiments had lined up along the Laotian border in late March, all of them aimed at the western rim of the Ring of Steel. Two weeks later Kroesen believed that the attacks just south of the demilitarized zone were "attempts to draw ARVN forces from the left flank and cover the movement of forces into positions for attacks from the west." FRAC now concluded that the primary aim of the North Vietnamese was to consolidate their hold on the area around Cam Lo and Camp Carroll, then link up with forces north of Dong Ha and along the Cua Viet River east to the sea. With that complete, the enemy could sweep south to Quang Tri City.⁴

Although the North Vietnamese had an almost unbroken string of victories in the early weeks of the offensive, they still did not completely dominate the northern part of Quang Tri Province. Enemy efforts sputtered in both the north and the west, leaving the South Vietnamese holding a tenuous line along the Cua Viet River and just west of Highway 1. Theoretically, either side could take the initiative.

In Saigon, General Abrams hoped it would be the South Vietnamese who would turn the tide. On 11 April he flew into Danang for a conference with his advisers and the I Corps command staff. General Lam pointed out that the North Vietnamese had not advanced over the last few days and boldly predicted that the enemy was beaten. Morale was high among the troops,

Lam told General Abrams, and plans for a counteroffensive were under way. The plan was audacious, calling for a South Vietnamese sweep north across the Cua Viet River to retake the district capital of Gio Linh and the entire area north to the demilitarized zone. Lam believed that by doing this he would force the enemy to withdraw back into Laos and North Vietnam.[5]

Fortunately, the plan was rejected. FRAC advisers politely argued that a drive north neglected the western flank, where the enemy was strongest and most persistent. Even if Lam's counterattack worked, it would take forces away from the west, leaving a corridor through the Ba Long Valley to Quang Tri City wide open. After considerable debate, Lam was convinced to focus his counteroffensive westward. Code-named Quang Trung 729, the operation's spearhead consisted of three marine battalions (the 147th VNMC Brigade), three ranger groups, and two armored cavalry regiments, all under the operational control of the 3d ARVN Division commander, General Giai.[6] Although the division itself was still reeling from defeats at Camp Carroll and along the demilitarized zone, it was regarded as "combat effective" by American advisers. "3d Div[ision], 2d and 57th Regts [Regiments] have recovered fairly well from the initial shock of combat and should prove effective when called upon again," was General Kroesen's assessment on the eve of the counteroffensive. The regiments averaged 1,700 men each, down from a strength of 2,000 before the North Vietnamese offensive, so General Giai planned to use them sparingly.[7]

The goals of Quang Trung 729 were simple yet optimistic: extend the South Vietnamese perimeter back to the high ground previously held by bases such as Camp Carroll and Mai Loc. An important part of the plan was to reestablish a position on Firebase Holcomb so that the South Vietnamese could once again overlook the crucial Ba Long Valley, the route used by the North Vietnamese to resupply their western thrust south from Highway 9.[8]

Senior Americans at FRAC warned their counterparts against overoptimism, stressing that to be successful, Quang Trung 729 had to be "slow and methodical." General Kroesen was hopeful about the counteroffensive's chances of success, though he was noncommittal to Abrams. "Success achieved will determine whether or not the perimeter is to be further expanded to [Firebases] Fuller, Khe Gio, and Sarge," he cautiously surmised. If the operation was initially successful, the South Vietnamese would then sweep north of the Cua Viet River near Cam Lo and push back east to the China Sea.[9]

Despite serious planning and the commitment of troops to Quang Trung 729 by the usually cautious corps commander, there remained an unrealistic quality about the counteroffensive. The first sign came less than a day before the operation was to begin. General Lam planned to launch his counteroffensive at 1:00 P.M. on 14 April, but his horoscope predicted bad luck if the timing was not changed. Operation orders were quickly altered, pushing H hour up twelve hours, to 1:00 in the morning.

More serious was the manner in which Lam planned to commit his forces to the counteroffensive. The leading edge of Quang Trung 729 was composed of infantry with the two armored cavalry regiments held to the rear. Lam planned to use his tanks only if the North Vietnamese used theirs first. General Kroesen disagreed with this tactic, arguing that without the mailed fist provided by an armor spearhead the counteroffensive lacked a lethal punch. In addition, the South Vietnamese army, still badly demoralized by earlier disastrous encounters with enemy armor, would be better served if its own tanks were out in front rather than to the rear. But Lam demurred, forcing Kroesen to conclude that "this attack is definitely preliminary and might be better described as an aggressive defensive move."[10]

Quang Trung 729 pushed off on schedule, with South Vietnamese troops moving cautiously forward. Only the 5th Ranger Group ran into opposition—a North Vietnamese battalion, which was overrun with the loss of only a single ranger. On the second day, 15 April, scattered contacts all along the western front line confirmed that the North Vietnamese were concentrating much of their effort there. The South Vietnamese inflicted moderate casualties on the enemy but became bogged down as the fighting intensified. By 17 April they had moved less than a mile—General Kroesen called it "almost nonreportable"—and in some sectors had even retreated slightly.

On 18 April the North Vietnamese were concentrating most of their efforts against Quang Trung 729, and all South Vietnamese units found themselves in combat four or five times a day. The 304th NVA Division, the 308th NVA Division, and the 204th Tank Regiment all committed units to halting the South Vietnamese counteroffensive in its tracks, and intelligence warned that the 201st NVA Tank Regiment, stationed just inside North Vietnam, was on its way south to reinforce the front. But tanks were not part of the enemy's first attempts to break up Quang Trung 729. Not until the evening of 18 April did they appear, and then it seemed that they were used in concert all along the South Vietnamese line. The 1st Ranger Group, 3d VNMC Battalion, and 2d ARVN Regiment all reported tanks moving in from the west.

Well aware of the effect tanks had had on his troops in the past, General Giai declared a tactical emergency and called for additional air strikes. The

U.S. Air Force responded with forty-eight sorties; the South Vietnamese air force added about a dozen more. One aerial forward controller watched as tanks raced toward the marines. Rolling down for a closer look, the pilot radioed for tactical air strikes. Realizing that they would not reach the marines in time, he switched frequencies and called for artillery fire from Ai Tu and Quang Tri. Within minutes, rounds whistled overhead, and the tanks turned tail and ran to the west. At midnight the tactical emergency was lifted.[11]

The three-hour bombing frenzy disrupted the North Vietnamese attack and offered the South Vietnamese their best chance to move onto the offensive, or at least to replace combat-weary units with fresh ones. But still the South Vietnamese failed to move. General Giai rationalized his division's lack of progress, saying that all units were diligently "searching every possible enemy hiding place as they move." General Lam was satisfied with this explanation, deluding himself into thinking that the situation in Quang Tri was under control. But the I Corps commander ignored the movement of North Vietnamese artillery units, which turned their attention to the stalled South Vietnamese counteroffensive. On 20 April "all units received a heavy volume of indirect fire." The North Vietnamese appeared to have backed off to give the artillery full advantage; during the entire day only the marines were attacked by infantry.[12]

General Lam received further encouragement on 21 April when captured enemy soldiers and documents revealed that the 308th NVA Division was supposed to attack Dong Ha between 15 and 17 April with tanks and infantry, and the 304th NVA Division was to have hit Quang Tri Combat Base at the same time. Lam believed that his counteroffensive was responsible for upsetting the North Vietnamese timetable, so he ordered General Giai to launch Phase II of Quang Trung 729 the next day.[13]

Not much changed during Phase II. South Vietnamese units failed to move forward, and the only offensive action was initiated by the enemy. As usual, the South Vietnamese disengaged and called for air support. The air force responded with forty-eight sorties, while U.S. Navy ships offshore added their guns to the battle. It probably was this aerial pounding that was responsible for dampening the enemy's offensive tempo, not the limited advances made by South Vietnamese troops on the ground, as General Lam claimed. Sustained strikes along the front edge of South Vietnamese lines in support of Quang Trung 729 effectively severed North Vietnamese logistical lines in the lowlands west of Quang Tri City. General Kroesen observed, "Allied air strikes have greatly deterred the enemy's offensive capability by hampering his efforts to resupply and reequip his forward elements." Even so, the North Vietnamese managed to move artillery along the coast to hardened positions, some of them containing mobile radar units.[14]

Despite the pounding, the North Vietnamese moved over onto the offensive on the morning of 23 April. In three separate actions, enemy tanks and infantry struck South Vietnamese positions west of Highway 1. The 1st Armored Brigade was hit by twelve T-54 tanks, while the rangers suffered some losses from infantry attacks. The American adviser with the armored brigade reported that the South Vietnamese tankers refused to move forward because Arc Light strikes had not first "softened up" the area into which they were to advance. This overreliance on air support had reached critical proportions at a point when North Vietnamese gains on the ground around Quang Tri were threatening the city's survival.

General Giai tried hard to develop some momentum in his stalled counteroffensive. At 8:00 on the morning of 23 April, the 3d ARVN Division command center in Quang Tri City ordered all units to push west. Instructions were vague, however, and many units hesitated. The marines at Ai Tu Combat Base were the "freshest" unit; the 147th VNMC Brigade had just relieved the 258th VNMC Brigade that morning. The brigade's two infantry units, the 3d and 6th VNMC Battalions, were to go to Hue for replacements and replenishment. The 3d VNMC Battalion had been in almost continuous combat near Dong Ha and around Ai Tu since 2 April, and 500 men out of a total of 700 had become casualties.[15]

The 147th VNMC Brigade had been roughed up during the retreat from Firebase Mai Loc, but after almost two weeks in Hue it was considered at full strength and combat ready. Now it was called upon to fight again. The new garrison at Ai Tu received the order to push west, but the commander, Colonel Nguyen Nang Bao, worried that if his units advanced westward he would be unable to adequately secure Ai Tu Combat Base, his main responsibility. Two units, the 1st and 8th VNMC Battalions, were to advance, leaving only the 4th VNMC Battalion at Ai Tu. That would leave Colonel Bao with no way to reinforce his forward elements. General Giai responded to Bao's objection by giving the 2d ARVN Regiment, positioned immediately south of the marines, responsibility for filling the "void between the perimeter [at Ai Tu] and the units to the west." This was no solution, argued Colonel Bao. Placing the 2d ARVN Regiment between the marine brigade headquarters and the forward battalions left the marines without operational control over their own forces, but there was no alternative.[16]

The disagreement highlighted a serious command problem that plagued the 3d ARVN Division during the Easter Offensive. General Lam placed his commanders, particularly General Giai, under serious operational constraints. By mid-April Giai held operational control over the remaining two regiments in the 3d ARVN Division, two marine brigades, four ranger groups, one armor brigade—a grand total of nine brigades, or thirty-three battalions. On top of all this, he was responsible for the territorial forces in Quang Tri Province and the corps-level artillery and logistical units still in Dong Ha. At first Giai was honored that the corps commander placed such high trust in him, but it soon became clear that there was too much to handle.[17]

General Lam was content to leave responsibility in the hands of his subordinate. Despite the overwhelming load he had placed on Giai's shoulders, Lam never visited the frontline troops or personally observed the 3d ARVN Division line of defense. His only contact with the battle was over the radio, leaving many of his subordinates with the impression that their corps commander did not think the situation was serious. But while Lam let Giai take responsibility for the battle, he did not grant him any real authority. From Danang, Lam personally interceded at all levels, sometimes going so far as to personally issue orders by radio to individual brigade commanders without notifying the division operations center. Both Giai and his division advisers often learned of the new orders only as they were being carried out. The inevitable result was that Giai's control over his unwieldy command slowly melted away.

Without a successful resolution of the command problem, the marines had no choice but to move forward. On the morning of 24 April the 1st and 8th VNMC Battalions, supported by two armored cavalry troops, pushed forward with little resistance. By nightfall both battalions reached their assigned positions and set up a thin arc from the railroad tracks south of the Vinh Phuoc River down to the dirt road east of Firebase Pedro. Unfortunately, other South Vietnamese units did not do so well. The rangers to the north and elements of the 2d ARVN Regiment to the south did not come on line before dark, leaving the marines vulnerable to infiltration by enemy units. During the long night the marines stayed on full alert, but the only attacks came from a few 82mm mortars in the distance. For the next two days the marines patrolled from their new positions, while the rangers and the 2d ARVN Regiment slowly moved forward.[18]

Giai tried hard to maintain control over his unwieldy command. As the beleaguered general turned from one trouble spot to another, his subordinate commanders began to lose confidence in their ability to carry the fight to the enemy. They devised many excuses for why they could not advance; logistical problems, personnel attrition, and fatigue were the most prevalent. The result was a stagnant front that provided a stationary target for North Vietnamese artillery. As the days wore on, casualties climbed and morale plummeted, but General Giai could not prod his men into action. One observer commented, "Quang Trung 729 did not resemble an offensive, but rather had settled into a costly battle of attrition in place in which the ARVN battalions were steadily reduced in strength and effectiveness by the enemy's deadly artillery fire."[19]

Although few American advisers in FRAC were surprised by the poor showing during Quang Trung 729, General Kroesen was subdued in his criticism of the counteroffensive. "In Quang Tri Province 3d ARVN Div[ision] elements appeared to lag in their offensive operations," he generously observed. "Enemy resistance was relatively light, however ARVN made only small advances." This was a polite understatement. Colonel Metcalf, the 3d ARVN Division senior adviser, later reported, "The front line trace had not changed by more than 500 meters in any one direction since the offensive had begun." For all practical purposes, Quang Trung 729 was over on 24 April, although General Lam insisted that the South Vietnamese army still held the initiative.[20]

Three factors doomed Quang Trung 729 from the onset. First, the thinly arrayed South Vietnamese front lacked the strength to break through the enemy forces in the west. The soldiers themselves sensed this at the time, realizing that if they left their bunkers and foxholes, North Vietnamese artillery would catch them in the open. Second, the corps-level logistical system lacked the resources to carry an attack back to the pre-April status quo. Finally, the command structure impeded rather than aided the counteroffensive. In the final analysis, the South Vietnamese lost badly during the counteroffensive. After ten days the 3d ARVN Division added to the already heavy equipment losses, further burdening the I Corps logistical resupply system. The figures were sobering. As of 25 April the division had lost eighteen 155mm and forty-seven 105mm howitzers, 37 tanks, and 89 armored personnel carriers. More than 240 vehicles of all types had been destroyed or captured. No one knew how many South Vietnamese soldiers had been killed, wounded, or deserted.[21]

On the positive side, the counteroffensive formed a single distinct front line against which most of the North Vietnamese forces involved in the attack on Quang Tri City were arrayed. For the first time in almost a month, American airpower was presented with a solid, almost stationary target. Earlier in the month General Giai, working in concert with American advisers, developed a series of Arc Light target boxes covering the area from Dong Ha south to Quang Tri City and west to a line running south from

Cam Lo to the Ba Long Valley. The boxes—over 200 of them—were arranged like overlapping scales, each one with a number. Strikes were simply called in by the numbers when the ground commander believed North Vietnamese troops had moved into the boxes. General Giai made frequent use of this system, and according to the air force, "Most of the Arc Lights were extremely effective due to the numerous concentrations of NVA and the capability for last-minute target changes."[22]

Senior American advisers at FRAC were less sanguine. General Kroesen felt that control of air assets was too far away from the action to be completely effective. The main problem stemmed from the fact that airpower "is not directly responsive to the tactical commander." In Kroesen's opinion, placing direct authority for air control in Danang "creates a system in which the controller is far removed from the situation and therefore inflexible and unresponsive to the immediate requirements."[23]

Grateful advisers on the ground were not so critical, though many were directly affected by the inflexibility of the air support system. "The only minor problem was that it seemed the air force always wanted everything in fifteen minutes or less," observed a U.S. Marine adviser. "Needless to say, it was done. We would have given them anything to continue the great support we were getting."[24]

This flawed system had a direct impact on the battle, however. During the South Vietnamese counteroffensive of 14–24 April, Kroesen reported that "130mm gun locations just north of the DMZ were submitted . . . and they have not been struck. These guns are a major force to be reckoned with and there is no explanation satisfactory to Gen[eral] Lam concerning the reason they have not been destroyed." The total number of air strikes also declined beginning on 21 April, precisely when the South Vietnamese needed them most.[25]

Although FRAC believed the air war could have been conducted more efficiently, from the enemy perspective the rain of bombs was deadly. But despite terrible losses, the North Vietnamese kept up the pressure, slowly pushing the South Vietnamese back on Quang Tri City. The cherished objective of capturing a provincial capital was within sight.

EIGHT

THINGS FALL APART

The morning of 27 April dawned gray and misty, perfect weather to screen the North Vietnamese assault. Enemy troops struck all along the thin South Vietnamese front from the Cua Viet River on the coast to Firebase Pedro in the southwest. The American advisers had seen it coming. "The enemy may be attempting to regain the initiative by capitalizing on adverse weather conditions, and the slowness of the ARVN forces to launch their expected counteroffensive," was the assessment sent back to Saigon by the American advisory team just prior to the attack.[1]

To the east of Highway 1 the South Vietnamese continued to hold back the enemy, retreating slowly south in good order. On the sandy flats along the Cua Viet River delta east of Dong Ha, a loose confederation of Regional Forces militiamen and soldiers from the 5th Ranger Group held off repeated attacks by North Vietnamese amphibious PT-76 tanks. Lieutenant Colonel Ngo Minh Huong, a battalion commander, tirelessly drove his men on as they cleared out enemy foxholes and blew up tanks. The diminutive officer was festooned with talismans and small Buddha figurines, though he believed that fierce fighting, rather than luck, would prevail in the end. But Huong knew that the enemy was determined to punch through the South Vietnamese positions. "One prisoner told me his group didn't have the strength to attack, but as they had not been told to withdraw, they were staying and fighting," Huong recounted with obvious respect for his enemy. "That's what they do—stay and fight."[2]

Ranger and armor units to the west of Dong Ha did not fare as well. Part of the 3d Troop, 20th Tank Regiment had all its officers killed by 9:00 in the morning. Six tanks, most of them aflame from rocket hits, broke and fled. The 4th Ranger Group, under the operational control of the 1st Armored Brigade and relying on the firepower of the 20th Tanks, was battered by attacks all day long with virtually no armor support. By midafternoon the rangers were pushed back some two miles. The 33d Ranger Battalion was ordered to reinforce the 30th Ranger Battalion, but by the time it was in position the 30th Ranger Battalion had fled to the east. The lone battalion fought on without support until nightfall, when it "also broke contact and withdrew to the east."[3]

Convinced that his defensive plan was sound, General Lam was furious when he heard that the rangers had retreated. He blamed the ranger group commander, Colonel Khoai, for the debacle, but the American ranger advisers believed there had been no alternative. "There was no question that the friendly situation had deteriorated and that ARVN soldiers, including Rangers were in dissarray [*sic*]. However, to place the responsibility on any single unit seemed unreasonable," concluded the advisory team.[4]

Some ranger units were at fault, however. The 43d Battalion panicked and broke, fleeing headlong toward the east. A handful of ranger officers, along with the armored brigade commander and his adviser, confronted the retreating soldiers and threatened them at gunpoint. Seeing that they faced certain death at the hands of their own commanders, the rangers turned back and looked for a place to make a stand. At least against the enemy, they might come out alive.[5]

The rangers fell back to a position straddling Route 604—little more than a narrow dirt road—at the point where it snaked east out of the low foothills onto the sprawling lowlands. The rest of the 4th Ranger Group formed up in a long, thin line stretching north from the road to a position about one mile south of Dong Ha Combat Base near the Mieu Giang River. Two weakened battalions held an area two and a half miles long against an unknown number of North Vietnamese troops. It was not enough. The enemy began to squeeze around the south edge of the rangers, threatening to cut them off from the south. At 6:40 P.M. the rangers and supporting armor from the 1st Armored Brigade were ordered to move north to Dong Ha Combat Base under cover of darkness. There they would link up with the 57th ARVN Regiment.[6]

The tired troops found the base empty, but the enemy was hot on their trail. South Vietnamese tanks barreled on to the east toward Highway 1, then turned south and raced to the 20th Tank Regimental command post just north of the Vinh Phuoc River. On the way the tanks were fired on by pockets of soldiers from the broken 57th ARVN Regiment, which thought they were enemy armor heading south. No one was injured, though some of the armored personnel carriers were shot to pieces. Once at the river, the tanks guarded the northern approach to the last major bridge north of the Thach Han River and the gates of Quang Tri City. The rangers, still at Dong Ha, followed behind as best they could.

The North Vietnamese lashed out with 122mm and 130mm artillery barrages in an attempt to force the South Vietnamese out of Dong Ha. If the enemy took the town and the combat base to the south, their forces on the northern perimeter could easily support those to the west and move to sur-

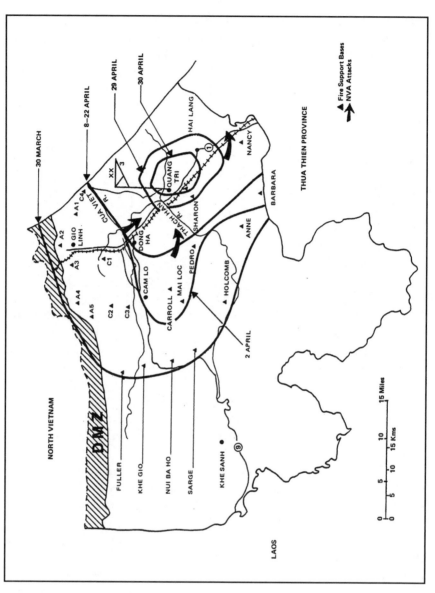

The shrinking 3d Infantry Division AO, Quang Tri Province

round Quang Tri City. In concert with the attacks to the north, the enemy also struck hard around Firebase Pedro southwest of Quang Tri City. The 2d ARVN Regiment was mauled by North Vietnamese armor and infantry, forcing General Lam to commit the 18th Armored Cavalry Regiment, one of the last reserve units, to the battle.[7]

Once again, General Lam was partly responsible for the ongoing collapse north of Quang Tri City. His poor command judgment and lack of tactical sense were an additional burden for General Giai to bear. Even as the defense of northern Quang Tri Province fell apart before his eyes, Lam ordered Giai to divert forces to help push logistical units through blocked roadways between Quang Tri City and Hue. The 3d ARVN Division commander was forced to divert an armored cavalry squadron from the front lines to conduct operations to the south. Lam's orders almost exhausted fuel and ammunition supplies just as the need was most desperate.[8]

Whereas General Lam misread the seriousness of the situation, FRAC saw it in crystal-clear terms. "Reports are fragmentary at this time but intelligence indicates that the objectives are the capture of FSB Nancy and to establish a blocking force on the Quang Tri/Thua Thien border," wrote General Kroesen. "Other NVA forces will then assume offensive operations to capture Quang Tri City."[9]

Lieutenant Colonel Huynh Dinh Tung was a tired man. As commander of the 2d ARVN Regiment, he had seen his unit stretched to the limit, then pierced by a superior North Vietnamese force. At noon on 27 April the 2d ARVN Battalion was overrun by a strong enemy force along the north bank of the Quang Tri River southwest of town. The survivors moved back to the bridge, where they were ordered to stand and defend the river's western approach. From the regimental command center at Ai Tu, Tung gave orders to his subordinates as he responded to the bewildering array of instructions coming from division headquarters in the citadel, and a few from corps command in Danang. The situation got worse during the early afternoon when North Vietnamese artillery intensified, much of it raining down on the command bunkers. One of Tung's main concerns was the Quang Tri Bridge to his rear. Spanning the Thach Han River just north of Quang Tri City, the bridge was crucial to both sides. The North Vietnamese needed it in order to surround Quang Tri City; the South Vietnamese had to keep it secure so they could withdraw in good order into the citadel when the time came. From Lieutenant Colonel Tung's perspective, his position was weak. He turned to his adviser for help checking friendly positions along the river.

Lieutenant Colonel William Camper, the same adviser who had escaped from Camp Carroll following its surrender on 2 April, was in the bunker. At Tung's request he dashed out of the bunker into the deadly shower of shrapnel. Major Brown, Camper's deputy, emerged right behind him and raced for new cover. Camper hoped to get a firsthand look at the battle so he could report back to Colonel Tung; then they could develop a plan to hold the bridge.

Suddenly, sharp bursts of small-arms fire erupted along the riverbank. Puzzled, Camper returned to the bunker to look at a map. No one was sure what units were in the area; North Vietnamese units were not reported that close. Camper, Brown, and a handful of South Vietnamese soldiers moved slowly along the bank until they reached the railroad bridge paralleling Highway 1. As they approached the bridge, enemy artillery again opened up. A stray round landed in the treetops, spraying the advisers with razor-sharp shrapnel.

Camper went down, his face and neck a bloody mess. Brown examined the wounds; Camper's vocal cords were partly severed, and huge chunks of flesh had been ripped away. Blood flowed into his nasal cavity, threatening to drown him. Brown turned Camper over so the blood would flow out of his face and onto the ground. Camper was conscious the entire time. Later he vividly recalled "lying in the dirt, in some kind of potato patch, so that my mouth, nose, and face would drain."[10]

Brown knew the wound was serious and that help was needed immediately. He tried to flag down groups of retreating South Vietnamese soldiers to aid the wounded man, but no one stopped. Desperate now, Brown radioed the 3d ARVN Division command center in the citadel to report that he was alone—"ARVN GONE" was the entry placed in the division daily journal. Two Americans, an army sergeant and a navy corpsman, volunteered to help the wounded adviser. They commandeered a South Vietnamese armored personnel carrier and forced the frightened driver to take Camper across the river to safety. From there he went back to the States for medical treatment. Major Brown departed with Camper, leaving the 2d ARVN Regiment with no American advisers.

Lieutenant Colonel Camper's evacuation seemed to herald the beginning of the end for the defense of Quang Tri City. By the morning of 28 April all South Vietnamese positions around the city were in desperate shape. Enemy units had pushed to within a mile of Quang Tri City in places, and on each of the past two days North Vietnamese artillery had dropped an average of 7,000 rounds in and around the town and surrounding firebases. General Giai's troops had taken a serious beating. The 20th Tank Regiment had only eighteen M48 tanks left in action, and the 17th and 18th Armored Cavalry Regiments had lost more than one-third of their fighting vehicles. The rangers were practically out of action. The 4th Ranger Group had one entire battalion rendered combat ineffective and only 800 men fit for action, while the 5th Ranger Group had two battalions out of action with only 600 men combat ready. The 57th ARVN Regiment, which had twice fled the battlefield after encounters with the enemy, could muster fewer than 1,400 men.[11]

South Vietnamese armor units in particular bore the brunt of the action on 28 April. After the retreat of the 57th ARVN Regiment the previous day, the 1st Armored Brigade became the northernmost South Vietnamese position along Highway 1. Colonel Nguyen Trong Luat, the brigade commander, had a temporary headquarters beside the road on a flat expanse of grassland about two miles south of Dong Ha, but merciless pounding by North Vietnamese artillery drove him back to the Vinh Phuoc River early in the morning. As refugees and South Vietnamese army stragglers streamed down the highway to escape the enemy bombardment, Colonel Luat's tanks took up positions on either side of the bridge. The aggressive officer disliked being on the defensive, but the flow of events had passed the point where he could do much about them.

It was not long before the North Vietnamese came south to do battle. The first enemy tanks were spotted a few minutes past 7:00 A.M. on Highway 1 near the abandoned Dong Ha Combat Base. Air force jets bombed the armored column, and half an hour later thirty tanks were reported burning. Three T-54s were chased by South Vietnamese M48 tanks and destroyed in a running gunfight, one of the few such battles during the offensive. In the face of further enemy assaults, Colonel Luat ordered part of his armor and elements of the 5th Ranger Group back across the bridge, but by 10:30 none of the units had set up positions south of the river.

Fearing that he would be cut off from the south, Colonel Luat ordered the rest of the tanks across the bridge. Only half of them made it. A salvo of 130mm artillery pounded the bridge, dropping part of one span into the water and bringing the rest of the column to a grinding halt. The lead vehicles still north of the bridge belonged to Colonel Luat and his adviser, Lieutenant Colonel Louis Wagner. Wagner had stayed with the armored brigade since the opening shots of the offensive and had grown closer to Luat with each passing day. Now it looked as though they might die together.

With no other option in sight, Wagner's driver gunned the engine, and the vehicle surged forward, jumping over the small gap in the bridge and coming down with a bone-wrenching thud on the other side. But they made

South Vietnamese civilians flee the fighting in northern Quang Tri Province. (U.S. Army)

it. Luat's armored personnel carrier followed close behind, but it had just cleared the gap when a North Vietnamese rocket slammed into it, spraying hot metal throughout the inside. Ammunition stored inside the vehicle cooked off, shredding Luat's leg as he scrambled out the hatch. Miraculously, the armor commander was not seriously wounded, though he would need to be evacuated to the rear.

Six armored personnel carriers and one M48 tank were left stranded north of the river. The crews still north of the river abandoned their vehicles and scrambled over the shattered bridge on foot. No one took the time to disable the weapons and engines, leaving seven perfectly good pieces of armor for the North Vietnamese. Lieutenant Colonel Wagner leaped from his vehicle to help his counterpart, then called in an air strike on the abandoned armor north of the river. Taking advantage of a break in the clouds, fighter planes swooped on the stationary targets, blasting them with hard bombs.[12]

The 1st Armored Brigade began to stream south in disorder. Wagner reported to division headquarters that "without the commander present, there was no motivation among the officers and men to organize and fight effectively." The acting commander of the 1st Armored Brigade, Lieutenant Colonel Tran Tinh, lacked the vigor and aggressive spirit of his wounded superior, and as he watched Colonel Luat leave for Quang Tri on a stretcher, Tinh seemed to lose confidence. Lieutenant Colonel Wagner tried to boost his morale, but he could see that his new counterpart had rough times ahead. Wagner characterized Tinh as "cautious, but competent; an officer who relied on his advisers and expected air support to come to the rescue." As a commander, Lieutenant Colonel Tinh was the rule, not the exception, among much of the South Vietnamese officer corps.[13]

The brigade moved southward in disorder until it came up against a roadblock just north of Ai Tu Combat Base. The marines refused to let it pass, and the mass of humanity and vehicles swelled until it threatened to break through the barrier of barbed wire and sandbags. Lieutenant Colonel Tinh set up a hasty defense about one mile long just south of the damaged bridge, a poor choice for a stand. A broad, flat plain covered with low scrub offered little concealment for the tanks, while low hills just to the north concealed enemy movement. To make matters worse, North Vietnamese artillery bombarded the highway, killing dozens of civilians and soldiers and panicking the survivors.

While soldiers milled around Ai Tu and the South Vietnamese tanks held their thin, vulnerable line, the marines continued to refuse entry to the base. Lieutenant Colonel Wagner radioed the 3d ARVN Division command post at Quang Tri and requested that a senior officer be sent up to impose order, but no one came. Sensing an impending disaster, Tinh and Wagner jumped into a jeep and drove to the citadel to talk with General Giai. The division commander decided to hold at Ai Tu, but he seemed unwilling to order the marines to open the gates.

Upon returning to their unit, Tinh and Wagner held a conference with Colonel Bao, the 147th VNMC Brigade commander, inside the beleaguered base. Major James Joy, the senior U.S. Marine adviser, was also there. Since the retreat from Mai Loc earlier in the month, Major Joy had remained with the brigade and once again found himself on the leading edge of a desperate defense. During the conference, Bao and Tinh decided that the gates must be opened to allow the milling mob to filter through to the south rather than let them remain and "destroy the tactical integrity of the northern perimeter." Wagner believed the marines had no choice considering the worsening situation: "The traffic jam was finally cleared up . . . more as a result of incoming artillery rounds than as a result of positive action by ground commanders." By 4:00 in the afternoon Highway 1 north of Ai Tu was mostly clear.[14]

But Ai Tu was no longer in a strong position. North Vietnamese attacks to the south threatened to cut Ai Tu off from Quang Tri City and trap the marines. To make matters worse, on the previous evening, enemy artillery fire struck the base ammunition dump, sending 2,000 artillery rounds, powder, and fuses into a powerful—and deadly—fireworks display. Under a pall of acrid smoke the dump continued to burn for several hours. Advisers at the 3d ARVN Division command post in the citadel two miles to the southeast reported seeing the flames. Major Joy decided that the risk was great enough to warrant splitting up his advisory team. Three advisers were sent back to Quang Tri City, leaving only Major Joy, his assistant (Major Emmett Huff), and the liaison officer in Ai Tu.

At 5:00 P.M. on 28 April, new orders came in to the 1st Armored Brigade. The 4th and 5th Ranger Groups and the 20th Tank Regiment were detached from the brigade and told to remain in place north of Ai Tu. The brigade itself was ordered to disengage and move southeast of Quang Tri City, where it would take up position with what was left of the 57th ARVN Regiment, the 17th Cavalry Regiment, and one platoon from the 18th Cavalry Troop.

The plan quickly fell apart. The 1st and 2d Battalions of the 57th ARVN Regiment, which had been streaming south near Highway 1 all day, reported that they were at the spot where the Vinh Phuoc and Thach Han Rivers merged. They never made it across. By nightfall the battalions, about 250 soldiers, had splintered and were never again reconstituted. The regimental adviser left the unit, and the division noted that "the 57th Regiment was assessed as totally ineffective by the regimental senior adviser."[15]

The 1st Armored Brigade succeeded in racing down the highway and through the city. At 8:00 that night Lieutenant Colonel Tinh established the new brigade headquarters a mile south of Quang Tri, just northeast of the 17th Armored Cavalry Regiment, with the tanks fanned out in a diagonal line across Highway 1.[16]

The night was peaceful, as was most of the next day, a welcome respite after two days of constant fighting.

The 2d ARVN Regiment was not so lucky. Beginning late in the day on 28 April, enemy tanks closed on the Quang Tri Bridge, the central point of the regiment's area of responsibility. An hour past midnight on 29 April, the regiment's 2d ARVN Battalion was attacked, and two hours later the 3d ARVN Battalion reported contact. Battle updates were spotty, and because the unit had no advisers, Team 155 could not accurately sort out the garbled reports. Colonel Metcalf convinced General Giai to send 2d Troop,

18th Armored Cavalry Regiment up to the bridge to reinforce what was becoming the central focus of the North Vietnamese assault.

The tanks arrived just after first light. Moments later the cavalry commander called on the radio, his voice betraying terrible tension. There was no infantry to be seen, he reported. The entire regiment seemed to have fled. Scanning the highway to the west, the commander could make out "a large number of soldiers mingled with the civilians moving south." A detachment of local province forces were dispatched to stop the retreating soldiers.[17]

General Giai was incredulous, but the cavalry's assessment was soon borne out. The command center intercepted a radio message from a North Vietnamese commander saying that he was moving along the road toward the bridge and there were no defending forces in sight. The enemy came up hard against the tanks from the 18th Armored Cavalry Regiment, and by 10:00 that night the tankers broke off to the east. The commander reported that he had no infantry support and had lost two M113 armored personnel carriers to enemy fire.[18]

It fell to the marines to reopen the bridge before the enemy consolidated new positions along the north bank of the Thach Han River. Colonel Nguyen Nang Bao, commander of the 147th VNMC Brigade, ordered two companies from the 7th VNMC Battalion to open the bridge (the 7th Battalion was part of the 369th VNMC Brigade, but it was assigned to Ai Tu by Giai). Backed by armor from the 20th Tank Regiment, the marines rolled up the North Vietnamese, rooting them out of defensive bunkers near the bridge's north entrance. Twelve enemy soldiers were killed, and two were captured.[19]

To the south of the city fighting was light. Although there was plenty of confusion, most of it was caused by mounting panic, not North Vietnamese troops. The steady flow of refugees was swelled by an increasing number of soldiers—many of them from the broken 2d ARVN Regiment—trying to flee south. Concerned by this trend, General Giai ordered a Regional Forces company to stop them. It was unsuccessful.

The confusion was compounded by a steady flow of civilians fleeing down Highway 1. The province senior adviser noted that most of the traffic on the road was military, but mixed into the confusion were hundreds of bicycles and motorcycles, plus scores of pedestrians. An American armor adviser witnessed the carnage. As South Vietnamese troops cleared a small bridge of debris, the flood of refugees broke free and streamed down the highway, only to be dammed again by another blocked bridge about a mile farther south. As they milled about along the bank, the North Vietnamese unleashed a fierce artillery barrage that, in the estimation of the province senior adviser, "killed hundreds." The stream of humanity reversed course back up the road, only to be hit again by the merciless artillery.[20]

At the close of day, the 3d ARVN Division was clearly in trouble, though poor communications prevented a precise assessment. The 57th ARVN Regiment was down to a single battalion—fewer than 300 men—while the 18th Armored Cavalry had only fourteen tanks and twenty-one other vehicles, all manned by 200 soldiers. Unit commanders reported that fuel and ammunition shortages were compounded by North Vietnamese artillery, which seemed to seek out and destroy every stockpile in the area. Shortages were not always consistent, however. The 33d Artillery Battalion had over 4,000 105mm rounds—but only 400 fuses; the guns inside Ai Tu itself had fewer than 1,000 rounds remaining. As artillery batteries ran out of rounds, some crews destroyed their guns, believing that they would receive no more. Colonel Metcalf felt the frustration and believed that this was one of the most important factors in the continuing decline of the South Vietnamese defense. "Every time the troops got a little ammunition . . . the NVA would rocket, mortar or artillery the damn place and it would go up in flames. We had a damn ammo dump or fuel dump going up every night for the last six, seven nights we were there."[21]

At noon on 30 April the 1st Armored Brigade was ordered to link up with marines pushing up from the south. Almost immediately the brigade took fire from North Vietnamese artillery, panicking some of the tanks, which fled in disarray. Some of the advisers were left behind; they made their way back to the citadel alone. Those tankers still in formation made it to the Nhung River Bridge, about six miles southeast of Quang Tri City, only to find that the North Vietnamese were already there. After a short battle the enemy was driven off, but the bridge remained blocked by burning vehicles. As the tanks tried to clear a path, North Vietnamese gunners struck with antitank rockets. Artillery followed, and the brigade, by this time mixed up with streams of refugees, turned back north.[22]

The unit the 1st Armored Brigade was supposed to link up with was the 5th VNMC Battalion. Colonel Pham Van Chung sent the battalion, part of the 369th VNMC Brigade, north to clear the highway to Quang Tri City. The task would not be easy.

"My God, have you seen the road?" asked one marine adviser as he drove back into the brigade compound after a scouting trip. "There are thousands of people coming down the highway from Quang Tri. As far as you can see north and south the road is covered with refugees." Most of the unfortunate souls were not soldiers but civilians. Another adviser observed that "only the very old, very young, the sick, the blind, the wounded" were on the road. "Women were toting their few possessions in one basket which was balanced on the other end of a carrying stick by their babies."[23]

The marines moved north against the flow of humanity. Mounted on tanks and armored personnel carriers, they plunged up the highway to the O Khe River Bridge before taking heavy fire from the riverbank. The marines dismounted and continued on foot to the south bank of the river, "driving the enemy skirmishers back," recalled Major Donald L. Price, senior adviser to the battalion. Moments later he heard the cough of a tank engine starting up on the north bank. He could not see it, but the enemy owned the other side of the river. Suspecting a tank ambush, Price began a "duel between forward observers." From the south bank he called naval gunfire onto the elusive noise. The North Vietnamese responded with 122mm and 130mm artillery fire, but in the end the marines won—or believed they had, because after an hour of air strikes and naval bombardment, a rapid burst of secondary explosions told the marines that their fire had found its mark. They climbed back into their tanks and armored personnel carriers and cautiously edged over the bridge and up the road, firing their machine guns into suspected ambush positions as they went.[24]

Almost immediately the marines were fired on again, this time from an old French fort on the north side of the river. Thinking the fort might be manned by nervous Regional Forces militia, the marines held their fire and called back to brigade headquarters. Colonel Chung asked for air strikes, but the marines advised him that friendly forces might be firing on them. Chung did not believe that. "Regional Forces don't shoot at marines," he snapped. "They are VC. Please get air."

Chung was correct. After the dust from a massive strike cleared, the marines walked into the fort and counted 234 bodies, all wearing North Vietnamese uniforms. They were part of the 27th NVA Regiment; wounded prisoners explained that they had found it abandoned by Regional Forces the previous night.[25]

Another bottleneck appeared south of Hai Lang, about seven miles south of Quang Tri City. The enemy was holed up in abandoned South Vietnamese bunkers along the highway, just waiting for a relief column to come north. The marines again stopped short of the ambush and called for support; the first to arrive was an AC-130 Spectre gunship. Converted from a C-130 cargo plane into a flying weapons platform, Spectre flew along the trench line, pouring 30mm Gatling gun fire and 105mm howitzer rounds on top of the North Vietnamese. Close on the gunship's heels came a flight of Phantoms, dropping high-explosive bombs and napalm on the bunkers.

Major Price watched enemy soldiers stream from their bunkers and run from the aerial bombardment, only to be shot down by the waiting marines.

The bottleneck broken, hundreds of refugees surged southward away from the fighting, clogging the road and ensuring that the marine battalion would never make it to Quang Tri. The commander ordered his men back to the O Khe Bridge, where they would keep the highway open for a break-out by South Vietnamese units from the north. North Vietnamese artillery fire increased, scattering the helpless civilians trapped on the road. A marine adviser witnessed the horror: "North Vietnamese gunners, for reasons I'll never know, opened fire with their large artillery guns on the column. . . . Any respect I had for the North Vietnamese military, I lost that day. His forward observers, who were directing this withering hail of fire, were close enough to determine that these were mostly civilians and not a military force."[26]

More than 500 vehicles were destroyed along the highway, and the Red Cross placed the death toll at 2,000, including patients from the Quang Tri hospital who were being evacuated south to safety.[27]

Despite the marines and armor to the south, the present South Vietnamese defensive posture was untenable. The division and its attached forces were divided between Quang Tri City and Ai Tu Combat Base to the north. Both positions were separated by the Thach Han River, which at the point where Highway 1 crossed it was almost 100 yards wide. A single bridge spanned the river, making retreat for those forces on the north side impossible if the enemy seized it. It made more sense to consolidate south of the Thach Han and use it as a natural barrier against North Vietnamese units to the north.

In the face of impending disaster, Giai called his commanders into the citadel and laid out his plan to withdraw from Ai Tu and gradually move south until the situation stabilized. Initially, the plan was kept secret for fear that if subordinate commanders learned of it they would move too early and telegraph the move to the enemy. Giai probably also realized that if he played his hand too soon, General Lam might step in and counter-mand the order.

Most of the commanders made it to the citadel on the morning of 30 April for the conference. The plan was simple, and with signs of another North Vietnamese attack against the sore point southwest of Ai Tu, it was timely. A grim and tired General Giai told the gathered officers that all units were to move south of the river, where they would draw up in a defensive line along the bank. Division headquarters would withdraw south along Highway 1 to My Chanh, a little town twelve miles down the highway on the southern provincial border. Like Quang Tri City, My Chanh was on the southern bank of a confluence of several rivers, providing a natural barrier behind which the South Vietnamese might make a stand. But twelve miles was a long way to move under the threat of enemy artillery. Some of Giai's subordinates were openly critical, a sure sign that the chain of command was breaking down. The general held his own, however, candidly telling the gathering that if they could not withdraw in good order, all Quang Tri Province was lost.

The crux of the plan involved the marines. The 147th VNMC Brigade was to move back from Ai Tu and take responsibility for defending Quang Tri City itself, while the rest of the South Vietnamese forces withdrew. The 1st, 4th, and 5th Ranger Groups were to line up west of Highway 1, the 1st Armored Brigade and the 57th ARVN Regiment—what was left of it— on the east side. On the surface the plan was sound, but up to this point the division had proved incapable of an orderly withdrawal of any kind. For the plan to be accomplished, the South Vietnamese would have to funnel across a single bridge. But with few other options, Giai ordered the move to begin immediately, stressing that no one was to move until the marines were in place south of the river. "I acknowledge your brave actions," said Giai in closing. "Our Fatherland and people will remember you forever." After the conference, Giai called Lam to inform him of the plan. The corps commander agreed with the idea in principle but never gave his official approval.[28]

The marines moved first. At noon on 30 April Colonel Bao got the final word to move the 147th VNMC Brigade from Ai Tu across the river to Quang Tri City itself. Because the South Vietnamese communication system was in such a bad state, he could not radio his deputy, Lieutenant Colonel Nguyen Xuan Phuc, to give him the order for fear that the North Vietnamese might be listening. Instead he told the officer to drive down to the citadel, where he could be told in person. In the meantime, after a quick reconnaissance of the area, Bao decided to use the old province advisory team site—called the tiger pad—for his new command post. Situated just outside the citadel walls, the position controlled access to the highway while using the river as protection against enemy assaults. Colonel Bao decided to remain at the site, sending his deputy back to Ai Tu to supervise the withdrawal.

Driving through a curtain of artillery fire is no one's idea of fun, but Lieutenant Colonel Phuc had little choice. For the second time that day he found himself winding between shell craters, sitting in an open jeep with only the wits of his driver, an M16, and fate to protect him from sudden death. Just ahead, Phuc saw the southern gate of Ai Tu Combat Base—home at last.

Without warning, an artillery round struck nearby. A deafening roar was followed by a geyser of smoke and dirt, and the jeep careened off the road. The driver was killed, but Phuc miraculously escaped unhurt. Diving for cover, he radioed for assistance, but it would take time to get someone down to help. In the meantime, the brigade command center was without leadership.

Major Emmett Huff was the deputy senior adviser, and in Major Joy's absence he found himself in virtual command of the brigade. Colonel Bao was still in Quang Tri, the brigade operations officer was nowhere to be found, and now the deputy commander was stranded at the southern edge of the base. In Joy's opinion, the situation should never have arisen. He objected to Colonel Bao's decision to remain in Quang Tri, arguing that it was "imperative that the brigade commander return to Ai Tu and supervise the execution of the withdrawal." But Bao disagreed, and now that the deputy commander was holed up in a ditch without driver or jeep, Joy could only mutter some form of "I told you so" under his breath while he radioed Ai Tu on the secure adviser net with instructions for the withdrawal.[29]

There was a new air of urgency among the marines. As Lieutenant Colonel Phuc was crawling out of his wrecked jeep, Colonel Bao was again summoned to the 3d ARVN Division bunker, where he was told that new intelligence predicted a division-sized attack on the city itself sometime that very night. The withdrawal from Ai Tu was to begin immediately.

Leading the way out of the base was the brigade headquarters, the artillery battalion, and the 1st VNMC Battalion; the 8th VNMC Battalion was to guard the western flank while the 4th VNMC Battalion brought up the rear. As the marines saddled up, Major Huff and his assistant advisers stacked all classified and sensitive material in one corner of the bunker. After pulling the pins, the advisers stuffed their incendiary grenades into the piles and watched as flames consumed the paper, then climbed into the timbers of the bunker itself. Satisfied that the bunker would burn to the ground, the advisers joined the column of retreating marines. Major Huff stayed behind just long enough to call in a titanic barrage of naval gunfire and air strikes on the base itself.

Under a threatening cloud of enemy artillery fire, the marines' withdrawal was "executed smoothly." But their luck did not hold for long. As the marine artillery battalion approached the main bridge into the city, it discovered that South Vietnamese engineers had prematurely destroyed it, leaving the marines stranded on the wrong side of the Thach Han River. Stunned by this turn of events, the artillery commander plowed his trucks into the fast-moving river, trusting that the water was shallow enough to ford. He was mistaken and, after the lead trucks bogged down, ordered the destruction of all eighteen howitzers, plus twenty-two vehicles. Firing mechanisms were disabled, tires shot out, trucks set ablaze, and amidst the choking haze of black smoke the officers worked out a new plan.

There was really only one option—swim. In less than an hour almost 2,000 marines were lined up at the old vehicle fording site ready to take the plunge. They walked out as far as possible, then swam the final fifty yards to the other side. The 4th VNMC Battalion stayed behind as a security element while Major Huff continued to man the radio, working the curtain of naval gunfire and air support up and down the river bank.

The last into the water were the advisers. Stacking radios and weapons on air mattresses, they swam for the south bank. At the deepest point, a floundering South Vietnamese marine grabbed Captain Earl Kruger, one of the brigade advisers, and climbed onto his shoulders. Already straining under the heavy load of ammunition, helmet, and flak jacket, Kruger could not handle the weight of a soaking wet, panicked marine. He went down toward the bottom, saved only by a radio handset cable attached to Major Huff's radio. As the stricken marine went under, Huff held tight to the radio and pushed his air mattress toward Kruger, who finally grabbed it and hung on for dear life. All three Americans finally made it to the far shore, as did most of the South Vietnamese marines, though a few drowned and others lost much of their gear.

Another episode highlighted the deepening chaos. Sometime around 5:00 P.M. an order came from somewhere along the 3d ARVN Division chain of command "to execute a night withdrawal to the south along the highway and to destroy all equipment without an amphibious capability." Curious about the order, but unable to check back up the chain of command, the troops complied. Twelve of the 17th Armored Cavalry Regiment's M41 tanks and eighteen 105mm howitzers from the 33d Artillery Battalion were destroyed despite an order from the 3d ARVN Division command post rescinding the previous order. One marine adviser was startled by the event. "You could hear a boom! boom! They're blowing the guns, and while the guns were being blown there was an air drop. All of a sudden we looked up and these parachutes were coming down with pallets of artillery ammunition." It was too late. In this time of crisis the South Vietnamese were adding to their troubles by destroying their own equipment.[30]

By nightfall the marines were in place around Quang Tri City. The 1st

Enemy soldiers find the 3d ARVN Division's base at Ai Tu abandoned. (Vietnam News Agency)

VNMC Battalion guarded the western approach, the 4th VNMC Battalion formed an arc from the eastern plain down to the south, and the 8th VNMC Battalion dug in along the riverbank to the north. The brigade headquarters set up in the citadel alongside the 3d ARVN Division command post.

Part of the 20th Tank Regiment was also hindered by the blown bridges, though it did not fare as poorly as the marines. Detached from the 1st Armored Brigade on 28 April, the tanks operated near Ai Tu in support of the marines. Only eighteen M48s remained in the regiment, and as they approached the Thach Han River they lost two of them. The first hit a mine, and the second was struck by a round from a recoilless rifle as the enemy closed in from the north and west. Sixteen tanks made it across the river and lent their guns to the defense of Quang Tri City.

The marines were understandably angry when what should have been a routine withdrawal turned into a swim for life. Communications had broken down, and many blamed the 3d ARVN Division. "The brigade's desperate decision to swim the Thach Han River was but another instance of confusion and needless loss of life and equipment because the 3d ARVN Division failed to provide coordination among its units," wrote Lieutenant Colonel Turley, the marine adviser who found himself stranded at Ai Tu during the early days of the offensive. Still angry from what he perceived as improper command procedures earlier in the month, Turley criticized the flow of conflicting orders and counterorders and the general lack of command presence. "There had never been a sincere effort made within the division staff to venture out into the forward battle positions to supervise and assist the difficult execution of the division's tactical orders."[31]

While the criticism was valid, the real culprit was General Lam. Giai's decision to withdraw south from Quang Tri City was sound and may have saved what remained of the division. But he never got the chance. At around midnight, just as the maneuver was to begin, an official message from corps headquarters came up to Giai, with copies for each subordinate commander. General Lam had changed his mind. The division was ordered to remain in place and "hold at all costs." No one was to give another inch of territory to the North Vietnamese. There were no additional orders: no unit was allowed to maneuver without specific approval from Lam himself. Giai took the news stoically, then calmly told Colonel Metcalf to call all the advisers and tell them to inform their counterparts that the original order was canceled; "we will stay where we are," he said pointedly.[32]

The countermanding order was vintage Lam. Insensitive to the immediate needs of his tactical commanders in the thick of battle, he remained in close touch with political machinations in Saigon. Lam's fateful move was probably an uncritical parroting of a recent proclamation by President Thieu that the South Vietnamese army would not give up in the face of blatant aggression from North Vietnam. What Lam did not recognize was that while Thieu's speech played well with diplomats in Paris, the soldiers on the bloody fields of Quang Tri Province were in no position to comply. It was an unrealistic order. But Lam did not possess enough knowledge of the tactical situation to make such a judgment. As South Vietnamese units splintered and virtually disappeared, he continued—in the words of American advisers—"to appear confident that the enemy cannot launch his attack." This wishful thinking prevailed despite warnings from FRAC that "it is doubtful that the 3d Division will be capable of a continued defense of Quang Tri."[33]

If Lam was not aware that his poor judgment was contributing to losing the battle, his American counterpart was. General Kroesen reported to his superiors as follows:

> The ARVN defense of Quang Tri is being hampered by command and control difficulties. Gen[eral] Giai . . . believes LTG [Lieutenant General] Lam has so restricted him tactically that he no longer possesses the

flexibility and maneuverability required to adequately handle the tactical situation in the Quang Tri area. This situation has, in fact, adversely effected Gen[eral] Giai's ability to influence the conduct of defense.

Kroesen had "frank discussions with LTG Lam in regard to this matter," but the situation did not change.[34]

Lam's decision was the final blow. The entire province north of Quang Tri City was in enemy hands, and the only thing preventing the North Vietnamese from crossing the river was a constant curtain of naval gunfire and tactical air strikes that pulverized the far bank. To the south, individual soldiers as well as entire South Vietnamese units fled down the highway. Colonel Metcalf described the division as being in a "precarious position."

Four North Vietnamese regiments and about sixty tanks had moved to within 500 yards of the city and were poised to strike before dawn. North and west of the city, angry streaks of antiaircraft tracers flashed skyward like flaming claws, seeking out the little air control planes that tirelessly circled the battleground guiding air strikes. South Vietnamese soldiers near the walls watched in fear as shadows danced across the barren ground, sometimes revealing the shapes of tanks and trucks just across the river. But late that night the artillery batteries in Quang Tri City announced that they had no more illumination rounds to light the battlefield for air strikes. As the last parachute flares sputtered out and plunged the grassy plain into darkness, North Vietnamese tanks and infantry again crept forward toward their prize.

NINE

THE CITADEL

General Giai's subordinates could not believe the news. First they were told to withdraw; now they were to stand and die. But it was too late for that. Orders had been issued and units were on the move. The marine brigade commander, Colonel Bao, was the first to rebel. Storming into the bunker, he told the exhausted general that the marines were leaving—with or without him.

Bao may have been bolstered in his insubordination by no less an authority than Lieutenant General Le Nguyen Khang, the Marine Division commander. At some point during the day, Khang had called Lam and protested that his marines were being used fruitlessly in a defensive role rather than as assault troops. Angered by the unexpected complaint, Lam reportedly replied that the marines had been placed under his command by Saigon, and they would be used as he saw fit. "I am involved in combat, and I must use what I have the best way I can," he said, then slammed down the receiver. Although Khang was not in the chain of command, he refused to let the matter rest. What followed is unclear, but according to one account Khang called the 147th VNMC Brigade, countermanded all 3d ARVN Division orders, and told Colonel Bao to pull back to a position south of Quang Tri City.[1]

Other South Vietnamese officers were also in the bunker and were clearly prepared to follow Bao's lead. Giai knew he had to seize the moment. Asking for calm, he called General Lam on the radio and informed him of the situation. Lam exhorted each officer one by one, but none admitted that he planned to leave. Yet when Lam signed off, it was as if nothing had changed. The officers defied Giai, saying that they were retreating.[2]

For Giai it was the last straw. Though he was a brave and competent officer, the stress of the past month was too much to bear. Giai fell heavily into a chair, placed his head in his hands, and cried. Metcalf stood nearby, uncertain of how to react, and waited quietly.[3]

There were no other options. In the face of Lam's eleventh-hour blunder, there was no time to organize a new defense, or even to stop the disintegration of the old plans. The disorganization and panic prompted the American advisers in Quang Tri to think about escape. Colonel Metcalf

In anticipation of the final North Vietnamese assault, a U.S. adviser burns classified documents in Quang Tri. (Frank Brown)

and his senior advisers developed plans "for possible evacuation by any means to include by foot," but it was already too late.

Through it all Giai remained in his bunker, numbed into inaction by the events of the past few hours. His initial depression changed to rage as he more fully realized his predicament. Some advisers watched as Giai "began throwing temper tantrums because he didn't have control over his own people." At noon Giai decided that continued defense was hopeless.[4]

In Hue, FRAC heard the news and knew that the city was lost. "The final deterioration of the situation in Quang Tri occurred when BG Giai was abandoned by his subordinate commanders," read one report from the front. "Following a meeting, they presented him with an ultimatum that he withdraw or be left alone in the citadel, a threat they then proceeded to carry out."[5]

Colonel Metcalf called FRAC with the latest battle information, but General Kroesen cared mostly about getting the Americans out of the citadel. What did the advisers intend to do? he asked. For the time being, nothing, replied Metcalf. Helicopters could not come into the citadel without being mobbed by South Vietnamese desperate to leave. "It would be a fight for who was going to get aboard," argued Metcalf as he and Kroesen sorted out options. As long as chaos reigned, there would be no evacuation. "I'll tell you when I think we might be able to pull it off," said Metcalf as he signed off.

Actually, there was a semblance of a plan. Metcalf believed that the panic in the city would empty the citadel within an hour, leaving the Americans on their own. Then the helicopters could come in. He was right. At 2:00 Metcalf called FRAC and said, "Begin your plan."

Still in the grip of depression, Giai succumbed to the panic around him. As troops streamed south, he gathered his staff and headed for the bunker door. Metcalf recalled that Giai "had lost all control. With his officers gone and the world falling apart around him, Giai panicked and ran from the bunker." Eighteen officers fled with him. Swarming aboard three armored personnel carriers, they left the citadel, hoping to join marine and ranger units about a mile to the south. They never made it. Within forty-five minutes Giai was back inside the citadel, thwarted by enemy forces that by this time had surrounded the city. Metcalf walked over to the general and told him there was a flight of rescue helicopters on the way. "Sir, I am planning an extraction and if you so desire, I'll take you out with me." Giai nodded gratefully.[6]

Originally, the air force wanted to land about 1,000 yards southeast of the citadel in an open field, but Colonel Metcalf doubted that the advisers could survive the artillery. Instead, they asked for the helicopters to fly into the citadel itself. While the rescue team readied, the Americans feverishly burned documents and destroyed radios, anything that might be of value to the enemy. Everyone remaining in the citadel was organized into three groups. Metcalf had the advisers search the compound and account for everyone. "I didn't want the helicopter to come in and then suddenly find a hundred or so Vietnamese coming out of the walls," he recalled. But there was no one else, only piles of abandoned weapons, which the advisers tried to smash into pieces. As a final precaution, a truck was wedged into the citadel gate so no one could even walk by—"nothing could get in or out of the citadel as far as we were concerned."[7]

Major David Brookbank stayed on the radio as liaison with the air force rescue operation. He flipped through frequencies searching for a friendly voice but could find only silence. "I sure hope I haven't screwed this up because I can't get them on the frequency," he said only half jokingly. Major Glenn Golden, the marine ANGLICO officer, rolled his eyes. "Goddamn it Dave, this is not the time," he thought to himself.[8]

The rest of the advisers waited nervously for the helicopters. The group that was to leave on the first chopper—which included General Giai and his staff—waited in the clearing near the landing zone; the second group was lined up along the citadel wall; and the final group, containing most of the American officers, stayed near the bunker. Arrayed in the open, the groups presented an easy target to the North Vietnamese, who were now in the town itself. Major Golden saw flashes of sunlight off the binoculars of forward observers holed up in nearby buildings. Yet there was very little shooting. North Vietnamese artillery was largely silent, and only a few bursts of small-arms fire sounded outside the walls. No one was quite sure why the enemy backed off and allowed the evacuation. The North Vietnamese certainly could have stormed the citadel as the advisers waited for helicopters, or they could have concentrated artillery fire inside the walls. There are a few possible explanations, though none are entirely convincing. First, the North Vietnamese may have been surprised by the rapid deterioration of South Vietnamese defenses and were unprepared to move on the citadel. Second, the ferocious air strikes along the river may have unhinged plans for a final attack. Finally, they may have been under orders to allow the escape. The humiliation of losing dozens of advisers might have triggered a fierce reaction by the Americans, who still had hundreds of marines waiting in ships offshore. That possibility may have been an escalation the North Vietnamese were unwilling to risk. Not that there weren't a few tense moments inside the citadel. As fighter planes continued their bombing runs along the river, some North Vietnamese artillery crews managed to fire into the walls. A 105mm round thudded into the ground just five yards from an adviser guarding the south wall. He was lucky. The soft dirt absorbed the explosion, leaving him dazed but unhurt.

But while the North Vietnamese did not seem anxious to launch an all-out attack on the advisers inside the citadel, they did take a heavy toll on aircraft in the area. At least three U.S. aircraft, two A-1E Skyraider ground support planes and a forward air controller, were shot down in the hours leading up to the rescue. The Skyraider pilots were rescued, and the forward air control pilot managed to parachute into the city, where he linked up with the marines and made his way out on foot.

Airborne rescue operations were an art form honed to perfection by the U.S. Air Force after years of practice. Usually they were designed to pick up downed pilots in hostile territory, but there was no reason why the same system could not be used on beleaguered army advisers. Seventh Air Force received the evacuation request from FRAC early in the day, and by 2:00 P.M. the Joint Rescue and Coordination Center in Danang had approved the plan. By 3:30 all helicopters were orbiting over the South China Sea east of

Quang Tri City "feet wet"—meaning over the water in combat aviation parlance. Three FACs were assigned to monitor the situation, each with four "sets" of fighter aircraft that could be used at will to suppress enemy fire.

At 4:30 they used them, guiding the fighters along the west bank of the Thach Han River in one of the heaviest bombing strikes of the offensive. The bombs landed close to the citadel. "The tactical situation dictated that normal safe distances for much of the ordnance be waived so we could do nothing but watch, wait, and thank God for the U.S. Air Force," wrote Major Brookbank.[9]

As the Phantoms swept back and forth, FACs called for the rescue helicopters. Four HH-3s, called Jolly Green Giants by the air force, left their orbit over the ocean and headed one by one for the citadel. The Jolly Green was tailor-made for rescue operations. Developed in the mid-1960s, it had a range of 640 miles, could fly at nearly 200 miles per hour, and could climb to 12,000 feet. Combined with machine guns and a jungle-penetrating cable hoist, the Jolly Green was a formidable machine with a proud history of plucking downed pilots from harm's way.

The first helicopter, Jolly Green 71, began its low-level approach to Quang Tri at 4:30 P.M. Flanked by A-1E Skyraiders flying cloverleaf fire suppression patterns, it flew straight toward the city from the northwest. Twenty minutes later Jolly Green 71 lumbered over the citadel walls, sending a whirlwind of dust and debris spiraling into the air. A small group of enemy soldiers took aim at the huge target, but the tailgunner fired a long burst, scattering the soldiers before they could do any damage.

The pilot put down near the south wall just in front of the burning advisory team bunker. General Giai and his staff brushed aside lower-ranking South Vietnamese soldiers so they could be the first on board, an uncharacteristic act of selfishness by the division commander who had bravely stood against overwhelming odds for exactly one month. Two minutes later the helicopter was airborne, carrying thirty-seven grateful soldiers.

Those still inside the citadel walls scanned the horizon for signs of the next helicopter. Jolly Green 65 appeared from the northeast at 4,000 feet flanked by a buzzing Skyraider. Black smoke continued to obscure the landing zone, but the pilot put the helicopter down and within a few minutes was back in the air rotoring toward Hue with forty-seven passengers. Jolly Green 21 came in right behind, picking up the last forty-seven advisers, among them Colonel Metcalf and Major Golden. The two men hesitated momentarily, vying to be the last American out of the citadel. Golden recalled that they both stepped onto the ramp at the same time, ensuring equality between the army and the marines.

A fourth helicopter flew into the citadel, but everyone was gone. Peering out from over the back ramp, a crewman scanned the scene. Only burning bunkers and blasted houses could be seen, and he gave the pilot the all-clear signal. The Jolly Green roared into the air, then turned south following the same route as the first three. As the helicopter climbed skyward, the doorgunners spotted a group of North Vietnamese soldiers running toward the citadel wall. The soldiers stopped and fired, but the chopper kept on its course toward Danang.

A total of 132 survivors were plucked from the citadel by the air force, 80 of them Americans. Within thirty minutes they were out of the war zone and in Danang, a city still relatively untouched by the enemy offensive. In the words of Colonel Metcalf, "Quang Tri City belonged to the enemy."[10]

Not all American advisers were safe in Danang. Those attached to the 57th ARVN Regiment, the 1st Armored Brigade, and the 147th VNMC Brigade were not whisked to freedom by Jolly Green Giants. As the officers of the 3d ARVN Division flew overhead in helicopters, their battle over, other South Vietnamese still had to fight their way to safety.

Lieutenant Colonel Louis Wagner could not have left with the 3d ARVN Division staff even if he wanted to. His unit, the 1st Armored Brigade, was three miles southeast of the citadel, just inside the tightening cordon of North Vietnamese troops encircling Quang Tri City from the south. Lieutenant Colonel Tinh, the brigade commander, heard the call and was frantic at the news that his advisers might be evacuated. Wagner assured him that he was staying and that the tanks could fight their way to safety.

The armor began an assault along the old railroad tracks south of Highway 1 on the morning of 1 May, but lack of air support and the discovery that a crucial bridge had been knocked out blunted the thrust. Within an hour the tanks were struggling toward the east in an attempt to break away from the enemy. Rockets, artillery, and machine guns pounded the South Vietnamese, forcing them back. Wagner radioed back to the citadel for orders, but no one answered his calls. The only friendly voice came from marine advisers with the 369th VNMC Brigade to the south. Dug in around a bridge over the O Khe River, the marines refused to allow anyone—friend or foe—to pass through their lines from the north. They reinforced their determination with recoilless rifles and a string of mines along the riverbank, and the 1st Armored Brigade was forced to stop for two hours while Wagner convinced the marines that his tanks needed to move south. Even so, they required the tanks to stop 300 yards north of the bridge while Wagner walked to their positions and personally accounted for each tank that passed by.

Wagner was not amused by the ritual. "By the time this agreement was made," he reported, "the enemy had reacted to the situation by placing antitank weapons [less than a half mile to the northwest]. Several vehicles were lost attempting to move toward the bridge and attempts to silence the antitank weapons by artillery fire and air strikes were not successful."[11]

By late afternoon many of the tanks were still north of the river. Disorganized South Vietnamese infantry units were now mingling with the armor as they flowed aimlessly south. Among them were two regimental commanders and a handful of battalion commanders riding in armored personnel carriers, but none could be persuaded to get out and organize the retreating rabble. Faced with total chaos, Lieutenant Colonel Tinh, the brigade commander, halted the charade of squeezing his tanks one by one through the marine defenses. Instead, the brigade settled down for the night while North Vietnamese artillery serenaded it with "very heavy" shelling.

At dawn the enemy was already moving in. Nine PT-76 amphibious tanks were skulking a few thousand yards to the west, while from the south and east the sound of additional—though unidentified—tanks could be heard. The brigade saddled up and again moved south toward the O Khe Bridge but ran into a curtain of artillery. It was the final straw. Tanks and armored personnel carriers fled in all directions, some of them crashing into each other in the confusion. What was left of the brigade fled north to Hai Lang, a once-sleepy town on Highway 1 halfway between Quang Tri City and My Chanh, where they stopped while officers tried to regain control of their tanks. They failed. Part of the 11th and 17th Armored Cavalry Regiments succeeded in crashing through the enemy encirclement, then headed south toward My Chanh, but the brigade headquarters element was attacked by six PT-76s before it could join the breakout. Four were destroyed as the South Vietnamese raced toward the east, the only direction open to them. "The move to the east was solely to save the unit," admitted Wagner. "There was no tactical advantage to it."[12]

At 11:00 A.M. they broke through the ring of heavy machine-gun and rocket fire near Hai Lang, though there was not much finesse to the maneuver. Tanks and armored personnel carriers were covered with South Vietnamese troops fleeing the battle, making it impossible for the tanks to fight back against the pursuing enemy. "Many infantrymen were killed when they fell off and were run over by other tracked vehicles," reported Wagner. In fact, they were safer on the ground because "it appeared that most of the enemy fire was directed at track vehicles rather than infantrymen who were walking."[13]

During the retreat many vehicles became stuck in the mud and were abandoned, but by noon the command group had reached the bridge at My Chanh, where they again encountered marines who were unwilling to allow anyone to pass south of the river. From My Chanh south, it was smooth going.

By 2:00 P.M. the surviving tanks of the 1st Armored Brigade reached Camp Evans. Six tanks had been lost that day, all of them bogged down in rice paddies and abandoned by frightened drivers who were not paying attention to where they were going.

The marines also missed out on the helicopter evacuation. During the confusion at the citadel on the morning of 1 May, the 147th VNMC Brigade prepared to move from its positions outside the walls toward more secure ground to the south. Early in the afternoon, Major Joy, the brigade senior adviser, got a call from the advisory team in the 3d ARVN Division compound. "The ARVN are pulling out," radioed Colonel Metcalf. "Advisers may stay with their units or join me." Joy declined the invitation, saying that his advisers would remain with the marine brigade. Metcalf said nothing about the pending helicopter evacuation.[14]

Six marine advisers remained with the brigade as it prepared to leave the city and join the 3d ARVN Division command staff to the south. There was a new urgency in the air as the advisers burned classified documents and radio equipment. As in a scene from an old war movie, the brigade moved off to the east, then turned south after passing wreckage and bodies clogging the highway. At 2:00 P.M. the column ran up against a deep river crossing, where it lost two M48 tanks in the treacherous water, though most of the marines made it across without incident.

As the marines continued south, they watched as, one by one, four HH-3 Jolly Green Giants dipped into the citadel, then rotored south toward Danang. "This was the first indication that helicopters were coming to extract the group," recalled Major Joy. Metcalf had not informed the advisers outside the citadel of the impending evacuation. The marines were alone, the northernmost South Vietnamese presence in Quang Tri Province.

As fighter planes continued to pulverize the far bank of the Thach Han River some two miles distant, the brigade turned toward Hai Lang District headquarters, six miles southeast of Quang Tri City. Just before sunset the North Vietnamese attacked the front of the column, which by this time was less than three miles north of the 369th VNMC Brigade along the My Chanh defensive line. Colonel Bao gathered his battalion commanders for a conference, but no one could agree on what to do, so the brigade stopped for the night. Major Joy argued against the decision, pointing out that it made more sense to punch straight through to My Chanh before the enemy could concentrate its forces. But Bao was not swayed, and as darkness fell the marines stayed where they were.

The night was quiet. Refugees continued down the highway despite the darkness, many of them stopping outside the marines' perimeter for safety. Then, at 5:00 on the morning of 2 May, sentinels heard tanks to the west near the 1st VNMC Battalion's area—"this seemed to spook the whole column," observed Major Joy. An hour later no one had seen any armor, but the 8th VNMC Battalion heard more rumblings to the south near the O Khe River, precisely the spot where the brigade planned to cross and run for My Chanh. The marines were surrounded.

North Vietnamese infantry backed by recoilless rifles and some tanks attacked from the north, west, and east. Advisers tried to calm the brigade staff, which had joined the general confusion by climbing on top of armored personnel carriers as they prepared to flee. Major Joy reminded the frightened officers that the tanks could not fight while the marines remained on top, but no one seemed to be listening. Tankers from the 20th Tank Regiment, which was still under the operational control of the 147th VNMC Brigade, fled in all directions without firing a shot. Only six of the original forty-two M48 tanks that had met the first enemy armor assault at Dong Ha on Easter Sunday remained.

Joy and Major Huff, the deputy senior adviser, were in the rear of the command vehicle when it broke and ran. Major Charles Goode and Major Thomas Gnibus, two other advisers, were on top of an armored personnel carrier when it bolted back to the north. They jumped off, along with an American civilian communications technician, Gerry Dunn, who had been caught up in the retreat from Quang Tri and had nowhere else to go. Two U.S. Army advisers with the 20th Tank Regiment stayed with what remained of their unit as it fled over the low dunes to the southeast. After days of fighting, the 147th VNMC Brigade had crumbled. During the rout, marines dropped weapons and shed uniforms as they ran from the enemy attack. Even Colonel Bao fled. Six advisers and one civilian were all that remained of the brigade command element.

Joy continued to call for air strikes, but time was no longer on their side. The advisers now found themselves at the rear of the retreating column, separated from their counterparts and out of touch with the brigade headquarters. "The advisory effort was over," concluded Joy, who decided that now was the time for extraction. Major Huff radioed the request to a circling air controller and stressed that "there are NVA on all sides and it appears that we have about five minutes before the enemy is on top of us."[15]

As they waited for a helicopter, the tiny group kept a lookout for enemy troops but saw only refugees and South Vietnamese deserters. "Every time we would look over a sand dune some place we would see naked or semi-naked Vietnamese, former soldiers who had stripped off all their clothing," said Major Goode. "They carried no weapons."[16]

The advisers wished they had more weapons. Of the six marines, two had M16s, the rest only pistols. Major Goode found only six magazines and a handful of grenades, which he distributed evenly. Then a small enemy patrol bumped into the little group. "We had a sharp little shoot-em-up with about six of them just on the edge of Hai Lang," recalled Major Goode. "I shot off about two magazines and we were down to about sixty rounds." The advisers reasoned that the enemy soldiers now knew where they were. Even if they did not, surely they could see the growing crowd of deserters skulking near the advisers. They knew it would not be long before a helicopter came to the Americans' rescue. But the chosen pickup spot offered the best defensive terrain around, and the advisers were not about to move. Major Joy had found a small, dried-up rice paddy flat enough for a helicopter landing yet guarded on all sides from direct fire by rolling sand dunes.

At 9:45 A.M. one of the marines saw a helicopter. Major Joy popped a colored smoke grenade and held his breath as the Huey dropped down. "The helicopter landed in an inferno," Joy recalled. "Direct fire, mortar, .51 caliber machine-gun and small-arms fire were all engaging the helicopter." But the Huey made it in and landed almost on top of the Americans. For the moment it was shielded from the North Vietnamese guns.

Captain Stanley A. Dougherty, U.S. Army, was at the controls. He kept the rotors spinning fast, ready to jump back into the sky at a moment's notice, while the advisers scrambled aboard. Major Goode went in face down, and before he could sit up, Gerry Dunn, the civilian, jumped in on top of him. Looking up from the floor, Goode noticed the shiny star of a brigadier general on one of the uniforms. It belonged to none other than General Thomas Bowen, the deputy senior adviser at FRAC. Bowen was in the air over My Chanh when he heard the marine advisers' distress call, and since his chopper was closest, he took the mission. "I thought it was awfully nice that he came to get us," joked Goode.[17]

Not everyone got aboard so smoothly. Major Huff and Captain Skip Kruger were elbowed aside by a mad rush of South Vietnamese stragglers who clambered inside. The helicopter shuddered as it began to lift into the air, and, thinking they might be left behind, the two advisers found the strength to fight through to the open door. As the chopper slowly rose, Huff found himself straddling one skid, hanging on to Kruger by the wrist. Upon clearing the top of the sand dunes, the advisers were greeted by two PT-76 tanks with guns leveled directly at the helicopter. One fired, but a rising helicopter—even an overloaded one—is a difficult target. Seeing Huff and Kruger dangling from one skid, the pilot dropped back to the ground so they could get on board.

So did the South Vietnamese still near the landing zone. The Americans kicked and punched at the Vietnamese, knocking most of them to the ground. General Bowen helped, striking out at one persistent soldier hanging onto a skid. "I could see the general kicking this Vietnamese right in the groin," said Major Goode. "His leg was going like a piston." From his position pinned to the floor, Goode kicked at the knees of one soldier, and another adviser repeatedly smashed a Vietnamese in the face with the butt of his pistol.

Still, it looked as if the helicopter would not make it into the air. The four-man crew, plus General Bowen and his aide, six marines, one civilian, and four tenacious South Vietnamese soldiers was too much weight for the Huey. But the pilot revved the engine to the danger line and slowly lifted into the air. Bullets filled the sky as the enemy turned every available weapon on the straining helicopter, yet the pilot managed to stay airborne. Suddenly, Captain Dougherty swung south, diving for the ground in an attempt to gain speed. Just above the treetops, he leveled out and raced for safety—with no time to spare. As the helicopter sped away, the marines saw North Vietnamese tanks and infantry less than 100 yards from the little landing zone.

They were lucky. Only Gerry Dunn was injured, and he only sustained a bloody gash from a bullet that creased his head. Captain Dougherty knew his helicopter had not escaped unscathed, and he constantly looked out the window for signs of damage. As they flew over My Chanh, an adviser with the 369th VNMC Brigade called and reported that they were streaming fuel and there was someone clinging to a skid. Rather than risk trying to fly all the way to Camp Evans, the pilot put down on Highway 1 well south of the North Vietnamese and called Phu Bai for another helicopter. He counted several holes in the rotors, engine, and stabilizing bars.

The new helicopter arrived, and the marines and General Bowen climbed aboard. But it, too, was overloaded and could not lift off. Bowen and his aide climbed out and ordered the pilot to take the battle-weary advisers to safety. All were pronounced exhausted but healthy by the medical staff at Camp Evans, except Gerry Dunn, who got twenty-four stitches in his head as a souvenir of the Easter Offensive.[18]

By the afternoon of 2 May only one organized unit of South Vietnamese troops remained in Quang Tri Province—the 369th VNMC Brigade. Dug in at My Chanh, just north of the Tach Ma River, it occupied the last sliver of the province. Everything else was in enemy hands. Colonel Pham Van Chung, the brigade commander, watched as thousands of South Vietnamese army stragglers and civilians made for My Chanh, the only gateway into relatively peaceful Thua Thien Province just over the river. Drawn like moths to a lantern, the refugees swarmed toward the bridge.

Major Robert Sheridan, Chung's senior adviser, stood nearby. "Well, sir, it looks as if everyone else is heading south," he said. "Are we to follow or stand here?"

Colonel Chung stared defiantly ahead, unwilling to acknowledge the possibility of retreat. "No, no, we will not go south," he answered angrily. "We are a good brigade and if you and your marines will stand with us, no communist will cross the river and live." Born in northern Vietnam, Chung refused to refer to the enemy soldiers as "North Vietnamese," preferring to call them "communists" or "VC."[19]

Looking back at the past few days, Sheridan must have thought Chung's boast an idle one. Given the overwhelming strength of the North Vietnamese, not to mention the momentum gained by capturing Quang Tri City, it was unlikely that the lone marine brigade could halt the offensive. Nor had the marines accomplished their original mission. Chung's brigade had been ordered to clear the highway south of Quang Tri and prevent the North Vietnamese from surrounding the citadel, but it had failed, and now Chung counted on the fearsome power of American air support to destroy the enemy.

Despite the brigade's difficulties over the past two days, it had somehow managed to remain an organized fighting unit. As the U.S. Army advisers left the citadel by helicopter on the afternoon of 1 May, the 369th VNMC Brigade was still south of the O Khe River Bridge about two miles northeast of My Chanh. For some reason, Colonel Chung did not receive word of the citadel's evacuation until late that night. "Very bad, very bad," he said upon hearing the news. "Quang Tri has fallen. Tomorrow we will have a big battle. Now we must prepare and plan."[20]

Chung had little time to plan. The North Vietnamese had at least two regiments at Hai Lang, a mere three miles north of the marines' position at the O Khe Bridge, and they were still moving south. Chung placed the 9th VNMC Battalion south of the O Khe River and the 5th VNMC Battalion two miles to the south just north of My Chanh. Behind them was a battery of 105mm howitzers, their tubes lowered to provide direct fire support to the front lines. Both battalion commanders knew the terrain well. Operating in the area since April, the brigade had identified all likely enemy avenues of approach. Major Sheridan registered the coordinates of probable North Vietnamese troop concentrations and, through an airborne forward air controller, radioed ANGLICO in Hue to report that everything north of the O Khe River was enemy territory. The big naval guns offshore could fire at will. In preparation for the expected attack on 3 May, Colonel Chung asked that the Americans reserve all the air support possible to fend off the North Vietnamese. Sheridan passed on the request and was told that they would get what they needed at first light.

Chung's prediction of a major assault was no exaggeration. During the night the marines heard the ominous sound of approaching tanks. Under the glare of parachute flares the advisers called in naval gunfire, but they could not be certain that they were hitting anything. Just before first light on 2 May, enemy artillery opened up on the marines; in Major Sheridan's words, "our whole world came apart." For almost an hour the big guns pounded the brigade, prompting Sheridan to wonder if anyone would be left alive to throw back the inevitable armor and infantry assault after the bombardment lifted. Vehicles, bunkers, friendly gun emplacements—even entire villages—were blown apart by the unerring accuracy of the enemy gun crews. "All we could do was dig deeper—and pray," Sheridan recalled.

As had happened so many times before over the last month, the North Vietnamese suddenly ceased fire, and the ground attack began. Eighteen T-54s headed straight for the 9th VNMC Battalion lines. Major James Beans, the battalion senior adviser, called for air support, but in the smoke and haze the forward air controller could not tell the difference between friendly and enemy forces and would not authorize strikes close to the brigade's forward edge.

For a crucial thirty minutes the marines were on their own. Five tanks managed to break through the brigade command position, forcing the officers to scurry for new cover. Colonel Chung dashed from the bunker with Sheridan right on his heels. The North Vietnamese crashed through the rows of abandoned buildings—"we looked like Keystone Kops running in and out of homes trying to get away from the tanks," recalled Major Sheridan. Finally, the T-54s were all destroyed with LAWs.

Major Beans lay on top of a dirt berm and watched as the attack unfolded. Despite the smoke, the North Vietnamese armor column was now clearly visible in the morning sun, and Beans called for air strikes. The swarming fighters pounced, killing at least three T-54s. Marine 105mm howitzers destroyed five more; only a single tank escaped the marines.

But the enemy was not yet ready to give up. Rarely did the North Vietnamese use armor and infantry well together, and this was no exception. Not until after the tanks were beaten did the enemy commit its infantry, and even then the soldiers charged in a human wave across open ground, directly into the guns of the waiting marines. Major Beans and Major Donald Price, senior adviser to the 5th VNMC Battalion, witnessed the carnage and later reported that hundreds of enemy soldiers died under a curtain of naval gunfire and tactical air strikes that left the ground looking like a "cratered moonscape." Within an hour it was over, and the remaining soldiers of two North Vietnamese regiments were scurrying for the cover of the Hai Lang forest.[21]

Victory, such as it was, allowed the marines no respite. Reeling from the previous night's artillery bombardment and from the enemy's massive frontal attack, the brigade fell back across the Tach Ma River to defend My Chanh (although the river was named Tach Ma, most Americans referred to it as the My Chanh River). Colonel Chung intended to keep his vow that "no communist will cross the river and live."

Although remnants of the 3d ARVN Division, the 1st Armored Brigade, and the 147th VNMC Brigade were still north of the river, Chung ordered the My Chanh Bridge destroyed. Fearing that enemy units might manage to slip through his lines in the confusion, he decided to force friendly troops to cross to the west where the river narrowed. South Vietnamese engineers set charges under the bridge but failed to destroy the center span. Worried that the enemy could easily repair the damage, the marine advisers siphoned gas from vehicles, doused the timbers, and set it ablaze with signal flares. Smoke from the fire lingered for days, giving forward air controllers and fighters a clear landmark for their bombing runs.

For the rest of the day the 369th VNMC Brigade had all the power of the U.S. Air Force and U.S. Navy at its disposal. As North Vietnamese troops consolidated their new positions south of Quang Tri City, Major Sheridan called in air and naval gunfire strikes on armor and infantry columns in the distance north of the river. With the enemy controlling an entire province and threatening to move south on Hue, all the rules of fire control went out the window. Air controllers called in strikes right up to the riverbank, even though South Vietnamese marines were less than 300 yards to the south. During one B-52 strike, the bombs fell so close that the ground trembled, knocking Sheridan to the ground as he talked on the radio. Colonel Chung's bunker partially collapsed under the impact, but he emerged covered with dirt and unperturbed. "That was very good," he said with a smile. "Do it again."[22]

A vanguard of North Vietnamese soldiers enters Quang Tri City on 29 April. (Vietnam News Agency)

General Lam took the news of the fall of Quang Tri Province quietly. He said nothing to his staff in Danang, nothing to General Kroesen. Lam only asked if he could borrow the FRAC jet for a trip to Saigon. On the morning of 2 May, as the 369th VNMC Brigade was still fighting near My Chanh, Lam flew to see President Thieu in a secret round of talks about the continued defense of I Corps. The Corps headquarters staff knew nothing of Lam's plans or even of his impending departure. Officers milled about, not knowing how to proceed while the fighting continued to the north. Kroesen made the most of the situation by working directly with the operations and intelligence staffs, streamlining their organization and generally keeping them busy in the face of Lam's unexplained desertion. It was as if the corps commander had forgotten that the North Vietnamese were still on the offensive.[23]

It was General Abrams himself who had prompted Lam's recall to Saigon. Concerned that poor leadership was fueling the crisis in I Corps, Abrams arranged a formal meeting with President Thieu. On the morning of 2 May, the MACV commander and Ellsworth Bunker, the U.S. ambassador to South Vietnam, drove to the presidential palace, where they met alone with Thieu for an hour. Abrams pulled no punches, telling the president that the ineffectiveness of his commanders was largely responsible for the defeat in northern I Corps, as well as the continuing problems in the Central Highlands and in III Corps. All that had been accomplished over the past four years was now at stake, and only the field commanders could influence the outcome, argued Abrams.

Thieu looked solemn, but he listened intently, then summoned his executive officer and ordered that all corps commanders be called to Saigon for a meeting—immediately. Abrams was relieved that the president took his observations seriously. "This was a very candid meeting," recalled Abrams, "but at no time did President Thieu show either irritation, impatience, or disagreement." General Lam received the order to fly to Saigon that day.[24]

Lam returned as mysteriously as he had departed. On the morning of 3 May he flew back to Danang, rushed from the plane, and disappeared into his quarters. Not until late that afternoon did he reappear and inform the FRAC advisory staff that he had been recalled to Saigon to serve in the Ministry of Defense. Other corps commanders, most notably Lieutenant General Ngo Dzu in II Corps, would simply be sacked, but Lam managed to call in political favors and get himself kicked upstairs in Saigon's military hierarchy. In an ironic twist, General Lam was made chief of the Ministry of Defense's anticorruption campaign.

At a meeting held later that evening, Lam told his surprised staff that he was leaving I Corps and that Lieutenant General Ngo Quang Truong, the IV Corps commander in the Mekong Delta, was coming north to relieve him. From his chair in the back of the briefing room, Kroesen noticed that "Lam was a changed man. The weight of the world had been lifted from his shoulders." Lieutenant General Hoang Xuan Lam, the commander who could never resist meddling in the chain of command, issued no orders that evening. He slipped back to his room and remained there in seclusion until he was whisked off to Saigon the next morning. There was no fanfare, no formal change of command, only the echo of artillery to the north and the steady stream of refugees fleeing the battlefront.[25]

Not until Lam was in Danang did he vent his feelings about the loss of Quang Tri. "I told them to stay, stay, stay," he told some of his closest contacts in the press corps. Shaking a clenched fist in the air, he blamed his subordinates. "They withdrew without orders. Quang Tri had not been hit yet." The fact that he had failed to give his officers flexibility to properly defend Quang Tri in the first place still did not occur to Lam, though he did finally accept the consequences. "I didn't fulfill the mission given to me," Lam said with tears in his eyes. "That is very bad, and it was very bad to lose Quang Tri. So I take my responsibility."[26]

Lam would not be remembered well in history, nor were his contemporaries kind to him. General Cao Van Vien, chairman of the Joint General Staff and the top military man in the South Vietnamese army, believed Lam was ill equipped for the job of corps commander:

> Looking back on that difficult period of time, I can now see that it was perhaps unrealistic to expect perfection from a corps commander. The kind of training and experience, the influence of politics on officers of General Lam's generation and their very background did not contribute to the cultivation of military leadership required by the circumstances.[27]

In hindsight, General Vien recognized another flaw in Lam that colored his effectiveness, one that had a direct impact on the outcome of the battle: "He would not report bad news or was very slow to do so." When the North Vietnamese first attacked on 30 March, Lam failed to report fully on the situation for fear of angering his superiors. In fact, Lam's initial battle report during the first days of April had been quite positive. "They [the North Vietnamese] made an all-out attack and we stopped them," said the general, though he knew the situation was far from secure. "It was a big defeat for the North Vietnamese. . . . They will try some more, but we have stopped them." As a result, for a few crucial days the Joint General Staff in Saigon did not know the magnitude of the enemy invasion. This trend continued. During April Lam consistently downplayed enemy advances and overstated South Vietnamese capabilities. On 30 April, the day before Quang Tri City fell, Lam told Saigon that the North Vietnamese had spent their fury and were incapable of crossing the Thach Han River. He knew better, but to report the truth risked upsetting the general staff.[28]

General Truong, the incoming I Corps commander, also had no respect for Lam's brand of leadership, and he was blunt in his criticism. "I had served in I Corps under General Lam [two years earlier] and the disaster that occurred there was no surprise to me," wrote Truong. "Neither General Lam nor his staff were competent to maneuver and support large forces in heavy combat."[29]

Now it was Truong's turn to take command and salvage a potentially disastrous situation. From his post far away in the Mekong Delta, Truong—undisputably the best officer in the South Vietnamese army—had watched the unfolding battle in Quang Tri. Truong's long history as a combat soldier free from the political corruption so prevalent among his colleagues made him a natural choice to take command of the beleaguered I Corps. Born in 1929 in Ben Tre, he was educated in French schools before attending the Thu Duc Officer Candidate School and the Command and Staff School at Dalat. When South Vietnam was created in 1954, Lieutenant Truong joined the 5th Airborne Battalion as a platoon leader; by 1963 he was battalion commander. In 1965 Truong was promoted to chief of staff of the Airborne Division, a noncombat position that might have stagnated his career. But a reputation for bravery and fairness got him noticed by top military brass in Saigon. General Cao Van Vien called Truong "one of the best commanders at every echelon the Airborne Division ever had." American officers also respected Truong. In the spring of 1966, Buddhist activists took to the streets of Hue to protest military control of the government, and the 1st ARVN Division, the unit stationed in the imperial city, proved incapable of handling the situation. As a young lieutenant colonel with a solid reputation as an officer—and a Buddhist—Truong was made acting commander of the 1st ARVN Division in June 1966.

Though grateful to be given a chance to command a division, Truong was uncomfortable presiding over a military unit operating to quell a civil disturbance. But he performed well at his new post, and Saigon made the position permanent. With his hands-on style of command, Truong quickly built the demoralized 1st ARVN Division back into one of the best units in the South Vietnamese army. Truong remained in command of the division until August 1970, when he took command of IV Corps. His performance was noticed by MACV commander General William C. Westmoreland, who observed that Truong "would rate high on any list of capable South Vietnamese leaders." Other U.S. commanders so admired Truong that they "would trust him to command an American division."[30]

General Truong expected the appointment, and when the call came, he already had a staff packed and ready to go north. Within the hour the new commander flew from IV Corps headquarters in Can Tho to Hue, where he met his new officers and American advisers and reacquainted himself with a region he had grown to love in years past. "My arrival in Hue was not unlike the return of a son among the great family of troops and fellow-countrymen of this city whom I had the privilege of serving not very long ago," Truong later wrote. "I was gratified to discover that the trust they had always vested in me was still lingering. This reassurance was what I needed most in this bleakest hour of history."[31]

But there was little time for reminiscence. Truong briefed his new officers, then met with his American advisers, the FRAC staff. In person, Truong did not appear to fit the robust image that preceded him. A quiet man with a stooped, paper-thin physique, Truong chain-smoked cheap cigarettes and seemed always to be concentrating on something besides the matter at hand. He lacked the hard persona and unflinching demeanor of some of his more colorful American counterparts, but any sign of weakness was only an illusion. Truong possessed a single-minded devotion to duty, fierce loyalty to his subordinates, and indefatigable energy, all qualities badly needed if the South Vietnamese were to hold the line in I Corps. Kroesen summed it up best when he observed, "I believed Truong could re-establish an offensive spirit."[32]

The sun dropped behind the western mountains on the evening of 3 May, mercifully concealing the death and destruction left behind in Quang Tri. Among the casualties was the entire 3d ARVN Division. "The division is totally ineffective as a unit and could not be rebuilt merely by furnishing personnel and equipment," concluded General Kroesen as he surveyed the damage reports coming into Hue and Danang. "Plans and directives to deal with the situation are incomplete and not coordinated."[33]

Even the best fighting forces were mauled. The marines were still considered "effective and reliable," although the 147th VNMC Brigade, which had seen most of the fighting during the final days of Quang Tri City, suffered heavy losses and had retreated in confusion, abandoning many of its weapons. FRAC estimated that it would take 1,000 replacements to return the marines to fighting shape.

The rangers were also badly battered. They wandered into Camp Evans in small groups, most of them without weapons. FRAC characterized them as "completely ineffective, unassembled and uncontrolled at this time," due to horrendous losses among their officers. One ranger group commander, two executive officers, and five battalion commanders were killed during the last two weeks of April, leaving the rangers badly demoralized. Many of them were on the verge of rioting, and the remaining officers could not control them. After a few tense hours during which the rangers set fire to the Dong Ba marketplace in downtown Hue, the "unruly" rangers were loaded onto trucks and moved to Phu Bai.[34]

The 1st Ranger Group was in the best shape, with only 14 percent losses. The 4th Ranger Group had lost almost 500 men, and it was estimated that it would be at least a month before the unit could be retrained. The 5th Ranger Group was in the worst shape. Besides losing most of its officers, it suffered more than 50 percent casualties within the ranks. At least 800 new recruits would have to be added before the unit was back up to strength. On top of that, equipment losses were called "enormous."[35]

The core units within the 3d ARVN Division—the 2d, 56th, and 57th ARVN Regiments—were in the worst shape. Stragglers from the 57th ARVN Regiment dribbled into Camp Evans, but very little of the 2d ARVN Regiment turned up. The 56th ARVN Regiment, part of which had surrendered at Camp Carroll on 2 April, was still retraining and conducting limited operations around Hue. After two weeks of refitting, it was in better shape than its sister units.

The 1st Armored Brigade was almost nonexistent. Combat losses were compounded when tanks and armored personnel carriers ran out of fuel and were abandoned or destroyed by their crews. Only a single M48 tank drove into Camp Evans under its own power, and a mere six M41 tanks and fifteen armored personnel carriers were accounted for out of a force of three armored cavalry squadrons and one tank regiment. During April the brigade recorded 1,171 men killed, wounded, or missing out of a total strength of just over 2,000. Lieutenant Colonel Wagner, the brigade senior adviser, counted 403 vehicles lost, 197 of them tanks or armored personnel carriers. Very little artillery was salvaged from Quang Tri Province, and none from the city itself.[36]

As the North Vietnamese had certainly intended, the loss of Quang Tri and the partial destruction of the South Vietnamese army in the battles leading up to it had dealt a severe blow to Vietnamization and America's plans for a smooth withdrawal from Vietnam. When the city fell, many senior U.S. officers expressed their gloom over the poor performance turned in by many South Vietnamese units. "They've got to get over the mental attitude that the great American silver bird is going to do it all for them," said an unidentified colonel in Saigon. "In the end it's the guy on the ground with the M16 that makes the difference."[37]

And it was the guy on the ground who was getting the blame. In war, as in politics, someone must be held responsible for any disaster. So it was with the debacle in northern I Corps. Brigadier General Vu Van Giai, the battlefront commander, was found to be the guilty man in the debacle in northern I Corps, though by relieving General Lam, President Thieu implied that the corps commander also had something to do with it. But it was Giai who was forced to shoulder most of the guilt and shame of defeat; he was arrested for abandoning his post in the citadel and sent to prison.

The fall of Quang Tri and General Giai's subsequent disgrace smeared the 3d ARVN Division with a reputation for cowardice and incompetence. President Thieu wanted the division removed from the rolls—it was "bad luck"—and reconstituted as the 27th ARVN Division. However, many others felt that such denigration was undeserved. General Kroesen believed

Giai had done "the best he could with what he had." Nor did Kroesen subscribe to the theory that the 3d ARVN Division performed badly. "It did very well for a good period of time," he later recalled. "The 3d Division just ran out of steam." Kroesen was quick to admit that tactical blunders were made, but most of them lay with General Lam. Months later, in a letter to General Truong, Kroesen again defended Giai. "If it were my decision to make," he concluded, "I would return him immediately to the command of a division in the combat zone."[38]

Lieutenant General William J. McCaffrey, deputy commander of the U.S. Army in the Republic of Vietnam (USARV), told the division's advisory team, "I honestly think that the 3d ARVN Division conducted itself creditably during its 28-day battle at Quang Tri and history will eventually record this fact." McCaffrey credited the division with reducing the 304th and 308th NVA Divisions to "thirty or forty percent strength" and blamed its ensuing problems on the higher command levels rather than on the "poor little bastards fighting on the ground."[39]

Advisers who served with Giai during the offensive also stood behind the division. "I think it is remarkable and a tribute to General Giai's leadership that the 3d Division held together as long as it did under the pressures it faced," wrote Lieutenant Colonel Heath Twitchell, former senior adviser to the 57th ARVN Regiment. "I know of no U.S. division that was ever thrown into full scale combat within 6 months of its organization. . . . Under the circumstances, I doubt if *any* general, U.S. or Vietnamese, could have done much better."[40]

Even General Truong was sympathetic to Giai. "I would have been happy to have had General Giai resume command of the reconstituted 3d Division," commented the new I Corps commander. Truong held Lam, not the division, directly responsible for the debacle. "To put it briefly," he wrote, "the 3d Division failed because it was overburdened." Truong did not believe that any other South Vietnamese division could have held out against the onslaught in northern I Corps, and he had complete faith in the 3d ARVN Division's ability to return to battle after a period of refitting and retraining. But actions speak louder than words, and the 3d ARVN Division had failed to hold Quang Tri Province while losing men and matériel at an alarming rate.[41]

Dismayed by the incompetence of General Lam and the defeat in the north, General Abrams seemed to lose hope that the North Vietnamese could be stopped in I Corps. "I must report that as the pressure has mounted and the battle has become brutal, the senior military leadership has begun to bend and in some cases break," reported the disheartened

MACV commander to Secretary of Defense Melvin Laird in Washington. "In adversity it is losing its will and cannot be depended on to take the measures necessary to stand and fight. . . . In light of this there is no basis for confidence that Hue . . . will be held."[42]

This was a dramatic change from the cautiously optimistic outlook put forth only six days earlier. "The South Vietnamese government, its armed forces and its people are holding together in this crisis," Abrams had predicted even as the North Vietnamese were threatening Quang Tri City. "The fabric of what the South Vietnamese have built here with our assistance has survived its severest test. The qualities demonstrated by the South Vietnamese people, in my judgement, assure that they will continue to hold."[43]

In spite of Abrams's dreary assessment, FRAC was not ready to throw in the towel. General Thomas Bowen, deputy senior adviser for FRAC, refused to give the North Vietnamese much credit for capturing Quang Tri City. "You can take any place if you're willing to pay the price and take the sacrifice," Bowen scoffed to reporters. "The sacrifice doesn't seem to bother the enemy. Maybe Quang Tri's worth 3,000 men to him."[44]

General Kroesen was more circumspect, though he also remained cautiously optimistic. "The military situation in MR [Military Region] 1 is grave but not hopeless," he wrote on 2 May. In Kroesen's opinion, things could have been worse. The fall of Quang Tri should have heralded the end of Thua Thien Province and Hue, but the North Vietnamese were unable to pursue the retreating South Vietnamese southward. After many years of reflection and analysis, Kroeson concluded, "This situation created the golden opportunity for the enemy to realize a final conquest of Hue and Thua Thien Province. That he failed completely to take advantage of the moment must be classed as another great blunder of the Quang Tri Campaign."[45]

But for the time being, such conclusions were merely idle speculation. If the North Vietnamese had missed a "golden opportunity," they had not given up on the goal of capturing Hue. Beginning in early April, the North Vietnamese had attacked Thua Thien Province, though fighting there lacked the intensity of that of Quang Tri. Now there was nothing to stop the enemy from devoting all efforts toward the attack on Hue, a fact that North Vietnamese propaganda continually pointed out. Despite American aid to Saigon, the old imperial capital and all of Thua Thien Province were doomed, boasted Radio Hanoi.

TEN

THE IMPERIAL CITY

Anticipating the fall of Quang Tri City, the North Vietnamese began diverting forces from that front south, while also bringing in fresh troops from the north. As early as 29 April, FRAC intelligence noticed that "the enemy is resupplying and consolidating for further attacks, while other units bypass the city [of Quang Tri]. . . . It is anticipated that Thua Thien will be subjected to increased pressure as the enemy attempts to enter the lowlands along Route 547 to support the effort against Hue."[1]

Enemy movement was particularly heavy within the A Shau Valley. "This activity supports the theory that reinforcements, supplies, and equipment are now being concentrated for a campaign in Thua Thien Province," surmised General Kroesen. No one was really surprised by reports of enemy troops in the A Shau. Long a haven for North Vietnamese units and a heavily used logistical pipeline, the valley was a narrow, steep-walled gash running parallel to the Laotian border for twenty-five miles. Thick trees and brush clung to the slopes and the valley floor, and dark, rain-filled clouds cloaked the bordering mountaintops, some of which soared to 3,000 feet. Route 548, a glorified term for this narrow dirt road, wound down the valley from the abandoned base of A Luoi to the tiny town of A Shau. Despite its state of disrepair, Route 548 was of great concern to the South Vietnamese. Branching out of the valley near the village of Ta Bat, the road (now designated Route 547) meandered northeast for forty miles into the city of Hue. Without a doubt, the A Shau Valley was a dagger aimed at the heart of the ancient imperial capital.

The A Shau Valley was an unfriendly place for soldiers who chose to fight the North Vietnamese there. In March 1966 a Special Forces camp guarding the valley entrance was overrun by a couple of North Vietnamese regiments, and from then on the enemy held sway over the tangled wilderness. Not that the Americans simply let them. In the summer of 1967, U.S. Marines moved into the A Shau to sweep it clean, but they did not get far. By September, a combination of fierce resistance and bad weather pushed them back, never to return. In April 1968, on the heels of the communist defeat during the Tet Offensive, the 1st Cavalry Division launched Operation Delaware into the valley. Once again, North Vietnamese tenacity, rugged

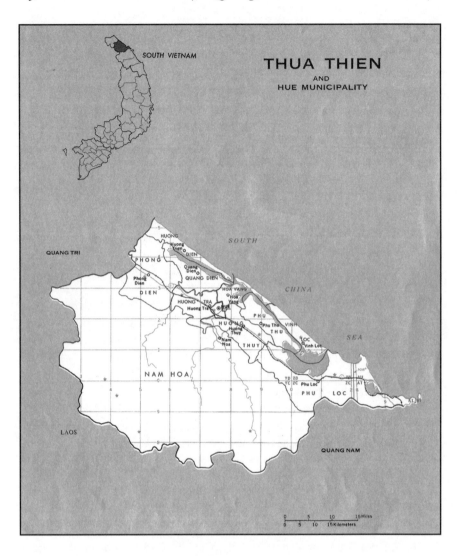

terrain, and atrocious weather joined forces to thwart the Americans, who left without seriously harming the enemy network. But General William Westmoreland remained obsessed with wresting the A Shau from enemy control. A procession of Special Forces reconnaissance teams were sent into the valley beginning in late 1968 to pinpoint North Vietnamese bases for destruction with B-52s; many were never heard from again. In 1969, limited operations kept the valley from being the exclusive domain of the North Vietnamese, but there was no attempt to permanently push the enemy out.

For the North Vietnamese, the A Shau was the terminus for Base Area 611, a logistical stockpiling and stepping-off point into South Vietnam. The overall command for the area was the B-4 Front, the virtual equivalent of the South Vietnamese Military Region 1, or I Corps. Before 1965 it had been called simply the Northern Front, but in 1966, in reaction to the massive U.S. troop buildup, it was made an independent military region, which reported directly to the high command in Hanoi. By 1968 the B-4 Front was also known as Military Region Tri-Thien-Hue (for Quang Tri Province, Thua Thien Province, and Hue) and had at its disposal between 50,000 and 65,000 troops. But one thing never changed—the B-4 Front existed to protect Highway 9 and the A Shau Valley, the two main spurs of the Ho Chi Minh Trail entering South Vietnam from Laos.

The commander of the B-4 Front was Trung Tuong (lieutenant general, a two-star rank in the North Vietnamese army) Tran Van Quang, a general little known to intelligence analysts, though he had commanded the B-4 Front since at least 1967. General Quang was both the military and the political leader, responsible for all troops and equipment funneled into central and southern I Corps from Laos. While Quang Tri Province was receiving most of the attention during the first month of the Easter Offensive, General Quang was applying steady pressure against Thua Thien Province. Without a doubt, Hue was his primary target. Few analysts doubted that the North Vietnamese prized the imperial city above all other South Vietnamese cities, save perhaps Saigon. Although the loss of Quang Tri City was a psychological blow, the city was only a poor province capital, a single stepping-stone from the demilitarized zone to Hue.

North Vietnamese units had been moving in from the west, hoping to employ the standard tactic of surrounding and then assaulting the city. During mid-March enemy forces were on the offensive near the line of firebases west of Hue, while North Vietnamese troops along the demilitarized zone and in Quang Tri Province were still building up. The railway between Hue and Danang was cut several times at the Hai Van Pass, and the 324B NVA Division was discovered setting up a wide arc around Hue from the A Shau Valley.

The difference between the situation in Thua Thien Province and northern Quang Tri was that the 1st ARVN Division, a well-seasoned unit, reacted promptly and effectively to the buildup, throwing the North Vietnamese off balance in several places. On 8 March the 1st ARVN Division reported, "The enemy is most likely attempting to develop the area [in the] vicinity of [Fire Support Base] Veghel as a staging area for future attacks on FSB Bastogne." Patrols in the area found the 29th NVA Regiment—part of the 324B NVA Division—moving east toward Hue along Route 547. The enemy soldiers had recently come south from their usual area near Khe Sanh; some of the dead wore scarves that read "Hero Warriors of Highway 9."[2]

Much of the 1st ARVN Division's success was due to its commander, Major General Pham Van Phu. Colonel Hillman Dickinson, senior adviser to the division, described Phu as "an excellent tactician" and one of South Vietnam's best officers. "Generally cautiously optimistic, he maintains an outward optimism in the roughest situations," Dickinson reported to MACV. "He is obviously respected and admired by his subordinates because of his ability, experience, and reputation for fairness." Phu also held the ear of President Thieu, who often called Hue and asked for the division commander's opinions on tactical matters.[3]

For the time being, however, General Phu's sole concern was the enemy buildup around Hue. Activity near Firebases Veghel and Bastogne indicated that trouble was afoot in the west, a conclusion that became clear well before the North Vietnamese launched their offensive on 30 March. Part of the 1st ARVN Division's area of responsibility, Veghel and Bastogne faced west toward the traditional North Vietnamese staging areas near the Laotian border. As early as 22 February the division pushed out from its bases and hit the North Vietnamese as they prepared for the Easter Offensive. In Operation Lam Son 36/72, the 54th ARVN Regiment, from the 1st ARVN Division, launched an aggressive search-and-destroy mission in response to North Vietnamese probing around two other small firebases, Anzio and Rifle. According to the regiment's orders, the mission was to "destroy the enemy and to prevent infiltration to the lowlands from the mountainous areas," broad instructions that the unit carried out with surprising success. By 28 February the operation was over, and although the North Vietnamese were not badly hurt, they were forced to contend with the bothersome sweep.[4]

Still, the North Vietnamese continued to build up their forces. Ground sensors recorded increasing activity along all routes, particularly the lower A Shau Valley. This activity, plus traditional North Vietnamese offensives in the area, left little doubt as to enemy intentions. Intelligence summaries unequivocally stated, "Enemy forces . . . have the ultimate mission of disrupting pacification in the lowlands of Thua Thien and seizing Hue. For them to accomplish this mission they must first neutralize FSBs such as Barbara, Rakkasan, Bastogne, and Rifle."[5]

The 1st ARVN Division continued to stay on the offensive with a series of operations, the largest of which was Lam Son 45. On 5 March, still concerned about enemy activity in the A Shau Valley, the 1st ARVN Division lunged south and west from Firebases Bastogne and Rakkasan in preparation for even bigger operations by the entire division. Behind a barrage of 175mm artillery fire, battalions from the 1st and 3d ARVN Regiments were airlifted from Camp Evans to a series of six landing zones along Route 547. Intelligence sources believed that the 803d and 29th NVA Regiments—both from the 324B NVA Division—plus the independent 6th NVA Regiment were massing in the mountainous Dong Cu Mong area at the mouth of the valley for an attack against Hue. Extra B-52 strikes were laid on, and a curtain of artillery again rained down on the gathering enemy.[6]

The 3d ARVN Regiment met immediate resistance from the entrenched enemy, a sure sign that a buildup was well under way. In the past, the North Vietnamese had fought hard only if they intended to protect something, such as supply stockpiles; otherwise they fought rearguard actions and melted away into the wilderness. This time the enemy stood and fought, and from 9 March through 11 March it succeeded in slowing the South Vietnamese, though only for a time. On 16 March the 3rd ARVN Regiment captured Dong Cu Mong, then held it for a time in the face of a determined enemy counterattack. The South Vietnamese were finally forced to withdraw in the face of superior enemy forces, but not before more than 200 North Vietnamese were killed. The 1st ARVN Division considered Lam Son 45 a severe blow to the enemy.[7]

Just how badly the North Vietnamese were hurt is difficult to gauge, but there can be no doubt that the operation upset their offensive timetable. It appears that the enemy planned to attack Thua Thien and Quang Tri Provinces at the same time and with equal ferocity, but Lam Son 45 caused the attack on Hue to falter. Some American advisers on the scene went even further, claiming that the preemptive strike saved Hue. Colonel Dickinson called it "the key to the enemy's failure to take Hue and Thua Thien Province."[8]

Nguyen Van Phuoc knew fear—a gnawing, piercing uncertainty born of long months in enemy territory, constantly moving to elude American bombers high overhead. Phuoc was a North Vietnamese soldier. His unit, part of the 324B NVA Division, had started south in February, reached the relative safety of the A Shau Valley in mid-March, then infiltrated to within seven miles west of Hue by month's end.

"Arty is firing a lot," Phuoc wrote in his pocket diary. Neatly penned entries lay within a tattered binding kept carefully inside Phuoc's pack. The diary, along with a picture of Ho Chi Minh, his marriage certificate, and a

Lao Dong Party membership paper, was his link to home and the peaceful life he had known before the offensive. But for now combat was the driving force in Phuoc's life. "Now is the beginning of the country campaign, and I must take a mortar to fix Hon Vuan."

The Americans called Hon Vuan Firebase T-Bone, a formidable compound about eight miles west of Hue housing the 6th ARVN Regiment as well as batteries of 105mm and 155mm howitzers. Phuoc and his mortar crews were assigned the difficult task of fixing the coordinates of T-Bone's artillery by firing a few quick mortar rounds, then plotting the range for bigger and more accurate bombardments once the heavy artillery moved up from the A Shau Valley. To do this, they had to elude sensors and booby traps sprinkled around the base and evade patrols sent out diligently by the South Vietnamese. To make matters worse, the North Vietnamese had to wait for their local Viet Cong comrades, who were supposed to have paved the way for the assault on T-Bone by providing flank security and blowing up the bridges along major South Vietnamese resupply routes. But the Viet Cong had not done their duty, and the North Vietnamese timetable was disrupted. "We must wait for help from the local forces," Phuoc wrote in his diary on 31 March. "The local forces could not organize the battlefield and our flank was open."[9]

Phuoc's impatience with the Viet Cong highlighted two new realities in the changing nature of the Vietnam War. First, the Viet Cong were no longer a factor as they had once been before the Tet Offensive of 1968. Unable to maintain high levels of support among the South Vietnamese population and increasingly harried by successful pacification programs, the Viet Cong spent most of their time simply surviving. Second, North Vietnam's newfound conventional military might lacked the refinement necessary to deal with battlefield vagaries. Unrealistic timetables, overly optimistic planning, and an idealistic belief in the power of the revolution in South Vietnam's countryside often offset the advantages of Hanoi's new armor and artillery assets. Although the North Vietnamese had startled their opponents with lightning successes in northern Quang Tri Province and had built up an undeserved aura of superiority, they still lacked the ability to defeat properly led and prepared South Vietnamese forces on the ground. But for Phuoc and his comrades, these were abstract considerations. All they knew was that every day they were forced to wait on the enemy's doorstep meant there was a greater chance that they would be discovered. The increasing fear was evident in Phuoc's diary.

4 April: "We moved to a new emplacement and dug all day long. This was a critical day as we were afraid of the enemy infantry searching. At

night we slept outside the bunker." (Only during the day, when South Vietnamese troops patrolled and U.S. warplanes flew overhead, did the North Vietnamese remain in their bunkers.)

6 April: "At 1700 hours we got an order to fire on Hon Vuan. We fired eight rounds from 2,600 meters to Hon Vuan. The enemy fired back at us three times."

7 April: "We continued to fire on Hon Vuan, ten rounds today. We are only afraid of the enemy infantry searching close to us."

8 April: "One more critical day passed. We were very scared. The enemy infantry is searching for us. We fired twelve rounds two time."

10 April: "We must remain in our position and fire three times with eleven rounds. The lookout reports back that he can hear the enemy moving around. I order the men to search out where he is."

12 April: "We fired twelve rounds twice. The enemy fired back immediately at our location. We ran away without firing back. We withdrew to the home base at 1800. Everybody was afraid."

13 April: "It is nine days since we had a bath and shave. It is a day for rest and satisfaction. The enemy is still searching. We are only two kilometers from the enemy."

Nguyen Van Phuoc made no more entries in his diary after 13 April. The following day his mortar crew was moving into a new position at the base of Firebase T-Bone when Phuoc tripped a claymore mine and was blown to bits. His riddled body was found on 15 April by a patrol combing the southwest slope of the firebase. These soldiers gave Phuoc's diary to the regimental intelligence staff, who added it to an ever-growing pile of captured documents for later analysis.

The life and death of Nguyen Van Phuoc was a microcosm of the enemy offensive in Thua Thien Province. Unable to gain the initiative as they had in Quang Tri Province, the North Vietnamese fell into a strategy of trading head-on assaults with the South Vietnamese, a deadly kind of warfare that they could not win.

"This is really sort of a sickening affair," said Colonel Hillman Dickinson as he watched the assault on Hue unfolding. "What we've got here is a long, bloody war of attrition."

Even so, by mid-April the North Vietnamese were only bruised, not beaten. In an attempt to break through South Vietnamese defenses along Route 547, they surrounded Firebases Bastogne and Checkmate, the most crucial points in the western defense of Hue. By the second week in April, both bases were cut off and had to be resupplied by air, an increasingly risky undertaking as the North Vietnamese brought up antiaircraft batteries. On 11 April the 1st ARVN Regiment attempted to clear Route 547 but was brought up short against determined resistance from the 24th NVA Regiment. Despite a sustained artillery barrage and constant B-52 strikes, the enemy held fast to its positions around Bastogne and Checkmate. During the last two weeks in April—the same time that Quang Tri City was threatened—the North Vietnamese again made a concerted effort to take the firebases. However, weather conditions improved, and tactical air strikes saved the base from being overrun.

But only for a week. Although the air force held the enemy at bay, North Vietnamese artillery units crept closer to Hue, and the shelling there increased daily. Then, on 28 April, the 29th and 803d NVA Regiments combined to attack Firebase Bastogne, the strongest bastion on Hue's western flank. Within three hours the enemy had the base, driving the South Vietnamese to the east. With this one victory the North Vietnamese also isolated Firebase Checkmate, which was evacuated that night. Now Hue was exposed to a direct thrust along Route 547, and intelligence indicated that the remainder of the 324B NVA Division was being reinforced for just such an attack.

The fall of Quang Tri City on 1 May enabled the North Vietnamese to shift even more troops toward Hue. As Firebase Bastogne was falling, FRAC observed that there was a "significant buildup" of men and matériel in the A Shau Valley, and the 66th NVA Regiment was reported moving in the area of Firebase Anne just north of the Thua Thien Province border. This was ominous news because the 66th NVA Regiment was part of the 304th NVA Division, a unit previously involved in the fighting north of Quang Tri City. Clearly, it was now making its way south to join the fighting near Hue.

North Vietnamese forces in Thua Thien Province were elated by the fall of Quang Tri and the consequent shift of troops to the south. Despite their losses west of Hue earlier in the month, the North Vietnamese believed they had turned the tide against the South Vietnamese. "The puppet 1st Division . . . was so badly mauled that it has now lost its fighting capability," heralded Liberation Radio, the communist propaganda broadcast run by the Viet Cong. "This shows that our people and armed forces' anti-U.S. national salvation struggle is entering a new and extremely favorable phase and is surging forward to score the greatest victories."10

General Phu was unperturbed by this premature prediction of his division's demise. Confident that the 1st ARVN Division was capable of holding back the North Vietnamese, he was however dismayed when journalists

An M113 armored personnel carrier guards the citadel in Hue. While fighting raged in Quang Tri, the city of Hue prepared for battle. As was the case during the 1968 Tet Offensive, the ancient imperial capital of Vietnam was a major communist objective. (U.S. Army)

and officials far from the battlefield believed the dire predictions. In his quiet, understated manner, the division commander pointed out that the North Vietnamese were often overrated, particularly General Vo Nguyen Giap, their legendary commander. "Giap maybe think we are paper tiger, not real tiger," Phu told reporters in broken English. "Maybe he make big mistake. We very much tiger."[11]

On 2 May enemy units south of Hue tried to surround the city, launching heavy rocket and artillery attacks against Firebase King and Camp Eagle, the headquarters of the 1st ARVN Division. The battle had reached a crucial juncture, one that would influence the course of continued American action. While the fall of Quang Tri City seemed to be a devastating loss, it was strategically unimportant. If Hue fell, however, the Saigon government would be in a strategically inferior position. The Nixon administration was well aware of this danger and prepared plans for "drastically intensified bombing" of North Vietnam if the enemy continued its drive on

Hue. "Hue is the crucial factor," a U.S. government official told reporters. "We'll wait and see about that before we decide what to do."12

Against this milieu of victory and defeat, chaos and order, General Truong set to work building a new defense for the region. From the beginning he was faced with the twin problems of defending Hue and retaking Quang Tri Province, neither of them easy tasks given the state of the South Vietnamese army in I Corps. He had to rely on his own imagination and the continued support of U.S. air assets. Though confident of his abilities as a commander, he did not resent American advice. Truong worked well with his counterparts at FRAC, most of whom respected him tremendously. General Kroesen quickly established a close working relationship with the new commander; although he had been satisfied with Lam's preference for working with General Bowen, this time he intended to have a traditional counterpart arrangement.

But while the Americans were more than ready to work with General Truong, there were other serious matters to attend to first. South Vietnamese soldiers fleeing south from Quang Tri City spread panic among the defenders in Hue, and before long other troops had joined the rout. It was Truong's first test, and he acted quickly and efficiently. On 3 May he issued an order that all troops return to defend Hue or be shot on sight and assigned 100 armored cars equipped with machine guns to back up the order. Truong's authority was also bolstered by President Thieu, who issued a shoot-to-kill order against looters and arsonists. "Responsible law enforcement agencies and military units are empowered to shoot on the spot elements committing these acts," read the order, which was broadcast nationwide. Such acts of anarchy, Thieu concluded, "must be regarded as acts committed by the communists infiltrating our ranks with a view to sowing chaos and thereby seizing power."13

Blaming faceless communist infiltrators for the anarchy engulfing Hue was a convenient propaganda tool, but it did little to assuage the fears of soldiers and civilians alike. The simple reality was that the social and moral fabric of the old city was disintegrating. Over a one-week period, almost 150,000 people fled south to escape not only the approaching enemy but also marauding South Vietnamese soldiers. Deserters from the battered 3d ARVN Division, as well as soldiers from ranger and even 1st ARVN Division units, roamed the streets of Hue like armed gangsters, looting, harassing, and firing on anyone who displeased them. Small-arms fire crackled throughout the town as rival deserters clashed with one another. Police could do little to quell the rampage, since the soldiers, armed with machine

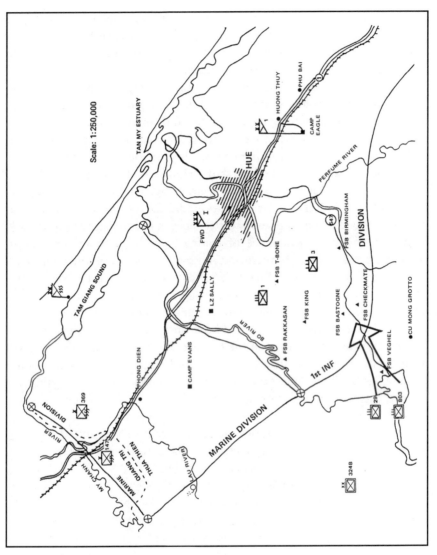

The defense of Hue, 5 May 1972

guns and grenades, easily outgunned them. On one evening, hundreds of drunken soldiers got into a wild gunfight, killing several bystanders. Reported one journalist: "South Vietnamese deserters from the 3d Division descended upon Hue like locusts, looting and carousing and inspiring panic among the city's population and the refugees streaming in from Quang Tri." Some of the soldiers later claimed they had rioted to express rage at their officers, many of whom had abandoned their men during the last days at Quang Tri. Even those officers who had stayed with their men seemed unable or unwilling to stop the chaos. "It's not our job," said one lieutenant as he sat astride a "liberated" Honda motorcycle. But General Truong considered it his job to stop the rampage, and his shoot-to-kill order, combined with his stellar reputation, did the job. By 10 May most of the rioting died down, and senior officers began to reorganize their units.[14]

After regaining a semblance of control over his demoralized troops, Truong turned toward restructuring command and control. In an effort to arrest the panic gripping Thua Thien Province, he moved the corps command from Danang to Hue, bringing along a staff he called "a rare assemblage of talents." Since artillery—the enemy's overwhelming use of it and the ARVN's inability to use it—had been the key weapon in the offensive, Truong quickly set out to even the balance. He established a Fire Support Coordination Center to streamline and coordinate all American and South Vietnamese artillery, concentrating them on counterbattery fire against the elusive enemy 130mm gun emplacements. A Target Acquisition Element was also organized "to exploit the tremendous power of the U.S. Air Force and U.S. Naval gunfire." Truong clearly saw that this organized and concentrated approach to artillery tactics was the core around which all South Vietnamese counteroffensive plans must be built.[15]

If artillery was the foundation, then the marines were certainly one of the pillars, and Truong was quick to realize this. For the first time since the Easter Offensive began, the marines were assigned their own division area of operations. Since they were considered an elite unit, the move may have seemed a natural one, but the reality was that in the scheme of Saigon's military hierarchy, the marines lacked political clout. It took the collapse of a division and the loss of a province to force President Thieu to remedy this situation, but on 4 May he appointed marine commandant Lieutenant General Le Nguyen Khang to the Joint General Staff, the first time a marine officer had held such high military office. Colonel Bui Thi Lan was promoted to brigadier general and made acting commandant. But with this privilege came a warning. Thieu's order of the day was that the My Chanh line would hold; there would be no further withdrawals.[16]

By 5 May Truong had a plan for the defense of Hue. Since there was not much left to work with, he concentrated on denying the enemy any more territory. The Marine Division's three brigades and two regiments of the 1st ARVN Division were the only South Vietnamese forces north of Hue. Truong arrayed them in a broad L-shaped line, with the marines responsible for northern Thua Thien Province south to the Bo River and the 1st ARVN Division defending from the Bo River south to Hue. The greatest threat came from the west, particularly the A Shau Valley, which the 1st ARVN Division watched particularly closely. Truong had a long perimeter full of holes, but it was all the South Vietnamese could offer. Truong's hope lay in his flexibility and a much-improved command system. Painfully aware of the consequences of Lam's quixotic chain of command, Truong kept his simple and straightforward, relying on clear-cut assignments to subordinate commanders in the field. All units had the flexibility to respond to the North Vietnamese as they saw fit. According to Truong:

Both divisions were given a free hand to conduct limited objective attacks in order to destroy enemy force concentrations in their sectors of defense. My concern at the time was to provide a defense in depth, to economize force, to create a realistic chain of command, establish strong reserves for each major unit, and integrate the regular and territorial forces, which so far had operated with little coordination, into the corps defense plan.[17]

Supplementing this "defense in depth" was a concept that Truong named Loi Phong, or Thunder Hurricane, "a sustained offensive by fire conducted on a large scale." Troubled by his forces' poor use of artillery and air assets, Truong made up for it by concentrating artillery, tactical air, Arc Light strikes, and naval gunfire into a single point aimed at seeking out and destroying "every worthwhile target detected," particularly the lengthening logistical lines of the North Vietnamese offensive. More than forty heavy guns, including a dozen 175mm self-propelled howitzers, made up Truong's Thunder Hurricane, which roared around the clock, pounding every major road and trail leading south toward Hue. One U.S. Marine adviser described it as "the heaviest artillery barrage I have ever heard." Most enemy artillery was silenced, though a few mobile 130mm batteries continued "light shelling" of the city.[18]

Reinforcements were also needed to bolster the South Vietnamese defense, but given the deteriorating situation in other regions of the country, there were not enough troops to go around. Still, General Truong did not want to become known as the man who lost the old capital, and President Thieu knew that his political life would end if North Vietnamese troops marched triumphantly into Hue. So Saigon's primary emphasis during May was on saving Hue. When Truong asked for reinforcements to make up for the loss of the 3d ARVN Division when Quang Tri fell, he got most of what he wanted. President Thieu released the 2d Brigade of the Airborne Division from III Corps on 8 May, and Truong promptly placed the paratroopers on the northern perimeter under the operational control of the marines. The marines also assumed control of the 1st Ranger Group, which had just finished reorganizing and refitting in Danang. Troop strength in and around Hue had climbed to around 35,000.

Truong also began an accelerated program of refitting and retraining the South Vietnamese units that had been so badly battered during the flight from Quang Tri. Although not technically part of the defense of Hue, this task was equally important if Saigon was to drive back the North Vietnamese in northern I Corps. The 1st Armored Brigade needed to replace 200 armored vehicles, half of them tanks, and the 3d ARVN Division had to be rebuilt from the ground up. All that remained after the rout from Quang Tri was a skeletal headquarters unit and remnants of the 2d and 57th ARVN Regiments. Artillery units had lost a total of 140 guns, the equivalent of ten South Vietnamese artillery battalions. Fortunately, the efficiency of the American logistical apparatus quickly filled the supply pipeline with replacements, particularly armor, artillery, and ammunition. Crucial matériel was rushed to Danang aboard U.S. C-141 and C-5A cargo aircraft, while the rest followed on supply ships. The most critical supplies included artillery rounds. Truong noted that the American system was so efficient that "no combat unit ever ran out of ammunition," and this despite the huge increase in the use of artillery under his Thunder Hurricane defensive strategy.[19]

In order to quickly restore units to combat readiness, Truong shortened the retraining process. A two-week "quick recovery" training program was conducted with each unit by South Vietnamese and American mobile training teams, usually at the battalion level, with all officers and noncommissioned officers attending. In addition to standard infantry tactics, the program also emphasized the use of antitank weapons, especially the new tube-launched, optically tracked, wire-guided (TOW) missile, which arrived from the United States on 21 May.

This was sophisticated technology, and the decision to give it to the South Vietnamese showed how serious the Pentagon believed the situation to be. General Abrams wanted to be sure the missiles would not be captured, so he ordered that they be distributed to the marines, though General Kroesen suggested they go to the Airborne Division. "When I have the personal assurance of General Truong that the Airborne will fight and will not abandon these weapons on the battlefield," replied Abrams, "I will consider authorizing their training." The MACV commander's anguish over the crumbling illusion of Vietnamization was clear, and he hoped to take steps to reverse the course. "All Vietnamese must understand clearly that the problem is not equipment," he told Kroesen. "It is men who will stand and fight."[20]

Some units, such as the 20th Tank Regiment and the 3d ARVN Division, had to undergo a complete retraining and refitting cycle at special sites located at Dong Da near Phu Bai and Van Thanh on the outskirts of Hue. The 3d ARVN Division was eventually moved south to Danang on 16 June to complete its reconstitution; within a month it assumed the defense of the city and a nearby airbase, relieving the U.S. 196th Infantry Brigade, which was drawing down in preparation for its departure from South Vietnam in late June. The new commander of the 3d ARVN Division, Brigadier General Nguyen Duy Hinh, was instrumental in his new unit's rebirth, and General Truong later said that the division's "return to the combat scene was truly a phenomenal achievement." General Hinh's accomplishments were also noticed in Saigon. A year later, in 1973, the 3d ARVN Division was rated by the Joint General Staff as the best of the South Vietnamese army divisions, and Hinh was the only division commander promoted to the rank of major general during the year.[21]

Although the period of retraining went on through the summer, by 8 May the defense was in place and the battlefront stabilized, though there was still fierce fighting to the west. "Life in the ancient capital began to return to normalcy," remarked Truong.[22]

Actually, Hue was far from normal. More than 100,000 refugees had converged on Hue since the fighting began, and the population, originally numbering around 200,000, was down to 50,000. Those who remained were frightened by what they had seen and heard, even though, after Truong's threat to kill looters, renegade South Vietnamese soldiers were no longer part of the problem. As a precaution, Truong placed Hue under martial law, kept the civil government on twenty-four-hour call, and ordered the police to round up more than 1,000 suspected communist agents living in the city. They were sent to jails in Danang, where they would be unable to help the North Vietnamese. Other measures included assigning the militia to dig defenses throughout the city—even in the immaculately manicured flower garden outside the American advisers' compound—and forming a 2,000-man "iron division" made up of teenagers and old men as a last-ditch defense should the North Vietnamese break through the regular forces.[23]

Much of Hue's populace was not reassured, however, though many chose to stay. The queen mother of Vietnam's last monarch, Emperor Bao Dai, elected to remain in the city as an inspiration to the people. "We shall stay in Hue, but we have great fear," said the frail eighty-three-year-old mandarin from her regal home near the outskirts of the city. "All Hue is afraid. The people of Hue have no more confidence in anything, in anyone."

Father Thuc, a Catholic priest, also decided to stay in Hue. Remembering the horror of the brief communist occupation of Hue during the Tet Offensive of 1968, when the North Vietnamese marched off and executed 1,800 civilians (282 of them from Father Thuc's parish), many Catholics chose to flee. Only a few families from Father Thuc's parish left, however. "The rest of us will remain," promised the priest. "This time we will not let them take our children. This time we fight to the death."

Ordinary people had the most to lose from the fighting. "People were beginning to be happy for the first time in four years," said one man sadly. For farmers, new seed strains, irrigation systems, and fertilizer, part of the government's pacification plan, had greatly improved rural life. "They were expecting an excellent harvest—only three weeks from now," said a farmer who stood to lose everything no matter who won.

A well-to-do woman from a respectable Hue family sent her relatives to safety in Danang but chose to remain behind because she feared for her property if she left. "If the ARVN do not steal our things, then maybe the Viet Cong will," she said, well aware of the stories about marauding South Vietnamese soldiers in Dong Ha and Quang Tri City. "If the rich leave, the poor will take what is left. In any case, nothing will remain."

Everyone feared both the North Vietnamese and the American retaliation that was sure to follow if Hue fell to the enemy. They remembered 1968 and the terrible damage wrought in the name of retaking the city. "Hue is dead," said one woman upon reflection of this sobering fact. "No," corrected another more optimistically. "Hue is nearly dead."[24]

But Hue had survived more than a decade of war, and it would survive again. The population was understandably demoralized after the dizzying pace of defeats to the north, but their pessimism was based on the performance of past military commanders. They had not counted on Truong's staying power and tactical skill. The new general intended to turn the tide.

ELEVEN

THE SLOW
MARCH NORTH

In mid-May General Truong felt strong enough to go onto the offensive. A series of operations, code-named Song Than (Tidal Wave), were planned to keep the North Vietnamese off balance, though Truong held out little hope that they would actually retake any territory. The first thrust—Operation Song Than 5-72—began late at night on 12 May when part of the 369th VNMC Brigade's reconnaissance company crossed the Tach Ma River. Although their mission was simply to establish a command and control site for the main operation to come, these marines became the first South Vietnamese troops to move north since the offensive began.

The main operation began at first light on 13 May. Helicopters from U.S. Marine squadron HHM-164 flew ashore from the USS *Okinawa* and picked up the 3d and 8th Battalions of the 369th VNMC Brigade for an assault on Hai Lang, about six miles southeast of Quang Tri City. As the marines loaded up, tactical air strikes and naval gunfire pounded Hai Lang in preparation for the attack. Flying nap-of-the-earth toward the target, the helicopters landed in a single wave in each of two landing zones, reducing the exposure time to North Vietnamese antiaircraft fire.

The first wave headed for its target, designated LZ Tango, behind a curtain of Cobra attack helicopters from the U.S. Army's Troop F, 4th Cavalry. The heavily armed escort poured rocket and minigun fire around the landing zone while the transport helicopters took evasive action in case the enemy was aiming at them. Major Donald C. Brodie, the operations officer of the marine helicopter squadron, recalled that despite the high-speed maneuvers there were no accidents. "Troop F would adjust their flight paths as necessary to avoid us and attack the targets or areas of potential threat," he observed. "With our 'jinxing' flight and their escort service, I always thought it looked like snakes crawling through a kettle of spaghetti."[1]

The Vietnamese marines unloaded on LZ Tango at 9:30 in the morning with no opposition. The helicopters returned to their ships to refuel, then flew back to shore to pick up the second wave of marines. This time the flight in was not so peaceful. As the helicopters headed for the second landing zone—LZ Delta—they were greeted by small-arms fire. Major David J. Moore, the squadron executive officer, radioed that the "LZ is hot from here on in." Army Cobra attack helicopters escorting the assault got the word and shifted south, pounding the enemy with rockets until it was safe to land. Still, the North Vietnamese managed to hit three CH-46 helicopters and damaged a CH-53 so badly that it had to be left behind at LZ Delta. After the crew had loaded aboard another helicopter, the Cobras destroyed the crippled CH-53 to prevent its capture.

With all the marines on the ground by noon, the two battalions swept toward My Chanh, where they planned to link up with another unit, the 9th VNMC Battalion, which had crossed the river. Between the pincers was the 66th NVA Regiment, which was caught completely by surprise. Captain Richard W. Hodory, one of the U.S. Marine advisers with the 3d VNMC Battalion coming down from the north, moved with the Vietnamese as they assaulted across 400 yards of open rice paddies toward enemy positions. He recalled that the enemy was driven back by the aggressive action, but as the marines regrouped, they were hit by mortar and automatic weapons fire. Friendly artillery quickly broke the enemy resistance, and the marines continued the attack.

Although Operation Song Than 5-72 lasted only one day, it gave General Truong the breathing room he sought. The North Vietnamese could no longer expect uncontested gains on the ground, nor could they rest easy in their defensive positions. But they did not intend to take the attacks lightly. On 21 May the enemy launched a three-pronged armor attack against the My Chanh line. The marines had expected some sort of retaliation, but this time the North Vietnamese did not follow the usual pattern. There was no preassault artillery barrage, and instead of going cross-country, the enemy thrust straight south along the coastal highway. Regional Forces set up along the front heard the tanks coming and quickly broke ranks, allowing the North Vietnamese to almost completely encircle the 3d and 9th VNMC Battalions. Both units were forced to withdraw, and the enemy penetrated almost three miles into the marines' positions. But with the aid of heavy air strikes and a South Vietnamese army armor cavalry unit, the marines managed to push the attackers back over the river by nightfall.

The next morning the North Vietnamese attacked again and pushed all the way to the 369th VNMC Brigade command bunker. The marines used LAWs and newly acquired TOW missile systems to push back the assault. Vietnamese marines cheered as the first TOW missile ever launched in combat sought out and destroyed a PT-76 tank in a ball of flames. Another demolished a machine-gun nest. A total of five enemy armored vehicles came within

The horror of war: A North Vietnamese tank crewman killed during the battle for Quang Tri. (U.S. Army)

400 yards of the command bunker before being destroyed by the TOWs, and by 9:30 that morning ten tanks and armored personnel carriers lay in ruins on the battlefield. Shortly before noon the 8th VNMC Battalion counterattacked and scattered the North Vietnamese. After two days of fighting, the enemy suffered 542 killed, while the marines reported light casualties.[2]

Not to be outdone by the marines, two regiments of the 1st ARVN Division left their defensive positions on 15 May and began clearing the high ground south of Firebases Birmingham and Bastogne, two strategic positions abandoned to the enemy almost three weeks before. The next day a couple of platoons of volunteers launched a heliborne assault directly into Firebase Bastogne, catching the North Vietnamese stationed around the base by surprise. By nightfall the elements of the two regiments sweeping along the ground to the south had reached Bastogne, and the firebase was securely in South Vietnamese hands.

For the next ten days the division widened its control, and on 20 May another firebase, known as Checkmate, was recaptured. The defeat must have been a bitter pill for the previously victorious North Vietnamese, one made more distasteful because it came on the eve of Ho Chi Minh's birth-day, 19 May. Artillery and air strikes kept the pressure on, and at the end of May the 29th NVA Regiment withdrew to the west.

Neither the retaking of Bastogne and Checkmate nor the limited coun-teroffensives by the marines were ends in themselves. Rather, Truong was striving to enlarge the defensive lines around Hue and deny the enemy time and space to maneuver. "We were fighting for elbow room," said one ad-viser, noting that reoccupying Bastogne was not as important as striking at enemy forces massing in the area. Another U.S. official watching from the sidelines said that if Truong could keep the South Vietnamese moving, "then he can spoil lots of the enemy's plans before they are even set in ac-tion." This sort of mobile warfare was a radical departure from General Lam's earlier static defense to the north, which in early April had allowed the North Vietnamese almost two weeks after their initial successes to re-group before launching their final thrust toward Quang Tri City. Whereas Lam continued to disbelieve reports of enemy strength and capability, Truong took them seriously and tailored his tactics accordingly.[3]

This difference proved to be profound. Truong's continued aggressive ac-tion, as well as accurate and sustained artillery fire, began to wear down the enemy troops, as they themselves had once worn down the South Viet-namese. Intelligence analysts believed that the 324B NVA Division in par-ticular was taking a beating—"suffering from a severe personnel shortage" was how FRAC characterized it. "The division may be withdrawn to Laos for refitting due to morale problems and high personnel losses," predicted General Kroesen cautiously. As FRAC saw it, Hue was largely out of dan-ger, and the North Vietnamese would concentrate on spoiling attacks, aimed particularly at cutting Highway 1 between Hue and Danang.[4] Within days, intelligence reports confirmed that the combination of limited South Vietnamese offensives, artillery, and air strikes resulted in the with-drawal of the 29th NVA Regiment from the area, which analysts consid-ered "a considerable reduction in pressure in the area of responsibility."[5]

Although the marines were successful in holding the My Chanh line, the enemy attacks so concerned the Joint General Staff in Saigon that it decided to commit the 3d Brigade of the Airborne Division to I Corps, reinforced with a regiment from the 2d ARVN Division, stationed in Quang Ngai Province in southern I Corps. It arrived on 22 May. Now most of the Air-borne Division was stationed near Hue, allowing a new reorganization of General Truong's units. He relieved the marines of their operational con-trol of the Airborne Division and assigned the division an area of respon-sibility northwest of Hue, between the 1st ARVN Division and the marines.

Airborne Division headquarters was located at Landing Zone Sally north-west of the city. Although the marines now had fewer troops under their control, the command shuffle allowed them more flexibility for offensive operations.

In fact, the marines were already planning for the next Song Than operation even before the dust had cleared from the last one. This time the 147th VNMC Brigade, which had largely recovered from its retreat from Quang Tri, provided the troops for the offensive, which would be an amphibious landing. On 23 May the 7th VNMC Battalion was trucked to Tan My Naval Base on the coast northeast of Hue, where U.S. Navy landing craft were waiting to take the marines out to ships waiting offshore. Aboard the USS *Blue Ridge,* the marine officers and their advisers put the final touches on Song Than 6-72, a combined seaborne and helicopter assault at Wunder Beach, a few miles south of Quang Tri City. This was the fabled "Street Without Joy" region made famous in the writings of historian Bernard Fall during the days of the American buildup. But the U.S. Marines were gone now, and their Vietnamese protégés were attempting to follow the footsteps of the corps.

Interestingly, the U.S. Marines and their Vietnamese counterparts had little in common. Although South Vietnam's Marine Corps had evolved into a division modeled after the Americans, complete with organic artillery support units, it had never executed an amphibious combat operation, the raison d'être of the U.S. Marine Corps. Song Than 6-72 would be its first.

The battalion itself was divided between two landing ship transports (LSTs), the *Cayuga* and the *Duluth,* part of the U.S. 9th Marine Amphibious Brigade, where it prepared to board amphibious landing craft. As they awaited final orders, the Vietnamese stretched out on the deck and ate rations while curious U.S. Marines from the amphibious brigade tried to start up conversations. But most of the men thought about the next day and tried to sleep.

At 7:50 on the morning of 24 May, Operation Song Than 6-72 stepped off. Artillery, air, and naval gunfire strikes pounded Red Beach and Landing Zone Columbus, the two designated strike zones. Amphibious tractors loaded with the 7th VNMC Battalion waited at the rendezvous point 3,600 yards offshore for the signal to hit the beach. When it came, the boats surged forward. One of the U.S. Marines watching from the deck of the *Cayuga* was struck by the spectacular sight of power and technology headed shoreward. "It was a beautiful day for a landing, nice and clear," he observed, though he was probably glad to be watching and not participating.[6]

There was another dimension to the landing that added both danger and security to the incoming marines. Part of the plan included timing a B-52 Arc Light strike to hit the beach just as the amphibious tractors approached a point 2,000 yards from shore. This took impeccable timing, but the air force pulled it off. The nervous marines were greeted by a deafening roar as the huge bombs thundered across the beach. For fighting men feeling alone and vulnerable in fragile boats, the sight must have filled them with confidence and pride.

The battalion hit the beach in two waves of forty amphibious tractors and seized the objective. North Vietnamese mortars opened up on the marines, but after the beating they had taken from the B-52s, their fire was ineffective. As the tractors backed into the sea like giant turtles, the marines moved over the sand dunes and fanned out toward their objective. Reports sent back to headquarters claimed the assault killed fifty of the surprised enemy and captured caches of weapons, ammunition, and food.

The second part of the operation was a heliborne assault by the 4th and 6th VNMC Battalions. At 9:40 A.M. eighteen helicopters carried the marines to Landing Zone Columbus at the junction of Routes 555 and 602. The cargo helicopters landed behind a curtain of smoke laid down by artillery to mask the landing, and like the Song Than operation two weeks earlier, U.S. Army Cobra gunships raced back and forth over suspected enemy positions, firing rockets and miniguns. It seemed to work because the North Vietnamese did not contest the landing, though both marine battalions did run into elements of the 18th NVA Regiment (part of the 325C NVA Division) the next day. Two captured enemy soldiers said that their regiment had just arrived near My Chanh and was preparing for an attack when the marines launched their operation. If true, Song Than 6-72 probably helped save the day.[7]

The South Vietnamese had actually discovered the tip of a new and very large iceberg. The 325C NVA Division was a brand-new unit that had been given orders on 7 May to move into northern I Corps and add its weight to the battlefield. The 18th NVA Regiment was the first unit to deploy. It took fifteen days, read one communist history, "amidst earth-shattering B-52 bomb runs and violent enemy artillery barrages," to move south to Quang Tri City. "A number of the division's cadre and soldiers spilled their blood and gave their lives before they even entered the battlefield."[8]

Although they did not fully realize the new threat they faced, all three marine battalions withdrew to the My Chanh line by 31 May. The conclusion of the operation marked the second time in a month that General Truong had used the marines to show the enemy that its sea flank was vulnerable and that innovative airmobile tactics could be used almost at will.

But while the North Vietnamese were thrown temporarily off balance in the north and east, the western flank was quickly back in action. On 25 May, while the marines were winding up Operation Song Than 6-72, the enemy hit the 258th VNMC Brigade. For three days infantry and armor from the 324B NVA Division threw themselves at the My Chanh line, committing more tanks to the action than during any other single attack of the Easter Offensive. But the assault was poorly conceived and badly executed. Troops massed during daylight, allowing South Vietnamese artillery and air strikes to take a deadly toll, and when the attacks finally began, North Vietnamese infantry and armor did not work well together. Still, on 26 May a battalion (probably from the 66th NVA Regiment) hit hard against the 9th VNMC Battalion's positions, driving the marines back over 1,000 yards. Captain Robert K. Redlin, a U.S. Marine artillery officer who had been assigned temporarily to the battalion as an infantry adviser, was with the Vietnamese marines as they pulled back. His knowledge of artillery was perfect for the situation. Throughout the day, Captain Redlin called in air support and coordinated naval gunfire against the enemy. By nightfall the attack was broken, and the North Vietnamese retreated, leaving behind their dead.

The 1st VNMC Battalion was also having problems. Two battalions from the 88th NVA Regiment, supported by tanks and artillery, almost managed to push through to the marines' command post. Another U.S. Marine adviser, Captain Lawrence H. Livingston, the same officer who had helped turn back the enemy attack on Firebase Pedro in early April, called in air strikes to shore up the breach in the battalion's line. After losing over 200 soldiers in their bid to capture the command post, the North Vietnamese were again pushed back, the momentum of their attack against the South Vietnamese western flank finally spent.

The month of May had proved to be costly for the North Vietnamese. More than 2,900 of their soldiers were killed, 1,080 weapons captured, and sixty-four armored vehicles destroyed or captured. But for all their losses, the North Vietnamese had failed to capture Hue; in fact, they had gained no ground at all. All along the My Chanh line the marines saw their morale rise as it became clear that they were turning the tide. But they had no more resources to throw into the fight if the situation again turned bad. By the end of May more than 15,000 Vietnamese marines—basically the entire division—were in I Corps.

President Thieu was pleased by the continued good news from the northern front. On 28 May he flew to Hue and addressed the troops, giving special praise to the marines. On the Emperor's Walkway in front of the Imperial Palace, Thieu personally thanked Colonel Lan, the Marine Division commander, and promoted him to brigadier general. After almost two months of successive defeats and setbacks, the president could go back to Saigon with good news.

June began with more offensives, each one bigger and bolder than the last. On 8 June all three marine brigades committed four battalions to Operation Song Than 8-72, a spoiling attack across the Tach Ma River into North Vietnamese forward positions. The marines advanced under a canopy of artillery and B-52 strikes, which thundered along the broad plain less than a mile to the front. Despite the bombardment, the enemy managed heavy resistance along Route 555, a narrow two-lane road running along the coast. But the marines prevailed, killing 230 North Vietnamese soldiers and destroying seven tanks while losing only nine of their own men. Unlike in previous operations, this time the marines stayed north of the river, setting up defensive positions while South Vietnamese army engineers built pontoon bridges and brought up tanks and artillery to support further infantry attacks.[9]

The marines did not stay put for long. On 18 June Operation Song Than 8A-72 began with elements of all three brigades again moving north in what was basically a continuation of the last operation. The 1st VNMC Battalion advanced along the beach, meeting only light resistance, while the 5th VNMC Battalion took the area near Highway 1. In the middle was the 6th VNMC Battalion moving along Route 555. Once again the North Vietnamese threw infantry and tanks against the marines moving up the middle road, and once again the attacks were poorly coordinated. Artillery made short work of the tanks, though on one occasion the enemy attacks broke through the perimeter and threatened the battalion command post. Timely B-52 strikes and naval gunfire beat back the attack after about eight hours, and the advance continued. Nine days later, on 27 June, Operation Song Than 8A-72 ended with the marines successfully establishing a new defensive line almost three miles north of the My Chanh line. In the process the enemy had lost another 761 soldiers and eight tanks.[10]

With the enemy's stranglehold on Quang Tri Province loosened just a little, a picture of what life was like under the conquering communist army emerged. Civilians who had not run from the advancing North Vietnamese told tales of terror and forced labor. One farmer, who said that the communists immediately told the people they would be shot if they tried to flee south, recounted how the invaders forced people to carry supplies and build fortifications. Those who were not pressed into service as ammunition bearers for the North Vietnamese were moved north. Entire villages were forcibly evacuated, apparently to create a cordon sanitaire between the two sides. The 2,000 civilians freed from North Vietnamese occupation by the marines' advance were the lucky ones; they were sent south to My Chanh and then to Hue and Danang. Although life as a refugee would not be easy, at least it would be safer.[11]

The slowly improving fortunes of the South Vietnamese military in I Corps coincided with a change in the top levels of the U.S. advisory command. On 30 May Major General Frederick J. Kroesen, the senior FRAC adviser, was replaced by Major General Howard H. Cooksey, an armor officer with only limited experience in Vietnam. For six months during 1968, General Cooksey had served as assistant commander of the Americal Division before cutting short his tour to take command of the U.S. Army Training Center at Fort Dix, New Jersey. During World War II Cooksey had fought with the 158th Regimental Combat Team during the Luzon campaign in 1944–45, and during the Korean War he was a captain in the 7th Infantry Division. During both wars Cooksey was decorated for valor. Now, during the closing months of American involvement in the Vietnam War, General Cooksey was in I Corps as the last commander of FRAC.[12]

At MACV headquarters in Saigon there was also a change of command. On 30 June General Creighton Abrams, who had faithfully served in Vietnam since 1968, would leave Vietnam to take over as army chief of staff. He was following the path of his old commander, General William Westmoreland, who had also served as chief of staff when he left Vietnam in 1968. The change-of-command ceremony marked the mood of the country at the time: somber and furtive. Abrams's departure was marked only by the presentation of a medal by President Thieu. There were no farewell parties, no public ceremonies, and heavy security kept reporters and curious bystanders at bay.

Abrams left Vietnam with mixed feelings. He had presided over a retreating army and had faithfully followed the Nixon administration's plan of Vietnamization (a word Abrams never liked) and drawdown, and he left with his career unblemished by a war that touched many others with controversy. Even so, Abrams had ridden a roller-coaster ride of emotions as the South Vietnamese edged to the brink of defeat, then slowly struggled back from the abyss. But by the time he left, Abrams once again felt that Saigon was going to come out on top. "There's going to be some rough days ahead still, and we might lose some more places," the general was quoted as saying during a staff meeting as General Truong was beginning his push north from Hue, "but they're [the North Vietnamese] beaten. They've failed."[13]

The man who would try to keep the South Vietnamese on the path toward victory was Abrams's deputy at MACV, General Frederick C. Weyand. A tall, cool soldier with an unflappable demeanor, Weyand was

The slow South Vietnamese push toward Quang Tri City resulted in the capture of enemy heavy weapons, such as this 130mm howitzer. (U.S. Army)

known by top civilians in Saigon as the "sophisticated general." During World War II he was called to active duty as a second lieutenant in the army, where he served in China and Burma as an intelligence officer. During the Korean War, Weyand commanded a battalion in the 3d Infantry Division and was part of the bloody retreat from North Korea in late 1950. When Vietnam became America's first military priority, General Weyand commanded the 25th Infantry Division when it deployed from Hawaii. In 1968 he commanded II Field Force, then went to France in March 1969 as part of the U.S. delegation at the Paris peace talks. In September 1970 Weyand was back in Saigon as deputy commander of MACV. Perhaps more than any other MACV commander, Weyand came to Vietnam with a well-rounded understanding of the war.

Compared with the explosive events that marked the Easter Offensive during April and early May, South Vietnamese advances during late May through June must have seemed paltry to outside observers. While the North Vietnamese had taken an entire province in a little more than a month, the South Vietnamese had regained only about four miles in two months. But momentum is crucial in battle, and in I Corps the enemy had lost his, while the South Vietnamese were rebounding. General Truong's leadership, Saigon's support, and the improved fighting abilities of the marines, the 1st ARVN Division, and the Airborne Division staved off the capture of Hue and focused attention on retaking lost ground. Quang Tri City was the center of Saigon's attention, though from a military perspective it was unimportant. During almost a decade of fighting, the North Vietnamese had never captured an important city and held it. Hue had fallen temporarily during the 1968 Tet Offensive but was recaptured, and now President Thieu could not afford to let the enemy keep Quang Tri.

On 14 June Thieu ordered General Truong to present his plan for a counteroffensive at a meeting in Saigon with the Joint General Staff. The president listened intently as Truong outlined his strategy, but he was clearly not pleased. Taking a purple grease pencil in hand, Thieu marked a map with arrows showing a less ambitious series of spoiling attacks much like those of the past month. Discouraged, Truong folded his map and flew back to Hue. where he complained to General Cooksey about Thieu's timidity. Cooksey agreed and reported to Abrams that "the attack must be a bold one that reaches the very rear area as quickly as possible."[14]

Truong brazenly decided not to present any further plans to Saigon. "If they wanted me to do anything," he later recalled, "they should give me a Vietnamese translation of whatever plan they wanted me to execute and I would comply." Truong's subtle stubbornness worked. Thieu called the next morning and asked him back to Saigon. After a little wrangling, the president approved Truong's original plan, though he told the general to expect no further reinforcements except the 1st Airborne Brigade, which would be transferred from An Loc, where it had already seen heavy fighting. General Truong now had his orders: recapture Quang Tri Province.[15]

TWELVE

RETAKING QUANG TRI

The North Vietnamese reconnaissance patrol must have been puzzled by its discovery. Near the side of the road lay four hastily hidden parachutes and a dead body. A search of the corpse showed it to be the leader of a secret team from the Strategic Technical Directorate, the South Vietnamese side of the Studies and Observations Group (SOG), a covert action unit that had been launching highly classified missions into Laos, Cambodia, and North Vietnam since early 1964. During the Easter Offensive, some of the teams were pulled back into South Vietnam to use their intelligence-gathering capabilities in behind-the-lines missions. This particular team was operating along Route 548, the traditional North Vietnamese infiltration road through the A Shau Valley.[1]

There was something else on the body–a codebook detailing the radio frequencies and passwords for other team drops in the area. It meant nothing to the North Vietnamese reconnaissance team, but when their superiors received it, they must have been elated. With only a little effort, enemy codebreakers deciphered the book and began monitoring South Vietnamese radio broadcasts. On 12 June, one day after the codebook was captured, the enemy began picking up messages sent to two other teams, one on Highway 9 west of the old U.S. Marine base at Khe Sanh, the other west of Dong Ha. The codebreakers were startled to learn that both teams were well behind North Vietnamese lines, broadcasting information about enemy troop movements, artillery emplacements, and bomb damage caused by air strikes.[2]

On 19 June the plot thickened. Using information gleaned from listening in on South Vietnamese radio broadcasts, teams of North Vietnamese soldiers intercepted two agents dropped into the A Shau Valley to reinforce the very team that had lost its leader and the codebook. The captured operators turned out to be North Vietnamese defectors from the 304th NVA Division who had willingly joined the Strategic Technical Directorate. Captured in a separate drop near Khe Sanh were bundles of food, radio batteries, medical supplies, and ammunition.

Six days later the North Vietnamese intercepted messages to the secret team near Dong Ha ordering it to coordinate with combined airborne and amphibious landings beginning on the morning of 27 June. North Vietnamese agents confirmed that the Airborne Division was preparing for an assault, and the marines were gathering amphibious craft at the Tan My naval base. Elements of the Airborne Division were planning to parachute into a landing zone about two miles northwest of Dong Ha, part of an operation code-named Lam Thuyen. Just before dawn, forty paratroopers took off from Phu Bai airfield in two C-47 aircraft headed for the drop zone. They were to be the lead element, with the main wave to follow one hour later, but at the last minute the operation was canceled due to bad weather, and the planes returned to Phu Bai.

In concert with the airborne, the marines planned to launch Operation Ngoc Tuyen, an amphibious landing near the mouth of the Cua Viet River. On the morning of 27 June one marine company and a battalion of Regional Forces militia stormed toward shore in landing craft behind a curtain of naval gunfire and air strikes. Like the airborne, which was in the air at the same time, the operation had to be aborted because of bad weather. Both missions were rescheduled. If successful, the twin operations would establish a major South Vietnamese salient well behind enemy lines and would threaten to cut off reinforcement and resupply to North Vietnamese units around Quang Tri City.

All this must have been viewed with alarm by North Vietnamese military commanders, especially when added to the other persistent and innovative attacks being launched by General Truong from My Chanh. But in reality it was all a deception, part of a plan to conceal the real South Vietnamese plan, a much less ambitious operation code-named Lam Son 72. The teams were real, but the codebook, the radio messages, and the resupply missions were phonies—even the corpse and the empty parachutes were part of the ruse, placed by the road to fool the enemy. General Cooksey had come up with the idea, backed by General Truong and supported by the best planners in MACV. General Abrams had approved of the plan in principle a month earlier.[3]

MACV had deception plans on the books going back several years, though there had been no need to use them until the Easter Offensive. During the North Vietnamese buildup in early 1972, Admiral John S. McCain, commander in chief of the Pacific Fleet and General Abrams's boss, had proposed an elaborate plan launched deep into North Vietnam from the Gulf of Tonkin. The plan, said McCain, would "inhibit NVA flexibility to deploy ground resources into RVN [Republic of Vietnam]." Other possibilities presented during April as the enemy was sweeping through Quang Tri Province included threatening to land U.S. Marines along the Cua Viet

River, or even in one of several towns along the narrow North Vietnamese panhandle. None were approved because they included the use of American troops, even though the marine detachment on Okinawa had contingency plans for a division-strength landing at the town of Vinh in southern North Vietnam dating back to the early 1960s. In fact, as late as 1965 the Vinh landing was the graduation staff problem at the U.S. Marine Corps Command and Staff College.[4]

Whether or not the North Vietnamese were completely fooled by the deception operation is unknown, though General Cooksey reported to Abrams that the mission was executed "on schedule with apparent good success." At the very least it seemed they were forced to keep troops in the rear that otherwise would have been put into the attack on Hue or thrown at the marines and airborne troops on the My Chanh line.[5]

With or without the deception plan, the North Vietnamese were losing ground. FRAC intelligence analysts reported that enemy troops were cracking under the strain of long months of constant fighting. One report to MACV observed, "Further signs of the enemy's decreasing morale and unwillingness to fight were evidenced yesterday [26 June] when an estimated four NVA companies reportedly broke contact and fled the battlefield when engaged by friendly forces north of My Chanh."[6]

General Truong decided to act quickly while the enemy was faltering. On 28 June Lam Son 72 began, the first corps-sized offensive operation ever executed by the South Vietnamese military. The primary objective was Quang Tri City, which planners expected to take within nine days with little opposition from the enemy. Their prediction proved to be wildly optimistic—the battle to recapture Quang Tri would become the longest of the entire war.

Behind a ferocious bombardment from B-52s, tactical air, and artillery, the South Vietnamese moved forward. Progress was to be measured by how far the South Vietnamese advanced along preset lines drawn on the map, called phase lines. There were three in all: Phase Lines Blue, Brown, and Gold, each marking a slice of enemy-held territory north to the Cua Viet River. Phase Line Blue marked the northernmost boundary of the advance.

The task organization for the counteroffensive was composed of the Airborne Division's three brigades and the Marine Division backed by both units' armor and artillery assets, the 1st Ranger Group, and the 7th Armored Cavalry. Around Hue the 1st ARVN Division would continue to push out to the west, while the 57th ARVN Regiment (reconstituted after the destruction of the 3d ARVN Division) guarded Danang and conducted limited offensive operations in Quang Nam Province. Corps reserve forces consisted of the 4th Regiment of the 2d ARVN Division, the 51st Independent Regiment, and the 17th Armored Cavalry Regiment. In addition to recapturing Quang Tri, Lam Son 72 was also aimed at destroying as many enemy forces as possible.[7]

The Airborne Division's 2d Brigade led the assault. Quang Tri City itself lay within the paratroopers' area of responsibility, and Colonel Tran Quac Lich, the brigade commander, was proud of the honor bestowed on his unit. So confident were his paratroopers that the top officers carried a neatly folded South Vietnamese flag and a bottle of champagne to celebrate the retaking of the city. With spirits soaring, the brigade—about 2,500 strong—surged forward, protected on both flanks by marines and rangers, which were also advancing north.

What they did not know was that the enemy was expecting them. A leak in the South Vietnamese high command (whether it was a case of poor operational security or a spy on the general staff is not known) placed all the plans for Lam Son 72 in North Vietnamese hands. American and South Vietnamese counterintelligence learned of the breach when sophisticated radio monitors intercepted communications between Hanoi and its units in the field. Despite the leak, South Vietnamese planners decided it was too late to alter the operation and ordered Lam Son 72 to proceed.[8]

It is unlikely that the North Vietnamese were able to make much use of their intelligence coup; there was not enough time. To alter defensive plans would risk being caught in midchange, as the South Vietnamese had been caught on the opening day of the Easter Offensive. So the enemy remained dug in behind three lines of defense. The first was a set of four old forts along Highway 1, the second consisted of a bunker complex on the southern boundary of Quang Tri City, and the third was the citadel itself. Rather than oppose the airborne at the center of the South Vietnamese line, the North Vietnamese chose to hold these three lines, sending limited counterattacks against the oncoming flanks—the marines and rangers.

Although there was little serious resistance from the North Vietnamese, it took more than a week for the 2d Airborne Brigade to advance the eighteen miles between My Chanh and the outskirts of Quang Tri City. The slow pace was born partly of caution and partly from a desire to use the array of available firepower to break down potential enemy positions before the infantry moved in. Before the paratroopers advanced into villages or potentially dangerous areas, they would call in air and artillery strikes to pummel the target.

Colonel Lich and his paratroopers arrived at the four forts on 4 July, pausing only to call in air strikes. The North Vietnamese made no attempt

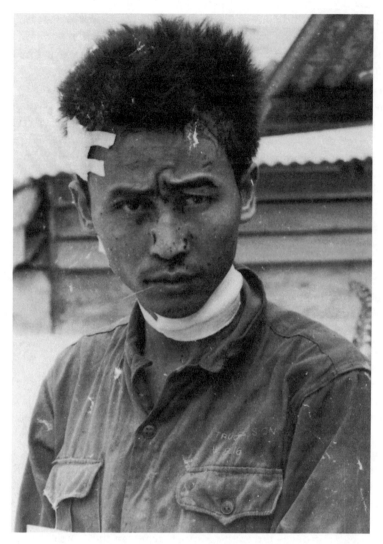

A captured North Vietnamese soldier remains defiant. (U.S. Army)

to defend the forts, falling back toward Quang Tri City in the face of the terrible onslaught. Two days later the 2d Brigade entered the suburb of Mai Linh, still without much resistance. Colonel Lich paused once again, this time to take stock of enemy defenses in the city itself. Although resistance had been light up to this point, he could only guess what lay in wait near the citadel. In a bold move, a reconnaissance platoon was helicoptered into the city, where it scouted the defenses, then made its way back to the brigade. With the intelligence from the patrol, Colonel Lich began his attack on 8 July. But this time the North Vietnamese fought back. Mortars and artillery rained down on the paratroopers, stopping them in their tracks.

For the next two weeks the 2d Airborne Brigade engaged in the deadly art of urban fighting. Using close-air support and tanks, the paratroopers fought house to house until they were within fifty yards of the citadel walls. In preparation for a final assault, air strikes blew three breaches in the walls, but the brigade could go no farther. The North Vietnamese were determined to stand fast and trade blows—to the last man if necessary.

The failure of the 2d Brigade to take the citadel marked the beginning of a new phase in the fighting. Mobile warfare turned to siege warfare as the South Vietnamese encircled the city in much the same way as their enemies had done back in late April. But unlike the North Vietnamese assault on Quang Tri, the paratroopers deliberately left a wide gap in the lines west of the city to give the defenders a way out. General Truong believed the battle would be less costly if the enemy was allowed to escape. Instead, the North Vietnamese used the open corridor to reinforce the citadel, moving about two battalions into the city by the end of July. The enemy paid heavily for this decision, however. During the day, wave after wave of tactical aircraft and B-52s dropped their payloads on the citadel, forcing the North Vietnamese to dig in deep. During the month of July, U.S. aircraft flew 5,461 tactical sorties and 2,054 Arc Light strikes, the largest total of any month during the entire Easter Offensive. The Arc Light strikes were particularly devastating. General Cooksey observed, "Time after time I saw the enemy concentrate his forces for attack only to be slammed by a B-52 strike." But airpower alone was not enough to win the battle.[9]

Actually, the North Vietnamese tried to shift the focus of the battle as a way of diverting airborne troops from Quang Tri City. For a time it worked. Attacks along Highway 1 south of the city placed the airborne in danger of being outflanked and cut off, forcing it to divert all but two units, the 7th and 11th Airborne Battalions, back south to deal with the problem. The 11th Battalion, which was supported by tanks, remained in position about two miles south of Quang Tri City; the 7th Battalion was stalled just to the east.

The confusion caused by shifting battle lines highlighted another crisis emerging in Saigon: a crisis of credibility. As had happened so many times before during the war, the observations of the media were at odds with official government versions of events. Reporters accompanying the airborne filed stories about the stalled drive, only to be criticized by Saigon, which asserted that Quang Tri was largely in government hands. Accusations flew, and on 7 July the commander of the Airborne Division, Lieutenant General Du Quoc Dong, barred newsmen from traveling north on Highway 1 toward the city. However, a handful of reporters were already on the outskirts of Quang Tri, and they continued to send back stories indicating that Saigon was misleading the public. In the end, Saigon was forced to change its claim that three-fourths of the city had been recaptured, though officials would not admit that the airborne troops were stalled. It turned out that the public affairs bureau was only following President Thieu's lead. During a radio address on 6 July, he had boasted of victory. "Today Quang Tri City has been recaptured," said Thieu. "I believe this is the starting point of the complete and final failure of the northern communist invaders." Thieu's optimism was premature, yet his subordinates were simply following their leader's example.[10]

As the paratroopers bogged down, U.S. advisers feared they had lost the fighting spirit. Intelligence estimates of enemy strength inside Quang Tri City indicated that the defensive positions were manned by militia and replacement units, not regulars. The main force, the 304th and 308th NVA Divisions, was believed to be dispersed west of the city to avoid being decimated by American airpower. The unfortunate soldiers left to man the defenses inside the city took the brunt of air strikes. North Vietnamese soldiers later described the slaughter. "The new recruits came in at dusk. They were dead by dawn," recalled one participant. "No one had time to check where they were from, or who was their commander. . . . No one could count how many lives were lost." Other North Vietnamese soldiers called the assault a "senseless sacrifice" and referred to Quang Tri as "Hamburger City."[11]

Still, the North Vietnamese held on. Artillery fire, particularly from the feared 130mm emplacements scattered around the city, rained down on the paratroopers as they crawled forward. On the evening of 9 July, part of the 7th Airborne Battalion was pinned down by a barrage of more than fifty of the big shells, plus a steady rain of mortar fire. Although it took few casualties, the airborne was once again stopped in its tracks.

Suddenly the North Vietnamese switched over to the offensive. Reacting to gains made by the marines to the northeast, the enemy attacked the airborne troops on the southwest side of Quang Tri City. It was a move General Truong had feared because it might be an attempt to circle behind the South Vietnamese and strike south at Hue. But the attack turned out to be limited. Several hundred enemy troops spearheaded by about two dozen tanks punched into South Vietnamese lines, driving the paratroopers from

South Vietnamese marines use a TOW antitank weapon to hunt enemy armor near the My Chanh River in southern Quang Tri Province. (U.S. Marine Corps)

hilltop positions and occupying the newly constructed outposts. Tactical air strikes once again saved the day, pounding enemy infantry as they massed and firing TOW missiles into tanks. At least nine T-54s were reportedly knocked out.[12]

Because it seemed that the South Vietnamese momentum might be falling away, U.S. tactical air support was increased. American planes zeroed in on North Vietnamese positions near the citadel, flying more than 1,000 tactical sorties and hundreds of Arc Light strikes, the highest two-week total of the entire offensive. The air force also used new technology to great effect on the Quang Tri battlefield. One fighter plane managed to drop a 2,000-pound laser-guided bomb squarely on the old fortress wall, blowing open a gaping hole that paved the way for a South Vietnamese assault. But as a spokesman for the South Vietnamese command was quick to point out to the press, the breach in the citadel wall was "only a preparation for our troops" and did not signal an imminent ground attack on the heavily fortified city center.[13]

The emphasis on airpower highlighted the lack of progress by the Airborne Division. For more than a week the paratroopers had been within

200 yards of the citadel, yet they were unable to reach gaps blown in the walls. "We are moving inch by inch, foot by foot, house by house," observed Captain Gail Furrow, an adviser with the 11th Airborne Battalion. "We are advancing nearly two blocks a day, but we are moving forward." Furrow had stayed with the paratroopers since the beginning of the offensive almost three weeks earlier. During the drive he called in air strikes and naval gunfire from a position maddeningly close to the citadel walls, yet unreachable. With a bottle of Coke in one hand and a field radio handset in the other, Furrow talked to the forward air controller high above.

"Give us more air strikes," he yelled over the roar of exploding artillery rounds. "We need that air support bad." Air force jets screamed overhead in an almost unbroken stream as they bombed enemy positions a mere 400 yards away. Next to Furrow sat Major Le Van Me, the battalion commander. The two officers were outside the remains of a cement house that had once been painted a garish blue, though now it was mostly gray from the bullets and shrapnel that had chipped away the paint. Retreating enemy soldiers had written in chalk on the battered walls: "We are determined to defeat the American aggressors" and "We will always remember Chairman Ho Chi Minh."

While their officers called in air strikes and planned for the next ground attack, the men lay around in hammocks or cooked food. Two soldiers fed wandering pigs with powdered rations captured from the North Vietnamese. But despite the outward calm, the paratroopers were ready to dive into nearby bunkers if the enemy began bombarding. For the moment they were content to let the warplanes fight the battle, but each man knew he still had to make it that last 200 yards to the citadel before the battle was over.

Captain Furrow and Major Me were also worried about a trap. It seemed too easy to just walk into the citadel and take over. "We're moving up slowly and bringing in reinforcements from the rear," said the airborne adviser, "because we know the communists might be slipping away from our main force in order to lay a trap." Another adviser feared a different trap. "If they let us bring our troops into Quang Tri almost unopposed," he said, "you know they have something big planned for us. Those 130mm guns they have in the mountains could hit us hard."14

On 16 July MACV suddenly called off all air strikes inside Quang Tri after it was discovered that many civilians were still living in the city. Planners had believed all residents had long since left the rubble, but American advisers began reporting seeing dazed and wounded peasants along the road. One adviser estimated that more than 1,000 inhabitants of the nearby village of Xuan Duong were killed by a combination of U.S. air strikes, naval gunfire, and North Vietnamese artillery. Those refugees lucky enough to survive the ordeal were moved south to camps near Hue.[15]

Naval gunfire filled in where the air strikes left off. The U.S. Navy began pouring fire—considered more accurate than bombs—into the citadel and on specific targets nearby. The destroyer *Eversole* hit a north Vietnamese ammunition dump three miles north of Quang Tri City, causing hundreds of secondary explosions as ammunition blew up. Navy ships also destroyed several barges loaded with war matériel from China southwest of Hon La, an island about thirty miles north of the North Vietnamese coastal city of Dong Hoi.[16]

That same day, a company of airborne troops managed to break through to the inner part of the city, and it looked as if the South Vietnamese might gain a foothold. But the eighty men were soon surrounded by an enemy battalion, and for two days other airborne units tried to rescue their badly mauled comrades. Ironically, the paratroopers were trapped in an old U.S. advisory compound, which was perhaps also fortunate because the well-made bunkers provided good shelter against enemy attacks. The paratroopers managed to break out two days later and returned to friendly lines with only seven dead.[17]

Word that new enemy units were heading for Quang Tri was reported on 16 July by MACV intelligence. Two divisions were moving toward the city: the 325C NVA Division, which was Hanoi's only reserve unit left in the North, and the 312th NVA Division, which had spent the entire war in Laos. The 325C, a heavy division with organic armor and artillery, had begun moving down the North Vietnamese panhandle in mid-April, bombed mercilessly by U.S. planes as it advanced. The 312th, a light division consisting of only two regiments rather than the usual three, had better luck, escaping most of the bombing to enter South Vietnam virtually intact. The appearance of these units highlighted Hanoi's determination to hold on to something after all the blood and treasure expended since the Easter Offensive began. Neither Saigon nor MACV was surprised by the move, however. On the morning of 16 July more than two dozen B-52s flew across the demilitarized zone, dropping 600 tons of bombs on North Vietnamese staging positions and infiltration routes.[18]

Unwilling to wait for reinforcements that may or may not reach Quang Tri, the North Vietnamese counterattacked on 19 July. Just after midnight an artillery barrage of more than 300 rounds marked the beginning of a ground attack by ten tanks and an estimated battalion of infantry. But the paratroopers were lucky; an enemy soldier stumbled into a trip wire and ignited a perimeter flare, warning of the impending assault. House-to-house fighting in the southern sector of the city raged until dawn, when South Vietnamese artillery was able to push the North Vietnamese back across the Thach Han River. Enemy losses were reported as 295 killed and two tanks destroyed. The airborne suffered 27 killed and 131 wounded.[19]

The bold use of tanks worried the Airborne Division command. After almost a month of fierce fighting and thousands of tons of ordnance, the fact that the enemy could still field armor meant that the fight was far from over. South Vietnamese intelligence estimated that despite claims that more than 100 enemy tanks had been destroyed since 28 June, there were still many more hidden in ruined buildings inside the city and in camouflaged bunkers in the hills to the west. This ability to mount continuing counterattacks raised fears that the North Vietnamese might try to sever Highway 1 behind the advancing airborne troops, cutting them off from resupply. Although not entirely convinced this would happen, FRAC pointed to increased enemy probes near the highway some eight miles southeast of Quang Tri City, near the old My Chanh defensive line. Some units were reported within 200 yards of the road.

By the end of July it was clear that the Airborne Division had gone as far as it could go. As the South Vietnamese advance bogged down and the North Vietnamese dug in deeper, questions were again raised regarding the wisdom of taking the city. In Washington, Secretary of Defense Melvin Laird argued that the South Vietnamese should forget the province capital and try to control as much territory as possible with the fewest losses. Other U.S. government officials analyzed the situation along more conventional lines, seeing the capital as a bargaining chip. "Quang Tri is obviously going to be discussed," said an unidentified American diplomat in Paris, "and when it is discussed, we want to have it in our hands."[20]

More correctly it would be in the hands of the South Vietnamese, since it was their blood being shed to take the citadel. And it was the battlefield, not Paris, that concerned General Truong. In Saigon there was talk of sending a division from the relatively unscathed delta region in the southern part of the country to reinforce I Corps, but the plan was impractical. Truong knew he would have to cope with the enemy using the forces already at hand. He was initially against assaulting the citadel, opting instead to bypass that part of the city and cut off its supply lines, then take it at a later date. But politics prevailed, and Truong focused on the citadel. "My final assessment was that we could not withdraw again from Quang Tri without admitting total defeat," he later wrote. "Our only course was to recapture the city. Therefore, I directed a switchover of zones and assigned the primary effort to the Marine Division."[21]

The marines also played a large role in Operation Lam Son 72 from the beginning (the marine portion of the counteroffensive was called Operation Song Than 9-72). When the counteroffensive stepped off on 28 June, the 3d, 5th, 7th, and 8th VNMC Battalions moved north along the coast on the east side of Highway 1 side by side with the Airborne Division. But unlike the paratroopers, the marines met stiff resistance from the first day. Elements of the 304th NVA Division had built overlapping rows of bunkers along the coast and, despite the initial unopposed advance by the airborne directly to the west, showed no inclination to withdraw.

Brigadier General Bui The Lan, the Marine Division commander, planned a heliborne assault behind enemy lines to relieve pressure on the attacking marine battalions. On 29 June the 1st and 4th VNMC Battalions, supported by the U.S. Marine Amphibious Brigade still off the coast of northern South Vietnam, landed along the coast near Wunder Beach at two landing zones named Flamingo and Hawk. Only scattered North Vietnamese forces opposed the 1,450 marines, mostly in the form of isolated armor attacks along the beach in an attempt to surround the landing forces before they could deploy. The tactic was a costly one because American warships positioned 4,000 yards offshore used their big guns to make short work of the enemy tanks.[22]

By the end of June the operation had relieved some pressure on the Airborne Division to the south and had forced the North Vietnamese to give up more ground as they rushed troops to deal with the marine assault on their flank. The combined marine and airborne operations resulted in 1,515 enemy soldiers killed during the month of June and eighteen armored vehicles destroyed.[23]

The two weeks following the thrust behind enemy lines were less dramatic. The marine battalions consolidated their positions but were reluctant to push forward as long as the airborne drive was stalled to the south. Concerned that his flanks would be exposed, General Lan decided instead to move one battalion by helicopter across the Vinh Dinh River to a position just northeast of the city while two battalions would assault enemy positions from east to west. The mission was to block North Vietnamese supply into Quang Tri City from the north.

After the usual softening-up bombardment by B-52s, tactical air, naval gunfire, and artillery, on the morning of 11 July the marines took off in thirty-four U.S. Marine helicopters from the *Okinawa* and *Tripoli*, again supported by U.S. Army Cobra gunships. The mission was basically identical to the last heliborne assault except that it landed about four miles farther north at two landing zones named Blue Jay and Crow.

Despite six hours of bomb and artillery strikes, the North Vietnamese were still able to put up a ferocious resistance. The U.S. Marine pilots flying the helicopters endured surface-to-air missiles and heavy machine-gun fire during much of the eight-mile flight to the landing zones. The lumbering CH-46s and CH-53s mustered all possible speed and clung as close to the earth as they could without crashing. Still, there were disasters. One CH-53 was hit by a SA-7 and burst into flame in midair, killing most of the fifty-five South Vietnamese marines on board. Two of the American crewmen were killed outright, and a third was badly wounded. The remaining two crewmen, plus a combat photographer, took shelter in a nearby bomb crater and watched as marauding North Vietnamese soldiers poked through the helicopter wreckage. At dusk a South Vietnamese marine patrol picked up the Americans and took them back to friendly lines. Another helicopter was downed by machine-gun fire with heavy loss of life, stranding the crew until a rescue team from the U.S. Army's Troop F, 4th Air Cavalry, braved enemy antiaircraft fire and rescued them.[24]

There were also a few near disasters. One pilot landed practically on top of a North Vietnamese T-54 tank. As the (equally surprised) enemy gunner turned his turret to obliterate the helicopter, an alert Cobra darted in and fired a TOW missile, knocking it out. Another chopper landed on the roof of a North Vietnamese command post.

After remaining on the ground for ten long minutes while the South Vietnamese marines disgorged, the helicopters took off and returned to the safety of the ships. The final tally found that three U.S. Marine helicopters had been shot down and another twenty-eight were damaged. Of the six Cobra gunships flying support for the assault, five sustained damage. Two U.S. Marine crew members were killed and another seven wounded. Despite the losses, U.S. Marine observers believed the attack was executed with precision and superb coordination. Lieutenant Colonel Gerald Turley, now the operations officer for FRAC, commented, "The execution was beautiful; lift-off, staging, coordination, control, communications, prep fires—everything went on schedule—never looked more beautiful."[25]

Once on the ground the 1st VNMC Battalion, commanded by Major Nguyen Dang Hoa, ran into heavy fire and began taking casualties. Although the marines did not know it at the time, they had encountered part of the 48th Regiment, 325C NVA Division, which was dug in just west of the landing zone. Major Hoa personally led his men against the entrenched enemy, overrunning two trench lines and securing the marines' perimeter. The move resulted in 126 enemy soldiers killed and succeeded in flanking the North Vietnamese position.

American advisers were also caught up in the action. The senior U.S. marine with the 1st VNMC Battalion, Captain Lawrence H. Livingston, found himself under fire from the moment he stepped off the helicopter. Livingston was the same adviser who had distinguished himself at Firebase Pedro during the early days of the offensive. Heavy resistance from the enemy at the landing zone pinned down the marines, but Livingston managed to form them into an assault force and stormed a North Vietnamese trench line. During the charge Livingston was knocked off his feet by an exploding round, but he managed to get back up and continue on. The North Vietnamese defenders sallied forth and met the charging marines in hand-to-hand combat, but the marines prevailed. Captain Livingston was awarded the Navy Cross for his bravery.

Just to the west the 7th VNMC Battalion slowly pushed North Vietnamese defenders from their positions and even managed to overrun an enemy armored regimental command post. The surprise move resulted in the destruction of several North Vietnamese tanks, armored personnel carriers, and trucks.

By 14 July the marines had cut the enemy's main supply route into Quang Tri City, and the enemy slowed its attacks, apparently to conserve supplies and ammunition. For the first time, medevac helicopters were able to fly in and pick up the more than 150 casualties sustained since the beginning of the offensive. Among the wounded was an American ANGLICO adviser, Lieutenant Stephen G. Biddulph, who had been wounded within minutes of leaving his helicopter during the initial heliborne assault on 11 July. Now Biddulph lay on the floor of a UH-1 helicopter with wounded and dead South Vietnamese marines stacked all around.

"A litter patient lay squarely across my wounded legs and I held another patient around the body to prevent him from falling out," recalled Lieutenant Biddulph. "We still had to make it over the heads of the enemy to get back."[26]

The helicopters did make it back to safety, but the casualties were a grim reminder that neither the South Vietnamese nor the Americans had an inexhaustible supply of manpower. United States Marine advisers were in such short supply that replacements had to be flown in from Camp Pendleton, California. On 17 July the first of them arrived in Saigon, where they underwent familiarization courses and prepared to move north. By the end of the month the South Vietnamese marines and their advisers were at peak strength, and morale was high.

The Quang Tri front remained constant until 22 July, when the marines launched another combined assault against the North Vietnamese north

North Vietnamese soldiers prepare to defend Quang Tri citadel during July and August 1972. Although little more than a pile of rubble, the citadel became a symbol of victory or defeat to both sides. (Author's collection)

and east of the city. In an attempt to sever lines of supply and communication, two battalions of the 147th VNMC Brigade launched an armor-tipped thrust north of their lines. The plan called for the tanks and infantry to link up with the brigade's 5th VNMC Battalion, which was air assaulted to two landing zones—code-named Lima and Victor—about three miles to the northeast. The helicopters flew in with little resistance, but one of the battalions assaulting on the ground ran into stubborn enemy defenders before the linkup was completed. By midday on 22 July, however, the brigade was back together, and the North Vietnamese had been pushed back to the north toward the Cua Viet River. For the next two days the marines mopped up, netting 133 enemy soldiers killed, five armored vehicles destroyed, and a 100-bed hospital overrun.[27]

It was at this point that the Airborne Division faltered. Until the end of July the paratroopers had kept abreast of the marines right up to the outskirts of Quang Tri City. But now, exhausted and depleted from hard fighting south of the city, not to mention previous battles near An Loc and in the Central Highlands, they could not muster the strength to recapture the citadel. The 2d Airborne Brigade was moved south to Firebase Sally due west of Hue, where it became the I Corps reserve. The rest of the division moved west and northwest to guard Highway 1 and provide security for the marines' left flank.

The Marine Division was ordered to relieve the airborne as the lead element in the battle for Quang Tri. At 9:30 on the evening of 27 July, elements of the 258th VNMC Brigade replaced airborne units at the front, and the fighting continued unabated. Between the marines and the citadel walls remained 200 yards of no-man's-land, the same strip of ground that had proved to be such a deadly killing field for the paratroopers. Could the marines do any better?[28]

During August, little changed. Quang Tri City remained in enemy hands, although the North Vietnamese were being bled dry by air strikes and ground assaults. Still defending the city was most of the 325C NVA Division, bolstered by elements of 308th and 320B NVA Divisions. The 325C NVA Division was comparatively fresh, but the other two units had paid a terrible price for defending Quang Tri City so persistently. During the month of July alone, the enemy suffered more than 1,880 dead, along with the loss of fifty-one armored vehicles and at least eleven artillery and anti-aircraft pieces.[29]

What was left of the North Vietnamese army in northern Quang Tri concentrated most of its force on the 147th VNMC Brigade north of the city, for this salient was the biggest threat to the enemy. Since the marines blocked Route 560, the only passable road leading into the city, the North Vietnamese were now forced to ferry supplies across the Thach Han River. This was both time-consuming and dangerous because it exposed supply convoys to air attack. During the month the 325C NVA Division hurled all three of its regiments, as well as the 27th Independent Regiment, at the marine brigade, but the South Vietnamese held.

North Vietnamese soldiers had endured much, yet the fighting became still more desperate. "The tempo of bombing and shelling reached such a level that it was not possible to distinguish individual explosions," recounted one official communist history. "In the province capital the walls of the old citadel were collapsing in big chunks." Bunkers caved in under the bombardment, while the shock waves from explosions sought out even the most well protected. "Although one might be sitting inside a bunker and not be struck with shrapnel," continued the account, "one still suffered bleeding from one's ears, nose, and mouth." Another account admitted that North Vietnamese forces were "seriously worn out" and that there were not enough reinforcements to replace casualties. Still, the exhausted soldiers "disputed each mound of earth, each portion of the wall, and each section of the trenches with the enemy. Some detachments fought to the last man and the last bullet."[30]

To the south of the city, the 258th VNMC Brigade's four battalions fought house to house, closing in on the citadel with the same bloody slowness as had the Airborne Division before them. The 3d VNMC Battalion attacked from the northeast, the 6th and 9th VNMC Battalions from the southeast, and the 1st VNMC Battalion from the southwest. But although the North Vietnamese were almost completely surrounded, artillery positions hidden outside the city continued to pound the marines. Air strikes were never able to completely destroy them. During the month of August, FRAC received reports of 720 enemy artillery strikes (called attacks by fire)—over 50,000 rounds—in and around the city. The single worst day would be 22 August, when over 3,000 mortar and artillery rounds fell on marine positions. One adviser characterized the barrages as "ceaseless," observing that the South Vietnamese were forced to "burrow into the ground like gophers."[31]

Despite the bombardment, the marines tried an all-out assault on the citadel on 3 August. For forty-eight hours South Vietnamese artillery launched its own barrage, pouring 2,000 rounds into the citadel. At dawn the 3d and 5th VNMC Battalions moved simultaneously on the northeast and southeast corners of the citadel, while the 9th VNMC Battalion attacked along Highway 1 toward the river. Standing in the way were four small forts, all still held by the North Vietnamese. But the attack faltered before it began when an argument between the marines and the airborne broke out. It seemed there was some confusion over whose area of responsibility the forts lay in, though the debate was moot, since the paratroopers had pulled back several thousand yards during the last few days of July. The enemy took advantage of the delay, attacking the exposed marines with recoilless rifles and mortars. As the offensive floundered, one marine adviser wrote in his journal: "The euphoria of last week was gone, as we realized a long, hard task lay ahead."[32]

A hard task indeed, but for the North Vietnamese the situation was rapidly deteriorating. A conference of B-4 Front officials held on 9 August admitted that the South Vietnamese counterattack had resulted in the "relatively rapid attrition" of North Vietnamese forces around Quang Tri. Even the 325C NVA Division, which was in the best shape of all the North Vietnamese units, had seen the number of men in each of its battalions drop from "approximately 400 to only 50–60 men," with 85 percent of the casualties "caused by enemy bombs and artillery." Despite the horrifying losses, the B-4 Front turned over defense of Quang Tri City to the 325C NVA Division.[33]

Yet there was still plenty of fight in the defenders. For three more weeks the marines failed to loosen the enemy's grip on the pile of rubble that was once the citadel. Both sides settled back into a series of artillery duels, with little progress on the ground. Then, on 22 August, the North Vietnamese broke the stalemate. After enduring an unusually heavy artillery bombardment, marines from the 8th VNMC Battalion looked out of their bunkers to see enemy infantry advancing behind a screen of tanks. Surprised by the bold move after the long period of static warfare, the marines sallied forth and pushed the North Vietnamese back into the citadel. Intelligence analysts later surmised that the failed attack was an attempt by the North Vietnamese to break out of what they correctly saw as a slowly closing trap.

Mounting pressure from Saigon added another dimension to the battle in northern I Corps. Clamoring for results after months of public criticism, President Thieu and the Joint General Staff demanded that the citadel be retaken—soon. General Truong would have happily obliged, but there were other factors to consider. General Lan, the Marine Division commander, was reluctant to commit his reserve force, the 369th VNMC Brigade (which remained nine miles southeast of Quang Tri City), to a final assault on the citadel. Lan argued that although the North Vietnamese were in desperate shape, they still had portions of five divisions in Quang Tri Province. General Truong agreed, and he was also worried that the poor condition of the Airborne Division made his exposed western flank vulnerable. The choices were clear. On the one hand, adding the brigade to an assault on the citadel would certainly break the back of the North Vietnamese defense. On the other hand, without reinforcement the stalemate at the citadel might well go on for months. In typically imaginative fashion, General Truong found a solution. On 8 September he ordered the 1st Ranger Group's three battalions to relieve the 147th VNMC Brigade of its blocking positions north of Quang Tri City. This enabled the marines to use two brigades in an assault against the citadel, even though both were battle weary, and still leave the third brigade in reserve.[34]

The move marked the beginning of the last stage in the battle to retake the citadel. Behind a curtain of B-52 strikes and naval gunfire, the amphibious troop ship *Juneau* steamed to a position near the mouth of the Cua Viet River loaded with 400 South Vietnamese rangers. As the B-52s ended their high-altitude runs along the shoreline, the North Vietnamese emerged from the smoke to meet the South Vietnamese on the beach. To their surprise, however, all they encountered was well-aimed naval gunfire from destroyers offshore. There was no amphibious landing; the move was yet another diversion designed to throw the North Vietnamese off balance, and once again it worked. The enemy shifted units north to the Cua Viet River, causing a noticeable decrease in the intensity of artillery fire directed at the marines at Quang Tri.

Just to the south, at the citadel, the marines quickly took advantage of the ruse. The 258th VNMC Brigade attacked from the south, while the 147th VNMC Brigade struck the northern half of the fortress. Near the southeast corner of the citadel, Lieutenant Colonel Do Huu Tung, commander of the 6th VNMC Battalion (258th VNMC Brigade), moved his men to the base of the battered walls. Tung, who had never before been to Quang Tri City, even during more peaceful times, was struck by the strength of the citadel. Despite bombardment by artillery and air strikes, many sections of the thirty-inch-thick walls still stood. But there was little time to admire the nineteenth-century workmanship. A flight of F-4 Phantom fighter planes screamed in from the coast and dropped their ordnance on the citadel walls. Some of the bombs missed the target and landed among the marines. Fortunately, only five were wounded.[35]

Although the marines were within a few feet of their objective, progress remained slow because the North Vietnamese had dug an intricate system of trenches, tunnels, and bunkers throughout the citadel. The marines did not know how extensive until the night of 9 September, when a handpicked squad from the 6th VNMC Battalion crept into the fortress for a look around. Upon their return the marines reported on the defensive network and pointed out that there were very few enemy soldiers left inside the walls. There would never be a better time to storm the citadel.

A few hours before midnight on 10 September, Lieutenant Colonel Tung launched a night attack against the southeast corner of the citadel and gained a tiny foothold at the top of the wall. Early the next morning a platoon of marines fought through dogged North Vietnamese resistance and set up a perimeter inside the citadel. Within hours, the 6th VNMC Battalion had moved in a company to strengthen the position.

To the west, the 1st VNMC Battalion secured the bridgehead where Highway 1 crossed the Thach Han River and held it against several fierce North Vietnamese counterattacks. From 11 to 15 September the 2d VNMC Battalion fought its way to the river, closing the gap between the 1st and 6th VNMC Battalions. North of the citadel, the 3d and 7th VNMC Battalions fought their way through the city streets, reaching the citadel on the morning of 15 September. That afternoon the North Vietnamese again struck back, calling in a massive artillery barrage to stop the marines closing in on the western walls. It failed, and by 5:00 in the evening the marines had control of the citadel.

South Vietnamese marines and an unidentified U.S. adviser (left) stand victorious near the ruins of the Quang Tri citadel. It was recaptured on 16 September 1972. (U.S. Marine Corps)

But the fighting was still not over. Throughout the night and into the next morning, the marines attacked across the 500-yard-square interior of the citadel, the 3d and 7th VNMC Battalions from the north, the 6th VNMC Battalion from the south. The onslaught was too much for the North Vietnamese defenders. They put up a stiff fight, but by noon on 16 September all enemy soldiers inside the citadel were either dead or captured. Jubilant marines scaled the crumbled walls and raised the scarlet and yellow South Vietnamese flag over the west gate while officers broke out the bottles of champagne they had carried all these months for a celebratory toast.

Although the South Vietnamese did not know it at the time, the enemy did not plan to simply give up. Even as the marines were storming the citadel walls, the B-4 Front had ordered the 18th NVA Regiment, a reserve unit, to "cross the Thach Han River to aid the forces in the ancient citadel." Because of the heavy artillery fire and the fact that their crossing points had all been destroyed, only a few of the soldiers were able to make it across to the southern bank. They, too, suffered heavy casualties, and that afternoon were ordered to withdraw.[36]

Although the cost of retaking the citadel had been high, and the need to recapture it questionable, the marines' American advisers were proud of the accomplishment. Lieutenant Colonel Turley saw the battle as a worthy addition to the glory of the corps. "Vietnamese marines," he later wrote, "short in stature, rich in courage, and full of determination, stood tall in the eyes of all marines." In order to attain that reputation, the South Vietnamese marines suffered more than 5,000 casualties since June, 3,658 of them during the seven-week battle to recapture the citadel. Almost one out of every four marines in the entire division was wounded or killed.[37]

General Truong was the hero of the hour. He had saved Hue and turned the tables on the most successful North Vietnamese offensive of the war. After five and a half long months of defeats, his troops had recaptured Quang Tri, denying the enemy the cherished goal of holding a province capital. In recognition of the victory, President Thieu flew to Hue and honored Truong, then helicoptered to the front lines north of Quang Tri City, where he personally thanked General Lan, the Marine Division commander. Still ebullient over the victory, Thieu visited the 147th VNMC Brigade headquarters, then drove a jeep to the 6th VNMC Battalion command post, where he congratulated Lieutenant Colonel Tung for his part in retaking the citadel.[38]

The North Vietnamese, though badly bloodied, remained defiant. Ignoring the fact that they had initiated the full-blown conventional attack, the North Vietnamese once again fell back on guerrilla warfare rhetoric. In an English-language propaganda organ, Hanoi bragged that "the liberation forces again hashed up" the best units in the South Vietnamese military. The communists also charged that using "modern technology and weapons and a maximum of firepower, the U.S. had schemed to level this area and turn Quang Tri into a land of death with no place for the revolutionary forces." The North Vietnamese conveniently overlooked their own considerable role in the destruction.[39]

Even after years of reflection, Hanoi remained convinced that the North Vietnamese army's combat performance at Quang Tri was "a shining example of revolutionary heroism." As is typical with Vietnamese communist military analysis, Hanoi's historians are unwilling to admit to mistakes, though they will acknowledge some shortcomings. According to one historical account, "From this battle our army had gained much experience in positional defense." It was a lesson learned the hard way, with few of the "students" surviving to pass on their experiences.[40]

With the recapture of Quang Tri City, the heart went out of the North Vietnamese offensive. Hue was out of danger, many of the firebases to the west of Highway 1 were recaptured, and the marines continued to push north toward the demilitarized zone. By the end of October the situation in I Corps had stabilized and hopes were high for a negotiated cease-fire. The North Vietnamese made a desperate push to take more territory before a cease-fire took place, but they were thwarted by South Vietnamese forces. "The enemy jumped the gun," reported General Cooksey, the senior American adviser in I Corps. "He . . . came out into the open to claim territory and people. Friendly forces seized the opportunity and dealt severe blows to several enemy local force units." But although the cities and populated rural areas were retaken by Saigon's forces, about half of I Corps, most of it unpopulated mountains, remained in North Vietnamese hands.[41]

The people of South Vietnam had paid a terrible price for beating back the North Vietnamese, and they recognized the sacrifices of the military, particularly the Airborne and Marine Divisions. General Truong later summed up the feelings of his nation when he observed, "These exploits remained forever engraved in their minds."[42]

PART TWO
Divide and Conquer:
The Battle for II Corps

THIRTEEN

SETTING THE STAGE

The sign over the old bunker said "Ben Het and loving it." It did not mean much in the spring of 1972, but during the heyday of U.S. involvement in Vietnam, every Special Forces trooper worth his green beret knew it was a reminder of the border battles fought back in 1969. Launched from the tri-border area where South Vietnam, Laos, and Cambodia converged, this series of North Vietnamese attacks was meant to force the Americans out of their mountain perches, blinding them to enemy activity in the western highlands. The enemy hit hard, and for three months beginning in March the Special Forces defenders were subjected to artillery bombardments, infantry attacks, and probes by PT-76 light tanks. The joke among those who endured the attacks was "I've been hit, and I ain't loving it," but after the North Vietnamese retreated back over the border, the motto "Ben Het and loving it" became a tribute to their own survival.

Ben Het was built in the fall of 1967 as one link in a chain of surveillance camps strung through the northern Plei Trap Valley in Pleiku Province in South Vietnam's Central Highlands. Special Forces teams and their Montagnard allies watched over the network of trails used by the North Vietnamese to bring supplies and troops into South Vietnam. By mid-1968 Ben Het was an important launching point for cross-border operations by the highly classified Studies and Observations Group. After the 1969 border battles ended in defeat for the North Vietnamese, and the United States began its withdrawal from Vietnam, Ben Het became a lonely place, home to just a handful of Montagnard soldiers and their American advisers. Then, in late 1971, when the North Vietnamese began to build up for the Easter Offensive, Ben Het again became important—and vulnerable.

In February 1972 Ben Het was manned by the 72d and 95th Ranger Battalions advised by two Americans. But in reality the battalions were little more than reinforced companies made up of Montagnard tribesmen living with their families in the run-down camp. Still, reports that the 320th NVA Division was in the vicinity did not disturb them.

"Boredom bothers us more than danger," said Lieutenant Ho Xuan Tinh, a ranger officer. "Think of having to stay in this base all the time.

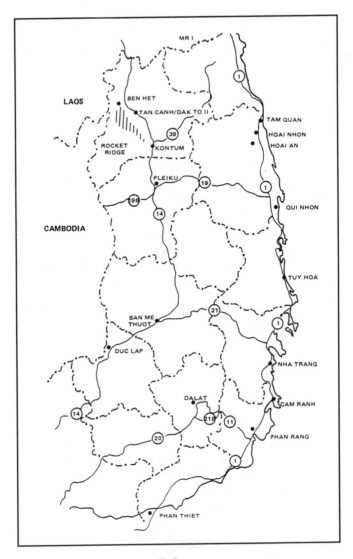

II Corps

What can you do to fill such emptiness?" His philosophy on the coming of-fensive was simple, almost fatalistic: "When they shell, they shell. When they don't, they don't. Why be afraid?"[1]

The Americans were not as apathetic about the enemy buildup, but none of them were scared either. Sergeant Irvin Dorward, an adviser at the camp, said, "I've got thirty days to go in this country. If I thought they could take us I wouldn't stick around." Sergeant Dorward spent most of his time making sure that the trenches were shored up and the sandbags filled.

In the valley below, signs of the enemy buildup were everywhere. Scanning the jungle with binoculars, the rangers could make out so much traffic on the nearby Ho Chi Minh Trail that they began calling it "Interstate Charlie." The North Vietnamese were so bold that supply trucks did not even bother to hide when spotter planes appeared overhead; they knew they could travel for several more minutes before the bombers showed up. Only then did they pull off into the jungle to hide. No one who had served previous tours in Vietnam could remember anything like it. The Ho Chi Minh Trail had become a highway, and as one adviser joked, "The only thing they don't have is stoplights."[2]

The South Vietnamese never felt completely comfortable operating in II Corps. The region was rugged and underpopulated, but crucial to the war effort. It constituted almost 50 percent of South Vietnam's total land area, yet only 3 million people lived there, or about one-fifth of the nation's population. Much of the area was covered by the Central Highlands, the western portion of II Corps stretching from Ban Me Thuot in Darlac Province north to Kontum Province and the southern border of I Corps. This vast area, more correctly known as the Annamite Mountains, occupied about 5,400 square miles of rugged jungle-clad hills, most of it sparsely populated by Montagnard tribesmen.

The highlands had seen its share of fighting going back to the First Indochina War. In 1954, at the twilight of their involvement in Vietnam, the French had felt the fury of Viet Minh attacks. As Viet Minh general Vo Nguyen Giap was planning the Battle of Dien Bien Phu, he was also striking out at French forces in the Central Highlands. On 2 February 1954 Viet Minh battalions struck French outposts strung out north of Kontum. On 7 February, after savage fighting in and around Kontum, the French abandoned the city and regrouped in Pleiku.

In the 1960s the Americans took their turn in the Central Highlands. As had been the case during their fighting with the French, the North Vietnamese saw the Central Highlands as crucial to the conquest of South Vietnam. Spurs from the Ho Chi Minh Trail carried soldiers and supplies into Cambodia, resulting in a troop buildup that immediately attracted the attention of American war planners. In the early days of American involvement, U.S. Army Special Forces established almost sixty outposts and trained Montagnard tribesmen to fight the communists. The camps were designed to thwart North Vietnamese infiltration, and although they had some success, the communists had little trouble building up their forces inside II Corps.

Not content to rely solely on the Special Forces to defend the Central Highlands, in August 1965 MACV deployed Task Force Alpha (later renamed I Field Force Vietnam) to control U.S. combat operations in II Corps. Headquartered at Nha Trang, Task Force Alpha had enormous resources at its disposal. Facilities at Cam Ranh Bay, Vung Ro, Qui Nhon, and Nha Trang provided men and matériel for battle.

American combat troops quickly followed the logistical buildup. In July 1965 the 1st Brigade of the 101st Airborne Division was deployed to II Corps, followed by the 1st Cavalry Division in September, a brigade of the 25th Infantry Division in December, and the 4th Infantry Division in August 1966. In November 1967 the 173d Airborne Brigade rotated into the region, replacing the brigade from the 101st Airborne Division. South Korea also deployed two divisions to II Corps, one in October 1965 and the other one year later.

Fighting came close on the heels of the first deployment of American troops. The 1st Cavalry Division headed into the western hills of the Central Highlands to thwart North Vietnamese designs on Pleiku. In November 1965, in the Ia Drang Valley, the first major engagement between American and North Vietnamese troops took place. In January 1968 the 1st Cavalry Division left for I Corps, then redeployed to III Corps as U.S. forces retrenched in 1969. The 4th Infantry Division left Vietnam in December 1970. I Field Force closed down in April 1971, and the 173d Airborne Brigade departed in August of the same year. All that remained in the Central Highlands were South Vietnamese troops, a handful of U.S. aviation units, and about 2,800 American advisers.

The American advisory structure in II Corps paralleled that in the other three corps areas. Each South Vietnamese officer from corps commander down to regimental commander was advised by an American officer. With the exception of ranger and airborne units, no Americans operated below the regimental level. But it was the top of the II Corps advisory structure that was unique. Instead of a commanding general, the advisory group—called Second Regional Assistance Group (SRAG)—was commanded by a civilian.

The position was held by John Paul Vann, a man with a long and distinguished career in Vietnam. He had gone there as an army officer in 1962, an adviser to the 7th ARVN Division in the Mekong Delta. Despite official American claims that the war was going well, Vann believed otherwise. A combination of personal and professional problems persuaded Vann to re-

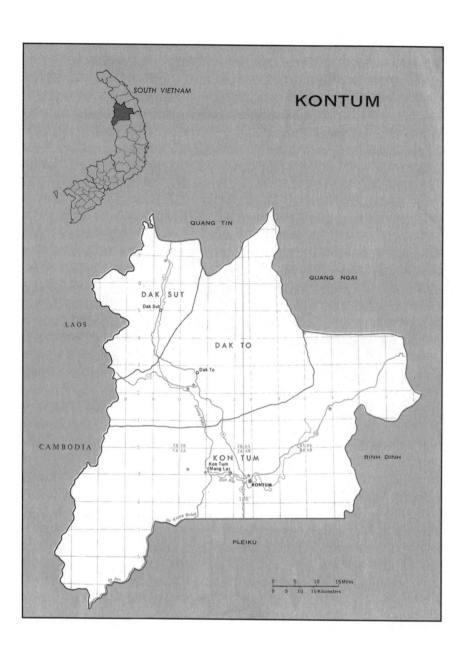

John Paul Vann's helicopter on the landing pad at SRAG headquarters in Pleiku. (Jack Finch)

sign his commission, but the crusade in South Vietnam was in his blood.
Vann returned in 1965 as a State Department official with the Agency for
International Development, but his maverick behavior and outspokenness
continued to put him at odds with superiors. Talent and ability overcame
most of Vann's personal difficulties, however, and he steadily climbed the
ladder of authority, landing a position on the III Corps pacification staff in
1966 and later serving as director of Civil Operations and Revolutionary
Development Support (CORDS) in IV Corps.

In May 1971 John Paul Vann attained his dream. All his life he had
wanted to command units in battle, and now he was in charge of all American advisers remaining in II Corps. As a civilian, Vann was officially called
"director" of SRAG, but his authority was no less than that of his military
colleagues in I Corps and III Corps. There were some who resented having
a civilian in a leadership position over military officers, but Vann's experience as a military officer and his long relationship with Vietnamese affairs
made him a good choice. Critics pointed out Vann's autocratic style and gi-

gantic ego. From an operational perspective, some felt Vann had lost touch with the concept of counterinsurgency he had once espoused, relying instead on the American technology and firepower he had once disdained. "He sits out there on Mount Olympus and brings down the thunder and lightning," observed one unidentified critic, "but he has forgotten the political dimension of the war on the ground." So, despite some animosity, Vann had risen to the equivalent rank of general almost a decade after shedding his army uniform and leaving the military.[3]

Vann's counterpart was Lieutenant General Ngo Dzu, a man better known for malleability and meekness than for command experience. Dzu was a Catholic from Qui Nhon, the son of a government province official, educated in a French Catholic boy's school in Hue. General Dzu had held few combat command positions, and his political connections with President Thieu were not considered strong. Yet in August 1970 Dzu found himself promoted to II Corps commander, a position in which he did not feel entirely comfortable.

Outside observers considered the top military leadership in II Corps to be the worst in the country, a potentially disastrous situation, since the North Vietnamese traditionally launched some of their biggest offensives at the Central Highlands. "This has had the lousiest leadership in any corps," complained one American adviser. "It's like having a deadhead as pointman on the lead platoon in attack."[4]

Vann believed Dzu was competent, however, though his reasons for cultivating him were devious and partially based in Dzu's shady past. General Dzu had long been suspected of trafficking in heroin, although for the record General Abrams and other American officials denied the allegations. Army investigators had firm evidence that Dzu's father was involved in dealing heroin, and his younger brother, a South Vietnamese air force pilot, was thought to fly loads of heroin in and out of Laos in a government C-47 cargo plane. Vann had evidence that the charges were true, but he chose to defend Dzu and virtually blackmail him into doing Vann's bidding. Dzu did not seem to mind, however. He tended to overreact to crises and preferred depending on American advisers rather than his own staff.[5]

Vann quickly discovered that Dzu wanted no conflict with his American advisers and would rather acquiesce completely to their wishes than face a disagreement. Dzu was propelled out of a series of low-profile jobs at the Joint General Staff and into the front lines when he was suddenly given the job of acting commanding general of IV Corps in the spring of 1970 after his predecessor, Brigadier General Nguyen Viet Thanh, was killed in a midair helicopter collision. Vann was the deputy for pacification in IV Corps

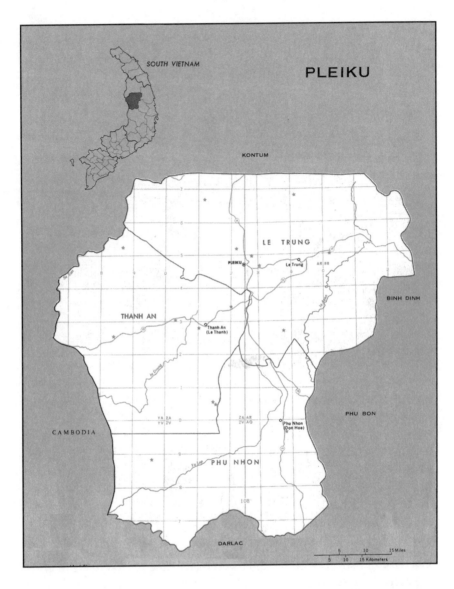

when Dzu arrived, and the two began planning an operation aimed at Viet Cong strongholds in the rugged Seven Mountains region of Chau Doc Province in western IV Corps. Dzu gave in to all Vann's suggestions, a situation Vann found to his liking. He could hide behind the facade of Dzu's command while pulling all the strings and calling the shots.[6]

A few months after Dzu became II Corps commander, his American military adviser left Vietnam. Vann hinted that he wanted the job and asked

Dzu to suggest his name if asked by Saigon. Dzu loved the idea, relieved that he would have a strong American personality to conceive and execute plans for him. By May 1971 the two men were back at work together, this time at the top of the leadership heap in II Corps.

The selection of John Paul Vann to head the American contingent in II Corps was the latest and best example of the man's political clout and military savvy. But in order to select Vann for the position, the military had change the rules. The Second Regional Assistance Command (SRAC) was changed to Second Regional Assistance Group to get around the legal questions behind having a civilian in a position of military command. A civilian cannot invoke a military court-martial, the legal basis behind issuing orders in the military. Vann was officially "deputy for military functions," although he was also the ranking man on the staff. This meant he was to be assigned a military deputy who would actually issue orders and call in air and artillery strikes, none of which would be done without Vann's order.

The man assigned as Vann's deputy was Brigadier General George Wear. Vann had hoped for a major general in the position, a move that would have given him three stars and made him the highest-ranking senior corps adviser in South Vietnam. But Vann had to settle for being equal to his colleagues in the other three corps.

General Wear was nearing the end of his second Vietnam tour. In a way, he was at home in the Central Highlands. He had grown up in the mountains of Colorado and understood the difficulties of fighting in hill country. Yet he found his main problem would be not battling the enemy but keeping up with Vann. The civilian general was a never-ending bundle of nerves and energy. He slept only a few hours each day and wrote most of his messages and reports late at night, spending the rest of his time in the field or, more properly, over the field. Vann was a helicopter pilot, and although he had his own personal pilot, he preferred to take the controls much of the time.

The stage was set. Vann was in command of the American contingent in II Corps on the eve of the biggest campaign of the Vietnam War. All that remained was to second-guess the enemy on where and when it would spring the attack.

FOURTEEN

INTELLIGENCE PICTURE

Late in November 1971 John Paul Vann and General Wear were summoned to a meeting in Saigon with General Abrams. They discussed the military situation in II Corps and what was expected out of the North Vietnamese in the early part of the coming year.

As the two left the meeting, Wear found himself wondering at the unreality of it all. The North Vietnamese were massing for an attack, and no one seemed concerned about whether or not the South Vietnamese could cope with it. All that seemed to matter to the intelligence people and to the MACV staff was whether or not they could predict the coming offensive with enough precision. Everyone remembered the aftermath of the Tet Offensive of 1968 and the way the press had crucified the military for failing to predict it. Of course, the finger-pointing had been premature; the military had predicted the offensive, though not with complete accuracy. Imprecision and puzzle solving are the true nature of intelligence and war, but the military was unwilling to run through the public-opinion gauntlet again. This time MACV wanted to be sure it made the right call, with nothing left to guesswork. The result was a perverse preoccupation with dates and numbers, none of which would matter much once the bullets started flying. When Tet 1972 came and went without an enemy offensive, the press would chastise the military for crying "wolf" and once again question American intelligence capabilities. It was a lost cause; the military in Vietnam could not win any battle with the media.

Vann seemed not to notice any of this. As he and General Wear walked across the tarmac at Tan Son Nhut toward their waiting plane, Vann was lost in thought. The slowly sinking tropical sun and the blinking lights on the runway could have been part of a scene at any of a dozen tourist spots around the world. But moments after becoming airborne, Vann and Wear were back in the war zone. The plane climbed rapidly to avoid snipers. Within the hour they would be back in Pleiku, in the center of a brewing offensive before which all others would pale.

Wear often felt Vann was unconcerned with details. They were ancient history. Times had changed, and he was in charge. Vann had something to prove, and he would move heaven and earth to win whatever battle lay ahead. In December 1971 Vann went back to Washington for briefings and refresher courses at the State Department, leaving Wear to continue watching for signs of the coming offensive. He did not have to look far.

The meeting in Saigon had come at the tail end of a long series of indicators of an enemy buildup around the Central Highlands. As was the case in I Corps and III Corps, American and South Vietnamese intelligence in II Corps had strong signs of the coming offensive and were surprised more by the timing and intensity of the attacks than by anything else. It is difficult to keep troops at full alert for months at a time without losing combat efficiency and morale. Such was the case in the Central Highlands. South Vietnamese troops had been warned so many times about an impending attack that they were weary and demoralized.

All of this led intelligence officials to stick with their prediction of a major North Vietnamese campaign in the Central Highlands sometime during the approaching dry season. Large enemy forces were reportedly moving into northern Kontum Province from Cambodia, and it was feared that the North Vietnamese were once again attempting to link up with their comrades in eastern II Corps and shear South Vietnam in half.

Interrogations of prisoners and reports from *hoi chanh* (defectors) had convinced American intelligence that something big was afoot. They even had the North Vietnamese battle plan, which told everything—particularly dates and places. What intelligence analysts did not know was that the timing had been pushed back a few months, partly because American bombing inside Laos and Cambodia had upset North Vietnamese supply lines, and also because the logistics involved in running a conventional war were new to Hanoi, and the communists had overestimated their ability to adhere to the timetable.

Intelligence sources and prisoner interrogations revealed that the coming campaign would be a three-phase affair. Phase one would last from 27 January to 7 February and would concentrate on the district towns of Tan Canh (known as "Tango Charlie" to the Americans) and Dak To, both sites of regimental-sized firebases north of Kontum. Phase two was to go from 7 February to 14 February, during which time the North Vietnamese would mop up the firebases west of Kontum. The final phase would last through the end of February and would concentrate on the population centers of Kontum City and Pleiku City. In addition, various Viet Cong units in southern II Corps and on the coast in Binh Dinh Province would pressure South Vietnamese forces in an attempt to turn their attention away from the main targets in the Central Highlands. The final goal was to sever II Corps and discredit the Vietnamization program.[1]

There it was. The North Vietnamese were about to spring the biggest offensive of the war, and Saigon knew exactly what the enemy was going to do. The only thing missing was strong evidence that the North Vietnamese planned to make extensive use of armor. But February and the Tet holidays came and went—with no offensive. No one was about to say the North Vietnamese had called it off, but by delaying their timetable the North Vietnamese had kept the South Vietnamese army at almost full alert, a state it could not maintain for long.

Aerial reconnaissance conducted throughout January and February 1972 confirmed the buildup. On 25 January American Cobra gunships reported firing on two enemy tanks in the Plei Trap Valley just west of Rocket Ridge, a massive heap of tangled rock jutting above the forest east of the triborder area where Laos, Cambodia, and South Vietnam meet. The North Vietnamese had made Rocket Ridge a stronghold, which they called Base Area 609, a place where many American and South Vietnamese soldiers had died over the years.

In early February U.S. air cavalry pilots observed the tracks of at least an armor company, but Vann was unimpressed by the reports and refused to put much credence in them. He even went so far as to tell his pilots and advisers to stop telling stories about tanks unless they could drag one in as proof. However, Vann did quietly report to General Abrams that North Vietnamese tanks had been observed by credible American pilots.[2]

Whether or not North Vietnamese tanks were really prowling the jungle trails near the border, Vann was convinced that the offensive was coming. In early February, patrols mounted by South Vietnamese border ranger groups located 122mm and 130mm artillery in the triborder area. Vann directed B-52 strikes against as many reported artillery concentrations as the air force could handle, while the South Vietnamese kept the border rangers on alert. As a result of ground and aerial reconnaissance, Vann was able to establish targets for over sixty B-52 strikes during the month of January.

In early February, captured documents confirmed that the North Vietnamese had committed two entire divisions in western II Corps—the 320th and the 2d—plus supporting artillery and the 203d NVA Armored Regiment. The strength of each division was estimated to be about 10,400 men. On the coast, the famous and feared 3d NVA Division, the "Yellow Star," bolstered local and main-force Viet Cong units, which traditionally had opposed South Vietnamese control in Binh Dinh Province. Intelligence estimates placed total enemy strength in II Corps at around 50,000.[3]

Facing the enemy, the South Vietnamese could muster two divisions, the 22d and 23d, plus two armored cavalry squadrons and the 2d Airborne

Brigade. Vann argued that in order to mount an adequate defense, Kontum needed a minimum of two battalions. But Dzu could not provide them. Uncertain of where to turn, Vann resorted to subtle begging. "While always reluctant to ask for assistance outside the Corps area," he reported to MACV, "I feel the stakes are too high to err on the side of optimism with regard to the capabilities of the II Corps forces." Vann hoped that Abrams could convince Saigon to send an additional airborne brigade "as soon as possible and not later than 1 April." In late March he got his wish when the Joint General Staff ordered the 3d Airborne Brigade to Kontum. Still, the defense would be tenuous. In addition to the airborne brigade, there were only two Regional Forces companies to defend Kontum City and only a single South Vietnamese army battalion in Pleiku as a reserve force.[4]

But Vann never intended to hold II Corps with South Vietnamese ground troops. He was well aware of the South Vietnamese reputation for lack of aggressiveness, and his strategy was tailored to bypass this weakness. "I'm enough of a realist that I'm not going to ask the ARVN to do what they won't do," he commented to reporters. Instead, Vann felt the South Vietnamese could thwart an enemy offensive with artillery and airpower. He was so confident, in fact, that he predicted the North Vietnamese would lose one-fifth of their attacking force—about 10,000 men.[5]

Although the signs of mounting enemy activity abounded, U.S. intelligence picked up only a fraction of North Vietnamese moves. Decreasing American manpower was partly to blame for the intelligence shortfall; aside from the few signs picked up by units in the field, MACV relied almost exclusively on satellite photos and electronic eavesdropping. South Vietnamese ineptness was another factor. Vann complained about unreliable intelligence reports, citing reconnaissance units that repeatedly reported no sign of the enemy after patrolling areas known to be swarming with North Vietnamese. Vann concluded that the intelligence reports were "highly suspect."[6]

North Vietnamese battle preparations went on day and night. Advisers in the firebases near the Cambodian border reported seeing headlights and hearing bulldozers to the east. The North Vietnamese were widening old trails into roads and building virtual highways in the forest. Right behind them were trucks laden with ammunition and supplies and towing heavy artillery.

South Vietnamese patrols were confronted by increased enemy action as well. While checking out the damage done by a B-52 strike near Rocket Ridge, the 23d Ranger Battalion found itself surrounded by a larger enemy force. It took a flight of tactical bombers to pull the surprised rangers out of danger. Another ranger unit, the 95th Border Ranger Battalion, came up hard against a regiment of the 2d NVA Division north of Ben Het, and the soldiers from the 2d Airborne Brigade were engaged by the enemy as they tried to patrol near Rocket Ridge. The size and intensity of the engagements were a final confirmation of a buildup that could only mean a major enemy offensive.[7]

Vann knew that his day on the battlefield was close at hand. He wrote with obvious anticipation of the coming test of South Vietnamese military mettle. "It appears that the enemy will launch his attack during the first days of April. From that time on through early June, the Vietnamese forces in this Corps will be involved in their largest and most important action they will have had in the last ten years."[8]

Publicly Vann was also optimistic. "I welcome a communist offensive," he said during a press conference. "For after the enemy expends himself and loses many of his men, he has to stay quiet until next year and gives us a chance to expand our control." Vann's superiors in Washington squirmed at his bravado, prompting Secretary of Defense Melvin Laird to privately ask General Abrams "if what this guy says is right or wrong."[9]

From SRAG headquarters in Pleiku, Vann continued working on a strategy he hoped would back up his bold words. He doubted that the South Vietnamese could fight toe-to-toe with North Vietnamese regulars, but he believed they "could fight rather well from defensive positions such as their fire support bases." The plan, rammed through by Vann with very little input from Dzu, was aimed at stopping the enemy north of Kontum. To do this Vann was forced to continue leaving Kontum relatively unguarded. Only the Airborne Division headquarters and one other airborne brigade defended the city. They had been taken from the general reserve during the first week of April.[10]

In order to take the fight to the enemy north of Kontum, Vann convinced Dzu to put about 10,000 men—the equivalent of almost a division—in Tan Canh. The headquarters of the 22d ARVN Division, composed of two infantry regiments plus separate battalions and the better part of two armored cavalry regiments, were moved north from its base at Pleiku.

Vann intended to stand and fight at Tan Canh, but he did not have the unqualified support of his staff. General Wear strongly disagreed with the move from a military standpoint. He believed the best strategy was the basic military concept of defense in depth. Wear argued that the South Vietnamese should seek to exhaust the enemy by defending and then withdrawing from successive positions as North Vietnamese pressure grew too great. That way the enemy would be forced to pay for each small victory. Vann vetoed the plan because it meant that the South Vietnamese would give up Dak To and Tan Canh after light fighting and move slowly south—which was tantamount to retreat, in his mind. The understanding was that they would take the area back at some point in the future. Wear believed the enemy could not ignore any point along the major roads heading toward Pleiku, so it would have to attack every defensive position thrown up by the South Vietnamese.

Vann and Dzu were indeed in a strategic quandary when it came to troop placement. Both the northern towns of Dak To and Tan Canh and the province capital of Kontum were important targets, but not all could be guarded adequately. The key to the problem was Rocket Ridge. It ran from north to south just to the west of Highway 14, the major road in the area, and sat almost exactly centered between Tan Canh and Kontum. Enemy troops used it as a staging area, giving them the freedom to pick and choose which of the cities to attack first. Vann firmly believed the North Vietnamese could not leave Tan Canh and Dak To unmolested. But he bet on the South Vietnamese holding out there and badly bloodying the enemy soldiers so they could be finished off with B-52 strikes. Besides, Vann told a skeptical General Wear, "If they get surrounded up there, they'll have to fight."

In early April, when fighting had broken out in I Corps and III Corps and was beginning slowly in II Corps, Vann went down to Saigon for a strategy meeting with General Abrams. "I will pass on your views to the MACV staff," Vann told Wear as he revved up his helicopter. He wanted to appear democratic to his second in command, but Wear later found out Vann had given Abrams the impression that the II Corps military staff was in complete agreement with the plan to defend Dak To.[11]

General Dzu did not like Vann's plan either, though not because he had any firm ideas of his own on how to meet the enemy threat. As was his style, Dzu began moving troops back and forth, from firebase to firebase, hoping he had guessed where the enemy intended to strike, then changing his mind. Dzu also pestered Wear for more B-52 air strikes. Wear ran himself ragged calling back and forth, trying to get bomb strike coordinates changed for the wavering Dzu and at the same time checking out the bomb requests to make sure the South Vietnamese were not planning to drop them on some population center because they suspected the enemy might be nearby.

Caught between Dzu's paranoia and Vann's workaholic habits, General Wear found his health beginning to fail. He had picked up a fungus in his lungs, and it was gradually wearing him down. Although he tried to ignore it, Wear would eventually have to be ordered home from Vietnam just as events were coming to a climax in the Central Highlands.

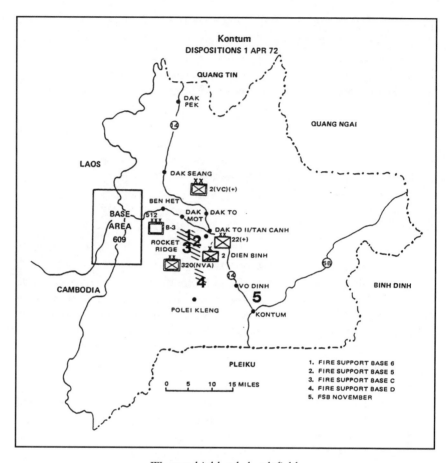

Western highlands battlefield

But for now there was work to be done. The North Vietnamese were clearly building, but intelligence could not pinpoint their numbers or location. By March U.S. intelligence knew that the 320th NVA Division sat just over the border in Laos. It also pinpointed three independent enemy infantry regiments and one artillery regiment attached to the B-3 Front, North Vietnam's command for the Central Highlands, farther south in the rugged hills west of Pleiku. A formidable force, it was only part of the picture. Unknown to the Americans and the South Vietnamese, the 2d NVA Division had penetrated into South Vietnam, setting up just west of Dak To. This represented ten enemy regiments of about 28,000 men in the Central Highlands alone. North Vietnamese units fell under the command of

Hoang Minh Thao, one of North Vietnam's best generals. Thao knew his enemy and the terrain well, having commanded the B-3 Front since 1967. Now he planned to throw his forces at the South Vietnamese in concert with communist attacks in I Corps and III Corps.[12]

This would be a new type of warfare for the North Vietnamese. In the past, their strategy in the highlands had been to draw their enemy out of the populated areas and fight in running battles over rough terrain in an attempt to inflict casualties. In the words of an official communist history of the conflict, "We were very familiar with tricking the enemy into venturing outside fortified positions and experienced in annihilating large forces in the field. Now that the enemy had fallen back on the defensive, would this experience still be applicable? Could it be that the only way to annihilate the enemy now was to storm his fortifications?" The bottom line, Hanoi's analysts concluded, was that "to liberate territory, it is important to annihilate forces."[13]

The key to the enemy offensive in the Central Highlands was clearly Rocket Ridge. The South Vietnamese had four firebases perched on top of the natural fortress, but Dzu was unwilling to have the troops patrol to the west in search of the enemy. Vann finally persuaded Dzu to turn his attention from Dak To long enough to order South Vietnamese units into action around Rocket Ridge. Near the end of March the 2d Airborne Brigade and part of the 47th Regiment of the 22d ARVN Division patrolled the southwestern edge of Rocket Ridge, hoping to draw out the enemy.

They were not disappointed. On 2 April, North Vietnamese troops struck the prepared South Vietnamese soldiers and paid heavily for their action. After losing almost 100 men to small-arms and machine-gun fire, the North Vietnamese drew back, only to be pounded by B-52s and tactical air strikes.

Vann believed the beginning of the offensive had finally come. "The enemy has apparently launched his offensive in the highlands," he reported to MACV. But Vann was not worried about the prospect. "I see the current situation as an outstanding opportunity for the GVN [government of Vietnam]," he wrote, though his enthusiasm was tempered by the knowledge that the opportunity might be missed because of "inadequate leadership and motivation from the Corps commander on down."[14]

Vann hoped to use B-52s and his own command skills to compensate for what he regarded as "inadequate leadership." "Our best hope of blunting his [the enemy's] offensive power or of delaying or even causing him to cancel it is the continued employment of B-52 strikes on the best targets available," he had written to Abrams earlier in the month in an attempt to keep the big bombers flying frequently over Kontum. But in early April, enemy troops roared across the demilitarized zone into I Corps and III Corps, scattering South Vietnamese troops before them, and Vann had to share air assets with other commanders who needed them even more desperately.[15]

In fact, enemy action in II Corps was subdued. North Vietnamese troops eased into the offensive with few attempts to mask their movements. Vann thought he knew why the North Vietnamese were holding back in their attack on the Central Highlands. In a memo to General Abrams he reasoned that the enemy was waiting until the withdrawal of one of the last American air cavalry troops, an aerial weapons company, on 7 April. When it was gone, Vann reported, the North Vietnamese would begin their attack in earnest. To counter this, he asked that the air cavalry's stand-down date be pushed back to 20 April. Abrams had no intention of altering the drawdown schedule, and the American helicopters went home as planned.[16]

It was idle speculation, however, because North Vietnamese action in II Corps—slow though it was—set the battle in motion, and there was no more room for maneuver. For the time being, enemy movement in western II Corps was quickly countered. B-52s and aggressive action by ranger and airborne units cut an attacking force from the 320th NVA Division to pieces as it assaulted the firebases on Rocket Ridge. Intelligence estimated that four or five enemy battalions were rendered combat ineffective. Prisoners taken during the fighting confirmed that their units had been shredded, mostly by air strikes. However, they offset the good news with bad by revealing that fresh reinforcements were infiltrating into South Vietnam daily and that the units would soon regain their original strength.[17]

At the same time, the 42d and 47th ARVN Regiments were heavily engaged by the enemy northeast of Dak To by part of the 2d NVA Division and the independent 66th NVA Regiment. This was the first confirmation that the 2d NVA Division was in the area, and its presence spooked General Dzu. To make matters worse, another North Vietnamese prisoner reported that the 2d NVA Division planned to attack the airfield at Dak To II, a base just southwest of Tan Canh. The division had also been ordered to seize the headquarters of the 42d ARVN Regiment at Tan Canh and destroy South Vietnamese artillery along Provincial Route 512. The prisoners were familiar with the layout of the Tan Canh headquarters and admitted that North Vietnamese reconnaissance units had successfully penetrated the compound in preparation for the attack. The prisoners did not know when the attack would take place, but they were sure it was coming.[18]

General Dzu was frantic over the news. Convinced he did not have enough troops to defend Tan Canh and Dak To, he impulsively ordered nine battalions from Binh Dinh Province on the II Corps coast. That would leave the province undefended save for a handful of territorial forces. Vann persuaded Dzu to cancel the order and instead proposed that the 23d ARVN Division area of operations be shifted to include Kontum. The move would leave two regiments in Binh Dinh Province and still allow Dzu to keep his troops near Dak To and Tan Canh.[19]

The South Vietnamese now had thirteen infantry battalions attached to the 22d ARVN Division—including ranger battalions—plus six airborne battalions, about sixty-five artillery pieces, and fifty tanks spread out between Pleiku and Ben Het. Most of the strength was north of Kontum in the Dak To area. Only some 2,000 troops were actually stationed around Kontum. But the weakest link in the defense chain was logistics. Only Highway 14 led into the area, and it was vulnerable to an enemy encirclement north of Kontum. General Dzu ignored these problems, concentrating instead on spreading his troops throughout the region, probably because President Thieu had ordered his corps commanders to hold territory at all costs.

Forcing Dzu to shift his troops between Binh Dinh and the Central Highlands was precisely what the North Vietnamese intended with their two-pronged attack in II Corps. When Vann convinced Dzu to leave his troops in Binh Dinh Province, he thwarted North Vietnamese attempts to weaken the South Vietnamese either on the coast or in the Central Highlands. The enemy could wait no longer. Besides, the countrywide offensive was over a week old, and the North Vietnamese in II Corps could not stay put and risk being discovered and bombed into oblivion.

Despite the serious threat building in the Central Highlands, the North Vietnamese offensive in II Corps opened on the coast far from the mountains where most of the attention was focused. And like the buildup in the Central Highlands, North Vietnamese preparations for battle on the coast had been going on since the fall of 1971.

FIFTEEN

OPENING SHOTS

As darkness fell over Qui Nhon on 8 January 1972, a troop of Vietnamese youngsters paraded into the town square. This was to be a public event, and the children wore yellow and red scarves around their necks to signify allegiance to the government of South Vietnam. It was a special occasion, to be sure, but was like others that had occurred many times in the past. A new chief had been assigned to the coastal province of Binh Dinh on the American New Year, one of many over the past decade. Would this one prove to be an able leader? In Binh Dinh Province he would have to be; the communists had long enjoyed a high level of support from much of the province's population outside the capital of Qui Nhon. Before the Easter Offensive began, Saigon claimed that only seven hamlets in all of South Vietnam—about 6,000 people—were completely dominated by the communists. All of them fell within Binh Dinh Province.[1]

The man on the podium was Colonel Nguyen Van Chuc, a South Vietnamese army engineer (who would later become chief of the corps of engineers) with a passion for yoga and a vigorous work ethic more in keeping with that of his American counterparts than his Vietnamese colleagues. Chuc had built a reputation as an honest, aggressive, and dynamic leader, and he had a habit of publicly denouncing corruption within Binh Dinh. No political or military official was safe from his muckraking. During his six-month tenure as province chief, Chuc fired six of the nine district chiefs for corruption and incompetence. Perhaps Chuc was too zealous; in July he would be replaced.

As Chuc spoke of things that needed to be done and the increasing strength of the government, the people listened, some bored, some hopeful. Before he could finish, an explosion ripped through a nearby building. Colonel Chuc escaped with only minor wounds, but many others died or were seriously injured in the blast.[2]

It was no accident. The Viet Cong had hoped to kill Colonel Chuc. This incident was only one of many as the communists stepped up terrorism in anticipation of an attack sometime during the new year. Yet Tet came and went without the predicted communist attacks. In fact, the first three months of 1972 passed without much of an increase in enemy activity save

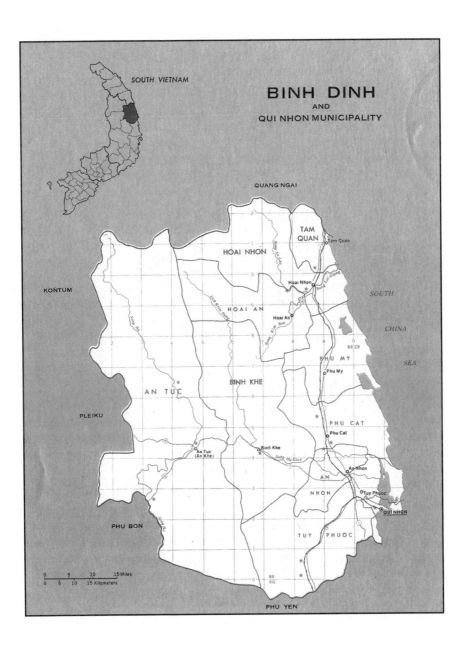

SOUTH VIETNAM

BINH DINH
AND
QUI NHON MUNICIPALITY

QUANG NGAI

TAM QUAN
Tam Quan

HOAI NHON

KONTUM

Hoai Nhon

SOUTH

HOAI AN

Hoai An

CHINA

PHU MY

Phu My

SEA

BINH KHE

AN TUC

PLEIKU

PHU CAT

Phu Cat

An Tuc
(An Khe)

Binh Khe

An Nhon

AN

NHON

Tuy Phuoc

QUI NHON

PHU BON

TUY PHUOC

0   5   10   15 Miles
0   5   10   15 Kilometers

PHU YEN

more frequent incidents of isolated terrorism. Somehow the inactivity seemed hollow, unreal.

On 5 April the bubble burst. North Vietnamese troops in their bases in northern Binh Dinh Province attacked South Vietnamese positions along the coast. Vann reasoned that the enemy had waited the extra week since the offensive had begun in I Corps because it hoped the South Vietnamese would redeploy forces from Binh Dinh to deal with the rising crisis in the Central Highlands. The South Vietnamese had done this in the past, particularly during the 1968 Tet Offensive, and Dzu tried again. "General Dzu is under the impression that he is faced with a threat of attack from the 2d NVA Division north of Dak To," reported Vann to MACV. "To counter this, he wishes to withdraw some of the nine ARVN battalions from Binh Dinh." Over Vann's objections, Dzu did move one battalion from the coast.[3]

Vann believed that the North Vietnamese intended to strike both Binh Dinh and the Central Highlands independently, and that neither attack was coordinated with the other. In fact, Vann was so certain that he made the prediction to General Abrams: "I have pointed out to him [Dzu] that the three NVA regiments in Binh Dinh have not yet launched their attack, and are undeniably waiting for him to thin out his forces there."[4]

Vann was correct. Beginning on 4 April, the North Vietnamese pushed south and east from strongholds in Binh Dinh's tangled interior, quickly overwhelming the demoralized South Vietnamese army and territorial forces in the northern two districts of Hoai Nhon and Tam Quan. The enemy had come from the An Lao Valley, a swath of forested flatlands carved by the An Lao River from the rugged mountains west of Highway 1 in Binh Dinh Province. The valley had long been home to the 3d NVA Division—the Yellow Star—a unit well known in Binh Dinh by both the South Vietnamese army and its American predecessors. In 1966 the U.S. 1st Cavalry Division had fought running battles with soldiers from the Yellow Star in this very place, and now the South Vietnamese would face them once again.

They did not have to wait long. After easily overrunning the lightly defended northern portion of Binh Dinh, the 3d NVA Division, along with the 303d, 306th, and 20th Sapper Battalions (which had infiltrated south from Quang Ngai Province), struck South Vietnamese positions at Landing Zones Pony and Orange situated next to the district capital of Hoai An. Pony, the first to fall, was abandoned on 9 April.[5]

With the fall of the northern bases, the South Vietnamese government's tenuous hold on most of the district hamlets was all but broken. Government troops refused to venture into the area, and the magnitude of the enemy force facing them remained unknown for weeks. On one of the few patrols sent out by the local Popular Force, the 300th Popular Forces Platoon, the militiamen ambushed and killed the deputy commander of a Viet Cong local force unit in Hoai An District. Documents on his body identified the Viet Cong local force order of battle.[6]

Although communist control of northern Binh Dinh Province had been strong, local cadre were wary of government pacification programs and the occasional South Vietnamese army operation. The spring offensive brought many of the communist cadre out into the open. While the North Vietnamese kept government forces on the defensive, Viet Cong propaganda teams openly exhorted villagers. Those who did not cooperate had their houses burned. In the town of Hoai An, the campaign to regain political dominance was carefully orchestrated. Soldiers tried hard to appear neat and clean, and to treat the peasants with respect. "Do not worry," the new political cadre told villagers, "continue to work the fields." Teenage schoolchildren were symbolically presented with AK-47 rifles and told, "We shall all be liberators." Some soldiers borrowed Honda motorcycles and raced up and down the streets as the villagers laughed. Other soldiers rounded up pigs and cattle, slaughtered them, and threw a huge party for everyone.

Everyone, that is, except those considered dangerous to the Communist Party. A house-to-house search by North Vietnamese soldiers netted almost 600 men. "Many of you have committed crimes against the people," exhorted one North Vietnamese officer. "The police have been the biggest offenders. Village leaders have committed the second greatest offenses. Government cadres have been the third biggest offenders. The crimes of local soldiers, forced to fight, have been the least grave." The unfortunate men were roped together and led off into the hills. The villagers were told they would be "re-educated."[7]

The main target of the Viet Cong was the National Police. Operations carried out by the police against the Viet Cong political infrastructure under the guidance of the American-run Phoenix program had in some cases successfully decimated Viet Cong political ranks. The communists meant to use the offensive to turn the tables. The police chief in Bong Son Village was captured, and the remainder of his men fled south toward Qui Nhon. The Viet Cong flushed out many government informers and agents by coercing the local pacification officials into informing on the local government cadre. In Hoai Duc Village the Revolutionary Development Cadre chief was seen pointing out local South Vietnamese civilian officials to the Viet Cong. Some South Vietnamese pacification officials were "turned" and used by the Viet Cong. Either they had always secretly worked for the communists or they had been persuaded to change sides. The village chiefs of Bong Son, Hoai Tan, and An Hao managed to keep their jobs after the communists overran the area, although the American district senior adviser reported that the three former South Vietnamese officials had a reputation for blatant corruption and it was unlikely that the Viet Cong would keep them around for long.[8]

While the communist cadre consolidated their hold on villages and hamlets of northern Binh Dinh Province, North Vietnamese main forces turned their attention to the remaining South Vietnamese bases. The only major unit that far north in Binh Dinh was the 40th ARVN Regiment, stationed at Landing Zone English some ten miles northeast of Landing Zone Orange. The base was crucial because it sat astride Highway 1 north of Bong Son, a tiny pinpoint of South Vietnamese army control thrust into contested territory. Landing Zone English was nothing to trifle with. Ringed with razor wire and bristling with artillery and protective bunkers, the base served double duty as home of the 40th ARVN Regiment and as the Hoai Nhon District capital. Soldiers brought their families up to live with them, and a virtual town had sprung up around the base perimeter. English could be quickly supplied with men or equipment; a huge airfield capable of landing C-130s ran along the edge of the base.

Timing played against the South Vietnamese, however. In early April, before the big enemy push into Binh Dinh Province, Colonel Tran Hien Duc, the commander of the 40th ARVN Regiment, decided to move part of his regiment from its base at Landing Zone English down Route 3A to Landing Zone Orange for an operation in the mouth of the An Lao Valley. Colonel Duc enjoyed the favor of both General Dzu and John Paul Vann. Dzu had promoted Duc in March, largely at the urging of Vann, who believed Duc would prove a capable leader.[9]

Only one American adviser, Lieutenant Colonel David Schorr, was attached to the 40th ARVN Regiment. Lieutenant Colonel Schorr knew the territory. He had been with the regiment since his tour began in July 1971, and he had seen the situation evolve in Binh Dinh. The signs of continuing enemy action were ominous. Streams of refugees came down from the mountains carrying all their belongings. Schorr had often seen civilians fleeing Viet Cong depredations, but nothing on this scale. As the people passed the army outpost, they repeated, "Beaucoup VC, beaucoup VC." Soon afterward, a battalion based at Landing Zone Pony reported heavy enemy fire and withdrew from its position. Another battalion set out between Pony and Hoai An as a blocking force reported sightings of North Vietnamese troops, and soon no one doubted the nature of the threat before them.[10]

Colonel Duc was devastated. It quickly became clear that Vann's faith in Duc's fighting ability was misplaced; Duc made no attempt to retake Pony. Withdrawing into a shell of depression and despair, Duc refused to respond to his adviser's words of encouragement. Vann even flew into Hoai An, braving North Vietnamese mortar attacks that had begun to seek out the paralyzed regiment, in an attempt to bolster Duc's confidence. Nothing worked. Nor could the 40th ARVN Regiment expect much help from the rest of the division over in Pleiku. As Hoai An came under attack, the situation was worsening north of Kontum, and attention was not easily diverted eastward.

The rocket and mortar attacks on Hoai An became even heavier, and within a few days the addition of direct fire weapons indicated that the North Vietnamese were closing in. Lieutenant Colonel Schorr had found two American companions in Hoai An, Major Gary Hacker and Lieutenant Thomas Eisenhower, serving as district advisers. Both officers confirmed that pacification in the surrounding districts was falling apart and the communists seemed destined to take over the northern part of the province.

Schorr and Duc planned to begin an orderly evacuation of Landing Zone Orange back to English at noon on 19 April. Artillery was laid on, U.S. Air Force F-4 Phantoms circled the outpost bombing and strafing anything that moved, and the U.S. 17th Cavalry planned to send helicopter gunships to cover the evacuation. Schorr felt optimistic and did not believe that the North Vietnamese were strong enough to oppose the move.

Just before the evacuation was scheduled to leave, Duc lost control. A few mortar rounds landed in the compound, and he raced toward a handful of M113 armored personnel carriers parked near the perimeter wire. "We go now," Duc said to the startled Schorr as he strode across the hardpacked dirt. Schorr tried to stop him, but Duc would only repeat over and over, "We go now."

The armored personnel carriers left the compound as startled South Vietnamese soldiers watched in confusion. Schorr could see the spirit drain from the men as their commander drove down a hill and out of sight. Schorr radioed to his superiors advising them of the situation. His message was more of a statement than a request: "Friendly troops may bug out at any time. Request guidance. If friendlies bug out before guidance arrives, will bug out with them."[11]

The Americans did not have to wait long. South Vietnamese soldiers began dropping their weapons and tearing off their uniforms as they raced for the wire and out into the countryside. Soon only the three advisers, the wounded, and two Kit Carson Scouts remained in Landing Zone Orange.

Seeing the defenses crumble before them, the North Vietnamese concentrated their fire on the retreating armored personnel carriers and the fleeing South Vietnamese soldiers. For the moment they ignored the handful of men remaining inside the perimeter wire. Schorr used what he knew was only a temporary breathing space to radio for helicopters to evacuate them.

The group was forced to leave the wounded and move down the hill outside the base. Schorr picked up an M79 grenade launcher in addition to his M16, loaded up with extra ammunition, and led the men into the rice paddies at the base of the hill. The North Vietnamese seemed to be giving only halfhearted pursuit. The Americans could see them, but there did not seem to be more than a platoon or so. They ran through the mud, pausing to shoot at their pursuers, then moving again.

Lieutenant Colonel Schorr moved up on an embankment and suddenly felt his leg give out. He knew he had been shot, although there was little pain and not much blood. Schorr dropped back into the mud beneath the embankment and radioed for help as Hacker fired at the closing North Vietnamese. About an hour later a helicopter arrived to get them. A voice came on the radio calling himself Ruthless Six, the call sign for Lieutenant Colonel Jack Anderson, the commander of the 7th Squadron, 17th Air Cavalry. On his second tour in Vietnam, Anderson liked a good fight and could never resist dropping his helicopter into a tight situation.

As the helicopter began to descend, Anderson quickly became the center of attention for every North Vietnamese gunner in the area. But this Huey was well equipped to fight back. Instead of the 7.62mm machine guns typically mounted in the doors of a UH-1 helicopter, Anderson had placed .50-caliber machine guns. They hammered away at North Vietnamese soldiers as close as twenty-five yards while Schorr, Hacker, Eisenhower, and the two Kit Carson Scouts clambered aboard. They reached Landing Zone English safely; upon landing the crew could find only nine bullet holes in the helicopter.

Lieutenant Colonel Duc and part of his regiment also made it back to English, where they waited for the North Vietnamese to attack again. A pair of new American advisers were shipped up to English, but the 40th ARVN Regiment was already doomed. On 2 May Landing Zone English would fall, though not through any action on the part of the North Vietnamese. Against the advice of his advisers, who believed that English could have held out longer, Duc chose to give up without a fight. Vann was not pleased when the landing zone was abandoned, but he reasoned that "the salvaging of over 2,000 troops by the evacuation will help the longer term situation in those six districts still held by the GVN."[12]

For the next two weeks the North Vietnamese swarmed over Hoai An

District and northern Phu Yen District. By the end of April the communists held 200,000 people in Binh Dinh Province under their sway. Eastern II Corps was in dire danger. With the buildup of enemy activity in the Central Highlands, there was little likelihood of reinforcement for Binh Dinh. Yet Landing Zone English was important. When it fell, only a handful of small South Vietnamese positions remained between the enemy and the provincial capital of Qui Nhon. If the capital fell, the North Vietnamese would have completed step one in their plan to sever South Vietnam through the Central Highlands. But they lacked the force to continue south until more gains could be made around Kontum.[13]

After the fall of Landing Zone English, momentum shifted west to Kontum. "The campaign door had thus been thrown wide open in the west," stated a communist history of the campaign. "The [B-2] Front's command . . . realized that it was no longer necessary to draw the enemy out as initially planned. . . . Instead, it decided to quickly implement the third stage, namely to attack and liberate the Dak To-Tan Canh area."[14]

John Paul Vann had correctly guessed that the North Vietnamese considered Binh Dinh secondary to the Central Highlands. At the same time, he upset North Vietnamese plans by preventing Dzu from shifting troops away from the coast. Now that all the feints and deceptions were out of the way, the enemy threw its weight down Highway 14 toward Kontum.

SIXTEEN

CLOSING IN
ON THE HIGHLANDS

In the weeks immediately preceding the fighting in Binh Dinh, North Vietnamese activity in the Central Highlands also escalated sharply. During most of March the enemy avoided contact, fighting only when South Vietnamese patrols threatened their communication lines or supply caches. During the first week of April, however, the North Vietnamese went over onto the offensive. Vann knew his time of reckoning was at hand. "Indications are that the long expected offensive . . . will probably begin within the next seven days," he reported to MACV at the end of March.[1]

Despite the ominous events of late March, the first week in April proved to be subdued compared with action on the coast or in I Corps and III Corps. Just south of the demilitarized zone the North Vietnamese were threatening the northern half of Quang Tri Province. In III Corps the district town of Loc Ninh was in danger, and the enemy clearly intended to take the province capital of An Loc. But pressure was building slowly in the Central Highlands, too. Although the North Vietnamese had not yet committed the bulk of their forces to battle, the South Vietnamese were clearly on the defensive. "The enemy continues to press the attack, has the initiative, and is forcing II Corps to react," wrote a frustrated John Paul Vann.[2]

The firebases on Rocket Ridge suddenly found themselves under attack by part of the 320th NVA Division, which had set up headquarters just west of the southernmost spur of the ridge. Manned by a battalion of airborne troops, this strategic high ground guarded the approach to Vo Dinh and ultimately Kontum. At dawn on 3 April, Firebase Delta, the southernmost outpost on Rocket Ridge, was probed by enemy artillery and infantry. The North Vietnamese were seeking to engage the best soldiers the South Vietnamese army in II Corps had to offer.

By chance, John Paul Vann was in his helicopter near Firebase Delta as day broke and the North Vietnamese began their attack. He was on his way to pick up the crew of a Chinook helicopter that had been shot down while resupplying the South Vietnamese and their American advisers four days earlier. The crew was waiting impatiently in Firebase Delta, hoping a rescue helicopter would reach them before the North Vietnamese did. It looked like the race would be close.

Vann got word from his advisers that the enemy troops had punched through the northern perimeter of Firebase Delta and were slowly working down the trench lines rooting out the stubborn paratroopers as they went. With him were three Cobra helicopter gunships, loaded and spoiling for a fight. The slim, fast, and heavily armed hunters darted back and forth, up and down, looking for targets on the ground. The pilots reported seeing fighting below; then they swooped down on the enemy, firing rockets and miniguns and lobbing 40mm grenades from automatic launchers.

Seeing that the situation was grim for his advisers in Firebase Delta, Vann began directing AC-130 Spectre gunships and fighter-bomber aircraft at the North Vietnamese troops massing to pour into the firebase perimeter. Bullets from the Spectre gunships' cannon and miniguns gushed forth in a steady stream, pouring onto the enemy below. With Vann's guiding hand, the air support destroyed every attempt by the North Vietnamese to reinforce their foothold inside Firebase Delta. It was the break the paratroopers needed; they counterattacked and wiped out the hundred or so North Vietnamese who had become stranded inside the perimeter. By noon the base was safe, but it could not last long without more ammunition and supplies.

Vann decided to do the job himself. The airborne battalion commander and his American counterpart, Major Peter Kama, looked around outside the firebase at the streams of antiaircraft fire periodically ripping up the sky and radioed Vann that he was crazy to try. Vann ignored them and planned his mission.[3]

Flying back to Vo Dinh, Vann prepared for his resupply mission. His pilot that day was Chief Warrant Officer Paul Acrement, a Cajun from Louisiana. He flew much of the time, but Vann sat in the copilot's seat so he could take the stick and fly if the mood struck him—which it often did. In one of the passenger seats was Lieutenant Huynh Van Cai, Vann's aide. Cai spoke fluent English, and Vann reasoned that it made more sense to use one trusted Vietnamese than to pick a U.S. Army officer and an interpreter.

As Acrement and Cai supervised the loading of supplies into the helicopter, Vann jotted down on a map the positions of enemy antiaircraft emplacements he had seen from the air. Just before they left, he sat down with Acrement and made sure they both understood the safest way through the deadly maze of antiaircraft machine guns.

In the haze of early afternoon, Vann, Acrement, and Cai took off in their overloaded OH-58 Kiowa helicopter. Called a Ranger by those who flew it, this bird was the latest in observation helicopters, and Vann fell in love

John Paul Vann's personal helicoper, an OH-58 Kiowa, better known as a "Ranger."
(Jack Finch)

with it at first sight. The Ranger's power and handling would come in handy for this mission.

Soon they were in sight of Firebase Delta, and the helicopter darted down to the treetops, hugging them until the last second, then sweeping over the perimeter clearing. Acrement held the Ranger motionless in midair as Vann and Cai tossed bundle after bundle of ammunition and supplies to the swarm of thankful paratroopers below. Then Acrement flicked the control stick, spinning the helicopter back onto the path it had just come in on, and headed back to Vo Dinh for another load. Vann and his little rescue team made six runs to Firebase Delta before dark. By then the paratroopers had enough ammunition to throw at the enemy until an airborne battalion sent to relieve them could arrive the next morning. Once again, John Paul Vann had taken action into his own hands, placing himself squarely in front of the firing line. Most important, he had taken some pressure off Dzu, who was rapidly unraveling as the North Vietnamese turned up the pressure.[4]

Vann felt he had personally won his first battle, and he was convinced that this small victory was a sure sign that the South Vietnamese would prevail against the North Vietnamese invasion. Taking time out from the battle, Vann wrote a long memo "To my friends" on 12 April in an attempt to solidify his perceived position as master strategist and battlefield prophet. Always searching for approval and recognition from those in higher positions, Vann made sure that copies of the memo made their way into the hands of men like Secretary of Defense Melvin Laird, conservative columnist Joe Alsop, and international counterinsurgency expert Sir Robert Thompson.

"It is my judgement that the enemy has made a desperation attempt to coerce the U.S. into making a concession in Paris," Vann wrote confidently. "It is quite predictable that their regular forces will both be defeated and will suffer such heavy casualties and losses of equipment as to be ineffective for the next one or two years." Vann also made optimistic predictions about the situation in II Corps, predictions he would be unable to live up to. "We expect to hold our major positions, to include Dak To . . . and Tan Canh, but it is going to be a difficult fight and a lot of soldiers are yet to die." He was half right—a lot of soldiers would die.[5]

Although the enemy attacks along Rocket Ridge were clearly only small probes compared with what was in store, the Joint General Staff in Saigon chose to pull troops out of II Corps and throw them into the worsening situation in I Corps, where Quang Tri City and Hue were in danger. On 20 April Dzu was notified that the 2d Airborne Brigade and the Airborne Division field headquarters were leaving, to be replaced by the 6th Ranger Group from Hue. The Rangers were worn out from almost a month of fighting in Quang Tri Province and near firebases around the A Shau Valley west of Hue, and as far as the soldiers in II Corps were concerned, they were a poor exchange for the tough airborne troops. But the survival of Hue was more important at the moment. President Thieu realized that at this point his political survival was at stake in I Corps, not the Central Highlands. Vann and Dzu would also make up for their manpower loss by tasking the 53d ARVN Regiment, part of the 23d ARVN Division, with taking over part of the airborne units' former area of operations along Rocket Ridge.[6]

Vann's plan to defeat the North Vietnamese at Tan Canh was not proceeding as planned. Constant vigilance through aggressive patrolling was crucial to success. He had to know where the enemy was. But the 22d ARVN Division commander, Colonel Le Duc Dat, was not cooperating. He sat on the high ground around Tan Canh, refusing to maneuver and even ignoring calls for reinforcements by units in trouble.

The senior adviser to the 22d ARVN Division, Colonel Phillip Kaplan, could do nothing to budge Dat, though not for want of trying. Kaplan held his temper whenever Dat refused to listen, reminding himself that the Americans would soon be gone and it would no longer matter. Particularly galling to Kaplan was Dat's fatalism. His stock reply to Kaplan's needling was to say that his troops could not maneuver against the North Vietnamese. If they did, they would be enveloped and annihilated. In his mind, the North Vietnamese were simply superior soldiers. Like most other South Vietnamese army officers, Colonel Dat sat back and hoped his men could hold out until American airpower could come and save the day.[7]

Vann had had trouble with Dat in the past, and it is surprising that he would hinge his plans on the performance of a man who had already proved himself untrustworthy. In 1967, as a province senior adviser in III Corps, Vann helped unseat Dat from his job as province chief. Dat's corruption had links all the way to the presidency, but because his patron Nguyen Cao Ky had fallen from political power, he was unable to hold on to his province seat. Not until 1970 did he regain influence, this time as deputy commander to the 22d ARVN Division. When the division commander slot opened in February 1972, Vann tried to convince Dzu to recommend against him, but Dzu was unwilling to risk offending so powerful an officer, even though Dat was subordinate to Dzu.[8]

To make matters worse, Vann's deputy, General Wear, had finally crumbled under the strain. The fungus in his lungs refused to be beaten, and medical facilities in II Corps were inadequate to handle the problem. Wear had to be evacuated, but at first he refused to go. Vann walked into Wear's office, got down on his knees, clasped his hands as if in prayer, and looked up at his friend. "George, please go away and rest. I'm going to need you later to help with Kontum." Wear reluctantly agreed, and on 22 April he went back to Saigon and boarded a plane for Clarke Air Base in the Philippines. After a few days he returned to Vietnam, checking in to a hospital in Saigon, but the fungus had advanced too far; he would not be back to help Vann with Kontum. Wear was ordered back to the States, devastating news for a dedicated officer. This had been his fight as much as it was John Paul Vann's, but for Brigadier General George Wear the war was over.[9]

There was no time to worry about personnel problems, however. During the evening of 21 April, the North Vietnamese finally overran Firebase Delta on Rocket Ridge. The remaining company of airborne troops and the new ranger reinforcements simply could not withstand the pressure. Only a handful of soldiers and their one American adviser managed to elude the surrounding enemy and escape to the south. Firebase Charlie, the next firebase north of Delta along Rocket Ridge, had been evacuated on 14 April, leaving most of the strategic high ground west of Dak To in enemy hands. Dak To itself was surrounded, and the North Vietnamese had increased the artillery bombardment from between 20 and 50 rounds a day to about 1,000 rounds by the beginning of the second week in April.[10]

The loss of the last firebases on Rocket Ridge opened the way for North Vietnamese trucks carrying supplies to troops preparing for the attack on Tan Canh. The South Vietnamese defenders grew more terrified daily as they gazed out across the valley and watched the buildup. Every night the trucks streamed along trails hacked out of the jungle by North Vietnamese engineers, oblivious to the threat of air strikes. "For a while it looked like the Los Angeles freeway," recalled an American adviser positioned just south of the town. "All across the ridgeline I could see a glow from the trucks' headlights."[11]

On 23 April the offensive in the Central Highlands began in earnest. Most of the 2d NVA Division plus the better part of four independent regiments from the B-3 Front slammed into Tan Canh's defenses. Standing in the enemy's way was the 22d ARVN Division, which was not as potent as it seemed on paper. The division was split between Binh Dinh Province and northern Kontum Province, and only the forward command post, the 42d ARVN Regiment, and one battalion from the 41st ARVN Regiment could be spared to defend Tan Canh itself—about 1,200 troops in all. Across the road at another small outpost called Dak To II, the 47th ARVN Regiment, along with an armor company and an airborne battalion, held down the fort. Vann worried about the 47th ARVN Regiment, which was commanded by Colonel Tran Huu Minh, an entrenched protégé of Dzu's who was, in Vann's opinion, "the most incompetent of the seven regimental commanders." Dzu had wrangled an early promotion for Minh, then consistently assigned his regiment to the "least difficult part of the battlefield. . . . The relationship of Minh to Dzu is known and disapproved of throughout the II Corps hierarchy." Though Vann had tried to get Minh replaced, he failed, and now it was too late for any leadership changes.[12]

Bad news continued to dampen Vann's optimism. With Rocket Ridge no longer part of the South Vietnamese defensive line, the enemy turned its attention northward. Beginning on 19 April a large enemy force had hit Dak Pek, an old U.S. Army Special Forces camp that was now the northernmost outpost of Kontum Province's defense. Populated by 4,500 Montagnard civilians and manned by an understrength border ranger battalion and a handful of militia platoons, the base fought back hard, killing 130 North Vietnamese and capturing sixty-six weapons. Despite their early success, however, the defenders were outnumbered and outgunned. Besides a pair of 105mm howitzers at Ben Het, Dak Pek was out of range of all friendly artillery, and American helicopter pilots reported that the enemy was setting up additional artillery and antiaircraft batteries south and west of the base. Vann believed the commander, the most capable of the ranger battalion leaders, "can hold out indefinitely."[13]

Dak Pek did hold out, but only because the North Vietnamese elected to bypass the tiny base. While North Vietnamese forces attacked there and on Rocket Ridge, Vann prodded Dzu to coerce his regimental commanders to beef up northern Kontum Province's defenses. However, neither Dzu nor Vann held out much hope that they would be successful. Dzu was "absolutely convinced that the 22d Div[ision] will not fight," and Vann secretly reported to Abrams that MACV "should be prepared for the loss of Dak To District within the next week."[14]

From his vantage point on top of a bunker, Captain Raymond Dobbins watched for signs of enemy movement. One of his jobs as acting senior adviser to the 42d ARVN Regiment was coordination of American fire support. Despite the growing danger, Captain Dobbins continued to do that job. The 22d ARVN Division command post outside Tan Canh was the target of a concentrated North Vietnamese artillery barrage, and rounds poured down around the hapless bunker in an unbroken roar of explosions. Dobbins tried to ignore the bomb bursts and calmly radioed targets for air strikes. The job was complicated by a battalion from the 42d ARVN Regiment, along with four M41 tanks, which Dobbins knew was trying to disengage from contact with an overwhelming enemy force near the perimeter. It had to move before the jets could drop their payloads. As he watched the action, one of the tanks stopped to unload a wounded crewman. Suddenly there was a brilliant flash, and the tank coughed smoke from a gaping wound below the turret. Scratch one South Vietnamese tank. Dobbins radioed the advisers in the command bunker that the tank had been destroyed by an enemy B-40 rocket-propelled grenade, a common, shoulder-fired antitank weapon manufactured in the Soviet Union and China.

Inside the bunker Major Jon Wise, the division operations adviser, acknowledged the report but thought it was a little strange. So did his boss, Colonel Phillip Kaplan. Kaplan was hunched over a pile of maps with Colonel Dat, alternating his time between marking off coordinates for air strikes and trying to bolster Dat's flagging spirits. As the senior adviser to the 22d ARVN Division, Kaplan had his hands full.

Colonel Kaplan moved from his cluttered table to talk to Major Wise. The two officers agreed there was no way a B-40 rocket could have destroyed that tank. The range of a B-40 was about 200 yards, and over 500 yards of flat ground with little cover lay between the tank and the nearest enemy position; it was unlikely that anyone could have sneaked closer without being spotted.

Kaplan suspected a new weapon had been introduced on the battlefield. Calling to his deputy, Lieutenant Colonel Terrence McClain, and Major George Carter, the senior adviser to the 14th Armored Cavalry Regiment, Kaplan headed out the bunker door. The three men paused to check the situation, then dove into a nearby ditch, using it for cover as they dashed to the smoking tank carcass. As Kaplan talked to a South Vietnamese soldier who had seen the tank destroyed, another rocket whooshed overhead and crashed into the side of a tank about 150 yards away. Lieutenant Colonel McClain spotted a thin wisp of copper wire along the missile trajectory. Picking it up, he wound about thirty yards of it arm over arm. Kaplan discovered a neat round hole in the tank and the fin section of a small rocket lying on the ground. Two copper wires hung broken from the fins.

The strange weapon was an AT-3 antitank rocket, better known as a Sagger. This sophisticated tank-killer weapon was a wire-guided missile that could be steered to its target with a set of controls manipulated by a soldier up to a mile away. The weapon was state-of the-art Soviet technology that before the Easter Offensive had not appeared on the battlefield in South Vietnam. But Kaplan and his officers could not take much time out to ponder the consequences of their discovery; there was a battle to be fought, and artillery continued to rain down, making life precarious for those above ground. The three men ran back to the bunker.

Later that morning yet another Sagger was launched, this time directly at the command bunker. It struck the sandbag wall at its weakest point, slicing through the sand and burlap, and exploded inside the radio room. Fire and smoke billowed from the creosote support timbers as men scrambled, coughing, to protect the remaining communications equipment. Lieutenant Colonel McClain shook the fog from his ringing head and staggered to his feet. Kaplan was also on his feet, but Major Wise lay still on the ground, blood flowing from a serious head wound. The other American advisers seemed unhurt, but about twenty South Vietnamese soldiers were sprawled dead and wounded among the debris. Kaplan started to throw

The latest in Soviet antitank technology, the AT-3 Sagger wire-guided missile, made its first battlefield appearance during the Easter Offensive. (U.S. Army)

water from a coffee pot on the roaring flames but quickly realized his time and energy would be better spent evacuating the bunker.[15]

"Get everybody out of here!" ordered Kaplan. As men stampeded out the door, the timbers gave way, collapsing in a heap of smoldering sandbags and showering sparks. After a quick head count, Kaplan called for a medevac helicopter. Colonel Dat was unhurt, but about ten of his staff were wounded. Major Wise was still bleeding heavily. As they waited for the helicopter, the Americans set up shop in the 42d ARVN Regiment's bunker. The North Vietnamese artillery did not seem as heavy as it had been earlier that morning, but it could rain down again any second. More important, the division was practically helpless without communications gear, which provided a lifeline to the South Vietnamese defensive network north of Kontum and to American air support.

About an hour before noon John Paul Vann swooped his helicopter into the compound. He supervised as the wounded were thrown onto medevac choppers and talked with Kaplan about the deteriorating situation in Tan

Canh. Scattered artillery rounds exploded nearby, and soldiers threw themselves to the ground. Some of the wounded were dropped as litter bearers dove for cover. Vann did not even flinch. He continued lecturing Kaplan, oblivious to the death and destruction around him. The wounded, he pointed out, were being evacuated exclusively by American medevac helicopters, not South Vietnamese helicopters as they properly should have been. Vann also observed that the South Vietnamese artillery batteries were silent in the face of the enemy bombardment. They seemed to be hiding in their bunkers.

Kaplan agreed that the South Vietnamese were falling apart. The Saggers had destroyed the soldiers' morale by reinforcing the fatalistic belief held by many South Vietnamese soldiers that the enemy was superior and would inevitably win. Since the collapse of the division bunker, Colonel Dat had taken to sitting in a chair and staring at nothing. "We will be overrun tomorrow," he told Kaplan.

Vann had already given up on Dat, and he shifted the conversation to planning an escape for the Americans if the base was overrun. If things got too bad, the advisers would gather at an abandoned helicopter pad near a minefield on the west side of the compound. From there they would wait for extraction. Vann finished his conference with Kaplan and climbed back into his helicopter.

The rest of the day and much of the night were spent remaking the division operations center. The North Vietnamese capitalized on the confusion within the compound by firing Saggers at the remaining M41 tanks hiding nearby. By afternoon most of them had been abandoned by their crews, but the monsters made perfect stationary targets for the enemy gunners. By evening only one was left undamaged.

That night the North Vietnamese concentrated their rocket fire on the airfield and the ammunition dump. Several direct hits ignited the ammunition, sending a billowing sheet of flame and smoke into the sky. Stray rounds cooked off in the heat, throwing lead in all directions. The advisers looked on in glum resignation. The defense of Tan Canh had been dealt another devastating blow.

At about 10:00 that night a voice crackled over the radio. It was that of the pacification adviser for Dak To District, Captain Richard Davidson. Kaplan looked up from his maps and listened. "There are tanks out here. We hear them all around." Davidson's voice was electric with fear. All he had to defend his tiny compound just west of Dak To District headquarters was a platoon of Popular Forces militiamen. Many of them were Montagnard tribesman with little real allegiance to either the government or the communists. They might bolt at any minute.

Captain Davidson requested an AC-130 gunship for air cover. Kaplan relayed the call to Pleiku, and within the hour Spectre was on the way. The gunship's infrared sensors and night vision equipment went to work hunting enemy tanks. "There are eleven of them down there," the pilot radioed to Kaplan. Spectre dropped a flare, and the column of Soviet-made T-54 tanks was bathed in light. The men in the district compound could see the tanks coming straight at them. Davidson froze behind a sandbag wall. But the tanks rumbled by without pausing or firing a shot.[16]

These were the first tanks seen in the Tan Canh area. A few tanks had been used on 21 April during the final enemy assault on Firebase Delta astride Rocket Ridge. Before their appearance Vann had refused to believe in their existence, although he had modified his view somewhat when tanks stormed into Loc Ninh in northern III Corps two weeks earlier. Despite his skepticism, Vann had made sure the 22d ARVN Division was equipped with hundreds of M72 LAWs and had seen to it that Colonel Dat placed soldiers trained to use them in each company. The South Vietnamese also found some of their big guns squarely in position to meet the enemy tanks. A 106mm recoilless rifle sat in a sandbagged position directly astride the road the tanks were moving along.[17]

The North Vietnamese tanks first encountered a platoon of Popular Forces militiamen on a bridge. They had LAWs, but when faced with eleven growling tanks, they broke and ran. Farther down the road the recoilless rifle crew also fled without firing a shot. Kaplan pleaded with Dat to order tank-killer crews into action, but when the soldiers refused to leave their foxholes, Dat simply shrugged in resignation. Kaplan could scarcely conceal his disgust.

Two bridges, including the one abandoned by the Popular Forces militiamen, were the only barriers remaining between the tanks and Tan Canh. Kaplan had been led to believe they were rigged with explosives and could be demolished instantly if that became necessary. It seemed necessary now, but to his shock Kaplan found he had been deceived. There were no explosives in place on either bridge. The tanks rolled on toward Tan Canh.

South Vietnamese artillery crews, virtually silent in the face of the enemy onslaught, were finally coaxed out of bunkers and back to their guns. They fired a few rounds onto the advancing tanks, but fierce North Vietnamese counterbattery fire sent the gunners scurrying back into their bunkers in terror.

The North Vietnamese tankers were confident in the face of their enemy's meek defense. "Our T-54 tanks roared down Route 14 like fierce tigers," recounted an official history. "Once in a while the steel hulls of the

T-54 tanks sparkled as they were hit by shrapnel exploding nearby. Inside the tanks, looking through the thick glass of their periscopes, the combatants still caught a glimpse of the infantrymen amid the smoke of exploding bombs."[18]

The one piece of good news for Kaplan was that Spectre still circled the sky above the tanks. The gunship had been rigged with 105mm howitzers and a sophisticated computer targeting system designed to track and fire at moving targets on the ground. High-explosive rounds belched from Spectre's cannon, and the pilot reported six hits. Unfortunately, the T-54 tanks were tough enough to withstand hits from above. Each round that struck home damaged the armor and shook up the crew but failed to stop the tank. One crew was so rattled by the unexpected hammering from above that it stopped near a bridge and abandoned its tank.

Colonel Dat had already hit rock bottom, and the news that nothing stood between Tan Canh and the North Vietnamese tanks had no impact on him. He sat in a folding chair, staring into space with his head in his hands. Colonel Kaplan had no luck breaking him from his depression, so Captain Dobbins gave it a try—with no more success. Dobbins did convince Lieutenant Colonel Thong, commander of the 42d ARVN Regiment, to deploy one company as tank hunter-killer teams. Within the hour they had good news to report: two enemy tanks had been destroyed on the western edge of town.

Then Spectre came back on the air with more bad news. Ten enemy tanks had split off from the main group headed for Tan Canh and were moving to the high ground north of the 22d ARVN Division compound toward the airstrip. The rest were coming toward Tan Canh from the west.

"That's all I can do for now," Spectre continued. "I'm low on fuel and ordnance, but I'll be back." The advisers did not have to wait long. In the pitch-black sky above the beleaguered compound, they heard the droning of another AC-130 gunship coming to stand guard until dawn. This one had only 20mm and 40mm cannon, insufficient to destroy the T-54 tanks below. Instead, the new gunship turned its attention on enemy troop concentrations pointed out by an American adviser, Captain Ken Yonan, from his vantage point atop an abandoned water tower.[19]

North Vietnamese armor and infantry were in position for the final assault on Tan Canh. Captain Dobbins and Lieutenant Colonel Thong had taken up positions on the east side of the perimeter, near the main gate. At 6:00 A.M. they watched as the tanks roared forward in a concerted attack. Actually, they heard them first. Then, out of the morning mist came the lead tanks. They raked the front line of bunkers clustered near the main

A North Vietnamese tank leads infantry in an attack on an outpost near Tan Canh. (Author's collection)

gate with machine-gun fire while the ten tanks near the airstrip charged down from the north. Both attacks were perfectly timed, and the advisers had no doubt that the North Vietnamese had learned to effectively coordinate their attacks with radios. Even more ominous was the enemy's use of infantry. Yonan and Dobbins could clearly see North Vietnamese soldiers scurrying behind the tanks in the half-light of dawn. In the past, particularly in I Corps and III Corps, the enemy had been unable to coordinate armor and infantry and had paid dearly for the mistake.

Dobbins got on the radio and told Kaplan of the news. Kaplan did not need this information to see that things were falling apart. The sound of rumbling tanks and screaming enemy infantrymen was too much for the demoralized South Vietnamese soldiers. The Americans watched helplessly as the remaining 900 members of the 22d ARVN Division—most of them support troops and engineers rather than combat troops—dissolved into a mass of panicked humanity. They ran in all directions as the North Vietnamese tanks continued advancing straight at the main gate.

Dobbins and Thong stood their ground, hoping their example would rally the troops, but it was too late. Kaplan called Dobbins on the radio for a status report. "They're at the gate and no one is left to stop them," Dobbins yelled over the battlefield din. As he spoke, three tank rounds slammed into the command bunker, blasting away the communications antennas. Silence. Dobbins was cut off from the other advisers.

Dobbins put down the receiver. He had to assume the worst—that his fellow advisers were dead or captured, and it was now every man for himself. Dobbins and Lieutenant Colonel Thong stared silently at each other, each knowing that the odds for survival were bleak. But they decided to stay until the bitter end. The two men worked feverishly to shore up the crumbling defenses and bolster the morale of the few remaining South Vietnamese soldiers. Some of the defending troops initially remained at their posts near Dobbins and Thong, but the constant artillery barrage wore them down. North Vietnamese gunners had pounded the center of the Tan Canh compound continuously during the morning attack, safe from U.S. air strikes behind the drizzling rain and dense clouds.

By dawn on 24 April the North Vietnamese were poised for the final kill. A North Vietnamese history of the battle sets the stage:

> At 0510 . . . three colored flares shot up in the sky, tracing dimly lit curves in the morning mist. From various directions, our troops charged simultaneously. When the man in front fell, the one behind him took his place. . . . Our tanks violently fired on both flanks of the enemy, creating favorable conditions for ground troops to charge toward the interior of the base. One after another enemy bunkers were collapsed by our tanks' fire, B-40 rockets, and infantry hand-held explosives. Several gun nests that put up resistance were crushed by our tank tracks.[20]

Fighting was fierce all along the northern perimeter. North Vietnamese tanks first punched through in the northeast, with North Vietnamese infantry close on their heels. On the northwest front an enemy infantry battalion had opened a gap in the line, allowing a platoon of T-54s to pour through. To the south a North Vietnamese battalion had been stopped by a courageous South Vietnamese reconnaissance company. They were finally overrun by sheer weight of numbers, though not before over 100 of the enemy had been killed. When the weather finally cleared just after first light, Dobbins relayed coordinates to the forward air controllers, who buzzed in to mark the targets with smoke. Artillery emplacements, antiaircraft batteries, and enemy armor were all fair game for the little darting aircraft as they fired phosphorous rockets from wing pods.

As the fighter planes did their work, Dobbins and Thong moved from bunker to bunker, taking cover where they could as they tried to assess the state of their shattered defenses. By 10:00 that morning Thong had lost all contact with his troops, and the two men decided they had to get out. Thong led Dobbins through the rain of artillery to his quarters in the center of the perimeter. Dobbins paused to look back and noticed about twenty South Vietnamese soldiers following along.

Thong dashed inside his hut and knelt down over a square piece of board on the floor. He pulled it back, revealing a trapdoor covering a hidden underground bunker. Thong, Dobbins, and the twenty soldiers squeezed inside, closed the trapdoor, and waited. In the darkness they could hear the fighting above. All day long tanks rumbled and creaked overhead, men screamed, and bombs from air strikes shook the ground, showering dirt on the men in the hidden bunker. Although the bombs often came too close for comfort, they were a welcome risk, for U.S. airpower was the only thing left between them and a North Vietnamese victory.

Back in the command bunker Kaplan knew the situation had become critical. Defense of Tan Canh was out of the question; it was now simply a matter of survival. He ordered all the American advisers to prepare for escape. Kaplan hated to abandon his position, but the handful of advisers in Tan Canh could no longer influence the battle's outcome. It was time to leave—if they could.

Gathering all the radios and weapons they could carry, Kaplan, McClain, and seven other advisers left the bunker. Colonel Dat and several of his advisers followed, but seeing the swirling battle outside, they returned to the false safety of the bunker. Captain Yonan, the young adviser in the water tower, was ordered to move to the prearranged extraction point. Yonan waited a few minutes before coming up on the radio. In a low voice he said there were enemy tanks all around, and any movement would mean death. He would try to join them later. Suddenly two loud explosions came from Yonan's position. Two T-54 tanks had fired point-blank into the water tower; one of them settled into a fixed position directly underneath the tower.

Yonan was still there, however. He radioed back that he was unhurt and would meet the rest of the Americans when he could. But it was not to be. Dobbins repeatedly tried to contact Yonan throughout the morning, but he was never heard from again. The mystery was solved in January 1973 when Captain Kenneth Yonan's name appeared on a prisoner list released by Hanoi. However, he was not among the prisoners returned to the United States following the 1973 cease-fire.[21]

Dodging artillery, Kaplan's group ran to the western perimeter, where they were brought up short by tanks moving along the road. As they crouched behind a pile of wreckage, a burning T-54 barreled down the road from the north. Kaplan figured small pockets of South Vietnamese soldiers must have refused to run and were taking a toll on the enemy. A second tank came down the road, and Lieutenant Colonel McClain, Kaplan's deputy, readied a LAW. It malfunctioned, and the tank rolled on by.

Fortunately for the advisers, there was no enemy infantry in the area, so they rushed across the road toward the minefield Kaplan and John Paul Vann had agreed upon as an extraction site. Dead and wounded South Vietnamese soldiers lay all around. As they had fled the North Vietnamese tanks, many of the panicked soldiers ran directly into the minefield, blowing themselves to bits. Kaplan and the advisers huddled near the edge of the minefield, looking for a way across.

At 6:30 A.M. Vann got the call that his advisers had pulled out of Tan Canh. He had been up most of the night writing messages to General Abrams in Saigon but had managed to grab a few hours' sleep. As Vann pulled on his clothes, he had his pilot, Chief Warrant Officer Robert Richards, start up the helicopter. Richards was a country boy from Georgia who had learned to fly helicopters at the height of the Vietnam War, when pilots were at a premium. He had survived when others had not, and Vann picked him because he was one of the best. Even General Dzu, who normally was reluctant to fly in helicopters, would go anywhere in one as long as Chief Warrant Officer Richards was at the stick.22

A second Kiowa scout helicopter joined Vann as he took off toward Tan Canh. It was piloted by Captain Dolph Todd, a crack flyer who had volunteered to be Vann's backup pilot. He had heard rumors of Vann's fearlessness, but he was unprepared for what he was about to witness.

The two helicopters rotored along close to the treetops. Vann was able to contact Kaplan as his chopper climbed high over Tan Canh. He circled the battlefield, surveying the situation and looking for the best spot for a rescue. Vann could see that Colonel Kaplan's original rendezvous point at the clearing across the minefield was impractical. Two North Vietnamese tanks had taken up position there, and enemy infantry was moving in on all sides. One of the advisers, Staff Sergeant Walter Ward, and a wounded South Vietnamese soldier found a path through the minefield and away from the tanks. Ward came back and led the other Americans to an old road that ran through a shallow ravine in the center of the minefield. Kaplan ordered his men to lie down and wait for the rescue helicopter, hoping it could land in the ravine, where it would be partially shielded from enemy fire.

Vann's helicopter swooped over the clearing and headed for the ravine. But all the pilot saw was three North Vietnamese tanks with their guns pointed right where he was about to land. Richards was scared half to death, but he came in anyway. The helicopter dropped like a stone to the ground. Richards did not bother to flare before landing; the maneuver would only leave him exposed for an extra split second. Todd's helicopter was right behind. Kaplan sent three advisers into each of the nervously waiting birds while he, Lieutenant McClain, and Captain David Stewart, the division signals adviser, remained behind. Stewart knew the communications equipment better than anyone, and he carried one of the portable radios.

The helicopters lifted off with their human cargo. Richards was convinced one of the three tanks would blast them to bits as they rose above the lip of the ravine, but none fired. Only sporadic small-arms fire seemed aimed at the helicopters. A handful of South Vietnamese soldiers ran forward and grabbed onto the skids as the helicopters took off. They hung on for dear life as the helicopters climbed into the sky.

Vann was certain the soldiers would fall to their deaths, so he ordered Richards to fly to Dak To II a few miles to the southwest. He reasoned that the North Vietnamese had not yet overrun the small base. They had not, but some enemy troops were taking up position for the attack, and they saw the helicopters coming in. Both choppers landed and dropped off the South Vietnamese soldiers and the six Americans. Vann radioed a nearby Huey, which came in to Dak To II from the southwest, following a course outlined by American advisers on the ground. For some reason, however, the pilot ignored the instructions and lifted off toward the northwest— right into the main concentration of North Vietnamese antiaircraft positions. The Huey flew less than a half mile before it ran into a cross fire of antiaircraft guns and vanished in a flash of bright orange flame. The advisers still in Dak To watched in horror, then sadly radioed the news back to Kontum, reporting there were no survivors.

They were wrong. Of the ten men aboard the Huey—six advisers and four crewmen—five had survived. They began a thirteen-day ordeal right in the middle of a battle in some of the most rugged country in South Vietnam. Three of the advisers and the two helicopter doorgunners managed to crawl from the flaming wreckage to temporary safety in a tangled hollow. Major William C. Warmath, Captain John Keller, and Sergeant Walter Ward found themselves in a worse situation than the one they had just left. One of the doorgunners had a fractured leg; most of the other men were also injured. Given their physical condition and the battle unfolding around them, the group was forced to stay near the wreckage.

The North Vietnamese paid no attention to the shattered helicopter, even when the survivors caught catfish and cooked them over a fire. Would-be rescuers did not notice either. Major Warmath tried signaling aircraft overhead using the tops of C ration cans. He also stripped the white nylon linings out of flak jackets and arranged them on the ground to spell out an SOS. Nothing worked.

About a week after the crash Captain Keller and Specialist Charles Lea, one of the doorgunners, set out on a fruitless search for food. They spotted an abandoned sampan and floated down river, where they miraculously found a field radio—apparently discarded by South Vietnamese soldiers—and contacted Pleiku. A helicopter was sent to pick them up, and they guided a second chopper to their wounded comrades. On 7 May, thirteen days after the crash, all five of the initial survivors made it safely back to Pleiku.23

Vann ordered Richards back to Tan Canh for the last three American advisers. As he climbed into the sky, some enemy soldiers who had seen the helicopters land opened up on the departing birds. Rifle fire raked the helicopter's nose, showering the cockpit with Plexiglass shards. Richards jerked back the control stick, and the chopper shuddered into a steep climb. Bullets came through the aluminum floor, but no one was hit. Fuel spurted from holes in the tank as Richards headed back to Pleiku, hoping he could make it before the fuel leaked away or before some lucky North Vietnamese soldier hit them with a tracer round. He made it, but the remaining advisers at Tan Canh still had to be picked up. Captain Todd made the flight, retrieving Kaplan, McClain, and Stewart without incident.

As soon as Todd landed in Pleiku with the three grateful advisers, Vann jumped aboard. His aid, Lieutenant Cai, came with him on this trip. Todd flew them back to Dak To II to rescue a lone American airborne adviser trapped near the base airfield. The usually brave paratroopers were beginning to panic, and it was clear that Dak To was going the way of Tan Canh. As the helicopter landed among the milling South Vietnamese soldiers, the American and his wounded interpreter were loaded aboard. Frightened troops also tried to climb aboard. Vann screamed to Todd to take off as he frantically clubbed the frightened South Vietnamese soldiers with his rifle. The overloaded chopper groaned slowly into the air, then sank back down to one side until the spinning rotor dug into the ground. The rotor splintered into thousands of pieces as the helicopter flipped over. The invincible Vann jumped clear of the wreckage; seeing that Cai was pinned underneath, Vann pulled him out.

The enemy was closing in, and Vann radioed to a handful of Cobra gunships for help. They slashed in for the kill, raking the advancing North Vietnamese with cannon fire and rockets. Vann was not content to sit and watch the Cobras do all the work, however. He fired away with his M16, slamming home fresh magazines until the rifle barrel was too hot to touch. An American Huey helicopter managed to run through the gauntlet of

North Vietnamese fire and pick up Vann, Cai, and Todd, as well as the American airborne adviser and his interpreter. This time the helicopter was able to take off without the extra weight of South Vietnamese soldiers clinging to the skids. It flew to Kontum, where Cai was delivered to the local hospital. Once again Vann had escaped almost certain death to fly and fight another day.[24]

Down in the dark bunker beneath Lieutenant Colonel Thong's hut, Captain Dobbins and the frightened South Vietnamese soldiers waited. The battle had moved over them and only a few isolated pockets of small-arms fire could be heard above. Dobbins slowly opened the trapdoor, raised his head, and looked around. He saw no movement, but the moon bathed the tortured landscape with a flat glow. Dobbins cursed under his breath. He had forgotten about the full moon, which would make escape that much more difficult.

It was 8:00 at night; they had been below ground for many hours, waiting for nightfall to mask their movement. The twenty soldiers were divided into groups of three and briefed on the escape plan. It was not much of a plan; they would simply try to sneak through the wire in small groups without being seen by the North Vietnamese. As the first few groups ran toward the treeline on the southwest side of the perimeter, they were spotted by the enemy, who opened fire, killing four South Vietnamese soldiers. The rest scurried to a nearby pigpen and huddled together wondering what to do next.

At midnight Dobbins decided to try again. As the men moved across open ground, a Spectre gunship firing on targets nearby dropped an illumination flare, bathing the men in bright, flickering light. Dobbins froze, but the North Vietnamese quickly saw the little group and again opened fire. Several more South Vietnamese soldiers fell to the ground. Dobbins, Thong, and the survivors remained at the pigpen until the moon dropped below the trees just before dawn.

It was time to move again. If the men were caught this time, the game would be up. Daylight was coming, and they would stand no chance without the cover of darkness. But tanks were still on the prowl throughout the area; a handful could be seen off near the treeline. Then Dobbins noticed something peculiar. Whenever a forward air controller flew overhead, the tanks blew smoke into the air to conceal their telltale shapes from the watchful airborne eyes. The smoke also blinded the tankers to movement on the ground around them. As another forward air controller came on the scene, the tanks released their camouflage, and Dobbins and the others ran. This time they made it. After reaching the relative safety of the jungle just before the gathering dawn, Captain Dobbins and Lieutenant Colonel Thong rounded up the small group, and together they walked south for several kilometers until they were spotted by American helicopters and picked up the next day.[25]

Within hours after Tan Canh came under attack on 23 April, Dak To II was also hit. The little hamlet of Dak To and its nearby firebase—Dak To II—sat along Route 512 about four miles west of the Tan Canh compound. Both bases were situated to stem North Vietnamese troops and supplies coming into South Vietnam from over the Laotian border to the west. This was a particularly important area because Route 512 was the only true road through the rugged hills and forests of northern Kontum Province. To get the job done, the bases had at their disposal over fifty 105mm and 155mm artillery pieces, along with 106mm recoilless rifles and over a hundred M72 LAWs brought in during the weeks before the offensive. Vann had been correct in predicting that control of Route 512 was vital to the North Vietnamese offensive in II Corps. But the overwhelming number of enemy troops meant that South Vietnamese troops in the area were doomed to defeat.[26]

The attack on Dak To II was part of the greater North Vietnamese offensive against northern Kontum Province. Since Tan Canh and Dak To II were only a few miles from each other, the enemy sought to knock them both out in a single blow and had the forces necessary to do it. The attacking North Vietnamese units were the same as those that were attacking Tan Canh—part of the 2d NVA Division, along with battalions of the 1st and 141st NVA Regiments and elements of the 203d Tank Regiment.

While enemy coordination between the attacks on Tan Canh and Dak To II was efficient, the South Vietnamese defense of the two bases was not. Dak To II was defended by a separate unit—the 47th ARVN Regiment—composed of fewer than 800 soldiers. The 22d ARVN Division headquarters was supposed to coordinate the 47th ARVN Regiment and its sister unit, the 42d ARVN Regiment in Tan Canh, but once the battle was joined, the two units were virtually on their own.

The North Vietnamese used the same attack plan as they had against Tan Canh. Armor and infantry circled the base to the south and east, simultaneously striking the nearby airfield. Colonel Dat had foolishly placed most of his armor—two armored cavalry troops—at Ben Het, an isolated firebase about twenty kilometers northwest of Dak To II along Route 512. The tanks were so far away from the bulk of his forces that they were out of the battle before it began. The North Vietnamese simply bypassed them and headed for Tan Canh and Dak To II.

As the enemy surrounded the two bases, Dat ordered the tanks and an infantry platoon from Ben Het firebase to reinforce Dak To II. They hurried east only to be ambushed by North Vietnamese forces on the high ground east of Dak Mot Bridge. Enemy antitank gunners destroyed all the South Vietnamese M41 tanks and scattered the hapless infantry platoon. These were the last possible reserves for Tan Canh and Dak To II.[27]

South Vietnamese defenses in Dak To II crumbled almost immediately when the enemy struck. But that might have been expected. Although the division was combat ready on paper, it was heavily sprinkled with logistics troops, and most of them were in Dak To II. The American advisers assigned to the 47th ARVN Regiment knew what they were in for, but no one anticipated a North Vietnamese attack of such magnitude. Because of John Paul Vann's unwillingness to accept previous sightings of enemy armor, they were especially surprised by the tanks. The result was a unit largely unprepared for its role as frontline spoiler for the North Vietnamese offensive in the Central Highlands.[28]

The American advisers in Dak To II had less time to plan an escape than had their compatriots in Tan Canh. Lieutenant Colonel Robert Brownlee, the senior regimental adviser, and his deputy, Captain Charles Carden, were surrounded and fighting for their lives when Vann flew into the base with the first group of advisers evacuated from Tan Canh. With the North Vietnamese swirling around the perimeter, they had watched in horror as the Huey taking those same advisers had been shot out of the sky by enemy antiaircraft gunners. It was Captain Carden who had radioed that there were no survivors.

By midmorning Carden found himself the lone American in the compound. After getting separated from Lieutenant Colonel Brownlee during the fighting, he returned to the tactical operations center, only to find it deserted. As he looked around wondering who was running the South Vietnamese side of the battle, two T-54 tanks rumbled onto the airstrip a few hundred meters away. One of them turned quickly on its treads and began firing into the meager defenses surrounding the operations center. Carden threw himself to the ground and watched as the tank fired round after round into the bunkers. Two South Vietnamese M41 tanks—the only remaining operational armor in the area—wheeled around one side of the enemy T-54 and fired three rounds apiece into the unsuspecting tank. Carden saw direct hits, but the enemy was not knocked out. Smoke billowed from the engine and turret, but the tank recovered and turned to face its attackers. Flame belched from its barrel as a round struck one M41 under the turret. A second round finished it off. Turning on the second South

Vietnamese tank, the T-54 fired one well-placed round and destroyed it. As Carden watched, the North Vietnamese—some of them obviously wounded—calmly opened the hatch and abandoned the burning tank. Their discipline and training were first-rate, thought Carden.

The ill-fated assault on the lone T-54 was the last "counterattack" by the South Vietnamese anywhere in Dak To II. Other actions consisted mostly of South Vietnamese troops fighting sporadically as they retreated from the advancing enemy. As the South Vietnamese fled, Captain Carden realized that he would be completely isolated if he stayed where he was. He slipped away from the regimental bunker and soon found Lieutenant Colonel Brownlee. After a quick conference held under the constant rain of artillery, the two Americans decided the compound was lost and they had better leave. Soldiers from the 47th ARVN Regiment and the 9th Airborne Battalion were still fighting from their isolated positions, but a total lack of leadership left their efforts uncoordinated. The final blow came with the news from Tan Canh that all the American advisers had been evacuated and the airborne troops had left.

Brownlee and Carden watched as South Vietnamese soldiers streamed out of the compound, many of them mowed down by enemy fire as they ran. There was nothing more to be done. The two Americans gathered up their radios and a few supplies, burned all the documents, and moved out of Dak To II toward the southeast. Only their Vietnamese interpreter and driver remained with them.

A small river, the Dak Poko, flowed along the southern edge of the compound perimeter. Because it was away from the heaviest fighting, it seemed to offer the best opportunity for escape, so the four men headed in that direction. They decided to cross at a small footbridge but found that what was left of the airborne battalion and some soldiers from the 47th ARVN Regiment were pinned down there by a large enemy force. The river was clogged with the bodies of dead and wounded who had been cut down while trying to cross the bridge. From their vantage point just above the fighting, Brownlee and Carden saw it was impossible to cross there, so they moved westward along the bank until they found a shallow ford about 700 yards upstream.

Without hesitation Carden and the two South Vietnamese dashed into the river, with Brownlee right behind. The enemy had anticipated escape along the river, and troops near that point opened up on the small group. As fire from small arms tore the air and mortar rounds thumped into the water beside them, the men struggled for the opposite bank. Carden scrambled up a steep incline on the other side. He reached the top and looked back to see Lieutenant Colonel Brownlee struggling at the bottom of the embankment. Carden started back to help his commander, but more North Vietnamese fire forced him to abandon the position and move about 100 yards downstream. After the firing slacked off several minutes later, Carden crept back to the riverbank in search of Brownlee. He was not there. After a search both up and down the river, Carden gave up. Along with the two South Vietnamese soldiers, he headed south toward Fire Base Vida, where they were picked up two days later. Lieutenant Colonel Robert Brownlee was never seen again and was listed as missing in action.[29]

By nightfall on 24 April the North Vietnamese were firmly in control of Tan Canh and Dak To II. Small pockets of South Vietnamese resistance continued over the next two days, but the enemy had already turned its attention back to Rocket Ridge and the eventual target, Kontum. Aside from basically eliminating two entire South Vietnamese regiments and capturing the northern portion of Kontum Province, the North Vietnamese managed to make off with thirty artillery pieces, including seven 155mm howitzers, and 14,000 rounds of artillery ammunition. They dragged them away from the abandoned South Vietnamese compounds and into the jungle, where they could be hidden from the American air strikes that would surely follow the evacuation of Tan Canh and Dak To II.[30]

The B-2 Front was proud of its feat of arms. "The Dak To–Tan Canh victory marked the first time the Highland's People's Armed Forces launched a fast, large-scale coordinated attack," concluded the official communist history of the campaign. "Within ten hours, they knocked down an entire force equivalent to a reinforced division."[31]

Indeed, Dzu and Vann had to face the fact that the 22d ARVN Division had crumbled and would probably be out of action for months to come. In fact, military advisers estimated that its combat effectiveness was "near zero." Most of the division's officers at Tan Canh had been killed or wounded, and the equipment destroyed or abandoned. All that remained of the division elements were small groups of South Vietnamese soldiers who managed to break through the tightening North Vietnamese noose and flee headlong down Route 14 toward Kontum. They ran so fast that Montagnard villagers living along the road dubbed them the "rabbit soldiers."[32]

Back at the doomed compound in Tan Canh, Colonel Le Duc Dat and his remaining staff finally emerged from their bunker late in the afternoon of 24 April. The sky had darkened, and a steady rain poured from the gray sky. Taking advantage of the worsening weather, Dat radioed General Dzu in Pleiku, pleading for a helicopter to come pick him up at the bunker. That was impossible, Dzu replied. Resigned to his final fate, Dat destroyed his radios and codebooks.

Colonel Le Duc Dat was never heard from again. One South Vietnamese captain later reported that Dat had triggered an antipersonnel mine while trying to escape the doomed base. Dat's deputy, Colonel Ton That Hung, escaped to Kontum and later reported a different story. According to him, Dat and a few members of the 22d ARVN Division staff managed to make it most of the way to Dak To II. Dat was wounded on the way there, and he may have committed suicide with his pistol as he lay dying rather than fall into North Vietnamese hands.[33]

SEVENTEEN

DESIGNING A DEFENSE

With the fall of Tan Canh and Dak To II, nothing remained between the enemy and Kontum except a handful of South Vietnamese positions on Rocket Ridge. On 25 April General Dzu decided to abandon the precarious footholds at Firebases Five and Six. He had no real choice. Although those bases were the only high ground along Highway 14, and therefore strategic positions, they were doomed. Better to save his men for the battle around Kontum.

From the North Vietnamese perspective the final fall of Rocket Ridge was an even more important victory than the capture of Tan Canh and Dak To II. Artillery manhandled up the mountain could dominate Highway 14 and force the South Vietnamese to abandon any other positions along the highway.

But the North Vietnamese sat on their laurels, failing to pursue the defeated and demoralized South Vietnamese down Highway 14 and into Kontum, a mere twenty-five miles to the southeast. Only a handful of troops remained in the city, easy prey for the victorious North Vietnamese. Yet they remained in place north of Kontum for three weeks, allowing Dzu to reinforce his precarious position.

The reason for the delay remains a mystery. An official North Vietnamese history of the Central Highlands campaign says only this: "Judging that although the enemy in Cong Tum [Kontum] were showing weak spots . . . we were not in a position to develop our attacks expeditiously and vigorously." Therefore, the "Standing Committee of the Central Highlands Force's Party Committee decided to urgently attack open routes for the transportation of supplies and the movement of forces."[1]

This explanation lacks clarity, but it does indicate that the North Vietnamese believed they were not yet ready to do battle in Kontum. Perhaps their intelligence underestimated Dzu's strength in Kontum and decided to wait until they had a clearer picture. Or the 2d NVA Division may have been ordered to wait for the 320th NVA Division to consolidate its position around Rocket Ridge. Perhaps the most plausible explanation lies in the inflexibility of North Vietnamese tactics. In North Vietnamese doctrine, orders are rarely changed in midstride to compensate for fluctuating battlefield conditions. Infantry and armor maneuver to surround the enemy, and attacks are preceded by heavy artillery bombardments. Only then are orders given for the final and crushing assault. On 24 April Kontum had not yet been "prepared" according to the rigid doctrine. It had not been encircled, and the artillery was not yet in place. No North Vietnamese commander was willing to risk a headlong charge down the highway and into the city without orders from the top, and those were unlikely to come.

Whatever the reason for the North Vietnamese pause, Dzu prepared for the worst. He believed that no matter what he did, Kontum could not hold. Demoralized over the defeat of the 22d ARVN Division and haunted by the fate of Colonel Dat, Dzu became increasingly ineffective. John Paul Vann watched as his counterpart withered before him, but rather than allow the instability caused by his counterpart's waning capabilities to hinder operations, Vann gave up all pretense of South Vietnamese command, took over himself, and openly issued orders. One of his first was to place most of the responsibility for the defense of Kontum in the hands of 23d ARVN Division commander, Colonel Ly Tong Ba.

Vann and Ba had worked together since 1962. Ba was better than most South Vietnamese officers, and he had not followed the trail of corruption to reach his position of command. Vann had seen to it that Ba fell under his influence and in January 1972 had maneuvered Ba into command of the 23d ARVN Division. Thus Ba owed his present status to John Paul Vann, a fact that Vann would exploit to the fullest. Ba would be the facade behind which Vann could pull the strings in the final battle at Kontum. Many South Vietnamese officers called Ba "Mr. Vann's man," and Vann preferred it that way. The fall of Tan Canh and Dak To II had badly tarnished his reputation as the civilian general, and he intended to put the luster back in his stars.

But Colonel Ba was also his own man. Over the past decade he had risen through an undistinguished officer corps to become one of the best commanders in the army. The road had been rough, however. Ba owed his low rank (he was one of the few division commanders who was not a general officer) to his unrepentant opposition to the corruption and incompetence that riddled both the Thieu regime and the South Vietnamese military. His reputation among American advisers was also lukewarm, discredited by an unfortunate incident that was partially beyond his control. In January 1963 Ba's armor unit was mauled by a small force of Viet Cong regulars near a village called Ap Bac. The insignificant battle became a symbol of both South Vietnamese ineptitude and American inveracity when public affairs officials tried to cover up the defeat by lying to the press. Unfortunately for

Colonel Ly Tong Ba, commander of the 23d ARVN Division, briefs Saigon officials on the situation in Kontum. (Author's collection)

MACV's reputation, a handful of reporters had witnessed the fighting firsthand. After being implicated in a failed coup attempt in September 1964, Ba was relieved of his armor command and later sent to Binh Duong to serve as province chief. But despite all setbacks, nine years later Ba was a division commander on the sharp edge of Kontum's defense. "Colonel Ly Tong Ba is faced with a real test of his leadership," wrote Vann on the eve of the attack on Kontum. "I am confident, however, that he is the best qualified commander available to do the job."[2]

The shift of power also upset the American division advisory staff. Colonel Ba had never liked his counterpart, Colonel Robert Kellar. Kellar was considered a good adviser, but other Americans noticed that he did not seem comfortable working in an equal relationship with a South Vietnamese officer. Whatever the case, Ba wanted him out. Kellar left suddenly, replaced temporarily by Colonel John "Jack" Truby, a roving officer in charge of coordinating all the small advisory detachments around the province into a reserve force. Truby had suggested to Vann that he round up advisers in the far reaches of II Corps not affected by the enemy offensive and place them in and around Kontum for the coming battle. Instead of heeding the advice, Vann made Truby Ba's temporary counterpart. The decision amazed many of the other advisers with the 23d ARVN Division. They knew Truby as a gentle, intellectual man without the bravado and outward confidence needed to interact with South Vietnamese officers. However, given the circumstances, there was nothing else to do, and Colonel Truby bravely stepped into his new job.

Both Vann and Ba really wanted Colonel R. M. Rhotenberry to fill the 23d ARVN Division senior adviser slot. Rhotenberry, known as "Rhot" to his friends, hailed from Texas and had all the habits and mannerisms to prove it. A bulky and brash man, Rhotenberry had seen so many tours in Vietnam—four of them—that he was known as "the soldier of fortune" by some South Vietnamese officers. Rhotenberry had first met Vann in 1962 when the two had shared a room in Cholon. He had also commanded a battalion of the U.S. 9th Infantry Division. Vann felt he would be perfect for the job, and, best of all, Colonel Ba agreed. So Colonel Rhotenberry was called over from the States, but he would not arrive until 14 May, at the height of the North Vietnamese assault on Kontum.[3]

Another personnel change worked in Vann's favor. When Brigadier General George Wear left Vietnam, Vann requested Brigadier General John Hill to fill the slot. Hill had just finished a second tour in Vietnam by overseeing the closure of the huge American-built port facility at Cam Ranh Bay. Vann first met Hill while both men were Reserve Officers' Training Corps (ROTC) instructors after the Korean War, and he found that their similar experiences during that war formed a common bond. Best of all, Hill was a fighter. Vann left him alone to organize aviation assets, naval gunfire support, and artillery. Vann would have his hands full with the ground units.[4]

Although most of the problems at the top of the II Corps chain of command had been solved, Vann still had to contend with traditional bickering below division level. As 23d ARVN Division commander, Colonel Ba really had only one unit, the 53d ARVN Regiment, at his disposal in Kontum before 28 April—plus operational control over ranger and airborne units, and two cavalry squadrons. Most of these units were commanded by colonels, and they resented taking orders from another colonel. To complicate matters further, each ranger and airborne commander—considered the elite of the South Vietnamese army—followed a chain of command separate from that of the regular army. If they did not like their orders, they could ask for confirmation down their own chain of command to Saigon. On a number of occasions senior officers would not show up for coordination meetings, making it impossible to adequately plan for the defense of Kontum.

This problem had reached critical proportions in I Corps, but in the Central Highlands Vann managed to overcome it by sheer force of personality. He suggested that Dzu and his deputy, Major General Phong, as well as Brigadier General John Hill, fly to Kontum every morning at 8:00 to preside over staff meetings. The presence of senior South Vietnamese and American officers strengthened Colonel Ba's position, ensured perfect attendance by the more junior officers, and silenced open criticism.[5]

At the lower advisory level, Vann received total commitment to the coming battle. Nonessential advisers, such as clerks and logistics specialists, were evacuated, but all combat advisers—about thirty-five men—remained in Kontum. That commitment played well with the South Vietnamese. "We're afraid," said one young soldier, "but if the VC come here we're ready for them. We'll listen to the Americans. If they tell us to stay and fight, that's what we'll do." An adviser with a team of Montagnard special forces took the commitment even further. "If you've ever heard a Montagnard say 'You die, I die,' you know how we feel. No, we're not running out on them."[6]

Vann wanted to confine the dying to the enemy, but before that would be possible he had to come up with a new strategy. A quick look at the order of battle figures showed that his options were limited, however. Of the twenty-four battalions assigned to the 22d and 23d ARVN Divisions and the II Corps Ranger Command, ten were considered ineffective, including the entire 40th and 42d ARVN Regiments. Ten other battalions were considered "marginal"; only the 44th ARVN Regiment was at "an acceptable level of effectiveness."[7]

Part of the blame for the dismal statistics lay with Vann himself. He had staked much of his reputation on placement of the 22d ARVN Division in northern Kontum Province and had failed. Now he wanted Ba to take all the survivors from that debacle, along with one regiment of the 23d ARVN Division, one ranger group, and the remnants of the 1st Airborne Brigade, and defend Kontum, leaving the rest of the 23d ARVN Division in reserve. Vann did not want to risk the only remaining division in the Highlands on an all-or-nothing defense of Kontum.

Colonel Ba did not agree, arguing that this was a hodgepodge solution to a pressing problem. The airborne brigade was exhausted and demoralized from its losing battle on Rocket Ridge, and none of the units now in Kontum were capable of fighting together as a cohesive unit. It made more sense, Ba countered, to utilize the overall strength of the 23d ARVN Division as the core of Kontum's defense. The 23d ARVN Division was originally based 100 miles to the south in Ban Me Thuot, where it was the spear point of South Vietnam's defense of the southern highlands. As the offensive heated up in mid-April, Vann had convinced Dzu to shift one regiment to Kontum.

Vann knew Ba was right, but he hesitated. To commit the entire 23d ARVN Division to Kontum meant there would be nothing left to defend the rest of the Central Highlands if the city went the way of Tan Canh and Dak To. Ba assured him he could hold it. Vann had no choice, so he let the rangers and airborne go back to the general reserve (they were soon shifted to reinforce I Corps), and by 28 April most of the remaining two regiments of the 23d ARVN Division had been airlifted into Kontum. The last regiment, however, arrived on 12 May, only two days before the North Vietnamese struck Kontum.

As the bulk of the division was preparing to move to Kontum, Vann and Ba worked out the details of their plan. An outer defensive ring circled Kontum about four miles from the city center, and a single blocking force straddled Highway 14 two miles north of the defenses. Inside Kontum were forty-eight artillery pieces (only four of them 155mm howitzers), enough, Colonel Ba hoped, to allow the defenders to mass their fire at any single point along the perimeter. All South Vietnamese forces in Kontum Province would come under Ba's command, including four battalions of rangers drawn up in blocking positions across the Dak Poko River along the northern and western sectors of the city. The 53d ARVN Regiment would be the core of Kontum's defense and had responsibility for the eastern and southern sectors. The 22d Ranger Battalion moved to Polei Kleng, an isolated airstrip below the southern tip of Rocket Ridge, to reinforce border rangers already in position. The rangers would form the initial blocking force against enemy movement from the west.[8]

To make up for the loss of the firebases on Rocket Ridge, Vann targeted B-52 strikes in and around the evacuated positions. If the North Vietnamese planned to use Rocket Ridge, they would have to find new positions. Vann would have liked to have used more strikes, but thousands of refugees, missing American advisers, and remnants of the 22d ARVN Division prevented their indiscriminate use. Instead, Vann relied on pinpoint tactical air strikes. Because of the growing importance of the battle for the Central Highlands, Vann was given most of what he asked for. Between 24 and 26 April alone, over 180 sorties were flown.[9]

Since the initial loss in northern Kontum Province, Vann had stayed awake day and night to patch together a new defense. An overhauled command, shuffled units, and an infusion of American airpower quickly bolstered the South Vietnamese position in Kontum. But the main battle was not yet joined, and Vann realized that his dream of victory at the head of an army in battle might yet be dashed. He admitted his mistake in committing most of his strength at Tan Canh. Now there was nothing left to fall back on. "My credibility is at stake," he told Colonel Rhotenberry one day.[10]

Vann's doubts went much deeper than just his reputation, however. He also secretly cabled General Abrams and warned that the South Vietnamese collapse in northern Kontum could have deep repercussions throughout the region. "Given the state of the ARVN defenders after their defeats in April," Vann wrote, "I feel that there is a reasonable chance that the enemy will achieve his aims even though there are numerically sufficient troops in the area to prevent the loss of Kontum." It would be best, Vann continued, to prepare for the partial evacuation of Pleiku. Twenty-five hundred American advisers and support personnel remained in the city, and Vann suggested that they be moved out in a three-phase withdrawal. Even the outwardly optimistic Vann saw the possibility of defeat just around the corner.[11]

Another major problem needed a solution before Vann could concentrate all attention on defending Kontum. South Korean troops stationed near Qui Nhon on the coast were huddled in their defensive positions, refusing to venture forth to engage the enemy. Their role was vital in keeping open South Vietnamese supply lines to the Central Highlands.

South Korean soldiers had been part of the fighting in Vietnam since December 1964. Starved for international support for the American war effort, President Lyndon Johnson struggled to re-create the worldwide cooperation that had existed during the Korean War. Although the United Nations did not back the American commitment, the war in Vietnam became nominally international in scope. In response to President Johnson's call for "more flags," five nations—Australia, New Zealand, the Philippines, Thailand, and the Republic of Korea (ROK)—sent military personnel to South Vietnam, while dozens of others provided nonmilitary aid.

South Korea provided the largest commitment. By 1968 just over 50,000 South Korean soldiers, better known as ROKs, were stationed in South Vietnam. The first Korean contingent was an engineer construction support group sent to assist the South Vietnamese pacification effort by rebuilding war-damaged areas. In September 1965 the Capital Division, better known as the Tiger Division, deployed along the coast between Qui Nhon and Binh Khe in Binh Dinh Province. The 2d Marine Brigade—the Blue Dragons—arrived two months later at Cam Ranh Bay but quickly moved to Tuy Hoa in Phu Yen Province. In early 1966 the South Vietnamese government formally requested more troops from South Korea, a request that was quickly granted. In September 1966 the 9th Infantry Division (White Horse) marched into Ninh Hoa, Khanh Hoa Province, an important crossroads where Highways 1 and 21 intersected. All three regiments of the 9th Division would operate along the coast of southern II Corps, from northern Phu Yen Province to southern Ninh Thuan Province.

The Korean military position in South Vietnam was largely defensive. MACV commander General William Westmoreland reasoned that the use of Korean troops to guard major roads in II Corps made sense for two reasons. First, if they were thrown into combat and took heavy casualties immediately upon arrival, the South Korean government might begin calling for withdrawal. Second, Korean troops lacked air assets, heavy artillery, and resupply capabilities to sustain long operations. Thus the ROKs remained on the coast and mounted operations within their own areas of responsibility.[12]

Both friend and foe rated the ROK contingent highly. General Westmoreland ranked the soldiers as very efficient and on a par with U.S. troops. South Vietnamese commanders grudgingly praised them. Perhaps most important, the enemy agreed that Korean soldiers were not to be taken lightly. A captured Viet Cong document stated that "contact with the Koreans is to be avoided at all costs unless a [Viet Cong] victory is 100 percent certain." That was high praise indeed. But General Abrams best characterized Korean performance in Vietnam, diplomatically praising the ROKs while backhandedly pointing out their flaws. When asked by Vice President Spiro T. Agnew about Korean performance vis-à-vis the South Vietnamese, he replied: "The kind of war that we have here can be compared to an orchestra. It is sometimes appropriate to emphasize the drums, or the trumpet, or the bassoon, or even the flute. The Vietnamese, to a degree, realize this and do it. The Koreans on the other hand, play one instrument—the bass drum."[13]

Perhaps the greatest problem with Korean troops was their relationship with other friendly forces in South Vietnam. Attitudes of racial and cultural superiority, combined with natural aggressiveness and competitiveness, made the ROKs difficult to work with and sometimes resulted in potentially dangerous situations. Part of the Koreans' unruliness was born of frustration. By the time of the Easter Offensive the war was clearly winding down, but Korean troops were not being pulled out of Vietnam as quickly as American troops. At the close of 1971, there were still 45,700 ROK troops on the ground in South Vietnam. That represented a decrease of about 4,300 soldiers since the high point of Korean involvement in 1968. During the same period American troop strength had fallen from 536,000 to 158,120. By the end of 1972 there would actually be more

ROK troops than U.S. troops in South Vietnam: 36,790 Koreans to 24,000 Americans.[14]

The Koreans felt they were left holding the bag while the inexorable American drawdown continued, and they resented it. When the Easter Offensive opened, most Korean units shut themselves in their bases and refused to come out, the result of secret instructions from Seoul to avoid casualties. As the early fighting on the coast north of Qui Nhon threatened to cut off supplies moving up from Saigon, the Koreans ignored their responsibility to keep the roads open. On the morning of 13 April, South Vietnamese convoys began running into enemy small-arms fire on Highway 1 north of the Vung Ho Pass. A Korean regiment refused to provide protection to a Vietnamese repair crew on its way to move disabled trucks from the road. Only a personal request from Vann brought the Koreans out of their bunkers.

The main threat was in the An Khe Pass, a major choke point along Highway 19 in Binh Dinh Province that fell within the Koreans' area of responsibility. Two battalions from the 3d NVA Division—the Yellow Star—had moved into the An Khe Pass in mid-April, bringing resupply convoys to a virtual standstill. The fighting north of Kontum consumed more than 10,000 rounds of ammunition daily, not to mention fuel and general supplies. Keeping the fight going required around 200 truckloads of supplies per day. As long as the An Khe Pass was closed, the South Vietnamese were hard-pressed to keep up with the demand. While the Koreans sat, South Vietnamese troops and American advisers were forced to rely on aerial resupply and a long, precarious overland route from Nha Trang, which could also be severed at any moment.

On 13 April, after three days of planning, the ROKs made a halfhearted attempt to clear the pass but were turned back after losing three helicopters. Korean commanders complained continually that they did not have enough artillery, helicopters, trucks, or armor; according to the ROKs, everything was in short supply. Yet the Korean regimental commander seemed unconcerned with the battle progress; he reportedly did not leave his bunker during the entire operation.[15]

The following day a combined force of Koreans and South Vietnamese pushed toward the pass but were smashed back by a battalion of North Vietnamese. In the confusion, the ROKs accidentally fired on the South Vietnamese, killing four and wounding twenty. The Koreans fell back, calling on U.S. fighter and gunship support but refusing to use their own artillery in the interest of saving ammunition. Vann was exasperated by the Koreans' matériel pettiness and operational incompetence. "The ROKs appear to have no plan to clear the pass other than massive quantities of fire support," he reported to General Abrams.[16]

The MACV commander shared Vann's pessimism and reported to Washington that the An Khe Pass was unlikely to open anytime soon, "because of their [ROK] inflexibility and reluctance to become deeply involved in high threat areas." He hinted to Secretary of Defense Melvin Laird that official action at the highest levels might provoke action from the Koreans.[17]

But from his embattled position on the ground, Vann could not afford to wait for high-level diplomacy to take effect; instead, he tried some of his own. In a polite letter to Major General Kang Won Chae, commander of Korean troops in South Vietnam, Vann inquired as to when he could expect a Korean operation aimed at clearing the enemy from the pass. "Today marks the seventh straight day that the pass has been closed and this has resulted in an extremely critical supply situation in the Central Highlands," Vann wrote. "Highway 19 must be reopened soon and must be kept open. I cannot see the justification for continuing any other mission within the Tiger Division area than those which are related to the defense of the Korean installation, and to the opening of the An Khe Pass." Korean troops were making short forays from their strongholds during the day, but at nightfall they returned to safety behind the barbed wire. Vann considered the tactic useless. "The history of the enemy effort . . . has been one wherein ambushes are moved in during the hours of darkness," Vann observed. Fighting during the day was barely a nuisance to the North Vietnamese.[18]

The letter brought few results. An Khe Pass was still closed the next day, though Vann sarcastically noted that any movement was an improvement. "At least there is a little progress after six days," he wrote. But Vann resented this diversion from the more pressing problems in the Central Highlands, and his anger was compounded by the fact that the 44th ARVN Regiment, in the process of being transferred from the 22d ARVN Division to the 23d ARVN Division, was still on the wrong side of the An Khe Pass. Stationed in Binh Dinh Province, the 44th ARVN Regiment, considered one of the best units in the South Vietnamese army, was to form the backbone of Kontum's defense—if it could get through the pass. The 44th ARVN Regiment had originally been sent to Binh Dinh to replace another South Vietnamese regiment that had been withdrawn in disgrace. Prior to the enemy offensive, the Viet Cong and North Vietnamese sappers had managed to blow up a command post, a few bunkers, and some airplanes while all the guards slept. The 44th ARVN Regiment set up a temporary headquarters near an old airstrip formerly used by the 1st Cavalry Division. Part of an aviation company, including a handful of Cobra gunships, was all that remained of the massive American military presence.[19]

As enemy pressure on An Khe Pass came to a climax on 17 April, an American lieutenant colonel went to the Koreans and literally begged for help. A Korean colonel—who spoke English but refused to speak to a mere lieutenant colonel face-to-face—slowly spoke through his interpreter. Seeing that nothing fruitful was going to come from the discussion, the American adviser walked away.

That afternoon Vann flew to An Khe to personally break the impasse. His helicopter rushed overhead, then turned on its tail and hurtled for the ground. As was his way, Vann pulled up on the stick at the last second and settled the helicopter onto the center of the highway. Americans, Koreans, and South Vietnamese alike stared as Vann strode from the helicopter toward the Koreans, oblivious to the firing going on around him. The enemy had heard the chopper coming over the treetops and began shelling the road in anticipation of his landing. Most of the advisers prudently dove for the nearest ditch. The Korean colonel tried hard to imitate Vann's bluster by standing up straight in the face of mounting artillery fire, and under the circumstances he seemed to think it best to agree to all Vann said in the interests of getting the meeting over quickly.[20]

By itself, Vann's bravado on the highway probably did not persuade the Koreans to act, but the next day ROK units began moving out of their encampments toward enemy positions on the pass. Following up on his conversation with the Koreans, Vann fired off a cable to General Abrams explaining the lack of cooperation from the Koreans. After eight days of inactivity the Koreans were only just beginning to move against the North Vietnamese and open the pass. On 17 April, after seven American tactical air strikes against a key hill just south of Highway 19 at the top of the pass, two ROK companies were still hunkered down in their positions a mere 400 meters from the bombardment. They insisted on more strikes before assaulting the hill. Helicopter gunships rotored in and raked the enemy with rockets and minigun fire. Still no movement from the Koreans. General Dzu offered the use of a South Vietnamese armor unit west of the pass to pour direct fire into the North Vietnamese position. The Koreans knew they were losing face, so they reluctantly accepted the offer.

Vann quickly saw that part of the problem was the "extreme ineptness" of Korean artillery and an overreliance on U.S. air support. At one point the Korean generals demanded that Vann order American helicopters to resupply and medevac Korean soldiers holding a knoll near An Khe Pass. From a hill nearby, North Vietnamese troops poured machine-gun fire into the ROK position. The enemy had shot down three American helicopters the previous day and seriously damaged a fourth, but Vann promised to get the Korean soldiers out if the generals would pour suppressing artillery fire onto the enemy-held hill. The Koreans agreed.

Vann dashed into his Kiowa scout helicopter and darted along the treeline, flashing up over the besieged Korean soldiers, then repeating the stunt he had performed so spectacularly on Rocket Ridge a week before. As the helicopter hovered briefly, bundles of supplies were heaved out the door to outstretched hands below. The Koreans fired about ten artillery rounds into the North Vietnamese position, not enough to silence the antiaircraft guns, so the medevac had to be canceled.

Vann's move sparked the Koreans to action. To not respond to his fearless flight into the jaws of North Vietnamese guns on An Khe Pass would be a severe loss of face for the Koreans. They were forced to respond with offensive action of their own. On the evening of 18 April, Korean troops began to move against the North Vietnamese on An Khe Pass. "After eight days of the pass being closed, the ROKs finally came up with a tactical plan to move against the enemy and open the pass," wrote Vann in grudging acknowledgment of the Koreans' move.[21]

But optimism was premature. For the next ten days the Koreans got nowhere, and they even lost ground when a North Vietnamese company pushed them off a hill on the southwest side of the pass. An American liaison officer with the ROKs estimated that they suffered at least 100 casualties. General Lee, the Korean division commander, decided to reinforce his forces at the top of the pass and sweep down from the high ground. "This, of course, is what should have been done from the first day," commented Vann upon hearing the news. The Koreans claimed to have killed over 200 enemy soldiers, but there was no independent confirmation, and Vann doubted the body count's validity.[22]

Not until 27 April did the Koreans clear An Khe Pass. That morning the ROKs broke out their M113 armored personnel carriers—virtually unused during the offensive—and rumbled toward the enemy. Unfortunately, the infantry did not follow, and the North Vietnamese promptly knocked out two armored personnel carriers at point-blank range from positions along the roadside. The Americans were forced to divert scarce aviation assets from the Central Highlands to bolster the cautious Koreans, even though, in Vann's opinion, the obvious solution was to bring in Korean helicopters from areas away from the fighting. But the ROKs were unwilling to risk their own helicopters in battle, and the only way to get them to act was to lead the way.

Several of the armored vehicles were mounted with flamethrowers. They rumbled forward, stopping occasionally to spit forth long tongues of liquid orange flame. The enemy retreated quickly in the face of this concentrated assault. "The An Khe Pass is reported open, convoys plan to operate from Qui Nhon today," General John Hill, Vann's deputy, told Abrams. After sixteen days of fighting, the Koreans claimed to have killed 705 enemy soldiers—an unlikely total—with a loss of only 51 ROKs.

But the North Vietnamese had never intended to hold An Khe Pass, only to disrupt supplies to the Central Highlands. Their mission was accomplished.

EIGHTEEN

CRISIS AT KONTUM

The North Vietnamese army could smell victory. It had badly mauled the 22d ARVN Division around Tan Canh and Dak To, and Kontum seemed to lie well within grasp. But despite South Vietnamese military disarray around the city, geography hindered the enemy buildup and would become a key player in the coming battle.

Kontum was situated within a valley carved from the surrounding hills by the Dak Bla River, which flowed from Cambodia. Before attacking the city, North Vietnamese troops had to mass in the hills, under the watchful eyes of American reconnaissance aircraft. The results were deadly. In the week before the attack on Kontum, the U.S. Air Force unleashed its full power on the concentrated enemy troops. B-52 bombers and all the tactical air strikes that could be spared dumped their loads on the milling enemy.

John Paul Vann wielded the bombers like a sword, and the more strikes he was allotted, the more he wanted. As Vann lay down the patchwork defense of Kontum, he wove together an interlocking web of B-52 strike boxes. Traditionally the air force flew the B-52s single file down the box, but Vann wanted better bomb coverage. He convinced the air force to fly them in echelon, with the wingtips of the two outside planes brushing the sidelines of the box. That often meant bombs fell uncomfortably close to friendly troops. But Vann waved aside all objections, and many strikes fell well within the five-eighth-mile limit prescribed by the air force.[1]

On a map, strike boxes were drawn all around Kontum like scrambled pieces from a jigsaw puzzle. When the enemy walked into one, the coordinates were radioed back to Pleiku and then on to the air force. The B-52s dropped their bombs into the target box with uncanny accuracy, thanks to new technology and experience gained from long years of war in Vietnam. But the effect of the bombers was largely unknown because most South Vietnamese units had long since given up sending patrols out to survey the carnage caused by the bomb strikes. American advisers often wondered whether the strikes had hit anything but trees and rocks.

When he was not too busy plotting Arc Light boxes, Vann flew out to personally survey the damage. He would hover his helicopter just outside a scheduled Arc Light box and wait for the bombs to drop silently from the sky. When the smoke cleared, Vann would dart in and scan the tortured landscape for mangled body parts, sure signs that the strikes were effective. Just to be sure no one did survive, Vann would sometimes spray bullets from his M16 into bomb craters.[2]

B-52s became the lifeblood of Vann's defensive strategy. He once graphically described the deadly efficiency of the high-flying bombers: "Any time the wind is blowing from the north where the B-52 strikes are turning the terrain into a moonscape, you can tell from the battlefield stench that the strikes are effective. Outside Kontum, wherever you dropped bombs, you scattered bodies."[3]

North Vietnamese timing was also a factor in Vann's ability to effectively play his B-52 card. The enemy waited three weeks from the time Tan Canh fell until they were in position around Kontum. By 14 May, when the first serious assault against Kontum began, the worst of the fighting in I Corps and III Corps was over, and a majority of the B-52s were free to concentrate on the Central Highlands. The result was devastating for the North Vietnamese. After laboriously moving forty or fifty T-54 tanks down the Ho Chi Minh Trail, they were only able to bring a dozen or so to bear on Kontum. In addition, countless hundreds of soldiers died in the rain of bombs without ever firing a shot at the South Vietnamese troops defending Kontum.

Although Vann was not certain of the damage wrought by his bombers, he knew it must be heavy. "The success of many of these strikes is unquestioned," Vann told General Abrams. "Those of the past week have been the most lucrative I've seen in the past six years." Limited patrolling turned up mass graves of North Vietnamese dead, and one ranger squad discovered ninety-two bodies inside a strike box northwest of Kontum.[4]

Vann fully believed that B-52s would win the coming battle for him. In his opinion, the conventional tactics currently used by the enemy represented Hanoi's weakness, not the final rung on Mao's ladder of successful revolutionary warfare. To Vann, the North Vietnamese had lost the war in 1968 during their ill-conceived Tet Offensive, and now they were forced to try and overwhelm Saigon with conventional force. The B-52s were Vann's answer to Hanoi's strategy. "Kontum will break the back of the North Vietnamese army," he predicted as he continued to plot strike boxes. "In six months there will be no more North Vietnamese army left."[5]

As Vann manipulated the B-52s, the infantry shuffle continued. The South Vietnamese corps command—with Vann's encouragement—formally decided to stand and fight at Kontum, using Colonel Ba and the 23d ARVN Division as the defensive backbone. For his part, Ba had managed to cobble together a defense for Kontum despite the fact that the Joint General

North Vietnamese soldiers ride a tank into position before the battle for Kontum. (Author's collection)

Staff had taken most of his reserves to bolster the worsening situation in I Corps. By the end of April, Quang Tri was in danger of falling, but the real North Vietnamese prize—the old imperial city of Hue—was still sufficiently safe to allow some of the reserves to return to II Corps. The 6th Ranger Group, still weary from heavy action outside Hue, arrived at Firebase Bravo just north of Vo Dinh to reinforce the airborne brigade. The next day the rangers were hustled aboard trucks and moved to Firebase Lam Son, just north of Kontum, and the airborne brigade moved back to Saigon to rejoin the general reserve.[6]

Major James Givens, the senior adviser to the 6th Ranger Group, was in a perfect position to watch the North Vietnamese close in on Kontum. Firebase Lam Son sat on a long, high ridge with a commanding view of Highway 14 north of Vo Dinh. To the south Givens could see the northern outskirts of Kontum. From his bunker he had listened to the fall of Tan Canh on the radio, hearing the cries for help from fellow American advisers, most of whom he had never met. But the anger and frustration were still there. His comrades were fighting and dying, yet there was nothing he could do. Givens also watched as remnants of the 22d ARVN Division straggled south toward Kontum, most of them with no weapons. He noted there was not a single crew-served weapon in the entire procession. Captain William H. J. Vannie, the deputy senior adviser, later observed that the retreating South Vietnamese showed no signs of panic; they simply walked along in groups of five to fifteen, like "Sunday strollers."[7]

By 27 April Firebase Lam Son was taking increasingly heavy shelling. There were few casualties, but the North Vietnamese gunners had the range—several rounds slammed directly into the command post. Although the base was not in any immediate danger, Colonel Ba decided to make the 6th Ranger Group part of Kontum's defense. The American advisers and the ranger command element were airlifted to Firebase November while the combat elements remained at Lam Son. Major Givens felt the move was poorly conceived, and he made his objections well known. The command unit was needed where the action was at the moment, not in Kontum.

The two remaining ranger battalions slowly unraveled under the unceasing artillery pounding. At 5:00 on the morning of 1 May, four M41 tank crews abandoned their positions just outside the firebase perimeter, leaving their vehicles to the enemy. A South Vietnamese officer was alert enough to call an air strike on the abandoned tanks before they could be driven off. South Vietnamese fighter planes and an American AC-130 gunship plastered the sitting tanks with bullets and ordnance until there was nothing left for the enemy to use.

By evening the artillery units were abandoning their guns and trying to break out of Firebase Lam Son. Major Givens asked his counterpart, Lieutenant Colonel De, what was happening, only to be told that there had been no contact with the besieged base. Givens later discovered that De had ordered his two infantry battalions to withdraw. Since the artillery was not part of his ranger group, De felt no responsibility to even notify it of what he planned. When the artillerymen discovered that they had been left alone without even minimal infantry protection, they abandoned their guns and fled.

Here was a clear example of the difficulties facing the field commanders. Few of the units involved in the defense of Kontum had any command relationship with the others. Therefore, they felt no responsibility to support or even consult each other about tactics. This time, however, General Dzu was outraged enough to take action. On 4 May he relieved Lieutenant Colonel De for incompetence.

John Paul Vann also stepped in to put a stop to bickering within the chain of command. He convinced Dzu to bring the two remaining units of the 23d ARVN Division—the 44th and 45th ARVN Regiments—into Kontum to replace the 6th Ranger Group. The move involved some precarious troop shuffling, but if it worked, Kontum's defense would be stronger. Unfortunately, the two regiments were at the far corners of II Corps, the 44th ARVN Regiment in Ba Gi in Binh Dinh Province near the coast, the 45th ARVN Regiment to the south in Pleiku. Moving either unit was risky. Binh Dinh Province was still in danger of being overrun by the 3d NVA Division, and removing the 45th ARVN Regiment from Pleiku left II Corps' southern flank less protected. Although Dzu was reluctant to take the risk, Vann persuaded him that Kontum was the real target. If the enemy troops could be forced to mass, they could be held and destroyed with B-52s and an infantry counterattack. Of course, Vann had also used this reasoning in his decision to defend Tan Canh.[8]

Despite pressure from B-52s, enemy artillery stepped up the bombardment of ranger camps north and west of Kontum during the first week of May. Two isolated firebases, Ben Het and Polei Kleng, bore the brunt of the shelling because they sat astride North Vietnamese supply routes and troop assembly areas. By noon on 6 May over fifty rounds per hour were falling inside Polei Kleng before concentrated U.S. air strikes drowned out the bombardment. Forward air controllers circling high above the firebase fired phosphorus rockets into enemy artillery positions, marking the spot for fighter planes roaring in from the east. At about 3:15 P.M. the little spotter planes left their stations, convinced that the enemy had been subdued. Within moments after their departure the shelling resumed, and by nightfall another 500 rounds had pounded Polei Kleng.

Two American advisers inside the firebase had directed the air strikes from the ground. Captain Geddes McLaren and Lieutenant Paul McKenna called enemy artillery positions up to the FACs and watched with satisfaction as bombs dropped with uncanny accuracy and silenced the gunners. But neither man was foolish enough to think the North Vietnamese were going to pull back and go home. Less than two hours after the air controllers and fighters returned to the base, the artillery began anew. Most of the rounds landed within a few yards of the command bunker; a few were direct hits. One round collapsed the walls and blew out the heavy wooden door. Smoke, dust, and debris showered down on the stunned men, but most survived the blast.

McLaren and McKenna dug their way free of the rubble and stumbled to the top of the destroyed bunker. Crawling across the open ground under the continuing bombardment, the two Americans scrambled into open foxholes near the perimeter wire. It seemed safer there because the North Vietnamese had obviously targeted the command bunker and were dropping most rounds right on top of it.

South Vietnamese artillery fires back at the enemy as the North Vietnamese close in on Kontum. (Jack Finch)

Within minutes everything above ground level was pounded into rubble. Buildings, bunkers, and radio antennae were all destroyed as eagle-eyed enemy forward observers relayed targets back to the artillery positions. Demoralized rangers cowered in their foxholes, afraid to move in the face of the accurate shelling. Lieutenant McKenna left the dubious safety of his foxhole to search for the ranger commander, only to find that he had managed to flee the compound.

Dodging and crawling back to the foxhole, McKenna noticed brief flashes of red light beyond the perimeter. With a sinking feeling, he realized they came from North Vietnamese officers, who were signaling their men to prepare for an infantry assault.

Rescue came just in time. At 7:00 P.M. an OH-6 light helicopter darted through the enemy antiaircraft ring and touched down inside Polei Kleng. McLaren and McKenna scrambled aboard, and the helicopter rushed back into the sky and away from the tightening North Vietnamese noose. The news they brought with them was grim: the ranger commander and his deputy were so incapacitated by fear that he could not exercise command.[9]

The rangers held out for three more days. B-52 bombs blanketed the ground outside Polei Kleng's perimeter as enemy troops massed for the final attack. Sixteen Arc Light strikes made the capture of the little firebase an expensive undertaking for the North Vietnamese. One dazed enemy prisoner later attested to the accuracy of the bombers, telling his captors that his company of about 100 had lost over 40 men, with many more wounded.[10]

Before dawn on 9 May, however, Polei Kleng fell as a wave of North Vietnamese tanks and infantry swarmed over the base. General Dzu flew over the area, reassuring the defenders at other small bases that the worst was over. He then reluctantly declared the entire area around Polei Kleng a free-fire zone and carpeted the fallen base with artillery fire and air strikes. He could only hope that the survivors of the enemy assault had managed to make their way to safety before friendly shells and bombs began to rain down.

At nearby Ben Het ranger camp, the scenario was much the same. Hundreds of artillery rounds rained down on the huddled soldiers as the North Vietnamese softened up their victim for an all-out assault. Some of the rangers cracked almost immediately. On 7 May the 71st Ranger Battalion mutinied, demanding that the commander order the unit's extraction within forty-eight hours. The revolt came too late. Although the commander gave in to the rangers' demands and began the evacuation, the North Vietnamese put a stop to it all by tightening their antiaircraft ring around the camp.

At dawn on 9 May the South Vietnamese were greeted with an unusual sound. Exhausted after three sleepless nights in fetid foxholes, some of the soldiers thought the noise was a figment of overwrought imaginations. Yet there it was: yelping dogs, dozens of them. The North Vietnamese had turned them loose to trip mines and booby traps set around the perimeter. A few went off, and an hour later the enemy launched an all-out assault spearheaded by eight PT-76 light tanks. Though not as deadly as the big T-54s, the PT-76 still managed to strike fear in the hearts of many South Vietnamese soldiers. Advisers reminded them over and over that the thin-skinned amphibious fighting vehicle could be pierced by well-placed heavy machine-gun bullets, and an M72 LAW would turn the little tank into an inferno.[11]

Two PT-76s supported by a couple squads of infantry headed straight for the main gate. Two alert rangers popped out of foxholes and fired off two LAWs, striking both tanks. The flaming PT-76s groaned to a halt, guns silent. The supporting infantry milled about behind the stricken vehicles, not certain what to do. Other rangers opened fire, killing or scattering the North Vietnamese.

After a short rest of about half an hour, the enemy tried again, this time attacking the camp's east perimeter. Five PT-76s followed by infantry crashed into the wire, flattening the defenses and sending the rangers running to new positions. Two tanks were knocked out, but the North Vietnamese settled into foxholes and trenches abandoned by the rangers. The three surviving PT-76s scurried back to their original staging area, out of LAW range. Seeing the tanks retreat emboldened the rangers, who threw all their dwindling strength against the enemy soldiers entrenched inside the wire. By midafternoon they had killed most of them; only a few survivors escaped. The attackers lost over 100 soldiers and most of their tanks in the failed assault. Although the North Vietnamese continued to shell Ben Het and probe the defenses with small infantry attacks, they were unable to mass a force sufficient to drive the rangers out of the camp. Ben Het held out for the remainder of the offensive, a tiny speck of South Vietnamese control in an ever-widening blanket of communist victories.

The North Vietnamese were also active south of Kontum, holding out the possibility of a major attack at Pleiku. It made little sense to strike so far down Highway 14 without first eliminating Kontum, but Vann could not assume it was only a feint. About five kilometers north of Pleiku sat Firebase 42, a tiny outpost next to Highway 14. As firebases go it was nothing special, just four 105mm howitzers and a half dozen heavy mortars. Before the offensive, Firebase 42 had been the regimental headquarters for the 44th ARVN Regiment, along with some elements of the 45th ARVN Regiment. Now the 2d Airborne Battalion, recently pulled out of Kontum, occupied the firebase and prepared to open the road north of Pleiku.

On the night of 5 May the enemy began to shell Firebase 42. Just after midnight on 6 May, the North Vietnamese began the assault. But instead of firing with everything they had and advancing straight at the firebase, they sneaked in silently through the barbed wire and minefields. The South Vietnamese defenders suspected nothing until explosives began going off inside the perimeter. The airborne commander called in heavy artillery support from Pleiku, and a Spectre gunship appeared overhead. But the sappers had made it in, and they headed straight for the command bunker, placing charges all around it. The bunker went up in flames—but no one was inside. The South Vietnamese had moved the staff to another bunker a few nights previously. Lives were saved, but the attack destroyed all four of the defenders' howitzers, along with a number of trucks and machine-gun emplacements.[12]

Fighting went on for five hours before the North Vietnamese were repulsed. But the damage was done. A handful of sappers had continued to draw attention from the brewing battle in Kontum by stepping up pressure on Pleiku. With a small manpower and supply investment, the enemy managed to keep Highway 14 between Pleiku and Kontum closed to major traffic, although Firebase 42 remained in South Vietnamese control. By striking at a wide range of targets in II Corps, the North Vietnamese ensured that the South Vietnamese would defend along an extended front. The enemy still called the shots.

During the first week in May, enemy artillery began shelling the center of Kontum, a barbaric tactic considering that only civilians were in the city. The 23d ARVN Division was dug in around the outskirts. When Dak To fell on 24 April, civilians and routed South Vietnamese soldiers clogged Highway 14 as they fled south. But Kontum was not safe either, and the city soon became a milling mass of panicked humanity seeking a way farther south to Pleiku.

Among the hardest hit were the Montagnards, primitive ethnic minorities caught between communist strong-arm tactics and age-old discrimination by the Vietnamese in general. Seeking peace and the freedom to continue their way of life, the Montagnards clung to the mountains of the Central Highlands, living by hunting and subsistence farming. The Easter Offensive magnified their problems with deadly intensity. As North Vietnamese tanks ground their homelands under steel treads and communist political cadre tried to organize their villages into Marxist camps, the Montagnards found themselves with nowhere to turn. The South Vietnamese were unsympathetic to their plight, and now American B-52s were raining bombs on their villages. Entire tribes abandoned their traditional territories, fleeing down Highway 14 carrying baskets packed with their few possessions.

Kek, a young Sedang tribal leader from Kon Horing, a village north of Kontum, led his people south only to be told that North Vietnamese tanks blocked the way. Many of Kek's people chose to stay in their familiar village rather than risk the wrath of the North Vietnamese. That night Kek heard the dreadful thunder of a B-52 strike in the vicinity of Kon Horing. When he reached the village the next day, he found it completely demolished, the wreckage splattered with the mangled bodies of his people. Kek sadly left for Kontum, only to find that the city was not much safer than the countryside.

Kek was just one of hundreds of Montagnards stuck in Kontum as the North Vietnamese began shelling the city. Rumors that the American advisers were about to flee the city set off waves of panic, but in reality only "nonessential" MACV personnel and pacification officials were leaving. As the staff left their command compound on the north edge of town, South Vietnamese soldiers burst in and threatened the Americans. Bald-faced bluffing and a few brandished rifles prevented violence as the Americans retreated to the airstrip. Angry at being deserted and looking for revenge, the soldiers looted the compound and some surrounding houses, taking everything of value. An American official who remained behind witnessed their depredations:

> The soldiers ran around the abandoned buildings looting hi-fi sets and other possessions left behind. They drank all of the alcohol in the abandoned clubs, then vomited everywhere and went on a rampage of destruction, smashing everything in sight. As the last of Kontum's officials and police left, soldiers began looting the downtown and shuttered houses.[13]

Mutiny was the exception, however. Most South Vietnamese soldiers were reassured by Vann's decision to keep a "hard core" of advisers inside the besieged city to share the fighting. The Americans "would stay with them [the South Vietnamese] to the last in the defense of Kontum City," promised Vann, though he warned that if their counterparts left, the advisers would be immediately evacuated.[14]

Civilians were not expected to remain behind, however, and people fled to the airstrip and to the sports stadium, where helicopters occasionally landed, all the while looking frantically skyward for salvation. Even the medical staff at the hospital fled, leaving patients to fend for themselves. Many made it out of Kontum, though not all. Military sources reported that by late April 10,000 people had been taken south by plane, helicopter, or truck. Typically, the Americans ran most of the evacuation while South Vietnamese corruption hampered the entire operation. Journalists reported that South Vietnamese air force helicopter pilots were charging $240 a head for the twenty-minute trip south to Pleiku.[15]

Despite extortion from some South Vietnamese helicopter pilots, the evacuation continued. Civilian trucks filled with refugees jammed the roads heading south to Pleiku, but as often as not they would be back again by nightfall, their drivers grim-faced. "Beaucoup VC, no can do Pleiku," one said sadly.

The plight of South Vietnamese refugees was heartrending. American advisers, especially those who had formed close ties with their units, tried to do what they could to get families out of the threatened city. One adviser brought a truck into Kontum to evacuate the families of some of his soldiers. People from all over came forward to get on the truck, but the adviser told

A South Vietnamese soldier (right) and a U.S. Air Force officer help an old woman board a waiting C-130 aircraft for evacuation. (U.S. Air Force)

them that only the soldiers' immediate families could be evacuated. He pulled a few small boys, crying, from the truck. "Tell them I'd like to take them all out," the American emotionally told an interpreter, "but I can't.... I wish I could take them all out. Come on, let's get out of here. I feel sick."[16]

Vann was also concerned, but he kept the faith as the enemy closed in. On the morning of 2 May, Vann and Ba flew from besieged Kontum to SRAG headquarters in Pleiku, where Vann persuaded General Dzu to allow a personal pep talk to his commanders. Exuding confidence, Vann emphasized that the South Vietnamese had the strength not only to hold Kontum but also to destroy the attacking enemy forces. "The overall reaction to this talk appeared to be good," Vann later told General Abrams. "For the first time, all commanders, including Dzu, were smiling." Vann's confidence was based on more than just happy faces, however. As he left to go back to Kontum and the brewing battle, Vann noticed that "there was an air of cohesiveness and cooperation" within the South Vietnamese chain of command.[17]

NINETEEN

TIGHTENING
THE NOOSE

Despite the North Vietnamese buildup around Kontum, Colonel Ba remained among his soldiers, eschewing the bunker mentality demonstrated by so many of his South Vietnamese military colleagues. He personally walked the entire perimeter, talking to the troops, criticizing weak positions, and praising good work. Ba was particularly concerned about the presence of enemy tanks. He was well aware of the devastating effect their appearance had on soldiers in Tan Canh, and he took steps to ensure his men would not be cowed. Old tank hulks were dragged into positions outside town, and soldiers took turns firing LAWs into them. After hearing the explosions and seeing huge holes blown out of the sides and turrets, the South Vietnamese began to realize that the steel monsters were not invincible. Colonel Ba also reinforced their confidence by passing around photographs of victorious South Vietnamese soldiers posing beside destroyed T-54s in An Loc. The battle down in III Corps was largely over by this time, and many of the enemy's tanks lay broken and burned, mute testimony to their ultimate vulnerability.

To further reinforce the point that the North Vietnamese could be defeated, Major General James Hollingsworth, the senior adviser in III Corps, flew up to Pleiku to share his experiences from the An Loc siege with the SRAG staff. Although An Loc was still in very real danger, it had already survived several major North Vietnamese assaults and appeared to be holding. Vann was grateful for Hollingsworth's visit because it showed both the South Vietnamese and the Americans in the Central Highlands that they were not alone in the struggle. "I very much appreciate the valuable information provided to us by your staff," Vann wrote in a letter to Hollingsworth. "Continue to give them hell there, and we'll do our best to do the same here. I am confident of the final results."[1]

Not completely confident, however. Dzu's virtual paralysis following the fall of Tan Canh and Dak To still cast a pall over the entire strategic situation, and it worried Vann. "General Dzu flashes hot and cold, leaping from pits of depression to peaks of joy over relatively minor matters," observed

Vann, who doubted his own ability to continue buttressing Dzu's flagging spirits. To limit damage to morale, he saw to it that Dzu was isolated from his field commanders as well as from the American advisers. Vann kept only his superiors at MACV apprised of the troubling developments. "General Dzu complained that he is being set up by the president to serve as the fall guy when and if Kontum falls," Vann secretly wrote to Abrams. But the corps commander's fears went even deeper. During frank conversations with Vann, Dzu revealed that he expected to be court-martialed by Thieu as a means of deflecting attention from the national government and placing blame on the corps commanders. After all, the president had done just that in I Corps after the fall of Quang Tri. Displaying what Vann called "an overall despair of a beaten and betrayed man," Dzu increasingly grasped at face-saving ploys in an attempt to salvage what he could of his honor. Believing that he could limit his punishment by getting out of the battle, Dzu tried to get relieved so he could be blamed only for the loss of Tan Canh and Dak To. Pleading illness, Dzu asked to be called to Saigon. Vann agreed that the political maneuvering going on at the highest levels of military command was counterproductive and that it was up to Thieu to quickly solve the problem. "I believe the president needs to either get quite solidly behind him [Dzu] or to relieve him ASAP," recommended Vann. Until such a time, however, Vann intended to "continue supporting Dzu to the hilt."[2]

President Thieu had already been looking for Dzu's replacement. He contacted a handful of senior South Vietnamese generals and asked if they would accept the "promotion," but the situation in II Corps looked bleak, and none wanted to take over a losing battle. Not until 10 May was Dzu officially replaced.

The man chosen to fill the breech was Major General Nguyen Van Toan, an armor commander serving as assistant operations commander in I Corps. Toan had fallen under the same cloud of disgrace as his boss, Lieutenant General Hoang Xuan Lam, who was largely to blame for the fall of Quang Tri Province on 1 May. He had little choice but to accept the command. A large man known for his impulsive laughter, Toan was one of South Vietnam's most undistinguished senior officers. Toan first came to reporters' attention as a division commander when he was investigated by Saigon's feeble anticorruption inspectorate for shady dealings in the cinnamon business. In 1965 Toan was relieved of command when his retreating armor unit killed some two dozen South Vietnamese rangers in Quang Tri Province. Toan was able to return to favor when the officer who had relieved him, General Nguyen Chanh Thi, was exiled for his unpopular political views. Although he now found himself in a difficult situation, Toan was still close to the powers in Saigon. He quickly moved in to his new headquarters in Pleiku, bringing in plush furniture and draping military flags along the walls.[3]

Vann approved of the choice. Toan allowed Vann and Ba the latitude to shuffle troops without bureaucratic interference. All Toan cared about was results. Forced into the position by President Thieu, Toan knew that his career was over if Kontum was lost, so anything Vann and Ba could do to save the city was welcome. His first act as commander of II Corps was to ask Vann to accompany him on a tour of Kontum, a dangerous undertaking considering that the North Vietnamese were closing in. Dzu had flown into Kontum only rarely. Toan and Vann heard a briefing from Colonel Ba, after which Toan suggested that they stay in the city overnight—"for morale purposes."[4]

With Toan's encouragement, Ba streamlined infantry command and control. A problem plaguing most South Vietnamese units was lack of artillery support. The guns were there, but artillery commanders were often reluctant to lend adequate support to the infantry. Under Ba's orders, patrols—mostly South Vietnamese rangers—roamed out to the end of the artillery fan looking for enemy positions. Many missions resulted in timely intelligence that translated into devastating B-52 strikes.

The feverish preparation was still not proceeding fast enough to satisfy John Paul Vann. Enemy units were closing in, yet some South Vietnamese units were still not in place. On 12 May, a mere two days before the first all-out assault on Kontum, the last of Ba's division moved into position astride Highway 14 about three miles northwest of the city. The soldiers were confident as they settled into foxholes and bunkers.

The 53d ARVN Regiment, in place for a few weeks, defended the airfield northeast of the city. Northwest of Kontum, just a mile or so north of the Dak Bla River, the 45th ARVN Regiment held the left flank. Center stage went to the 44th ARVN Regiment, one of the best infantry units in the South Vietnamese army. It would take the brunt of the enemy attack. Regional and Popular Forces militiamen guarded the southern approaches to Kontum along the Dak Bla River, the least likely avenue of attack.[5]

Colonel Jack Truby, the division senior adviser, had been down to review the militia defensive positions the previous day. He returned to the bunker hoping with all his heart that the North Vietnamese would not do the unexpected and attack from the south. The militia, known as "Ruff-Puffs" to the Americans, had done little to prepare for the assault. Instead of deep foxholes the Ruff-Puffs had scooped shallow depressions in the ground, barely deep enough to conceal a man from infantry fire, let alone tanks. Worse, the Ruff-Puffs' attention was not fully on the coming battle. Concerned for their families, who lived in the area, the militiamen had brought them to the front lines. Their welfare was much more important than maintaining proper military defensive positions. All Truby could do was radio the province chief and ask him to tighten up the discipline. He had no illusions about the chances that anything would change on the southern perimeter, however.[6]

New enemy movement to the north quickly overshadowed Truby's concern for the Ruff-Puffs. The North Vietnamese had long since thrown aside secrecy and stealth. Masses of infantry and armor moved into final staging areas, braving U.S. air strikes as they prepared for the final assault. At 7:00 on the morning of 13 May, American advisers in the command bunker were besieged by enemy radio messages from North Vietnamese officers to units in the field.

There was no guesswork left—the attack would clearly come the next morning. But in many ways the buildup had been out of character. North Vietnamese units had tried to encircle Kontum, which was standard procedure, but there had been no heavy artillery bombardment. Vann was surprised enough by the lack of shelling to initially question his advisers' prediction of an attack the following morning. But the B-52s had taken their toll, and North Vietnamese commanders probably felt that to delay longer was to risk destruction from the air. Besides, much of the enemy's artillery had likely been destroyed during the weeks of air strikes. A few South Vietnamese units had been subjected to sporadic barrages, but they were nothing compared with the blasting taken by the 22d ARVN Division at Tan Canh.

With hindsight we know that the North Vietnamese hesitated because they had overestimated the South Vietnamese defenses and lacked confidence in their own offensive preparations. "[South Vietnamese] troops in Cong Tum [Kontum] were encircled, their roads cut," said an official report. But despite this advantage, North Vietnamese planners were concerned about the "numerous solid interconnected fortifications" in the town itself. "The enemy in the city was in dire straits, but not yet exhausted; for this reason, conditions for a breakthrough were not yet ripe" was the conclusion. Clearly the North Vietnamese believed that Kontum would be a harder nut to crack than Tan Canh.[7]

All trepidation aside, the battle was clearly coming. Shortly before midnight one battalion from the 44th ARVN Regiment near Firebase November reported lights moving south along Highway 14 directly toward their position. That might mean the enemy was still moving supplies to the front, an indication that the attack would not come in the morning. Perhaps Vann

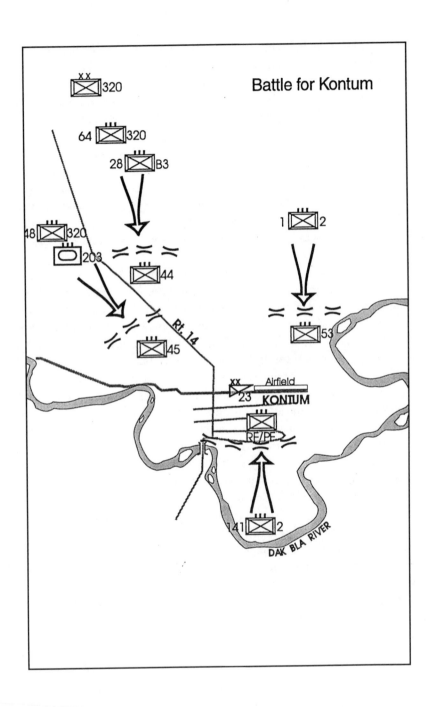

had been correct. But less than an hour later the battalion reported that the lights were from tanks, not trucks. Colonel Truby and the advisers huddled in the bunker were incredulous. The North Vietnamese were so inexperienced at moving tanks in the dark that they had risked destruction by turning on their lights to see the way.

Colonel Ba provided another bit of bad news. He ducked into the 23d ARVN Division command bunker waving a piece of paper. It was a message captured during a patrol that afternoon. The 320th NVA Division artillery commander had ordered all his guns to support an infantry assault beginning at 4:00 the next morning, 14 May. Colonel Truby sent word back to Pleiku, but Vann remained skeptical. Still, all available U.S. attack aircraft were laid on for missions at first light, and Abrams gave his approval to Vann's plan to use most of the B-52s for one twenty-four-hour period.

The predicted time of attack came and went. South Vietnamese soldiers nervously clutched rifles and peered into the darkness from sandbagged positions. American advisers prayed that Vietnamization was working and the soldiers would hold. There was no place to go if they did not, and the collapse of Tan Canh was on everyone's mind.

Suddenly Lieutenant Colonel Tieu, the division intelligence officer, rushed into the command bunker with word that new intelligence predicted the attack would be delayed for half an hour. Tieu's intelligence was precise—at exactly 4:30 A.M., North Vietnamese artillery opened up north of Kontum. The pounding continued for one hour, and then the attack began.[8]

John Paul Vann had been wrong. The enemy was acting contrary to standard procedure by neglecting the heavy use of artillery before an infantry assault. The conquest of Tan Canh had been so easy that North Vietnamese commanders apparently decided to forgo the customary artillery preparation and go straight for Kontum's heart. The three weeks that had elapsed between the fall of Tan Canh and the attack on Kontum probably also played a part in the decision. While the North Vietnamese waited, effective air strikes had taken a heavy toll on artillery batteries, and communist morale dropped dangerously. Another success was needed to bolster their spirits.

The enemy advanced down three main avenues. The 320th NVA Division rushed the 48th NVA Regiment, plus one company from the 203d Tank Regiment, down the west side of Highway 14. The 64th NVA Regiment, along with a second company from the 203d Tank Regiment, stormed south along the flatlands west of Route 58. Coming straight out of the north was the 28th NVA Regiment, an independent unit attached to the B-3 Front. The 141st NVA Regiment, part of the 2d NVA Division, probed the Ruff-Puffs south of the city.

South Vietnamese units braced for the impact. The B-52s were not yet over Kontum when the North Vietnamese hit the defenses north of the city, so Colonel Truby called the corps operations center at Pleiku for all the tactical air support he could get. Vann reacted by sending out a new weapon just sent over from the States—UH-1B helicopters mounted with TOW antitank rockets. TOW stood for tube-launched, optically tracked, and wire-guided, a new technology capable of steering missiles unerringly into tanks no matter where they tried to hide. Attached to the sight mechanism by a thin wire, the missile would fly to the target as long as the sight was locked on by the gunner. Basically, wherever the gunner looked, the missile flew. Three TOW helicopters, complete with mechanics and hardware, had arrived in the Central Highlands in late April. Each TOW ship was usually supported by two Cobra gunships, which suppressed antiaircraft fire while the TOWs went about their work. TOWs had been used to some extent in I Corps and III Corps, but they would get a real test from the helicopters flying toward Kontum. By the end of the offensive, TOWs were credited with forty-seven kills, twenty-four of them on tanks (only ten of which were T-54s). The rest were trucks, artillery and machine-gun emplacements, and bunkers. Considering their limited numbers, the results were good. Of eighty-five TOWs fired in combat, only ten were counted as misses. In the final analysis TOWs did not influence the tide of battle. There were not enough of them, and no American commander wanted to risk losing any to the enemy. They were morale boosters that showed up on the battlefield whenever events looked darkest.[9]

Artillery deserved the real credit for breaking the North Vietnamese attack, however. The South Vietnamese artillery commander, a graduate of the U.S. Army artillery school at Fort Sill, Oklahoma, had prepared his batteries by the book. When Colonel Ba and Truby asked if he could lay on concentrations of fire along the main avenue of enemy approach, the artilleryman answered, "Just tell me when and where you want it."[10]

He was true to his word. When North Vietnamese tanks came rumbling down Highway 14 on the morning of 14 May, they ran into a wall of death dropped down by the South Vietnamese. Enemy infantry, trying to support the onrushing armor, was forced to flee or die beneath the deadly barrage. It was the heaviest concentration of effective artillery fire put down during the Easter Offensive by any South Vietnamese unit in II Corps.

The lone tanks soon became easy prey for South Vietnamese tank-killer teams. Soldiers from the 44th ARVN Regiment initially cringed in their bunkers when the T-54s clanked into sight on the highway. The steel monsters seemed unearthly as they emerged from the wall of smoke and debris thrown up by the South Vietnamese barrage. But the ones that made it through the artillery curtain threatened to crash through the 44th ARVN Regiment's defenses and push on into Kontum. At first only a few soldiers rushed out of their holes to confront the tanks; more followed as they saw how effective the LAWs were at point-blank range. Within minutes two tanks had been killed, their carcasses burning in the half-light of early morning.[11]

As the North Vietnamese armor began to falter, more TOW helicopters swooped from the sky. One pilot spotted two T-54s moving across a stream just northwest of Kontum. A tank sat in the middle of the stream—a sitting duck—while the other prepared to enter the water. The pilot reported the sighting and rolled in for the kill. A thousand feet above, the pilot locked his optical sight on target and released the TOW missile. Trailing a thin wire thread, the rocket streaked earthward, striking the tank beneath the turret with a flash of flame and smoke. Another helicopter reported that the crew of the second tank was pouring from the hatches, hoping to abandon the vehicle before another TOW missile found its mark.[12]

Despite heavy artillery and air support, many enemy soldiers managed to close with Kontum's forward defense. Fierce hand-to-hand fighting raged up and down the front line as the North Vietnamese tried to "hug" South Vietnamese positions in an attempt to escape the murderous aerial bombardment. As the enemy began to consolidate, other units moved forward to reinforce the new positions.

At 10:00 P.M. another major assault against the 44th and 53d ARVN Regiments threatened to break through. In the confusion caused by darkness the two regiments failed to coordinate interlocking fields of fire, and a North Vietnamese battalion quickly punched a hole between the 44th and 53d ARVN Regiments. Suddenly things looked grim.

The senior adviser to the 44th ARVN Regiment, Lieutenant Colonel Thomas McKenna, had good reason to worry. The North Vietnamese had managed to pierce Kontum's northern defenses, threatening to cut off two South Vietnamese regiments. As bullets flew and artillery boomed in the background, McKenna and his deputy adviser, Major Wade Lovings, sat huddled in a foxhole wondering what would happen next.

"Do you think they're going to hold?" Major Lovings asked as he stared off into the darkness, seeing nothing, yet hearing the sounds of battle close by.

"I don't know, Wade. I just don't know," replied McKenna as he brushed dirt from his rifle.

An unspoken understanding suddenly passed between the two men. If the South Vietnamese did not hold, they had to have a plan to get out on their own. They had both walked the line with their counterparts, checking foxholes and gun emplacements to make sure the soldiers were ready. Everyone said the 44th ARVN Regiment was one of the best units in the army, but the Easter Offensive was unlike anything it had faced in the past. Up to this point in the offensive, the entire South Vietnamese army's battle record had not been very good.

McKenna pulled out his flashlight while Lovings stretched a poncho over the foxhole to keep the light inside. They were not concerned about being seen by the enemy but by the South Vietnamese soldiers around them. If they knew the American advisers were planning an escape, there was no telling how they might react. The Americans picked a stream a couple of kilometers to the rear as the rendezvous point if the defensive line should break.[13]

McKenna and Lovings never had to play out the escape plan. As the situation deteriorated, all American advisers turned their attention to coordinating air support, always a last-ditch lifesaver. Major Lovings called the division operations center requesting a Spectre gunship to work over the area surrounding the 44th ARVN Regiment. The AC-130 arrived on station and circled the perimeter. North Vietnamese units—Lovings estimated about three battalions—were attacking the front, eastern flank, and rear. The American advisers looked up to see a wall of tracer bullets pouring down like red rain from Spectre's guns. Suddenly it would cease, and only the gunship's droning propellers were heard. Then came the deadly rain again, this time in another place. This went on for over an hour.

At the 23d ARVN Division headquarters in Kontum, Colonel Truby convinced Colonel Ba to try a daring plan. The only way to blunt the North Vietnamese attack seemed to be with B-52 strikes. Two were already preplanned for later that night, but friendly units were too close to the target box. Truby proposed that the 44th and 53d ARVN Regiments fall back to Kontum one hour before the strikes. The move would be risky for two reasons. First, in those days, any battle maneuver performed at night stood a good chance of failure because communications and orders often became mixed. Second, because the enemy had closed with the South Vietnamese, a fallback risked opening a temporary gap through which the North Vietnamese could surge toward Kontum. To compensate, Ba ordered his artillery to blanket the area forward of the retreating South Vietnamese units. If the plan worked, the B-52s would catch the enemy in the open.

Truby called Vann and requested approval. He was concerned over the

South Vietnamese ability to handle the complex coordination involved, but in the end he agreed to the plan. The next three hours were spent holding the North Vietnamese in place. The 53d ARVN Regiment committed its reserve to block penetration in the eastern sector. In the center, the 44th ARVN Regiment continued to rely on Spectre to hold its own against North Vietnamese forces attacking on three sides. At about 1:00 on the morning of 15 May, the order came down to pull back. For an hour South Vietnamese artillery concentrated on backing the maneuver. Both regiments held together and withdrew in good order to new positions a mile or two to the south.

The bombers arrived just in time. Lieutenant Colonel McKenna and the rest of the 44th ARVN Regiment did not even know exactly when they were coming. Far above the battlefield, out of sight and sound, the bombers loosed their cargo on the North Vietnamese. The ground trembled under the impact, trees snapped, and huge rocks flew through the air as if they were pebbles. Dirt crumbled from the sides of foxholes and bunkers, showering the men taking refuge there. When the attack was over, an eerie silence clung to the killing ground. South Vietnamese soldiers rose unsteadily from their holes. Blood flowed from the noses and ears of some; others simply shook their heads, trying to clear the roaring sensation. The calculations had been correct, though almost too close; B-52s had dropped their bombs well inside the safety margin, but no South Vietnamese had been killed.

The enemy was not so fortunate. At first light the 53d and 44th ARVN Regiments moved back to their former positions of the previous night. The carnage was sobering. Hundreds of bodies lay scattered, most of them in pieces. Sandals and parts of green uniforms—most of them still covering torn and bloody limbs—hung from shattered trees. The ground itself was torn and broken; one adviser thought it looked like the surface of the moon. The air strike had also caught some artillery support units. Howitzers and rocket launchers sat silent, the crews dead beside them. McKenna and Lovings counted over 200 bodies surrounding the 44th ARVN Regiment position. Major Richard O. Perry, senior adviser to the 53d ARVN Regiment, reported 189. Seven tanks were also part of the debris.[14]

While searching the twisted earth where the B-52s had struck, a South Vietnamese battalion discovered a clump of twenty-three corpses. One of them moved. A single soldier had survived the bombing. He told his captors that his company had been whittled down to only twenty-five men on the eve of the attack. The order came to begin the attack, and as the company surged forward, they walked under the falling bombs.

The first battle for Kontum was over, and the South Vietnamese had won. It had been a struggle. Early on 14 May, events seemed to favor the South Vietnamese; by nightfall the tide had shifted, and it looked as if the enemy would take Kontum by morning. A bold plan by Truby and Ba, well-disciplined fire and movement by South Vietnamese infantry, and a timely B-52 strike had snatched victory back from the North Vietnamese. However, General Toan and Colonel Ba saw their victory for exactly what it was: a timely reprieve borne on the wings of B-52 bombers. A serious reappraisal of South Vietnamese defenses was clearly in order.

TWENTY

REGROUPING

John Paul Vann and his staff at II Corps headquarters took stock of the situation. Two facts had become clear during the course of battle. First, the North Vietnamese were using their experiences in I Corps and III Corps to shape the attack on Kontum. Although tanks had not been decisive in any confrontations during the Easter Offensive, they had invariably struck fear into South Vietnamese troops who had never before encountered them. Vann concluded that the North Vietnamese were trying to save time by throwing their armor at Kontum instead of opening with an artillery barrage. But the lesson that tanks were vulnerable had been slowly learned until most South Vietnamese soldiers no longer feared them. In addition to the T-54s destroyed by TOW helicopters, South Vietnamese troopers armed with LAWs claimed eleven tank kills. This time they had stood and fought. Second, fewer than 3,000 enemy troops had taken part in the first attack on Kontum. The 320th NVA Division had been hacked to pieces by air strikes and artillery before it could close with the South Vietnamese north of the city. Vann knew that the 2d NVA Division, the unit that had taken Tan Canh and Dak To, was still intact. It numbered around 10,000 men, all within striking distance. A second major thrust was expected within days.

Colonel Ba ordered a limited counteroffensive aimed at finding remaining concentrations of enemy troops and fixing them until new artillery and air strikes could be ordered. The North Vietnamese were definitely still out there. All advancing South Vietnamese units were fired on by mortars and automatic weapons. Helicopter reconnaissance flights picked up activity on the northeast, west, and southeast sides of Kontum.

The buildup south of the city was very disturbing. Colonel Truby recalled the disorder he had seen a few days earlier among the Regional Forces and Popular Forces guarding the south side of the city. At the time he let it pass because no enemy troop buildup had been reported in that sector. Now it was a different situation. The Ruff-Puffs habitually left their positions at night, going into town to be with their families. The North Vietnamese certainly knew of this and could infiltrate into Kontum virtually undetected.

North of Kontum, Colonel Ba also shifted his troops. His units had been spread too thin, and the oversight had almost cost him the battle. An efficient staff had made up for most of the gaps in the defense with sound coordination and communication, placing artillery on enemy troops whenever they sought to exploit a weak point. Ba tightened the perimeter, then moved the 44th ARVN Regiment back into the city, placing it in reserve around Kontum's hospital. The 45th ARVN Regiment moved up to take its place. John Paul Vann and General Toan paid a visit to Kontum to review the troop shuffle. Ba's plan was sound.[1]

On 15 May Vann took advantage of the brief respite to step up an airlift of civilians still inside Kontum. Montagnard families were coaxed onto airplanes and flown south to Pleiku. Most of the men remained behind. They were armed with rifles and sent to bolster militia units south of the city. By mid-May 30,000 civilians had fled the area north of Kontum for the relative safety of southern II Corps.[2]

The respite ended just after midnight on 16 May when the North Vietnamese reverted to their habit of turning up the level of artillery fire. Colonel Ba thought this might be the second phase of the offensive, especially when some of the shelling on Kontum was reported as coming from the 100mm guns of T-54 tanks. If true, this could only mean that the enemy had moved in close enough to use direct fire, something it would not risk unless ready to again commit to an all-out assault.

An American ground TOW team inside Kontum was sent to investigate. It had arrived in the city on 14 May fresh from Fort Bragg, North Carolina. Antitank specialists in crisp new olive green fatigues complete with 82d Airborne Division patches on their sleeves, the crews were a surprise to almost everyone. They drove through the streets in American jeeps with TOW rockets mounted on the back as American advisers and South Vietnamese soldiers alike paused to stare. Was the U.S. Army coming back to South Vietnam? If it was, no one had said anything about it.[3]

The decision to employ ground TOWs on the battlefield was a risky one. TOW gunships were one thing—they were highly maneuverable, and the antiaircraft environment around Kontum was not as dangerous as it had been around Quang Tri City and An Loc—but jeeps could be trapped on the ground and captured by the enemy. TOW technology was state-of-the-art, and if the North Vietnamese captured it, Washington would be deeply embarrassed. On the other hand, the presence of TOWs on the ground was a morale booster, and they took pressure off the air force, which had bombing obligations in the other corps areas and especially in North Vietnam. John Paul Vann promised that the South Vietnamese would not operate the weapons; only American crews would do it, and they would be well protected.[4]

The ground TOWs were only marginally effective in the overall battle, but they broke up the North Vietnamese attack on the morning of 16 May. The jeeps drove through the streets in the northern part of the city looking for targets. They destroyed one tank and fixed the positions of five others, relaying the information back to division headquarters.

During the afternoon the enemy turned much of its attention toward the 53d ARVN Regiment stationed at the airfield northeast of Kontum. Artillery fire increased, and helicopters coming in to refuel received the full attention of North Vietnamese mortar crews. Three helicopters were damaged, and two sitting South Vietnamese air force C-123 cargo planes were destroyed on the ground. Some fifty rounds fell onto the airfield itself, pitting the runway and making landing dangerous. The runway was closed that evening and not reopened until early the next morning. Repair crews used the cover of darkness to fill in the holes.

North Vietnamese infantry did not have the same success as their artillery brethren. In fact, their timing could not have been worse. A probe against the 53d ARVN Regiment north of the airfield was launched at 10:40 P.M. on 16 May, but the unfortunate enemy walked right under a load of bombs dropped from B-52s high above. The enemy dissolved right before the defenders' eyes. Sporadic fire continued along the northern perimeter, but by midnight all firing had ceased.

Despite the pounding, the North Vietnamese refused to give up on the airfield. An American C-130 cargo plane landed during the afternoon of 17 May. As the plane disgorged its load of supplies and ammunition, mortar rounds again began to fall nearby. The pilot panicked. He gunned the engines, heading the plane down the airstrip with the back ramp still down. Sparks showered as the steel ramp scraped the tarmac, sending bewildered soldiers scattering as the plane lumbered down the runway. The pilot barely reached takeoff speed before running out of tarmac. He jerked the nose skyward, but the plane's belly scraped the roof of a building at the end of the runway. The C-130 went out of control; the right wing dipped and struck the ground, and the plane cartwheeled. A helicopter scrambled out to the crash, rescuing two crew members from the wreckage. Vann reacted to the disaster by banning all fixed-wing daylight flights into the airport.[5]

That same day Colonel R. M. Rhotenberry arrived in Kontum to take over the position as senior adviser to the 23d ARVN Division. A grateful Colonel Truby said good-bye to his fellow advisers and headed back to Saigon, then home to the States. Rhotenberry's first day in the war zone

The wreck of a C-130 transport plane sits on the Kontum airfield. (Jack Finch)

was a quiet one. Only a few artillery rounds landed on the airfield; almost nothing hit Kontum. An intelligence briefing in the command bunker indicated that the lull would be a short one—the enemy planned a major artillery bombardment as the North Vietnamese army celebrated Ho Chi Minh's birthday. The prediction did not come to pass. Throughout the day on 18 May, there was no significant artillery bombardment, although beginning at about 5:30 P.M. around 200 rounds of mortar and artillery peppered the city center. Rhotenberry quietly wondered about his tactical intelligence people. If they could not get this right, what about crucial order-of-battle intelligence?[6]

For Lieutenant Colonel McKenna, the failure of the expected artillery barrage to materialize brought little relief. His regiment was probed by tanks during the late afternoon. Seven T-54 tanks appeared near the forward elements of the 44th ARVN Regiment, but a forward air controller spotted one of the tanks skulking near the treeline and called in tactical air support. A lone fighter plane quickly roared in from the east, fired its rockets, and reported one dead T-54. The other tanks remained about two miles away from the South Vietnamese defensive positions. McKenna reasoned that the enemy was reluctant to expose its armor to the increasingly accurate South Vietnamese antitank fire.

The circling air controller did not stop working when the fighter planes appeared to take on the tanks. He continued circling the battlefield, looking for signs of the enemy presence. The advisers below appreciated the voice on the radio. It was an invisible bond with the security of American firepower. Even when the situation seemed darkest, the air controllers held the key to rescue. With a single radio call they could summon the deadly accurate rockets and bombs of fighter planes as they sprinted low over the treeline or the awesome power of the high-flying B-52s.

The air controller came through once more. He discovered two 130mm artillery pieces firing on Kontum from the vicinity of Polei Kleng. The formidable guns were ringed with 23mm antiaircraft batteries. Although the North Vietnamese artillerymen realized they had been discovered, they continued firing on the city. A flight of fighter planes screamed in from Pleiku and silenced the troublesome battery.

Despite their reluctance to engage, the North Vietnamese had spent the past week studying weaknesses in Kontum's defense. Sapper units infiltrated the city from the south through the poorly trained Ruff-Puff defensive positions. They stayed quietly in place, waiting for the final attack. Other reconnaissance units managed to penetrate the city disguised as civilian refugees and South Vietnamese soldiers. These spies—called *noi cong,* or "inside forces"—helped North Vietnamese commanders piece together an accurate picture of the city's defenses. Kontum's weakest point, they discovered, was the junction between the 45th and 53d ARVN Regiments. But before they could attack there, the North Vietnamese had to weaken the strong point in the defense—the 44th ARVN Regiment.[7]

Shortly before midnight the enemy stepped up its bombardment of Kontum as a prelude to another armor and infantry assault. The enemy thrust straight at the strongest part of the South Vietnamese defense—the 44th ARVN Regiment holed up in the hospital compound in northern Kontum. Colonel McKenna had seen to it that the defenses were ready. Claymore antipersonnel mines had been planted all along the perimeter in anticipation of an assault. As the 48th NVA Regiment surged forward, the South Vietnamese set off the claymores, tearing gaping holes in the wall of attackers. South Vietnamese artillery to the rear also opened fire, sending round after round into the enemy. Then came the B-52s. Fifteen minutes past midnight on 19 May, an Arc Light strike carpeted the killing zone just forward of the 44th ARVN Regiment's front lines, decimating the remaining North Vietnamese attackers. The assault was over.

Throughout the day the North Vietnamese sat back and licked their wounds. The only significant activity occurred late in the evening when enemy troops closed with the northern perimeter and fired tear gas canisters into frontline bunkers, then dashed forward hoping to overrun the teary-eyed defenders. Accurate artillery fire put a quick end to the poorly planned assault.

A surprise gain for the North Vietnamese came early in the morning of 20 May when three successive assaults against the 53d ARVN Regiment on the northeast part of the city managed to push the unit out of its positions. Some charitable observers stated that the regiment's retreat in the face of moderate enemy pressure was caused by weariness after three weeks of fighting. This was certainly partly true, but the regiment's senior adviser, Major Richard Perry, had few kind words for his South Vietnamese counterparts. He felt the men were willing to fight, but the officers could not—or would not—lead.[8]

The counterattack to retake the lost position seemed to bear out Perry's criticism. Throughout the day on 20 May, the South Vietnamese pushed against the enemy, who dug in their heels in a bid to keep their limited gains. On several occasions during the day, South Vietnamese commanders falsely reported they had recaptured the lost positions. Yet by nightfall the enemy was still firmly entrenched. Sappers had even managed to dig tunnels to within twenty meters of South Vietnamese positions, too close to use air strikes to dislodge the stubborn enemy.[9]

Inaccurate battle reports from the 53d ARVN Regiment worried Colonel Rhotenberry. From his command bunker in Kontum he sent an adviser up in a helicopter to survey the situation with every false report of success by South Vietnamese field commanders. Colonel Ba became incensed by his subordinates' perfidy. Because of the confused situation, he had been reluctant to commit his armor and infantry reserves to the fray. Ba decided to go to the front, where he lashed out at his commanders for both their inability to fight and their inaccurate reporting.

As was his way, John Paul Vann appeared just as the situation reached crisis proportions. He swooped into Kontum in his helicopter and dashed into the command bunker for a conference with his advisers and Colonel Ba. Vann argued that the only remedy lay in committing the division reserve. He was right. The 53d ARVN Regiment finally succeeded in retaking its former positions when nine M41 tanks supported by Cobra gunships supported the counterattack. The tanks provided direct fire support, while the Cobras slashed at enemy soldiers as they tried to dig in deeper.

All was calm throughout the night of 20 May. Vann and Toan prepared to execute a counterattack they had planned days earlier. The following day, 21 May, they planned to send three ranger units to open the highway at Kontum Pass. The 6th Ranger Group would attack on foot, with two battalions from the 2d Ranger Group air assaulting onto the Rock Pile just to the east. The plan optimistically called for road crews to begin work clearing the road by 23 May. Vann was convinced it would work. He wired General Abrams to report that "the plan is a bold and imaginative move by the new corps commander [Toan]. I consider that it has a good chance for success and that, if successful, can turn the tide of battle for Kontum."[10]

The counterattack sputtered, however, because just before dawn the next day the enemy assaulted the city again, this time with greater intensity across a broad front. The 44th ARVN Regiment, scheduled to be replaced by the 45th ARVN Regiment, began taking heavy artillery fire. Under cover of the barrage, a North Vietnamese sapper battalion sneaked in behind the 3d Battalion of the 44th ARVN Regiment and cut Highway 14 a mile and a half northwest of Kontum. A more serious attack occurred at the point where the 45th and 53d ARVN Regiments' defensive positions met. One enemy battalion managed to wedge itself between the two South Vietnamese units while attention was turned toward the sappers sitting astride the highway.

Lieutenant Colonel McKenna thought this attack was the last straw. His regiment had held time after time against some of the fiercest assaults the North Vietnamese had to offer. But the ease with which the enemy had punched between the two South Vietnamese units boded ill for the beleaguered defenders.

As McKenna peered through the firing slits of the regimental bunker, he saw a terrifying sight. A mere 100 meters away squatted a T-54 tank, its black muzzle scanning back and forth looking for targets. As McKenna stared, transfixed by the deadly sight, the gun barrel came to rest directly on the bunker. A puff of smoke and belch of flame heralded an oncoming round, and everyone in the bunker threw themselves to the ground. The bunker shook under the impact, showering dirt and wood fragments to the floor. Other tanks joined in, their guns issuing a distinctive crack, much different from the dull boom of artillery pieces.

As McKenna brushed himself off, he noticed his South Vietnamese counterpart yelling into the radio. Looking to his interpreter for a quick translation, McKenna saw that the soldier was not quite willing to give an exact rendering. It seemed that the commander was ready to abandon the bunker.

"He says we go," the interpreter said, his voice betraying deep fear. With the battle raging outside, McKenna knew they would not make it out the door. Major Wade Lovings, McKenna's deputy adviser, was resigned. He hoisted the field radio onto his back and prepared to leave with the South Vietnamese. McKenna reached for the handset and called the division command post.

"My counterpart is getting ready to flee the regimental bunker," he said matter-of-factly.

"What do you intend to do?" came the pointless reply. McKenna and Lovings exchanged incredulous looks at the question.

"If he goes, I'll go with him," McKenna said. Colonel Rhotenberry promised to send help to get them out of the area safely, but McKenna told him to forget it. With more than a little irritation in his voice, he pointed out that simply keeping in touch with the command bunker would be difficult, so linking up with a relief team was probably out of the question. On the other end Rhotenberry knew his regimental adviser's assessment was correct. He gave a silent prayer for his men and went back to work plotting air strike coordinates.

Everyone started for the bunker entrance. The regimental commander continued yelling nonstop into the radio. Suddenly the door opened, and a breathless South Vietnamese junior officer rushed in. It seemed the tide had turned, and most of the North Vietnamese had been driven from the compound. The regimental commander slumped down onto an empty ammunition crate and slowly took off his helmet. He knew how close he had come to death. McKenna later charitably reasoned that the commander had planned to leave the bunker so he could die in the open rather than being flushed out of his hole like a rat. Whatever the reason for his decision, the regimental commander did not use the lull to venture outside and bolster his troops; they were on their own to fight or die without adequate leadership.[11]

Lieutenant Colonel McKenna was unaware of the big picture. All he knew was that the situation surrounding his bunker looked grim. He did not know that even though his little area was safe for the time being, the North Vietnamese had managed to drive a wedge between his unit and the 53d ARVN Regiment. Nor did he know about the enemy attempt to cut Highway 14.

The South Vietnamese counterattacked immediately. The 3d Battalion of the 44th ARVN Regiment struck south. A second battalion from the regiment, along with one battalion for the 45th ARVN Regiment, moved north along the highway, hoping to catch the enemy in a pincer movement. Spectre gunships and tactical fighters provided air support. The two forces linked up and cleared the road after over an hour of fierce fighting, but the wedge between the two regiments remained. The North Vietnamese had probably planned the attack on the highway as a diversion. Their earlier assessment of South Vietnamese defensive weaknesses pointed toward the junction between the two regiments, and they had exploited the soft spot.

Colonel Ba was worried. He called for a priority-one air strike on the enemy salient, hoping to dislodge the North Vietnamese before they dug in. As friendly artillery whistled overhead, U.S. Air Force fighter planes shrieked over the treetops, dropping napalm and high-explosive ordnance. Ba was convinced that this was the crucial point in the fighting. If the North Vietnamese managed to hold the salient, Kontum was lost. He tightened the chin strap on his helmet, pulled his flak jacket a little tighter around his thin frame, and stepped out of the bunker into the raging fight above. He and a few staff members made their way to the point where South Vietnamese units were preparing to counterattack. Their presence was an inspiration to the demoralized soldiers, and Vann later wrote that Ba's personal intervention had been a key factor in the counterattack's success.[12]

The enemy was reluctant to retreat from its hard-won salient. North Vietnamese commanders quickly ordered another assault to regain the position, but their luck had run out. While the South Vietnamese frantically dug in to consolidate their recaptured ground, the North Vietnamese stormed back in a counterattack. As they did, a South Vietnamese air force AC-47 Spooky gunship sent up from Pleiku arrived on the scene. Spooky was the old version of the AC-130 Spectre gunship, a much less sophisticated, though still deadly, model. Armed with three 7.62mm miniguns, Spooky could churn out thousands of rounds per minute. The gunship took up its station above the battlefield and circled for about thirty minutes, spewing lead down on the hapless North Vietnamese as they milled about in the open. Spooky's timely arrival spelled disaster for the assault.

Within the next two hours the North Vietnamese attempted two more counterattacks. Again their timing was unfortunate. As they massed for the attack, B-52 strikes rained down and squashed the attempts. Then, at 4:00 on the morning of 21 May, the enemy launched a desperate final attack. One company managed to close with the South Vietnamese, who by this time had managed to dig back into their old positions. Fierce hand-to-hand fighting ensued as Vietnamese closed with Vietnamese in a wild melee of swinging rifle butts, point-blank duels, and screams of bloody terror. The South Vietnamese were the first to break, but only along one small sector of the front line. The enemy quickly exploited the opening, but the penetration was much smaller than the previous day's salient.

Major Lovings saw the South Vietnamese fall back and called for air support. The first units on the scene were Cobra helicopter gunships. They raked the North Vietnamese for almost half an hour as more airborne aid winged its way to the battlefield. Two Arc Light strikes rained down to the north of the attacking enemy company, drowning out all attempts by the

North Vietnamese to reinforce their gain. The Cobras, which had hovered outside the Arc Light box just prior to the strike, darted back in to finish off the survivors. There was little work left to do. One pilot reported seeing bodies thrown several feet into the air by the exploding bombs.[13]

The North Vietnamese had launched five assaults to retake the wedge they had driven between the 44th and 53d ARVN Regiments on the morning of 20 May. Although the South Vietnamese had fought bravely, they could not have prevailed without the massive air support from B-52s, tactical air, and gunships. B-52 support alone amounted to at least one strike somewhere along the northern edge of Kontum every hour for almost twenty-four hours.[14]

Although the South Vietnamese infantry only narrowly escaped defeat on 20 and 21 May, huge gains were made in the battle to keep Kontum resupplied. American C-130 aircraft had begun landing at Kontum airfield while the North Vietnamese were busy throwing themselves against the 44th and 53d ARVN Regiments. They were the first fixed-wing aircraft to land in over forty-eight hours. During the night of 21 May, twelve C-130s made it into Kontum airfield. In addition to delivering their valuable cargo of food and ammunition, the planes replaced the two 10,000-gallon fuel bladders destroyed on 17 May. By dawn the fuel was in place and fully operational.

TWENTY-ONE

ARVN ON
THE OFFENSIVE

General Toan was pleased with the previous day's results. The 23d ARVN Division had lost over 100 men, but the North Vietnamese had probably lost over 1,000. The South Vietnamese had held, thanks largely to American airpower, and supplies were again flowing into the city from Kontum airfield. The time was ripe to move onto the offensive. For the first time since the siege of Kontum had begun over one month ago, the South Vietnamese were ordered to take the initiative. The first objective was to clear the road between Kontum and Pleiku to the south. If successful, the counteroffensive would allow more supplies into beleaguered Kontum City.

From his command center in Pleiku, Toan gathered his staff and outlined his plan for a counteroffensive. "This will be the first offensive action in a long time," Toan told his audience. "I'm sure it will be successful." In Toan's opinion, the enemy had lost the initiative, and his weaknesses could be exploited. "After this offensive we will have another offensive," he predicted cheerfully. Vann did not completely share his counterpart's enthusiasm, however. "My major reservation is that this operation will take place at a time when the situation in Kontum City could become critical," he confided to General Abrams. Even so, Vann believed the risk was worth taking.[1]

Toan was true to his word. On 21 May South Vietnamese troops headed south in a limited counteroffensive. A task force composed of the 2d and 6th Ranger Groups and the 3d Armored Cavalry Regiment began clearing operations along the stretch of Highway 14 running south toward Pleiku. Although supply by air to Kontum had been restored, the city still needed truck convoys to bring in matériel. Again, the South Vietnamese were not up to the task of dislodging the enemy without massive air support. During the fighting of the past few days the 95B NVA Regiment had taken up positions astride the highway as it ran through the Chu Pao Pass. B-52 strikes and fighter planes loaded with cluster bombs pounded the enemy before the South Vietnamese rangers moved in.

As the infantry approached, the North Vietnamese picked up the tempo. Armored personnel carriers from the 3d Armored Cavalry Regiment clattered along the road toward the enemy positions only to be brought up short by B-40 rocket-propelled grenades. Two days later there was little progress to report. Vann praised Toan's efforts, but privately he was critical. "The Corps commander has been advised to consider using his armor . . . and to hit him [the enemy] from the rear," wrote Vann to MACV headquarters. "It has been pointed out to him [Toan] that his drive thru the pass has lost its momentum." But Toan remained cautious, and the North Vietnamese held their original positions.[2]

The South Vietnamese had better luck north of Kontum City. As Toan's counteroffensive stalled to the south, Colonel Ba ordered the 23d ARVN Division reconnaissance company airlifted six miles northwest of the city. As the helicopters landed in a clearing, the soldiers jumped out and headed south to link up with a battalion from the 45th ARVN Regiment that was moving north on the ground. The terrain they passed over looked as if it had been through a meat grinder. B-52s had turned the landscape into a twisted mass of rock, dirt, and shattered trees. About thirty broken bodies lay in the killing ground, and evidence of other casualties lay strewn about. After reporting back to the 23d Division headquarters, the reconnaissance company returned to base, and the rest of the 44th and 53d ARVN Regiments moved out to inspect the area forward of the perimeter. Light contact with scattered enemy units made the going slow, and by evening the South Vietnamese ceased their operation and returned to Kontum. They had accomplished little, and John Paul Vann was disappointed in their lack of progress.

American air cavalry scouting patrols also confirmed the extent of damage done to the enemy by air strikes. One helicopter reported seeing enemy troops pulling bodies out of underground bunkers. The bombs had been so powerful that they had killed men dug into the earth from sheer concussion. It was a sobering thought.

Because the 44th ARVN Regiment had been under constant pressure since the beginning of the siege, Ba shifted it back into a reserve position. The move began on the evening of 21 May, after the North Vietnamese were thrown out of their wedge in the South Vietnamese front lines, and it took the better part of the next two days to complete. Light probes by the North Vietnamese harassed the unit, but there was no serious challenge to the redeployment. The closest call came at dawn on 23 May. Sappers breached defenses and planted explosives, but tactical air support prevented enemy infantry from exploiting the confusion. At first light a small reconnaissance team counted between twenty and thirty bodies strewn about beyond the wire.

Given the fact that the North Vietnamese fought without benefit of air support, it is surprising that they held up as long as they did. Yet only a few hundred soldiers surrendered to the South Vietnamese during the offensive. One soldier staggered into South Vietnamese lines following a B-52 strike on 23 May. He claimed he was from the 48th NVA Regiment, and he revealed the terrible toll exacted by American airpower, telling his interrogators that most companies in his battalion had been whittled down to about ten men during the weeks of B-52 strikes. Many of their supplies had been destroyed en route to the front lines, and food and medicine were in short supply. Stockpiles of artillery rounds were running low, possibly the reason why the North Vietnamese had failed to employ their standard heavy artillery barrage before the last infantry assault.

The prisoner knew little of his unit's battle plans, but he did know that another major thrust was planned for sometime during the next few days. Intelligence experts reasoned that the ferocity of any preassault artillery barrage would depend largely on the enemy's ability to resupply. Air strikes were siphoned away from Kontum's perimeter for use on suspected logistical lines behind the North Vietnamese positions. To the delight of American advisers in the command bunker, the prisoner was able to pinpoint the location of the 48th NVA Regiment's command post. It was in for a brutal pounding as soon as the B-52s received the coordinates.

The fighting had exhausted both sides. Colonel Ba took advantage of a lull in the action on 23 May to give his men some rest. During the entire day the usual sounds of battle were subdued, punctuated only by the occasional incoming artillery round and the distant thunder of U.S. air strikes. Then, on 24 May, the battle begun anew with Ba sending his forces onto the offensive.

At 10:45 in the morning one battalion from the 44th ARVN Regiment was airlifted about four kilometers north of Kontum along Highway 14. A second battalion landed just to the east, and both units were ordered to attack southward. They would meet a blocking force inserted in front of the enemy north of Kontum.

Another operation involved most of the 53d ARVN Regiment. It struck northward toward a small village that had been captured by the North Vietnamese two days before. By just past noon all units, both those involved in the hammer-and-anvil operation to the north and the 53d ARVN Regiment, reported light resistance. By dark all objectives were in South Vietnamese hands.

Colonel Ba reflected on the day's success, and John Paul Vann sent his congratulations. Vann had been content to allow Ba control of the battlefield while he concentrated on directing air support. But both Vann and Ba knew the failure of the North Vietnamese to conquer Kontum up to this point did not mean they would give up. Ba predicted that the next attack would be a furious, all-out assault characterized more by desperation than by cunning. Time now worked against the enemy, who had to either achieve a quick victory or withdraw completely and rebuild. The annual monsoons would soon drench the Central Highlands, turning roads and jungle trails into an impassable quagmire. Simple battlefield attrition also worked against the enemy. After almost two months of constant fighting in II Corps, the North Vietnamese were on their last legs. Constant casualties had whittled down enemy strength to the point where artillery barrages and frontal assaults could not carry the day. Vann correctly reasoned that this was the enemy's last gasp. The North Vietnamese were gambling everything on one final assault. So the question was not if the enemy would mass for another attack, but when.

The assault came sooner than expected. Late at night on 24 May the enemy bombardment picked up, and just past midnight the city was once again hammered by North Vietnamese artillery. But this time the pressure came from the south, with additional thrusts at the Kontum airfield to the northeast. At 3:00 in the morning demolitioneers from the 406th and 10th NVA Sapper Battalions crept through the meager defenses at the south end of Kontum and took up positions inside the city. As U.S. advisers had observed earlier, Ruff-Puffs responsible for the city's southern defenses were less than vigilant. Now the enemy knew that and took full advantage. Behind the demolitioneers came squad-sized sapper units, some dressed in the captured uniforms of South Vietnamese soldiers. It was later found that many of the uniforms had once belonged to South Vietnamese soldiers of the 22d ARVN Division, the one decimated at Tan Canh.[3]

The North Vietnamese took up positions near the airfield and in a Catholic seminary that also served as the residence of the French bishop of Kontum. Although the quality of the Ruff-Puffs in the area was generally poor, some did respond well, engaging the superior North Vietnamese forces in fierce firefights. The South Vietnamese managed to contain the penetration into the city's southern sector, but once again the North Vietnamese had gained a foothold. At the airfield, alert sentries surprised some enemy sappers and killed twenty of them.

North Vietnamese artillery concentrated on silencing South Vietnamese batteries before they could return fire. The 53d ARVN Regiment's artillery received especially heavy fire, which destroyed two 105mm howitzers. Lieutenant Colonel Norbert C. Gannon, who had replaced Major Perry as regimental senior adviser, suggested the remaining artillery be moved to another position. A sound idea, but the enemy had capable spotters watching every move. No sooner were the guns set up in their new positions than the North Vietnamese adjusted fire and landed a test round within fifteen yards. The next salvo destroyed another 105mm howitzer. The 53d ARVN Regiment's artillery was not being singled out by enemy gunners; all batteries in and around Kontum were targeted. By 3:00 in the afternoon virtually all of the 23d ARVN Division's artillery had been neutralized.

At Kontum's hospital complex, the 44th ARVN Regiment was particularly hard hit by the bombardment. It occupied the center position in the city's defenses, so the North Vietnamese kept up a steady stream of artillery rounds on the exhausted soldiers. During the firing, Major Wade Lovings, the regimental assistant senior adviser, thought he heard something strange. The boom of artillery did not sound normal. He was used to the crump of 105mm howitzers amd the deeper cough of Soviet- and Chinese-made guns, especially the distinctive roar of the 130mm howitzer. An artilleryman by training, Lovings knew an American-made 155mm howitzer when he heard one. That weapon was not supposed to be in the North Vietnamese arsenal.

During a lull in the shelling, Major Lovings rushed out of his bunker, searching for craters made by impacting artillery rounds. He found them everywhere. By measuring crater diameter, Lovings calculated that only an American-made 155mm howitzer could have been responsible for some of the huge holes. The South Vietnamese must have been chagrined to learn that some of their own guns had joined in the attack. The enemy could only have acquired the big guns when it had captured Tan Canh over one month earlier.[4]

From SRAG headquarters in Pleiku, Vann declared a tactical emergency. He was not concerned that this might be the thrust that pushed the enemy into the city so much as he wanted all available aircraft at his disposal to finally squash the North Vietnamese offensive. As usual, airpower held the enemy at bay. Vann wielded his favorite weapon with finesse and precision. Fighter planes and bombers danced and swirled through the sky, striking out at targets called in through forward air controllers, or from the regimental bunker in Kontum. Perhaps more than on any other day during the siege of Kontum, air support was the single most important factor in the battle. With the virtual elimination of South Vietnamese artillery, the infantry could do little but wait in foxholes and bunkers until the enemy was close enough to engage with small arms. That was no way to fight a battle. But the South Vietnamese did not have to; the U.S. Air Force saved them. For the rest of the day the planes held the North Vietnamese at bay.

Another early victim of the artillery barrage was Kontum's supply line. Despite massive American air support, South Vietnamese infantry was consistently unable to prevent the enemy from pinching off both the highway and the approach to the airport. Once again fixed-wing aircraft could not use the runway, but a soccer field in the city center was modified to take CH-47 Chinook helicopters. The big twin-bladed cargo ships looked like ungainly grasshoppers as they winged their way through enemy machine-gun fire to land emergency supplies and evacuate the seriously wounded. Hueys from the South Vietnamese air force then picked up the supplies and shuttled them to beleaguered troops around the city.

From his vantage point above the city, Vann took stock of the situation. By his estimation the ferocious air bombardment had kept the North Vietnamese from consolidating their gains around the southern part of Kontum, but the situation around the airfield was still uncertain. Vann radioed Colonel Rhotenberry in the 23d ARVN Division bunker that he estimated there was still at least one battalion of enemy sappers near the airfield. Any future combat would probably occur near that area. "Be ready for anything," Vann cautioned. "I'll support you with air, but tell those Vietnamese to fight for their lives."[5]

Vann was right once again. One hour past midnight on 26 May, the North Vietnamese began the traditional all-out bombardment. Every minute for almost an hour, dozens of rounds slammed into Kontum and the nearby airfield. Then the firing stopped, and the Americans peered through the bunker firing slits, searching for the tanks they were certain would lead the attack. They were not disappointed.

Three or four infantry teams led by tanks stormed down from the north under cover of the artillery bombardment. As they had done on 22 May, the North Vietnamese smashed into the 53d ARVN Regiment, right at the point where it butted up against the 45th ARVN Regiment. The South Vietnamese fought hard, holding the enemy to a small penetration where the two South Vietnamese regiments overlapped. At first light, Cobra gunships and TOW-mounted helicopters streaked in to relieve some of the pressure. Two T-54 tanks went up in flames, their crews pouring out of the burning hulks. Smelling blood, the Cobras slashed in with miniguns blazing. Most of the fleeing tankers died in the hail of bullets.

Colonel Ba ordered one battalion from the 44th ARVN Regiment, reinforced by eight South Vietnamese tanks, to counterattack. It may have been one of Ba's best moves. The North Vietnamese were slammed back, their progress halted to only a small salient. As the enemy fought hard just to maintain the penetration, Cobras savaged reinforcements and supplies moving up from the rear. But as had been the case on 22 May, the South Vietnamese were unable to completely push the tenacious enemy soldiers from their hard-won positions, although the situation seemed to stabilize by nightfall.

While part of the 44th ARVN Regiment was battling desperately near the airfield, other South Vietnamese troops inside the city were panicking. A month of fighting had taken its toll. Uncertain supplies and uniformly poor leadership combined to keep morale low. If the North Vietnamese had not totally surrounded Kontum, desertions would certainly have reached an intolerable level. As it was, disgruntled or cowardly South Vietnamese soldiers simply sat in their holes, refusing to obey orders relayed from officers buttoned up inside bunkers. Soldiers fled to the soccer field, where they pushed aside badly wounded men and scrambled aboard helicopters. The situation got so bad that American soldiers accompanied each flight. Their sole job was to beat any South Vietnamese soldier who tried to board a helicopter.[6]

As night fell the North Vietnamese poured more artillery fire on the 45th and 53d ARVN Regiment command posts. Infantry attacks against the 45th ARVN Regiment were particularly heavy. Three battalions from the 64th NVA Regiment had worked through the salient and around the rear of the South Vietnamese. The 45th ARVN Regiment was almost completely surrounded. Vann diverted all tactical air to support the embattled regiment, but the situation looked grim. The senior adviser on the ground, Lieutenant Colonel Grant, radioed Colonel Rhotenberry at the 23d ARVN Division bunker and pleaded for B-52 strikes. Rhotenberry agreed, and two Arc Lights were laid on to support the 45th ARVN Regiment; they arrived at 2:30 in the morning.

The bombs hit hard, a mere 600 to 700 yards from friendly troops. But the North Vietnamese were right under them. Lieutenant Colonel Grant gratefully noted that the ferocity of the attacks slacked off noticeably following the strike. To keep the South Vietnamese company for the rest of the night, the U.S. Air Force sent a Spectre gunship to cover the 45th ARVN Regiment's positions. It prowled back and forth, spitting a curtain of lead between the beleaguered South Vietnamese and the attacking enemy.

Trouble was not confined to the 45th ARVN Regiment, however. Just to the south, inside Kontum, the 44th ARVN Regiment came close to disaster. Although the unit was considered the best in the area, and it had participated in almost every counterattack for over a month, a serious judgment error almost erased all that. When the 44th ARVN Regiment moved from north of Kontum back to a reserve position in the city's hos-

Lieutenant Colonel William Bricker, operations adviser to the 23d ARVN Division, stands beside his demolished quarters in Kontum. (Jack Finch)

pital compound on 22 May, no security element was placed out front to soften enemy assaults. The regimental commander had mistakenly assumed that the 45th and 53d ARVN Regiments would perform that function.

Early on the morning of 27 May, one regiment of the 320th NVA Division, along with the 66th NVA Regiment and one company of armor, pushed south along Highway 14 toward Kontum. A second regiment from the 320th NVA Division, along with the 52d NVA Regiment, which had succeeded in surrounding the 45th ARVN Regiment the previous night, thrust from the northeast. The result was a coordinated attack against the 44th ARVN Regiment, which sat secure behind its wire and bunkers assuming that any assault would first have to come up against friendly troops just to the north. But there was no warning.

Lieutenant Colonel McKenna and Major Lovings settled down for yet another sleepless night on the dirt floor of the regimental bunker. As was typical in Kontum, sleep in the damp bunker was made more difficult by the constant crash of incoming artillery. McKenna had been on the radio most of the night, following the progress of action on the northern perimeter, up near the 45th ARVN Regiment. The news had not been encouraging. Enemy units were creeping around behind the embattled 45th ARVN Regiment and threatening to break through into the northeastern part of the city.

Suddenly, even fitful sleep became impossible. "Tanks and infantry in our wire!" shouted one adviser. Lovings glanced at McKenna, unspoken amazement written on his face. He ran to the bunker entrance to see for himself. It was worse than he imagined. Just outside the door—a mere fifty yards away—rumbled a T-54, the lead tank in the assault. A battle flag fluttered defiantly from its radio antenna in the morning breeze.

Before Lovings could react, the blast of an M72 LAW blocked his view of the oncoming tank. The clang of metal on metal rang out over the din of battle—a direct hit. Through his binoculars Lovings could see a gaping hole in the slanting front plate of the tank. One dead tank, but there was no telling how many were left to go.

A second tank was spotted across the hospital compound. The crew members apparently witnessed the destruction of their brother tank because this T-54 tried to turn around in the narrow street and retreat. As it turned broadside, an alert South Vietnamese soldier shouldered his LAW and placed a rocket under the turret. In the space of a few moments, Major Lovings had seen two enemy tanks turned into helpless chunks of steel. Satisfied with the performance of the South Vietnamese infantry, he turned back into the bunker to help Lieutenant Colonel McKenna call in air support.

General Hill, Vann's deputy, watched the unfolding North Vietnamese assault from his helicopter. He had taken off from Pleiku before first light, the lead ship in a team of Cobra gunships. Hovering overhead, Hill radioed down to Lovings and reported six tanks moving across an open field north of the hospital. All around them enemy infantry scurried like ants between the ruined buildings. Lovings replied with the bunker coordinates, adding that everything north of the line was fair game. The Cobras swooped down, concentrating their deadly fire on the infantry. Within minutes the North Vietnamese had scattered, leaving the tanks alone and vulnerable. Seeking shelter from the gunships, two T-54s scooted into a pair of deserted buildings. They were safe for the time being, but the battered walls effectively prevented them from firing their main guns.

A second wave of helicopters made short work of the remaining tanks. A flight of TOW-mounted Hueys had taken off from Pleiku right behind the Cobras, and by 6:00 in the morning they were on target. The pilots must have been delighted by the terrain below. The country to the north of the 44th ARVN Regiment was perfect tank-hunting ground—open and flat, with few trees or buildings. The enemy tanks were like fish in a barrel. With a whoop of excitement the flight leader ordered the attack, then darted in for the kill. Two quick hits left two T-54s smoking and silent. With Lovings's guidance one TOW ship spotted a tank hiding inside an abandoned building. The pilot swooped down, hovered briefly to get a fix, then unleashed a missile. It flashed through the air trailing the thin guide wire, then disappeared through a hole in the building. A flash and a loud roar told the gunner his aim had been true. Scratch one more North Vietnamese T-54.

The enemy continued to pressure the 44th ARVN Regiment's defenses, throwing tanks and infantry at the South Vietnamese from the northeast. At about 7:15 in the morning the defenders were hit with another cruel break. The main ammunition dump near Kontum airport was struck by an enemy mortar round, probably the work of sappers sneaking in close for just such a mission. Exploding rounds flew everywhere in a massive and deadly fireworks display, but the most immediate problem came from tear gas. Hundreds of pounds of the chemical agent billowed into the air, paralyzing friend and foe alike. Many of the South Vietnamese had gas masks, but the enemy had nothing. For almost an hour the fighting stopped as soldiers on both sides struggled to clear their eyes and throats of the burning gas.

To make matters worse, a stray round from the exploding ammo dump arced over and plunged into a nearby petroleum pump. A huge orange ball of flame billowed forth, spewing black smoke across the city. The scene was macabre. Furtive figures dashed back and forth against a backdrop of dull orange while a curtain of smoke dropped down, swirling amid the ruined buildings and still bodies. Above the din of screaming men, rumbling tanks, and crackling bullets was the roar of thousands of gallons of fuel burning, which lit up the morning sky.

North Vietnamese artillery destroyed one of the 23d ARVN Division's ammunition dumps early in the battle, causing it to burn for several days. (Jack Finch)

With the help of tactical air strikes, the helicopters had blunted the assault. By 10:00 A.M. only a few tanks could be seen, and they confined themselves to skulking out beyond the regimental perimeter. North Vietnamese infantry remained a threat, however, occupying pockets throughout the hospital compound and near the airfield. On the southern and eastern edges of the city the Ruff-Puffs also held out against increasing attacks.

At the hospital compound, fighting slacked off at about noon. McKenna and Lovings decided to take the jeep to the division compound for a shower, shave, and change of clothes. After over a week in the bunker, both men were covered with sweat and dirt. The sky outside was bright and cloudless, and the two men found it difficult to believe there was a war going on. After taking the shower and changing into a clean uniform, McKenna looked at his grimy flak jacket with disgust; he was so clean, it was difficult to shrug back into the dirty vest. As the two advisers drove back into the hospital compound, John Paul Vann was driving out. He turned the jeep sharply around and followed them to the bunker.

Major Wade Lovings (left) surveys damage to the 44th ARVN Regiment's command post after a North Vietnamese assault. An enemy tank (center) was destroyed at the bunker's doorstep. (Author's collection)

Vann chided McKenna about his squeaky-clean uniform and smooth-shaven face. "I bring a reporter out here to see real soldiers in combat and you're off taking a shower," he joked good-naturedly. Vann introduced the reporter and then drove back to the division bunker.

McKenna pointed the reporter toward the northern edge of the hospital compound, where some enemy soldiers were holed up in an abandoned building. The South Vietnamese were planning an attack to root them out, a good story for any news-hungry journalist.

From behind a pile of rubble, McKenna and the reporter waited for the firefight to begin. The South Vietnamese fired tear gas into the building, then opened fire. Much to everyone's surprise, however, the enemy retaliated by lobbing mortar rounds back at their attackers. McKenna, the reporter, and a handful of South Vietnamese officers dove for cover. McKenna spied an empty foxhole and ran for it. Before he reached its safety, a giant force slammed him to the ground. Rolling over and over toward the hole, McKenna saw blood and felt a pain deep inside. Something was very wrong.

Shrapnel from the exploding mortar rounds had ripped into McKenna's upper shoulder. He staggered to his feet and gasped for air. The bunker was less than a city block away, but McKenna was not sure he could make it. He staggered along trailing blood, not caring whether or not more mortar rounds rained down. Along the way he could see South Vietnamese soldiers watching his torturous progress with indifference. None lifted a hand to help. McKenna finally reached the bunker, where his interpreter called for a medevac helicopter. He left Kontum on a stretcher and never saw Major Wade Lovings or the reporter again; Lovings became senior adviser to the 44th ARVN Regiment. The fighting seemed to wait for McKenna to leave Kontum, because his helicopter had little trouble coming in or going out. Then the firing closed in once again.[7]

Reporters seemed to bring bad luck to everyone that day. At the 23d ARVN Division command bunker, another American officer was assigned to take a journalist out to see the fighting firsthand. A United Press International writer, Matt Franjola, had come in on a helicopter on its way up to Kontum to pick up some North Vietnamese prisoners for interrogation back in Saigon. Arriving about noon, he asked Rhotenberry where the action was. Between calls on the radio, he replied that the situation just north of the compound could probably provide some excitement. Just the day before, the North Vietnamese had occupied the area, but a sharp counterattack had pushed them back. "I'll get somebody to meet you up at the old division headquarters at the north edge of town," bellowed Rhotenberry as he stared down at one of many maps on the scarred table. "You can't miss it." Franjola headed out of the bunker and toward the sound of gunfire.

At the front, a young American adviser sat in a bunker, peering through binoculars at enemy movement in the treeline. He was Captain John "Jack" Finch, an intelligence officer assigned to the 23d ARVN Division advisory team. Most of his duties were centered around calling in air strikes, a job that occupied most of the hours in a day. Today, however, he was putting in time as an infantry observer.

In the air above, American helicopter gunships flashed back and forth over the advancing enemy, firing rockets as fast as the pilots could identify targets. From over the horizon U.S. Air Force fighters rushed in low, dropping high-explosive bombs on the advancing enemy. Suddenly a long burst of machine-gun fire riddled two soldiers nearby. Finch was jarred by the closeness of sudden death, but a radio call from the division bunker broke his concentration. "Get back to the bunker," crackled a voice over the receiver. "We've got a new job for you." Finch dashed back to the command post.

When Finch arrived inside the bunker, Lieutenant Colonel James Bricker, the division operations adviser, told him he was to accompany Franjola along the battle lines to get some "combat pictures." Since Finch was the only American who had been outside the bunker lately and knew about where the enemy was, he got the job. Finch and Franjola left the bunker at approximately 8:30 A.M. and toured the usual assortment of burned-out bunkers, destroyed tanks, and combat-weary troops resting at the rear. Franjola's camera was still clicking when they arrived at the airborne soldiers' compound, situated about 1,000 yards from the nearest fighting. Earlier that morning the airborne unit had been attacked from the east, and the compound was still buzzing with activity. Soldiers dashed back and forth, carrying water and extra ammunition to foxholes and bunkers.

Speaking passable Vietnamese, Franjola asked a group of lounging soldiers what the situation was outside the perimeter. They replied that the road had been cleared of the enemy, but it was mined. Finch told Franjola not to worry; he had helped place the mines, and they were antitank, not antipersonnel. Men walking down the road were not going to trigger an explosion. Finch shouldered his M16, Franjola strapped on the radio and hung his cameras around his neck, and the two started gingerly down the road.

Not far along, the two ran into a group of South Vietnamese tankers who told them not to go on. "Beaucoup VC," they warned. Franjola's experience with South Vietnamese soldiers told him that they always said that, and they were usually wrong.

Not this time. Less than 100 yards farther on, Finch and Franjola ran into a group of enemy sappers who had slipped through the forward South Vietnamese elements; Finch later estimated there were about sixty of them. Bullets zipped overhead and grenades exploded nearby. Finch and Franjola dove for a nearby ditch.[8]

The two men found mud and water waiting for them at the bottom of the ditch, but it was preferable to the firing above. Reaching for the radio, Finch found that the handset had been soaked in the dive; it was useless. He put a bullet through the frequency setter just in case the enemy found it. Above them the South Vietnamese had opened up on the enemy, and Franjola and Finch found themselves caught in the crossfire. Looking frantically around at the situation, Finch was sure a grenade would roll into the ditch and finish them off. Options were few. If they ran toward the South Vietnamese, they would surely be shot by mistake. If they stayed, the enemy would probably make for the ditch, since it was an obvious point of cover. Finch pictured his final seconds on earth: bayoneted by some twenty-year-old North Vietnamese soldier. There had to be a better way to go.

Finch finally found a wide spot in the ditch near the South Vietnamese perimeter. Expecting the worst, Finch gave Franjola his pistol and a couple of grenades, keeping the rifle and another grenade for himself. Then, lying flat against the bank, he placed his helmet atop his rifle barrel and slowly raised it above the bank. It looked like something out of an old war movie. But unlike in the cinema, Finch's helmet did not turn into Swiss cheese from enemy fire, though it did attract the attention of a South Vietnamese M41 tanker. Instead of realizing that there were Americans in the ditch, he opened fire with the tank's .50-caliber machine gun, narrowly missing Finch with the heavy bullets.

The South Vietnamese started zeroing in on the movement in the ditch, convinced that the enemy was using it for cover. Bullets came closer, and Finch once again waited for a grenade to pop down next to them. He started yelling at the top of his lungs, "Covan my" (American adviser). No one heard, and the bullets kept flying. He tried "Toi la nguoi my" (I'm an American), and "Viet-Nam cong-hoa muon nam" (long live Vietnam), all to no avail.

Finally, a South Vietnamese soldier slowly raised his head above his bunker and saw Franjola. In his hands was an M79 grenade launcher, and for a moment Franjola thought he was going to fire a round into the ditch. But recognition showed in the soldier's eyes, and soon the firing stopped. Franjola wanted to get up and run toward the South Vietnamese, but his pants had crept down low on his hips; he was afraid that as soon as he stood, they would fall down and trip him. He later recalled that he thought he was going to "trip and die from Communist gunfire with my pants around my ankles. Ridiculous."

Finch had a better idea. They would crawl through the five coils of barbed wire while the South Vietnamese covered them. Forty-five minutes later the two men were safe inside the perimeter. Looking at the sheepish soldiers, Franjola indignantly asked why they had fired at them. "Oh, we thought you were North Vietnamese," one soldier replied. "We thought you were killed hours ago."

Indeed they had. The advisers at the bunker told Finch they had given them up for dead and had radioed back to Pleiku that two Americans were missing in action. Finch got permission to fly down to Pleiku and phone his fiancée and tell her he was safe, just in case she heard otherwise.

Matt Franjola went on with his work. After cleaning his cameras and finding they still worked, he turned in the film and later published a picture of Captain John Finch peering above the ditch with a helmet perched on his rifle barrel. It received wide attention, and Finch's parents in Delray Beach, Florida, saw it in the newspaper. They were just glad to see their son alive.

Despite the little fight outside the northern compound, most of the action remained around the Kontum hospital. Air strikes were stepped up after South Vietnamese air force spotters noticed a large group of enemy troops massing for an attack near the hospital compound. They radioed through their own channels for a tactical air strike but were told none was available. In exasperation the South Vietnamese resorted to what everyone else did: beg for U.S. air support. A flight of American fighters streaked in low and dropped their ordnance right on top of the massing North Vietnamese. Sixty of them died, and the rest scattered for cover.[9]

Not all South Vietnamese pilots turned in pitiful performances. Near the embattled airport A-1E Skyraider jockeys made pass after pass at antiaircraft positions, exposing their slow, propeller-driven fighters to deadly ground fire. They managed to silence several machine guns and at least one 23mm antiaircraft gun that was foolish enough to reveal its position.[10]

Late in the afternoon Vann and Colonel Rhotenberry managed to cajole the South Vietnamese air force into shuttling supplies from the soccer field to the various regimental command posts. Lieutenant Colonel Gannon, the senior adviser to the 53d ARVN Regiment stationed near the airport, supervised the operation. He organized the South Vietnamese into teams and ordered them to run out to the drop zone and pick up the bundles after the helicopters dropped them off. The soldiers were reluctant to brave North Vietnamese artillery, but they must have figured that was safer than bucking Gannon. The American adviser got the job done, but he was wounded in the process. Shrapnel gouged Gannon's upper thigh as he was running back to the command bunker.

At the 23d ARVN Division headquarters Colonel Ba reassessed the situation. There seemed no alternative other than to tighten up the city's defenses yet again, so Ba ordered his units to disengage and move toward the city center. The main maneuver entailed withdrawal of the 45th ARVN Regiment from its position at Firebase November to new defenses southward inside Kontum itself. Ba reasoned that while he would lose some of his buffer to the north, it was preferable to allowing the North Vietnamese more and more tiny footholds inside his lines. He called General Toan, the corps commander, and asked permission to also move the 53d ARVN Regiment away from the airport and incorporate it in the greater defense of Kontum. The maneuver was "going to be ticklish," predicted Vann, but it would allow the division "to maintain greater integrity."[11]

Reluctantly, Toan agreed, probably after subtle coercion from Vann. General Toan was uneasy about any change in tactics because he realized he was in the spotlight. By late May the North Vietnamese offensive was largely over throughout the rest of South Vietnam, and all eyes were turned toward the Central Highlands. To lose another province capital (Quang Tri City had fallen in I Corps on 1 May) would be politically disastrous, so Toan remained overly cautious.

Ba was correct to move back on the city center. By late afternoon on 27 May, the North Vietnamese infantry had wormed its way to within forty meters of South Vietnamese positions in the hospital compound. Both sides spent the night staring at each other over gun barrels; only a few mortar rounds disturbed the uneasy quiet. In the distance the South Vietnamese could hear the comforting whirring roar of Spectre gunships, backed by a handful of South Vietnamese air force AC-47 Spooky gunships, making the rounds.

Then, about two hours before dawn on 28 May, all hell broke loose. Between 300 and 400 enemy artillery rounds dropped all along the northern defensive perimeter until dawn. North Vietnamese sappers struck the compound where the 14th Armored Cavalry Regiment kept its tanks. Just to the west, in the hospital compound, the 44th ARVN Regiment was hit yet again.

And once again the U.S. Air Force flew in to the rescue. A steady drizzle and low-lying clouds prevented effective use of tactical air support, so Sky Spot strikes were flown instead. For eight and a half hours the planes struck every twenty minutes along the battlefront.

Despite the heavy ground pressure, some of the South Vietnamese units managed to counterattack. Part of the 44th and 53 ARVN Regiments, supported by tanks from the 8th Armored Cavalry Regiment, threw themselves at enemy positions to the north. At the same time the Ruff-Puffs at the south end of Kontum doggedly fought from house to house in an attempt to dislodge North Vietnamese troops there. The Ruff-Puffs had risen to the occasion, transforming themselves from undisciplined militia to determined soldiers.

Trouble was brewing not far from the 23d ARVN Division command bunker. North Vietnamese soldiers had managed to scale a water tower and set up a heavy machine gun. From their new vantage point—the highest structure in Kontum—they could fire on approaching troops and aircraft at will. Within minutes the North Vietnamese gunners had downed an unsuspecting A1-E Skyraider. Colonel Ba took only a moment away from his other concerns to order the machine-gun nest taken out of action. The rest was up to the soldiers. But the task was easier said than done. A handful of South Vietnamese soldiers lay dead near the water tower, mute testimony to the mission's difficulty. A pair of M41 tanks tried their luck, but the tower's reinforced concrete posts resisted even direct hits from the main guns.

Captain John Finch tried to resolve the emergency. After his ordeal with the journalist the previous day, Finch was trying to catch some sleep in the damp and noisy bunker, but this turned out to be futile, so he went outside for a breath of fresh air and a look around.

Scoping the scene with his binoculars, Finch quickly saw what was happening. South Vietnamese soldiers in the area were milling about, and from the confusion Finch reasoned that either their radios were not working or they did not know how to use them. Either way, many of them were going to get killed if they did not straighten out the situation. Finch managed to round up about ten soldiers and convinced them to follow him in an assault on the water tower. They hoped to get close enough to the tower so the enemy machine gun would have a difficult time angling straight downward to reach them.

What Finch did not know was that the North Vietnamese had another machine-gun crew on the ground waiting for just such an attack. The gunners in the tower spotted the advancing South Vietnamese and radioed down to their comrades on the ground, who opened fire. By the time Captain Finch made it to within fifty yards or so of the tower, he turned around and noticed only three men still behind him. The rest lay dead or dying in the field, victims of the enemy machine gun. Finch realized that these three remaining soldiers must be very brave—or very foolish. They had followed a strange American, one with little infantry training, into the teeth of a well-defended enemy machine-gun nest.

As the wounded screamed behind him, Finch called for artillery support, remembering at the last moment that there was none left. To his surprise, a lone 155mm howitzer opened up. Finch adjusted fire and called for a medevac helicopter to come pick up the wounded.

The howitzer came from nearby, so Finch called for the minimum powder charge. The idea was not to overshoot the water tower and endanger other South Vietnamese positions. Two rounds landed on the tower, knocking out the machine gun. Finch then called for air strikes to finish off the tower. From over the horizon came a TOW gunship.

"Mark the target," came a voice crackling over the radio. Finch wondered if the pilot was really talking to him. After a brief moment he answered. "Are you kidding? It's the only water tower in Kontum all full of holes. Hit the damn thing." On came the helicopters, and within a few minutes the top of the water tower lay twisted and smoking.[12]

Despite success all around Kontum's shrinking perimeter, the North Vietnamese were beginning to falter. In what John Paul Vann interpreted as a desperation move, enemy artillery opened up on the city center, diverting

Soldiers from the 44th ARVN Regiment survey their battered compound. For several days they were fired on by enemy situated in a nearby water tower (center). The tower was finally destroyed by 155mm artillery fire and U.S. air strikes. (Jack Finch)

precious ammunition from militarily important targets such as the airfields and the regimental command posts. The business district, already damaged by successive bombardments, was virtually destroyed, as were many of the residential areas. Over 100 civilians were killed, probably the highest single-day total of the entire offensive.[13]

Colonel Ba threw more reinforcements into Kontum at about noon. The 3d Battalion of the 47th ARVN Regiment moved in from Pleiku, while the 45th ARVN Regiment was ordered back into the defensive perimeter. They encountered stiff resistance from North Vietnamese troops entrenched just inside the city and were unable to break through until the next day.

By nightfall the situation was still touch and go. No North Vietnamese units had been pushed out of their new positions, and the 23d ARVN Division only barely managed to prevent the enemy from making more gains inside the city. But the sheer weight of American and South Vietnamese air assets was beginning to tell on the attackers. Countless strikes reduced North Vietnamese troops to a fraction of what they needed to maintain the offensive. Resupply was also difficult. Hourly B-52 strikes forced the enemy to store food and ammunition far away from Kontum, and keeping the troops supplied became both difficult and risky. Supply lines were often spotted by sharp-eyed forward air controllers who called in air strikes. Transportation units probably suffered higher casualties than soldiers near the city for the simple reason that they received most of the attention from the B-52s. The freedom of the U.S. Air Force to strike at will at any target it could identify reduced the North Vietnamese timetable to a simple equation: win swiftly or retreat to the hills and resupply. They had already stretched the acceptable limit, and the soldiers were feeling the squeeze.

The 23d ARVN Division was also feeling the pinch of the on-again, off-again resupply system. The airfield had proved to be an unreliable drop-off point, and the South Vietnamese air force was either unable or unwilling to fly helicopters into the city much of the time. As usual, the U.S. Air Force came to the rescue. Late in the day a C-130 cargo plane air-dropped crates of ammunition, about 75 percent of which was recovered.[14]

On 29 May the South Vietnamese began to sense that they were at the end of what had been a very long ordeal. Light sniper fire and sporadic mortar attacks dominated the action; only about thirty artillery rounds landed in the city by midafternoon. But it was enough to thwart all South Vietnamese attempts to dislodge enemy troops from their positions. For twenty-four hours enemy soldiers had dug in, strengthening their bunkers against air attacks. Sixty sorties destroyed thirty-nine of the bunkers, but it was not enough. By nightfall the South Vietnamese had to settle for a stalemate.[15]

Just after midnight on 30 May, the 44th and 53d ARVN Regiment command posts came under attack, mostly from heavy mortars. Two AC-130 Spectres and an AC-119 Stinger gunship happened to be on station at the time, and they quickly put some of the mortars out of action.

Another North Vietnamese attack started along the northeastern perimeter, a final attempt to link forces with comrades south of the airfield. Between the attacking North Vietnamese and the defenders lay the old ammunition dump, which had exploded three days before. Another mortar round landed in the ashes—and it went up with a roar. Apparently, plenty of ammunition had survived the first inferno. But this time the maelstrom of lead and shrapnel played against the attackers. The ammunition exploded just as the bulk of enemy troops passed nearby, killing scores and breaking up the attack. It marked an ironic beginning to the last North Vietnamese gasp in Kontum.[16]

At dawn on 30 May, all units of the 23d ARVN Division counterattacked the northern positions occupied by the enemy. Fierce fighting, much of it brutal hand-to-hand combat, raged between the bunkers. Hand grenades flew, and rifles fired point-blank. It was the only way for the South Vietnamese to win the battle. Air strikes had failed to destroy the reinforced bunkers, and they were too close to friendly units to allow the use of B-52s. It was ironic that in the final hours of the battle for Kontum airpower was unable to defeat the North Vietnamese, although it had done so much to blunt their offensive. No one would deny that airpower had saved the Central Highlands, but it took infantry to punctuate the victory.

The final indication that the battle for Kontum had been won by the South Vietnamese came at exactly 2:30 P.M. on 30 May. Over the treetops from the south winged a helicopter flanked by snarling Cobras. In the Huey was South Vietnamese president Nguyen Van Thieu, coming from Saigon to visit the troops in beleaguered Kontum. Amid sporadic mortar and small-arms fire, Thieu jumped out of the helicopter and strode straight up to a sheepish-looking Colonel Ba. Blinking in the bright sunlight—which he had seen little of over the past few weeks—Ba mumbled his thanks for the visit. Thieu responded by promoting the colonel to brigadier general, pinning the new rank insignia to Ba's collar as guns rumbled close by.

Vann had arranged and promoted the entire event. When Thieu flew to Pleiku on the afternoon of 30 May for a briefing, Vann encouraged other officers to suggest a presidential flight to Kontum. When Thieu agreed, Vann quickly rounded up available journalists and flew them to Kontum so they would be in position when the president arrived. But although the event was well choreographed, it was dangerous. Three 122mm rockets

Colonel Rhotenberry (left), senior adviser to the 23d ARVN Division, and Colonel Ba (center), the division commander, stand beside the wreckage of a North Vietnamese tank. (Author's collection)

landed within 300 yards of the president, and sniper fire whistled constantly overhead. Still, Thieu wandered among the troops in their foxholes and bunkers, congratulating them on a job well done. Vann reported, "Overall, it was an extremely impressive performance and a great morale boost to the forces in Kontum City."[17]

As Thieu chatted with the men, other South Vietnamese soldiers slowly but surely pushed the tenacious enemy out of its positions. Two T-54 tanks lurking near the hospital met destruction at the hands of South Vietnamese infantrymen wielding LAWs. Snipers were routed from their positions all around the city. As the 44th ARVN Regiment prepared to move north in a general counteroffensive, reconnaissance units reported large groups of enemy soldiers retreating to the northeast. That was the safest escape route because South Vietnamese troops were counterattacking from all other sides. American air cavalry units also reported enemy soldiers leaving the battlefield in droves. Air strikes pursued them, but it was clear that North Vietnamese commanders had issued a general retreat from the area. Only a few stragglers were unable to get away. By the end of the day a few pockets of enemy resistance inside Kontum fought on, but they could no longer hold on in the face of South Vietnamese pressure.

At noon on 31 May John Paul Vann declared that the battle was over. As he flew over the ruined cityscape, Vann could see hundreds of North Vietnamese bodies among the wreckage of T-54 tanks. Fighting would go on for weeks, but only in small pockets on the city's outskirts. Almost 4,000 North Vietnamese dead littered the battlefield, the debris left from an expensive experiment in conventional warfare.

TWENTY-TWO

MOPPING UP

While fighting in the Central Highlands held the headlines, there were other battles still to be fought. By early June Kontum was out of danger, but all was still not well in II Corps. As the North Vietnamese grudgingly abandoned their goal of capturing Kontum and melted away toward the Cambodian border, fighting again flared in Binh Dinh Province. Communist successes on the coast in the early days of the fighting had pushed the South Vietnamese out of their bases and down toward Qui Nhon. At the end of May only one major base remained as a South Vietnamese toehold north of Qui Nhon, an old American enclave called Landing Zone Crystal. Like the abandoned bases to the north, Crystal straddled Highway 1 and was tasked with keeping the road open south to Qui Nhon. The base sat just outside the district center of Phu My about thirty miles north of Qui Nhon.

Crystal was home base for the 41st ARVN Regiment. Like the 40th ARVN Regiment at Landing Zone English, it was part of the 22d ARVN Division, which had been defeated at Tan Canh. The 41st ARVN Regiment had gamely held on to its tiny spit of territory as the offensive raged. Throughout April and May the unit sat in its base, sending occasional patrols out into the countryside. As the northern part of the province gradually fell throughout April, Crystal found itself the northernmost bastion of Saigon's influence in Binh Dinh.

The ranking American at Landing Zone Crystal (there were only two) was Lieutenant Colonel Donald Stovall, senior adviser to the 41st ARVN Regiment. Stovall had been there since the beginning of his tour in July 1971, and he was familiar with the unit and the terrain. When the 40th ARVN Regiment was hit at Landing Zone English in April, Stovall had monitored the situation. He was prepared to step in to help if the situation grew dangerous. It did.

The two remaining battalions of the 40th ARVN Regiment quickly crumbled before the North Vietnamese attack. Lieutenant Colonel Duc, commander of the 40th ARVN Regiment, again proved incapable of handling the situation; he sat despondently in his bunker as artillery rounds rained down and his men waited for orders. None came, and the two American advisers placed a frantic call to Landing Zone Crystal asking to be evacuated. Seeing no reason to risk their lives in a futile defense, Stovall went in with U.S. helicopters to pick up the two men.

Two slicks and four Cobra gunships raced to the beleaguered firebase. As the Cobras fired rockets and machine guns into the surrounding enemy, the Hueys swooped in. Stovall's helicopter shuddered as 12.7mm machine-gun fire raked the front and sides. The pilot took four hits in his armored breastplate, and the doorgunner was hit and seriously wounded. Stovall was nicked in the leg. As the advisers scrambled aboard, the helicopters climbed back into the air. Seeing their quarry escaping, the North Vietnamese turned up the volume of fire. When Stovall's chopper landed back at Crystal, the crew counted seventeen bullet holes.

Rumor had it that Landing Zone English had struck a deal with the North Vietnamese. In other cases where the South Vietnamese had been defeated, they had fled headlong from the battlefield, throwing down their weapons and casting off their uniforms. At English the 40th Regiment—which had no U.S. advisers by this time—neatly packed its equipment, formed into units, and marched out of the base to the coast. There the soldiers loaded onto landing craft and made their way down the coast to Qui Nhon. The circumstances were indeed suspicious. Worse, from the perspective of the defenders at Landing Zone Crystal, the 40th ARVN Regiment left behind its artillery, including the potent 155mm howitzers. Before air strikes could bomb fallen Landing Zone English into oblivion, the North Vietnamese managed to drag at least a few of the big guns out of the base. South Vietnamese defenders at Crystal would be fired on by these guns in a matter of weeks.[1]

Landing Zone Crystal was clearly next in line. During late April and into May, South Vietnamese units on reconnaissance patrols reported increased enemy activity north of the base. To step up the pressure on Crystal, enemy units moved down from Landing Zone English and periodically dropped mortar rounds and rockets into Crystal's perimeter. The defenders watched and waited.

The big break for the defenders at Crystal came on 1 June when a soldier from the 3d NVA Division was captured by a South Vietnamese patrol. He told his captors that a full-scale assault was planned for just after midnight on 2 June. There was no time to double-check the story; the defenders were told to prepare for the worst. Each soldier was given extra water, three cases of grenades, and extra ammunition and was told to stay in his foxhole.

At midnight nothing happened. The hour came and went, and the North Vietnamese did not attack. No one in Crystal moved, however. They all secretly hoped that the report of an impending attack was false, yet they knew that faulty timing may have caused the delay.

Six hours later the North Vietnamese struck. Artillery and mortar fire rained down on the defenders, immediately blowing up the ammo dump and the helicopter fuel bladders near the base. Three 82mm mortar rounds landed directly on the advisers' compound, wounding five of the men inside. For five days the enemy threw artillery bombardments and infantry assaults at the defenders. But with the aid of massive air support, Landing Zone Crystal held.[2]

During the night of 4 June, the North Vietnamese seemed to turn the tide against the beleaguered firebase. As enemy troops closed on the wire, a U.S. Air Force AC-130 Spectre gunship appeared in the black sky over Crystal. As the night wore on, Spectre circled the base menacingly, spitting fire from miniguns and cannon onto the enemy below. At dawn Spectre called to the Americans below, saying it was low on fuel. Stovall implored the gunship to stay long enough to take out one particularly troublesome recoilless rifle about 500 yards outside the wire. Spectre complied, firing some well-placed 105mm rounds into the enemy position. The gun fell silent, and Spectre rumbled away over the jungle to pick up more fuel.

Not all close-air support missions ended so well. The next day an air force F-4 Phantom from Phu Cat Air Base was on a bombing run outside Crystal when it slammed into the ground while diving on a target. No one was sure why the plane augered in; there was no enemy antiaircraft fire at the time. The next morning, during a lull in the fighting, Lieutenant Colonel Stovall and one company of armored personnel carriers went out beyond the wire looking for the remains. Both bodies were found near the wreckage a mere 400 yards outside the wire.[3]

By 6 June the battle was over. Despite the intensity of the fighting, the defenders inside Landing Zone Crystal suffered only minor casualties. That day a handful of new American advisers, including a marine gunfire liaison officer, arrived at Crystal. Flying them in to their new assignment was John Paul Vann. He commended the two original American advisers on a job well done, pointing out that Lieutenant Colonel Stovall had single-handedly controlled naval gunfire, tactical air, Spectre gunships, South Vietnamese artillery, B-52s, and air cavalry gunships. In typical perfectionist fashion, however, Vann found a flaw in the advisers' performance in the battles for Landing Zones English and Crystal. As Stovall supervised South Vietnamese soldiers stacking the hundreds of communist small arms gathered from the battlefield, Vann chastised him for making the decision to pull the advisers out of Landing Zone English. "You pulled them out too early," Vann said.[4]

President Thieu was less critical. On 7 June he made a five-hour visit to Binh Dinh Province, including a stop at Crystal. Obviously pleased by the successful defense of the base, he exhorted his troops to move onto the offensive. In Binh Dinh, Thieu demanded the recapture of Tam Quan, Hoai Nhan, and Hoai An Districts, though he realized that North Vietnamese occupation of the Bong Son Pass made a northward sweep risky. Instead he called for either an air assault or an amphibious landing at Tam Quan, the northernmost district, followed by a sweep south, thereby cutting off enemy positions in Bong Son. Observers noticed that the president seemed confident and pleased, a dramatic change from the dark days of May when both the coast and the Central Highlands were in danger.[5]

But incompetent commanders and low troop morale prevented quick action. As the threat in the Central Highlands dissipated and Binh Dinh Province was gradually retaken, attention turned to the critical supply routes between the Highlands and the coast. Most important was Highway 19, the main artery running between Pleiku and Qui Nhon. North Vietnamese forces had cut the road in several places during the offensive, most seriously at An Khe Pass in mid-April. But they had also occupied the strategic pass at Mang Yang, a tangle of green-clad hills rising abruptly from the rolling plateau about fifteen miles east of Pleiku. South Vietnamese troops had been unable to clear Mang Yang, but by mid-June the corps commander, General Toan, had more troops to devote to retaking it. Toan was skeptical about occupying the pass, however, arguing that his soldiers were battle-weary and in dire need of retraining.

After prodding from MACV advisers, Toan agreed to push a heavily armed convoy through the pass on 13 June. The Americans did not feel this was adequate, though they understood the problems facing Toan. "Believe me, no one could try harder than he has," said SRAG headquarters in defense of Toan against criticism from Saigon. However, they conceded, "his troops move slowly at best." Toan personally confronted his subordinates over their lack of progress, then relieved two of them on 10 and 11 June for lack of progress in clearing Mang Yang Pass. The Americans were amazed by Toan's anger over his commanders' lack of imagination. "I thought he was going to shoot one of his officers right there on the battlefield," reported one adviser to General Abrams. But despite Toan's threats, Mang Yang Pass was not opened for another week.[6]

At the end of June the new 22d ARVN Division commander, Colonel Phan Dinh Niem, moved his headquarters from Pleiku to Qui Nhon. He also brought with him the 42d and 47th ARVN Regiments, which had spent most of the offensive in Pleiku awaiting an attack there. The move marked a shift in priority from the Central Highlands to the coast.[7]

With the new headquarters in place, the 41st Regiment sallied forth from

Crystal and retook Landing Zone English. It was not a difficult task. The North Vietnamese chose not to contest English and risk bringing down the wrath of renewed American aerial firepower. They slowly retreated, leaving a rearguard force of Viet Cong main-force and local-force units to bear the brunt of the counteroffensive.

Beginning on 19 July the four South Vietnamese regiments plus the 2d and 6th Ranger Groups from Kontum began to work their way north, pushing the North Vietnamese from the northern districts. On 21 July the district capital of Hoai Nhon was recaptured, on 23 July the enemy was driven from Tam Quan, and on 26 July Hoai An and Landing Zone Orange were once again occupied by South Vietnamese troops.[8]

With supplies running low and the probability that more U.S. air assets would be diverted to the coast as Kontum came out of danger, the 3d NVA Division moved into the rugged An Lao Valley for retraining and refitting. Although the enemy had been pushed out of all towns taken in the early part of the offensive, intelligence indicated that they still retained the capability to conduct regimental-sized attacks against the three northern districts. The most the South Vietnamese could claim even after retaking lost district towns was a return to the status quo. Even in defeat the communists remained a potent force in Binh Dinh.

The recapture of the three communist-occupied district capitals in Binh Dinh Province signaled the end of the major North Vietnamese onslaughts in II Corps. The enemy broke off engagements more rapidly and completely than in I Corps and III Corps, possibly because of the late date. By June 1972 An Loc in III Corps had broken free of its siege and the North Vietnamese had lost the initiative throughout northern I Corps. More troops were available to reinforce the Central Highlands or the Binh Dinh coast if need be.

To observers both in Vietnam and back in the States, John Paul Vann was the central figure in Kontum's fight for survival. It was Vann who wielded the bombers, Vann who conceived battle strategy, Vann who kept his South Vietnamese commanders in line. He was in his element during the Easter Offensive. Vann had spent his entire career—in and out of the army—climbing to the point where he could command men in battle.

The Easter Offensive represented the pinnacle of his life. The North Vietnamese sallied forth and did battle, something they had been largely unwilling to do in the past. But by doing so, Hanoi exposed its troops to the full fury of American technology and firepower, both of which John Paul Vann was more than willing to apply. And he applied them with relish.

Vann tried to inflict maximum destruction on the North Vietnamese because, after almost a decade of duty in Vietnam, he believed that communism was an evil that must be resisted in the South. He had seen that the United States was unwilling to do what was needed to win, so by attacking south of the demilitarized zone in April 1972, the North Vietnamese provided Vann with an opportunity to vent his moral outrage both at the enemy and at the policy makers in Washington.

John Paul Vann often fought with abandon. He risked death daily, yet he managed to live through it all. His performance was an inspiration to all Americans in his command. One adviser called Vann "the heart and soul" of Kontum's defense, an epithet few would have disagreed with. When Vann declared Kontum out of danger on 31 May, it represented more than just an end to the offensive. It also validated John Paul Vann's position of command. He had succeeded.

But only barely. On 9 June John Paul Vann was killed in a helicopter crash, the highest-ranking official to die in Vietnam that year. The timing was uncanny, as if now that the battle was over and his place in history secure, Vann could return to the world of mere mortals, where taking risks often ends in death. The odds simply caught up with him. That very day he reported to Abrams, "The last enemy pocket in Kontum City has been cleared. The interior of the city has been secured." It was his last message.[9]

Vann flew to Saigon on the morning of 9 June to see his deputy, Brigadier General John Hill, awarded the Legion of Merit by General Abrams. Hill was going home to continue his career as Fifth Army chief of staff at Fort Sam Houston. Vann remained for a strategy meeting with the MACV commander and other senior corps advisers, then flew back to Pleiku with Hill and Colonel Robert Kingston, Vann's new deputy. After a farewell dinner for General Hill, Vann climbed into his helicopter for the flight to Kontum. Since the siege began, Vann had managed to fly into Kontum at least once every day, and although the offensive was over, he did not intend to break his streak. Vann even planned a party with some of his advisers and General Ba.

At a little after 9:00 P.M., Vann took off with his new pilot, First Lieutenant Ronald Doughtie, and copilot Captain John P. Robertson. Nervous at the idea of flying with instruments through low-hanging clouds and light rain, Doughtie cautiously eased his OH-58 Kiowa helicopter into the sky over Pleiku. He had heard stories about the eccentric and fearless John Paul Vann, particularly his propensity for asking pilots to fly into weather that made more reasonable men think twice. But Doughtie's reputation as a pilot—he was called "levelheaded and a very capable pilot" by fellow flyers—was meant to offset Vann's recklessness.[10]

They went down fifteen minutes outside of Kontum, near the Chu Pao Pass. There was no distress call. A South Vietnamese ranger, Sergeant Nguyen Van Loc, saw the helicopter veer left from its course, then crash into a hillside. Part of a road-clearing mission along Highway 14, the rangers called in the accident sighting, though it took another half hour for the U.S. 17th Aviation Group at Pleiku to determine that only one helicopter was reported in the air at that time—John Paul Vann's.

A search-and-rescue team of three helicopters raced to the scene, but the team's powerful searchlights were unable to penetrate the darkness and thick vegetation. Even the aerial flares from an AC-130 Spectre diverted to the crash site failed to brighten the gloom. Finally, the command ship, flown by Lieutenant Colonel Jack Anderson, the same pilot who had rescued advisers from certain capture or death in Binh Dinh Province during the early days of the offensive, landed in a clearing. The team quickly located the shattered fuselage, then found Vann's battered and broken body several yards from the wreckage. Sporadic rifle fire in the distance spooked the rangers, who threatened to leave, forcing Anderson to fly away carrying only Vann's body and a piece of the main engine. The other bodies were not recovered until the following day.

At midnight, General Hill identified Vann's body, an unpleasant ending to an evening that had begun as a celebration. Fate had finally chased down the man who routinely tempted death. Few would have predicted that this warrior who routinely flew into the teeth of enemy guns would fall victim to a flying accident. Yet it may have been Vann's own devil-may-care attitude that killed him. He was probably at the controls when the helicopter crashed, and a post-crash investigation concluded that he was "intoxicated," though not enough to impair his flying. According to one American officer present at the dinner, Vann "had full control of his faculties." The autopsy report noted that Vann had not been wearing a helmet. But the probable cause of the crash, according to the accident board, was that the pilot became disoriented in the murky sky and lost control of the helicopter.[11]

Few who knew Vann were surprised that fate had finally caught up with him. In the early days of the offensive, a friend had written a few words of caution to Vann as he prepared to do battle: "Your reputation for guts [is] well-established and your primary value is in thinking and advising rather than personal feats involving excessive danger. Remember all you would miss should your goddess of good fortune be on a coffee break at the wrong time."[12]

Vann's goddess of good fortune had turned away this time, but he died knowing that he had won. Most of his advisers in the Central Highlands were stunned by the news; they had come to believe him invincible. Command of U.S. advisers in II Corps went to Brigadier General Michael "Iron Mike" Healy, a Special Forces officer who was not particularly fond of John Paul Vann and his brand of civilian leadership. Since a military officer was now in charge, SRAG was changed to SRAC—Second Regional Assistance Command—and mopping-up operations went on undisturbed.[13]

Enemy resistance in the Central Highlands continued through the rest of the year, though at a low level. On 5 June the B-3 Front had concluded that "the conditions for completely annihilating the enemy in [Kontum] no longer existed," and the front's Party Committee "decided to order a pullback." The North Vietnamese offensive in the Highlands was over, and they had not prevailed, but communist officials believed that they had made great strides in "annihilating the enemy's strength and liberating territory, thereby making an important contribution to the common victory."[14]

The North Vietnamese decision to withdraw from the area allowed the South Vietnamese to rapidly go on the offensive. In June their operations concentrated on opening Highway 14 between Kontum and Pleiku and in clearing enemy troops from pockets north of the city of Kontum. Areas that had fallen to the North Vietnamese in the early days of the siege were heavily fortified and riddled with tunnels, forcing the South Vietnamese to move slowly and deliberately.

Opening Highway 14 was the most difficult. Fourteen South Vietnamese battalions were thrown at the entrenched enemy, and at first the North Vietnamese fought fiercely. But by the end of June heavy casualties and dwindling supplies tore down their will to resist. On 26 June the South Vietnamese won the high ground east and west of Highway 14, and on 30 June the highway was deemed safe enough to risk sending a military convoy from Pleiku on up to Kontum. Thirty-six trucks drove the entire stretch of road without incident. On 6 July the road was opened to civilian traffic.[15]

In Pleiku Province the North Vietnamese continued to harass traffic and tie down South Vietnamese units. In August, small, sharp engagements prevented either side from gaining the upper hand, but during September the enemy regained enough strength to strike at the road once again. On 19 October the North Vietnamese again closed the road by blowing up a huge culvert twelve kilometers south of Kontum. Traffic was effectively stopped for a few days until South Vietnamese road crews repaired the damage. On 22 October a bridge in Kontum Pass was demolished. South Vietnamese engineers moved in to rebuild the bridge, but enemy sniping and small-unit action prevented them from working. Operations by the 23d ARVN Division took a heavy toll on the North Vietnamese, but not enough to stop them from interfering with the bridge repairs. On 8 November the bridge was finally reopened.

Territory lost to the enemy north of Kontum was the central focus of the counteroffensive. On 7 June President Thieu had ordered that Tan Canh be retaken, although he was pragmatic enough to realize that this could not be an immediate priority. Heartened by Thieu's speech and emboldened by the North Vietnamese retreat, the South Vietnamese army launched a series of operations aimed at the fleeing 320th NVA Division as it retreated to Tan Canh and Dak To. What was left of the 2d NVA Division retreated into Quang Ngai Province and began the slow process of recuperating from its wounds.[16]

By mid-June, however, the 23d ARVN Division, weakened by the fighting in Kontum, was in no position to beard the North Vietnamese in their new defensive positions around Tan Canh. Instead, they relied on small airmobile operations to keep the enemy off balance and create a psychological impact on the people living in communist-occupied areas. The first assault took place on 17 June, a limited raid code-named Cuong Than 23/8. One reconnaissance company air assaulted north of Tan Canh, then swept south through the town. The surprised enemy lost twenty-four men at a cost of only a single soldier wounded on the South Vietnamese side. An enthusiastic General Healy called the operation "a complete success," even though the South Vietnamese were forced to leave after three hours. They flew back to Kontum, taking with them thirty-seven civilians and nine South Vietnamese soldiers who had been stranded since Tan Canh fell in April.[17]

A few months later they tried the operation again, this time on a larger scale. Two companies air assaulted into the area near Tan Canh and Dak To but were partially driven out by superior enemy forces. About a week later another company was sent in, but the North Vietnamese chose not to fight. On 12 November the South Vietnamese declared victory and withdrew.

Because Tan Canh had been largely destroyed during the fighting, the North Vietnamese settled in Vo Dinh, a small town about twenty kilometers north of Kontum on Highway 14, an area that had been bypassed by the early fighting. The enemy was in among the population, causing American and South Vietnamese officers to think twice about bombing the town into oblivion. When the January 1973 cease-fire took place, the South Vietnamese had advanced no farther than ten kilometers northwest of Vo Dinh.[18]

Although Saigon permanently lost part of the sparsely populated territory north of Kontum, the North Vietnamese could not have been satisfied with the final outcome. Unable to take Kontum and incapable of holding Tan Canh and Dak To, the enemy dispersed its forces, leaving the 2d NVA

Division in the rugged mountains near the border and sending the 320th NVA Division back to its sanctuary in Laos. General Hoang Minh Thao, commander of North Vietnamese forces in the Highlands, the B-3 Front, reportedly reprimanded both division commanders for their failure to capture the province capital. Thao later admitted, "We could not take Kontum City because the ability of the commander and the campaign staff to organize and command campaigns was still insufficient." Still, Thao did not concede defeat, arguing that a North Vietnamese "victory" was secured because "the enemy in Kontum City were not as strong as in the past." He also credited a strategy of deception with causing the South Vietnamese forces to be "dispersed to the other key theaters."[19]

What is indisputable is that Hanoi's battle in the Central Highlands was costly. American intelligence estimated that the North Vietnamese lost between 20,000 and 40,000 soldiers killed in the Central Highlands alone, not to mention the loss of perhaps a hundred tanks as well as an immeasurable quantity of supplies.[20]

From a strictly military point of view, South Vietnam defeated the enemy attack in II Corps. By any definition, North Vietnam had failed to obtain a single objective in the entire region. Far from cutting South Vietnam in two across the Central Highlands, the North Vietnamese did not capture a single province capital, and they had failed to decisively defeat any major South Vietnamese combat units. Even the 22d ARVN Division, badly beaten at Tan Canh and Dak To, was still considered partially combat effective and would soon be refitted and retrained. On the other hand, the North Vietnamese had been mauled by repeated bombings, and their supplies and manpower reserves had been severely depleted.

But what had the South Vietnamese "won"? An optimist would say they had won time. But with the continuing American withdrawal and mounting international indifference to South Vietnam's final fate, time did not mean much.

PART THREE
Besieged:
The Battle for An Loc

TWENTY-THREE

HELL IN A VERY INSIGNIFICANT PLACE

When Bernard Fall called the Battle of Dien Bien Phu "hell in a very small place," he had no idea that America's final months in Vietnam would come to a climax much like the final months for the French—in a small, insignificant patch of ground surrounded by enemy artillery and battered by infantry assaults. But while the French met their Vietnam Waterloo at Dien Bien Phu, the United States managed to bolster South Vietnamese forces at the provincial capital of An Loc and turn back the North Vietnamese offensive in III Corps. In the end the South Vietnamese won, though their victory over the communist forces did not stem purely from their own military might. American air support turned the tide and made the final difference between winning and losing. Yet by all accounts, the Battle of An Loc was a bitter struggle, and certainly the largest siege of the entire war.

As the enemy offensive unfolded in I Corps and South Vietnamese troops in Kontum and Pleiku braced for the worst in the Central Highlands, advisers with the Third Regional Assistance Command (TRAC) stationed in Long Binh did not know what to expect. Intelligence coming primarily from Cambodia indicated a buildup of North Vietnamese forces in the area, though there was little specific information heralding communist intentions.

Assuming that the attack in I Corps was the main thrust of the North Vietnamese invasion, the South Vietnamese command in Saigon ordered units from the other corps to reinforce north of Hue. III Corps lost the 18th Cavalry Regiment, the 5th and 6th Ranger Groups (part of which would return as the attack on An Loc intensified), and the 4th Ranger Group, which was on loan from IV Corps.[1]

The importance of the enemy offensive in III Corps was unclear at the time. Was it a diversion meant to take attention away from the main thrust of the attack in I Corps? Or was the opposite true? Were North Vietnamese actions in I Corps ultimately aimed at diverting reserves away from Saigon so as to open the way for the real thrust into III Corps? In April 1972 the South Vietnamese Joint General Staff did not regard An Loc as the central focus of the offensive. This had always been regarded as a

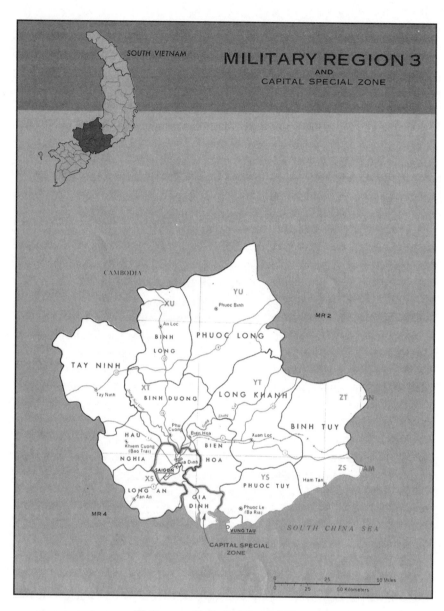

III Corps and Capital Special Zone

potentially dangerous sector, but because of its distance down the Ho Chi Minh Trail from Hanoi, irregularities in supplies and reinforcements made a large-scale invasion problematic. On the other hand, the unoccupied country to the west near the Cambodian border was honeycombed with sanctuaries and base areas.

The few North Vietnamese sources on the subject are somewhat contradictory on the importance of III Corps in the offensive. According to one official history, the communist politburo first chose "eastern Nam Bo [the region around Saigon] as the primary direction of attack, but later on, in March 1972, we shifted to the Tri-Thien area [Quang Tri and Thua Thien Provinces in northern I Corps] as the primary direction."[2] However, another account maintains that I Corps was always the primary focus of attention. In January 1972 a military commission within the Party Central Committee determined that I Corps would be the main battlefield, and attacks in II and III Corps would be "in coordination" with the principal attack.[3] Yet another history of the North Vietnamese army is more ambiguous, indicating that all three fronts were of equal importance, with perhaps a bit more emphasis on the I Corps front simply because of its proximity to North Vietnam.[4]

The thinking behind the North Vietnamese attack in III Corps may have been to probe and then see what happened. If initial attacks were successful, they could be easily reinforced. If not, units could be withdrawn to base areas or ordered to the front in the Central Highlands or in I Corps. The flexible nature of this option was probably what the North Vietnamese had in mind when they attacked the tiny rubber plantation town of Loc Ninh in northern Binh Long Province during early April. Because they were initially successful, the assault was carried through to An Loc. Had the enemy been turned away from Loc Ninh, the story might have been altogether different. There may also be a short-term explanation for the importance of An Loc to the communists. By the middle of April the attack in I Corps had slowed, and some analysts speculated that Quang Tri would not fall; Hue was certainly not seriously threatened at that time. If Hanoi believed it could not take a province capital in I Corps, then II Corps or III Corps seemed like a logical place to try, and North Vietnamese troops north of An Loc were in the best position to capture a city.[5]

Whatever the real motives behind Hanoi's strategy, the significance of the battle for An Loc was overblown by both policy makers and the press. The city itself became a symbol all out of proportion to its true importance. An Loc was a town of fewer than 15,000 residents sitting in the midst of an underpopulated province. But because it was only some fifty miles northwest of Saigon, its capture was rightly regarded as unacceptable. Yet even if the city did fall, the loss would be more symbolic than real. True, if the South Vietnamese relinquished the province capital, the flagging prestige of the military would fall further. But the North Vietnamese could never hold An Loc. Once the enemy had established its provisional government center, the fearsome power of American B-52s would soon unseat the North Vietnamese. As one U.S. Air Force officer observed, "They'd have to sleep under a B-52 blanket, and that can be scratchy."[6]

As in the rest of the country, South Vietnamese units in III Corps found themselves filling large American shoes. Long Binh, the sprawling U.S. base in Binh Long Province, had been headquarters for USARV and the U.S. II Field Force. In 1968, at the height of the American troop buildup, III Corps was the operational home of the 1st Infantry Division, the 25th Infantry Division—the Tropic Lightning—along with the 199th Infantry Brigade, 11th Armored Cavalry Regiment, two brigades of the 1st Cavalry Division, and one battalion of the 17th Air Cavalry Regiment. It was a formidable force, even when compared with other distinguished American fighting units in the rest of South Vietnam. By December 1971, however, the drawdown was in full swing, and U.S. troop strength was reduced to one squadron of the 17th Air Cavalry, the 1st Aviation Brigade, one squadron of the 11th Armored Cavalry Regiment, and a battalion of combat engineers. By June 1972 all but the 1st Aviation Brigade and the 3d Brigade of the 1st Cavalry Division had left for home.[7]

In their place the South Vietnamese attempted to secure III Corps with three divisions. From Cu Chi the 25th ARVN Division occupied its traditional haunt, operating in Tay Ninh, Hau Nghia, and Long An Provinces. The 18th ARVN Division was stationed in Xuan Loc and was responsible for the provinces of Bien Hoa, Long Khanh, Phuoc Tuy, and Binh Tuy. On the northern side, the 5th ARVN Division was positioned in Lai Khe and watched over Phuoc Long, Binh Long, and Binh Duong Provinces. The corps headquarters at Long Binh retained the 3d Armored Brigade, 1st Airborne Brigade, 3d Ranger Group, and 43d Infantry Regiment.[8]

This order of battle had only recently been patched together, however. Since early 1971 South Vietnamese forces supported by U.S. helicopters and artillery had operated mostly inside Cambodia, keeping the main North Vietnamese units outside of South Vietnam. The III Corps commander, Lieutenant General Do Cao Tri, had been an advocate of operating aggressively inside Cambodia to keep the enemy off balance. Then, in February 1971, General Tri was killed in a helicopter crash. His replacement, Lieutenant General Nguyen Van Minh, preferred a strategy of setting

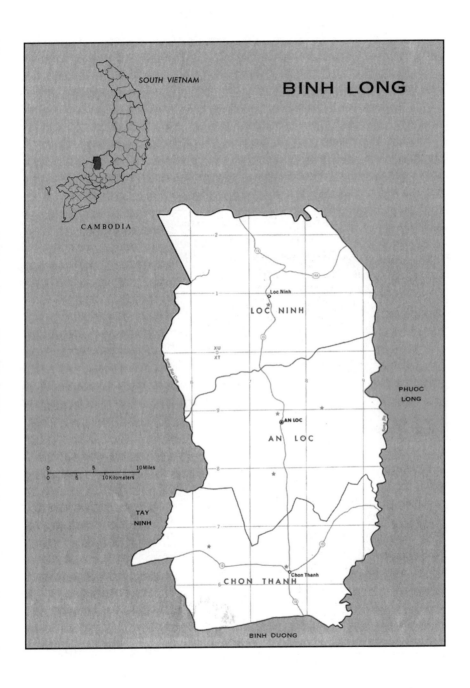

SOUTH VIETNAM

CAMBODIA

BINH LONG

2

LOC NINH

Loc Ninh

XU
O
XT

6

1

2

8

9

9

AN LOC

AN LOC

PHUOC
LONG

8

7

CHON THANH

Chon Thanh

TAY
NINH

BINH DUONG

his troops astride the border in standoff defense instead of operating in Cambodia. Minh thought he could strike a decisive blow to North Vietnamese troops in the border region, hoping to throw the enemy into disarray and then retire over the border back into South Vietnam.[9]

General Minh was a relative newcomer to the game of political appointments, though he had been in the military since 1950, when he served as an airborne officer under the French. After backing the wrong side in an unsuccessful coup against then-president Ngo Dinh Diem in November 1960, Minh was banished to An Giang Province in the Mekong Delta, where he served as province chief until after Diem's death in November 1963. A year later he became deputy commander of the 21st ARVN Division, still in the delta, where the insurgency had reached dangerous proportions. In 1965 Minh was promoted to brigadier general and given command of the division. In early 1966 the American deputy senior division adviser noted that the successes of the 21st ARVN Division were "due primarily to the leadership and skill of the division CG [commanding general] Major General Nguyen Van Minh. This division is an aggressive fighting force, and extremely well-led." General Minh was also instrumental in developing an effective airmobile capability for the division within eight months of taking command.[10]

But as a corps commander, Minh was out of his league. Despite the overblown evaluation of his American counterpart, Minh was in reality an able and energetic administrator, not a fighter, and the responsibility of handling both the military situation in the field and the political games in the capital proved to be a crushing weight. To make matters worse, Minh was also responsible for the security of Saigon, which, although it fell inside III Corps, was considered a separate administrative zone.

Minh's uneasiness in the highest levels of command and his limited sense of strategy quickly became apparent. During a battle between the Airborne Division and the 141st NVA Regiment in December 1971, an entire enemy battalion was all but wiped out. General Minh was elated and believed the enemy threat to the border area to be over. On 26 December he ordered all South Vietnamese troops out of Cambodia and released the Airborne Division to the general reserve. Other South Vietnamese units were redistributed to their original positions throughout III Corps, leaving a buffer zone of rangers to act as sensors for any further enemy movement. Without lifting a finger the North Vietnamese were able to remain in place inside Cambodia, secure in the knowledge that the South Vietnamese would not pursue them. Beginning in early 1972 the North Vietnamese were allowed to prepare unmolested for the coming offensive.[11]

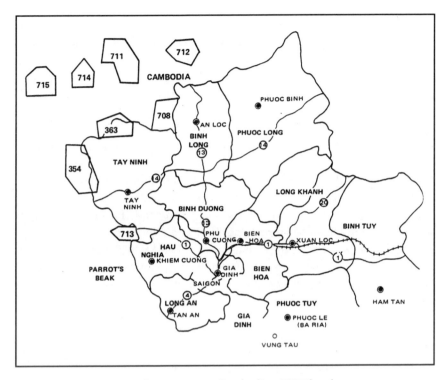

Enemy base areas on Cambodian-RVN border

Over the border inside Cambodia, the North Vietnamese maintained three divisions. The 5th VC Division was perched less than twenty miles northwest of Loc Ninh on Highway 13, the 7th NVA Division waited north of Tay Ninh Province in the Dambe rubber plantation, and the 9th VC Division operated to the west of Tay Ninh Province in the Chup rubber plantation.[12]

South Vietnamese intelligence first detected the presence of the 5th VC Division in January 1972 in a sanctuary region the North Vietnamese called Base Area 712, near the Cambodian town of Snoul. The division had previously been operating around the rubber plantation town of Krek, where it had attacked firebases and outposts. Its presence on Highway 13 as it entered South Vietnam in northern Binh Long Province indicated a change from the usual North Vietnamese strategy of dispersing divisions into regiments or smaller units and operating close to the traditional base areas.

While the encroaching enemy units were ominous, the South Vietnamese actually outnumbered everything the North Vietnamese could throw into III Corps. Hanoi was well aware of this. "In terms of the comparison of forces committed to the campaign," notes an official communist history, "we were outnumbered by the enemy. . . . However, this comparison was only relative, because our forces and weapons were concentrated in a number of definite directions, chiefly on [Highway] 13, while the enemy's Armed Forces were dispersed throughout the eastern Nam Bo theater."[13]

The North Vietnamese could not have picked a better time to attack in III Corps. The beginning of April marked another milestone in the drastic drawdown of U.S. military personnel in the region, forcing many advisers to shuffle or double up responsibilities. Some South Vietnamese units went without advisers entirely. Those Americans who did remain as advisers operated within Third Regional Assistance Command. Headquartered just outside the provincial town of Long Binh at a compound called the Plantation, TRAC was the distilled remains of II Field Force and III Corps Advisory Group. Following the drawdown of American troops that had begun in mid-1969, the region had seen U.S. combat units dwindle to almost nothing. The sharpest decrease had taken place between February and April 1972, when 58,096 troops returned to the United States. This was the single largest troop reduction of the entire war, and it could not have come at a more inopportune time. As the North Vietnamese built up for the Easter Offensive, the Americans built down.[14]

Basically, the advisory system in III Corps for 1972 was the same as that throughout the rest of the country—a skeleton team sprinkled throughout the top of the South Vietnamese army officer corps. In combat units, advisers interacted with counterparts only at the corps, division, and regimental levels. In elite units—airborne, rangers, and marines—advisers were used down to the battalion level. Besides limiting the quantity of expertise advisers could provide, the scaled-down system also hamstrung the dissemination of intelligence. American advisers tended to be clustered around the headquarters, with only a handful out in the field with combat units. No longer could advisers rely on information coming from American units operating in the field or from U.S. intelligence reports. What information that did come in was from Vietnamese units, and it was not always accurate. For the most part, American advisers continued to fill the role of supply conduit and air support coordinator for their counterparts.[15]

In December 1971 TRAC came under the command of Major General James F. Hollingsworth. Perhaps no one was more out of place in these days of drawdowns. Hollingsworth was a hands-on commander, not a manager, preferring to lead men in battle, not supervise them as they withdrew from the field. Yet that was what General Hollingsworth had been sent to Vietnam to do. Known as "Holly" to his admirers, he had graduated from Texas A&M in 1940 with a bachelor's degree in science and an ROTC commission as a second lieutenant. Caught up in the patriotism of the day, Lieutenant Hollingsworth marched off to battle under the command of such men as Eisenhower and Bradley. Hollingsworth's military career was shaped by his experiences as a tank commander under General George Patton during World War II. In 1966–67 Hollingsworth served as deputy commander of the 1st Infantry Division, and in August 1971 he returned to Vietnam for one last fling as deputy commander of XXIV Corps. By the end of the year he was on his way to Long Binh to command the last American advisers in III Corps.

An irreverent and brash style of command modeled unabashedly after that of General Patton became Hollingsworth's trademark as a senior officer. He was profane and unforgiving yet also a talented tactician with a genuine and deep-seated concern for the welfare of those who served under him. Hollingsworth made it a point to learn the first names of every officer in his command, and he never failed to inquire about their families. Upon taking command of TRAC, Hollingsworth sent personal letters to the children of his advisers, telling them he was sorry their fathers could not be home with them but that they were doing supremely important work, and he needed them in Vietnam.

Hollingsworth was a close friend of General Abrams; they had served together as tankers during World War II. While Hollingsworth was not above calling on his personal relationship with the MACV commander, he did not always get his way. As the offensive deepened, the two generals found themselves in several disagreements that could not be erased by friendship. Caught up unwillingly in the swirling tide of international diplomacy, Abrams had to play to Washington's tune, despite his true feelings about the seriousness of the situation in South Vietnam. Hollingsworth, on the other hand, only saw that politics was getting in the way of fighting. At one point in the middle of the offensive, Hollingsworth, frustrated with the incompetence and inactivity of the senior South Vietnamese military leadership, let fall the facade of Saigon's control of the battle when he told reporters, "I'm going to kill them all before they get back to Cambodia." Hollingsworth also made the mistake of letting his emotions get the better of him, telling reporters that it felt "real good to be killin' hell out of the communists." Infuriated that Hollingsworth had given the impression that he—and not the local South Vietnamese commanders—was personally in charge of the situation, Abrams told Holly to "shut his mouth."[16]

Like all American senior officers still in Vietnam in 1972, Hollingsworth knew some sort of North Vietnamese attack was in the wind. The question was where and when. Intelligence was spotty, and what there was came from Vietnamese sources, which were not always reliable. In an attempt to get a feel for what was happening in the field, Hollingsworth would often require briefings at TRAC headquarters. Many advisers dreaded these briefings because no one knew who would be singled out by the outspoken general. Many a young officer tried to sit in the rear of the room, hoping not to be noticed, only to hear Hollingsworth bark, "What do you have to say, major? You've been here for a month now, and I haven't heard a god-damned word out of you yet. Are you just ignorant?"

And pity the poor man who tried to paint a rosy picture or confuse the situation with statistics. During a typical briefing a major was explaining to Hollingsworth how the South Vietnamese regiment he was advising had recently located and destroyed an enemy weapons cache as well as two tons of rice. Hollingsworth listened quietly before breaking in. "Two tons of rice? How can you destroy two tons of rice? The only way you can destroy two tons of rice is to throw it in a river, and I know you don't carry a river around with you." General Hollingsworth was sarcastic, but he never failed to communicate to his subordinates exactly what he felt.[17]

One link down the chain of command was the deputy TRAC commander, Brigadier General John R. McGiffert. An artillery officer, McGiffert had served a tour in Vietnam with the 1st Infantry Division in 1966 and 1967. As deputy TRAC commander, a position he had held since June 1971, he served as an extension of Hollingsworth's presence. Since Hollingsworth could not be everywhere at once, McGiffert filled in the gaps. Between the two of them, there was a general flying over most of the hot spots in III Corps at all times. General McGiffert presented a stark contrast to Hollingsworth. A quiet and thoughtful man, McGiffert would listen and then act only after he felt all the facts were on the table. His calm exterior and academic bearing provided a perfect balance to Hollingsworth's emotional antics and brash style.

Out in the field the key advisory position was occupied by the division senior advisers. The three South Vietnamese divisions in III Corps—the 5th, 18th, and 25th ARVN Divisions—each had one senior adviser with a small staff under him. First and foremost it was the division senior adviser's task to "advise" his counterpart regarding troop movement and deployment, a particularly crucial job during the drawdown because the South Vietnamese army was spread thinly over areas previously covered by both American and South Vietnamese troops. The adviser also pulled together intelligence from units in the field and sent it back to TRAC headquarters for analysis. However, as far as the South Vietnamese were concerned, the senior adviser was most valuable in his role as air support provider. As a result, much of the senior adviser's time was spent plotting air strikes and coordinating them with TRAC headquarters.

As the battle for An Loc unfolded, the 5th ARVN Division would play the crucial role. The division senior adviser, Colonel William Miller, stayed in the city with his fellow advisers as the North Vietnamese hurled themselves against the defenses. It was Colonel Miller who bolstered his counterpart with sound advice on troop placement and made sure that air strikes came on time and on target. After the battle, few would deny that Colonel Miller had been instrumental in saving An Loc during that critical first month.

Miller had the experience of two previous wars to prepare him for Vietnam, though some would argue nothing could prepare a person for Vietnam. An enlisted man during World War II, Miller was awarded the gold bar of a second lieutenant in time to go to yet another war, this time in Korea. During the Vietnam War he served three tours, the first as an adviser to Nguyen Van Thieu, at that time a general in President Ngo Dinh Diem's army. In 1966 and 1967 he fought as a battalion commander with the U.S. 25th Infantry Division. Returning to the war yet again in June 1971, Miller advised the 5th ARVN Division as it conducted operations near the Cambodian border. Like his commander, General Hollingsworth, Miller was a personable officer. He spoke with a calm, down-home southern patois and an easy backwoods sense of humor that made everyone around him feel at ease, even when the situation seemed darkest. Colonel Miller was first and foremost an infantryman, and he knew that the battle for An Loc would be decided on the ground, in the trenches. But just to be safe, he wanted the B-52s flying overhead.

Before the North Vietnamese surged into III Corps, Miller and his fellow advisers had devoted themselves to gathering intelligence on future enemy intentions. Because the South Vietnamese knew the enemy was out there and that some sort of attack was imminent, intelligence-gathering became their single most important task.

Although the South Vietnamese in III Corps expected an invasion, they misread the time and place. As in the rest of the country, an attack was expected during the Tet holidays, but when it failed to materialize, no one really expected that the threat had passed. American intelligence had learned from the 1968 Tet experience and now looked carefully for similarities between the enemy buildup before Tet in 1968 and current North Vietnamese preparations. It found little in common.

"An analysis of all source information available at this time, the enemy's capabilities both prior to and during aggressive operations currently being conducted to pre-empt future enemy plans, and the current disposition of divisional elements in Cambodia, suggests that another TET 68 in level and intensity within MR 3 is unlikely," concluded the official TRAC intelligence summary in mid-January. The main difference seemed to be the emphasis of the North Vietnamese buildup. During early 1968 the enemy had stressed preparations around major population centers, including Saigon. In 1972 analysts concentrated on outlying areas such as district headquarters and military outposts, evidence that winning territory and defeating South Vietnamese main-force units were to be the primary goals of the coming offensive. Clearly, the North Vietnamese had not forgotten the failed "popular uprising" of 1968.[18]

Although TRAC intelligence accurately read the big picture in III Corps, it was less successful in predicting the thrust of the coming North Vietnamese offensive. Beginning in February 1972, U.S. intelligence stressed that Tay Ninh was the most likely target of a North Vietnamese offensive in the region. "Within MR 3, the level of enemy activity is expected to increase during the period 19–25 Feb[ruary] 72 probably focalized in the Tay Ninh area," concluded one report. This was an interesting observation considering that just one month before, TRAC intelligence was giving equal importance to both Tay Ninh and Binh Long Provinces.[19]

A combination of factors led intelligence analysts to alter their assessment. First, Tay Ninh was the most vulnerable to attack; second, the North Vietnamese wanted them to think Tay Ninh was the primary focus. Past experience indicated that North Vietnamese attacks into western III Corps were staged out of a tangled woodland known as Base Area 708 northwest of Tay Ninh Province. Although this was a traditional staging area for North Vietnamese attacks from eastern Cambodia, the discovery of the 5th VC Division north of Binh Long Province along Highway 13 was strong evidence that the enemy was about to try something new. South Vietnamese ranger patrols along the Cambodian border detected increased enemy activity in late February and early March. A number of North Vietnamese soldiers were captured, and all of them told of large troop movements concentrating around Binh Long Province.[20]

Then, on 13 March, a South Vietnamese Mobile Strike Force made up of the 3d Armored Brigade and the 3d, 5th, and 6th Ranger Groups took part in a three-part operation aimed at North Vietnamese troop and supply concentrations in Base Areas 354 and 708. The Mobile Strike Force overran the enemy Sub-Region 23 headquarters and turned up strong evidence of an impending enemy offensive operation. One enemy depot contained more than 1,000 tons of rice, 300 to 500 tons of 107mm and 122mm rockets, and several hundred tons of 82mm and 120mm mortar rounds. The total weight of small arms and 12.7mm antiaircraft ammunition was estimated at about 300 tons, along with more than 5,000 rifles and machine guns. There were so many supplies carefully stacked away that the corps commander air assaulted a regiment from the 25th ARVN Division and a battalion of 105mm artillery into the depot area to assist in its destruction.[21]

The North Vietnamese were very clear in their own minds as to where their main thrust would be. "The central, decisive area of operations of the campaign would be from the Route 17 intersection to north Chon Thanh, including the town of Binh Long [An Loc]."[22] In fact, specific intelligence pointing toward an enemy offensive in Binh Long Province fell into South Vietnamese hands on 16 March. Elements of the 25th ARVN Division occupying Firebase Pace captured three North Vietnamese soldiers while on a routine patrol. An old outpost from the days when the 1st Cavalry Division roamed the border area, Firebase Pace crouched near an abandoned village called Xa Mat. Little more than a shell of broken-down huts and burned-out buildings, Xa Mat was the terminus of a major North Vietnamese infiltration route near Route 22 in northwestern Tay Ninh Province.

One of the captured enemy soldiers was the executive officer to the 272d Regiment of the 9th VC Division. The officer was carrying documents indicating that the 9th VC Division had prepared base camps east of the Saigon River and west of An Loc. They were to be occupied by North Vietnamese troops on 24 March. In combination with the discovery of the 5th VC Division north of Binh Long Province, this provided strong evidence that An Loc, not Tay Ninh, was the real target.

Near the end of March, South Vietnamese patrols captured an enemy document during an operation in Tay Ninh Province. A high-level directive from COSVN, the document partially outlined North Vietnamese plans for the coming spring. Among the most important revelations were three points. First, the 9th VC Division was to move from inside Cambodia to Base Area 708 on or around 24 March; one element of the division was to assemble southwest of the base. Second, the 9th VC Division was ordered to coordinate future actions with the 7th NVA Division, an indication that a large campaign was planned for the near future. Finally, it was revealed that some enemy units in the area had completed urban combat training, a

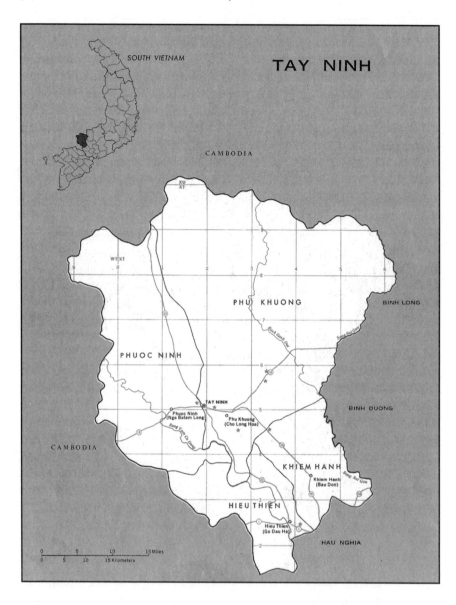

significant factor because such training had been discontinued in 1969 and resumed in late 1971 for only a few main-force units.[23]

Yet American intelligence was slow to react. Daily intelligence reviews continued to stress Tay Ninh Province, with hardly a mention of Binh Long even when more firm evidence of enemy intentions fell into the laps of the intelligence analysts. On 27 March a North Vietnamese scout from a 7th

NVA Division reconnaissance team rallied to the government and revealed his mission. His unit had been ordered to reconnoiter a route from Tay Ninh to Binh Long in preparation for the division's next move. In support of the rallier's story, South Vietnamese patrols began reporting increased enemy reconnaissance activities in the area between Tay Ninh and Binh Long.

Finally, on 1 April—two days after the offensive broke in I Corps—patrols from the 7th ARVN Regiment began engaging small enemy elements on the Cambodian border north of Binh Long Province. A handful of North Vietnamese soldiers captured during a short firefight revealed more information that pointed toward a conventional offensive. Some of the prisoners were signals personnel who told their captors that they were laying telephone wire for a large-scale operation. A couple of others had been surveying possible artillery firing positions; the North Vietnamese wanted their big guns pointing down Highway 13.[24]

These pieces of information were not enough, however. Neither the Vietnamese nor the American intelligence mind-set could shake itself free of the traditional pattern of enemy incursions into III Corps. In the past they had come through Tay Ninh Province, not Binh Long. The reasons were fairly clear. First, Binh Long was farther from the enemy's traditional base areas than was Tay Ninh, and attacks there were more difficult to support. Second, as a military and political prize, Binh Long was insignificant. Binh Long had a population of 60,000, compared with Tay Ninh's 300,000. But the nature of the war had changed. North Vietnam was fighting for real estate, not hearts and minds, and land grabbing was a primary objective. The fewer people who stood in the way, the better.[25]

Still unknown to the South Vietnamese, the enemy had its goals spelled out in great detail, although the timetable was overly optimistic. On the broadest dimension the North Vietnamese planned to disrupt Vietnamization and pacification, hoping to discredit the American effort in South Vietnam on the eve of its final departure. On a secondary level the communists planned to take large chunks of South Vietnamese territory within III Corps and, in a best-case scenario, topple the government in Saigon. To accomplish these objectives the North Vietnamese outlined a complex plan. Two independent regiments—the 24th and 271st—were unleashed in northern Tay Ninh Province against forward elements of the 25th ARVN Division. The attack would look like the real thing but would be only a diversion to mask the movement of the 7th NVA and the 9th VC Divisions through Base Area 708 and into Binh Long Province. The 9th VC Division was to be given the honor of capturing An Loc. According to the plan, this was to be done in five days, certainly no more than ten. The timetable called for the establishment of a new communist capital at An Loc on 20 April 1972. The 7th NVA Division was to block Highway 13 to the south between An Loc and Lai Khe, choking off all reinforcements and supplies to the besieged city. To the north, the 5th VC Division would destroy South Vietnamese units defending the district capital of Loc Ninh, the sole obstacle standing between the Cambodian border and An Loc.[26]

Loc Ninh was expected to fall within a day or two. The victorious 5th VC Division would then fall into line with the 24th and 271st NVA Regiments and contain the 25th ARVN Division. This was to be done by 1 May. With the 25th ARVN Division neutralized, these units would turn their attention to Tay Ninh Province, cutting it off from IV Corps to the south and Saigon to the east. By mid-May the North Vietnamese would turn their attention toward the capital. All units would pour down Highway 13 and the Saigon River corridor and storm into Saigon.

Although the communist plan of attack was clearly set forth, American and South Vietnamese intelligence was largely unaware of its scope and suspected a ruse. Still, the South Vietnamese did not concentrate all efforts in Tay Ninh; they also took steps to reinforce northern Binh Long Province. III Corps headquarters created Task Force 52 on 21 March and ordered it to move from Xuan Loc in Long Khanh Province to the 5th ARVN Division forward headquarters at An Loc. On 28 March the task force was sent north to the junction of Highway 13 and Route 17, about five miles southwest of Loc Ninh.[27]

Task Force 52 was created out of one battalion from the 52d ARVN Regiment and one from the 48th ARVN Regiment, along with one artillery battery and a 155mm artillery platoon. A total of about 1,000 men plus three American advisers, Task Force 52 was to block enemy infiltration into South Vietnam from the west. The 9th ARVN Regiment in Loc Ninh would guard against an attack down Highway 13 from the north.[28]

As the North Vietnamese forces stormed into the northern part of South Vietnam on 30 March, General Hollingsworth and his advisers remained unsure about enemy intentions in their region. During the afternoon of 31 March, Hollingsworth reported to Saigon, "Enemy activity is expected to remain at a relatively low level throughout the forthcoming 24 hours." The North Vietnamese were indeed quiet, although the corps commander, General Minh, was concerned that the enemy might launch an attack during the night of 31 March. In a fit of nervousness he planned to insert four ranger teams into Base Area 354, a North Vietnamese training and staging area near the Fishhook inside Cambodia north of Binh Long Province. Hollingsworth tried to calm Minh, pointing out that the rangers would simply be committing suicide. Yet Hollingsworth still had no evidence that a North Vietnamese attack was close at hand. "We have no information or indicators which would tend to confirm any enemy high point at this time," he cabled Abrams after convincing Minh to countermand the order.[29]

On the morning of 2 April the North Vietnamese struck into III Corps. Playing on the suspicions of South Vietnamese intelligence, the North Vietnamese threw their initial forces against Tay Ninh Province. The 24th NVA Regiment, supported by tanks, attacked Firebase Lac Long, an isolated post on the Cambodian border about thirty-five kilometers northwest of Tay Ninh City. The base was defended by one battalion of the 49th Regiment, 25th ARVN Division. With the help of a few tanks, the North Vietnamese routed the South Vietnamese by midday.[30]

It was clear that the isolated outposts in the frontier along the Cambodian border were sitting ducks. Orders came down to abandon the firebases and form a perimeter around Tay Ninh City. Only a single battalion of rangers remained at Tong Le Chon. The battalion commander was convinced that his unit would be ambushed if he tried to evacuate. He held out at the lonely outpost throughout the offensive.

The defenders at Firebase Thien Ngon were not so lucky. As the South Vietnamese pulled back from the outpost about twenty miles north of Tay Ninh City, they were ambushed by elements of the 271st NVA Regiment and lost many of their artillery pieces and vehicles. Reinforcements from the 25th ARVN Division arrived at the ambush sight the next day, only to find that the enemy had made no attempt to drag off the artillery for later use. In fact, the North Vietnamese seemed to have disappeared back toward the Cambodian border rather than advancing on Tay Ninh City.

At the 5th ARVN Division forward headquarters in An Loc, Colonel William Miller, the division senior adviser, was not convinced the North Vietnamese were showing all their cards. He believed the Tay Ninh attacks were a ruse designed to draw attention from Binh Long Province. It simply made more sense to come down Highway 13 instead of traversing the jungle of western Tay Ninh Province. As the enemy hit isolated firebases in Tay Ninh Province, one of the III Corps intelligence officers called to rub it in.

"We told you the North Vietnamese were going to push into Tay Ninh. They hit a couple firebases this morning."

"Yeah?" Colonel Miller replied. "What have they done?"

"They've hit three or four outposts up there."

"They haven't taken them yet, have they? If they wanted to, they could overrun them. You call me back when the big units come into Tay Ninh," laughed Miller as he hung up the receiver.[31]

The big units never did come into Tay Ninh Province. It was becoming clear that both the South Vietnamese and their American counterparts had been deceived. It would not be until a few weeks later that intelligence pieced together the story, but by then the point was academic. A majority of North Vietnamese units were concentrating the attack on northern Binh Long Province.

General Hollingsworth and his advisory staff at TRAC headquarters eventually saw that the low intensity of the attacks did not match the immensity of the North Vietnamese buildup. Then there was the matter of the 5th VC Division perched on the Cambodian border north of Binh Long Province. What was the enemy up to? At this point it was clear that a real threat existed to the north. Hollingsworth was now reasonably sure that no matter what was happening in Tay Ninh Province, the enemy was about to attack straight south down Highway 13. That would place Loc Ninh, An Loc, and eventually Lai Khe in jeopardy.

Hollingsworth pressured General Minh to prepare for an attack in northern Binh Long Province. The first step was to consolidate the myriad outposts along the northern border into a single defensive position. The South Vietnamese could not hope to fight an entire enemy division. The most logical place for a stand was Loc Ninh.

TWENTY-FOUR

LOC NINH

Brigadier General Le Van Hung was devastated when the North Vietnamese opened the offensive in northern Binh Long Province. He had hoped he would be spared, that the enemy would strike outside his area of responsibility. All intelligence indicated that he would be safe. MACV expected the main thrust of the offensive to come in I Corps or the Central Highlands; even TRAC intelligence believed the III Corps thrust would bypass An Loc. But it was not to be. When the 5th VC Division moved on Loc Ninh, it became clear that his division would be at the center of the brewing offensive.

General Hung was no more prepared for this kind of war than any of his fellow officers, perhaps less. He came from a well-to-do family with all the social status necessary for command in the South Vietnamese army, and he disliked overbearing Americans who wanted the war fought according to American rules. This resentment had colored Hung's relations with U.S. officers since the early 1960s, garnering him a reputation as "anti-American." Hung was not an officer with a long history of command experience. Before being awarded command of the 5th ARVN Division in 1971 on the advice of his friend and mentor, General Minh, Hung was a province chief in the Mekong Delta. He came to III Corps as part of a clique of officers—the so-called Delta Clan—brought from the Mekong region to surround Minh with loyal minions. Hung was fairly tall for a Vietnamese, about five and a half feet. Even during the dark days just before the siege of An Loc, he remained an immaculate dresser, with his fatigues pressed, his insignia polished and straightened. He later returned to IV Corps as the deputy corps commander, and when South Vietnam fell in the spring of 1975, Le Van Hung and his commander committed suicide rather than surrender to the communists.[1]

As division senior adviser, Colonel William Miller got to know Hung better than any other American. But Miller himself never quite knew what to make of Hung. When he first came to the 5th ARVN Division in the summer of 1971, Miller reported to TRAC that "Hung displays outstanding leadership, is aggressive, organized, and forceful. He appears extremely knowledgeable, has confidence in himself and is quickly gaining the confidence of his subordinates." Either Miller was being less than candid with

Brigadier General Le Van Hung, commander of the 5th ARVN Division. (Author's collection)

his commander, or he had badly misread his counterpart. On the eve of the battle in III Corps, Miller's perceptions of Hung were more sharply etched.[2]

In one way the 5th ARVN Division commander was just like other South Vietnamese officers Miller had served with during previous tours; they all regarded their counterparts as a faucet to tap the wealth of supplies and ammunition flowing through the American logistical pipeline. But Hung was more aloof than most South Vietnamese officers. Although he respected Miller, Hung rarely sought out his advice and often did not inform him of tactical decisions. Hung was no coward, but like many other high-ranking South Vietnamese officers, he tried to refrain from making tough decisions. If possible he would wait and watch, hoping a bad situation would just go away.

This one would not simply go away, however, and Miller was concerned that Hung cared only that he might be called upon to fight, not about the critical situation throughout South Vietnam. Miller thought that Hung would probably be happy as long as he could sit and do nothing, even if the entire country burned around him in the meantime. But now the chips were down, and Hung's worst fears had come true. The North Vietnamese were putting his unit on center stage. The 5th ARVN Division would have to fight, and Saigon would be watching.

To Miller, the most immediate concern was Loc Ninh. Although it was the administrative center for the district of the same name, Loc Ninh was barely more than a speck on the map. Since the coming of the French in the nineteenth century, Loc Ninh had been a rubber plantation town, and most of its residents worked in the fields of the huge colonial rubber estates. In 1972 Loc Ninh had a population of about 3,000 people, most of them ethnic Montagnards. The town sat at the edge of a small valley along the Rung Cam River. A low hill separated it from its sister city, Loc Thien, another rubber town just to the southwest. Loc Ninh and Loc Thien were serviced by an all-weather airfield carved among the rubber trees about a half mile west of Highway 13. Just west of the airstrip sat the 9th ARVN Regiment. The base was really three small compounds arrayed parallel to the airfield. The northernmost compound belonged to the district pacification team and local police station, and the center perimeter housed the regiment's artillery. The 9th ARVN Regiment's headquarters sat at the southern end of the airstrip.

In Colonel Miller's opinion, Loc Ninh was "reasonably defendable." The troops were fresh—the 9th ARVN Regiment had just replaced the 7th ARVN Regiment on 11 March—and the position was strong. To the south lay open terrain offering clear fields of fire; to the west the thick vegetation and rubber trees had been bulldozed back about 300 yards. Across the runway to the east lay a gentle hill sloping away from the perimeter toward Highway 13. In theory, the base could defend Loc Ninh against a substantial attacking force—if the regiment was consolidated around the firebase. But only three infantry companies, plus the headquarters staff, were actually inside the wire near the command bunker. The next closest unit was the reconnaissance company stationed to the northwest. In the artillery compound sat two batteries of 105mm and 155mm howitzers in circular, sandbagged revetments; the 155mm guns could throw their shells almost to the Cambodian border.

Considering the small contingent of South Vietnamese troops in Loc Ninh, the American advisory component was large. Five advisers were assigned to the regiment, and two to the district pacification team. Lieutenant Colonel Richard S. Schott was the regimental senior adviser. His chief assistants were Major Albert E. Carlson and Captain Mark A. Smith. Two enlisted men, Sergeant First Class Howard B. Lull and Sergeant Kenneth Wallingford, rounded out the team. Over at the district compound on the north end of the airstrip, Major Thomas A. Davidson and Captain George Wanat bolstered the Regional Forces militia and the district chief, a South Vietnamese major recently transferred from a ranger battalion.

The regimental advisory team was a varied lot. Lieutenant Colonel Schott had recently transferred to Loc Ninh from a desk job in Saigon. He had a previous tour in Vietnam, and as an infantry officer he felt his place was in the field. Schott arrived at Lai Khe looking for work; he told Colonel Miller he "wanted to get out and get in the mud." Miller understood the feeling. Many officers tired of the bureaucratic existence of staff work at MACV headquarters; besides, without command time in the field, an officer's career could reach a standstill. Miller gave Schott command of the 9th ARVN Regimental advisory team, which was without an adviser because the regimental commander could not get along with the last one and had had him removed.[3]

Major Carlson was an artillery adviser counting down the final days of his last tour in Vietnam. While processing his paperwork in Saigon, he heard there was to be an informal ceremony in his honor on 4 April. Afterward he planned to meet his wife in Bangkok, Thailand, then leisurely head back to the States. As Carlson left for Loc Ninh, Miller gave him money and asked Carlson to pick up some jewelry in Thailand. He would never see either the jewelry or the money.

Captain Smith had plenty of experience in Vietnam, most of it as a Special Forces officer. He returned to Vietnam in 1971 to the only slot left that held out some promise of action—an infantry adviser on the front lines. Sergeants Lull and Wallingford were specialists with experience in communications.

Colonel Miller liked his advisory team. What concerned him was the regimental commander. Lieutenant Colonel Nguyen Cong Vinh commanded the 9th ARVN Regiment, but his only real qualification for the job was his friendship with the division commander. Vinh's leadership did nothing to inspire his troops to action. Captain Mark Smith remarked that Vinh was an officer who was "liked by all, respected by none," a characteristic honed during decades of coping with unceasing warfare. Like many other South Vietnamese officers, Lieutenant Colonel Vinh learned to be a survivor. During the First Indochina War, Vinh served in the French colonial army; he was captured by the Viet Minh in the early 1950s and spent years in a communist prisoner of war camp. After partition in 1954, Vinh again marched to war, this time in the army of Ngo Dinh Diem, the first president of South Vietnam. For the next eighteen years he fought sparingly, convinced that caution was the better part of valor and inactivity preferable to death or capture.

Colonel Miller knew that Vinh was unsuited to command a regiment on the front edge of the division's area of operations. In March Vinh had phoned Miller privately and asked him to come up to Loc Ninh. Miller flew up immediately. The regimental commander looked harried, "much older than his age; he was tired and worn out," recalled Miller. As they walked to the command bunker, Vinh spoke of the old days, but Miller knew something else was bothering him. Vinh asked if American ground troops would come back if the North Vietnamese attacked in force. That was unlikely, replied Miller. Besides, he continued, the South Vietnamese army was now equal to the North Vietnamese in equipment and personnel, plus it had an air force, something the enemy lacked. This did nothing to settle Vinh's fears, however. He reminded Miller that Saigon had relied first on the French and later on the Americans; it seemed unlikely that the South Vietnamese could now stand alone. Vinh would always believe that the North Vietnamese were superior in the art of war. And one day, he warned, the enemy would attack in strength, and the war would end—on Hanoi's terms. Miller's concerns were more immediate, however. Would the regiment fight if attacked? Yes, replied Vinh, but eventually it would have to succumb to the inevitable and surrender. The more it resisted, he argued, the worse it would be in the prison camp.

Miller felt as if he had been hit in the stomach. If the frontline units would not fight, what would it be like at An Loc after the enemy had momentum? As they walked back to the airstrip, Miller tried to raise the dejected commander's spirits, without much luck. His last words as he stepped into the waiting helicopter were, "Vinh, if the enemy comes, fight the son of a bitch."[4]

At Lai Khe, Miller decided not to tell General Hung the whole story of Vinh's confession, but he did tell him that he felt the regimental commander should be replaced. That was impossible, replied Hung. It would take too long, and to insist too loudly could possibly incur the wrath of someone in Saigon with political ties to Vinh. That would endanger Hung's position. Then the division commander launched into a tirade about interference in Vietnamese affairs by overbearing American advisers. Miller backed off and hoped Vinh would have a change of heart.

Hung and Miller also argued about the defense of the region north of An Loc. Miller hated relying on a series of small outposts and firebases sprinkled near the border. In his opinion, they only encouraged South Vietnamese commanders to parcel out manpower and artillery all over the map without gaining anything in return. This was a poor substitute for the old days, when American units occupied far-flung bases in strength. As it now stood, the enemy could still pick and choose its point of attack, threatening specific locations, such as Loc Ninh, while the South Vietnamese remained holed up in inconsequential outposts far removed from the action.

The situation in northern Binh Long Province perfectly illustrated this "outpost mind-set." The 5th ARVN Division was strung out from Lai Khe to Loc Ninh without sufficient artillery to mutually support each firebase. In Miller's opinion, the division could not mount an effective offensive operation, nor could it provide an adequate defense in its present posture. To mass the division would be a major undertaking that could not be accomplished in time to meet an enemy thrust. Miller tried to get Hung to concentrate on either an offensive or a defensive strategy; he could not do both.

Hung chose to do neither. The defense of Loc Ninh remained piecemeal—not strong enough to stand up to a division-strength attack, though it did tie up enough troops to seriously weaken the 5th ARVN Division if Loc Ninh fell. But that would not happen, argued Hung. In his opinion, the North Vietnamese would only launch limited attacks against border ranger camps along the Cambodian border. After all, that was all the enemy had done in the past.

Captain Mark Smith watched Lieutenant Colonel Vinh as he paced the regimental bunker. The man is a coward, thought Smith. He has no stomach for battle. Smith believed Vinh planned to surrender at the first hint of trouble. He thought back to an incident a few weeks earlier when the American advisers found a secret bridge built across a river near Firebase Alpha northwest of town. The bridge was made of stones just below the water surface, concealed from the casual observer, but providing easy access for troops and vehicles. Vinh was unconcerned, however. He simply waved his hands at the news and speculated that Montagnards probably used it to smuggle exotic wood from across the border in Cambodia. Vinh refused to order the bridge destroyed.

Other examples of Vinh's inaction also pointed to his unsuitability for command. The most obvious was the slipshod conduct of the regiment's operations around Loc Ninh. The North Vietnamese moved with impunity in the region just south of the Cambodian border, a fact borne out by South Vietnamese border ranger units in the area, and by the local French plantation manager. For years the French had been paying the communists to stay away from the rubber trees. True to their word, the enemy left the plantation alone, a fact well known by the 9th ARVN Regiment. Whenever possible, the South Vietnamese patrolled inside the plantation, knowing that the North Vietnamese were staying away from the rubber trees.

Although Vinh's lack of aggressiveness affected his ability to guess enemy intentions in the region, he continued to deny that his regiment was in danger. As North Vietnamese divisions struck northern I Corps on 30 March, South Vietnamese officers in Binh Long Province grew nervous at the possibility that tanks might be part of enemy plans in III Corps. Vinh was unconcerned, however. He casually read the latest copy of the American newspaper *Stars and Stripes,* which showed pictures of Soviet-made T-54 tanks moving south on the Ho Chi Minh Trail. When Lieutenant Colonel Schott asked how the regiment planned to deal with tanks, Vinh replied that he had nothing to worry about because the only tanks his unit might face were captured armored personnel carriers.

But even if that were true, the 9th ARVN Regiment would be unable to blunt their attack. An inspection of the ammunition dump by American advisers turned up only six antitank rounds for the regiment's single 106mm recoilless rifle. Vinh was unperturbed by the report; he told the advisers that he had requested more ammunition and expected it at any time.

Signs of the impending attack were all around. On 4 April Captain Smith and two other regimental advisers drove north from Lai Khe back to Loc Ninh. All along the way they encountered overloaded trucks carrying families and their belongings south, away from the North Vietnamese. The French plantation manager flagged down the Americans just south of town and told them to go back; it was too dangerous, and the South Vietnamese soldiers were abandoning their posts, he said.

The Americans continued on to Loc Ninh to find that the Frenchman was right. The village square was deserted except for a handful of drunken soldiers hanging around the local pub. Captain Smith confronted the men about their unsoldierly conduct, to which they replied that they were drunk today, for tomorrow they would die. Colonel Vinh's defeatism had rubbed off on his men.

Vinh made no attempt to raise the morale of his troops or to bolster defensive positions. Since intelligence indicated that the North Vietnamese would field at least one division—the 5th VC Division—the best defense lay in getting the 9th ARVN Regiment's disparate forces back to Loc Ninh. Colonel Vinh had placed Task Force 1-5, consisting of the 1st Armored Cavalry Squadron and two infantry companies, at Firebase Alpha. A small force of five armored personnel carriers and a single M41 tank was separated from the task force and left at the junction of Highways 13 and 14 about three miles north of Loc Ninh. This tiny force provided strong evidence that Vinh lacked the tactical skill to do battle with the North Vietnamese. A single armor unit split between two insignificant outposts would be easily swept away by the enemy.[5]

The North Vietnamese certainly recognized this weakness. Although

North Vietnamese troops fire a recoilless rifle near Loc Ninh. (Vietnam News Agency)

communist planners maintained a healthy respect for Loc Ninh's "solidly built fortifications and a relatively strong mobile force," they believed that any advantage from this was offset by "many weak points: the town was situated far from the puppet force's rear area [An Loc], thus it was difficult to get timely assistance from the rear. The defense forces were scattered over several areas far from each other."[6]

Vinh had a rationale for this haphazard defense. He believed that if he split up his forces the North Vietnamese might strike somewhere besides Loc Ninh and leave his regimental headquarters alone. He told the advisers that the regiment might "survive" if it provided the North Vietnamese with a variety of targets. Failing that, Vinh planned to surrender, and he reasoned that if he could point out to his captors how he had actually helped the enemy, things would go easier for him.

Two events on 4 April presaged the coming battle and sharply outlined the size of the enemy force arrayed against Loc Ninh. The first occurred early in the afternoon, when the 9th ARVN Regiment's reconnaissance company ran into what was believed to be the E-6 NVA Regiment west of Loc Ninh. Most of the company was destroyed in the battle, but a lone soldier managed to radio back to the compound that tanks and infantry "in large numbers" were moving toward Loc Ninh. The second warning came later in the day, when a South Vietnamese patrol south of Loc Ninh ambushed and captured part of an enemy squad. The prisoners said they were part of the 272d NVA Regiment and that their division, the 9th VC Division, was to bypass Loc Ninh and attack An Loc. The 272d NVA Regiment was assigned to provide a blocking force on Highway 13 to prevent the 9th ARVN Regiment from retreating south—if they could. The 5th VC Division was to devote all its attention to destroying the tiny district town.

Captain Mark Smith received this information just after midnight on 5 April. He walked to the situation map in the regimental bunker and placed the symbol for the E-6 NVA Regiment in the rubber trees to the northwest of the regimental compound. It was only a matter of hours before the attack began.

TWENTY-FIVE

TANKS IN THE WIRE

The inevitable shelling began three hours past midnight on 5 April. As round after round poured into the little district town, the South Vietnamese cowered in their bunkers and foxholes in terror. Bombardments of this magnitude were unprecedented in III Corps; the South Vietnamese had never before been subjected to such sustained artillery fire. Advisers at TRAC headquarters refused to believe that the North Vietnamese could have assembled much heavy artillery under the watchful eyes of U.S. airpower. Hollingsworth reported to Abrams that Loc Ninh was being subjected to "heavy fires" made up largely of 60mm and 82mm mortar fire—along with a few rockets for good measure. "There were also unconfirmed reports of 105mm howitzer and 76mm tank gun fires," the general pointedly observed, though at first he did not believe it.[1]

But armor was definitely part of the enemy order of battle at Loc Ninh. The first tanks were sighted by two companies positioned just west of Loc Ninh. Upon hearing the roar of their engines and the clank of treads, the soldiers withdrew into the regimental compound and frantically reported that they heard tracked vehicles on the move. On top of the constant artillery and infantry probes, the news that tanks were preparing to attack convinced the South Vietnamese they were doomed.[2]

Lieutenant Colonel Vinh got on the radio and ordered Task Force 1-5 and the rangers to evacuate Firebase Alpha and return to Loc Ninh. Lieutenant Colonel Schott told the frantic commander that it was too late; besides, they were safer inside the firebase, which had artillery and an antitank ditch. But Vinh ignored the advice, and within fifteen minutes the troops had left the safety of Firebase Alpha and were headed down the road to Loc Ninh.

At 3:35 A.M. the cavalry commander called Vinh to say he was going to surrender. The enemy had pounced on them as soon as they left the protected perimeter with a force that far outnumbered their own. Vinh nodded quietly, then told the cavalry commander that he understood.

Captain Smith snapped. He had watched Vinh's cowardly actions for days without comment, but now that the compound was under attack, he could stand it no longer. From the moment the fighting began, Smith be-

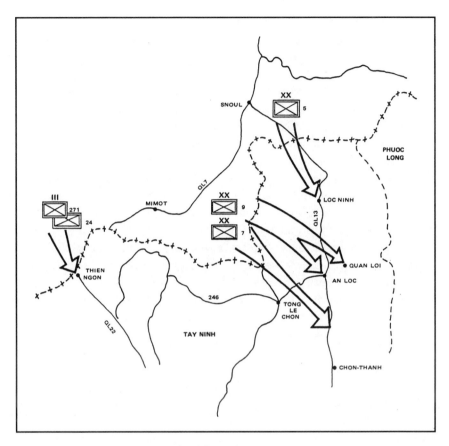

NVA plan of attacks in III Corps

came the point man for the advisory team. His knowledge of the Vietnamese language and his uncanny ability to call in fire on multiple targets
simultaneously were a godsend, and Lieutenant Colonel Schott was more
than willing to play a background command role. One of Smith's first acts
was to confront Vinh about the decision to allow Task Force 1-5 to surrender without a fight. Smith berated the desolate regimental commander
in front of the staff, but only the executive officer backed Vinh.[3]

Rushing to the radio, Smith called the task force commander, telling him
in Vietnamese that he would call in an air strike on his head if he did not
fight. The sullen voice coming over the receiver said he would try, but minutes later the rangers called and said they and the infantry company were
fighting through the North Vietnamese blocking force and heading for Loc

Ninh. However, the 1st Armored Cavalry had surrendered and was moving west with the enemy, willingly driving its tanks and armored personnel carriers toward the Cambodian border. Smith called the nearest forward air controller and ordered air strikes on anything moving in that area. An AC-130 Spectre gunship reported attacking armored vehicles west of Highway 13, but no one could tell if they belonged to the surrendered task force or if they were a column of North Vietnamese tanks.

The rangers and some of the South Vietnamese infantry made it to the intersection of Highways 13 and 14, where they found the lone M41 tank and five armored personnel carriers that had been left earlier by the task force. The grateful soldiers clambered on top of the tanks and headed south to Loc Ninh. Captain Smith requested that the Spectre gunship cover the withdrawal with its formidable firepower.

The splintered task force would be a welcome addition to Loc Ninh's defense—if the men made it back. But the North Vietnamese had set up a half-mile-long ambush across the highway just north of town. The rangers called the regimental bunker to report the firefight and asked their commander for instructions: Vinh told them to go back to Firebase Alpha! The rangers were only a few hundred yards from Loc Ninh; if they turned back, they would have to travel almost two miles along an enemy-held road back to a base that was probably crawling with North Vietnamese.

Overhearing Vinh on the radio, Captain Smith rushed over and jerked the handset away, telling the staff to disconnect his communications equipment. If Vinh wanted to talk to somebody, said Smith, he could get on the horn to An Loc and keep the 5th ARVN Division informed of battle progress. At least that way he would not be causing any more problems.

Air support was heavy over Loc Ninh. As the forward air controllers took their turns over the town, they learned that "Zippo"—Captain Smith's radio call sign—was calling the shots against anything that moved outside the perimeter. But even fighter planes could not stave off the inevitable. The North Vietnamese crept closer, setting up direct-fire weapons to shoot straight into the bunkers.

Suddenly, the South Vietnamese specialist manning the sensor boxes called out in alarm. All the little lights representing a group of motion sensors planted on trails and roadways around the town were lit up like a Christmas tree. The technician banged his fist against the side of the box, thinking the system it must be malfunctioning. But it was not a false alarm. The North Vietnamese were moving in on all fronts.

"Bomb them all," Smith radioed to a circling air controller, but before he could say more, the regimental bunker took a direct hit from a 75mm recoilless rifle round. Shrapnel and debris whirled through the air, wounding both Smith and Lieutenant Colonel Schott in the head and neck. High above Loc Ninh, Hollingsworth heard the pause in target coordinates from Zippo and called down to learn the problem. Smith curtly told him "to wait until I get the holes in my head patched up." Hollingsworth apologized.

Spying two tanks pulling into the tree line just to the west, Smith took Lieutenant Colonel Schott and Sergeant Lull and raced toward a small bunker on the outer perimeter. Major Carlson, Sergeant Wallingford, and Yves-Michel Dumont, a French photographer stranded in Loc Ninh before the battle, stayed in the command bunker. Smith's new position had the regiment's only artillery piece—a 106mm recoilless rifle—on the rooftop. Still watching the enemy tanks, Smith yelled at the cowering crew to get up and fight. Some did, and the recoilless rifle swung into action, slamming a round into one T-54 as it moved out of the tree line. The tank shuddered to a halt. A second tank was more of a problem. Still in the tree line, the gunners could not get a clear shot, so Smith called an orbiting air controller and asked for Spectre. The lumbering gunship appeared, peppering the evasive tank with hundreds of armor-piercing minigun rounds. Smith saw the bullets strike the back deck of the T-54 with a blinding sparkle as they pierced the hard shell and exploded inside.

Enemy artillery continued to pound the defenders throughout the day. With uncanny accuracy, rounds rained down on the compound, hindering movement and keeping the South Vietnamese pinned inside their bunkers. Captain George Wanat, the assistant district adviser holed up in the northern compound, climbed to the sandbagged roof of his bunker and saw North Vietnamese mortar crews firing from the swimming pool on the grounds of the old plantation house northeast of the perimeter. On the top floor of the house itself was a forward observer calling in fire and correcting errant rounds. Wanat radioed Smith with the information, then listened as Zippo called for Spectre to clean house. But General Hung, monitoring all air requests from his headquarters in An Loc, canceled the strike. Unwilling to allow the North Vietnamese sanctuary in the old house, Smith and Lieutenant Colonel Schott swung the recoilless rifle and blasted the enemy with canister. Like a giant shotgun, the round's flechettes tore into the walls and silenced the forward observer.

As the one-sided battle raged throughout the day, only American air support kept the attackers at bay. The mainstay of early tactical air support for the beleaguered town was a handful of A-37 Dragonfly jets flown by American pilots from the 8th Special Operations Squadron. The small fighters carried a heavy bomb load, and their slow speed allowed pinpoint low-level accuracy in support of ground troops. The squadron was based at Bien Hoa, from where it had previously flown missions in support of operations in Cambodia. When the North Vietnamese launched the Easter Offensive, the 8th Special Operations Squadron raced back to III Corps. There were only two dozen aircraft, but they were more than welcome at Loc Ninh.

The Dragonflies were tough little planes, able to fly long hours and take considerable punishment. Pilots flew six to eight missions per day during the height of the enemy offensive. When the fighting began in April, the A-37 pilots were assigned two or three sorties in a twelve-hour period. Eight aircraft were always on alert, ready to take to the sky within fifteen minutes. Some planes were loaded with "soft" ordnance—cluster bombs or napalm—others with "hard" ordnance such as high explosives. The planes were scrambled according to what the troops on the ground called for. If enemy soldiers were in the open, soft ordnance was on the menu; if they were holed up in buildings, high explosives were called on to blast them out.

Lieutenant "Skip" Bennett was one of the Americans thrown into the air over Loc Ninh. He had arrived incountry in November 1971, spending most of his time in the skies over Cambodia. Now he found himself embroiled in a high-intensity battle against some of the densest air defense south of the demilitarized zone. When word came that the North Vietnamese attack had begun, Bennett and his wingman were among the first scrambled for a mission near Quan Loi. As soon as they dropped their bombs and returned to base to refuel, they were sent back into the air. A group of American advisers under attack near the airfield at Quan Loi needed support, and the Dragonflies were the closest aircraft.

Then came the call from Loc Ninh. The A-37s were scrambling as fast as they could rearm and refuel. The operations phone rang in the ready hanger, telling the waiting pilots what type of ordnance was needed on target. As the first Dragonflies roared down the runway on the morning of 5 April, word came from the operations center that the target was tanks. Lieutenant Bennett listened to the tactical radio.

"OK, I'm cleared hot . . . oh my god, there goes another one." The pilots were up against more tanks than they could shoot. Armor had often been reported, but it always turned out to be PT-76 light tanks, or simply trucks. This time it was the real thing—Soviet-made T-54s. The first pilots soared over the treetops in time to see a group of tanks rumbling into town. The Dragonflies zeroed in on the easy targets, but machine-gun fire forced them out of the area before they could see the results of their first pass.

An A-37 Dragonfly from the U.S. Air Force 8th Special Operations Wing bombs North Vietnamese troops attacking Loc Ninh. (Author's collection)

Soon enough, Lieutenant Bennett took his turn in the air. That first day, tanks seemed to be everywhere around Loc Ninh. Bennett and his wingman zeroed in on a pair of T-54s and began their approach. The Dragonfly can fly over 500 miles per hour, but it had to slow down considerably before dropping its bombs. An unsophisticated system of fastening ordnance to the wings prevented smooth delivery at high speed. Napalm was particularly troublesome. When dropped at speeds around 300 miles per hour, the sleek pods would often be forced up over the front of the wing before tumbling backward. It was an unnerving problem. The solution was to approach at high speed, slow down to drop the bombs, then scream back up to speed.

Bennett rolled in from 6,000 feet into a thirty-degree diving pass. At the last moment he fired a rocket at a tank below before climbing back into the sky. He felt sure the rocket hit the tank—he heard the explosion roll across the ground—but he did not actually see it as he concentrated on the controls. Lieutenant Bennett and the Dragonflies had drawn first blood from the enemy's main thrust into northern III Corps.[4]

While the fighters swarmed, Hollingsworth stayed above Loc Ninh monitoring the battle. His call sign, Danger 79, became well known to air controllers and advisers alike as the little helicopter darted back and forth over the beleaguered town, dodging bullets that ripped the air around him. Hollingsworth had resurrected the call sign from his days with the 1st Infantry Division, hoping that the enemy might recognize it and remember the Big Red One. The general loved a good fight, but he was concerned about the situation his handful of advisers were facing. Tactical air support and some B-52 strikes kept the North Vietnamese at bay, but increasing numbers of antiaircraft batteries were making the bombing runs challenging. Hollingsworth reported that most of the antiaircraft fire he encountered on 4 April and early on 5 April was 12.7mm machine-gun fire. By the afternoon of 5 April, he reported encountering air bursts from 23mm and 37mm antiaircraft weapons. But the general knew that airpower alone would not win the battle; the South Vietnamese had to get out of their holes and fight back.[5]

Enemy artillery pounded Loc Ninh into the evening. Small contingents of infantry probed the perimeter while tanks were drawn up as fire support in the trees to the west. Later that night the shelling slacked off, and the advisers radioed that the situation had stabilized. More good news appeared in the form of two companies of the 3d Battalion, 9th Regiment. The units had been operating west of Loc Ninh when the North Vietnamese attack began. As the fighting eased off late in the evening, both companies managed to close to within supporting distance of the 9th Regiment command post, but they were pounced on and shredded by a North Vietnamese blocking force before they could reach the perimeter. Only twenty soldiers made it inside the wire. However, most of the five armored personnel carriers left at the intersection of Highways 13 and 14 made it back into Loc Ninh; the rest kept moving south to An Loc.

Late that night the pressure was still on Loc Ninh. Given the intensity of the North Vietnamese attack, it was a miracle that the little town had not fallen. The stress continued to unravel Lieutenant Colonel Vinh, who spent the day in a corner with his trusted officers. A few hours before midnight, Smith saw Vinh whisper something to his bodyguards, who then donned flak jackets and helmets and sprinted from the bunker. Not until after they returned did Smith find out that Vinh had ordered the perimeter gates opened. When confronted, Vinh explained, "We had to do this so we can run out easier." Furious at the regimental commander's blatant cowardice, Smith said he "seriously considered shooting Vinh there and then." But even this invitation did not prompt the North Vietnamese to attack; the night remained calm save for the usual smattering of artillery.

Did the lull mean that the enemy had spent its force in vain? Few of the advisers watching helplessly from outside Loc Ninh thought so. Despite his outward confidence, even General Hollingsworth was skeptical at the defenders' chances of survival. He credited the air force and the valiant efforts of Captain Mark Smith for Loc Ninh's continued survival. "There can be no question that Loc Ninh would have fallen in the hands of the enemy early in the day had it not been for the magnificent support of the 7th AF [air force] and the brilliant fire direction efforts of a young army captain," reported Hollingsworth. "As it now stands, Loc Ninh remains in friendly hands, and the enemy thrust has been blunted."[6]

Just before first light on 6 April, the North Vietnamese turned up the pressure. Captain Smith watched tracers rise lazily from the rubber trees, mentally noting their position as he called in air strikes. Around noon, the eastern perimeter reported that civilians from the village were walking up the road toward the base. Schott and Smith ran to the wire in time to see, in Smith's words, "one of the most pitiful sights I have ever witnessed." The North Vietnamese were forcing women and children toward the compound; one poor soul was waving an American flag as he walked. Smith fired a burst in front of them, forcing the crowd to break and flee back to the village.

The enemy continued to probe Loc Ninh, mostly from the west, but also from the southeast, where Hollingsworth suspected that the 174th NVA Regiment had reinforced positions in preparation for a new assault. In response to warnings from the high-flying general, Schott and Smith, with the help of the regimental doctor and two soldiers, crawled into the western wire and placed claymore mines and white phosphorous grenades along the perimeter. After wiring the ensemble, they retreated to the bunker and waited for the attack. It came during the afternoon.

A battalion backed by tanks raced for the wire, but Spectre was waiting. Running from north to south, the gunship concentrated on the tanks, forcing them to turn and run for the forest. Alone at the edge of the perimeter, the infantry struggled through the wire. "I saw hundreds of NVA standing in the wire, and the ARVN soldiers staring at them," recalled Smith. He detonated the mines in a blinding explosion of dirt and debris. "It was brutal. As if coming out of a daze the ARVN soldiers began firing. The NVA battalion was decimated."

From the southeast, a company from the E-6 NVA Regiment stormed the front gate, running amok inside the wire before Smith could muster air support to drive it off. Calling for cluster bombs inside the perimeter, he watched from the bunker as fighters scattered the attackers with the deadly bomblets. But both attacks left groups of North Vietnamese soldiers inside the regimental base. A lone tank was stopped in its tracks by Spectre. As the crew members ditched the motionless hulk, South Vietnamese soldiers picked them off like ducks in a shooting gallery. Later, the tank was gone. Smith asked a young soldier what had happened and was told that two other tanks had come out of the woods and dragged it off. Why did no one act to stop its escape? "The tanks were not shooting and I didn't want to make them mad," said the soldier. Smith could only shake his head and pat the young Vietnamese on the shoulder. He knew what it was like to tackle armor with only a handheld M72 LAW.

Spirits rose at TRAC headquarters when news of the beating administered by the air force came over the radio. "I estimate that the better part of a regiment operating southwest and west of Loc Ninh has been blown away by TAC air strikes," reported a jubilant General Hollingsworth. Although the North Vietnamese must have taken horrendous casualties, Hollingsworth's boast was certainly an exaggeration.[7]

The regimental compound was surrounded by silence. At least it seemed like silence compared with the terrible shelling of the past few days. Only a few shells exploded outside the bunkers, but there were no infantry or armor attacks. In the command bunker, Vinh distributed bottles of warm soda to the officers and men slumped on the floor along the walls. It was an almost laughable sight. Clutching a bottle of soda, Vinh wandered around the bunker stripped down to his white undershorts and T-shirt, telling his men they would have to surrender. Officers could give up, said Vinh, but enlisted men would be shot by the North Vietnamese. The border rangers faced the worst fate. Most of them were recruited from Montagnard, Cambodian, and Nung ethnic minorities and could expect no mercy from their captors. They were told to slip out the gate and make their way as best they could to the south.

Captain Smith knew none of this. His attention was held by bright lights that appeared along the open ground about 500 yards to the south. In the darkness he could see them bouncing along; what could they be? He found out just before midnight when two 240mm rockets slammed into the compound. The North Vietnamese had driven a battery of rocket launchers within point-blank range of the base. Notoriously inaccurate most of the time, the rockets found their mark on this occasion. One struck the hospital bunker, killing every wounded soldier inside; the other flew straight into the ammunition dump in the artillery compound, obliterating guns, crews, and artillery rounds. In his helicopter high above, General Hollingsworth saw the blast and said, "It looked like a nuclear explosion."

A half hour before midnight, the enemy launched another major assault. There was no variation, just a repeat of the earlier attack as infantry and tanks stormed the compound from the west and southeast. The ever-present air force bombed the North Vietnamese as they stormed the wire, while defenders used all their remaining 106mm canister rounds repelling the charge. Smith and Schott spent the rest of the night moving along the perimeter, checking defensive positions and talking to orbiting air controllers on the radio. Though the advisers did not witness the battle on the perimeter, the fighting must have been desperate. An American helicopter pilot flying over the area the next morning reported seeing bodies—friend and foe alike—entangled in the wire.

Just after midnight on 7 April, the artillery bombardment died down to only a few isolated artillery rounds. Smith took advantage of the lull to call in additional air strikes west of the compound and cleared a Spectre gunship to again fire on the plantation house to the north. At 5:30 A.M. the defenders heard the clank and rumble of armor in the half-light of dawn. A little more than an hour later the tanks moved in from the southwest, and from the town of Loc Ninh itself to the north.

By this time the 9th ARVN Regiment headquarters had lost touch with most of the units outside the command bunker. It was every man for himself. The American advisers noticed that Lieutenant Colonel Vinh sat in the corner surrounded by his loyal bodyguards, but he made no move to find out the status of the battle. Suddenly, at about 8:00 A.M. Vinh dashed out of the bunker, followed by his executive officer and the bodyguards. Smith watched until he saw the executive officer pulling the gold and scarlet South Vietnamese flag down from the flagpole.

Vinh was surrendering! Smith dashed from the bunker in time to see the officer stripping off his white T-shirt and tying it to the flagpole. He grabbed the rope from the cowardly officer, throwing the white symbol of surrender onto the ground. Smith glanced around, noticing that other soldiers were stripping off their shirts. The confrontation had reached a crucial moment, and Smith had to act immediately and decisively, so he tore up the white "flag" and berated the officer in front of his men. In the face of Smith's withering rage, the soldiers donned their shirts and skulked back to their defensive positions.

In the bunker the advisers mulled over their short list of options. Only Smith, Lieutenant Colonel Schott, and Sergeant Lull remained in the command center; Major Carlson, Sergeant Wallingford, and the French photographer were still holed up in another bunker. There was really only one thing to do: retreat from the bunker and sneak through enemy lines. It was a fateful moment. Smith told the others it was time to get away as best they could, but Lieutenant Colonel Schott's head wound had become worse, and he did not believe he could keep up.

"Leave me," said Schott. No, Smith replied, if they could not all go, they all would stay. North Vietnamese soldiers were all around the bunker, and some began throwing satchel charges in the door. There is disagreement over what happened next, but only one man lived to tell about it—Captain Mark Smith. According to him, Schott took the hero's way out by sacrificing himself for his men. Realizing that there was no time to argue, Schott calmly placed a .45-caliber pistol to his forehead and pulled the trigger. Though horrified and saddened at the time, Smith later said the "action was not an act of fear, Dick Schott died to save Sergeant Lull and myself. . . . His was an act of sacrifice, not personal desperation."[8]

General Hollingsworth climbed into his helicopter and rushed to Loc Ninh in the darkness. From the reports coming from his besieged advisers, Hollingsworth figured this was the beginning of the enemy's final all-out assault. He only hoped he was not too late. In the half-light of dawn, Hollingsworth could just make out the tanks rolling toward the south compound, their progress marked by belches of smoke as the main guns fired. Major Thomas A. Davidson, the Loc Ninh District adviser, was pinned down at the north compound. He came on the radio and frantically reported that tanks were attacking his police post as well. He told Hollingsworth that there were twelve of the monsters bearing down on him, but when the general's helicopter sped over the area, he could count only five. The discrepancy was lost on Major Davidson, however, and his police panicked and broke before the onslaught. Within minutes the district adviser found himself with only forty or so police and militia forces to defend the compound.[9]

A forward air controller came up on Davidson's radio net. "Samba 66, this is a last-ditch defense, but I need to know how strong your bunker is," called the forward air controller using Davidson's call sign. "Can it take hits from TAC air?"

"The bunker can probably withstand 100 pound bombs," replied the nervous adviser. The thought of getting bombed by his own planes was not reassuring, but other options were fading fast. Yet there was another possibility. "Samba 66, what is your exact location within the compound?" queried a nearby Spectre gunship. Davidson replied that he could not give an adequate description, at least not one that would allow pinpoint bombing.

Spectre came back with a strange suggestion: "Start up a vehicle anywhere in your compound. Will fix on its silhouette as a marker." Although Davidson did not know exactly what the pilot meant, he was aware that the sophisticated location gear aboard the AC-130 could detect heat given off by vehicles. He managed to start up a jeep, and Spectre locked on, hosing down the compound and killing most of the North Vietnamese infantry supporting the armor attack. Fighter planes finished off the tanks.[10]

Within forty-five minutes most of the enemy armor inside the district compound was destroyed. Again the tide of battle seemed to turn, but bad luck quickly shifted it back again to the enemy. For a crucial thirty minutes the air force was unable to provide tactical air strikes over Loc Ninh. Someone—probably General Minh, the corps commander—had ordered a B-52 strike within two miles of Loc Ninh without first checking the tactical situation. Though usually a welcome weapon, B-52s could not bomb close enough to friendly positions to affect a close-quarters battle. At this point in the battle, most of the attacking North Vietnamese were within 200 yards of the defenders, but the fighters and gunships were ordered out of the area while the big bombers winged in from Thailand. The forward air controllers protested, but the order was not rescinded, and all aircraft reluctantly left the battlefield.[11]

Enemy tanks rumbled into the compounds near the airfield, this time unopposed. They rushed in close to the bunkers, firing point-blank into the structures. Chunks of dirt and jagged wooden splinters were torn from the bunkers, which trembled under the impact of the tanks' main guns.

Some aircraft did make it to Loc Ninh during the lull in tactical air support, however. A single OH-6 helicopter appeared suddenly over the treetops, careened toward earth in a breathtaking drop, then flared at the last moment and hovered a few feet from the ground. Captain John Whitehead, a crackerjack pilot from the 1st Cavalry Division, was at the controls. He hoped to pull the Americans out, but the swirling melee prevented a rescue. Instead, South Vietnamese soldiers rushed the helicopter as Captain Smith ran from the bunker armed with an M60 machine gun. Better somebody gets out than no one, thought Smith as he sprayed bullets at some nearby North Vietnamese infantry. The chopper lifted off with South Vietnamese soldiers hanging out the door and clinging to the skids. Captain Whitehead saw Smith shot down by enemy troops crossing the airstrip to the east, and he later reported that North Vietnamese soldiers yanked him to his feet, presumably to take him prisoner. But Smith was not captured; the "captors" were South Vietnamese rangers, not enemy soldiers, and as the helicopter swung away over the rubber trees, they pulled him to safety.

Above it all Hollingsworth's helicopter spiraled, evading the .51-caliber antiaircraft fire that zipped up from the ground. In despair, the general watched as North Vietnamese tanks ground Loc Ninh under their treads. Hollingsworth swore into the radio, begging and cajoling the air force to hurry. Then at about 10:00 A.M. the jets reappeared, screaming in from the horizon to the southeast.

Among the fighters arriving on station were the little Dragonflies from the 8th Special Operations Squadron. Lieutenant Skip Bennett and his fellow pilots flew around the clock in support of Loc Ninh, and every time it seemed the town would fall, the air force turned back the enemy tide. This time it was close. Lieutenant Bennett looked down at the battle through his plastic bubble canopy and saw a cluster of buildings—probably the old plantation complex a few hundred yards to the northeast. As far as he could tell, some advisers were hunkered down in one of the bunkers, radioing for all the air support they could get. Aircraft were stacked up overhead, waiting for word to move in from the forward air controllers.

"They're on top of us," radioed Zippo from the ground. "Drop your stuff on us. They're in the bunker and we want to get rid of them. Tear the damn thing down!"

Lieutenant Bennett's plane was on line, and the air controller cleared him to sweep in. He eased the Dragonfly into a level pass over the flat, dark green expanse of rubber trees outside town. Bennett could see sparkling points of orange spitting bullets as he rushed in. But enemy gunners were shooting at his wingman, precisely what Bennett hoped they would do. A standard deception tactic was for the wingman to slash downward in a steep dive, then fire rockets from high altitude. That got the gunners' attention, but while they fired at the wingman, Bennett swept in and dropped his sleek bombs right on target. Dirt and debris covered the bunker as the Dragonfly broke east and headed for home.[12]

Major Davidson also called for air strikes on his own position. Over the radio he "urgently begged for CBU and gunfire inside the compound, with napalm and hard bombs on the outside." The air force complied, but as the jets unloaded their ordnance and headed for home, the pilots reported that there were still a few tanks inside the compound.[13]

By midmorning most of the North Vietnamese tanks were driven from the two compounds; a few were left shattered and smoldering near the bunkers they had mangled. But the defenders paid a bitter price for their small victory. Both compounds were largely destroyed, and the South Vietnamese had suffered heavy casualties. By noon only about fifty soldiers from the 9th ARVN Regiment remained at their posts in the south compound, while the strength of the northern compound was down to about thirty district militiamen.[14]

Throughout the day the North Vietnamese assaulted positions around the town and at the north and south ends of the airfield. They hugged the defenders closely, hoping to find safety from the waves of tactical air strikes that decimated their ranks with every pass. Then, at 7:00 P.M., radio contact with the American advisers abruptly stopped. The last message was received by an air force forward air controller coordinating air strikes for Loc Ninh.

Earlier in the day the same air controller had reported seeing a white flag fluttering over the 9th ARVN Regiment's headquarters. Captain Smith later recalled that the white shirt pulled down after he confronted the regimental executive officer was up the flagpole for only five minutes or so. That could have been the surrender flag seen by the air controller. However, Smith could not say for certain that other South Vietnamese soldiers did not run white flags up the pole sometime afterward. Another report heard by the 5th ARVN Division at An Loc speculated that a few South Vietnamese soldiers and the surviving American advisers had evacuated most of the defensive positions earlier in the morning and had tried to take up a position on the east side of the runway just south of town.

Some weeks later a South Vietnamese artilleryman who had been captured and later escaped from a North Vietnamese prisoner of war camp reported that the artillery had all abandoned their positions as early as 7:00 on the morning of 7 April. He also said that the infantry supporting them had fled east as enemy tanks had attacked from the west. It soon turned into a rout, with most of the panicked soldiers ending up in the district compound north of the airfield. A few Regional Forces and some police were still resisting from their positions, but most had fled toward Loc Ninh Village to the northeast. Many of the routed South Vietnamese soldiers followed them. If the account told by the South Vietnamese artilleryman was true, the enemy had routed most of the South Vietnamese defenders by 7:30 A.M.[15]

A postbattle communist radio broadcast reported that 1,300 South Vietnamese had been taken prisoner in Loc Ninh. The few escaping soldiers confirmed this report, estimating that around 1,000 had surrendered. For the division advisers in An Loc to the south, the real story would remain a mystery until after the war. With the exception of Davidson, the Americans did not make it out of Loc Ninh. Six advisers were listed as missing in action.[16]

But luck was with Major Davidson as the North Vietnamese tightened the circle around Loc Ninh. Along with a handful of district troops, he slipped through a hole in the perimeter and initially tried to head toward town. They quickly ran into enemy patrols, and after several firefights Davidson found himself alone with his Vietnamese interpreter. During the next four days they walked, crawled, and swam through heavily populated enemy-held territory. During one particularly close call, the two men retreated into a marsh when they heard a large patrol coming their way; the North Vietnamese passed within five yards of their hiding place. On another occasion an enemy patrol burst into a house where Davidson was hiding. Thinking the game was up, he was surprised when the patrol seemed unaware that there was anyone else in the house. Davidson and the interpreter sneaked out the back and climbed a tree to hide until the patrol left.

Unfortunately, the North Vietnamese decided to make camp there, and for the rest of the day the fugitives nervously watched as the enemy set up tents and dug trenches. At one point Davidson recalled that fifty soldiers "walked by so close we could have tripped them." After dark the two slipped away and continued south. On 12 April Davidson and the interpreter stumbled into the northern perimeter of An Loc, where they were taken to safety by some South Vietnamese rangers. When asked how he kept his courage up in the face of overwhelming odds, Davidson replied that he just told himself over and over, "I will not surrender. I will not die all balled up with my hands tied behind my back."[17]

Considering the weakness of Hung's defenses at Loc Ninh, Colonel Miller was not surprised when he heard his advisers were gone, though he felt the full weight of their loss. Once the battle began, Miller did what he could, flying his helicopter to Loc Ninh to monitor the situation and ensure that Captain Smith got all the air support he needed. "We burned up two or three tanks of gas over Loc Ninh," Miller recalled. Since his earlier confrontations with Hung over the misplacement of units north of An Loc, Miller had wanted to remove the advisers from Loc Ninh. But he had only threatened, not acted, and now it was too late. "I'll have that on my conscience for the rest of my life," he later said.

General Hollingsworth was also personally devastated when it became clear that he was going to lose his advisers at Loc Ninh. By the end of the day on 7 April, he was still unclear as to the final fate of Loc Ninh. "It appears that the forces at Loc Ninh fought valiantly, but the camp appears to have been overrun," read Hollingsworth's report to Saigon. "Some fighting continues. I have no estimate of the extent of friendly casualties within the Loc Ninh complex. I feel they must be heavy."[18]

The TRAC staff at Long Binh racked their brains for plans to rescue the advisers from Loc Ninh. American helicopters flew toward the besieged town on a couple of occasions, only to be turned back by intense antiaircraft fire. Hollingsworth assembled his downcast staff and laid out the facts. "I will save those people in Loc Ninh if there is any way possible," said the general with characteristic bravado, "but I won't send good people after dead ones." His words made perfect sense. Soldiers died during

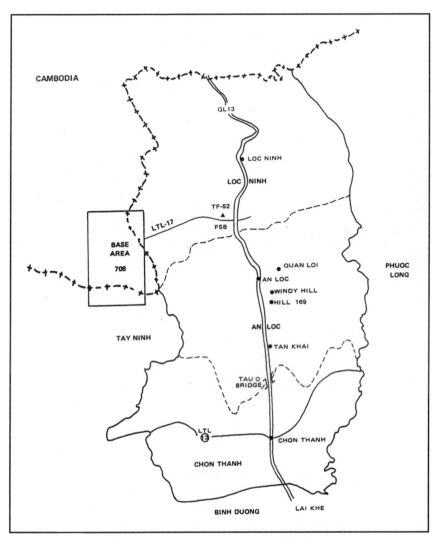

Key locations, Binh Long Province, III Corps

battle, but sacrificing live ones in heroic—though futile—rescue missions was counterproductive. Hollingsworth knew that in all likelihood the advisers in Loc Ninh were beyond his power to help. Yet the general felt the loss more deeply than he cared to show his subordinates. That afternoon he told General Abrams, "Those on the ground at Loc Ninh fought gallantly against insurmountable odds. . . . Dauntless and remarkable courage kept them going."[19]

Hollingsworth had done his best, as had the handful of courageous helicopter pilots who braved withering antiaircraft fire as they attempted to rescue the advisers at Loc Ninh. But not all the Americans were lost—at least not yet. Major Carlson, Sergeant Wallingford, and the photographer, Yves-Michel Dumont, were still in the command bunker. Outside, they could hear the sounds of tanks and yelling soldiers all around, though there was almost no shooting. The enemy must have taken the base, they correctly reasoned. Without warning, some North Vietnamese soldiers poured gasoline into the bunker's entrance and through the narrow firing slits. Horrified at the thought of being burned alive, the advisers surrendered, followed shortly by a handful of South Vietnamese who were also inside the bunker.

Captain Smith, too, was still on the loose. After the death of Lieutenant Colonel Schott, Smith shot his way out of the bunker and into a nearby trench line, where he tried to get the only three soldiers still there into some sort of defense. "Helicopter! Helicopter!" was all they could say. Little chance of that, thought Smith as he radioed yet again for air support. A North Vietnamese sniper ended the attempt when he fired a single bullet through Smith's backpack radio and into his lung.

Staggering back into the bunker, Smith found that the North Vietnamese were already there. He saw bodies all around, as well as three soldiers trying to cut the head off Schott's body. They had already cut off his rank insignia and name tag. Firing from the hip, Smith killed all three. In another part of the bunker he found Sergeant Lull and twelve South Vietnamese holed up in a corner in a last-ditch defense.

With the help of twelve South Vietnamese soldiers, Smith recaptured two bunkers on the perimeter and held out until 6:30 in the evening. A Spectre gunship made a run down the west side of the compound, and behind the deadly curtain of fire, the little team managed to slip outside the wire and through the minefield to the southwest. A squad of North Vietnamese spotted the men and opened fire, killing some of the South Vietnamese soldiers and wounding Smith in the groin.

Just after midnight on 8 April, Smith, Sergeant Lull, and several South Vietnamese, including the regimental surgeon, were still eluding the North Vietnamese. During the previous evening, the small group had headed south out of the compound. Smith's wounds were debilitating, and several times he had to stop and drain blood from his bowel. Sergeant Lull and the Vietnamese soldiers elected to push on; in Smith's words, "all but two of the ARVN soldiers chose to desert me." Almost immobile from his wounds, Smith was so physically and emotionally drained that he sank to the ground and cried. He could only watch as Lull and the soldiers ran off toward the south.

Alone with the regimental doctor and his loyal bodyguard, Corporal Hen, Smith tried to get up and walk. The little party managed to move about 500 yards to the south, where they came to a dry streambed. They were not the first to take cover there. South Vietnamese soldiers had tried to dig into the steep bank before they were blown to bits by an American bomb and napalm attack earlier in the day. Most of the soldiers were dead, but a few, gravely wounded, looked up imploringly. Smith and his small band could only stare back in horror. They moved on without saying a word.

During the night a massive air strike tore up the hills to the south, precisely where Sergeant Lull and his party had headed after leaving Smith. As thundering roars and blinding flashes ripped through the battered forest, Smith was certain that Lull and his following were killed in the inferno.

Actually, Lull may not have perished in the air attack. A South Vietnamese doctor later claimed to have linked up with Lull late in the day on 8 April—just before both were captured by the enemy. According to the doctor, Lull was executed near Highway 13 about six miles north of An Loc and buried on the spot. Lull's remains were never recovered, but the U.S. Department of Defense listed him as killed in action.[20]

On three occasions during the night Smith and his two companions ran into North Vietnamese patrols. After the third time the men were so exhausted and riddled with wounds that they could only crawl. At dawn on 8 April, Smith spotted a forward air controller droning a few thousand feet overhead; he signaled furiously with a mirror. The pilot might have seen it because later that morning a flight of fighters roared in and unloaded cluster bombs a thousand yards or so away. Smith was again wounded by shrapnel but was relieved that the North Vietnamese were caught in the middle.

The three men stumbled, crawled, and rolled toward a swath of rubber trees that had miraculously been spared by the bombing. It was the wrong way to go. As Smith scrambled up a low hill, he saw a North Vietnamese soldier eating a bowl of rice. Bringing his arm up, Smith shot the startled man with his pistol—his rifle had long since been lost—only to be knocked senseless by an unseen assailant. Smith's last recollection was of a bright orange flash and a terrific pain in his left leg.

When he came to, he recalled, "I had a great weight on my head. An NVA soldier was standing on my head. I saw them shoot my bodyguard dead. They were lining up the regimental surgeon when I forced my way to my feet." Pistol still in hand, Smith tried to shoot the executioner, but a soldier wrenched the gun from his hand. "Right or wrong, I intended to pre-serve at least one friend from the battle," recalled Smith. The doctor was spared, though he would spend years in a prison camp.

At the new North Vietnamese headquarters near Loc Ninh, Captain Smith was treated roughly by most of the enemy soldiers, especially when they discovered he was the infamous Zippo they had heard over the radio. One "distinguished-looking" officer ordered his wounds cleaned and dressed. Smith had more than thirty wounds, some of them serious. As a North Vietnamese doctor saw to Smith, an interpreter told him that he was a captive of the 72d Regiment, 9th NVA Division. Smith, he said, "was a guest of the 'Group Commander, Mr. Tra.'" Not familiar with the enemy chain of command, Smith asked if Tra was the regimental or the division commander.

"Mr. Tra has many divisions," replied the interpreter with a smile. Mr. Tra was none other than General Tran Van Tra, commander of the B-2 Front, the overall command for North Vietnamese troops in III Corps.

Smith was reunited with Major Carlson, Sergeant Wallingford, and the French photographer later in the day when a group of enemy soldiers drove up the road in an American jeep with the advisers tied up in the back. Carlson was wounded, but the others, save for a few scrapes, were in good shape. Smith was tied to the floorboards, and the jeep headed down the road toward Highway 13 a mile to the east. Smith was chagrined to find that the North Vietnamese crossed over the underwater rock bridge, the same bridge that Lieutenant Colonel Vinh had been so certain was nothing but a smugglers' pathway. The North Vietnamese knew right where it was.

On one occasion the jeep pulled over under some trees when the driver heard a Spectre gunship overhead. The soldiers leaped out, looking for cover, leaving Smith tied to the jeep with the engine still running. Knowing that Spectre could "see" the heat signature, he screamed to the North Viet-namese and strained at his bonds. "Turn off the engine," he yelled in Viet-namese. "Although I probably gave away a secret, I finally got them to turn off the engine," Smith recalled. When the gunship passed by, they clam-bered back into the jeep and continued north toward Cambodia. Along the way Smith saw several captured armored personnel carriers hauling gear for the North Vietnamese, a sight that made him furious when he thought of the cowardice displayed by many in the 9th ARVN Regiment.

At Snoul, a Cambodian rubber plantation town about twenty miles from Loc Ninh, Smith was given more medical attention while North Vietnamese photographers snapped pictures of the "merciful" treatment afforded the Americans. For the next ten months Smith, Carlson, Wallingford, and

Wanat (George Wanat managed to elude capture for thirty-one days before being turned in by wary villagers) were kept as prisoners of war in a fetid camp. Yves-Michel Dumont, the photographer, was released on 14 July 1972, Bastille Day, as a goodwill gesture to the French. Captain Mark Smith and his fellow advisers had to wait until the conclusion of the Paris peace talks for their freedom. On 12 February 1973 they went home.[21]

"The Binh Long victory is a proper answer to the bellicose and die-hard Nixon clique, a due punishment of their war escalation in both North and South Vietnam," crowed Liberation Radio, Hanoi's clandestine broadcasting station in South Vietnam. Considering that only a fraction of the province was actually "liberated," this was a bold claim. But in the early days of the Easter Offensive, even the smallest victory was followed by pronouncements of "popular uprising" and "people's victory." When Loc Ninh fell, it became the provisional capital for the communists' revolutionary government in South Vietnam.[22]

The fate of South Vietnamese army prisoners and civilians left behind under North Vietnamese control was typical of communist "liberation" policy. According to refugees fortunate enough to flee the new North Vietnamese–imposed government, the communists clamped down quickly. Teams of political cadre rode through town and the surrounding villages informing citizens through blaring loudspeakers that a provisional revolutionary government was now in place.

Former Saigon government officials soon felt the weight of communist occupation. On 8 April, the day after the fall of Loc Ninh, dozens of civilian administrators, teachers, and other "tools" of the government were rounded up. The head of the local self-defense militia, along with a sergeant and another militiaman, were publicly executed in the town square, shot outright without even the benefit of a "people's court." The rest of those arrested as "enemies of the people" were bundled into trucks and driven to a secure base near Snoul. North Vietnamese political cadre encouraged the population to cooperate by starting a "turn-in-a-friend" campaign. People sentenced to death were told they would receive amnesty if they located any government officials or soldiers hiding among the population.[23]

As a symbol of benevolence and confidence, the North Vietnamese conquerors allowed about twenty members of the local defense militia to keep their weapons and act as the local police force. All private vehicles, including motor scooters, were confiscated and driven to Snoul. They would be returned and "redistributed to the poor," the political cadre said, but few believed it.[24]

Viet Cong living in the countryside outside Loc Ninh and among the population had set the stage for the rapid political consolidation. An underground network had organized Loc Ninh's sympathizers along communist lines, with one cadre being responsible for five families. These cadre knew who sympathized with the government and who was loyal to the communists. With the North Vietnamese in town, there was no need for secrecy, and they openly strode the streets, pointing out "lackeys" of Saigon.

The saying "to the victors go the spoils" was not lost on the conquering North Vietnamese troops. They ransacked homes and plundered offices of both government officials and plantation employees. Among the most prized booty were half a dozen black-and-white television sets confiscated by the victorious North Vietnamese. The captured TVs were sent to COSVN headquarters over the Cambodian border, where high-ranking officers and cadre closed out each workday by watching programs broadcast from Saigon.[25]

The North Vietnamese expected to achieve victory through sheer military weight, but communist dogma insisted on predicting a "popular uprising." Although this was certainly not as crucial to victory or defeat as the one that failed to materialize during the 1968 Tet Offensive, communist political cadre must have been disappointed at the general lack of cooperation from peasants and townspeople in northern Binh Long Province. In Loc Ninh, two Saigon labor officials were reportedly stranded in the town for ten days after the town's capture but were given refuge and finally spirited out of the occupied zone by local plantation workers. When they returned to Pleiku, the two men happily told their superiors that the communists' heavy-handed occupation policies had won few sympathizers among the local population.[26]

The North Vietnamese had rapidly defeated South Vietnamese forces around Loc Ninh and just as quickly brought the population under communist political control. Yet the fall of Loc Ninh was only a small fragment within the scope of the battle in III Corps. By close of day on 7 April, Loc Ninh was no longer a factor in the defense of Binh Long Province. The North Vietnamese were inexorably moving south toward An Loc, the focal point of the campaign in III Corps.

TWENTY-SIX

PREPARING FOR THE WORST

As North Vietnamese tanks crushed Loc Ninh beneath their treads, Lieutenant General Nguyen Van Minh lost his composure. Along with news that the district capital was lost came a summons from President Thieu in Saigon to attend a meeting of the Joint General Staff and the other three military corps commanders beginning on 7 April. As Minh boarded his personal helicopter, doubts assailed him. Could he hold Binh Long Province in the face of the gathering enemy storm? Was he correct in making a stand at An Loc, or would the North Vietnamese somehow bypass him and head directly for Saigon?

General Minh was intimidated by the political power emanating from Saigon. As a division commander in IV Corps before the offensive, he had played the necessary political games to enhance his power base, but he was in the field with his troops, not at the source of the power elite. As he sat in Thieu's chambers with the top generals, many of whom had made their careers by currying political favor with the president, he was uncertain about how to proceed. But offense was the best defense, so Minh presented his case forcefully. Forgetting his previous conviction that the North Vietnamese meant to attack Tay Ninh in full force, General Minh asked for more troops to defend An Loc. Saigon, he argued, was in dire danger if An Loc failed to hold out against the North Vietnamese. Only Chon Thanh and Lai Khe stood between the enemy and Saigon once An Loc was out of the way.

But President Thieu and his generals had other defense considerations, and they overruled the request. At this time, they pointed out, I Corps was reeling from the enemy assault, and although II Corp had seen only light fighting, the buildup there was ominous. Minh was sent from the room while the other corps commanders remained with the council. The general was certain he had reached the end of his career for speaking his mind, but later in the day he was recalled and told that the 21st ARVN Division would move up from IV Corps to relieve An Loc. In addition, the 1st Airborne Brigade, one of the last uncommitted units left in the general reserve, was assigned to the defense of An Loc.[1]

The 9th ARVN Division had been offered as a possible reinforcement for An Loc, but Lieutenant General Ngo Quang Truong, at this time still the IV Corps commander, suggested the 21st ARVN Division be sent instead. He gave two reasons. First, it had a reputation as an effective unit while conducting mobile search-and-destroy operations in the U Minh Forest. Second, the 21st ARVN Division had previously been commanded by General Minh, so the unit was less likely to resent being moved out of its old stomping ground and placed under a new overall command.

As it turned out, the Joint General Staff had previously made the decision to deploy the 21st ARVN Division in I Corps in an effort to retake lost territory north of the Cam Lo River. But Lieutenant General Dang Van Quang, President Thieu's assistant for security, advised that losing a provincial capital so close to Saigon would be an unforgivable loss of face. Thieu agreed, and the decision was made to reinforce An Loc. The 21st ARVN Division would begin moving immediately by air to Chon Thanh. By 12 April the entire division was ready to advance up Highway 13.[2]

Back at Lai Khe, General Minh attended to the defense of An Loc. The 5th ARVN Division ordered the withdrawal of Task Force 52, a combined unit occupying two small bases between Loc Ninh and An Loc, and recalled South Vietnamese forces from the Cam Le Bridge south to the provincial capital.[3] Task Force 52 was demolished as it retreated south, but the South Vietnamese troops at the bridge managed to withdraw to An Loc in good order, though they were forced to destroy all their artillery. Their arrival heralded the first blows in the attack on An Loc.[4]

Another clear sign of the severity of the North Vietnamese threat to An Loc was the throngs of civilians heading south away from the North Vietnamese. Some reported that communist troops pressed civilians into service, dispersing them in their ranks so that when the South Vietnamese opened fire they would kill their own people. On 7 April workers from the rubber plantations near An Loc reported large North Vietnamese units in the vicinity. Other civilians reported that the enemy had stripped store shelves bare of canned and dried food. Intelligence interpreted this as a sign that North Vietnamese supply lines were not keeping pace with the advancing troops. Whatever it meant, the North Vietnamese were clearly closing in on An Loc.[5]

Several groups of locals and South Vietnamese soldiers told of enemy units advancing toward An Loc behind herds of cattle and civilians to activate mines and mechanical ambushes. Most ominous of all were reports that the enemy had already set tanks in position around the city. One adviser later recalled that doom was "written on all the faces of civilians and military alike." A South Vietnamese officer captured by the enemy at Loc Ninh later escaped and brought final word that the communists intended to press on; he said his captors told him they meant to take An Loc at any cost.

With Saigon firmly behind him, Minh poured what men and resources he could into the city. MACV and the III Corps advisory staff tasked American CH-47 helicopters with delivering ammunition and rations, and taking out refugees and wounded soldiers on the return flights. The North Vietnamese were very much aware of the feverish activity but were unable to do much about it. They were so anxious to win the battle that the commanders of the B-2 Front had met on the night of 6 April to assess the situation. "The enemy's position is deteriorating in all the South Vietnam theater," they reasoned. "The importance now is that we work against time to quickly seize Binh Long City [An Loc] instead of waiting until we are fully organized in order to attack." The North Vietnamese were willing to sacrifice the normal cautious preparation in favor of speed, but their troops could not break out of the mold. A second command meeting on 11 April concluded that "because of our failure to seize the opportunity at the beginning, the enemy has increased its forces, actively set up defenses, and intensified B-52 activities. The situation has become complicated and different. . . . The guideline now is to fight steadily but urgently."[6]

Part of the North Vietnamese plan was to harry reinforcements sent toward An Loc. As high-ranking communist officials were meeting, III Corps headquarters sent two battalions of the 3d Ranger Group north by helicopter to back the 5th ARVN Division inside the city. They ran up against North Vietnamese units about four kilometers northeast of the city.[7]

Early on the morning of 11 April, the 1st Airborne Brigade left Lai Khe for Chon Thanh in trucks. It was ordered to dismount just outside Chon Thanh and continue north toward An Loc on foot, sweeping the area of enemy patrols that might threaten the vital supply lanes. The defenders inside An Loc were elated at the news of reinforcements, but their hopes were dashed when the airborne troops were stopped in their tracks a mere three miles north of Chon Thanh—they were still nine miles from An Loc. A blocking force made up of a regiment from the 7th NVA Division was entrenched near Highway 13 north of Chon Thanh. The North Vietnamese were determined to cut off all reinforcements and supplies from the south.

An Loc itself had still not come under attack, but a mile and a half to the east the Quan Loi airstrip was hit by the North Vietnamese. Late in the evening of 7 April, an enemy frontal assault supported by artillery rolled over two companies of South Vietnamese soldiers defending the airstrip.

The attack was so fierce that the defenders were ordered to fall back, destroying their two 105mm howitzers as they retreated. It took them two days to reach An Loc. The city was now isolated from the outside by road. Only helicopters—those that could make it through the increasingly deadly antiaircraft ring—could keep An Loc alive.

Under a canopy of B-52 strikes the South Vietnamese frantically continued reinforcing An Loc. For two days, beginning late on 10 April, the 1st and 2d Battalions of the 8th ARVN Regiment and the regimental reconnaissance company were flown into the city by helicopters of the 1st Brigade, U.S. 1st Cavalry Division. This Air Cav unit was the last remaining legacy of the famous airmobile division still in South Vietnam. As Cobra gunships circled menacingly, the Air Cav flew troops and supplies into An Loc around the clock.

The enemy buildup was big. Air force forward air controllers reported heavy troop and truck movement, particularly to the north of the city. B-52 strikes were placed wherever a troop concentration was reported. For the most part, however, there was no way of telling how much damage the big bombers were doing because the South Vietnamese were not patrolling beyond the city limits. Sometimes the Americans saw signs of the carnage. On one occasion, as the Air Cav was ferrying South Vietnamese troops into the city, General Hollingsworth spotted the bodies of approximately 200 enemy soldiers killed in an air strike.[8]

Inside An Loc General Hung waited for the worst. As commander of the 5th ARVN Division, he had seen one of his regiments take a severe beating to the north in Loc Ninh, and he had every reason to expect the same would happen in An Loc. Colonel Miller had pushed Hung for the past week, prodding him to decide whether to defend at An Loc or reinforce the firebases to the north and west.

"If you're going to defend An Loc," Miller said, "do it fast and get dug in. Get your bunkers and overhead cover strengthened because this is conventional war, not little VC guerrillas." But Hung would not say a word. He knew that his indecisiveness angered his counterpart, but to knuckle under meant losing face. So Hung simply withdrew into his shell. When Hung finally acted, it was too late. He waited too long before deciding to pull back from the firebases and into An Loc. Hung's indecisiveness cost the 5th ARVN Division many of its artillery pieces, which were left behind by South Vietnamese troops ordered to evacuate their forward positions only hours before the enemy appeared at the gates.

General Hung was dealing with a bold but unimaginative enemy. The North Vietnamese were rarely creative in the planning and execution of at-

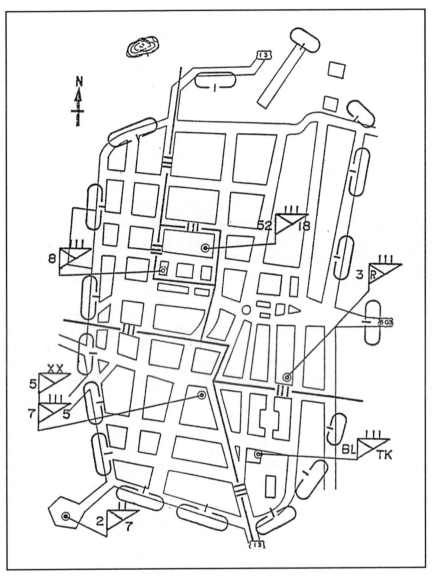

The defense of An Loc, 12 April 1972

tacks. The siege of An Loc was no exception. On 12 April the artillery barrage intensified, a clear indication that the attack was beginning. Then would come tanks and infantry. The enemy had been shelling An Loc since before Loc Ninh had fallen, but only sporadically. Now the artillery fire rained down in a rolling barrage. On that first day an estimated 1,000 rounds landed within the city.[9]

With the South Vietnamese committed to stand firm at An Loc, General Hollingsworth found himself in an unenviable situation. Like all American commanders remaining in South Vietnam he was under pressure to continue the drawdown and not endanger American lives. Yet withdrawing advisers from an increasingly dangerous situation would send a signal of uncertainty to the South Vietnamese. In their hour of need, such a move would certainly have weakened the defenders' resolve.

Hollingsworth chose to stand. However, he did not order his advisers to remain in An Loc; he evacuated those deemed nonessential and ordered Colonel Miller to pick his combat advisory team. Only a handful of Americans remained in the tactical operations center with Miller, Hung, and the 5th ARVN Division staff; Lieutenant Colonel William Benedit, the deputy senior adviser, and Major Allan Borstorff, the operations officer, had the highest ranks. A handful of advisers attached to ranger units, provincial forces, and air control teams also remained inside the tightening North Vietnamese noose.[10]

Hollingsworth still doubted North Vietnamese capability and commitment to an all-out battle for An Loc. Part of his skepticism was based on the natural tendency for every military tactician to suspect a ruse from his opponent, but most of Hollingsworth's doubts stemmed from a persistent underestimation of his foe and the belief that airpower, when wielded with appropriate ferocity, could thwart the North Vietnamese as they massed. Hollingsworth made his position known to General Abrams in one of his daily situation reports to Saigon. "The enemy has the determination and intention but is not capable at this time, to conduct sustained, all out 'win or die' attacks on friendly forces," he confidently reported to Abrams. "The enemy is particularly vulnerable to aggressive ARVN sweep operations, air strikes, and detection by VR [visual reconnaissance]." This was an optimistic conclusion considering that TRAC knew full well that An Loc was surrounded by at least two divisions of North Vietnamese troops, and that the South Vietnamese had long since given up patrolling outside the perimeter. Yet whatever variables remained, Hollingsworth knew that An Loc was the place for a showdown.[11]

Committed to the defense of the beleaguered provincial capital, General Hollingsworth called his deputy, Brigadier General John McGiffert, to meet him at the 5th ARVN Division base camp in Lai Khe. McGiffert had been flying over the An Loc area looking for enemy troop concentrations. He turned his helicopter around and dashed for home. The two generals walked off into the rubber trees near the base and discussed strategy. With most of the South Vietnamese units tied up inside the city, fire and maneuver was out of the question. Hollingsworth opted for the heaviest club in his arsenal—the B-52 Arc Light strike. He ordered McGiffert to draw a dozen Arc Light boxes around An Loc. The coordinates would be prearranged so the big bombers could pulverize the area whenever an enemy unit was reported inside one of the boxes. In a way, the desperate situation inside An Loc was preferable to the running retreat going on up in I Corps. At least here the enemy positions were more easily fixed—they were all around the city.

Seeing Hollingsworth and McGiffert sitting in the rubber trees, a casual observer would never have suspected the gravity of their informal council of war. But the lives of many American advisers were at stake, as was the prestige of South Vietnam's government. Failure at An Loc also meant failure of America's long road toward Vietnamization. A South Vietnamese defeat on the field of battle would shatter the illusion, carefully crafted by the United States, that Saigon's army had been adequately trained to stand alone.

After the meeting in the rubber trees, Hollingsworth flew off to MACV headquarters in Saigon to ask General Abrams for extra B-52 strikes the following day, 13 April. He argued that all signs pointed to an all-out strike by the North Vietnamese beginning at first light. He guessed that the enemy would be bunched up and vulnerable to a series of Arc Light strikes, which would decimate their ranks. Abrams agreed and ordered the diversion of strikes from I and II Corps. Satisfied, General Hollingsworth returned to Lai Khe and waited for daybreak and the inevitable North Vietnamese onslaught.[12]

Colonel Miller also waited, but not for long. Only fifteen minutes into the new day, South Vietnamese security elements west and southwest of the city reported the movement of large enemy units. At 4:00 in the morning, reports of tanks and heavy trucks came back. Thirty-five minutes later, an AC-130 Spectre gunship rumbled overhead and unleashed its fearsome fire on four trucks moving toward the city from the west. An hour later the North Vietnamese retaliated by intensifying their artillery bombardment, concentrating fire on the ammunition and fuel dump near the airstrip. After a few direct hits the defenders watched as great walls of angry flame shot toward the sky, punctuated by streaks of exploding tracer ammunition. Five hundred meters beyond the east side of the city, trip flares and claymore mines went off, revealing enemy tanks and trucks to the watching South Vietnamese soldiers. They fled their positions for the seeming security of the city center.

For better or worse, the South Vietnamese perimeter was set for the onslaught. On the north, along the north-south axis of Highway 13, were two battalions from the 18th ARVN Division. On the west flank the 7th ARVN Regiment manned its defenses. Facing east was the 3d Ranger Group, probably the best unit in An Loc. The soldiers could mark the advancing enemy by the swarm of aircraft overhead. The oncoming T-54s had been harried by American aircraft as they readied for the assault on An Loc, and many of them did not even make it to the outskirts of the city.

One group of prowling Cobras from F Battery, 3d Aviation Brigade, pounced on a column of tanks as soon as it emerged from the trees onto Highway 13. The gunships unleashed rockets and minigun fire on the surprised armor column, destroying two or three tanks. The burning hulks bottled up the road, and the last thing the Cobra pilots saw as they turned their helicopters back for home was a group of stranded T-54s, unable to pass the roadblock because the forest was too thick on either side of the road. A forward air controller called in fast movers to finish off the milling tanks. Still, many more made it to An Loc unscathed.

At 6:00 on the morning of 13 April, the battle was joined when North Vietnamese tanks slammed into the defenders' west flank. Fortunately for the South Vietnamese, the armor was not followed closely by infantry, a tactical failure probably brought on by an earlier COSVN decision to place all armor directly under the COSVN Military Command rather than with the divisions. The results were disastrous. The tanks operated completely on their own, with little communication with the infantry units. Armor easily broke through the South Vietnamese defenses around An Loc, but without infantry to follow up the attack the North Vietnamese could not hold their gains. Worse, after getting over the initial shock of seeing tanks, the defenders could knock out the tanks one by one as they hid behind buildings.[13]

The North Vietnamese tankers seemed to hesitate once inside the city. Although they had studied urban tank tactics, actually fighting on city streets was a new experience. Tanks were not meant to operate on narrow roadways and sharp street corners; around every curve and in every doorway, a single soldier with a handheld antitank weapon might be waiting. All it took was a single brave soldier to prove that armor was not invincible. And that was exactly what happened. The first contact on the west flank probed the local Popular Force militia contingent, considered the weakest point in the line. The main unit defending the west side of town was the 7th ARVN Regiment; the militia filled in the gaps. Overcoming his fear, a single brave militiaman stood up from his position, pointed an M72 LAW, and launched the round at a tank down the street. His aim was true, and the rocket struck the tank below the turret. With a flash and roar the tank sputtered to a stop, smoke billowing from its turret.

Word quickly spread that tanks were not invincible. As the South Vietnamese had discovered in I Corps two weeks earlier, a single soldier could stop one of the steel monsters with ease. Soldiers raced through the streets, trying to see who could kill the most tanks. But they had been lucky. The small North Vietnamese infantry contingent was easily driven back, leaving the hapless tanks to fend for themselves.

Although the situation looked good on the western side of An Loc, that was not the case elsewhere. The bulk of the attack was an armor-tipped thrust from the north, straight down Highway 13. The South Vietnamese defenders broke almost immediately, falling back through the city streets. At the tactical operations center in the center of town, Hung and Miller were pleased to hear the news from the western flank, but they knew that had been small compared with what was happening on the northern edge of town.

The North Vietnamese were well aware of the mistakes they made, and of their inadequacies fighting a multifaceted conventional battle in a built-up area. In a postwar history they freely admitted the problems they faced, noting that "some elements of our forces had reached Hung Vuong Street, a part of the local residential area. But . . . we did not have enough forces to develop the attack and fight a decisive battle to seize the entire military sector." North Vietnamese commanders remained optimistic, however, concluding that "our forces had moved close to their objectives and had created good jumping-off positions" and were quickly gaining "experience in combined-arms operations, street fighting, and attacking the enemy in strong fortifications. These were new factors ensuring the division's capability to develop its attacks and record even greater success."[14]

Within his private thoughts Colonel Miller was concerned. His anxiety level rose daily as he wondered whether the South Vietnamese troops would hold in the face of enemy tanks. During his many years as a soldier, Miller had often pondered his final fate. He accepted that he might someday be wounded or even killed on the field of battle, but it never occurred to him that he might one day be captured by the enemy. It was unthinkable. Yet for the first time in his career, Colonel Miller faced up to the possibility. He was trapped in a city surrounded by the enemy, "protected" by troops he did not command. By any estimation, the 5th ARVN Division was not the best unit in the South Vietnamese army, and Miller felt that fate had dealt him a cruel hand.

On the northern edge of town the South Vietnamese fell back in terror, throwing down weapons and equipment as they retreated. Tanks rumbled along behind them, almost oblivious to the fleeing soldiers. Someone counted forty-one tanks, but the figure was never confirmed. Whatever the final tally, they were a serious threat. One T-54 tank crashed through the South Vietnamese perimeter from the north and rolled all the way through town before it was destroyed outside the southern gates by a militiaman with an LAW.[15]

Another tank wandered through the city, stopping casually to fire at any target that moved. At one point the T-54 stopped, traversed its turret toward a nearby Catholic church, and pumped round after round through the front wall. One American adviser witnessed the grisly spectacle, later reporting that a large group of civilians was huddled inside praying for salvation from the terrible attack. Almost everyone inside was killed. After a few minutes the tank's gun fell silent. The crew, out of ammunition, climbed out of the turret, arms raised in surrender. In no mood to take prisoners, some nearby South Vietnamese soldiers ran up and emptied their rifles into the hapless enemy tankers.

Cobra gunships had been sent north from Lai Khe to engage the tanks. Called the Blue Max Squadron—formally known as the 79th Aerial Rocket Artillery, 3d Brigade, 1st Cavalry Division—these heavily armed helicopters were part of the last remaining U.S. gunship contingent in the 12th Aviation Group. They swooped into An Loc, wary of the antiaircraft batteries ringing the city, and pounced on the North Vietnamese tanks wandering the streets. For the most part the Cobras fired at whatever targets they identified. The sky was alive with antiaircraft fire, and the helicopters were forced to come in from high altitude and dive on their targets; even the briefest hover meant certain death. On one occasion a Cobra came up on Colonel Miller's adviser net asking for targets.

"Get the hell off my frequency," Miller retorted. "I'm fighting a damn war here and I don't know who the hell you are."

"Sir, I have two Cobras and we're looking for action." The voice belonged to the Blue Max commander, Major Larry McKay, a West Pointer who loved the excitement of flying, particularly if he could use his considerable skills to shoot rockets at something. And tanks made perfect targets.

Miller thought briefly about the danger, then decided he could use all the help he could get. "I'm not sure your helicopters can survive over this town."

"I'm willing to chance it if you want to commit me," came the reply over the radio.

Again Colonel Miller mulled it over. But there was no time to waste. "What are you carrying on those wing-pods, major?"

McKay said his gunships had high-explosive, antitank (HEAT) rockets. Miller nodded gleefully. That was exactly what was needed. "Come and get it," he told the Cobras. Then he turned to his deputy, Lieutenant Colonel Benedit. "Put all the tac air we have onto the air defense. When they beat it down I'm going to bring those Cobras in on the tanks." The fighters dropped their bomb loads on the enemy antiaircraft positions ringing An Loc. Then the Cobras rolled in on the attack, releasing twelve rockets from about 4,000 feet and striking a T-54 below.[16]

The Cobras went on to kill two more tanks, the last one as the enemy armor turned tail and ran for the cover of the forest. A rocket slammed into the lead tank's tread, spinning it sideways and blocking the road. The other tanks careened around the carcass, some of them becoming mired in the soft ground. Out of ammunition and low on fuel, the Cobras veered into a pillar of black smoke rising from the town and escaped to the south. They would be back.

The Cobras accounted for only a handful of enemy tanks. But when this number was added to the ones taken out of action by South Vietnamese soldiers with handheld LAWs, it became clear that the tide was turning. Without the support of infantry, the T-54s were helpless giants trapped inside unfriendly territory. The South Vietnamese soldiers on the buckled northern perimeter of the city began to take their cue from the militiamen and hunted down individual tanks with LAWs.

Inside the command bunker Miller watched as Hung and his staff faltered and withdrew into silent shells. They were fatalistic, convinced the North Vietnamese were superior fighters. So they froze and waited for the end. Miller was not yet ready to die, however. He pushed Hung into action, urging that he bend the ranger units on the east side of the city toward the center. Hung complied, sending one battalion to a new position astride the road leading into town from the north. The move was accomplished behind a curtain of precise tactical air support, which held the North Vietnamese momentarily at bay. One errant bomb would have resulted in many dead rangers. Finally the line began to hold, and by the end of the day every enemy tank inside An Loc had been driven out or destroyed.[17]

A Soviet-made T-54 tank burns in the streets of An Loc. The North Vietnamese made poor use of armor, attacking down city streets without infantry support. (Author's collection)

As the battle raged in swirling confusion, Miller continued to guide the war above An Loc. B-52s rained bombs down just outside the city, and tactical air strikes pounded supply vehicles behind the North Vietnamese units. General McGiffert was convinced the bombers had tipped the scales in favor of the defenders. The preplanned Arc Light boxes allowed strikes within 1,000 meters of friendly positions. "I really believe that without those the city would have fallen," McGiffert later told his boss. In his opinion the North Vietnamese infantry was prevented from joining the tanks in the attack because the B-52s had broken them up as they assembled outside of An Loc.[18]

General Hollingsworth was also elated. The North Vietnamese had massed and attacked in strength, something the Americans had tried to force them to do for the past seven years with very few successes. This time the enemy offensive allowed the full weight of U.S. firepower to be brought to bear, and for Hollingsworth it was a gratifying experience. "There was a great battle at An Loc yesterday—perhaps the greatest of this campaign," he wrote triumphantly. "I am most pleased with the outcome of the battle. . . . The enemy hit us hard all day long with everything he could muster—and we threw it right back at him."[19]

Hollingsworth's assessment was characteristically optimistic and definitely premature, but shortly after dark the fighting died down to isolated firefights all around the city. Early in the morning on 14 April, the North Vietnamese pulled back slightly, allowing their artillery to fire. For a couple of hours howitzer rounds and 122mm rockets poured into An Loc. At 7:45 the shelling slacked off, and tanks were again reported on the outskirts of town. Within an hour they had pushed to within 500 yards of the 5th ARVN Division command center. The tanks were again destroyed or driven off, but with each attack the South Vietnamese were weakening.

Responding to Hollingsworth's prodding, General Minh busily executed a plan to get reinforcements to the desperate defenders inside An Loc. The 21st ARVN Division remained just north of Chon Thanh. Still suspicious of enemy intentions, General Minh had ordered the division to block movement along the border between Binh Long and Binh Duong Provinces. Although An Loc was receiving the brunt of the North Vietnamese assault, there was still the possibility that they really intended to break off the attack once a majority of the South Vietnamese forces were committed in An Loc and head down Highway 13 for Saigon. Part of the 7th NVA Division was in the area south of An Loc, but Minh was not sure if it was the spearhead for a thrust at Saigon or a blocking force stopping reinforcements from the south.

The 5th ARVN Division urgently requested reinforcements to bolster the crumbling defenses around the city. III Corps headquarters complied by sending one of its last reserve units, an airborne brigade, north to An Loc, though Minh retained operational control from the III Corps headquarters. The airborne brigade had been recalled from the Tau O area to the south, reequipped and air assaulted with American helicopters to positions on Windy Hill and Hill 169, both less than two miles southwest of the city, on 13 and 14 April. There were now three airborne battalions along An Loc's southern perimeter.

First Lieutenant Ross Kelly sat in the open door of a Huey as it skimmed over the scarred landscape. This was it, he thought, the battle he had spent his short career training for. Lieutenant Kelly had come to Vietnam seeking combat, but the last thing he had expected was an all-out conventional invasion in these final months of American involvement in Vietnam. But that was exactly what had happened, and now Lieutenant Kelly found himself in the vanguard of a bold air assault against Windy Hill and Hill 169, two seemingly insignificant bumps south of An Loc.

Kelly was a gung ho officer on his first tour in Vietnam. Well aware that the army was drawing down as he neared graduation at West Point, Kelly wanted to see some combat before it was all over. Prior to shipping out, he pulled every string he could to be assigned as an adviser to an elite unit where he could be assured of at least some action. In November 1971 Kelly arrived incountry and was immediately assigned to the 6th Battalion, 1st Brigade, of the Airborne Division. He could not have been more pleased.

After the fall of Loc Ninh, the 6th Airborne Battalion was deployed to Lai Khe to prevent the North Vietnamese from cutting Highway 13 south of An Loc. From there it loaded onto helicopters and flew to Chon Thanh on 8 April, deployed west of the highway, and waited for the enemy. It did not have long to wait; North Vietnamese units engaged the airborne battalion in small running battles for three days. As Saigon firmed up plans to bring fresh South Vietnamese troops north along Highway 13 from IV Corps to relieve An Loc, the airborne soldiers were moved still farther north in an attempt to reinforce the besieged city. On the morning of 14 April, the 6th Airborne Battalion loaded into helicopters for an assault five miles southeast of An Loc. The battalion was assigned the mission of "securing the high ground to the immediate west of the landing zone to relieve pressure on the beleaguered town of An Loc."[20]

In the lead was Company B, with Lieutenant Kelly aboard one of the first Hueys. The helicopters raced low over a patchwork of farmers' fields, then landed in a shallow valley east of Hill 169. Airborne soldiers poured out and immediately stormed over the broken terrain at the base of the mountain.

The advisers knew the operation was risky. So risky, in fact, that they had elected not to saturate the area with air strikes and artillery before the assault. "We were told that there were unknown numbers of NVA investing An Loc at the time," recalled Kelly. "We knew we were going to be in a race with the enemy for the crest of Hill 169, so we didn't see any real point in prepping the LZ, except to tip off the North Vietnamese about what we were doing."

The scenario played out precisely as the advisers had feared. As the airborne moved up the eastern slope of Hill 169, the enemy was moving up the west. The timely support of Cobra gunships from Troop F, 4th Cavalry, helped even the race, but the North Vietnamese still managed to reach the top first. They raked the hilltop as the North Vietnamese dug in, but the airborne still had to root them out.

Knowing that the North Vietnamese were preparing to counterattack, Lieutenant Kelly crawled closer to the enemy positions, threw a smoke grenade to mark his position, and called in the cavalry to come to the rescue. As the enemy massed, the Cobras swooped in and broke up their ranks. Time after time the enemy tried to charge, only to be sprayed with the gunships' miniguns and forced to disperse.

It was still up to the ground troops to clean up the mess. "We did it the old-fashioned way—with an infantry charge," said Kelly. "I probably had the dubious distinction of leading the last bayonet charge of the entire war," he claimed. "We fought them in the trenches."

It was now or never, so the company commander ordered the charge, then stood up and raced for the enemy positions. Lieutenant Kelly followed close on his heels, killing one North Vietnamese soldier as he tried to lead a flanking move against the airborne company. The South Vietnamese quickly overran some of the trenches, driving the North Vietnamese into the open, where they were pounced on by waiting Cobras. The pilots were almost gleeful as they savored the "target-rich environment" on the hilltop.

As the fighting continued, a voice broke in on the radio. Kelly ignored it. "Boiler Whiskey, give me a sitrep," insisted the voice. "This is Danger Seven Niner." Completely unaware that Danger 79 was General Hollingsworth's call sign, Kelly gave an angry reply. "Danger Seven Niner, this is Boiler Whiskey. I don't know who the hell you are, but I'm putting in air right now—get the hell off my net." Danger Seven Niner seemed to understand. "Roger. I'll get back to you later," he said.

That evening, after things had quieted down, the voice came back on the air. "Hello, Boiler Whiskey, this is Danger Seven Niner. Have you got time to talk to me now?" Kelly looked through his codebook—something he had not had time to do during the fighting—and realized who he had brushed off. "Roger, I've got time," replied Kelly, trying to pretend that he had done nothing out of the ordinary. But Hollingsworth did not hold it against the beleaguered lieutenant. After the battle the general signed off on a Distinguished Service Cross for Kelly, the second-highest award for valor in the U.S. Army.

As the airborne company secured part of the hilltop, the rest of the battalion closed in behind. But unlike their compatriots on the summit, the soldiers found themselves harassed by mortar fire from enemy positions still in place on the hilltop. One of the first casualties was Major Morgan, the battalion senior adviser, who suffered a nasty leg wound. Lieutenant Kelly also had some wounded to tend to. As he carried one man down the hill for a medevac, an artillery round landed nearby, blowing him off his feet. A jagged piece of shrapnel gouged into his gas mask case, and another bounced off his helmet, leaving a fist-sized dent but no serious injuries.

That night, Kelly found himself to be the only American on top of Hill

169. He spent most of the night calling in support from AC-119 and AC-130 gunships that rotated in and out of the area. By dawn the North Vietnamese had had enough. Daybreak revealed that the enemy had taken its dead and wounded and retreated off of Hill 169. The airborne company had also suffered, though not badly. Kelly counted half a dozen South Vietnamese killed and about twenty wounded.

But the battle that had begun as a heroic charge and gained the South Vietnamese the most strategic high ground south of An Loc soon turned into a fight for survival. Although the North Vietnamese had retreated in the face of overwhelming aerial firepower, they had no intention of ceding Hill 169 to the South Vietnamese. As the airborne company clung to its vulnerable perch, the enemy reinforced and prepared to take back the hill. As the adviser report later noted, "The situation of the battalion in securing the key high terrain was fast becoming tenuous."

For the next three days the rest of the 6th Airborne Battalion mounted operations aimed at keeping the North Vietnamese off balance, but constant enemy artillery took its toll. In addition, the North Vietnamese brought up more antiaircraft weapons, making resupply, reinforcement, and air cover risky. On the evening of 19 April, the battalion headquarters retreated to the west, leaving only two companies to fight for Hill 169. The North Vietnamese sensed the changing initiative and closed in.

Inside An Loc the battle on Windy Hill meant nothing. The defenders were caught up in their own life-or-death struggle, and Colonel Miller did not think that the presence of the airborne south of the city would have a direct impact on the situation. As the 6th Airborne Battalion began to lose ground, the South Vietnamese inside An Loc fought on, trapped inside their crumbling defenses surrounded by a determined enemy backed by armor.

On 15 April the North Vietnamese attacked again from the northern part of the city with eleven tanks, but the defenders were ready and waiting. Throughout the day the South Vietnamese competed among themselves to see who could knock out the most tanks. Yet the enemy once again came close to taking the city center. A single T-54 came so close to the 5th ARVN Division operations center that it fired a round point-blank into the bunker. The blast wounded the South Vietnamese operations officer for Binh Long Sector and two other staff officers. When the dust had cleared at the end of the day, the South Vietnamese had destroyed nine of the eleven tanks. The rest managed to scurry to safety.[21]

The North Vietnamese were not pleased with the battle up to this point. The commander of the 9th NVA Division, General Nguyen Thoi Bung, reported to his superiors that American and South Vietnamese air strikes and artillery had succeeded in "strik[ing] hard at our assault formation. The commanders of the division and its regiments could not control the battalions because the communication lines were broken. Our infantrymen could not stay close to the tanks, and our artillery could not put its firepower to good account in support of the infantry." Four days later, on 19 April, North Vietnamese unit commanders would meet to review the first two phases of their attack on An Loc and, building on General Bung's observations, concluded that "we organized combat activities in a simplistic manner, and we were confused in dealing with contingencies." Because of this, "there had been no annihilation battle capable of causing a great shock wave. . . . The 13 and 14 April phase of attack was unsuccessful not because the enemy was strong, but because we did not fight well, and there was no close coordination between our infantry and our tanks."[22]

But despite these many problems, the North Vietnamese regrouped and prepared for the next assault.

TWENTY-SEVEN

THE SHELLING GAME

By 16 April most of the close-quarter fighting had died down. After three days of fierce combat the North Vietnamese had lost twenty-three tanks, most of them T-54s and the Chinese equivalent, the T-59. With crucial help from the U.S. Air Force, the South Vietnamese had held on in the face of constant terrifying assaults. But even so, the enemy had still managed to seize and hold the northern half of An Loc. Attackers and defenders looked at each other from positions on opposite sides of Nguyen Trong Truc Street, one of the main roads running east-west through the city. Worse, North Vietnamese units outside An Loc seemed to be tightening their grip. In fact, South Vietnamese intelligence reported there was the better part of five enemy regiments in and around the city. Friendly artillery was virtually nonexistent. The South Vietnamese had lost most of it in the first two days of fighting, and counterbattery fire could only be done with tactical air strikes—if anyone was lucky enough to get a fix on North Vietnamese artillery positions.

Inside his dusty bunker Colonel Miller was concerned about the situation, and he could find little good to say in his daily report to TRAC headquarters. On the night of 17 April he painted a grim picture for General Hollingsworth:

> Three days ago the enemy moved into An Loc with tanks. As a result his forces now hold half the city. The division is unable to retake lost ground. Yesterday, the northern 2–3 blocks of the city were destroyed by tactical air strikes. Last night the enemy reinforced his defenses in north An Loc and is now firmly entrenched with mortars and anti-aircraft artillery. Believe the enemy will get stronger in the northern part of town. The 81st Airborne Battalion [sent to reinforce] has not yet arrived and the city is now heavily ringed on 3 sides with antiaircraft guns. Believe that the enemy will use strangulation and starvation tactics—then attack in force. . . . The division is tired and worn out; supplies minimal—casualties continue to mount—medical supplies and coverage is low. Wounded a major problem—mass burials for military and civilian—morale at low ebb. In spite of incurring heavy losses from U.S. air strikes, the enemy continues to persist.[1]

As the siege dragged on, relations between Colonel Miller and General Hung worsened. Frustrated by Hung's lack of control, Miller tried hard to coax him into counterattacking while the North Vietnamese regrouped. But Hung hesitated, unwilling to risk his troops in open combat. Instead, he pleaded for more air strikes. Miller's frustration climbed higher as he watched Hung hesitate time after time. "The Division CG [commanding general] is tired—unstable—irrational—irritable—inadvisable—and unapproachable," he angrily reported to Hollingsworth. "When the chips are down he looses [sic] all of his composure. This operation exceeds his 4–6 hours per day routine. Unless the Airborne saves us I believe the enemy can take An Loc at any time."[2]

It looked bad for the defenders, but the enemy could not afford to sit on their laurels. Air strikes whittled away at the North Vietnamese, and every minute they delayed attacking resulted in more dead soldiers and destroyed equipment. Yet while the air support was welcome, it could also be troublesome. Colonel Miller grew angry as messages got mixed and missions went awry. As the North Vietnamese leaned close against South Vietnamese defenses north of town, Miller asked for cluster bombs instead of the usual high-explosive hard bombs. Ordnance was falling too close to friendly lines for comfort, and the exploding bomblets contained in cluster bombs were less likely to result in South Vietnamese casualties. But the order was never received, and hard bombs continued to fall.

Miller blamed the forward air controllers. In desperation he radioed Hollingsworth. "Stop sending those goddamned hard bombs. Request soft ordnance," he radioed. Hours later, high-explosive bombs were still raining down. Miller got back on the radio: "If we can't get this air situation straightened out I'm putting my three advisers on the perimeter with rifles where they can do some good," he threatened. The situation was finally resolved.[3]

The constant air strikes continued to pound the North Vietnamese, knocking them further behind schedule. It was time for a change of plan. First, additional antiaircraft batteries were put in place around the city. Second, the North Vietnamese command decided to support its next attacks on the city center with secondary assaults of the airborne troops on Windy Hill and Hill 169. Two regiments were assigned the task: the 275th of the 5th VC Division and the 141st of the 7th NVA Division. Their main goal was to knock out the 105mm howitzer battery that the 1st Airborne Brigade had placed on the hilltop. This was crucial. Because the North Vietnamese had knocked out most of the artillery inside An Loc, this single battery of howitzers was critical to the South Vietnamese defense. All three regiments of the 9th VC Division would again attack the northern sector of the An Loc perimeter.[4]

South Vietnamese soldiers stand near a captured 12.7mm anti-aircraft gun. By mid-April An Loc was ringed by enemy anti-aircraft weapons, making aerial resupply of the town dangerous. (Author's collection)

Yet by a stroke of good fortune the South Vietnamese managed to get a step up on the coming attack. They knew of the enemy plan. On 18 April a company from the 92d Border Ranger Defense Battalion patrolling the road between Tonle Cham, an area just inside Tay Ninh Province, and An Loc ambushed and killed a highly placed COSVN political officer. On his body was found a six-page letter from the political commissar of the 9th VC Division to COSVN headquarters outlining plans for yet another assault on An Loc, this one to be launched on 19 April—the next day. That the North Vietnamese planned the attack was well known. But the details were helpful to the South Vietnamese. The enemy had been so confident this would be the final attack that it announced over National Liberation Radio that An Loc would be taken on 20 April. From that day forward, An Loc would be the seat of the new communist government in South Vietnam. Many of the North Vietnamese attackers assumed the radio report meant that the battle was over. On at least one occasion the tankers had been told by their officers that An Loc had already been captured. All they had to do was drive into town and take over.

Another letter found on the dead man's body revealed new cracks in the seemingly impenetrable armor of the enemy offensive machine. The letter was a critique of North Vietnamese strategy and performance up to that point in time. The 9th VC Division and its commander, General Bung, were castigated for failing to take An Loc within the first few days of the attack.[5]

To live up to their political officers' prediction, the North Vietnamese soldiers struck hard beginning early on the morning of 19 April. The attack proceeded precisely as outlined in the captured document. An Loc came under the usual heavy preassault artillery barrage. As the defenders endured their daily dose of artillery rounds, the 275th and 141st NVA Regiments began hammering the airborne battalions on Windy Hill and Hill 169. On this occasion enemy armor and infantry worked well together. With six tanks leading the way, the North Vietnamese smashed through the 1st Airborne Brigade headquarters on Hill 169, forcing the 6th Airborne Battalion to destroy its 105mm howitzer battery and retreat. Two companies from the battalion and the brigade headquarters unit fell back to An Loc, while the remaining two companies found themselves cut off. After fierce fighting they were able to move south—away from An Loc—where they were eventually picked up by South Vietnamese air force helicopters and carried to Chon Thanh. All six of the North Vietnamese tanks were destroyed, but the enemy had the high ground atop Hill 169.

Lieutenant Ross Kelly knew the final enemy assault was imminent. Since the initial attack on Hill 169 on 14 April, he had stayed with the company as it was gradually whittled down by persistent enemy thrusts. As dawn broke on 20 April, about 800 North Vietnamese surged up the hill, backed by tanks and artillery. Nervous airborne soldiers opened fire with heavy machine guns, but they had little effect on the advancing enemy.

Kelly frantically called for all the air support he could get. Considered one of the best air support coordinators in the Airborne Division, Kelly could manipulate air controllers and handle multiple "sticks" of aircraft—anything from helicopter gunships to jet fighters—bringing them unerringly on target. All six of the tanks were destroyed, mostly by South Vietnamese soldiers with LAWs, but the assault took its toll. Dozens of dead and wounded airborne troopers further depleted the ranks, and the brigade commander, who was in An Loc at this time, ordered the company off the summit of Hill 169. The battered soldiers moved down the east slope to a partially wooded knoll in the hope that they could hold out for reinforcement or evacuation.

It was inevitable that the enemy would close in and destroy the dwindling battalion. Fewer than 100 men were still in fighting condition, and some of them were walking wounded. "We were easy pickings," recalled Lieutenant Kelly. "Most of the North Vietnamese east of An Loc pressed in to beat us up."[6]

Lieutenant Colonel Dinh, the commander of the 6th Airborne Battalion, was part of the problem. He ordered some of his men to dig a foxhole, then he climbed in, hunkered down, and refused to come out. The airborne soldiers milled about looking for cover and waiting for orders, only to be told that there were none. Dinh refused to discuss anything. The battalion operations officer, a man respected by Americans and Vietnamese alike, took Lieutenant Kelly aside and told him gravely, "Dinh has made his peace with dying."

Neither Kelly nor the operations officer had made such a peace, however. As they assured the men that all would be well, Kelly received a call from An Loc, where the rest of the airborne brigade was now holed up. Major Jack Todd, the deputy senior adviser, said that he had laid on a series of Arc Light strikes to give the 6th Airborne Battalion some breathing room so they could make good their escape. The time and place that the bombers would make their run were preset; it was up to the battalion to either break out toward An Loc or find some other way to safety. Kelly mulled over the choice and decided that getting into An Loc was no bargain; he was better off on his own. The South Vietnamese agreed. "We have to break out, sir," Lieutenant Kelly said over the radio. "I can't wait here. We're heading southeast toward Song Be." It was the last communication between the 6th Airborne Battalion and the rest of the brigade.

That night, one B-52 strike went in as planned west of An Loc. Although the battalion intended to move east, the object was to make the North Vietnamese think it was headed toward An Loc. A second strike followed five minutes later, this time to the east of Hill 169 along the path the airborne soldiers planned to use for their escape. The strike hit just as the North Vietnamese were massing for an attack.

"That's the signal," said Lieutenant Kelly to the battalion operations officer. "We have to move now." In the darkness they could see the flashes of bomb blasts and hear the roar of the explosions. "An Arc Light at night is like the jaws of hell opening up," Kelly recalled in awe.

The South Vietnamese moved out smartly, right through the area where the North Vietnamese had been blown apart by the Arc Light strike. Any survivors were summarily shot by the South Vietnamese. When the group stopped and regrouped a few miles farther along, Kelly made a head count. All that remained of the original 500-man battalion was about 60 soldiers, and many of them were wounded or shell-shocked.

On several occasions during the night the little group ran into North Vietnamese units. Kelly consolidated all the ammunition, giving it to the best soldiers. This little group of about twelve men stopped dozens of enemy attacks while Kelly concentrated on guiding a South Vietnamese air force AC-119 Stinger as it strafed their front and kept the North Vietnamese at bay. Throughout the night it was touch and go.

By dawn on 21 April they were low on ammunition, and the North Vietnamese were still pressing. Stinger continued to fire, and the air controllers radioed encouragement, but Kelly was losing hope. Fever and exhaustion set in, forcing the young lieutenant to struggle just to remain upright.

The little band reached a stream shortly after dawn, but as they filled canteens, a squad of North Vietnamese broke out of the woods on the far bank. Each side seemed as surprised as the other, but when the firing was over, three of the enemy soldiers lay dead. Certain that larger enemy units were now on the way, the South Vietnamese moved faster toward the south. Although Kelly and the remaining officers and sergeants tried to keep control, morale broke down, and the troops became unorganized and undisciplined. Finally, sometime during midmorning the little group fired its last M79 grenade round, then sat back and waited for the end.

Not until 5:45 on the evening of 21 April did they receive help. Kelly got word over the radio that they were to be extracted by helicopter at a clearing to the southeast. Just as it looked as if they were safe, a North Vietnamese patrol hit the tail end of the battalion as it moved toward the pickup point. Lieutenant Kelly broke the attack by placing timely air strikes within 200 yards of his position.

Without warning, a group of South Vietnamese helicopters appeared in a nearby clearing. They hovered over a muddy bog at about shoulder level, refusing to come closer. Only a few soldiers were still strong enough to climb aboard, but they managed to pull some of their weaker comrades up after them. Kelly reached down to help his radio operator, but the pilot panicked and the entire squadron pulled back into the sky, leaving about thirty soldiers on the ground. As the Huey circled upward, Kelly could see the soldier growing smaller below, his arms stretched toward the sky.

After all they had been through, Kelly was furious. He pulled his pistol and threatened to kill the pilot if did not go back, but the ordeal had taken its toll, and he passed out on the chopper floor. When he came to, Kelly was on a stretcher in Lai Khe. He later heard that the soldiers who were left behind managed to hide in the woods and waited until the North Vietnamese turned their attention back toward An Loc. They walked for another week until they ran into a Regional Forces post near Song Be.

As the North Vietnamese were driving the airborne soldiers out of their positions on the hilltops, the 9th VC Division again attempted to punch through South Vietnamese defenses in the southern part of the city. Aware that the 20 April deadline for capturing An Loc was quickly slipping away, the North Vietnamese launched a frenzied attack, dashing themselves against South Vietnamese positions. But the defenders clung doggedly to their foxholes and bunkers. They knew it was stand or die; there was no place to run.

Once again the attack failed. B-52s and tactical air strikes made the difference, pounding enemy positions in the northern part of the city with precise strikes that sometimes landed within 200 yards of friendly positions. Yet the South Vietnamese gratefully endured the close calls, clinging to the dirt inside bunkers and trenches as the earth rumbled and shook under the strain of tons of falling bombs. A few nosebleeds and broken eardrums from the pressure were well worth the final payoff. Some South Vietnamese peered through firing slits to see the carnage. Enemy bodies lay scattered and bleeding; few of them were whole. Bombings over the past week had decimated the attackers, accounting for perhaps 2,000 dead. Those who survived the terrible rain from above were cut down by machine-gun fire as they closed with the South Vietnamese.

Colonel Miller was jubilant, the first hopeful emotion he had experienced in weeks. "Indications are we are stacking the little bastards up like cordwood," he reported to TRAC when asked for a bomb damage assessment. The air strikes also seemed to assuage his bitterness toward General Hung. "Counterpart ti-ti [a little] cooler but worn out," Miller observed charitably. "Like good whiskey, [Hung] will improve with age." The entire 5th ARVN Division benefited from Miller's mood shift. "Nerves have settled down slightly, ARVN getting more conditioned to the environment," he reported matter-of-factly. "Pucker factor is high. Little ARVN has got to hold, there ain't no place to go. We'll do it." The division senior adviser signed his dispatches with a flourish that would become his trademark: "Hanging in there, Colonel Miller."[7]

Despite Miller's newfound optimism, the slaughter was not one-sided. South Vietnamese casualties mounted daily. No one seemed to be keeping track of the dead, but the scores of wounded provided strong evidence of the beating suffered by An Loc's defenders. The battle did not end for the wounded. Rarely were they evacuated from the embattled city. The few Vietnamese air force helicopters that braved enemy antiaircraft fire to bring supplies and evacuate the wounded were not enough to keep up with the casualties. Paradoxically, it was mostly the badly wounded who were doomed to remain in the city. When South Vietnamese helicopters did fly into An Loc, they generally hovered just long enough for the walking wounded to clamber aboard. On many occasions stretchers brought out to the hovering helicopters were dropped and left behind as the stretcher-bearers rushed aboard to escape the hell below.[8]

General Minh wanted his wounded out, but he knew the South Vietnamese air force was not up to the task, so he turned to Hollingsworth. Unwilling to lose face with his American counterpart, he argued that his helicopters lacked night-flying capabilities; would the Americans handle the job? "Request denied," answered Hollingsworth sharply. The South Vietnamese air force had the capability; it was simply unwilling—or afraid—to fly into An Loc. The wounded would have to wait.[9]

By nightfall on 20 April the attacks subsided. General Hollingsworth paced the floor at his headquarters in Long Binh until just before midnight. "Looks like they're not going to make it," he said, glancing at his watch. He was right. The North Vietnamese had thrown their full weight against An Loc, and although they had left the South Vietnamese bruised and bleeding, the city held. Better still, the defenders had won an important moral victory. By setting the 20 April deadline for capturing An Loc, the North Vietnamese had given the defenders an immediate goal to fight for. As that deadline came and went with the city still in South Vietnamese hands, the enemy became less invincible, and the fatalism plaguing the South Vietnamese army was partially lifted. A prediction had failed to come true.

Upon seeing that the northern front was not going to give way, the three assaulting regiments from 9th VC Division tried to disengage, move to the southwest to Highway 13, and attack An Loc from the south. The plan never materialized. Either orders became confused or the battered division lacked the mobility and supplies to comply. Whatever the case, the 9th VC Division remained in its positions within the northern streets of An Loc.[10]

Another possible factor in the 9th VC Division's inability to maneuver south was the movement of two South Vietnamese airborne units to the battle. On the morning of 21 April, the 5th and 8th Airborne Battalions reached positions in the rubber trees just south of the city. Both companies had been driven off Hill 169 on 19 April and had maneuvered their way to the city. The appearance of the airborne companies was a mixed blessing. The defenders appreciated the extra manpower, even though the para-troopers had been forced to abandon their artillery on Hill 169. On the other hand, when the 1st Airborne Brigade was driven from the hills south of An Loc, the defenders relinquished the last of the high ground. The North Vietnamese controlled all prominent terrain surrounding the city. The comparison with Dien Bien Phu was unavoidable, and many of the South Vietnamese officers were again plunged into despair.

At the end of the day on 22 April, the fighting simmered down. With the help of American airpower the South Vietnamese had taken everything the enemy could give and still managed to fight to a draw. Colonel Miller was glad to be alive, but he knew the battle was not yet over. His report to General Hollingsworth at TRAC again painted a gloomy picture of the battlefield:

> There is currently no change in the situation in the northern part of the city. The northeast corner is heavily fortified—unable to breach. . . . Airborne elements caused to divert resources to save remnants. 5th Airborne and 8th Airborne had solid contact south of An Loc at ap-proximately 1800 yesterday.[11]

Miller remained less than happy with the performance of tactical air sup-port. His concern was partly the perception of a desperate soldier in a tight situation and partly because of the overextension of U.S. air assets all over embattled South Vietnam. To Colonel Miller, "tactical air is too slow in re-sponse, FACs have little knowledge of the actual target. I detect a lack of urgency or a lack of realization—probably not intentional" on the part of U.S. Air Force pilots. Miller was clearly frustrated by the inability to com-bine air support with some sort of counterattack by the South Vietnamese on the ground. "Still need a maneuver force to break the stalemate," he complained to Hollingsworth about General Hung's unwillingness to move his troops out of their bunkers. "I'm still waiting for that dynamic spirit to take place."[12]

At TRAC headquarters, General Hollingsworth was able to see the big picture with more objectivity than his besieged subordinate. In particular he regarded the inability of the North Vietnamese to take An Loc by the 20 April deadline as a great psychological victory. Yet he also admired the enemy's single-minded determination. "We are still killing NVA with clean khaki uniforms in their packs that they were going to wear on the 20th to the inaugural ball!" Hollingsworth later told a gathering of U.S. military and civilian officials from Washington.[13]

Unlike Colonel Miller, Hollingsworth had only praise for the air support around An Loc, and he gave most of the credit for the 5th ARVN Division's successful stand to the pilots who flew missions around the clock. "The 7th air force reinforced by the USS *Hancock* and the tireless efforts of our heavy bomber squadrons is responsible in large measure for the failure of the enemy," Hollingsworth wrote to air force and navy commanders. "Their professionalism and dedication to duty has been an inspiration to me and the gallant soldiers in Loc Ninh and An Loc. Please pass on my highest regards and sincerest gratitude to all of the officers and men who have been participating in this great battle."[14]

Initiative shifted to the defenders after the failed North Vietnamese attack, though the situation on the ground had changed little. After 22 April the North Vietnamese seemed to lose the will to sustain the level of attacks of the previous ten days. In particular, air strikes had become unbearable. Intelligence reported that enemy units had dispersed into the country outside An Loc, seeking relief from the bombs. But the fight was far from over. The defenders, now numbering fewer than 4,000, were still trapped in An Loc, and the antiaircraft ring was as deadly as ever.

Artillery remained the single largest threat. Mimicking Soviet and Chinese doctrine, the North Vietnamese organized entire divisions of artillery, relying on them to precede ground attacks. At Dien Bien Phu they had dragged artillery pieces into the hills around the besieged French positions in the valley below. During the long years of American troop involvement in South Vietnam, the North Vietnamese were rarely able to use concentrated artillery. With the exception of the siege of U.S. Marines at Khe Sanh in 1968, heavy artillery played a relatively minor role in North Vietnamese offensives. In 1972 it had come full circle. During the Easter Offensive, artillery was a major factor in attacks in all three military regions of South Vietnam.

No one knew that better than the defenders in An Loc. From the day Loc Ninh had come under attack, An Loc had been subjected to daily poundings by North Vietnamese artillery. American advisers inside the city categorized incoming rounds as "light" up until 12 April; then they were said to be "heavy." By 20 April someone was counting them. The average num-

ber of rounds falling inside An Loc was around 1,000, with some days top-
ping 2,000. Although U.S. air strikes were aimed at suspected enemy artillery emplacements, they seemed to have little effect on the volume of fire.
During the entire siege of An Loc, artillery pressure remained fairly constant despite mounting air strikes.[15]

As enemy ground attacks subsided, Colonel Miller again hounded General Hung to go on the offensive and push the North Vietnamese from the
northern third of the city. His pleading was to no avail; Hung sat in his
bunker, maintaining only limited contact with his regimental commanders
and relying on U.S. airpower to save the day. The experience was frustrat-
ing for Miller. "I cannot get ARVN to push out, not even one single foot
from [the] perimeter," he complained. "I plead long for patrols, or any
form of security. . . . ARVN still lacking a sense of urgency in any quarter
and time does not seem to bother them."[16]

As the days slid by, the North Vietnamese dug in deeper and stepped up
their shelling of the city. On 25 April enemy artillery targeted and destroyed the city hospital. An Loc was left with no medical facilities except
for the various military medics and aid stations around the city. Both military and civilian casualties had to be treated on the spot, with almost no
possibility for evacuation. Worse, there was now no place to store bodies.
The streets were littered with dead, raising the specter of a disease epi-
demic. South Vietnamese soldiers were ordered to dig mass graves and bury
all the dead together.[17]

For the defenders, there was nothing to do but wait. Colonel Miller, still
concerned about his counterpart's unwillingness to take control of the situation in An Loc, looked for positive aspects of the battle up to this point.
On 28 April, as midnight approached, Miller sat in the dreary command
bunker writing his usual late-night missive to General Hollingsworth. Artillery fire was less intense than on previous days, and the battlefield
seemed downright quiet. "[I] believe we have chewed a sizable plug out of
his [the enemy's] ass," Miller penned before closing the journal. "He has
not withdrawn or broke, but surely he is slightly bent."[18]

Another phase in the battle for An Loc was over. The North Vietnamese
had been thwarted in their attempt to capture the city by 20 April, but as
Colonel Miller had pointed out in his report to TRAC, the enemy could
still resort to "strangulation tactics." Much of the remainder of the battle
would depend on the ability to resupply the besieged defenders.

TWENTY-EIGHT

AIR RESUPPLY

As the sun set behind the dark green carpet of rubber trees southwest of An Loc, eight North Vietnamese soldiers quietly left their makeshift bunkers and divided mortar tubes, base plates, and ammunition among themselves. They had spent the last several days below ground waiting out the thundering aerial bombardment that pulverized the earth around An Loc on a daily basis. But they could wait no longer. Headquarters had ordered teams of crew-served weapons—mortars and heavy machine guns—to set up around the south side of An Loc and zero their weapons in on the soccer field just south of the city where the big helicopters landed to drop off supplies to the defenders. More than a dozen mortar and machine-gun crews from the 9th NVA Division converged on the landing zone, many more than were needed, but headquarters reasoned that American bombs would destroy many of the teams before they were in place. If a few of the guns were successful, it would be enough to seriously hamper South Vietnamese resupply efforts.

The eight young communist soldiers moved furtively, constantly glancing skyward for signs of the deadly jets that could so easily snuff out their lives. All these soldiers had seen dozens of their comrades blown to bits by bombs during the days before the siege, and they feared the planes' awesome power more than all the South Vietnamese troops in An Loc. Gladly would they throw themselves headlong at the city's defenses if only the order would come. Instead, they were told to stay in the killing ground surrounding An Loc and brave the bombs. The assigned task, the political officers told them, was of the utmost importance. If they succeeded in smashing South Vietnamese efforts to bring in supplies, they would be people's heroes.

The closing darkness slowed the young soldiers down to a crawl. Though it was black as a tomb, they welcomed the night, for it meant that the spotter planes buzzing around in the sky above like bothersome insects had to return to their airfields. All the soldiers had to fear was accidentally walking into a prearranged Arc Light box, or a flight of fighter planes dumping their bombs at random spots in the rubber trees. At least the North Vietnamese need not worry about the South Vietnamese infantry; the Saigon soldiers rarely left their bunkers to run patrols in the forest.

Before first light the teams were in place. Three 81mm mortars and two 12.7mm machine guns pointed their muzzles skyward through the broad leaves of the rubber trees. As soon as the guns were in place, the North Vietnamese soldiers dug deep trenches in the soft earth for protection from the bombs that would surely come as soon as they fired the first round. Over the next few days they would harden their position, dragging thick branches from the forest to lay an overlapping roof of wood and dirt over their heads. When they were finished, the new bunkers would withstand all but direct hits from the bombs above. All that was left was to wait for the telltale thump of approaching helicopter rotors. As soon as they flared for landing, the mortars and machine guns would open fire, concentrating all their power on the landing zone.[1]

Resupply helicopters had no choice but to land in the open field. The center of An Loc was constantly subjected to a deadly rain of fire from North Vietnamese batteries to the north and west of the city, while enemy infantry concentrations ringed most of the countryside surrounding the city. Only the south side of town offered a practical landing zone, though it was also dangerous. But there was no choice. Beginning on 7 April, U.S. Army and South Vietnamese air force CH-47 Chinook helicopters began flying daily missions into An Loc. By 12 April they had flown forty-two re-supply sorties to the defenders. A few of the American Chinooks were hit as they hovered for the few brief seconds it took to dump the cargo, but none were shot down by the North Vietnamese mortar and machine-gun crews. Then, on 12 April, a mortar round scored a direct hit on a South Vietnamese Chinook. The hovering helicopter burst into a ball of flame, leaving the demoralized defenders to pick through the wreckage for any scraps left unscathed by the fire.[2]

After the Chinook shoot-down, only fixed-wing cargo planes attempted the dangerous flight into An Loc. But South Vietnamese air force responsi-bility for the resupply of its own troops inside the city came to a complete halt on 19 April after a C-123 transport plane was shot down. It was the second South Vietnamese resupply plane shot down; the first had been de-stroyed on 15 April. From that point on, the U.S. Air Force picked up the job. The Americans tried to put a good face on the development by pub-licly pointing out that the Vietnamese air force had done the best it could, "despite the hopelessness of their efforts."[3]

Actually, the U.S. Air Force was already preparing to take on the job of resupplying An Loc's defenders before the first South Vietnamese cargo plane was shot down. On 14 April the air force was directed by MACV to prepare for airdrops into the city. It responded by planning five daylight container drops using C-130 cargo planes—two on 15 and 16 April and one on 18 April.

Air delivery fell into three distinct phases. The first phase lasted less than two weeks—from 7 to 19 April—and for most of the period the South Vietnamese air force did much of the work. American CH-47 helicopters and South Vietnamese C-123s landed on the airstrip south of the city, unloaded the supplies, and took off again—all in as short a time as possible. During phase one, 301 tons of supplies were delivered to An Loc, none of which fell into enemy hands.[4]

Not until 15 April did the air force try to send in the first C-130 cargo planes. Two of the lumbering giants ran the gauntlet at first light, trusting their cargo to a computerized dropping system called computed aerial release point (CARP). Circling outside the city, the first plane received the go-ahead from a forward air controller and began the dangerous run. Instruments were not needed for the trip; pilots had been instructed to follow Highway 13 from the south as it headed into the city. Near the soccer field the computer would take over, releasing the supplies at the pre-arranged point. The first plane roared overhead as enemy guns opened fire. Pallets of food and ammunition crashed to earth, and the plane climbed back into the sky with only two bullet holes in its skin.

Fifteen minutes later the second C-130 began its high-speed run. This time the North Vietnamese gunners were ready. As the plane neared its drop point, a wall of machine-gun fire climbed into the sky just in front of its nose. The pilot grasped the controls tightly as the plane shuddered under the impact of dozens of bullets. A few rounds smashed through the circuit panel in the flight deck, killing the flight engineer and wounding the navigator and copilot.

In the cargo hold the situation was even more desperate. Incendiary rounds had torn through the plane's thin skin, igniting some of the pallets holding 155mm howitzer and 81mm mortar ammunition. Crewmen frantically broke out fire extinguishers and sprayed down the cargo, hoping to beat the flames to the ammunition crates. Another round ruptured a hot-air duct, sending blasts of 700-degree steam throughout the cargo compartment. As the crew worked, the pilot tried to jettison the cargo, but the automatic devices failed. The loadmaster stepped in and cut the ropes by hand. As the crates fell to earth, the wind extinguished the flames, leaving the ammunition intact. Fortunately, none of it fell into enemy hands. As the C-130 turned back toward home, another fire broke out in the cargo compartment, making for a tense ride all the way back to Tan Son Nhut Air Base.[5]

That night, transport pilots and forward air controllers met at Tan Son Nhut to discuss the mounting problems of aerial resupply. Clearly, the North Vietnamese could predict that more than one plane was coming in, so if they were surprised by the first aircraft, they would certainly be ready for the second. The enemy might also be listening in on the single frequency used by the pilots. The solution, reasoned the air force, was to vary the paths taken into the drop zone and maintain a series of five different radio frequencies. The CARP system was also abandoned because it required strict attention from the crew, which had too much else to do just flying the plane through enemy fire. Instead the crew would manually drop the load.

The next morning two more C-130s rumbled down the runway at Tan Son Nhut and climbed into the sky for the trip to An Loc. The lead plane was piloted by Colonel Andrew P. Iosue, commander of the 374th Tactical Airlift Wing. Colonel Iosue wanted to see firsthand the problems experienced by his pilots the day before. Both planes headed for An Loc, this time toward a clearing south of town and east of Highway 13. Although this alternate drop zone was still clear, it was rapidly becoming dangerous as North Vietnamese troops tightened their grip around An Loc.

Both C-130s came in at about 3,500 feet above the trees and bracketed the coordinates given to them by U.S. advisers outside the town. Although both planes were hit by enemy ground fire, they managed to drop 30,000 pounds of ammunition and supplies, all of it within an area controlled by the South Vietnamese. The cascading pallets were a welcome sight to the soldiers below, and to the air force pilots who managed to fly two successful missions right on the heels of the previous day's fiasco.

Airborne air controllers were the key to success during aerial supply drops. They watched for enemy gunners, kept the radio frequencies untangled, and told the big cargo planes when to begin their runs. But the air controllers had to be able to see the ground to be effective, and the deteriorating weather over An Loc beginning late on 17 April kept the little planes grounded. The situation inside the city was worsening by the hour, so on 18 April another C-130 resupply mission was authorized, this time back over the soccer field. Two air controllers monitored the air over An Loc that day, one high above as overall controller, the other down low watching out for enemy antiaircraft.

The lookout air controller was Captain Robert Shumway, a pilot with the 21st Tactical Air Support Squadron. As Shumway scanned for signs of North Vietnamese gunners, he watched the progress of the first C-130. As it roared in about 1,000 feet above a grove of trees south of the soccer field, the number-three engine suddenly burst into flames as it ran into a wall of bullets sent up by an unseen enemy antiaircraft gun crew.

Captain Shumway saw exactly where the firing was coming from. "Break south and west," he calmly told the pilot of the stricken cargo plane. "Dive for the deck and build up air speed."

The C-130 responded, plummeting toward the ground until it was only 400 feet off the deck. After jettisoning the cargo, the pilot headed due south. Looking out the cockpit window, he saw the control flaps burning as chunks of the wing tore away and streaked backward along the fuselage. Within minutes the entire right wing was burning brightly, and the controls were frozen. The plane began to roll to the right as the pilot struggled to keep the nose up. There was no way that the crippled C-130 was going to make it back to Saigon, so the pilot decided to crash-land in an open field near the town of Lai Khe. As the hard earth edged closer, the pilot forced the unwilling plane into a level attitude and nosed it belly first into a stretch of marshy ground covered with elephant grass. Within minutes, U.S. helicopters from Lai Khe were in the air, and the entire crew was rescued with only minor injuries.[6]

The cost of continuing this type of aerial resupply was simply too high. The air force had lost one C-130, damaged four others, and had one pilot killed. No one questioned the bravery of the pilots, but it was time for a change of plan. The planes would have to move higher into the sky to perform their airdrops. But after fourteen resupply runs at 8,500 feet, only two bundles landed in the drop zone. Nine fell into enemy hands, while three were considered recoverable. On 19 April the air force tried the same system from 6,000 feet with only marginally better results.

Intelligence sources indicated that the North Vietnamese were beginning to work the high percentage of bad drops into their battle plans. According to one report, the enemy was "counting on shortages of food and water," along with mounting numbers of South Vietnamese dead and wounded, "to undermine ARVN morale," making the defenders "vulnerable to political warfare appeals calling on ARVN troops to desert." The food was also a welcome change from the usual austere diet of a communist soldier. A North Vietnamese officer captured later in the battle asked his captors for fruit cocktail. Seeing the startled looks on the interrogators' faces, the enemy officer explained that he had become accustomed to eating it after wayward airdrops began falling into the hands of his unit. An American adviser watching this bizarre exchange found the episode "very depressing" after weeks of surviving on rice, canned fish, and brackish water.

Inside An Loc the botched resupply efforts were definitely taking a toll.

One adviser pointed out the obvious: "Needed supplies were in extremely short supply." Colonel Miller noted in his daily report that "the enemy enjoys observing no resupply. . . . Come hell or high water, supplies have to get through."[7]

The beginning of phase two on 20 April did not provide much relief. The air force relied on low-level parachute drops flown both day and night. Off and on over the next week, lumbering C-130 aircraft made the long approach flying just barely above the treetops. About three miles from the drop zone the plane climbed to about 500 feet, jettisoned the load, then dropped back to the relative safety of the treetops. The method was fairly safe for the big planes—none were shot down, although 60 percent sustained damage. Most critical, however, was the success rate. Of 845 tons delivered, only 45 tons fell inside the South Vietnamese perimeter. Another 231 tons was categorized as "possible recovery," which meant there was a roughly equal chance the supplies would be recovered by the South Vietnamese or by the enemy. The rest of the supplies—569 tons—probably fell into the hands of the enemy.[8]

The decision was made to climb higher into the sky and drop supplies by parachute while the air force worked on the problem of consistency. It quickly discovered a weakness in the system: South Vietnamese riggers had been packing the chutes, and many of them had failed to open. On 24 April, with a growing sense of despair, the air force returned to dropping containers into An Loc without benefit of parachutes.

For four days supplies continued to fall largely into enemy hands. Then it was discovered that a combination of army advisers and forward air controllers had given some of the C-130s the wrong drop coordinates. There were two open fields near Highway 13 south of An Loc, one on each side of the road. Briefers treated the soccer field as if it were an obvious landmark when seen from the sky, the only possible drop zone. Yet from the pilots' perspective either field might be the target. For some reason the error was not discovered for two days. During that time the army thought the drop zone was one field, but the air force thought it was the other. Every time the C-130s dropped their loads, the advisers would radio in and complain that the supplies were landing east of the field. The air force took all this into account and tried to be more careful on the next run. Not surprisingly, no matter how precise the pilots were, they could never get the drop on target. A South Vietnamese officer figured out the problem, and after he drew an overlay on a map of the city, it became clear that the army and air force were not reading from the same script. Two army advisers showed up in person at MACV headquarters in Saigon with a new set of drop zone coordinates.[9]

Although aerial resupply techniques were going nowhere, new developments inside An Loc took some pressure off the air force. According to current needs, it took 200 tons daily of supplies to sustain the 15,000-plus soldiers and civilians inside the city. The highest priority was small-arms ammunition and 105mm howitzer rounds. After the North Vietnamese wiped out all the 105mm artillery pieces in the first few weeks of the siege, this was no longer a factor. Need for the second-highest priority—water—was also reduced when a series of brackish wells were found inside the perimeter. Army advisers felt that the town could survive on 65 tons daily, less than one-third of the original estimate. However, even this minimum was rarely met.

With casualties mounting among air crews, the air force ordered that drops be attempted at night. This appeared to be a sensible solution, but in reality few of the crews were qualified to fly at night. Nevertheless, on the night of 24 April, seven C-130s headed for An Loc with all lights out. All made it in safely and dropped their loads, but accuracy remained elusive. Impatient with the continuing difficulties, General Hollingsworth told 7th air force commander General John W. Vogt that although the night drops had "a fair degree of accuracy," he preferred day drops because the pallets were more easily recoverable.

On the ground below, Colonel Miller was not at all satisfied with the drops, though he was resigned to continued inaccuracy. The defenders' problems were magnified by the need to round up errant bundles. "Uncertainty of drops creates a grab bag and a dog eat dog system," he observed following the air force's night drop. "Incoming [artillery] so heavy, not many volunteers to search for supply bundles. We need to know what, when, and where on drops. Aside from forementioned problems, situation normal."[10]

The next night eleven C-130s tried the same technique. This time the North Vietnamese were ready, and the planes ran into heavy antiaircraft fire. The first four planes rolled in for the drop zone, only to be hit by a rain of heavy bullets. Two of the loads were wildly off target, but two made it onto the drop zone. As the planes split off in separate directions like a covey of giant quail winging away from hunters, one was hit by dozens of rounds. It shuddered and lost altitude, then the pilot clawed the plane back into the air before losing control at the last minute. The C-130 pitched over backward, erupted into a giant fireball, and plummeted to earth a mere two miles south of An Loc. There were no survivors.

Air force planners were getting desperate. It made no sense to them that the enemy could maintain such a strong defensive capability beneath a blanket of uncontested air superiority. On 26 April the 374th Tactical Air Wing was directed to "fly a daylight 10 ship low level mission with fighter escort" to An Loc. The pilots who were to fly the mission were aghast at the suggestion. Such daylight mass-formation airdrops were generally successful, but they were never intended for use in high-threat areas such as An Loc. Even with fighter support, the mass of lumbering cargo planes would be easy targets for North Vietnamese gunners. Forward air controllers on station were also amazed at the decision. They were so convinced the mission would be a disaster that they planned to order search-and-rescue aircraft into the air before the ten-plane mission was launched. Fortunately for everyone involved, the idea was dropped in favor of continuing the low-level drops under cover of darkness.[11]

Night drops brought on other complications, however. Pilots could not see the soccer field in the darkness, especially on low-level runs. South Vietnamese soldiers on the ground were understandably reluctant to venture out and place flares, so for the first few nights the C-130 pilots had to navigate by the flicker of the burning city. The soccer field appeared lighter than the surrounding darkness of the rubber trees, though the contrast was slight. One pilot recalled that it was like looking at "a pencil drawing in black and brown." Dropping flares was one possible solution, but that only gave enemy antiaircraft gunners advance warning of the airdrop as well as perfect silhouettes of the big cargo planes.

The air force tried everything in the textbooks, but the best solution to the lighting problem happened by pure chance. AC-130 Spectre gunships lumbering around An Loc hosing down enemy troop concentrations with cannon fire used two-kilowatt lights with infrared filters to illuminate targets on the ground. When the filters were removed, the lights made acceptable beacons for the cargo planes. Beginning on the night of 25 April, the Spectres orbited the drop zone, turning on the bright lights when the C-130s were about four miles from the soccer field. Just as the big planes came to the cone of light, Spectre flicked it off, leaving the area in total darkness. The system was not perfect, but it worked. Although enemy gunners were warned of the coming C-130s whenever the bright lights went on, they were temporarily blinded when the lights went out.[12]

Still, most of the supplies were not getting into the defenders' hands. As Colonel Miller sat in the command bunker feverishly plotting air strike coordinates, he received word that another drop had fallen short of its target. He noted the event sarcastically in his daily journal: "At the close of this writing the air force just dropped a C-130 load one kilometer north of my location in the lap of Charlie." General Hollingsworth passed the word along to MACV, noting that "less than thirty percent was recoverable by friendly forces. . . . The system seems to be going from bad to worse."13

From the air force point of view, things were definitely getting worse. On the night of 2 May, another C-130 was lost when it nicked the treetops just beyond the drop zone and cartwheeled into a low ridge east of An Loc. No one saw ground fire, and there was some speculation that the pilot had simply miscalculated in the darkness. All low-level missions into An Loc were immediately canceled while the air force reexamined the situation. A report completed a few days later concluded that the combination of low drop success and high aircraft loss was "unacceptable." It was "mandatory to find a new tactic."

The air force had been working with high-altitude drops early in the battle for An Loc, but parachute drift caused many of the supplies to fall into enemy hands. An advanced high-altitude low-opening (HALO) system was in the experimental stages, but the air force lacked qualified personnel inside Vietnam to make it workable. A group of experts was flown in from Taiwan and worked around the clock to get the system ready. A series of cords allowed the parachute to partially deploy, slowing the drop rate to about 130 feet per second. Then, at 500 feet above the ground, the delay cord cut away, allowing the chute to deploy fully. This method allowed the C-130s to fly at 8,600 feet above the drop zone—well out of the range of most enemy antiaircraft fire. Accuracy was also improved by employing ground radar air delivery system (GRADS), a computer-monitored system that automatically plotted and released loads based on the aerodynamic characteristics of payload and parachute.

The first HALO mission to An Loc was attempted on 4 May. A flight of C-130s flying at altitudes varying from 6,000 to 9,000 feet dropped twenty-four bundles: twelve performed flawlessly, nine failed to open and crashed, and three opened prematurely. Even so, all but one was recovered. The next day eighty-eight tons of supplies were dropped, but only half recovered. By 7 May the record was steadily improving as air force technicians experimented with new methods. Two days later the success rate stood at 94 percent. The results were not always pretty, but most of the supplies were reaching the desperate defenders. During a drop on 8 May, all twenty-two bundles dropped onto the soccer field fell on target. Some of the rice bags and most of the cans of fruit broke open, but the hungry soldiers ate the food off the ground before it could spoil. Crates of small-arms ammunition burst all over the drop zone, but soldiers managed to scoop that up as well. During another drop the parachute on a one-ton bundle of canned peaches failed to open. The load hurtled toward the ground, landing squarely on top of one of the few operational jeeps in An Loc.

Two items that did not adapt well to HALO techniques were high explosives and medical supplies. Crates of 81mm mortar ammunition were particularly susceptible. On four occasions hard landings set off mortar rounds, causing sympathetic detonations lasting up to five hours. Medical supplies were delicate and rarely survived the impact of a high-velocity drop. Serious shortages were common, and both the South Vietnamese and the U.S. advisers were forced to rely on infrequent helicopter flights for medical supplies. But South Vietnamese helicopter pilots were rarely careful enough to make the system work. One helicopter flew into An Loc with a supply of whole blood and kicked it out the door fifty feet above the ground while flying at thirty knots.

Despite the inevitable problems, General Hollingsworth was pleased when Colonel Miller reported that seventy-nine tons of supplies had reached the defenders by 9 May. Three days later the TRAC commander told his boss, General Abrams, "This represents a 90 percent effectiveness rate and a significant improvement over past drops."[14]

The perfection of HALO cargo drops marked the beginning of phase three, the longest and most successful stretch of the resupply effort. It lasted from 4 May until aircraft could land near An Loc with some degree of safety on 25 June. During this phase the air force flew 230 sorties totaling 2,984 tons of supplies. The defenders received 2,735 tons; only 249 tons fell into enemy hands.[15]

Despite the improvements in resupply efforts, enemy antiaircraft fire remained deadly. During mid-April the North Vietnamese began moving additional 14.5mm and 23mm guns into place around An Loc. These highly maneuverable, rapid-fire weapons could easily track both slow-moving C-130s and fast fighters. They were a high-priority target for the air controllers. If one was spotted, all available fighters were scrambled to that point in an attempt to shut down the threat. On the morning of 9 May, an airborne spotter was concentrating on trying to locate a particularly troublesome 23mm antiaircraft site in the rubber trees southeast of An Loc. As he scanned the ground, air force F-4 Phantom fighters swirled through the space below the big C-130s flying at 9,000 feet searching for targets. After successive bomb runs over a particularly troublesome 23mm antiaircraft position, the air controller reported that they had missed again.

"They've still got incoming on the soccer field," he reported. The impatient voice of an F-4 pilot came on the air. "I've tried to kill that SOB twice now. I want to make sure." The fighter barrel-rolled back onto its attack line and ran back along the rubber trees to the gun emplacement. The pilot never knew whether he was successful.[16]

From a statistical viewpoint, the resupply situation went from terrible to excellent during the siege. But to the defenders inside the city, mere numbers meant little. By all accounts, civilians inside An Loc never had enough food. On the other hand, one American adviser recalled that although times were tough, nobody starved. "I never went hungry," recalled Captain Larry Moffett, deputy senior adviser to the 3d Ranger Group. "I always had plenty of rice and tuna and there were always plenty of bullets lying around. I don't think the resupply problem was nearly as bad as it was made out to be."[17]

TWENTY-NINE

SECOND ROUND

From the failure of the North Vietnamese attack on 22 April until 10 May, the tactical situation around An Loc remained basically unchanged. The South Vietnamese were unable to retake any lost ground, and the enemy seemed too worn out to press its gains. General Hollingsworth saw the enemy inactivity as an indicator of things to come. "Intelligence indicates that the enemy is tired and hungry. . . . Morale and disciplinary problems are beginning to appear within his ranks," Hollingsworth concluded. "Although he is determined to take An Loc, I do not feel he can hold up too much longer. His sustained, coordinated attacks have decreased in scope and intensity."[1]

Hollingsworth's prediction held for almost two weeks. By the beginning of May "there was no confirmed GAF [ground-to-air fire] larger than 7.62 cal. [*sic*] . . . and no confirmed tank sightings reported." The slack time was sufficient to allow the South Vietnamese to maneuver somewhat within their cramped perimeter and shift over to a limited counteroffensive. On 5 May the 81st Airborne Ranger Battalion exchanged positions with the 8th Regiment and was instructed to push north through the city streets, though it was unsuccessful in dislodging the enemy. On the North Vietnamese side only one significant action took place. After two weeks of constant probing on the western side of the city, enemy forces carved out a small salient of about two square blocks.[2]

The most important change in the battle came from within COSVN. On 5 May a North Vietnamese lieutenant from the 9th VC Division rallied to Regional Forces patrolling outside the city. He willingly told his interrogators that the North Vietnamese intended to renew the attack, but with a different order of battle. After missing the 20 April deadline for capturing An Loc, the 9th VC Division commander was officially reprimanded, and the job of capturing the city was handed to the 5th VC Division, the same unit that had taken Loc Ninh almost a month before. The 5th VC Division commander, Senior Colonel Bui Thanh Van, also made grandiose promises. He bragged that the city would be taken within two days, the same amount of time it had taken his division to take Loc Ninh. The 5th VC Division would attack from the southeast, coordinating the effort with the 7th NVA

Division. The disgraced 9th VC Division would continue its efforts from the north and northeast, but much of the support would be shifted away from that front. The only thing the defector did not seem to know was the precise timing of the attack, although he thought it would materialize within a week.[3]

With the 5th VC Division at the helm in the coming attack, the main battle would shift to An Loc's rear. The 5th VC Division had set up its headquarters south of the city on Hill 169; it had been there since pushing the 1st Airborne Brigade out on 1 May. Two regiments positioned themselves near Windy Hill, about three kilometers southeast of An Loc.

Inside the city Colonel Miller was largely unaware of all this. He knew the North Vietnamese were unlikely to simply give up and filter back into Cambodia, yet he felt there were some indications that the fight might be winding down. In a report to TRAC on 8 May, Miller noted the character of the bombardment had changed:

Enemy continues to shell An Loc with mortars and artillery. Mortar fire on the upswing; artillery possibly being reduced. Enemy mortars targeted heavily against troop concentrations while artillery fire is directed primarily against the division CP. . . . Overall, can't figure the enemy at this time. If he is gone, he left a hell of an indirect covering force. If he's utilizing an economy of force role, it is working well for him. I still give him the capability to attack if he so elects.[4]

As Colonel Miller would soon discover, the North Vietnamese were not gone, but they were indeed relying more on mortars. The reason for this remains unknown. One factor might have been U.S. air support. Large artillery pieces were more vulnerable than mortars, and the enemy either lost their big guns to air strikes or may have elected to try to save them by remaining silent. Perhaps they were simply conserving ammunition. The changing nature of the battle might also have influenced the North Vietnamese decision to emphasize mortars over heavy artillery.

By the end of the first week in May, the fluid battle lines had solidified somewhat into three zones of conflict. The northern third of the city was firmly controlled by the enemy, the southern third by the South Vietnamese, while the middle third was hotly contested. As the North Vietnamese consolidated their grip on the northern part of the city, mortar teams dug in deep looking for relief from the bombs. Those who survived long enough to construct hardened bunkers and tunnels were soon bombarding South Vietnamese positions inside the city.

From the air it was obvious what ground the enemy held. The northern third of An Loc had been so pulverized by air strikes that it could only belong to the enemy. One forward air controller, Major Robert L. Murphy, likened the scene to "acres of grey ash." Just beyond the battle zone stretched a green carpet of rubber trees. Despite a jigsaw puzzle of water-filled craters throughout the forest, much of the foliage had miraculously survived the pounding. Beneath the trees were enemy troops and tanks, hoping that if they remained out of sight of the buzzing spotter planes they might somehow escape the bombing. Whenever an air controller located a mortar pit or an antiaircraft position, he dove his frail little Cessna airplane straight toward the ground, releasing white phosphorous rockets to mark the position for the attack aircraft.

Major Murphy concentrated on the mortar positions in the northern third of An Loc. He fired three white phosphorous rockets at a handful of North Vietnamese bunkers, then radioed for a flight of Phantoms waiting high above. They screamed down, dropped their bombs, and climbed back into the sky. Smoke and debris cloaked the impact area, denying Major Murphy the privilege of seeing the results of his handiwork. He winged his way to another area and started all over.

On the ground below, Colonel Miller liked what he saw in the air over An Loc. "There's been a little spark of encouragement in last few days," he radioed to TRAC headquarters. "Godammit, I hope it stays that way." But Colonel Miller may have been trying to put a good face on things for his boss at TRAC headquarters. In reality the situation remained uncertain. Despite the bombing, the North Vietnamese infantry was positioned only 2,000 or 3,000 meters from the command bunker. As reports filtered in about enemy movement, the defenders' morale sank back to rock bottom. General Hung was again struck by a case of fatalism. He and some of his officers were convinced that this would be the last day of their lives. Colonel Miller tried to bolster the depressed men.[5]

At TRAC headquarters General Hollingsworth knew the coming few days would make or break An Loc. Unlike Colonel Miller, he saw the new phase of the siege as a challenge, an opportunity to deliver a sledgehammer blow to the North Vietnamese. He agreed with Miller's assessment that if the North Vietnamese were going to again attack in force, they had to mass; if they massed, Hollingsworth would unleash the B-52s.

In Saigon General Abrams had devised a plan to get the maximum effect out of his bombers. He proposed that for three days each of the northern three military regions be given the total strike capability of the B-52 fleet for a twenty-four-hour period. Normally, the B-52s were parcelled out at about eight strikes a day. Hollingsworth was thrilled by the idea of having total access to all B-52s, though he did not like the idea of relinquishing them to the other two regions for the next two days. Calling on his close friendship with the MACV commander, Hollingsworth convinced Abrams that a major assault on An Loc was imminent and that III Corps should get the first allotment of B-52 strikes. Abrams agreed and asked when the bombing should begin. Pleased that he had once again had his way, Hollingsworth replied that he would have the answer the following day.[6]

Although tactical air support was overshadowed by the B-52s, it was equally important. The big bombers had to fly in from bases in Thailand, or even farther away in Okinawa. Attack planes loaded with ordnance were available almost at a moment's notice from bases inside South Vietnam. Day after day they pounded enemy positions, called in by American advisers inside An Loc. As always, the connection between the fighter planes and the advisers on the ground was the airborne controller. Most performed admirably, though from the army advisers' perspective, there was often too much confusion in the air. Captain Thomas Hammons of the air force, one of many air controllers rotating in and out of the sky above An Loc, witnessed the frustration of an unidentified adviser, known to Hammons only by his weary voice on the ground inside the besieged city. Hammons learned to gauge the seriousness of the situation by the voice of his unknown compatriot down below. "When he's calm, he stutters a bit," Hammons later recalled. "When things are hot, he shoots those words out without a pause."

Captain Hammons circled An Loc in an O-2A observation plane day after day, reporting enemy positions and relaying strike coordinates to tactical air control. As the planes streaked in over the target, he guided them to the target. In any combination it was an intricate and unenviable job.

"I'd like napalm south of town, napalm and CBUs in town, and hard bombs seven klicks [kilometers] northwest of town," crackled the familiar voice over the radio. A flight of fighters roared in low over the tree line and dropped the bombs as ordered. The adviser's voice came back up on Hammon's radio, this time more than a little perturbed. "That was too close for us. Keep your stuff at least 600 meters to the east, OK?" Hammons did not take it personally. He knew that weeks of frustration and sheer terror brought on by being surrounded by enemy troops made the Americans on the ground edgy.

During another air strike, Hammons listened in as a Cobra pilot came on the radio complaining that his strike zone was being taken over by a flight of F-4 Phantoms that were low on fuel and had to dump their loads. Listening to the bickering from the ground below, the beleaguered adviser lost his temper. "We ain't playing no godamned game, boys. If you can't take it, you get your ass back to base until you cool off. You hear me, babe?"[7]

This sort of grinding pressure was a daily companion for everyone inside An Loc, but as the senior American adviser, Colonel Miller felt it acutely. After a month in the city the tension was grinding him down. Miller's isolation was compounded by an increasing sense of helplessness. These were not his troops; he had no real control over how they fought. Worse, Miller never knew whether they would break and surrender, allowing the enemy to sweep through the city from all sides. After all, he was only an adviser. Convinced that General Hung would not fight on the ground, Miller was resigned to using airpower to turn the tide. With intelligence reports firmly indicating an impending attack, Miller goaded TRAC headquarters for more strikes. He reasoned that if the bombers saturated the area around An Loc, there was a chance that they might "break up [enemy] troops before they are able to launch main attack."[8]

General Hollingsworth recognized the symptoms. No one questioned Colonel Miller's bravery—he had been largely responsible for the South Vietnamese stand up to this point. But the time had come to replace him. Miller was eligible to leave Vietnam at any time; he was slated to return Stateside and command a brigade of the 101st Airborne Division. Better to get a new adviser in before the next attack. The new officer chosen to stand in the breech at An Loc was Lieutenant Colonel Walter Ulmer, a West Pointer and one of the army's fair-haired boys; he arrived at Lai Khe in early May. Ulmer had served on the MACV staff in 1963 and 1964 before moving on to advise the 40th ARVN Regiment in the Central Highlands. In 1972, with the war winding down, Ulmer searched around for a path back into the action. He could not have known what he was in for.

Word came down that Ulmer might get a senior adviser slot either in I Corps or somewhere in III Corps. While he was in Saigon, TRAC decided it could use him, and Ulmer was whisked off to Lai Khe where Hollingsworth pinned a set of full colonel's eagles on his collar. The promotion meant more responsibility, and in his heart Colonel Ulmer knew he was headed for An Loc. Endless briefings at TRAC headquarters followed. Other than from media accounts, Ulmer knew little about the situation in An Loc. The term "Arc Light" meant nothing more to him than it did to the man on the street. Hollingsworth's staff briefed him on the intricacies of plotting B-52 target boxes and emphasized to him that the big bombers were his best weapon for destroying the attacking North Vietnamese.

Nothing was left to chance. As Ulmer packed—the staff even told him what to take—he got briefings on communications, the personalities of the advisers and their counterparts, how to communicate with the forward air controllers—"everything under the sun," Ulmer later recalled.

Brigadier General Richard Tallman, Hollingsworth's new deputy (General McGiffert joined the MACV staff in Saigon), took Ulmer aside in the mess hall one morning and painted a grim picture of the situation in An Loc. He said intelligence predicted a major armor assault against the besieged city within the next forty-eight hours. Ulmer mulled this over, reflecting on the larger implications of losing An Loc.

"Sir, what happens if things get really bad up there? Will America come to the aid of the advisers?" asked Ulmer.

Tallman replied with the simple truth. "No," he said without a trace of emotion. Ulmer appreciated the honesty.[9]

Hollingsworth was less blunt, but his manner made it clear that he, too, believed the battle for An Loc could go either way. Despite his outward bravado, Hollingsworth felt the weight of his responsibilities in the final months of America's barely dignified retreat from Vietnam, but he was not about to burden Colonel Ulmer with his feelings.

The time came to fly Colonel Ulmer into An Loc. He sat in a chair as a Vietnamese barber shaved his head down to a short stubble, listening intently to a last-minute briefing on how the helicopters would get through the enemy antiaircraft. It was decided that Ulmer would go in early on the morning of 10 May. The job fell to the pilots of the 12th Aviation Group, one of the last American combat units in Vietnam. Commanded by Lieutenant Colonel Jack Dugan, the Cav's helicopters were the only American link between the advisers in An Loc and the outside world.

Dugan was a scrappy Irishman who loved flying. After first seeing combat during the Korean War, Dugan briefly served as a New York City policeman before rejoining the army, this time as a cavalryman and an officer. To the annoyance of some of his noncavalry superior officers, Dugan usually wore the unauthorized cowboy hat and yellow scarf that were trademarks of old horse soldiers. Jack Dugan had also served a previous tour in South Vietnam. He had arrived for this tour in July 1971 and spent most of his time flying in support of the South Vietnamese operating inside Cambodia. After the Easter Offensive opened in Binh Long Province, Dugan and his helicopters had moved to Lai Khe, flying support missions in and out of An Loc.

The Cav went into An Loc prepared for anything. The ship that would make the actual run into the city was accompanied by another Huey and a handful of Cobra gunships. The Cobras suppressed enemy antiaircraft as the Huey flew just above the treetops, flaring at the last moment and settling on the landing pad. The extra Huey hovered outside the antiaircraft ring as a backup. If anyone was shot down, it would dart in and pick up the survivors.[10]

Dugan and his deputy for operations, Lieutenant Colonel Joe Newman, decided to fly Colonel Ulmer into An Loc themselves. A half dozen other helicopters, mostly Cobras, would fly shotgun. Although Ulmer thought they were going through a lot of trouble just to take him into An Loc, he did not know that Dugan and Newman generally flew into the city together. They operated under the principle that officers should not ask their men to do what they themselves would not do. In the case of flying into An Loc, Dugan and Newman often took the principle to extremes. Whenever a mission was flown into the city, the two men were somehow involved, either in a command and control ship or flying the bird that actually went in.

Before first light on 10 May, Ulmer climbed into Dugan's Huey. As the rotors whined during warm-up, last-minute supplies were loaded for the advisers already in An Loc. Radio batteries, mail from home, rations, and maps were stuffed into two duffle bags and thrown on. Dugan raised his helicopter into the dark sky, looking back to watch the line of snarling Cobra gunships waiting on the ground before takeoff. They looked like deadly sharks twitching in anticipation of the next kill.

The helicopters hugged the trees all the way to An Loc. Just as the sun edged over the horizon, the city came into sight. Dugan eased down on the stick, and the Huey banked along a strip of rubber trees near the landing field. The helicopter flared briefly, then the skids slammed into the ground. Ulmer dove out, with the duffle bags full of supplies heaved right behind him. The last thing Ulmer saw was Colonel William Miller diving into the helicopter as Dugan jerked the bird back into the sky and away over the rubber trees. The landing had taken less than a minute. It was 6:12 A.M.[11]

The moment the Huey landed, enemy artillery opened up. The North Vietnamese gunners had learned to bombard all possible landing sites as soon as the sound of rotor blades sounded in the sky above. But the helicopter pilots had also discovered a few tricks during the long siege, one of them being how to keep low over the tree line so the telltale slap of the rotors was concealed until the last moment.

Ulmer dashed across the fifty yards of open dirt to a bunker. Falling down the concrete stairs, he tumbled into the arms of an American ranger adviser. Safe at last, Ulmer thought to himself. Or at least as safe as he could be in An Loc.

Dugan and Newman breathed a collective sigh of relief as they darted their Huey out of the North Vietnamese antiaircraft ring. Newman took the stick, and Dugan looked back to check on Colonel Miller. He was a picture of contrasts, happy to be out of the hellhole he had called home for over a month, but guilty about leaving the job to another officer. When they landed at Lai Khe, Miller thanked Newman for the flight from An Loc. Out of sympathy for the tired soldier, Newman tried not to recoil, but Miller presented quite a sight—and smell. After six weeks in combat, his uniform was tattered and covered with red mud. As Newman helped Miller off the helicopter, he noticed that the tired colonel seemed relieved to be finished with the fight.[12]

He was also angry. Miller believed the situation in An Loc could have been handled better at all levels. Corps headquarters could have been more supportive, particularly when it came to funneling the latest intelligence down to the division level. "I expected to get something from higher, but I didn't get shit," he told an army interviewer less than a day after he left An Loc. Miller was also critical of his counterpart, General Hung. "The whole damn defense was half-assed from day one," he observed. "[I wish I could] say this little son of a bitch [South Vietnamese soldiers in general] is fighting like a tiger, all the officers are out there with drawn sabers hollering 'charge.' But the whole system collapsed. Leadership, maintenance, sanitation, discipline, everything."[13]

After a short stay at Lai Khe, Miller was on his way back to the States. In recognition of his brave stand at An Loc against incredible odds, Colonel William Miller was awarded the Silver Star. He later briefed members of Congress on the situation in South Vietnam, bringing particular attention to the role played by airpower. Though Miller gave credit to the B-52s and tactical fighters, he also emphasized the importance of the Cobra gunships. In a letter to Brigadier General James F. Hamlet, commander of the 3d Brigade, 1st Cavalry Division, he wrote, "Let me state in Doughboy-foxhole language what your command did to save me and a small handful of Americans, plus an ARVN Division. . . . [The Cobras] were the main stay in brunting [*sic*] the big tank attack, 12 to 15 April 1972. The exact number of tanks destroyed I am not sure, but whatever the number, it was sufficient."[14]

The morning of 10 May dawned with the usual artillery barrage. On the previous night the North Vietnamese had made strong probes with battalion-sized forays against various spots around the perimeter. One of the areas hit hardest was a position on the east side of town held by the 52d Ranger Battalion. In contrast with stands by ranger units earlier in the battle, the 52d Battalion immediately broke and ran. The men refused to fire their weapons, they claimed, because to do so would "give away their positions." Instead, they hurled all their grenades in the general direction of the enemy, than raced back toward the city center. The senior adviser later blamed the fiasco directly on the battalion commander, Major Thieu Ta Dau, arguing that he was "unfit for command because of his unwillingness to lead his unit personally." It was one of the few times that ranger units performed so poorly during the battle.[15]

About two hours before sunrise the North Vietnamese suddenly fell back to allow the artillery to open up. Hollingsworth used most of the morning to readjust his eighteen new Arc Light boxes. Since he had the flexibility of a full twenty-four hours of B-52 strikes, Hollingsworth decided to add seven more Arc Light boxes. The enemy, Hollingsworth said, would attack in full force sometime the next day. Early in the afternoon he called General Abrams and delivered the Arc Light information he had promised the day before. Hollingsworth wanted one Arc Light strike every fifty-five minutes for the next twenty-five hours beginning at 5:30 A.M. on 11 May. If the city held in the face of one last North Vietnamese onslaught, the worst would be behind them. If not, An Loc might go the way of Loc Ninh. Whatever happened, airpower would make the difference.

Beginning a half hour past midnight on 11 May, North Vietnamese artillery rained down with such intensity that the sound of exploding rounds melted together in a single rolling roar. Before the day was over, 8,300 rounds would fall inside the 5th ARVN Division perimeter, which had shrunk to a mere 1,000 by 1,500 yards. By any estimation the barrage was fearsome. One adviser philosophically summed up the experience: "Those were days when healthy men were taking anti-diarrhea tablets to keep from having to go outside. Nature's calls seemed a lot easier to resist." Another adviser was more circumspect: "This may seem facetious, but it may be that the best hope for An Loc is that the North Vietnamese will give out of shells sooner or later. They can't keep firing them at the rate they have without having one hell of a supply problem."[16]

In terms of numbers of rounds, it was the biggest barrage of the siege, although in deadliness the impact had subsided somewhat since the first weeks of the offensive. Rounds from heavy artillery had been responsible for much of An Loc's early devastation, but by early May most indirect fire came from mortars.[17]

Colonel Ulmer took to his new job like a man possessed. He had to. If intelligence predictions were correct, he had less than twenty-four hours

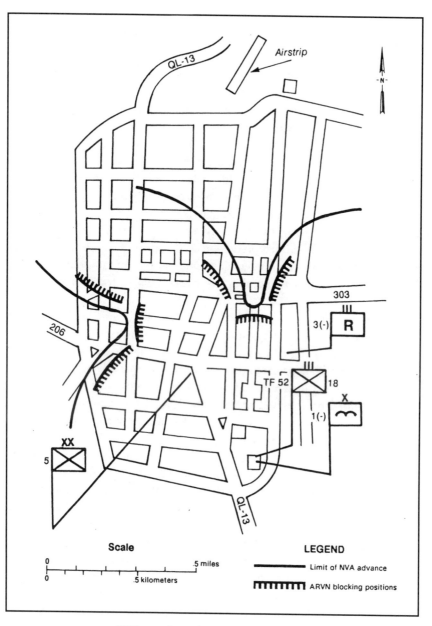

NVA attack on An Loc, 11 May 1972

before a major enemy assault was to be launched against An Loc. Like any good officer, Ulmer relied on his subordinates, most of whom had been in the thick of battle for the better part of a month and provided sound advice. He later recalled that to a man they were "professional, competent, and enthusiastic."[18]

Colonel Walter Ulmer was a very different sort of officer than his predecessor. Where William Miller was passionate and intimately wrapped up in the details of his relationship with the division commander, General Hung, Ulmer was detached and observant. While Miller was emotional and moody, Ulmer was rational and coldly calculating. The different styles were clearly revealed in the tone of daily correspondence traveling between the 5th ARVN Division command bunker in An Loc and TRAC headquarters. In one of his first messages Colonel Ulmer matter-of-factly outlined events and made cautious, qualified predictions. "It appears that enemy is making final effort," was his first understated entry in the division daily journal. Ulmer even continued to number his paragraphs in traditional military fashion.[19]

But Colonel Ulmer also feared that An Loc might not hold out much longer. Despite all the briefings and lectures before his harrowing flight into the besieged city, Ulmer was not prepared for the chaotic situation that greeted him. He glanced around at the dead and dying lying in the corridors of the command center and listened to the moans of men in agony. The scene had a profound effect on Ulmer's early hours inside An Loc. "I am quite concerned for U.S. [personnel] safety at this time due to enemy action," he radioed to General Hollingsworth. "I feel we must begin to prepare and think of possible extraction." TRAC agreed and began plans for a helicopter evacuation should the situation become critical.[20]

For the soldiers and civilians inside An Loc, the situation had long since become critical. Fear was palpable in the ravaged streets and in the battered bunkers, but nowhere more so than in the division command center. As Colonel Ulmer struggled to learn the techniques of calling for Arc Light strikes and Spectre gunships, he watched his counterpart. General Hung was aloof—as he had been with Colonel Miller—but Ulmer gave the harried commander the benefit of the doubt, considering that he had been under siege since early April and alone carried the responsibility for the defense of An Loc. Ulmer latter recounted how Hung seemed weary and cautious, but he was clearly in command. "Some of Hung's people were wringing their hands and were a little distraught; they were obviously fatigued and nervous," Ulmer recalled. "Hung never buckled, though he was clearly very concerned."[21]

Hung had every reason to be concerned. He had survived three major North Vietnamese assaults so far and knew that another—perhaps bigger—attack was coming within a few hours. Colonel Ulmer saw the general lose his composure a couple of times as the tension rose. He screamed into the radio at his regimental commanders, even to his superiors at corps headquarters, but Ulmer reasoned that it was just nerves, an understandable condition given the circumstances. As he watched the skittish South Vietnamese officers, Ulmer realized that he had shouldered more responsibility than just the welfare of his subordinate advisers. Hung's staff looked to the Americans as a barometer of events. If the advisers ran out, it was very likely that the South Vietnamese would regard that as a sign that the end was near and simply fold. "Our personal presence buoyed up the staff," Ulmer later pointed out. "There were as many [South Vietnamese] officers watching us as were watching Hung."22

Suddenly, a few hours before dawn, the heavy shelling stopped as abruptly as it began. Like all the American advisers in the city, Captain Moffet, a ranger adviser, had endured the beating inside his bunker. "It sounded like somebody was popping popcorn—shaking it just all over the city," he later recalled. "At about 4:00 or 4:30 [A.M.] it stopped—bam— just like somebody dropped a baton. Everything stopped at once." The defenders knew what the sudden halt heralded: the dreaded ground attack was about to begin.23

North Vietnamese infantry moved up behind the artillery bombardment, and when the shelling ceased, they attacked. The 5th VC Division, now the spearhead of the assault, pressed in from the north, while the 9th VC Division moved from the west. First into the town were three T-54s, which barreled along, crushing hasty barricades and firing rounds into buildings. According to the official communist account, Tran Van Tung, the leader of this North Vietnamese reconnaissance company, guided the tanks into place and pointed out targets. Within minutes, however, two of the tanks were disabled, while the third punched deeper into An Loc backed by the reconnaissance force.24

Tactical air and gunships had been standing by in anticipation of the attack, and now they thundered overhead, dropping ordnance and strafing anything that moved outside the city. But this time they faced an additional threat from enemy air defense: the SA-7 heat-seeking surface-to-air missile, the Strela, which had been in use in I Corps for the past two weeks. Most of the advisers knew it was only a matter of time before the weapon would appear around An Loc. The first Strela was spotted by a forward air controller just after midnight on 9 May, though TRAC was careful to treat the sighting as "unconfirmed." It knew the missile would change the face of helicopter tactics, but panic was something to be avoided.[25]

By the morning of 11 May, the reports became "confirmed," and the Strela lived up to expectations. Anything flying below 10,000 feet—the outside range of the SA-7—was fair game. The missile left a telltale trail of white smoke as it spiraled up toward its intended victim so an alert pilot could dodge the thing before it flew up his tailpipe. Or, in the case of forward air controllers, pilots could stay out of the Strela's range above 10,000 feet. But in the case of Cobra gunships, helicopter attack tactics were practically useless at that altitude. Few American aircraft were shot down by the SA-7, but the effect of tactical air support on the battle was somewhat diminished.

As Strelas added their smoking white tails to the snarling red and green tracers of conventional antiaircraft fire in the sky above An Loc, the battle in the streets below began to unfold. This time the North Vietnamese launched the attack with armor and infantry working in concert. Forty tanks supported by what was left of two North Vietnamese divisions tried to shove their way into An Loc. Coordination between armor and infantry remained poor, but the presence of both forces created a new strain on the defenders.

The North Vietnamese attackers pushed desperately toward the city center, hoping to use sheer weight to link up with each other and split the defenders into tiny enclaves. If they succeeded, all that would remain would be to search out and destroy the divided South Vietnamese. The attackers seemed to sense that this was their final chance. American air strikes were constantly eating away at their units, and supplies were becoming scarce. The base areas in Cambodia were being depleted to sustain the extended offensive, and it was a long way to North Vietnam for new supplies. This was the last gasp.

Inside An Loc the defenders seemed to sense the enemy's desperation. Despite the ferocity of the attack, the South Vietnamese held their ground. Perhaps earlier experience had taught the soldiers that well-aimed M72 LAWs could stop tanks dead. Or maybe the knowledge that there was no place to run gave them the determination to fight to the death.

They were also helped by a stupid mistake on the part of the North Vietnamese. Elements of the 271st Regiment, 9th VC Division, rushed toward the 5th ARVN Division command post—but they made a wrong turn. "Instead of attacking southeastward," reported a North Vietnamese after-action report, "the [regimental element] had attacked northeastward. . . .

This was a serious shortcoming." Instead of the command post, the assault force had an easy time overrunning the provincial public works service building, which offered little resistance. To make matters worse, the division commander did not discover the mistake for almost twenty-four hours. The North Vietnamese "had concentrated its forces on attacking an objective of no tactical value."[26]

Despite the mix-up, the North Vietnamese did come close to overrunning the town. On the northeastern and western sides of An Loc, enemy units managed to punch two salients into the South Vietnamese positions. The largest gain came in the northeast. The enemy came straight down two of the main roads running north-south through An Loc, Hoang Hon and Nguyen Du Streets. The two roads ran parallel, separated by only two small city blocks. For a tense hour or so it looked as if the North Vietnamese tanks might punch through, but General Hung ordered the 5th Airborne Battalion from the relatively secure southern perimeter into the fighting on the northeast. Their weight immediately turned the tide. The North Vietnamese armor was brought up short within this thin salient, blocked on three sides by South Vietnamese troops. On the west side of town the 7th ARVN Regiment finally held, also bolstered by the arrival of the airborne soldiers, allowing the North Vietnamese only a shallow penetration into the city from that quarter.

Colonel Ulmer called for increased tactical air strikes on the two enemy salients. Because of the narrowness of the northern wedge, the air strikes were not completed for fear of killing friendly troops. On the west, however, Vietnamese air force A-1E Skyraiders and American AC-130 Spectre gunships made pass after pass, methodically destroying the North Vietnamese before they could dig in. In all, 297 sorties of tactical air support were piled on enemy positions during 11 May. To make sure that the enemy remained off balance, General Hollingsworth added another 260 sorties on each of the next four days.[27]

Once again, the key role was played by the giant B-52 bombers. They began their prearranged runs at 9:00 in the morning, just as the intensity of enemy armor attacks peaked. During the action Hollingsworth had also managed to divert an additional five B-52 strikes from II Corps, bringing the Arc Light grand total to thirty strikes within a twenty-four-hour period.[28]

Coordination between the command bunker inside An Loc, TRAC headquarters in Long Binh, and the B-52s far above was also excellent. In fact, the Arc Light strike became arguably the most effective tactical weapon in the aerial arsenal. Cooperation between Strategic Air Command headquarters at MACV and General Hollingsworth's intelligence staff at TRAC was so close that B-52 strikes could be altered in flight anytime up to one hour before the bombers were scheduled to drop their payloads. General McGiffert, Hollingsworth's former deputy, later estimated that 90 percent of all Arc Light strikes were diverted from their original targets and dropped somewhere else. In one case a last-minute change saved a South Vietnamese unit from certain destruction, decimating the attackers instead. On the northeastern front the 81st Airborne Ranger Battalion was almost engulfed by a North Vietnamese attack. Hearing its call for help, the 5th ARVN Division command post diverted a strike and brought it down on top of the enemy attackers—a mere 600 yards from the rangers' position. The enemy regiment was virtually destroyed, its combat effectiveness ruined.[29]

By noon on 11 May it was over. The North Vietnamese had failed to take An Loc. Panicked enemy soldiers fled from air strikes, trying to disperse in the forests to the west. All they succeeded in doing, however, was make themselves more vulnerable to marauding fighter planes. On at least one occasion fleeing North Vietnamese soldiers were caught in the open and torn to pieces by tactical air strikes. Not a single enemy tank was reported moving anywhere near An Loc during the rest of the day, although many abandoned and destroyed hulks were counted. All forty of the tanks involved in the morning attack were dead on the battlefield. Some were smoking carcasses, others undamaged though abandoned. Some had even been left with engines still running.

Both sides seemed to sense that the battle was over and An Loc would remain in South Vietnamese hands. Yet despite the beating the North Vietnamese had received over the past month, they were unwilling to simply retreat. At 10:00 on the night of 12 May, they tried again, though the attack lacked the intensity of the previous day. A few tanks joined in, but they remained at a distance and fired their main guns from fixed positions. The infantry was reluctant to close with the defenders, instead devoting its efforts to sniping from positions just outside the South Vietnamese perimeter. General Hollingsworth brought in a few more Arc Light strikes, but he felt the worst was over.

North Vietnamese commanders probably agreed, though they were loath to give up. On 15 May the Party Committee of COSVN met to assess the battle and concluded that, despite the fact that units had conducted "several well-fought battles," they failed to overrun An Loc not "because the enemy was strong and unbeatable, but mainly because of our own shortcomings." The committee decided to change its strategy from frontal assaults to "besieging, wearing down, and destroying enemy personnel."[30]

COSVN's report to Hanoi was dour. On 17 May it reported to the politburo that "our failure to overrun Binh Long has limited our success and affected the development of the campaign." In addition to changing from assaulting An Loc to besieging it, COSVN also decided to send part of the 9th VC Division, which had performed so poorly in the fighting, to the south to help "in intercepting enemy forces trying to secure Route 13."[31]

THIRTY

RELIEF FROM THE SOUTH

As the North Vietnamese attacks surged against An Loc, a single glimmer of hope was held out to the defenders. Relief in the form of the 21st ARVN Division—affectionately referred to as the Bengal Tigers by its American advisers—had begun moving north from IV Corps to open Highway 13 and eventually reinforce the 5th ARVN Division in the city. Unfortunately, it never made it, and arguments about the South Vietnamese army's effectiveness began to settle not on the defense of An Loc but on the progress of this relief division.

The criticism was not completely fair, nor were all the facts adequately considered. First, although the 21st ARVN Division did not succeed in rescuing the soldiers at An Loc, it did relieve some of the pressure on the city. Two North Vietnamese regiments took part in the blocking action along Highway 13 south of An Loc, units that otherwise would have made their weight felt around the besieged city.

Second, the South Vietnamese did not do as poorly as has usually been portrayed. Although there were numerous examples of South Vietnamese military incompetence—mostly from officers—the soldiers generally fought well. There were more examples of bravery than of cowardice. According to Colonel J. Ross Franklin, senior U.S. adviser to the 21st ARVN Division, the soldiers fought when they were well led. "Those little Bengies are great soldiers," he told one reporter. But critics measured their progress in miles advanced, not damage done to the enemy. By that standard, the 21st ARVN Division was unsuccessful—it did not reach An Loc. Yet by June 1972 the 101st NVA Regiment had been so badly battered that it would be out of action for the next three months.[1]

Most of the 21st ARVN Division was moved to Lai Khe, some thirty miles south of An Loc, on 12 April, only six days after the fall of Loc Ninh. Its initial mission was not to relieve An Loc but to keep open the road between Lai Khe and Chon Thanh. An advance element of the relief force consisting of the 31st and 32d ARVN Regiments moved immediately north toward Chon Thanh. The 31st Regiment was air assaulted about two kilometers north of Chon Thanh to Suoi Tre Hamlet, while the 32d Regiment moved by truck into Chon Thanh itself. Both units arrived without incident, but the enemy either anticipated the move or had rapidly shifted forces to deal with the new front. Whatever the case, the 101st NVA Regiment appeared between the two South Vietnamese units and blocked the road ten miles north of Lai Khe.[2]

For eleven days the South Vietnamese made no move, allowing the enemy time to dig into positions along the road. Part of the Airborne Division's 1st Brigade was flown in and took up positions just north of Chon Thanh. The paired elite paratroopers and armor units congregating in the fields outside town seemed like a formidable team, but the North Vietnamese were unimpressed. During one firefight the enemy unleashed a barrage of rockets and mortar rounds, sending the armor crews scurrying for their tanks and personnel carriers. As the armored vehicles turned tail and dashed south, the paratroopers found themselves abandoned.

An American adviser shook his head in resignation; he had seen this same scene before. Armor and infantry units were under separate commanders, he told reporters, and there was no coordination between them. As he spoke, small groups of paratroopers staggered out of their positions dragging wounded comrades as the North Vietnamese continued the shelling. The reporters bravely drove up to the beleaguered soldiers and gave the wounded a ride to the rear. One of the injured paratroopers, a lieutenant, said that his men were unable to get help from other units. In particular, he said, they needed water. "We were not afraid of dying out there from fighting, but we were dying from thirst. I don't know why they couldn't come out and bring water to us. They had tanks." Then he slipped into unconsciousness. Other officers estimated that the North Vietnamese were keeping the road block with only a company of troops.[3]

Finally, on 22 April, the 33d ARVN Regiment—the part of the division still in Lai Khe—moved north while the 32d ARVN Regiment moved south, hoping to catch the enemy in a vice. The 31st ARVN Regiment settled into Chon Thanh to secure the division's northernmost position against attack from the rear.

The northward advance began with much fanfare. For one entire day soldiers from the 31st ARVN Regiment poured into Lai Khe from their original positions in the Mekong Delta. South Vietnamese troops decked out in pressed fatigues loaded onto trucks and moved out along the highway. Overhead, South Vietnamese air force helicopters buzzed around like insects.

"They'll never win this war as long as the Vietnamese let those guys fly choppers," observed one American adviser as he shook his head in disgust.

"These guys can't fight and won't fight. You'll never catch them in the air after 5:00 P.M." To emphasize the statement, he pointed to a poorly maintained Huey, its crew dozing inside.[4]

During the second week in April, the column moved thirteen miles north to Chon Thanh, a lazy town of tin houses and thatched roofs nestled about halfway between Lai Khe and An Loc. Despite the ominous threat looming to the north, the residents of Chon Thanh seemed to enjoy the show. "Some people are scared," confessed one restaurateur named Tu Ca, "but not enough to leave. Some of the rich have taken their children to Saigon, but all the regular people stay." Ca had no intention of leaving. His reputation for making the best *chao long* (meat, vegetable, and noodle soup) in town had to be upheld, war or no war.

The soldiers took up the jovial mood, almost giddy with prebattle optimism. Major Tran Ai Quoc, a battalion commander, sat in his sandbagged bunker on the south side of town. He reported that all was quiet, then eyed his junior officers and sergeants sitting listlessly around the bunker. It would be a disaster if the enemy chose this moment to attack, Quoc thought, because his men were mostly drunk from the town's free-flowing supply of Ba Muoi Ba beer and De Kuyper crème de menthe.

The next day Saigon's press corps flocked to Chon Thanh to watch the troops march off to war. They found a carefully choreographed show awaiting them on the highway just north of town. Senior South Vietnamese officers exhorted the troops for the benefit of the press, saying that the operation would be a triumphal march to relieve An Loc and destroy the enemy force. General Hollingsworth swooped down on the scene in his helicopter and added his optimism. "The North Vietnamese are trying to get back to Cambodia now," he lectured. "We are going to kill 'em all before they get there. These NVA are like mice in a haystack." An American adviser found the spectacle an ominous beginning. "This is just like the First Battle of Bull Run," he muttered to no one in particular.[5]

At the end of the oratory the troops moved out. The landscape was flat and covered with tall grass, withered brown from lack of rain. Only a few clumps of scraggly trees broke the terrain, a battleground tailor-made for U.S. airpower. Without cover of dense vegetation the North Vietnamese would be easy prey for American planes.

But the enemy had no intention of being caught in the open. Well aware of the road-bound nature of the South Vietamese army, the North Vietnamese turned their numerical disadvantage into a tactical advantage. Sappers mined the road in several places and blew up a huge culvert on Highway 13 about five miles north of Lai Khe—behind the advancing column of South Vietnamese troops. To the north, two patrols of airborne soldiers heading to the relief of An Loc were badly mauled by an enemy ambush. That meant that the 31st ARVN Regiment was between at least two North Vietnamese troop concentrations. The march north would not be so easy after all.

True to their guerrilla nature, the enemy soldiers stayed out of sight and sniped at the advancing South Vietnamese. Mortars thumped in the distance as solitary rounds aimed at the column made life miserable. South Vietnamese tanks accompanying the troops fired back furiously, although they could never see their targets. One South Vietnamese tank was hit by a B-40 rocket. Chunks of red-hot steel ripped from the stricken tank; the interior became a molten death chamber. Within a few minutes South Vietnamese air force Skyraiders appeared on the scene, followed shortly by American F-4 Phantoms and AC-119 Stinger gunships. The planes prowled back and forth, strafing and bombing, but nobody knew if they hit anything. At least the mortars stopped firing.

During the lull that followed, South Vietnamese troops dug in. A handful of troopers scavenged sandbags from a bunker blown apart during the enemy mortar bombardment. Other soldiers dug shallow foxholes and climbed in, staring sullenly across the waving fields of yellow grass. Over campfires fueled by empty ammunition crates, soldiers cooked homemade soup. "Beaucoup hot," commented one trooper as he gazed at the shimmering mirage up the asphalt road. The black surface was pitted and cracked from repeated artillery bombardments. "Beaucoup VC," replied another soldier philosophically.[6]

On the morning of 22 April, North Vietnamese soldiers attacked a civilian refugee column streaming south, killing dozens. In one instance a rocket-propelled grenade struck a blue bus, killing four and wounding another twenty. American advisers with the 21st ARVN Division named the opening engagement the Battle of the Blue Bus in memory of the innocent dead.

The actual battle took place two days later. On 24 April the 32d and 33d ARVN Regiments clashed with North Vietnamese troops seven miles north of Lai Khe. For five days the South Vietnamese, bolstered by massive air support, tried to root out the enemy from well-constructed bunkers and trenches. On 29 April the 32d and 33d ARVN Regiments linked up on Highway 13, catching the 101st NVA Regiment between them. One battalion from the 165th NVA Regiment reinforced the unit, acting as a stay-behind as the 101st NVA Regiment withdrew.[7]

But as the South Vietnamese enjoyed their limited gains against the enemy on Highway 13, Saigon pressured for more successes, exhorting General Minh to break the stalemate and achieve victory. On 29 April President Thieu delivered to all his corps commanders handwritten notes containing broad objectives and an implicit warning of political consequences should the battle turn out badly. General Hollingsworth was present when Minh opened his letter. Hollingsworth recalled that, in addition to blanket orders to "hold at all costs," the note contained specific instructions for General Minh: "Clear enemy from An Loc and Hwy 13 by 02 May."[8]

In the face of Thieu's admonition, the South Vietnamese had little time to sit back and savor success. Their victory at the Battle of the Blue Bus left the road between Lai Khe and Chon Thanh relatively clear, but small enemy units still lurked nearby, making movement along the highway risky. More important, the 165th NVA Regiment remained dug in about four miles north of Chon Thanh. For the first thirteen days of May, the South Vietnamese assaulted this next enemy position along the highway.

The 31st ARVN Regiment had sat out the Battle of the Blue Bus in Chon Thanh, providing a dual role of protecting the town and acting as a blocking force between the battle and enemy forces to the north. With the defeat of the North Vietnamese at the Blue Bus, the 31st ARVN Regiment was quickly air assaulted four miles north of Chon Thanh to engage the 165th NVA Regiment. Swarms of B-52s and tactical bombers preceded the assault, taking a heavy toll on the North Vietnamese. The enemy tried to get out from under the deadly rain by edging in close to the South Vietnamese troops—the so-called hugging tactic.[9]

As the North Vietnamese infantry reeled from the aerial blows, they relied heavily on artillery—sited in mobile positions to the rear—to engage the South Vietnamese. They also used the AT-3 Sagger wire-guided missile, although not effectively. The Sagger was primarily an antitank missile, but the North Vietnamese used it against regimental command posts and firebases to the west of Chon Thanh in much the same way as they had in the Central Highlands.

Sometime during the battle, probably within the first few days of May, the 209th NVA Regiment reinforced from the north. It arrived just in time. The 165th NVA Regiment had been shredded; most of its remaining units melted into the countryside to the west to rebuild. But even with one regiment decimated and the other still not firmly in position, the 31st ARVN Regiment, advancing behind a wall of air strikes and massive artillery support, was unable to uproot the enemy.

At first the North Vietnamese held their own in the face of air and ground attacks, but the South Vietnamese moved slowly forward. Then disaster struck. On 9 May the regimental commander was seriously wounded, and progress flagged. Control of the operation was handed over to the 32d ARVN Regiment on 12 May, although most of the fighting was still done by the 31st ARVN Regiment. After a short break in the action the South Vietnamese succeeded in overrunning enemy positions on 13 May. Highway 13 was open five miles north of Chon Thanh.

The defenders inside An Loc were not impressed by the little victories tallied by the 21st ARVN Division. During his last few days as senior adviser to the 5th ARVN Division, Colonel Miller expressed his displeasure over the slow progress to the south of An Loc. "I have never looked at these units as the savior of An Loc. We must save ourselves," wrote Miller. He saw An Loc itself as the key to victory in the entire region, and it should be treated accordingly by III Corps headquarters. "Without more heavy artillery than is presently allocated, the enemy is capable of reducing our current force and then turning all his might to the south," Miller warned. "Therefore request our fair share of the assets proportionate to the number of enemy confronted." He could barely conceal his disdain for the 21st ARVN Division's slow trek north.[10]

Even with the airpower and artillery diverted from An Loc, the North Vietnamese were not decisively defeated. The 209th NVA Regiment took up new blocking positions just south of Tau O Stream, another mile and a half to the north (about six miles north of Chon Thanh). For the next thirty-eight days the Battle of Tau O Bridge, as it was informally called, raged. Enemy soldiers had dug in deep, building bunkers with two feet of overhead cover to shield them from the bombs. North Vietnamese infantry on the front lines hugged South Vietnamese positions to within twenty meters, seeking respite from the air strikes.

The situation became desperate for the North Vietnamese. Cut off from their supply lines, the soldiers had to find food as well as fight. "At times we had to instruct our combatants to disguise themselves as enemy soldiers," recounted an official history of the campaign, "mingle with them, and try to overcome all perils to bring supplies to the forward blocking positions." In the end, however, it was all for naught. "We tenaciously held on to the stationary main blocking positions while organizing mobile ones to counterattack the enemy," continued the communist account, "but were still unable to repel them."[11]

Nor could the South Vietnamese root out the entrenched enemy. The 32d ARVN Regiment, still flushed with victory from the last two engagements, ran up against an immovable wall. North Vietnamese defenses were simply too much for the regiment to overcome, so it fell back and called for air support.

General Minh, concerned that he was losing face because he had failed to meet President Thieu's 2 May deadline for clearing the way to An Loc from the south, turned most of his attention away from the siege and onto the stalled 21st ARVN Division. He asked for both tactical air strikes and aerial resupply, both of which were still badly needed at An Loc. General Hollingsworth was unwilling to provide the resources. "I consider the use of C-130[s] . . . to be a misuse of assets," he argued. "There is no doubt that this unit is in need of resupply . . . however, the unit is neither cut off nor isolated. The use of hvy [heavy] drop is not only a very inefficient resupply system, but it also degrades the incentive for the 21st Div. to open Hwy 13." Hollingsworth diplomatically suggested that the South Vietnamese air force do its duty and fly supplies in by helicopter.[12]

Despite displeasure over the slow progress, TRAC headquarters was convinced that the 21st ARVN Division was having a positive effect on the unfolding battle. "At this time the enemy is more intent on preventing the 21st Div. from reaching An Loc than they are on defeating friendly forces around the provincial capital," Hollingsworth reported. "I believe that the enemy is incapable of applying pressure to both An Loc and Hwy. 13 simultaneously."[13]

Fortunately, Hollingsworth was correct—the enemy was forced to throw new units into combat along Highway 13 in a bid to keep the South Vietnamese from moving north. Yet it was a stalemate. After struggling for over a month, the South Vietnamese could not dislodge the North Vietnamese. On 21 June the 32d ARVN Regiment, which had taken about 40 percent casualties during the advance up Highway 13, was relieved by the 46th ARVN Regiment, a unit from the largely untouched 25th ARVN Division stationed at Cu Chi in Hau Nghia Province. It was a straight trade: the 32d ARVN Regiment became part of the 25th ARVN Division and redeployed to Cu Chi.

Although the cost had been high for the regiment, it had been worse for the North Vietnamese. The 209th NVA Regiment lost over 250 killed and had most of its crew-served weapons destroyed or captured, but still it remained in place north of the Tau O Bridge. One of Hanoi's propaganda publications trumpeted the stalled South Vietnamese drive as a victory for the "people's forces." "Nguyen Van Thieu had sworn to relieve Highway 13 before June 19, 1972—'the ARVN Day'—but now he still remains helpless," crowed the English-language propaganda magazine *Vietnam*. "Thus,

Highway 13 is not only the 'Road of Thunder,' but also a 'Road of Death' for Nixon's strategy of 'Vietnamization' of the war."[14]

For all practical purposes the drive up Highway 13 to relieve An Loc fizzled and died. The South Vietnamese troops had won some and lost some, although in the end they did not reach An Loc. But by late June it no longer mattered—An Loc was out of danger.

THIRTY-ONE

END SIEGE

On 12 May General Hollingsworth proclaimed that the worst of the fighting around An Loc was over. Perhaps so, but there was one last battle to be decided. Hollingsworth knew that although An Loc was holding its own, the perimeter inside the city was so small that a single crack within the South Vietnamese defense could turn survival into disaster overnight. For that reason some sort of ground relief had to reach An Loc.

On 15 May the 21st ARVN Division was still fighting at Tau O Bridge and was not expected to reach the city anytime soon. In Hollingsworth's estimation the South Vietnamese needed to place artillery in a position where it could support both the An Loc defenders and the embattled South Vietnamese soldiers at the Tau O Bridge. He persuaded General Minh to assault an insignificant hamlet called Tan Khai and set up a new fire support base.

Tan Khai was a largely abandoned hamlet sitting astride Highway 13 about seven miles south of An Loc and two and a half miles north of Tau O Bridge. It was in a perfect position to harass the enemy on two fronts—if it could be taken and held. The 15th Regiment of the 9th ARVN Division had arrived at Lai Khe from IV Corps on 12 May and was given the mission of securing Tan Khai. Early in the morning of 15 May, the 1st Battalion of the 15th ARVN Regiment and the 9th Armored Cavalry Regiment (Task Force 9th Cavalry) assaulted, bypassing enemy positions near the Tau O Bridge by moving east of Highway 13. At the same time the 2d Battalion of the 15th ARVN Regiment and the regimental command group air assaulted into Tan Khai.

Early the next day the command group was in position. The armor regiment and the 1st Battalion were delayed by rough terrain and did not reach Tan Khai until the evening of 18 May. Artillery began arriving as soon as the regimental command post was in operation. Vietnamese air force Chinooks and an American Sky Crane brought in three 105mm howitzers and a platoon of 155mm howitzers, which were set in place to fire at the enemy to the north and south. The 3d Battalion, 15th ARVN Regiment, and the 33d ARVN Regiment closed into Tan Khai on 17 May, presenting the North Vietnamese with a formidable force wedged between their positions.

The South Vietnamese also used this opportunity to attempt another break-through into An Loc. Two battalions of the 15th ARVN Regiment, two battalions of the 33d ARVN Regiment, plus the Task Force 9th Cavalry struck out north from Tan Khai to relieve An Loc. They would not make it for almost a month. On 24 May Task Force 9th Cavalry returned to Tan Khai with the wounded from the 15th and 33d Regiments, which continued to fight their way north. The enemy destroyed eighteen armored personnel carriers before the South Vietnamese made it back to the relative safety of Tan Khai.

The North Vietnamese were quick to realize the gravity of the new problem they were facing. Two battalions of the 141st Regiment, 7th NVA Division, reinforced by three tanks, turned away from An Loc and moved south to encircle Tan Khai. The enemy appeared to be desperate to dislodge the new firebase because they attacked during broad daylight, exposing themselves to tactical air strikes, which took full advantage of the opportunity.

For three days the North Vietnamese threw themselves at Tan Khai. Tactical air did most of the fighting, but the South Vietnamese fended off whatever enemy troops made it through the wall of airborne shrapnel. Despite the attacks, South Vietnamese artillery positioned at the new base began pounding enemy positions both in An Loc and near Tau O Bridge.

The fighting eased off somewhat after 24 May, but the North Vietnamese continued to attack Tan Khai through June. In Hollingsworth's opinion this split in North Vietnamese forces was significant in the face of mounting enemy losses. "I feel that what is left of the 5, 7, and 9 NVA Div[isions] is not capable of initiating and maintaining an attack of any significance," he concluded. "Consequently, I think they are continuing the withdrawal of 10 to 15 percent from the battlefield while leaving 85 to 95 percent never to fight again." Hollingsworth prodded General Minh to emphasize the destruction of shifting North Vietnamese base areas and lines of communication.[1]

Despite their diminishing strength, however, the North Vietnamese continued to cause trouble for the South Vietnamese, including the introduction of a new system of electronic radio jamming and, on one occasion, the use of nontoxic gas. Continued enemy pressure also accounted for another 100 South Vietnamese killed and 357 wounded after the siege was declared officially over on 12 May—many of whom were to remain in the hamlet until the end of the month. By the beginning of July, however, the South Vietnamese were still in Tan Khai. The move proved to be the final blow to the North Vietnamese siege of An Loc. By diverting part of the 141st NVA Regiment from around the city, the South Vietnamese at Tan Khai bought An Loc's defenders a much-needed respite.[2]

General Hollingsworth could scarcely contain his enthusiasm over this latest defeat handed to the enemy. No longer content to cautiously predict victory, he let it be known that he considered the victory to be complete and decisive. "I would think the enemy is fully aware of their total disaster," he wrote in a letter. "Two and two-thirds divisions [of enemy troops] is one helluva rent to pay for twenty-five percent of a small inconsequential province capital for less than thirty days occupancy by two battered companies."[3]

An Loc was a city no more. All that remained of the provincial capital was a twisted pile of iron and rubble. Strewn about in the wreckage was the flotsam of war—smoking hulks of burned-out tanks, broken weapons. Bodies piled upon bodies bore gruesome testimony to the violence wrought by two months of combat. Some corpses had been lying around until the rain and sun rotted away flesh and blood, leaving little more than skeletons. Others, not yet decomposed, lay twisted in the tortured poses of violent death. Hanging over it all was the stench, so foul on some days that breathing was difficult.

But there were also good omens amid the carnage. A statue of the Virgin Mary stood serene and unharmed among smashed and gutted buildings, and atop Dong Long Hill inside An Loc flew the gold and scarlet flag of the Republic of Vietnam, a symbol of Saigon's perseverance and Washington's continued military assistance.

Tired and shell-shocked, what remained of the 5th ARVN Division climbed out of bunkers and saw the fluttering South Vietnamese flag. They could hardly believe the sight. The shelling had died down somewhat, and there were no intermittent infantry attacks from the north and west. General Hung and Colonel Ulmer lost no time in moving the tired South Vietnamese onto the offensive, however. One of their first successes on the ground came late in May when a patrol successfully flanked North Vietnamese positions in the western salient, driving them from their bunkers. A few hours later a South Vietnamese ranger patrol captured a 57mm antiaircraft gun mounted on a T-54 chassis—the first Soviet-made ZSU-57/2 ever seen in III Corps.

By the last week in May, elements of the 5th ARVN Division were making limited patrols outside the city perimeter. They quickly discovered the magnitude of death and destruction that had rained down from B-52s and tactical aircraft. Literally hundreds of mangled and moldering bodies lay where they had fallen around the city, in some instances stacked in heaps.

As it became clear that the enemy lacked the strength to prevent the

South Vietnamese from pushing outward from An Loc, morale soared. The defenders knew the siege was over and that they had won. Inside the city the northern salient held by the enemy was gradually pushed back until, on 8 June, the last enemy troops were driven out. By 12 June remnants of the North Vietnamese western salient were mopped up by the 7th ARVN Regiment. A jubilant General Hollingsworth cabled MACV: "At 12:00 the ARVN reported the entire city of An Loc was under friendly control." But the best indication of the flagging North Vietnamese effort was the decrease in artillery aimed at An Loc. By 15 June it was so slight that the 5th ARVN Division began offensive operations outside An Loc, pushing out from all directions.

On 14 June one regiment from the 18th ARVN Division was air assaulted on American helicopters into An Loc, bypassing enemy blocking forces along Highway 13. Enemy antiaircraft fire would have made such a move impossible only a few weeks earlier. Over a two-day period 1,500 fresh troops streamed into the ruined town to the cheers of the haggard South Vietnamese defenders. Three days later, on 17 June, the 48th ARVN Regiment seized Hill 169, a key vantage point lost to the enemy almost two months earlier. From this high point the South Vietnamese spotted several enemy troop concentrations, which were quickly decimated with tactical air strikes. Small engagements continued around the city as the South Vietnamese systematically rooted enemy troops out of bunkers and trenches.

Even the timid General Minh felt An Loc was out of danger. On 16 June Hollingsworth coaxed the corps commander to fly to An Loc for a few hours of visiting with the troops. It was his first trip into the city since before the battle.[4]

On 18 June the situation was considered stable enough to return control of the 1st Airborne Brigade to III Corps command. The paratroopers marched out of An Loc for Tan Khai, where they were airlifted out the next day. General Minh marked the occasion by officially declaring the siege of An Loc over, an optimistic pronouncement considering that Highway 13 remained blocked around Tau O Bridge.

On 11 July the 25th ARVN Division began moving up Highway 13 to help the 21st ARVN Division clear the road of North Vietnamese positions. By 20 July the last pockets of resistance had been eliminated, and the road was declared open. However, travel remained risky because the enemy continued to shell the road from mobile artillery positions to the west. As a parting gesture they also sowed mines and booby traps, leaving the South Vietnamese with a formidable mine-clearing task before traffic could be resumed. Although the North Vietnamese did not completely withdraw until the end of the year, they were unable to do more than cling to tiny footholds near the highway.

Inside An Loc the price of victory was clear for all to see. Only six buildings remained standing, and none of them had a complete roof. Running water and electricity had long since disappeared. Vehicles lay scattered throughout the deserted streets, though not a single one had four tires; shrapnel and bullets had torn away the rubber. But that did not stop South Vietnamese soldiers and civilians alike from piling into them and driving on bare rims.

Those civilians remaining in An Loc had lived through hell. Many had holed up in the three-story Quoc Hoang School during the early stages of the siege. Then, in late April, the North Vietnamese battered the school with direct fire from a recoilless rifle, sending the survivors scurrying into the nearest bunkers. "We lived close to the soldiers," recalled Tran Thang Ung, a local civil servant. "We cooked and slept in our bunkers and relieved ourselves in tins and threw them out of the bunkers. No one worried about burying the dead, and the wounded were often left to die."[5]

As the North Vietnamese stranglehold on An Loc loosened, more refugees fled the dying city, joining up with thousands of others from I Corps and II Corps to descend upon new refugee camps springing up around Saigon. In early July fewer than 1,000 civilians remained in An Loc. During the horrendous artillery barrages and constant street battles of the previous month, about 1,000 civilians perished, while thousands of others became refugees as they fled south toward Saigon. Many had taken refuge in Phu Duc, a small village just east of the city that had been spared because it had no military value to either side. However, in their desperation to capture An Loc, the North Vietnamese seemed to turn to a strategy of cruelty. In May enemy artillery had destroyed the city's hospital, killing thirty people huddled inside, and since then most of the wounded civilians had been taken to a battered pagoda in Phu Duc. Whether from spitefulness at their inability to capture An Loc, or because they planned some new angle of attack, artillery rounds rained down on Phu Duc with increasing frequency, killing and maiming huddled civilians with every explosion.

By the end of June the pagoda had scores of civilians languishing with almost no medical care. There were no beds and only a few mats; most patients lay on the dirt floor or on bundles of rags. One little girl died of lockjaw because there was no tetanus medicine. After a few days her twisted body still lay under a shroud of filthy rags. Only a few feet away was an old woman dying of malnutrition, her face covered with flies she was incapable of brushing away. The woman had remained in her bunker for over a month, subsisting on boiled rice until her supply ran out. After that she ate bugs and leaves until she was found and taken to the dubious shelter of the pagoda.[6]

Even after enemy attacks subsided, the supply situation in the province remained haphazard. Authorities were either unable or unwilling to implement a system of rationing, even though rice was beginning to arrive from Saigon. Province officials simply sat behind a wire fence and tossed bags out to those strong enough to wrestle their way to the gate. One wizened old man with a wooden stump where his leg used to be hobbled up to where the rice had been dumped, but he could not find a way to both manage his crutches and shoulder a bag of rice. Since his family was either dead or gone south without him, there was no one to take pity on the man and lend a hand. He ended up taking only a few handfuls, all that he could fit into his tattered pockets. Province officials were not entirely to blame for the rice fiasco, however. On at least two occasions during the siege, South Vietnamese soldiers reportedly hijacked lorries carrying rice to refugees south and east of An Loc.[7]

The medical situation for South Vietnamese troops was equally bad. Their surgical facility was a small bunker, which had been pressed into service when the hospital had been destroyed. The military system of medical care consisted of laying critically wounded men on the bunker floor and assigning their less severely wounded comrades to clean, cook, and care for them. Cooking fires burned just outside the bunker, and greasy smoke curled inside, mixing with the dirt to destroy any semblance of cleanliness. Sterilization of surgical instruments was out of the question, although there were only a handful left to be sterilized. Dr. Nguyen Van Quy, one of An Loc's few remaining physicians, used threads taken from old sandbags as sutures to sew up the wounded.

South Vietnamese air force helicopter pilots remained unwilling to fly into An Loc to evacuate the seriously wounded, even though the fighting had died down to only a fraction of what it had been in the middle of May. A one-mile stretch of Highway 13 had become the helicopter landing zone since the closure of An Loc's air strip. In a way, it was safer to land on the highway than the airfield because North Vietnamese gunners could never predict precisely where the choppers were going to put down. The only trouble was that landings had to be coordinated so the defenders knew where to send their wounded for evacuation. When they did come, helicopters streaked in low over the highway, hovering a few feet off the ground just long enough for a few of the less seriously wounded to clamber aboard. The rest lay in their stretchers, where they had waited for hours

In appreciation of the successful defense of An Loc, President Thieu (right) awarded Brigadier General Hung for bravery. (Author's collection)

in the hundred-degree heat, only to receive a new coating of red dust on their wounds for their patience.

General Hollingsworth was outraged by the performance of South Vietnamese helicopter pilots. "Their performance as pilots during recent operations is unacceptable," he wrote. "Their helicopter operations are characterized by much planning and very little execution." Hollingsworth's solution to this problem was to get American pilots to lead the South Vietnamese helicopters in, hoping to set an example of bravery. They were only sometimes successful.[8]

While the suffering of civilians and soldiers in An Loc continued unabated, the politicians in Saigon considered the battle over and won. On 7 July President Thieu visited An Loc to honor the troops on whose shoulders he had placed such a momentous burden. Lieutenant Colonel Jack Dugan flew him in, surrounded by Cobra gunships to ensure that some stay-behind North Vietnamese gunner did not make himself a people's hero by shooting down the president's helicopter.

Brigadier General Hung waited for the president among the sandbag bunkers of the 5th ARVN Division operations center. Thieu smiled and hugged the division commander, then placed the National Order Medal Third Class with Gallantry Cross and Palm around his neck. Hung, smiling from the honor bestowed upon him but embarrassed by the publicity, led Thieu on a tour of the battlefield. With a handful of officers trailing respectfully behind, Thieu walked among ruined buildings, burned-out enemy tanks, and piles of captured weapons. Bursting with pride over the successful defense of An Loc, Thieu believed that his army had proved it could beat anything Hanoi could send south. Standing among the rubble and sandbags of the division compound, he explained to the small gathering the significance of their sacrifice:

> Binh Long is not the symbol of one battle. . . . Binh Long is a national as well as an international symbol. The Binh Long victory is not a victory of South Vietnam over communist North Vietnam only, the Binh Long victory is also a victory of the Free World over the theory of people's war [and the] revolutionary war of world communism.[9]

In the spirit of victory and celebration, Thieu decreed that all combatants who had taken part in the fighting in the beleaguered city were automatically promoted to the next higher rank—including Hung, who became a major general. As the president's party left the battlefield, Thieu laughingly told an aide, "Hung looked deceitful to me. Why do you think he kept constantly squinting and blinking his eyes?" Taken aback by the joke, the aide replied in all seriousness, "Why, Mr. President, General Hung has not seen sunlight for a long, long time."[10]

President Thieu had made the defense of An Loc into a showcase of South Vietnamese military might, a last stand that became a symbol of Saigon's prestige. The army, he argued, had held out against three North Vietnamese divisions in one of the biggest set-piece battles in post–World War II history. An Loc's defenders had done what the French had failed to do at Dien Bien Phu back in 1954—defeat the communists on a battlefield of their own choosing. Thieu emphasized that point frequently. "Dien Bien Phu fell once the Communists had broken through the defenses," bragged an official government postbattle pamphlet. "An Loc held—and held. Where Dien Bien Phu lasted 56 days before collapse, An Loc held on for 70 days before driving the Communists out leaving the town strewn with the wreckage of field guns and derelict Soviet T-54s." Most important, in Thieu's optimistic worldview, the "An Loc victory was not only that of the RVN Armed Forces over three enemy divisions, but also a victory of the free world's democracy over Communist totalitarianism."[11]

As the South Vietnamese celebrated, the handful of U.S. advisers in An Loc remained at their squalid posts. Though the fighting had been fierce, few Americans were killed during the siege. Ironically, one of the last Americans to die in An Loc was also the highest ranking. On 9 July Brigadier General Richard Tallman, the deputy commander of TRAC, put together a small entourage for a sightseeing tour of An Loc. Although the siege was officially over, North Vietnamese artillery continued to plague the defenders.

Over the objections of Colonel Ulmer and Lieutenant Colonel Dugan, the 12th Aviation Group commander, Hollingsworth reluctantly allowed his deputy to go. Dugan warmed up his helicopters and called for gunship support. As he had done countless times during the siege, Dugan flew fast and low into An Loc, dropping off his high-ranking passengers without incident.[12]

Colonel Ulmer was in the southern part of town near the province headquarters when the call came over the radio that General Tallman's chopper was on the way, and he walked to the landing strip to greet the staff.

"Walt, how are you doing?" greeted General Tallman. As the two officers exchanged pleasantries, a 105mm artillery round exploded some seventy-five yards away. Everyone scattered. Tallman and his party ran to the right; Ulmer dove left toward a little concrete bunker. The second round landed right in the middle of the general's party.

Ulmer looked up in horror at the gory scene. Rushing across the thirty yards of open ground, he knew there was little hope of saving anyone. The North Vietnamese gun crew had done its work very well, Ulmer remembered thinking. They must have had a spotter in close to get the rounds in so accurately.

The general was alive—just barely—as were a couple of others. The rest probably never knew what hit them. A few South Vietnamese soldiers ran over to help. They cut the web gear off the badly wounded men and carried Tallman into the province headquarters, where a South Vietnamese surgeon did what he could. The general had a deep gash in his leg and a penetrating wound in the back of his skull. Ulmer held the dying man's hand as he spoke reassuringly in his ear; he thought he felt the general squeeze his hand in recognition.

News of the tragedy quickly reached TRAC. A medevac helicopter volunteered to come in immediately, but Ulmer warned it off. "We've got a surgeon working on the general and the rest are beyond help," he said. "Hold off for awhile in case there's more artillery in the area."

In the sky above An Loc, Lieutenant Colonel Dugan was unaware of the carnage he had just missed. He learned the news from General

Hollingsworth, who radioed Dugan to pick up the bodies. He swung around and headed his helicopter back to An Loc, knowing how close Hollingsworth had been to his staff. It was a bitter loss at the end of a hard-fought battle.

Tallman was still barely alive when Dugan landed his helicopter. He was rushed from the bunker festooned with plastic tubes and bandages through the swirling dust just as the chopper's skids touched down. A group of South Vietnamese soldiers rushed the helicopter in an attempt to get out of town, a scene that had become all too familiar over the past few months. Ulmer helped fight them off as General Tallman was thrown on board. Dugan jerked the stick back, stood the bird practically on its nose, and roared back into the sky.

Ulmer watched sadly as they disappeared over the rubber trees. He knew in his heart that Tallman would not make it back alive. He was right. General Tallman became the highest-ranking American soldier killed during the Easter Offensive (John Paul Vann in II Corps, though in a higher position, was a civilian).

For the advisers inside An Loc, however, the battle was largely over. On 11 July the 18th ARVN Division replaced the weary 5th ARVN Division inside the city and continued pushing outward from An Loc. During August the division's primary task was to recapture Quan Loi and its airfield. The South Vietnamese quickly took control of the high ground east of Quan Loi but bogged down as they ran into enemy defensive positions around the airfield. Not until 4 September did the 18th ARVN Division breach the North Vietnamese perimeter and recapture the south end of the airfield. They were again stalled when the 52d Regiment, 18th ARVN Division, failed to secure the high ground north of Quan Loi.

In October the South Vietnamese prepared for another communist push in anticipation of a possible cease-fire at the end of the month. The positions around An Loc had solidified, and the enemy was unable to make any significant gains. On 29 November the 18th ARVN Division was replaced by the 3d, 5th, and 6th Ranger Groups, a total of nine battalions. The rangers settled in and blocked approaches into the city until the final cease-fire in January 1973. An Loc's residents were particularly fond of the rangers, though they were also grateful to the long line of South Vietnamese troops who had taken part in holding back the enemy offensive. As a token of their gratitude, the people erected a monument to one of the best units in the defense of An Loc, the 81st Airborne Ranger Group. "Here, on the famous battlefield of An Loc Town, the Airborne Rangers have sacrificed their lives for the nation," read the inscription. The monument watched over a small, well-kept cemetery containing the bodies of some eighty rangers. Five battered North Vietnamese tanks lay like slaughtered beasts around the graves, mute testimony to the rangers' ferocity. "The 81st never gave up an inch of ground, and they never left a single of their dead unburied, even under the heaviest artillery fire," said one of their advisers proudly.[13]

Ironically, it was the lowliest troops in An Loc who made the greatest sacrifice. The local militia—the Regional Forces and Popular Forces—in some cases proved to be "much more aggressive than the 5th Division regulars," according to province advisers. One American called their performance "dynamic." In the early days of April the militia knocked out more tanks than the regular army defenders, and they were responsible for mopping up many of the North Vietnamese units that managed to get into the city. Though they were stationed on the southern side of An Loc, an area under less pressure than the north and west, the militiamen consistently left their protective bunkers and closed with the enemy.

This led to horrendous losses. One of the worst incidents was caused by American bombs. During a counterattack against a North Vietnamese unit probing the southern perimeter, a bomb got hung up on the rack of a fighter providing close-air support and landed squarely in the midst of the militiamen. Tran Quoc Vy, the commander of the 212th Regional Forces Company, had both his legs blown off in the blast. A dozen other troopers were killed.[14]

The main reason for the militia's tenacity was good leadership. Its overall commander, Colonel Tran Van Nhut, the chief of Binh Long Province, was considered one of the best province officials in the country. Some American pacification officials remembered Colonel Nhut as calm and cool under fire. General Hung, the 5th ARVN Division commander, looked weak and indecisive by comparison. Another factor was the militia's unfamiliarity with close-air support. As local defense troops, they had never had access to the bombers and helicopters that routinely supported frontline soldiers in battle. Where South Vietnamese soldiers automatically called for air support when the tanks appeared in An Loc, the Regional Forces simply ran out of their holes and engaged the steel monsters with LAWs. Finally, the militiamen were defending their homes. Most were born and raised in Binh Long Province, and, although their families had mostly been evacuated, they felt they were fighting for their livelihood. The South Vietnamese army regulars were strangers and cared little for An Loc; they were simply following orders.

Among the regular soldiers at An Loc, the 5th ARVN Division suffered the most. With upward of 30 percent casualties, the division was basically combat ineffective when it reached Lai Khe in mid-July. Colonel Ulmer and his advisory team spent the rest of the year refitting and retraining the division. In September Brigadier General Tran Quoc Lich relieved General Hung as commander; Colonel Ulmer believed him to be "simply outstanding. He and the likes of him will save the country," predicted the senior adviser. In Ulmer's opinion the entire division was again ready for action by the end of 1972. "The 5th ARVN Division seems to enjoy a relatively good reputation within Military Region III," he wrote. "As a unit the division is more confident and effective than it was several months ago, and possibly is better than it ever has been." Colonel William Miller had lavished similar praise on the division when he first arrived incountry back in 1971.[15]

Though the South Vietnamese army in III Corps seemed to be bouncing back, it would take a long time to recover. The government reported that 8,000 South Vietnamese had been killed or woujded at An Loc, around 1,000 of them civilians. Both the 18th and 21st ARVN Divisions remained in fair shape, despite over two months of fighting. Unlike the 5th ARVN Division, North Vietnamese pressure on them had been uneven and generally affected only a few regiments or battalions at a time.

On the other hand, the North Vietnamese divisions in III Corps were devastated. American sources claimed that 25,000 North Vietnamese had perished, but no one could confirm that number. The North Vietnamese had fought a poor battle in III Corps, both strategically and tactically. At the highest level, Hanoi's military planners were criticized for their failure to understand the destructive potential of American firepower, particularly the B-52s. Critics also questioned the North Vietnamese preoccupation with terrain, specifically the city of An Loc. Why not simply surround and neutralize An Loc and then bypass it, sending armor and infantry down Highway 13 toward Saigon, they argued.

Tactically the North Vietnamese blundered as well, using tanks in city streets clogged with rubble and obstacles. As every tanker knows, these are the worst possible conditions for the employment of armor. Worse, the tanks were often sent in alone, without supporting infantry. In general, North Vietnamese commanders were unimaginative, relying almost exclusively on the Soviet doctrine of massed frontal attacks preceded by heavy artillery barrages. There was virtually no fire and movement. Hanoi later admitted that "more than half the tanks used in the battle were lost."[16]

In an official history written after the war, North Vietnamese analysts readily criticized their troops' performance but preferred to take a longer view, noting that the lessons learned from the battle served the North Viet-

namese army well in the future. The 9th VC Division, in particular, was singled out for criticism—and praise. "From using only infantry with limited
firepower in fighting, the division progressed to going out to a battle with
combined-arms forces and coordinated actions between infantry, tanks,
sappers, artillery," read one report:

> These were new aspects of the division's maturation regarding the
> quality of its fighting in the 1972 offensive, a year of hard and fierce
> fighting marked by the countless trials and sacrifices endured by all
> units and each cadre and combatant. . . . These victories and the mat-
> uration had been achieved at the price of blood and by organizational
> and command skills [and by the] will to win and to find ways to fight
> victoriously.[17]

Despite mistakes, the enemy managed to permanently hold the entire
western fringe of III Corps from southern Quang Duc Province to the
northern edge of the Parrot's Beak. Loc Ninh was never retaken by the
South Vietnamese, and the buffer zone along the Cambodian border was
forever lost. Another communist history noted that "for the first time eastern Nam Bo was able to liberate a vast region in the vital strategic direction north of Saigon, create liberated enclaves . . . and exert pressure on the
gateway to Saigon." From a strategic perspective, these "liberated" areas
were adjacent to the base areas in northeastern Cambodia and southern
Laos, making the resupply of troops on the battlefields west of Saigon
somewhat easier than before the offensive.[18]

All this occurred in a region where South Vietnamese military officials
had not believed such a battle was even possible. Early planning had virtually ignored III Corps, even though the threat to Saigon was clear. Pre-
offensive intelligence invariably predicted that the main North Vietnamese
emphasis would be on either capturing Hue or splitting the Central Highlands. No one predicted the magnitude of enemy efforts in Tay Ninh and
Binh Long Provinces. When the fighting reached high intensity in April, it
was American air support that saved the day, though the tenacity of South
Vietnamese soldiers fighting for their lives played an important part. Despite
blatant examples of cowardice and incompetence within South Vietnamese
units at An Loc, many individual acts of bravery helped turn the tide.

From his vantage point back in Saigon, President Thieu did not recognize the complex set of circumstances that stemmed from the battle. To him
the simple truth was that the South Vietnamese had won. During a speech
at an Armed Forces Day ceremony in Saigon on 19 June, he told a gather-

A jubilant President Thieu poses with soldiers from the 5th ARVN Division after the siege of An Loc was broken. (Author's collection)

ing of military officers his thoughts on the Easter Offensive. "I consider this a desperate phase, a risky action in the hope to salvage what is left of the [North Vietnamese] war of aggression," argued the president. "To date the communists must have realized that they have failed in their expectations . . . because our army is not destroyed. On the contrary, most of their own regular forces are weakened and are being decimated."[19]

Simplistic and ringing with fervent patriotism, Thieu's point was partially valid, though often ignored by critics of the South Vietnamese army.

They tended to brush aside the devastation suffered by the North Vietnamese army, concentrating instead on damage done to the South Vietnamese. "Perhaps the best that can be said is that the city died bravely," observed one reporter, "and that—in a year that included the fall of Quang Tri and Tan Canh—is no small achievement." The response typified American reaction to the battle. However, An Loc was not dead, only badly wounded. On the enemy side, many chose to ignore the thousands of dead North Vietnamese soldiers and the hundreds of burning tanks and trucks. To critics of South Vietnam any ground given by the South Vietnamese army was proof positive of Saigon's final weakness, while any losses suffered by the enemy were simply part of the give-and-take of war.[20]

This double standard was maddening to other observers, some of whom pointed out that the South Vietnamese were often held up to a standard that no army in the world could match. "How many American units would have held on as stubbornly and as heroically as the South Vietnamese did at An Loc?" asked columnist Joseph Alsop rhetorically. The *Paris Match* compared the South Vietnamese defense to "a Verdun or a Stalingrad in which the South Vietnamese army proved it could stand on its own feet and that Vietnamization was not some kind of trick."[21]

Perhaps this was an overly glowing tribute, and it certainly ignored the role of American airpower, but such praise did acknowledge the obvious fact that An Loc had not fallen, though the North Vietnamese had made no secret of their intention to take it. Both armies could lay claim to a pyrrhic victory: the South Vietnamese had held on, but only with the help of massive American air support, and the North Vietnamese claimed they had dealt a severe blow to Vietnamization.

But in war, as in law, possession is nine-tenths of ownership, and after the smoke had cleared, An Loc remained in Saigon's hands. Despite all the armchair analysis and polemical excuses, the North Vietnamese attack in III Corps had indeed been thwarted. As one anonymous American adviser observed, "The only way to approach the battle of An Loc is to remember that the ARVN are there and the North Vietnamese aren't. To view it any other way is to do an injustice to the Vietnamese people." General Hollingsworth was even more adamant in his assessment of the battle for An Loc. "I think it will go down in history as the greatest victory in the history of warfare," he bragged.[22]

PART FOUR
Suffering the Consequences

THIRTY-TWO

WAR IN THE DELTA

South Vietnam's jewel was the Mekong Delta. Twenty-six thousand square miles of verdant rice fields fed by the great Mekong River provided South Vietnam with 75 percent of its food. More than half of the country's 17 million people lived in the region's sixteen provinces (grouped together in a political entity known as IV Corps), cultivating their crops and using the vast network of rivers and canals to ship produce to Saigon. To both military and political planners, the Mekong Delta presented a conundrum—predominantly rural, it was heavily populated; economically tied to the Saigon regime, it boasted some of the most pro-communist provinces in the nation.

During the mid-1960s, the Americans chose not to follow the search-and-destroy strategy in the delta, opting instead for a more selective method of counterinsurgency. Pacification was paramount, with conventional units operating almost exclusively in support of "winning hearts and minds." This method was quite successful, though it was compromised by a six-month offensive launched by the U.S. 9th Infantry Division in January 1969, called Operation Speedy Express. By June, Speedy Express claimed 10,899 dead Viet Cong, though only 688 weapons were recovered from the bodies. The ensuing controversy over this discrepancy clearly showed that despite the emerging importance of pacification, the U.S. military was finding it difficult to leave behind its reliance on body counts as a measure of success.[1]

The Mekong Delta was also the hunting ground of U.S. Navy sea, air, and land (SEAL) teams, an elite special operations unit first formed in 1962 as part of President John F. Kennedy's penchant for counterinsurgency units. By the end of 1970 the SEALs had killed over 2,000 Viet Cong and captured about 2,700, many of them important members of the communist political infrastructure. So effective were the SEALs that the Viet Cong held them in awe, calling them "devils with green faces" in reference to the camouflage paint they daubed on during missions.[2]

The emphasis on pacification and on special units like the SEALs took a toll on the communist insurgency. By late 1970, guerrilla activity had fallen off dramatically, allowing the people to go about their business. Ninety-five

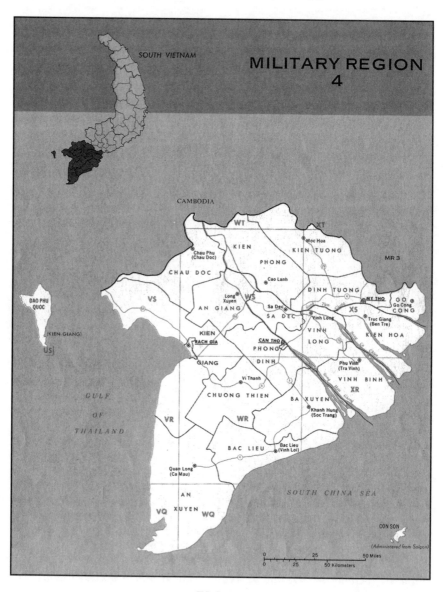

IV Corps

percent of the population lived in what the government called "secure" hamlets and villages; rice production had increased substantially; and education was available to all children. Political reform programs such as "Land to the Tiller" and "Hamlet Self-Development" were gaining momentum, and in March 1972 a separate plan to allow farmers more control over their profits was approved in Saigon. As an experiment in pacification, these programs were effective in curbing guerrilla activity. "Three years ago you couldn't even drive out of town," recalled Lieutenant Colonel John R. Meese, the senior adviser to the Mekong Delta province of Chuong Thien. "But then we made considerable progress on pacification. We had things under control."[3]

North Vietnamese strategy in the delta shifted frequently over the course of the war, but the most recent change occurred during 1970. A North Vietnamese directive issued in late 1969 highlighted the strategic importance of the Mekong Delta and proclaimed that it would become the "principal battlefield where the outcome of the war would be decided." These were not mere words. By early 1970 the 1st NVA Division headquarters and all three of its regiments infiltrated into the delta and dispersed to various sanctuaries. For the first half of the year, enemy attacks seriously threatened pacification and kept South Vietnamese forces off balance. Not until May 1970, when the Americans launched a massive incursion against North Vietnamese sanctuaries inside Cambodia, was the pressure relieved, forcing the enemy to withdraw from the delta. During 1971 the North Vietnamese remained in Cambodia, licking their wounds and planning for the next assault.[4]

South Vietnam also realized the importance of the Mekong Delta and devoted considerable military strength to its defense. As strategists in Saigon were fond of saying, "He who wins the battles in the Mekong Delta will win the war in South Vietnam." To back up the maxim, the Joint General Staff committed three infantry divisions, two mobile and six border ranger groups, plus 200,000 territorial forces throughout IV Corps. The 9th ARVN Division operated around the tangled Seven Mountains region along the Cambodian border, traditionally a North Vietnamese stronghold; the 21st ARVN Division harried enemy units in the U Minh Forest and northern Ca Mau Peninsula, South Vietnam's southernmost point; and the 7th ARVN Division held down Dinh Tuong and Kien Hoa Provinces, two of South Vietnam's most staunchly pro-communist areas. Lieutenant General Ngo Quang Truong, the delta regional commander, established a system of outposts along the border manned by border rangers to relieve pressure from his regular divisions, then slowly but surely rolled up the en-

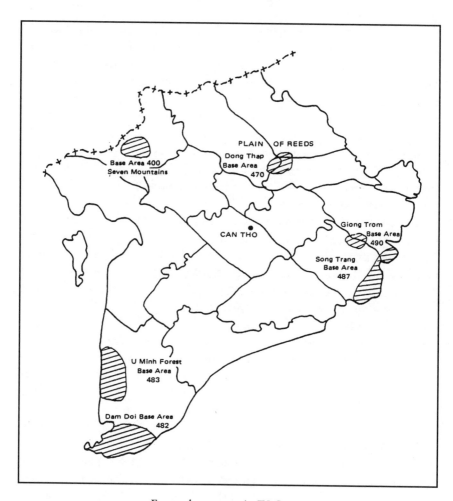

Enemy base areas in IV Corps

emy's "mini-bases" along the Cambodian border and squeezed off part of Hanoi's vast supply network.

Then came the Easter Offensive. In the Mekong Delta, the population held its breath while North Vietnamese units struck all three northern corps areas. As the fighting developed to the north during April 1972, the delta remained wrapped in a deceptive calm. Intelligence analysts knew full well that six North Vietnamese regiments operated piecemeal inside IV Corps, and the 1st NVA Division lurked just over the border in Cambodia. Two separate enemy regiments were also reported leaving the U Minh Forest and heading eastward into the delta heartland. General

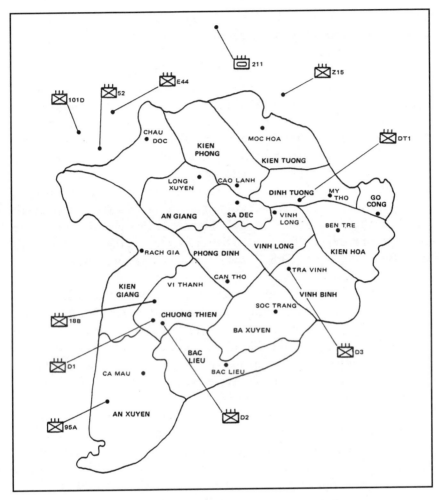

Enemy regimental dispositions in IV Corps, 1 April 1972

Truong correctly surmised that these moves marked the beginning of an enemy offensive.[5]

North Vietnamese strategy in the Mekong Delta during the Easter Offensive was two-pronged. Militarily, the enemy hoped to pin down South Vietnamese units inside IV Corps, preventing them from being deployed to other parts of the country. Politically, Hanoi hoped to destroy pacification's past advances and at the same time sever the region's economic connection to Saigon. Neither strategy was really new; throughout the war the North Vietnamese had adhered to Mao's guerrilla philosophy of surrounding the cities from the countryside. The only real difference in 1972 was that Hanoi was willing to risk all its considerable military strength in the delta on a single campaign.[6]

North Vietnam actually opened its delta offensive in Cambodia. On 22 March 1972 the South Vietnamese 42d Ranger Group uncovered a supply cache near Kompong Trach, a border town about ten miles north of the Chau Doc Province boundary. But rather than attacking in full strength, the 1st NVA Division threw only the 101D Regiment into action. When the South Vietnamese beat back the attack, the division committed another regiment, then finally the last, giving the South Vietnamese time to cope with each attack separately. Watching from the Delta Regional Assistance Command (DRAC) headquarters in Can Tho, the senior American regional adviser, Major General Thomas M. Tarpley, concluded, "The sum total of Kampong Trach was a defeat for the 1st NVA [Division]. This unit was kept out of South Vietnam where it was sorely needed in the Easter Offensive."[7]

While the battle at Kompong Trach raged, the North Vietnamese made their opening thrust into the Mekong Delta with a series of attacks on 7 April. Four Viet Cong units, the 18B, 95B, D1, and D2 Regiments, emerged from their strongholds in the U Minh Forest in an attempt to destroy South Vietnamese outposts and communication routes. Other enemy local-force units surfaced piecemeal and converged on South Vietnamese territorial forces militia in an attempt to disrupt the government's pacification program and form a wedge down the center of the delta at the Bassac River. DRAC noticed that "a pattern is beginning to emerge in that the enemy is hitting OPs [outposts]." Despite the wide-ranging nature of these early attacks, the North Vietnamese were effectively contained by the militia and did not affect any of the delta's urban areas. A correspondent for *Time* magazine called the offensive in the delta "a Graham Greene kind of war, of weak outposts overrun at night, of ambushes and infiltration, of contested villages and safe roads suddenly cut."[8]

While the militia bore the brunt of the enemy attack, South Vietnamese regular forces remained in the background, waiting for the main thrust of the enemy offensive. To help keep the North Vietnamese off balance, U.S. tactical air and B-52 strikes were called in, the first time airpower was used in the delta since late 1971. General Truong credited the air strikes with tipping the offensive in favor of the South Vietnamese. Without air support, claimed Truong, "it is doubtful that the ARVN ground forces . . . would have been able to defeat so decisively the large enemy forces engaged in these battle areas."[9]

Air strikes also allowed the South Vietnamese to maintain a defense at only partial strength on the ground. On 7 April—the same day as the opening North Vietnamese attack—the 21st ARVN Division was ordered to move north to Binh Long Province and relieve the deepening siege at An Loc. One month later the 9th ARVN Division's 15th Regiment was also sent to An Loc, stripping the delta of another few thousand soldiers. Despite the resulting overextension of remaining South Vietnamese units, the IV Corps command held the enemy at bay. Major General Nguyen Vinh Nghi replaced General Truong when he went north to command I Corps in May. A timid commander in the past, Nghi rose to the occasion, aided by General Tarpley's experience.

Throughout April, Tarpley watched as the North Vietnamese threw regiments at territorial forces outposts and avoided South Vietnamese regular units. At first he was puzzled by the strategy, suspecting a feint. "Many major units have not disclosed their muscle," Tarpley reported. By the middle of the month, he began to suspect that "the conservation of main force units during the first phase may indicate that the next phase will be characterized by their employment against ARVN units."[10]

Tarpley's assessment was correct. On 18 May elements of the 1st NVA Division's 52d and 101D Regiments attacked Kien Luong, a district town in northern Kien Giang Province. Enemy sappers opened the battle by blowing up a cement factory and setting up a defensive position in the rubble. For ten days the enemy held militia forces at bay before South Vietnamese ranger and armor units came to the rescue and drove the North Vietnamese back over the border into Cambodia. Just what the enemy hoped to accomplish at Kien Luong remained unclear, but after the battle, life in the provinces west of the Bassac River returned to normal. Four enemy local-force regiments left behind in the area found themselves battered by air strikes and were unable to move back onto the offensive.

As North Vietnamese forces were moving out of Kien Giang Province, another battle was brewing in northwestern IV Corps. Intelligence detected a buildup of enemy forces in the region known to Americans as the Parrot's Beak, a spit of Cambodian territory thrust into Vietnam just north of Kien Tuong Province. On 23 May South Vietnamese border ranger units bumped into the 207th NVA Regiment near the border town of Cai Cai south of the so-called Elephant's Foot in the western part of the Parrot's Beak, a wedge of Cambodian territory thrusting into South Vietnam south of Tay Ninh. The rangers pushed back what turned out to be only a tentative probe, capturing several important supply caches in the process. In one was a document containing plans for the infiltration of North Vietnamese troops into northern Kien Tuong Province, followed by attacks against the province capital at Moc Hoa. More information surfaced on 10 June when a prisoner disclosed that the 5th VC Division, which had failed to take An Loc in III Corps, was being redeployed to the Elephant's Foot and infiltrated into the Plain of Reeds, an enemy base area in the northern part of the province.

General Nghi believed that the high point of the offensive was looming. During a meeting with President Thieu back in Saigon, he predicted that he would not have enough troops to handle a serious enemy attack but vowed to do his best. However, there was no doubt that an attack was imminent. After losing in III Corps, North Vietnam's tired and hungry troops hoped to move into the food-rich Mekong Delta to build their strength. In an effort to prevent this, Nghi moved the 7th ARVN Division into the Elephant's Foot, while the IV Corps advisory team stepped up air strikes whenever an enemy troop concentration was located. The combined effort halted the North Vietnamese infiltration and gave Nghi more time to prepare a defense of the adjoining provinces of Dinh Tuong and Kien Phong.[11]

Fighting simmered near the Elephant's Foot for almost a month. The North Vietnamese positioned several batteries of antiaircraft weapons, including the SA-7 shoulder-fired heat-seeking missile, which cut down the Americans' efforts to bring on tactical air strikes and helicopter support to bear. Still, the 7th ARVN Division prevailed. Brigadier General Nguyen Khoa Nam, the division commander, pushed his soldiers forward with surprising speed, routing the enemy and securing the Elephant's Foot by 30 June.[12]

Searching for a way into the delta, the North Vietnamese shifted away from the border, pushing two regiments from the 5th VC Division, plus the 24th and Z18 independent NVA Regiments, deeper into the Tien Giang region east of the Mekong River. If successful, these units would join forces with the Z15 and Dong Tap 1 NVA Regiments already in the area.

Still inside Cambodia, elements of the 9th NVA Division, which also had been beaten during the siege of An Loc, converged on the town of Kompong Trabek, capturing it in mid-June. Acting in concert with local Khmer Rouge units, the North Vietnamese attempted to tighten their hold on the main highway running between Cambodia and South Vietnam. By early July, all but two towns were in communist hands. Since Cambodian government troops were unable to dislodge the enemy, South Vietnamese troops were sent over the border to retake Kompong Trabek. After twenty-two days of fighting, the communists were pushed out of the town and back east along the highway.[13]

Enemy attacks in IV Corps

But there were only so many South Vietnamese forces to go around, and while some of them were fighting in Cambodia, the North Vietnamese took advantage of the void to close in on Dinh Tuong Province, the delta's rice bowl and its vital supply line to Saigon. Two enemy regiments initially attacked three district towns—Sam Giang, Cai Be, and Cai Lay—beginning in late May, but they were pushed back by territorial forces with heavy losses. Mounting pressure caused General Nghi to redeploy the 7th ARVN Division to Dinh Tuong, leaving behind only one regiment to form a screen along the Cambodian border. In July the 9th ARVN Division's 15th Regiment, which had been sent to An Loc in May, returned to the delta and, along with two ranger groups, immediately reinforced Dinh Tuong Province. At the same time, B-52 strikes were launched against enemy base areas and other areas of reported troop concentrations.[14]

General Nghi was pleased with the performance of his troops, but the concentration of so many South Vietnamese units in a single province made command and control a nightmare. In early August, therefore, Nghi established a IV Corps forward command post and placed his operations officer, Brigadier General Nguyen Thanh Hoang, in charge. The restructuring seemed to work. Unencumbered by the usual top-heavy corps-level command structure, South Vietnamese forces fought several sharp actions with the enemy in Dinh Thuong Province. In early August the rangers cleared the banks of the Mekong River west of My Tho, the provincial capital, and rebuilt a chain of outposts previously destroyed by enemy attacks. By early September, IV Corps had sufficiently subdued the North Vietnamese in Binh Thuong Province to begin shifting its efforts toward Chau Doc Province, where intelligence reports predicted a reinfiltration by elements of the 1st NVA Division. Chau Doc's position along the Cambodian border had always made it ripe for enemy activity, but this time the South Vietnamese were able to shift their forces westward so quickly that the North Vietnamese assault fizzled and finally died out.

Not until October did the North Vietnamese manage one last offensive, probably as part of a last-minute land grab before an expected cease-fire was signed in Paris. Two regiments from the 1st NVA Division left their strongholds in Cambodia and southern Chau Doc Province, thrusting into Kien Giang Province and farther south to the Ba Hon Mountains near the coast of Ha Tien Province. East of the Mekong River, the 207th NVA and E2 Regiments raced down from Kompong Trabek and back into Kien Phong Province. South of the Bassac River, four local-force regiments launched scattered attacks, driving wedges into major South Vietnamese lines of communication and major population areas. However, when October passed with no sign of an agreement in Paris, the attacks died away. It proved to be the end of the Easter Offensive in the Mekong Delta.

The only significant action during the rest of 1972 occurred in early November when the 7th ARVN Division surprised the 207th NVA Regiment in Kien Phong Province and annihilated a battalion. After eight days of fighting the South Vietnamese took seventy-three captives, the largest single group of enemy prisoners taken during the entire war. Most were hungry and tired teenagers, some of whom claimed they had been abandoned by their officers "when the going got tough."[15]

More than in any other region, the North Vietnamese offensive in IV Corps was a failure. Hanoi, of course, did not see it that way. "For the first time in the Nam Bo [southern front] lowlands," claimed an official history, "we were able to combine the offensive and uprising strength of the armed forces . . . with the masses' forces in a large-scale campaign." This is wishful thinking. North Vietnamese and Viet Cong main-force units were mostly ineffective, and there was never any sign of a popular uprising.[16]

The bottom line was that the North Vietnamese failed in all their objectives. Despite repeated attempts, none of the delta's major roads were blocked for more than a few days, pacification was not disrupted, and the supply line to Saigon was never severed. No district town, not even the most remote, was captured by the North Vietnamese, and no areas of significant population fell into enemy hands. Analysts noted that "the overall rigidity of the enemy plan for the conduct of the war in the delta" prevented them from exploiting weaknesses in the South Vietnamese defense, while communication and coordination were "sorely lacking."[17]

If the enemy performed poorly in the delta, the South Vietnamese shone. Territorial Force militia units were in the forefront of almost every battle, routinely holding back North Vietnamese regulars until the South Vietnamese army arrived. The army also rose to the occasion. At the corps level, commanders overcame the traditional problems of an inefficient chain of command and unit immobility to fight a running battle with the enemy all across the delta. General Tarpley noted that "ARVN showed an excellent capability of moving units over extended distances within relatively short time frames to influence the outcome of a battle." Although their accomplishments were overshadowed by the big campaigns in Quang Tri, Kontum, and An Loc, the South Vietnamese army in IV Corps won its battles while sharing more than half of its forces with I Corps and III Corps. Airpower did play a decisive role in the victory, and in some cases the South Vietnamese became overreliant on B-52 strikes, but in the final analysis, American advisers believed they bolstered morale.[18]

When General Tarpley left Vietnam in early 1973, he was pleased with the performance of his counterpart and most of the units in the delta. "While they still have a long way to go before becoming top notch in every military area," he wrote in his final report, "they proved themselves considerably better than their opponents and, provided their will to continue the struggle does not falter, they are capable of eventually defeating the enemy."[19]

THIRTY-THREE

TAKING THE WAR TO HANOI

After almost four years of futile negotiations at the Paris peace talks, U.S. National Security Adviser Henry Kissinger could unfailingly predict the actions of his communist counterparts across the bargaining table. "In my experience the North Vietnamese were never more difficult than when they thought they had a strong military position," he later wrote, "and never more conciliatory than when in trouble on the battlefield."[1]

When Quang Tri City fell in May 1972, Hanoi seemed to be in a very strong military position, but Kissinger saw an opportunity to turn North Vietnam's aggression into an excuse to strike back hard and hand the communists a nasty battlefield surprise. Since November 1968 the United States had refrained from bombing North Vietnam, giving Hanoi a chance to strengthen its antiaircraft defenses and upgrade the logistical pipeline feeding its army in the South. But after Hanoi's blatant attack in the spring of 1972, Washington again had an opportunity to pressure the North Vietnamese by bombing their homeland. With that in mind, Kissinger traveled back to Washington after a particularly fruitless negotiating session to propose to President Nixon that the United States deliver a blow that would shatter Hanoi's confidence and bolster the South Vietnamese. Any such move, he argued, would have to be aimed at North Vietnam itself. The president agreed and promised that "the bastards have never been bombed liked they're going to be bombed this time."[2]

Actually, Nixon had begun bombing North Vietnam less than a week after the first North Vietnamese tanks crossed the demilitarized zone. Limited tactical strikes, code-named Operation Freedom Train, struck enemy storage areas up to the twentieth parallel in an attempt to hamper North Vietnamese logistical lines, followed by deeper strikes beginning on 16 April. As a signal of his determination, Nixon authorized seventeen B-52s to spearhead attacks against fuel sites near the coastal city of Haiphong. These were the first raids into the North Vietnamese heartland since the bombing halt in November 1968, and the first time B-52s had ventured north of the demilitarized zone.

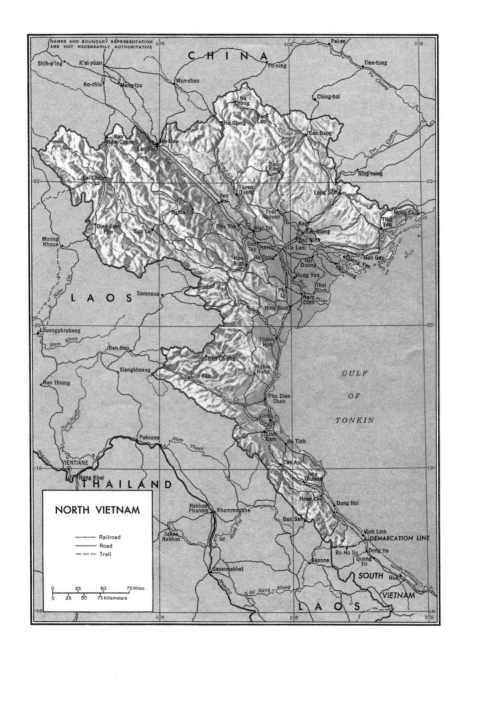

CHINA

Pai-se

Shih-p'ing   K'ai-yüan   Fu-ning   Tien-tung

Ko-chiu   Meng-tzu   Wan-shan

                                        Na
                                       Hang   Ching-hsi

                                    Bao
                                    Lac
                          Ha Giang

Ban   Ho-k'ou   Cao Bang
Nam Coum   Lao Cai
              Lao Cai

                                              Bac
                                              Kan
Lai Chau   Ning-ming

                                   Tuyen
                                   Quang
                        Yen   Lang Son
                        Bai

                  Nghia Lo   Thai   Mong
                                  Nguyen   Yen
Dien Bien   Phu Tho   Viet Tri   Kep   Tien
   Phu   Son La   Bac Giang   Yen
Muong   Bac Ninh
Khoua   Son HANOI Gia Lam
                         Tay
                    Hoa   Ha Dong   Hai   Hon Gay
                    Binh   Quang Yen
                                   Hung Yen   Haiphong

LAOS   Samneua   Phu   Thai
                              Song Wa Ly   Binh
                                        Nam   River
                                 Ninh Binh Dinh

Louangphrabang

Nam   Thanh
        Khan   Hoa
        Ban Ban   Ban Chiang
                                   Nghia   GULF
Xiangkhoang   Cua Rao   Hung

Ban Thieng   OF
                               Phu Dien
                               Chau   TONKIN

                               Vinh
Paksane   Nam
              Theun   Linh   Ha Tinh
                               Cam
VIENTIANE
Nong Khai   Tan Ap
THAILAND   Ma
                                   Thuong

                               Hoan Lao
Nakhon   Dong Hoi
Phanom   Khammouane   Ban Sah

Sakon   Vinh Linh
Nakhon   DEMARCATION LINE
                          Sil   Bo Ho Su Dong Ha
Savannakhet   Xepone Quang
                                       Tri   SOUTH
              Sil Bang Hieng   Hue
                               LAOS   VIETNAM

NORTH VIETNAM

—+—+— Railroad
————   Road
— — — Trail

0   25   50   75 Miles
0   25   50   75 Kilometers

At midnight, seventeen B-52s raced high over the North Vietnamese countryside, escorted by F-4 Phantoms from the 4th Tactical Fighter Squadron out of Danang. As the bombers approached their target, the sky lit up with tracers and the telltale white trails of SA-2 antiaircraft missiles. One exploded near a B-52, knocking out an engine and gashing the fuselage with shrapnel. The pilot broke formation and limped back to Danang, where he landed on five engines. More than 200 missiles were fired by the North Vietnamese, but except for the crippled B-52, no planes were hit. As the B-52s headed for home, an F-4 pilot observed that the bombs "left the target area in flames, and secondary explosions lit up the sky." Reconnaissance planes later confirmed that seventeen fuel storage areas, as well as nearby warehouses and rail lines, were destroyed.[3]

Six hours later, thirty-two air force F-4 Phantoms bombed fuel storage facilities northeast of Hanoi. Because of the earlier B-52 raid, the North Vietnamese managed to scramble four MiG-21 fighters to intercept the attackers. Three were shot down immediately, and the fourth crashed while trying to land. Unscathed, the Phantoms destroyed their targets and headed for home.

While the air force hit Hanoi, the navy sent A-7 Corsairs to bomb warehouses and an airfield near Haiphong. This raid was also successful, although two jets were shot down by SA-2 missiles. In Washington, Nixon received the news with satisfaction. "Well, we really left them our calling card this weekend," he told an aide.[4]

These raids were a mere shadow of what Nixon really wanted to inflict on North Vietnam, but he was concerned that a massive bombing campaign would halt the burgeoning détente with the Soviet Union. To have Moscow cancel the upcoming summit would be politically disastrous for Nixon, but, as Kissinger pointed out, "We could not fraternize with Soviet leaders while Soviet-made tanks were rolling through the streets of South Vietnam and when Soviet arms had been used decisively against our interests." On 3 May the White House sent Soviet leader Leonid Brezhnev a letter warning that the United States meant to strike at North Vietnam for its aggression in South Vietnam and for its bad faith at the bargaining table. Brezhnev warned that U.S.-Soviet relations "were likely to be in for a chilly period," but he made no threats and did not cancel the summit. The way was open for retaliation against Hanoi.[5]

History loomed large in White House planning. President Lyndon Johnson had launched Operation Rolling Thunder against North Vietnam in March 1965, but after more than three years of limited raids hamstrung by restrictive rules of engagement, Hanoi remained defiant. Nixon intended to ease the restrictions and apply full pressure on Hanoi rather than the "gradual escalation" practiced by the Johnson administration. "We have the power to destroy the enemy's war-making capacity," wrote the president in a memo to Kissinger. "The only question is whether we have the will to use that power. What distinguishes me from Johnson is that I have the will in spades."[6]

Nixon's first demonstration of will came quickly. In a surprise television speech on the evening of 8 May, he announced that U.S. planes would mine Haiphong harbor. The only way to stop North Vietnamese aggression, the president told the American people, was "to keep the weapons of war out of the hands of the international outlaws of North Vietnam." Closing off the harbors to foreign shipping that supplied those weapons, Nixon said, would cause Hanoi's offensive against South Vietnam to grind to a halt.

As Nixon spoke, the mines were already dropping into North Vietnam's harbors. Nine attack planes streaked off the deck of the aircraft carrier *Coral Sea* for the twenty-minute trip to Haiphong, slipping under North Vietnamese radar by skimming the waves at a height of less than fifty feet. Each pilot was handpicked from the *Coral Sea*'s three squadrons because the mission was expected to be dangerous. An 8,000-pound payload took away some of the planes' maneuverability, making them vulnerable to North Vietnamese fighters and antiaircraft batteries. In fact, mission planners predicted that three planes would probably be lost to enemy fire. It seemed the prediction might be fulfilled because as the jets flew toward their target, radar aboard the cruiser *Chicago* detected a flight of four North Vietnamese MiGs streaking toward the fleet from airfields near Hanoi. The cruiser fired a salvo of missiles at the MiGs, destroying one and sending the rest scurrying back to Hanoi.

Upon reaching Haiphong, the American planes split into two groups, then climbed to 350 feet and began their mining runs. The first wave flew straight down the channel and dropped the mines; a few seconds later the second wave flew across the channel and mined the harbor entrance. At 8:59 A.M. on 9 May (as President Nixon was delivering his television address—it is twelve hours earlier in Washington than in Vietnam), the first mine splashed into the sea; 120 seconds later all thirty-six 1,000-pound Mark 52 mines were in place, and the jets raced back to the fleet. None were hit, though the North Vietnamese unleashed a ferocious barrage of antiaircraft fire at them both coming and going.

Over the next three days other carrier aircraft laid 11,000 sophisticated mines in North Vietnam's secondary harbors, each containing sensors that monitored a variety of underwater signals such as a ship's magnetic field, engine and propeller noise, and decreases in water pressure from a ship's passage. Any of these signals would trigger an explosion powerful enough to rip a hole in the hull of a cargo ship. Not a single ship tried to run the gauntlet of mines, leaving North Vietnam's shipyards idle and its logistical pipeline empty. Twenty-seven Chinese and Soviet-bloc ships were already in Haiphong when the mines were sown; they remained there until after the Paris Peace Accords were signed in January 1973.[7]

As Kissinger had predicted, the Soviets did not cancel the summit following the mining of Haiphong. Hanoi called the incident an "insolent challenge" and demanded increased support from its communist allies, yet reaction from both Moscow and Peking was mild. The Soviets protested the mining but made no move to bring their mine-sweeping ships into Vietnamese waters. China registered its "utmost indignation" over the mining but took no action to reverse its new relationship with the United States. Disgusted by the big-power politics being played beyond its reach, Hanoi characterized the inaction of its communist brothers as "throwing life preservers to a drowning pirate." For Nixon, however, the lack of reaction meant that the gamble had paid off and the United States could react at will to North Vietnam's Easter Offensive.[8]

The mining seemed to have an immediate effect on Hanoi's ability to supply its army in South Vietnam. Three weeks after the closing of Haiphong harbor, U.S. intelligence detected no alternate supply routes and no significant increase in truck traffic from China to make up for the loss of sea routes. Eighty-five percent of North Vietnam's imports, particularly food and fuel, came by sea, and Hanoi would have to more than double its truck fleet overnight to bring the same volume over land. The result, claimed intelligence analysts, was that "virtually none of the 6,500 tons of military and economic imports it needs daily" were coming into the country.[9]

There was also an immediate impact on the battlefield in the South. Shelling by North Vietnamese artillery dropped off by more than 55 percent between 9 May and 1 June, and the firing of surface-to-air missiles dropped off dramatically. Still, the U.S. military was quick to point out that the slowdown was certainly not due to an immediate shortage of artillery shells, but rather to a desire to conserve ammunition for the future. Intelligence analysts had always believed the North Vietnamese army had enough supplies stockpiled in Laos and Cambodia to sustain campaigns in the Central Highlands and west of Saigon through the autumn of 1972.

Nixon did not stop there. Just prior to the mining of Haiphong, the president had urged his military commanders to "recommend *action* which is very *strong, threatening,* and *effective.*" In response, they proposed a full-scale attack aimed at cutting off overland supply routes between China and North Vietnam. Nixon concurred, and the operation was code-named Linebacker I. On 10 May the first strikes knocked out the Paul Doumer Bridge spanning the Red River on the northern outskirts of Hanoi using "smart" laser-guided bombs, a railroad switching yard at Yen Vien just north of Hanoi, and the Hai Duong railroad yard halfway between Hanoi and Haiphong. Eschewing the precedent set during Rolling Thunder, Nixon left tactics and timing to the air force, though he did reserve the right to approve targets. Civilian casualties were a primary concern from the onset, however. According to the original Linebacker directive, "It is essential that strike forces exercise care in weapons selection to minimize civilian casualties." Nixon also forbade the bombing of dams "because the results in terms of civilian casualties would be extraordinary." The air force took its instructions seriously. On one occasion a flight of F-4s armed with smart bombs destroyed the Lang Chi hydroelectric plant generator, leaving the dam fifty feet away unscathed.[10]

The raids spawned a storm of controversy in the United States about expanding the war. Most in the military felt the bombing was long overdue and credited it with accomplishing more in three months than Rolling Thunder did in over three years. On the civilian side, reaction was mixed. A public opinion poll showed that many Americans were outraged by Hanoi's blatant aggression, and 55 percent of those interviewed approved of bombing North Vietnam. Pundits were cautious in their endorsement, waiting on the sidelines to see whether or not the bombing brought about an agreement in Paris. Former Johnson administration official Leslie Gelb saw the situation as a clever ploy by the White House to take advantage of inherent Soviet weaknesses in Southeast Asia and force a showdown with Hanoi. "The Russians are in a box," observed Gelb. "They haven't got the force to confront us." Military historian S. L. A. Marshall went further, hailing Nixon's move as "the boldest action taken by an American war president in this century." On the other side of the ideological spectrum were the war protesters, whose position had not changed over the years. Typical of their reaction to the bombing was Democratic presidential candidate George M. McGovern's opinion that the action was a "flirtation with World War III."[11]

Hanoi responded quickly to Linebacker I by dropping some of its formally nonnegotiable positions at the Paris peace talks. The first to go was the communist demand that President Thieu be removed from power in South Vietnam and replaced with a coalition government. The White House was pleased by the progress, but Nixon announced that "there was to be no bombing halt until the agreement was signed." After four months of bargaining, Kissinger and Le Duc Tho approved a tentative agreement and planned to meet again in Paris for a formal signing on 30 October. As a reward for Hanoi's cooperation, Nixon ended Operation Linebacker I on 23 October, and Kissinger returned home proclaiming, "We believe peace is at hand."

Not surprisingly, Hanoi saw the situation differently. North Vietnamese "military victories on the battlefields" had brought about the agreement, claimed communist negotiators. "Caught in a losing position, the Americans were forced to agree to the provisions we set forth in the draft agreement." The North Vietnamese also claimed that all the difficulties in the negotiations originated in Washington and Saigon, not Hanoi, and that it was the Americans who "dragged their feet, refusing to sign the document."[12]

North Vietnamese pronouncements belied the military situation, however, particularly the damage done by the American air raids. During almost four months of bombing, U.S. planes dropped 155,548 tons of ordnance on North Vietnam. Although this was less than 25 percent of the total tonnage dropped during three and a half years of Rolling Thunder, two factors contributed to Linebacker's success. First, the bombing campaign's intensity was unprecedented during the war, and second, the nature of the war itself had changed radically. Unlike in the earlier years of guerrilla warfare, during 1972 huge quantities of supplies were needed to feed the North Vietnamese offensive in the South, and the logistical system needed to transport them was vulnerable to air attack. As British military expert Sir Robert Thompson observed, "You cannot refuel T-54 tanks with gasoline out of water bottles carried on bicycles."[13]

According to U.S. intelligence, the bombing decimated North Vietnam's overland supply system, cutting imports through China from 160,000 tons to 30,000 tons a month. By the end of the campaign American bombs had destroyed virtually all of North Vietnam's oil storage facilities and three-quarters of the country's electric-generating capacity. A journalist in Hanoi reported that "the industrial power plant for the city has been destroyed, and the electric current from the remaining power plant is feeble and subject to repeated failure." The Chinese themselves intensified Hanoi's problem by holding up supplies north of the border as a symbol to both the North Vietnamese and the Soviets that Beijing intended to remain an important player in the game. For three months after the opening of Linebacker I, the Chinese refused transport of Soviet supplies across their territory.[14]

Naturally, the fighting in South Vietnam was directly affected by the action taking place in the skies over North Vietnam and at the bargaining table in Paris. Anticipating a cease-fire, both sides launched land-grabbing attacks, hoping to improve their respective positions before it occurred. Washington responded by flooding South Vietnam with new military equipment under a program called Enhance Plus. Since the accords would allow only a one-for-one replacement of equipment, this augmentation immediately improved Saigon's offensive capability and provided a consistent pipeline for resupply even after a total U.S. withdrawal.

On 7 November 1972 Nixon overwhelmingly defeated Democratic Party nominee George McGovern for a second term as president of the United States, ending any hopes Hanoi might have held for a unilateral American withdrawal from South Vietnam (although the communists probably predicted early on that McGovern would lose). When Kissinger met with Le Duc Tho on 21 November, it quickly became apparent that North Vietnam's position had changed. A series of misunderstandings and miscalculations on both sides threatened to derail the talks, culminating in an attempt by North Vietnamese negotiators to secretly insert seventeen changes into the completed text on 13 December. American translators discovered the ruse, and Kissinger halted the talks. Upon returning to Washington, he told Nixon that the time had come "to turn hard on Hanoi and increase pressure enormously through bombing and other means."[15]

Hanoi was furious, and its histories consistently blame the Americans for all missteps. Kissinger's "ploy" to halt the talks, they claim, made the situation "very tense . . . owing to the premeditated, stubborn, underhanded attitude of the U.S. administration."[16]

In reality, however, Le Duc Tho's change of heart had little to do with American "stubbornness." Rather, it may have been born of a desire to stall until Congress reconvened in January. Hanoi believed—probably correctly—that Congress would cut off funds for the war and halt the flow of arms to South Vietnam. Fully expecting a resumption of the Linebacker I bombings to spur the negotiations, the politburo evacuated parts of Hanoi on 4 December. This was the height of North Vietnam's winter monsoon, and in the past, bad weather had prevented concerted and continuous air strikes. Once again, reasoned the North Vietnamese, they could weather the storm.

Hanoi's newfound intransigence may also have reflected a confidence in its recently beefed-up air defense system. North Vietnam, already considered by U.S. pilots to be one of the most "hostile" antiaircraft environments in the world, became even more dangerous between July and

December. Expecting increased air strikes against the North—to include B-52s—Hanoi ordered its Air Defense Forces to "urgently continue studies, developing plans for fighting B-52s, compiling training documents, and training troops in fighting B-52s in complicated circumstances." By early September new antiaircraft and missile batteries, many hooked up to sophisticated radar equipment, were in place around Hanoi and Haiphong, part of the "plan to counter the U.S. imperialist B-52 raids" that the North Vietnamese expected. The general staff ordered all preparations to be completed by 3 December.[17]

Hanoi's worries were well-founded. With Kissinger's promise of peace all but shattered, Nixon delivered an angry ultimatum to the North Vietnamese, warning them to return to Paris within three days. Hanoi refused, and Nixon again turned to airpower to persuade the communists that the bargaining table was more profitable than the battlefield. In a meeting with the Joint Chiefs of Staff, the president made it clear that all targets of military and economic significance would be fair game. "This is your chance to use military power to win this war," Nixon told the chairman of the Joint Chiefs of Staff, Admiral Thomas Moorer.

The result was Operation Linebacker II, an all-out bombing campaign aimed at military installations around Hanoi and Haiphong, as well as any facility that contributed to North Vietnam's war effort. On the surface this seemed identical to the previous bombings, but there was a significant difference: Linebacker I was an interdiction campaign, while Linebacker II was aimed directly at North Vietnam's will to resist. Between 18 and 29 December, U.S. Air Force and U.S. Navy planes battered North Vietnam's military and industrial capability until it lay in ruins. After ten days there were no legitimate targets left to strike. The attacks were so intense that, for the first time during the war, North Vietnam was unable to defend itself. During the last three days of Linebacker II, the attacking planes were hardly fired upon. "There were no missiles, there were no MiGs, there was no AAA [antiaircraft artillery]—there was no threat," recalled one American pilot.[18]

The bombing statistics were impressive. B-52s flew 729 sorties against thirty-four major targets, dropping 15,237 tons of bombs. Other air force and navy planes flew an additional 1,216 sorties, delivering almost 5,000 tons of ordnance. The bombs cut North Vietnam's railway system in 500 places and destroyed 383 rail cars, completely disrupting rail traffic within ten miles of Hanoi. Electric power generating capability fell from 115,000 to 29,000 kilowatts, and the raids reduced oil supplies by 25 percent. Finally, 191 warehouses containing an unknown quantity of supplies were demolished. Eleven days of concentrated bombing had ground North Vietnam's limited industrial capability to a virtual halt, something that three and a half years of air strikes under Operation Rolling Thunder failed to accomplish.[19]

This was not just Nixon administration rhetoric. In a briefing to its Soviet allies in December 1972, Hanoi secretly admitted that "the Americans struck our strategic and military targets and they were successful. . . . In four years of air war under [President] Johnson, the Americans had not achieved the type of results that were achieved during only one month under Nixon."[20]

Although the American media called the bombing indiscriminate and speculated on heavy casualties, the reality was quite different. By Hanoi's own admission, 1,318 civilians were killed and 1,216 wounded, a low total if the U.S. military had actually been engaged in "saturation" bombing. In fact, the figures bore out the Nixon administration's claim that strict rules of engagement, combined with new smart-bomb technology, had allowed devastating pinpoint bombing without significant "collateral damage." One journalist in Hanoi confirmed the raids' accuracy, noting that although many press reports left "the impression Hanoi had suffered badly in the war . . . in fact the city is hardly touched."[21]

Linebacker II was costly for the Americans as well. In eleven days the North Vietnamese fired more than 1,000 surface-to-air missiles, resulting in fifteen B-52s lost. However, unlike the previous Linebacker I bombings, MiGs were not a threat this time. The North Vietnamese used them as aerial scouts to report the bombers' speed and position to the SAM sites. No bombers were damaged by enemy fighters, while B-52 tail gunners managed to shoot down two North Vietnamese aircraft.[22]

But these figures and observations came to light somewhat after the event. At the time of the bombing campaign, criticism was intense. In an editorial, the *Washington Post* asked, "How did we get in a few short weeks from a prospect for peace that 'you can bank on' to the most savage and senseless act of war ever visited, over a scant ten days, by one sovereign people upon another?" The *New York Times* called the bombings "shame on earth," while across the Atlantic in Germany, *Die Zeit* observed that "even allies must call this a crime against humanity."[23]

If Nixon needed additional evidence of the bombing's unpopularity, he got it from Congress. Senator Edward Kennedy said the bombing "should outrage the conscience of all Americans." Senator William Saxbe of Ohio speculated that Nixon had "taken leave of his senses," while Senate Majority Leader Mike Mansfield called the raids "a Stone Age tactic." On 2

January 1973 the House Democratic Caucus voted to cut off all funds for military operations in Southeast Asia, followed two days later by a similar resolution from the Senate Democratic Caucus. Congressional outrage seemed to reinforce Nixon's belief that the bombings were his last chance to force North Vietnam back to the negotiating table.[24]

Hanoi claimed victory, of course. In public, communist leaders called the air defense campaign a "glorious victory," which showed that North Vietnam was "fully capable of completely defeating U.S. imperialist B-52 raids."[25] Rhetoric aside, however, Linebacker II clearly hurt badly, and the North Vietnamese must have reasoned that any future air raids might be even worse. Ironically, uninformed media hysteria probably helped spur Hanoi's fears. If Nixon was deranged, as several newspapers speculated, then he might really bomb the dikes along the Red River or even drop a nuclear bomb on Hanoi. A CBS news broadcast on 22 December raised just such a specter when it posed the question, "What higher bargaining cards do we possess?" Whatever the case, when Le Duc Tho returned to Paris, Kissinger noticed a change in his demeanor and pointed out that "it quickly became apparent that Tho had come to settle."[26]

And settle he did. By 13 January the basic agreement had been hammered out and tentatively approved by both Washington and Hanoi. Only President Thieu criticized the provisions, calling them a "surrender agreement." Unwilling to be railroaded by his own ally, Nixon used both carrot and stick to persuade Thieu. The United States would retaliate if North Vietnam broke the agreement, Nixon promised, but if Saigon refused to sign, then all aid to South Vietnam would be cut off. Thieu reluctantly signed, and on 23 January 1973 the Paris Peace Accords were formally ratified.

Although not the only reason for Hanoi's change of heart, Linebacker II was certainly one of the most important. Kissinger believed that Le Duc Tho's behavior at the negotiating sessions mirrored the effectiveness of the bombings. "What brought us to this point," Kissinger observed, "is the President's firmness and the North Vietnamese belief that he will not be affected by either congressional or public pressures." Never before had Hanoi seen such resolve from the United States.[27]

American military and civilian leaders agreed that the bombings brought a successful conclusion to the war. Nixon later observed that "the bombing had done its job," while Kissinger noted that Linebacker II "speeded up the end of the war." Admiral Moorer contended that "airpower, given its day in court after almost a decade of frustration, confirmed its effectiveness as an instrument of national power." Senator Barry Goldwater, one of the few congressional proponents of the war at that time, saw the bombings as a blueprint for the future. "Let us hope that the strategic bombing lesson of the 12 days in December does not escape us as we plan for the future," he said on the Senate floor. "Airpower, specifically strategic airpower, can be decisive."[28]

Not surprisingly, the U.S. Air Force concurred. One officer in the headquarters of the 8th Air Force called Linebacker II "the single, most important action in the Vietnam campaign which convinced the North Vietnamese that they should negotiate." Other officers called the bombings "long overdue" and pointed out that when finally applied with vigor, airpower brought Hanoi's war-making ability "to a grinding, screeching halt."[29]

But these opinions ignored crucial points about the evolving situation in Vietnam. Most important, the United States' goals in 1972 were very different than those of 1965. When America first entered the ground war in South Vietnam, it wanted to preserve the Saigon regime and persuade North Vietnam to cease its aggression. By 1972 Washington was satisfied with an end to U.S. involvement and a decent interval of survival for Saigon. Add to this the increasingly conventional nature of the North Vietnamese military and the shift in Soviet and Chinese support for Hanoi, and the goal became more easily attainable.

Neither Washington's concerns over a decent interval nor Soviet and Chinese geopolitical considerations interested Saigon, however. As far as President Thieu was concerned, his country was simply being abandoned by the United States. When asked what South Vietnam would do after the peace treaty was signed, he replied, "I suppose we'll fight until the last cartridge and that then the communists will conquer us. It's certain. There can be no doubt."[30]

THIRTY-FOUR

WINNERS AND LOSERS

In Greek mythology there is a story of a man named Sisyphus who cheated death and tricked the gods. But gods are immortal, and when men die, the gods get the last laugh. In Hades, Sisyphus was condemned forever to roll a rock up a hill, only to have it tumble back to the bottom when he neared the top. If Vietnam were Hades, then the U.S. advisers played the part of Sisyphus, constantly trying to push the South Vietnamese army toward military self-sufficiency, only to see it fall back down the hill of Vietnamization whenever Hanoi launched an offensive.

Part of the frustration sprang from the continuing troop drawdown imposed from Washington. As U.S. soldiers were pulled out of Vietnam even as Hanoi was clearly building up for a big offensive, many advisers saw a disaster in the making. Major General John F. Freund, MACV's director of training during 1966, summed up the situation with a chess analogy:

[W]e have elected to forfeit our "queen" (our overpowering infantry strength) without comparable loss to our opponent. This might not be so serious—in view of our much greater game experience—had we not in earlier moments of magnanimity given away a castle (continuous bombardment of the north), and a knight and bishop (the flexibility to operate with U.S. ground forces outside the borders of SVN).[1]

Indeed, if Vietnamization were a game, Saigon was still learning to move the pawns when Hanoi launched its biggest attack of the war. As the course of the Easter Offensive clearly showed, American advisers were an integral part of South Vietnam's survival. They had no command authority, but at their disposal was the awesome power of air strikes, artillery, even gunfire from ships offshore. This authority never changed, not even during the drawdown.

In 1968 U.S. Army advisory strength reached a peak of 9,430, then steadily decreased to around 1,000 during 1972. During the war, 378 U.S. Army advisers were killed in action, and another 1,393 were wounded. Five advisers earned the Medal of Honor, the nation's highest award for valor. As noted military historian Harry Summers observed, "If there is a criticism of this field advisory effort, it is that U.S. advisers were too good, for they inadvertently helped to create a dependency that was to prove fatal once U.S. support was withdrawn." But in the final analysis, advisers could not change the basic weaknesses in the South Vietnamese military system; they could only shore up the structure. As the U.S. Army's official history of advisers in Vietnam concluded, "Why, after all, should Americans force changes down the throats of the Vietnamese generals who, by 1968, ought to have known what was possible and what was necessary to ensure the survival of South Vietnam?"[2]

One area where the advisory effort was particularly successful was the rural counterguerrilla war, usually known as pacification, which began in earnest in the wake of the 1968 Tet Offensive. By 1971 most of the South Vietnamese countryside was considered "pacified." While certainly an exaggeration, there was much to indicate that it was at least partly true. The Viet Cong insurgency, decimated by the Tet Offensive, steadily declined in strength until it was no longer considered a credible threat. For example, in Kien Hoa Province in the rice-rich Mekong Delta, best known as the birthplace of the National Liberation Front, Viet Cong strength fell from over 12,000 in 1967 to 9,000 after the Tet Offensive, and then to under 2,000 in 1971. Communist recruiting in other parts of the country also fell dramatically as new government programs combined with strict security took affect. Another measure of Viet Cong impotence was the growing security of South Vietnam's roads. Once the roads were traveled only by armed convoys, but in 1971 an unarmed jeep could drive almost anywhere in relative safety.

In 1972 all that changed. Pacification is basically defenseless against the onslaught of a conventional assault. Indeed, turning back the gains made by pacification was one of Hanoi's primary goals. According to the U.S. State Department, "One of Hanoi's objectives was to force the GVN [Government of Vietnam] to deploy all of its combat resources to meet the major main-force thrusts. This, Hanoi calculated, would permit NVA/VC forces to return to former strongholds in the South Vietnamese countryside and thus regain a source of manpower and supply in the South."[3]

In February 1972, the last full month before the Easter Offensive, Saigon statistics showed only 3.7 percent of the population living under communist control, but by the end of July the figure had risen to 9.7 percent. More than 25,000 civilians died, and almost a million became refugees, 600,000 of them living in camps under government care. But while these figures looked grim, they were better than the aftermath of the 1968 Tet Offensive. In March 1968 a total of 4,093 hamlets were under communist control; in

July 1972 the figure was placed at 963, leading MACV to note that pacification during the height of the Easter Offensive suffered only a "small regression." The CIA concurred, pointing out that North Vietnamese troops paid less attention to taking over villages than their Viet Cong counterparts had during the 1968 Tet Offensive, preferring instead to concentrate on destroying South Vietnam's regulars. Because of this, concluded a CIA report, "The present Communist offensive has . . . caused less damage to the government's hold over the population [than expected]." While not exactly a failure, the impact of the offensive on pacification must have been a setback for North Vietnam. Captured documents indicated that Hanoi blamed the Viet Cong for failing "to create a 'country-wide uprising,'" leading the State Department to speculate that "the VC/NVA seem to have lost the optimism of the offensive's opening days."[4]

In fact, parts of South Vietnam were almost unaffected by the enemy offensive. Villagers in An Giang Province in the southern Mekong Delta were less than 200 miles from the fierce fighting at An Loc, but it might as well have been 200,000. While artillery, bombs, and the cries of unfortunate refugees sounded to the north, villagers in parts of the delta were unscathed. "The rice grows so fast here," one farmer noted, "you can almost hear it at night." Even at the height of the Easter Offensive, An Giang Province was rated as "100 percent pacified." Other provinces also escaped serious damage during the offensive, including Long An in III Corps and Tuyen Duc in II Corps.[5]

Although North Vietnam gained little valuable territory during the Easter Offensive, the ensuing upheaval rippled across South Vietnam. Much of the population was aware that Saigon had barely escaped defeat, and they decided to sit on the fence. "Until the current offensive the people became more and more committed to the GVN," wrote the senior American pacification adviser for Quang Tin Province in June 1972. "Now, many are measuring sides and their commitments waiting for the winner."[6]

In response to this uncertainty, President Thieu demanded that he be given the power to rule by decree for six months, a move reluctantly approved by the South Vietnamese National Assembly. Thieu attempted to create a sense of urgency in the country by declaring martial law on 10 May, followed the next day by a decree lowering the draft age to seventeen and wiping out most draft deferments. In June he increased the income tax rate, mandated the death penalty for some crimes, and ordered Saigon's newspapers to make large cash deposits as insurance against government fines or libel suits. In August Thieu went even further, abolishing free elections in South Vietnam's villages and giving the power to appoint local officials to the province chiefs. Many viewed this as the final destruction of grassroots democracy in South Vietnam, but Thieu countered by pointing out that many local officials had made deals with the communists during the Easter Offensive and threatened national security. Although not consulted in advance about Thieu's plans, American officials tried to put a good face on the situation by pointing out that the need for stability "at the extreme local level" during the offensive outweighed fledgling democracy during the offensive. Off the record, however, some at the U.S. embassy in Saigon said that Thieu had merely taken "the glove off the iron fist," and that democratic reform was merely window dressing for the benefit of Western observers.[7]

On the military side, the South Vietnamese effort during the Easter Offensive really proved very little—except that the army had survived one more round in the long war. Because of the massive injection of U.S. airpower, the offensive was not a conclusive test of Vietnamization; the real trial would only come when South Vietnam had to stand and fight on its own, and few doubted that Hanoi would try again in the years ahead. In the meantime, Saigon could do nothing but wait for the next offensive.

This defensive strategy had been the crux of South Vietnam's disadvantageous position throughout the war. While North Vietnam could prepare interminably for an offensive with little fear of a preemptive strike, and then pick the time and place of its attack, Saigon was forced to remain forever vigilant, maintaining a thinly spread defensive network all over South Vietnam. Casualty statistics for the Easter Offensive illustrated the weakness in this strategy: government figures claimed 10,000 soldiers killed, 33,000 wounded, and more than 2,000 missing in action. Over 1,000 of the deaths occurred during the first two weeks in April. Unofficial figures ran much higher, placing South Vietnamese combat deaths at almost 30,000, with 78,000 wounded and 14,000 missing, though these were never confirmed. American casualties paled in comparison. During 1972 all services reported 198 killed, most of them during the Easter Offensive. But there was good news as well. During the last week in September 1972, MACV reported that there were no U.S. combat deaths in South Vietnam for the first time since March 1965.[8]

But casualty figures told only half the story. Despite Vietnamization, the South Vietnamese army exhibited many of the same problems in 1972 as it had ten years earlier, a fact made painfully clear during the Easter Offensive. During 1971 and 1972 huge quantities of war matériel were dumped into South Vietnam, particularly offensive weapons such as tanks and artillery. But the U.S. military never taught the South Vietnamese army to fight an offensive war, opting instead to take on that role itself. As a result, despite the drawdown, Saigon continued to fight a defensive war of attrition along the lines of the departing U.S. forces, with the difference in numbers made up by U.S. air support. The Easter Offensive showed that this partnership could work, but only as long as American firepower remained abundantly available. Even General Abrams—a proponent of Vietnamization and the advisory effort—made no serious effort to coax the South Vietnamese out of their static area security mission and onto the offensive. Although cross-border operations in Cambodia and Laos in 1970 and 1971 demonstrated that Saigon's troops could fight offensively and leave area security to the Territorial Force militia units, concern for the South Vietnamese army's immobility was too little, too late.

So in 1972 the South Vietnamese army remained bogged down with territorial security responsibilities. For ten years it had performed small-unit operations in support of pacification, and most divisions were unprepared for conventional war. When the South Vietnamese did fight conventionally, it was to meet enemy "high points" rather than a nationwide offensive, and units were generally committed to battle piecemeal—a battalion here, a brigade there. Defenses were not organized in depth with sufficient fortification, and there was a lack of firepower coordination between the army, marines, and air force. Artillery was broken down into small elements confined to isolated firebases, which became good targets for enemy artillery. Finally, South Vietnam's reserves were woefully inadequate. Since all of South Vietnam's infantry divisions were deployed in static defense, each corps had only one ranger group as a tactical reserve. The strategic reserve—the Airborne Division and Marine Division—were insufficient to reinforce simultaneous attacks across the country. General Cao Van Vien, chief of the Joint General Staff, freely admitted that "Vietnamization still had a long way to go toward developing the self-supporting capabilities of the RVNAF [Republic of Vietnam Armed Forces]."[9]

Why, if Vietnamization had been going on since 1969, was improvement so difficult to discern? Clearly, progress was being hampered by something deeper than manpower and matériel. Indeed, at the beginning of the offensive the South Vietnamese army was among the best equipped in the world. By 1972 the United States had provided 640,000 M16 rifles, 34,000 M79 grenade launchers, 40,000 radios, 20,000 trucks, 200 tanks (including more than 500 state-of-the-art M48 tanks), 500 helicopters, and almost 1,000 fixed-wing aircraft. Such military power would seem sufficient to turn back Hanoi's aggression. "It's inconceivable that the South can't hold out against the North Vietnamese," commented one U.S. analyst. "They are just too good and well-equipped an army for that—unless the North Vietnamese are all Prussians and the South Vietnamese all Italians."[10]

Cultural generalizations aside, the South Vietnamese military was simply not as efficient as its northern enemy. At the root of Saigon's predicament was a failure to improve its officer corps. Tied firmly to the politics of patronage practiced by President Thieu, South Vietnamese generals were uniformly corrupt or incompetent—often both—and although advisers all the way up to general Abrams tried hard to get them replaced, very few ever were. The urgency of the Easter Offensive forced President Thieu to replace Generals Hoang Xuan Lam and Ngo Dzu, his worst corps commanders, but only after the enemy had taken the better part of two provinces. By South Vietnamese standards, this represented a dramatic and timely correction of a traditional problem.

Casualties among the lower echelons of the officer corps further contributed to the dilemma. By June 1972 there was such a shortage of field-grade officers that out of 104 South Vietnamese maneuver battalions, only 4 were commanded by lieutenant colonels. The rest were commanded by majors, captains—even lieutenants. By October the situation was worse, with only one battalion commanded by a lieutenant colonel. By the end of the year a new officer development program improved training, but the South Vietnamese officer corps never completely recovered.[11]

In the end, therefore, guns and tanks—of which Saigon had plenty— were not as crucial to South Vietnamese military effectiveness as intangible factors such as leadership and morale. The Easter Offensive revealed once and for all that the "strategy" of Vietnamization could never compensate for a lack of national will. Statistics bear this out. Despite heavy losses in manpower, MACV noted that "the RVNAF personnel replacement system seemed to function adequately . . . in that losses were replaced rapidly." Only during April, when the level of enemy attacks was highest, and September, when South Vietnamese forces were taking heavy casualties during the counteroffensive in Quang Tri, did replacements fail to keep up with losses. By the beginning of 1973 the South Vietnamese military had all but recovered from the Easter Offensive, boasting 566,996 regular forces and 549,909 in the territorial militia. Every battalion in both the army and the marines was at least 73 percent of authorized strength, with most of them over 90 percent. (The Airborne Division and the Marine Division, elite units that had been badly mauled during the Quang Tri counteroffensive, actually showed a net increase in total strength.) These statistics are more interesting in light of the fact that 70 percent of all manpower losses were from desertions, a figure that was 43 percent higher during 1972 than any previous year. Yet with all this, the South Vietnamese military remained inferior to the North's.[12]

The cease-fire agreement reached at the end of 1972 ended all direct U.S. military support to Saigon and rendered moot any speculation as to the success or failure of Vietnamization. Up to the last day, South Vietnam failed to face up to the new situation, leaving the United States to vainly hope that the final infusion of matériel would be sufficient. In the words of the official U.S. Army history of the advisory effort in Vietnam, "Until the end, Saigon remained an American protectorate in terms of foreign policy and military strategy."[13]

For North Vietnam the Easter Offensive had a mixed outcome. At the strategic level it was a military failure that marked the end of General Vo Nguyen Giap's long career. Although records concerning North Vietnamese decision making during the offensive are not yet available, it is safe to assume that in order to get a consensus in favor of invading South Vietnam, Giap had to promise spectacular results, and when these were not forthcoming, he paid the political price. In the early summer of 1972, Giap all but vanished from public view, leading many observers to predict his demotion, though it was unclear if he was personally blamed for the failure of the Easter Offensive. This view was confirmed in August when General Van Tien Dung, the ground commander during the Easter Offensive, was elevated to full membership in the politburo, followed a few months later by his promotion to commander of the North Vietnamese army. Giap remained as minister of defense until 1980, but it was a hollow title with little responsibility. When South Vietnam fell in 1975, it was Dung, not Giap, who was in complete control of the military.[14]

Giap's ouster was not surprising considering that his strategy was flawed from its inception. Rather than concentrating his forces for a single strike, or perhaps two, General Giap attacked on three fronts, and so lacked the strength to prevail in any of them. Given the history of South Vietnamese immobility, Hanoi could easily have converged on one or two provinces secure in the knowledge that Saigon would be unable to send reinforcements in time. Some observers believed that Hanoi launched its offensive not as a desperate, one-shot gamble to secure territory but rather as a means of "impressing on U.S. policymakers the reality of the military stalemate . . . [and providing] the impetus for a negotiated end of the U.S. military role in the war." According to this reasoning, Hanoi's intention was to tie down South Vietnamese forces at three main points and grind them down until they were combat ineffective, thereby forcing Washington and Saigon to negotiate from a position of weakness. Communist public pronouncements seemed to back this view. An article in *Tien Phong,* the Viet Cong's official press organ, explained that "our general offensive is designed to defeat the enemy's Vietnamization plan, force the enemy to acknowledge his defeat and accept a political settlement on our terms."[15]

Perhaps, but the simple fact is that the North Vietnamese army was exhausted and incapable of fighting more than a low-level guerrilla campaign for years to come. "Our cadres and men were fatigued," admitted General Tran Van Tra, commander of communist forces in the B-2 Front around Saigon, "we had not had time to make up for our losses, all units were in disarray, there was a lack of manpower, there were shortages of food and ammunition, so it was very difficult to cope with the enemy's attacks."[16]

And all this occurred despite the fact that North Vietnam committed fourteen divisions and twenty-six independent regiments—virtually its entire army—over three broad fronts and came away with not a single province. In the end it was the North Vietnamese army that was ground down to combat ineffectiveness thanks to a faulty strategy based on unimaginative frontal assaults. General Giap's preoccupation with fixed objectives like the towns of Kontum and An Loc was more characteristic of North Vietnam's traditional set-piece battles, such as Dien Bien Phu or Khe Sanh, rather than the mobile warfare Giap appeared to have been striving for during the Easter Offensive. As Lieutenant General Phillip B. Davidson, formerly head of MACV's intelligence section, observed:

An experienced armor commander would have loaded his infantry on the decks of the tanks and bypassed the two towns. The terrain and weather would have permitted it, and a sizable NVA armored force showing up in ARVN's rear areas would have panicked the already jittery South Vietnamese troops. . . . If an Abrams or a Hollingsworth had commanded NVA troops at Kontum or An Loc, those battles might well have gone quite differently.[17]

These strategic errors were compounded by tactical blunders committed by commanders in the field. First, infantry, artillery, and armor were poorly coordinated, particularly in Kontum and An Loc. Tanks were usually sent into action without adequate infantry support, bogging down in the rubble-strewn streets, where they were vulnerable to antitank weapons. North Vietnamese commanders used armor as moving artillery, wasting it on static battles rather than bypassing South Vietnamese strongpoints and pushing on toward Saigon. Second, North Vietnamese commanders negated their superior numbers by launching repeated mass attacks against a broad front rather than concentrating on breaking through at a single point.

Hanoi partially admitted these shortcomings. Setbacks on the battlefield, claimed the official history of the North Vietnamese army, were due largely to "limited organizing and command skills," which often meant that "our main-force troops were slow in switching to developing the offensive and attacking the enemy when he was retreating or in disorder, thereby missing good opportunities." But communist planners saw these flaws as lessons for the future, noting that their experiences during the offensive, as well as the Paris Accords that ended America's involvement in the war, provided a "new opportunity for our army and people to 'fight until the puppets topple.'"[18]

One mitigating circumstance helps explain these failures: the intrinsic weakness of the North Vietnamese logistical system. On the one hand, Hanoi's logistical pipeline was the picture of creativity and efficiency, expanding from a trickle in the early 1960s to a flood a decade later. According to North Vietnamese statistics, the volume of supplies reaching South Vietnam in 1972 was more than 600,000 tons, an increase of more than 275,000 tons over 1968, the next biggest year.[19]

On the other hand, even this was not enough to maintain a hard-fighting conventional army. Hanoi's pipeline could not adequately support several divisions in one place, nor could it move munitions from base areas to the battlefront fast enough to keep pace with mobile combat. Most important, any effort to stockpile the amount of supplies needed for a massive assault risked detection and destruction by air attacks. This same theory might also explain Hanoi's inability to maintain steady pressure against cities such as Kontum and An Loc. North Vietnamese troops, unaccustomed to fighting within the confines of conventional tactics, underestimated their consumption of food, fuel, and ammunition, causing them to outrun their logistical support and then pause, waiting for the supplies to catch up. At the same time, the supply lines were forced to function under a cloud of American aircraft. Traditionally, mobile warfare cannot be conducted in the face of enemy air superiority, yet North Vietnam tried to do it in the face of total domination by U.S. warplanes.[20]

Clearly, the single most important factor in the North Vietnamese defeat was U.S. airpower. During the sieges of An Loc, Kontum, and to a lesser extent Quang Tri City, South Vietnamese troops had either lost or abandoned their artillery and had to rely almost exclusively on air strikes. Simply put, without them the South Vietnamese would probably have lost on every front. Half of the estimated 85,000 to 100,000 enemy soldiers killed and 450 tanks destroyed during the offensive were credited to air strikes. British counterinsurgency expert Sir Robert Thompson put it best when he observed that while "it is untrue to say that the battles were won solely by American air power, it would be true to say that they could not have won without it."[21]

Naval gunfire should also get some credit. Two cruisers and five destroyers from the U.S. Navy's Seventh Fleet pounded targets in Quang Tri Province, firing 16,100 tons of ordnance between April and October, the biggest total since 1969.[22]

Hanoi's military blunders boiled down to three basic miscalculations. First, communist planners overestimated the North Vietnamese army's ability to wage conventional war and exaggerated the momentum that the attack could generate using heavy weapons such as tanks and artillery. Second, Hanoi underestimated the staying power of the South Vietnamese army and the determination of large segments of the population to resist the North's blatant aggression. Because of this, President Thieu gained temporary allies from former political foes. Third, North Vietnam failed to anticipate the vigor and depth of the American military response. Nixon's bombing of North Vietnam and the unprecedented air support given to the South Vietnamese army dealt a devastating blow to the offensive.

Political factors were a little less clear-cut. Hanoi misjudged the influence of U.S. antiwar sentiment on Washington's will to punish North Vietnam for its offensive, and it failed to anticipate the lack of response from China and the Soviet Union to the mining of Haiphong and the bombing of Hanoi. On the other hand, Hanoi's inherent political advantages in many ways overshadowed the military disadvantages. Washington's Vietnam strategy remained basically defensive, leaving Hanoi with the ability to strike South Vietnam at will, secure in the knowledge that the ground war would never expand north of the demilitarized zone.

In the final analysis, Hanoi took the long view of its performance during the offensive. For the communists, the battle did not end in July when all of their thrusts had been blunted, or even in September when the one tangible gain—the capture of Quang Tri—had been retaken by Saigon. The offensive continued until March 1973, when MACV closed its doors and left South Vietnam as per the Paris Peace Accords. Only at that point was the offensive over. And it ended in victory, they reasoned, because they were still there and the Americans were gone. Hanoi had said all along that its primary strategic task was, in the words of the official history of the North Vietnamese army, "fighting until the Americans flee," and despite North Vietnamese losses during the Easter Offensive, that had been accomplished.[23]

In Saigon, the picture at the close of 1972 was less than promising. True, South Vietnam's military was better equipped than North Vietnam's, and given the beating Hanoi had taken during the Easter Offensive, it seemed that Saigon had the upper hand. But by the spring of 1973 all foreign military troops had left, and South Vietnam's survival depended solely on its own abilities. The next two years would tell how well Saigon had learned the "lessons" of Vietnamization and the Easter Offensive. It seemed as if South Vietnam's destiny was no longer its own to control. As one veteran Vietnam-watcher pointed out, "Something always happens to save the South. The North runs out of supplies, the peasants don't revolt, or the army decides to fight one good stubborn battle. This may be Saigon's salvation time again."[24]

But "salvation" was really nothing more than stalemate, and from Washington's perspective it only needed to be temporary—just long enough to allow the United States a decent interval. Kissinger clearly saw this, but he rationalized the stalemate with the observation that by failing to achieve its objectives during the Easter Offensive, Hanoi would be unable to launch another offensive for at least two years. He was exactly right. In April 1975, after carefully incorporating its own lessons from the Easter Offensive, North Vietnam again attacked the South—in direct violation of the Paris Accords—and swept all the way to Saigon.

THE LAST PATROL

Vietnam's paradox in 1972 was that as Hanoi was building up for the biggest offensive of the war, Washington was building down at a dizzying rate. After almost a decade of fighting and dying for a regime considered vital to halting the spread of communism, suddenly it seemed that the United States could not leave South Vietnam behind fast enough.

From the demilitarized zone to the Mekong Delta, once-bustling military bases were deserted. In large sections of the countryside an American uniform was a rarity, and the U.S. trucks and jeeps that had once clogged South Vietnam's major roadways were outnumbered by South Vietnamese military vehicles. Even in the hustle and hype of Saigon's nightclubs, bar girls now outnumbered soldiers.

For those American soldiers remaining in Vietnam during 1972, however, those facts were trivial. They remained far from home, and the enemy was still very real. "Please don't say only one man was killed last week," said one sergeant when a reporter pointed out how light American casualties were in early 1972. "The 'only one' is one too many to these guys out here."[1]

Most soldiers resented Nixon's claims that the American combat role had ended. The Pentagon claimed those troops still in South Vietnam were part of a "dynamic defense," a term despised by most U.S. soldiers still there. "Defense, hell," said a private sitting out the last days of the war in an isolated firebase. "We'll be out of combat when we are 'back in the world,' not before."

That was the picture for the grunt on the ground. From Washington's perspective, the drawdown actually accelerated during 1972. In January of that year there were 104,500 U.S. Army ground troops in South Vietnam— 11 battalions compared with 115 in early 1969. Five months later there were 31,900 troops incountry, and by the end of 1972 there were less than 15,000. Like clockwork the number of soldiers ticked down, streaming out of Vietnam the way they had come, in shiny civilian aircraft ferrying between Saigon and Honolulu.

Even the Easter Offensive could not change the pace of the American withdrawal. As fighting raged across three fronts, the drawdown continued unabated. Soldiers boarded planes and left Vietnam behind; most of them gave no further thought to Vietnamization or to who would win the latest battle. For the Americans returning home, the booming artillery was no more dangerous than distant thunder, a storm that was too far away to present a threat.

Then the unthinkable became reality. As North Vietnamese troops swept over Quang Tri Province and threatened Hue, the decision was made to send U.S. troops back into harm's way. The numbers were insignificant—less than one battalion—but to the soldiers who had to go, Nixon's draw-down suddenly seemed like a bad joke. Instead of going home, they were headed for the combat zone. Suddenly the rumbling guns to the north seemed very dangerous.

The hard-luck unit was the 2d Battalion of the 196th Infantry Brigade, the last American ground combat unit in South Vietnam. Most of the brigade left for the States in early in 1972, but two battalions remained; one would leave Vietnam in June, the other—the 2d Battalion—would have to wait until August. The 196th Infantry Brigade had already endured six years of fighting.[2]

On 13 April about 400 soldiers loaded aboard C-130 transport planes in Danang and flew north to a little corner of the war where U.S. soldiers still had a stake in the fighting in South Vietnam. Here, American combat units supported by American artillery operated out of an American base supported by American logistics. Vietnamization had still not come to Phu Bai, a major installation located about ten miles down Highway 1 from Hue. Phu Bai had a long and colorful history during the war, but by 1972 all that remained was a sensitive radio intelligence center run by the supersecret National Security Agency. For the soldiers at Phu Bai during the Easter Offensive, going home was still a dream, and as the North Vietnamese closed in during mid-May, their duties became more intense.

"They will need to put the marines in to get us out of here if it gets bad," predicted one American soldier gloomily. He was not talking about the South Vietnamese marines; he meant American marines—1,500 of them floating offshore with the 7th Fleet. Those sentiments were shared by most of the men still in Phu Bai. Gung ho enthusiasm and unit esprit de corps had gone the way of American public support at home—straight downhill to almost rock bottom.

Low morale showed clearly in the performance of some units within the 196th Brigade. In February, before the Easter Offensive was launched, North Vietnamese troops holed up in caves southwest of Danang ambushed a U.S. patrol, killing one and wounding seven. The Americans withdrew without a fight, leaving the enemy in control of the heights. Even after air strikes pounded the caves, the unit would not go back. When asked about the patrol's performance, an army spokesman could only say, "We have no indication they sealed them [the enemy] off or went up there to find out if they killed anybody."[3]

The patrol's hesitance to engage the enemy was the rule rather than the exception in 1972. Every officer dreads the moment when morale drops so low that he cannot command his men. Yet that was precisely what happened on 12 April. During a routine patrol about three miles west of Phu Bai, Charlie Company abruptly refused to move. "We're not going!" shouted some of the men. "This isn't our war. We're not going out in the bush. Why should we fight if nobody gives a damn about us?"[4]

In the end, however, the frustrated soldiers moved out into the bush, but only after one platoon leader convinced the men that their disobedience would endanger another U.S. unit already in the field. Even then it took a virtual guarantee from the company commander that the patrol would not run into the enemy. The army tried to downplay this major embarrassment. A spokesman said that the soldiers did not disobey a direct order, so there would be no disciplinary action. But that did not mollify the men. "Man, the war stinks," said a soldier. "Why the hell are we fighting for something we don't believe in?" Another pointed out, "We're supposed to being doing defense, nothing else, not offensive. Going out on patrol, what's that?"

During the entire war there were very few examples of mass insubordination. Ironically, the most famous incident occurred in August 1969 when another battalion of the 196th Brigade—then part of the Americal Division—refused orders to move forward during an operation aimed at reaching the site of a helicopter crash thirty miles south of Danang. But back in 1969 most soldiers still believed the old basic training line that they were in Vietnam to stop communism. In 1972 even the dimmest soldier looked around and saw that Washington was reaching out to China and practicing détente with the Soviet Union, both countries that had supplied the weapons that killed so many U.S. soldiers during the war. Now they were leaving, and no one wanted to be the last American to die in Vietnam.

Yet the battalion could not simply sit behind sandbags and allow fate to take its course. Security for both themselves and the intelligence base meant patrolling outside the perimeter, keeping the enemy off balance. Lieutenant Tom Eaton, commander of 3d Platoon, Alpha Company, made sure that his soldiers got out into the heat and danger around Phu Bai on regular patrols. On the afternoon of 11 May the platoon was on a barren ridge looking west from Phu Bai, trying to escape the hot sun. Ponchos draped over branches were the only shelter as the soldiers waited for sundown and the beginning of their patrol. Darkness brought pouring rain, a quantum shift from the weather they had just endured, but no one found it much of a relief. The platoon moved off down the hill, leaving half the men to set up an ambush while the rest moved around to confuse any watching North Vietnamese observers.

To the south was the Hai Van Pass; to the southwest, tucked under the shadow of the mountains controlled by the enemy, was a line of South Vietnamese firebases—King, Birmingham, and Arsenal—the southern rim of Hue's defensive perimeter. It was between Firebase Arsenal and the Hai Van Pass that the U.S. battalion operated. Lying in the brush on their lonely hilltop, the ambush team could see the entire Hue battlefront unfolded like a giant map below them.

That night Firebase Arsenal was pounded by mortars. Within hours B-52s raced silently overhead, and the ground trembled and flashed under the impact of Arc Light strikes. Naval gunfire added its voice, and crashing rounds erupted in spouts of fire and dirt around the firebase. For four hours the bombardment continued as the American patrol watched from its secure perch. When it was over the men went into action. A Nighthawk mission—two helicopter gunships with searchlights and infrared detection equipment—clattered overhead in an attempt to flush enemy soldiers out of the brush. They did not have long to wait. North Vietnamese small arms cracked in the distance as they tried to shoot down the deadly helicopters. Lieutenant Eaton called in artillery from Phu Bai onto the North Vietnamese positions, then listened to the radio as Charlie Company, also on patrol, reported ambushing an enemy patrol.[5]

The next morning the platoon scoured the area, looking for signs of the enemy. Lieutenant Eaton spotted a cave on the mountainside and sent seven men to check it out. Sergeant Lee Thompson and three other men rappeled down on ropes, swinging into the entrance quickly to surprise any occupants. No one was there, but tracks and skid marks showed that something heavy—perhaps an artillery piece—had been dragged out sometime after the heavy rains of the previous evening.

As the sun climbed into the sky, the temperature again soared, and the platoon climbed under bushes to escape the heat. During the late afternoon a helicopter flew in a load of ice-cold Cokes to take the edge off the dust and heat, while "Doc," the platoon medic and a conscientious objector who carried a stick instead of a rifle on patrols, cooked up a batch of canned C rations. Unlike the American soldiers in years past, patrols from Phu Bai could not look forward to escaping the war in the bars and the PX that catered to GIs—they were all gone now.

The Americans silently worried about the situation. There was no way they could possibly fend off a concerted attack, even if the marines did storm ashore to assist them. Yet it was not beyond the realm of possibility that the North Vietnamese might make just such a move. If they did, they could strike a symbolic blow against the last vestiges of an American presence that, to the communists, represented years of imperialism and support for a decaying regime in Saigon. A concerted attack against the U.S. battalion at Phu Bai might trigger a reaction by the marines and would certainly raise the body count at a time when Americans were supposed to be coming home. "One hundred Americans in body bags and a fighting retreat by marines would demonstrate the old U.S. had been beaten," speculated one American officer. Fortunately, his doomsday scenario was not played out.

In the end the soldiers' fears were for naught. The North Vietnamese did not attack Phu Bai, and the withdrawal continued. In June most of the 2d Battalion was withdrawn from Phu Bai back to Danang. Along with what was left of the 196th Brigade, it was reconstituted as Task Force Gimlet and turned into a holding unit for soldiers left over from other recently inactivated infantry units. Some of the men had been with the 1st Cavalry Division and the 101st Airborne Division, but because they did not have enough "incountry time" they had to stay in Vietnam when their units went home. Others had extended their tours because they just did not want to leave.

Yet there were still times when combat patrols had to be sent into the bush. An unwritten rule in Vietnam had always allowed "short timers" to finish the last weeks of their tour working in rear jobs such as mail clerks or drivers. But what happened when the entire unit became short? Who went on patrol? Task Force Gimlet found itself in just such a quandary. On 5 August Delta Company, 3d Battalion, 21st Infantry, was assembled at its base camp outside Danang, affectionately called Camp Swampy, and ordered to sweep the nearby valley to root out enemy units that had been firing 122mm rockets into the city. For two days Delta Company did what American soldiers had done for the past seven years—humped the boonies. "Our last combat assault out to the bush was damn near like the first time for me," recalled Specialist Fourth Class Richard W. Miller. "The feeling in my gut, the sweat, and the fear. . . . Everybody knew you could die on the last [patrol] as quick as you can on the first." Another soldier summed up what everybody must have been thinking. "All I wanted to do was just get through this patrol in one piece and go home," he said.[6]

Although they did not run into the enemy, there were booby traps. One platoon triggered several mines, wounding two men. On 6 August, Specialist Fourth Class James McVicar became one of the last U.S. soldiers wounded in action during America's official involvement in Vietnam. But after only four days on patrol, Delta Company was ordered to head for the final landing zone, where they would be picked up and flown back to base. While waiting for the helicopters, the soldiers were met by a South Vietnamese unit that had been combat assaulted to take Delta Company's place in the field. The Americans were so elated that they gave their extra grenades and magazines to the South Vietnamese soldiers. As the helicopters landed to take Delta Company home, they all knew it was the last patrol.

Task Force Gimlet left Vietnam on 11 August. Lieutenant Colonel Rocco Negris, the task force commander, presided over a small ceremony and officially retired the unit colors. "As I reflect on that moment, I view with pride the men of Task Force Gimlet," wrote Lieutenant Colonel Negris after the war. "To the man, they were outstanding soldiers who carried out difficult and dangerous missions that included endless days in the field, frequent patrolling and daily helicopter and ground combat operations."[7]

The American ground war in Vietnam had come to an end.

NOTES

Prologue

1. Phillip B. Davidson, *Vietnam at War: The History, 1946–1975* (Novato, Calif.: Presidio Press, 1988), p. 650.
2. David Fulghum and Terrance Maitland, *The Vietnam Experience: South Vietnam on Trial* (Boston: Boston Publishing Co., 1984), p. 87.
3. Ibid.
4. Richard M. Nixon, *RN: The Memoirs of Richard Nixon* (New York: Grosset and Dunlap, 1978), p. 498; Lewis Sorley, *Thunderbolt: General Creighton Abrams and the Army of His Times* (New York: Simon and Schuster, 1992), p. 312.

Introduction

1. Fulghum and Maitland, *South Vietnam on Trial*, pp. 124, 127; Frank Snepp, *Decent Interval* (New York: Random House, 1977), p. 98.
2. Col. Peter F. C. Armstrong, "Capabilities and Intentions," *Marine Corps Gazette*, Sept. 1986, p. 40.
3. Shelby L. Stanton, *Vietnam Order of Battle* (New York: U.S. News Books, 1981), p. 333.
4. Davidson, *Vietnam at War*, p. 575.
5. Msg, Westmoreland to Moorer, CJCS [chairman of the Joint Chiefs of Staff], 1 Feb. 1972.
6. CIA Intelligence Memo, Enemy Strategy and Capabilities in Indochina Through May 1972, 7 Jan. 1972. Quoted in Gen. Bruce Palmer Jr., "Studies in Intelligence: U.S. Intelligence and Vietnam," vol. 28, no. 5, 1984, p. 91; State Dept. estimate in Memo, Amb. Bunker to President Nixon, 26 Jan. 1972.
7. Armstrong, "Capabilities and Intentions," pp. 42–43.
8. Ibid., p. 44.
9. Ngo Quang Truong, *The Easter Offensive of 1972* (Washington, D.C.: U.S. Army Center of Military History, 1980), p. 157.
10. Msg, Abrams to Moorer, 1 Feb. 1972, subj: Unnumbered COSVN [Central Office for South Vietnam] Resolution, pp. 6–7.
11. Ibid., p. 8.
12. Ibid., p. 5.
13. SPECAT msg, Abrams to CINCPAC [commander in chief, Pacific], 17 Jan. 1972; Msg, Abrams to CINCPAC, 20 Jan. 1972.
14. Palmer, "Studies in Intelligence," p. 92.
15. Armstrong, "Capabilities and Intentions," p. 45.

16. "Laird Saw No Likelihood of Wide Enemy Attacks," *New York Times*, 21 May 1972; "Extracts from Press Conference," Gen. William C. Westmoreland, Chief of Staff, U.S. Army, 31 Jan. 1972.

17. Msg, Lavelle to Abrams, 22 Mar. 1972, subj: Freedom Block, p. 4.

18. *Washington Post* news brief, 10 Feb. 1972.

19. XXIV Corps Periodical Intelligence Report (Perintrep) 4–72, 20 Feb. 1972; Msg, Lavelle to Abrams, 22 Mar. 1972, subj: Freedom Block.

20. Msg, Abrams to XXIV Corps, 7 Feb. 1972, subj: Enemy Ground Campaign; Msg, Abrams to Lavelle, 11 Feb. 1972.

21. XXIV Corps Perintrep 24–71, 14 Nov. 1971; XXIV Corps Perintrep 5–72, 5 Mar. 1972.

22. In fact, most North Vietnamese soldiers were drafted. Le Tien Kien's account is undoubtedly idealized, but it provides some insight into a soldier's life on the Ho Chi Minh Trail. Nguyen Dinh U, "Departure for the Front," *Vietnam*, no. 169 (1972): 12–13.

23. "Vietnam: The Anti–U.S. Resistance War for National Salvation, 1954–1975: Military Events," FBIS translation, 3 June 1982, p. 31.

24. MACV 1971 Command History, vol. I, p. III–45.

25. Vu Tien De's account comes from "A Meeting with a Hero of Truong Son," *Vietnam*, no. 169 (1972): 8–9.

26. COSVN Resolution 55 is quoted in Hoang Ngoc Lung, *The General Offensives of 1968–69* (Washington, D.C.: U.S. Army Center of Military History, 1981), p. 118.

27. "The Man Behind the Offensive," *Time*, 8 May 1972, p. 30.

28. Douglas Pike, *People's Army of Vietnam* (Novato, Calif.: Presidio Press, 1986), p. 339; "The Man Behind the Offensive," p. 30.

29. Qiang Zhai, "Transplanting the Chinese Model: Chinese Military Advisers and the First Vietnam War, 1950–1954," *Journal of Military History*, Oct. 1993, pp. 707–713; F. P. Serong, "The 1972 Easter Offensive," *Southeast Asian Perspectives*, summer 1974, pp. 13–14. Gen. Nguyen Chi Thanh was killed in 1967 while commanding COSVN, apparently during a B-52 bombing raid.

30. Harry G. Summers, *Vietnam War Almanac* (New York: Facts on File Publications, 1985), pp. 177–178; "If Giap Were a U.S. General," *U.S. News & World Report*, 3 May 1971, p. 35. Giap's comments on battle deaths come from Oriana Fallaci, *Interview with History* (Boston: Houghton Mifflin, 1977), p. 76.

31. Brian M. Jenkins, "Giap and the Seventh Son" (Santa Monica, Calif.: RAND Corporation, Sept. 1972), p. 4.

32. "The Man Behind the General in Hanoi," *Time*, 15 May 1972, p. 28.

33. Ibid. Pike also outlined Le Duan's shift of opinion in a U.S. Information Service paper entitled "The Power Struggle in North Vietnam," Apr. 1972.

34. Bui Tin, *Following Ho Chi Minh: Memoirs of a North Vietnamese Colonel* (Honolulu: University of Hawaii Press, 1995), pp. 132–133.

35. Quoted in "Hanoi's High-Risk Drive for Victory," *Time*, 15 May 1972, p. 26.

36. MACV 1971 Command History, vol. I, p. III-2; Davidson, *Vietnam at War*, p. 674.

37. MACV 1971 Command History, vol. I, pp. III-6, III-7.

38. Fulghum, *South Vietnam on Trial*, p. 120.

39. Ibid.

40. Ibid., pp. 120, 130–131.

41. Dept. of the Army Pamphlet 381-10, "Weapons and Equipment Recognition Guide, Southeast Asia," Jan. 1972, p. 311.

42. Davidson, *Vietnam at War*, p. 675; Fulghum, *South Vietnam on Trial*, p. 120.

43. *History of the People's Army of Vietnam* [*Lich Su Quan Doi Nhan Dan Viet Nam*] (Hanoi: People's Army Publishing House, 1990), p. 50; Pike, *People's Army of Vietnam*, p. 345.

44. A partial translation and analysis of the *Quan Doi Nhan Dan* article is in the Abrams Papers. Msg, Abrams to Moorer, CJCS, 22 Feb. 1972, subj: NVN Propaganda.

45. *History of the People's Army of Vietnam* [*Lich Su Quan Doi Nhan Dan Viet Nam*], p. 51.

46. Quoted in Stanley Karnow, *Vietnam: A History* (New York: Viking Press, 1983), p. 639.

Chapter 1. The Blazing Front Line

1. Truong, *The Easter Offensive of 1972*, p. 15.

2. Army Activities Rpt, Southeast Asia, NVA/VC Unit Locations, 26 Apr. 1972.

3 Senior Officer Debriefing Rpt, Lt. Gen. Melvin Zais, Commanding General, XXIV Corps, 23 July 1970, pp. 27–28.

4. Senior Officer Debriefing Rpt, Brig. Gen. Henry J. Muller, Deputy Senior Adviser, I Corps, 9 June 1970, p. 9.

5. The only detailed account of the formation of the 3d ARVN Division is Howard C. Feng, "The Road to the 'Ben Hai Division': An Analysis of the Events Leading to the Formation of the 3d ARVN Division in October 1971" (master's thesis, University of Hawaii, 1987).

6. Hoang Ngoc Lung, *Intelligence* (Washington, D.C.: U.S. Army Center of Military History, 1982), p. 155; G. H. Turley, *The Easter Offensive: The Last American Advisors, 1972* (Novato, Calif.: Presidio Press, 1985), p. 31.

7. Interview, author with William C. Camper, Senior Adv., 56th ARVN Regt., 14 Jan. 1994.

8. Rpt, Adv. Team 155 to COMUSMACV, undated, subj: Combat Operations After Action Report, Appendix 7 to Annex D, NVA Artillery Tactics.

9. Camper interview, 14 Jan. 1994.

10. Interview, Col. Donald J. Metcalf by Maj. Robert Flowers, 15 Sept. 1972, p. 1.

11. Turley, *The Easter Offensive*, pp. 31–32.

12. MACV captured document file, translation of NVA dispatch 72.176, "Mieu Bai Son Under Fire," 12 Apr. 1972.

13. Manh Nhieu, cameraman of the People's Army studios, "With a Shock Unit," *Vietnam*, no. 168 (1972): 15–16.

Chapter 2. Western Collapse

1. The VNMC commandant, Lt. Gen. Le Nguyen Khang, also acted as the division commander. His high rank disrupted the chain of command and ensured that

opcon command would not go lower than corps level. This problem was remedied in May 1972 when Bui The Lan, a brigadier general, was placed in command of the Marine Division. Rpt, CINCPAC for POLAD, Dept. of State, subj: "Command Histories and Historical Sketches of RVNAF Divisions," 6 Feb. 1973, part II.

2. Account of FSB Sarge is from USMC Oral History Interview, Maj. Walter E. Boomer, Senior Adv. 4th VNMC Bn., 8 Mar. 1983.

3. According to MIA-POW records, the two soldiers were later identified as Sp-5 Gary Westcott and Sp-4 Bruce Crosley Jr.

4. Account of Nui Ba Ho is from USMC Oral History Interview, Capt. Ray L. Smith, Deputy Senior Adv., 4th VNMC Bn., undated.

5. Project CHECO Rpt, "The NVA 1972 Invasion of Military Region I: The Fall of Quang Tri and Defense of Hue," by Capt. David K. Mann, undated, p. 10.

Chapter 3. Piercing the Ring of Steel

1. The intelligence disagreement was reported during the Easter Offensive in *U.S. News & World Report,* 15 May 1972.

2. Interview, author with Frederick J. Kroesen, Senior Adv., FRAC, 4 Dec. 1989.

3. USMC Oral History Interview, Col. Raymond R. Battreall, no. 2034, undated.

4. "Vietnamization—Russian Style," *Washington Post,* 7 Apr. 1972.

5. Memo, Col. Harold M. Hawkins to Brig. Gen. Thomas Bowen, subj: Trip Report, 3d FSB, 3 Feb. 1972.

6. Account of the fall of Alpha 2 is from USMC Oral History Interview, 1st Lt. Joel B. Eisenstein, OIC U.S. Naval Gunfire Spot Team, Sub Unit One, 1st AN-GLICO, undated; Rpt, OIC, Naval Gunfire Liaison/Spot Team 1-2 to Naval Gunfire Liaison Officer, FRAC, subj: After-action report, period 30 March–10 April 1972, 30 Apr. 1972.

7. Turley, *The Easter Offensive,* pp. 93–94.

8. Ngoc Thong, "Capture of Zoc Mieu Base," *Vietnam,* no. 169 (1972), p. 5.

9. Memo, 3d Inf. Div. HQ/G-3 to subordinate cmdrs., 1 Apr. 1972. English translation of General Giai's orders.

10. Battreall interview, p. 11.

11. Metcalf interview, quoted in Maj. Charles D. Melson and Lt. Col. Curtis G. Arnold, *U.S. Marines in Vietnam: The War That Would Not End, 1971–1973* (Washington, D.C.: U.S. Government Printing Office, 1991), p. 47.

12. The exchange between Metcalf and Turley comes from Turley, *The Easter Offensive,* p. 97.

13. FRAC G-3 daily journal, entry for 1 Apr. 1972; Turley, *The Easter Offensive,* p. 100.

Chapter 4. The Bridge at Dong Ha

1. Quoted in Melson and Arnold, *U.S. Marines in Vietnam,* p. 50.

2. Turley, *The Easter Offensive,* p. 121.

3. Ibid., pp. 127–128.

4. USMC Oral History Interview, Capt. John W. Ripley, no. 6032, 23 Apr. 72.

5. John G. Miller, *The Bridge at Dong Ha* (Annapolis, Md.: Naval Institute Press, 1989), p. 37.

6. Ibid., pp. 77–78.

7. Msg, Lt. Gen. Dolvin, CG XXIV Corps to Abrams, 29 June 1971, subj: M48A3 Tanks for ARVN.

8. Gen. Donn A. Starry, *Mounted Combat in Vietnam* (Washington, D.C.: Dept. of the Army, 1978), p. 204.

9. Armor Command Advisory Detachment, Combined Armor Bulletin no. 1, 22 Feb. 1972.

10. Battreall interview, p. 7.

11. Ibid., pp. 9–10.

12. Quoted in Melson and Arnold, *U.S. Marines in Vietnam*, p. 53.

13. Lt. Gen. William Potts, MACV J2, subj: The Tank Battles at Dong Ha, undated after-action summary; Rpt, Brig. Gen. Stan L. McClellan to Brig. Gen. George S. Patton, USA Armor School, Ft. Knox, 22 May 1972, subj: Activities of the 20th Tank Regt.; Maj. James E. Smock, "0-52-0," *Armor*, Oct. 1974.

14. Battreall interview, pp. 13–14.

15. Quoted in Melson and Arnold, *U.S. Marines in Vietnam*, p. 56; description of Sgt. Luom's heroism: Rpt, Ripley to Senior Marine Adviser, 14 Jan. 1973, subj: Evaluation of the NVA Easter 72 Offensive.

16. Battreall interview, p. 14; Turley, *The Easter Offensive*, p. 155.

17. 1st Armored Brigade after-action rpt, "Quang Trung 729/Defense of Quang Tri Province," undated, p. 5. Hereafter referred to as 1st Armored Bde. AAR.

18. FRAC Daily Journal, 2 Apr. 1972, entry for 0953 hours.

19. Maj. James E. Smock, Senior Adv. 20th Tanks, memorandum for the record, 19 Mar. 1976. This document, though written four years after the event, is more contemporary than almost all other documents regarding the incident. Ripley wrote a short report on 14 January 1973, but he only says that "instructions were received to destroy the Dong Ha bridge." He does not say he got them directly from Turley.

20. Maj. James E. Smock, memo for the record, 19 Mar. 1976; Interview, author with James Smock, Senior Adv., 20th Tanks, 20 Feb. 1991.

21. Quoted in Turley, *The Easter Offensive*, p. 155.

22. Smock, Memo for the Record, 19 Mar. 1976. For the most contemporary account of Ripley's actions, see USMC Oral History Interview, nos. 5089, 5090.

23. 1st Armored Bde. AAR, p. 5.

24. Battreall interview, p. 16; Skyspot order comes from I-DASC (Direct Air Support Center), air strikes submitted between 0600H and 2000H 2 Apr. 1972, 021610 Apr. 72. The mission on the Dong Ha Bridge came in at 1:24 P.M. and was given the call sign "Bibby."

25. Most accounts credit Combat Skyspots with destroying the bridge. 1st Armored Bde. AAR, p. 5; MACV 1972–73 Command History, vol. II, p. L-9; Adv Team 155 Daily Journal, entry for 1630H, 2 Apr. 1972; Rpt, Coastal Zone Intelligence Officer to COMNAVFORV, date unreadable. Although the U.S. Marines claim that the charges placed by Ripley demolished the bridge, Ripley himself stated

in his first interview that "almost anything could have detonated them [the charges]." Ripley interview, 23 Apr. 1972, p. 17.

26. There is a long paper trail "documenting" the destruction of the Dong Ha Bridge. However, all of it originates with Ripley himself and cannot be independently corroborated. The most contemporary documents, as well as interviews with U.S. Army armor advisers at the bridge, credit air strikes with detonating the explosives set by Ripley and Smock and demolishing the bridge. Events were further confused by two newspaper articles written after the fact by reporters (both former marines) who got their information secondhand (Holger Jensen, "Both Sides Dig in at Key River," *Washington Post,* 4 Apr. 1972; Peter Braestrup, "Destruction of Bridge Halted Communist Push at Dong Ha," *Washington Post,* 26 Apr. 1972). The attention made Ripley a hero, and the Silver Star medal recommended by Smock in April was upgraded by Secretary of the Navy John Warner in June to a Navy Cross, the nation's second-highest award for valor. Ripley's recognition, which was well deserved, diverted attention from the fact that others played equally important roles in the defense of Dong Ha and the destruction of the bridge: the Vietnamese marines held the ground south of the river, the 20th Tanks turned the North Vietnamese armor away, and U.S. air strikes finished off the bridge itself.

27. For the complete story of the Bat-21 rescue, see Dale Andradé, "SEALs' Shadowy Rescue," *Vietnam,* Dec. 1990, pp. 27–33; Darrel D. Whitcomb, The Rescue of Bat 21 (Annapolis, Md.: Naval Institute Press, 1998).

28. Melson and Arnold, *U.S. Marines in Vietnam,* p. 61.

29. Rpt, Maj. David Brookbank, USAF Air Liaison Officer, 3d ARVN Div, 31 July 1972, subj: VNAF TACS and the Fall of Quang Tri, p. 7.

30. Ibid.

Chapter 5. Surrender at Camp Carroll

1. Details of Lt. Col. Camper's experiences at Camp Carroll are from Memo for Senior Adv., MACV Adv. Team 155, 13 Apr. 1972, subj: Surrender at Camp Carroll; USMC Oral History Interview: William Camper, Senior Adv., 56th ARVN Regt., undated; Interview, author with William Camper, 20 Feb. 1990.

2. The message came in at 3:02 P.M. The 3d ARVN Division advisers remained unaware of the situation inside Camp Carroll until 3:20 P.M., when Lt. Col. Camper called back and requested evacuation by helicopter "because 56th Regt. commander is surrendering." MACV Adv. Team 155, Daily Staff Journal, 1520H 2 Apr. 72.

3. Turley, *The Easter Offensive,* pp. 145–146.

4. Accounts on Coachman 005 differ. According to Camper, the helicopter jettisoned its cargo short of Mai Loc when it ran into heavy antiaircraft fire. Turley writes that the ammunition had been delivered to Mai Loc before receiving word of the disaster at Camp Carroll. Turley, *The Easter Offensive,* p. 147.

5. The only account of this comes from a USMC artillery adviser at Mai Loc. His counterpart was apparently in contact with Bravo Battery just prior to the surrender. USMC Oral History Interview, Capt. George Philip, Adv. to the 1st Artillery Bn., VNMC.

6. Msg, Kroesen to Abrams, 16 Apr. 1972, subj: Combat Effectiveness, I Corps.

7. Adv. Team 155 Daily Journal, entry for 1806H 2 Apr. 1972.

8. Hanoi continued to insist that the National Liberation Front (NLF, or Viet Cong) was conducting the campaign, even though all the troops were from North Vietnam. Unofficial translation of broadcast made over Radio Hanoi on 3 Apr. 1972. Recorded by Maj. Gerald Wetzel and translated by Sgt. Vo Van Chi. Included in USMC Oral History Collection, Camper interview.

9. This is an interesting commentary, since it confirms that fewer than half of the 1,800 South Vietnamese in Camp Carroll actually surrendered. The rest managed to slip out of the base. However, the regiment was rendered combat ineffective. *Vietnam*, no. 169 (1972): 6.

10. Interview, author with Thomas W. Bowen, Deputy Senior Adv., FRAC, 13 Dec. 1989.

Chapter 6. Firebase Pedro

1. USMC Oral History Interview, Maj. Robert Cockell, Senior Adv., 1st Bn., VNMC, no. 5092, undated, p. 2.

2. Ibid., pp. 2–3.

3. Ibid., p. 5.

4. Melson and Arnold, *U.S. Marines in Vietnam*, p. 68; USMC Oral History Interview, Capt. Allen Nettleingham, Asst. Bde. Adviser, 258th VNMC Bde., undated, p. 17.

5. Rpt, Senior Adviser, 6th Infantry Bn. to Assistant Senior Marine Adv., 22 Apr. 1972, subj: Personal Evaluation and Comments on Easter 72 Offensive.

6. Ibid.; USMC Oral History Interview, Capt. William Wischmeyer, Asst. Adviser, 6th VNMC Bn., undated, p. 7.

7. Ibid., p. 8.

8. Ibid., p. 9.

9. Rpt, Senior Adv., 6th VNMC Bn. to Asst. Senior Marine Adv., subj: Personal Evaluation and Comments on Easter 72 Offensive, 22 Apr. 1972; Wischmeyer interview, p. 8; Cockell interview, p. 5; Nettleingham interview, p. 18.

10. Cockell interview, p. 6; Rpt, Senior Adviser 6th VNMC Bn. to Asst. Senior Marine Adv., 22 Apr. 1972, subj: Personal Evaluation and Comments on Easter 72 Offensive.

11. Quotation from Cockell interview, p. 6; it is not completely clear whether this figure is in addition to the tanks disabled by mines earlier in the day.

12. Melson and Arnold, *U.S. Marines in Vietnam*, p. 70.

13. Rpt, Senior Adv. 6th VNMC Bn. to Asst. Senior Marine Adv., subj: Personal Evaluation and Comments on Easter 72 Offensive, 22 Apr. 1972; Cockell interview, p. 7; Melson and Arnold, *U.S. Marines in Vietnam*, p. 70.

14. Rpt, Senior Adv. 6th VNMC Bn. to Asst. Senior Marine Adv., subj: Personal Evaluation and Comments on Easter 72 Offensive, 22 Apr. 1972.

15. MACV 1972–73 Command History, vol. II, p. L-11; "Hanoi's Heavy Defeat," *Washington Post*, 26 Apr. 1972.

16. Msg, Senior Adv. 3rd ARVN Div. to FRAC, date unreadable, subj: Significant Events, p. 2.

17. The official USMC history states that at Firebase Pedro the South Vietnamese marines "proved that individuals could indeed destroy enemy armor with their own antitank weapons." Melson and Arnold, *U.S. Marines in Vietnam,* p. 70. This was not the case. Capt. Wischmeyer, 6th VNMC Bn., said that "we sure as hell didn't hit any [tanks] with LAWs, at least that day." Maj. Cockell, 1st VNMC Bn., reported "I can't recollect that there were any tanks knocked out by LAWs." Wischmeyer interview, p. 10; Cockell interview, p. 6.

Chapter 7. Consolidation and Counteroffensive

1. Msg, Kroesen to Abrams, 10 Apr. 1972, subj: Enemy Situation.
2. Msg, Kroesen to Abrams, 16 Apr. 1972, subj: Combat Effectiveness, I Corps.
3. Msg, Kroesen to Abrams, 12 Apr. 1972, subj: Commander's Daily Evaluation; Msg, Kroesen to Abrams, 13 Apr. 1972, subj: Daily Commander's Evaluation.
4. Ibid.
5. Truong, *The Easter Offensive of 1972,* p. 36.
6. The 57th ARVN Regt., still weak from its retreat from the demilitarized zone earlier in the month, was tasked with maintaining the front along the Mieu Giang-Cua Viet River from the coast to a few miles short of the town of Cam Lo.

Quang Trung 729 order of battle (from north to south):
    1st Armored Brigade (including 20th Tanks)
    4th Ranger Group
    5th Ranger Group
    147th VNMC Brigade
    2d ARVN Regiment
    1st Ranger Group

7. Msg, Kroesen to Abrams, 16 Apr. 1972, subj: Combat Effectiveness, I Corps.
8. MACV 1972–73 Command History, vol. II, p. L-13; 3d ARVN Div. AAR.
9. Msg, Kroesen to Abrams, 13 Apr. 1972, subj: I Corps Offensive Operation.
10. Ibid.
11. Msg, Kroesen to Abrams, 15 Apr. 1972, subj: Daily Commander's Evaluation; Msg, Kroesen to Abrams, 19 Apr. 1972, subj: Daily Commander's Evaluation; 3d ARVN Div. AAR; MACV 1972–73 Command History, vol. II, p. L-13.
12. Msg, Kroesen to Abrams, 18 Apr. 1972, subj: Commander's Daily Evaluation; 3d ARVN Div. AAR.
13. MACV 1972–73 Command History, vol. II, p. L-13.
14. 3d ARVN Div. AAR; Msg, Kroesen to Abrams, 22 Apr. 1972, subj: Commander's Daily Evaluation.
15. Truong, *The Easter Offensive of 1972,* p. 255.
16 . Maj. James Joy, Memo for the Record, 3 May 1972, p. 2, USMC Oral History Collection.
17. Truong, *The Easter Offensive of 1972,* p. 33.
18. Joy, Memo for the Record, 3 May 1972, p. 3; Turley, *The Easter Offensive,* p. 257.

19. Truong, *The Easter Offensive of 1972*, p. 37.

20. Msg, Kroesen to Abrams, 22 Apr. 1972, subj: Commander's Daily Evaluation; Col. Donald J. Metcalf, "Why Did the Defense of Quang Tri Province, SVN Collapse?" (Carlisle Barracks, Penn.: USAWC Research Essay, 23 Oct. 1972), p. 18.

21. MACV 1972–73 Command History, vol. II p. L-13.

22. CHECO Rpt, "The NVA 1972 Invasion of Military Region I: Fall of Quang Tri and Defense of Hue," undated, pp. 21–22.

23. Msg, Kroesen to Abrams, 24 Apr. 1972, subj: TAC Air Support in MR1.

24. CHECO Rpt, "The NVA 1972 Invasion of MR1," p. 22.

25. Msg, Kroesen to Abrams, 24 Apr. 1972, subj: TAC Air Support in MR1.

Chapter 8. Things Fall Apart

1. Msg, Kroesen to Abrams, 27 Apr. 1972, subj: Daily Commander's Evaluation.

2. "The Miscalculation Is Mutual," *Newsweek*, 1 May 1972, p. 52.

3. Rpt, Maj. Kenneth Teel, Senior Adviser, 5th Ranger Gp to Senior Adv, III Corps Ranger Command, 4 Amy 1972, subj: Activities Report, 5th Ranger Group, 19 Apr.–4 May 1972, p. 2.

4. Rpt, Maj. Edward F. McGushin, Ranger Group Staff Adv., 11 May 1972, subj: Situation in Quang Tri, 27 Apr.–1 May 1972.

5. 1st Armored Bde. AAR, p. 13.

6. Ibid.

7. MACV 1972–73 Command History, vol. II, p. L-15.

8. Truong, *The Easter Offensive of 1972*, p. 41.

9. Msg, Kroesen to Abrams, 27 Apr. 1972, subj: Daily Commander's Evaluation.

10. Incident recounted from Camper interview with author, 3 Jan. 90; USMC Oral History Interview, Lt. Col. William C. Camper, Senior Adv., 56th ARVN Regt., 18 June 1983; Turley, *The Easter Offensive*, p. 263.

11. MACV 1972–73 Command History, vol. II, p. L-15.

12. Interview, author with Louis Wagner, Senior Adv., 1st Armored Bde., 25 Nov. 1991.

13. 3d ARVN Div AAR, Annex F, p. 11; Wagner interview, 25 Nov. 1991.

14. Joy, Memo for the Record, 3 May 1972, p, 6; 1st Armored Bde., AAR, p. 14; Melson and Arnold, *U.S. Marines in Vietnam*, p. 78.

15. 3d ARVN Div. AAR, p. 11.

16. 1st Armored Bde. AAR, pp. 14–15.

17. MACV Adv. Team 155 Daily Journal, 0535H 29 Apr. 1972.

18. 3d ARVN Div. AAR, p. 11.

19. One account claims that eleven NVA were killed, but the marines say it was twelve. 3d ARVN Div. AAR, p. 13; Arnold and Melson, *U.S. Marines in Vietnam*, p. 79.

20. Quang Tri Province report, April 1972, p. 2; MACV 1972–73 Command History, vol. II, p. L-16.

21. 3d ARVN Div. AAR, p. 13; Metcalf interview, 15 Sept. 1972, p. 5.

22. 3d ARVN Div. AAR, p. 14.

23. Turley, *The Easter Offensive*, pp. 286–287.

24. Melson and Arnold, *U.S. Marines in Vietnam,* pp. 79–80.

25. Turley, *The Easter Offensive,* p. 288.

26. Ibid., p. 290.

27. CHECO Rpt, "The NVA 1972 Invasion of Military Region I: Fall of Quang Tri and Defense of Hue," undated, p. 27.

28. Giai's instruction was presumably dated 29 April, though it is not specified on the actual order. English translation is included in 1st Armored Bde. AAR, Enclosure 4, "Special Message," p. 2.

29. Joy, Memo for the Record, 3 May 1972, pp. 11–12.

30. USMC Oral History Interview, Col. C. G. Goode and Maj. Wells, "Brigade 147's Withdrawal from Quang Tri City," undated, p. 13.

31. Turley, *The Easter Offensive,* pp. 278–279.

32. Truong, *The Easter Offensive of 1972,* pp. 44–45; Metcalf interview, p. 7.

33. Msg, Kroesen to Abrams, 30 Apr. 1972, subj: Daily Commander's Evaluation.

34. Msg, Kroesen to Abrams, 29 Apr. 1972, subj: Commander's Daily Evaluation.

Chapter 9. The Citadel

1. F. P. Serong, "The 1972 Easter Offensive," *Southeast Asian Perspectives,* summer 1974, p. 33.

2. Interview, Flowers with Metcalf, 15 Sept. 1972, p. 9.

3. Interview, author with Metcalf, 18 Dec. 1991.

4. UPI wire dispatch, by Arthur Higbee, 1 May 1972.

5. Msg, Kroesen to Abrams, 2 May 1972, subj: General Assessment: MR 1.

6. Interview, Flowers with Metcalf, p. 11.

7. Ibid., p. 13.

8. Melson and Arnold, *U.S. Marines in Vietnam,* p. 84.

9. Rpt, Maj. Brookbank, ALO 20th TASS, 3d ARVN Div., 31 July 1972, subj: VNAF TACS and the Fall of Quang Tri, p. 18.

10. CHECO Rpt, "The NVA 1972 Invasion," endnote no. 107; 3d ARVN Div. AAR, Annex F, p. 14.

11. 1st Armored Bde. AAR, p. 17.

12. Wagner interview.

13. 1st Armored Bde. AAR, p. 18.

14. Joy, Memo for the Record, 3 May 1972, p. 16.

15. Ibid., p. 20; Turley, *The Easter Offensive,* p. 296.

16. Col. C. J. Goode and Lt. Col. Wells, "Brigade 147's Withdrawal from Quang Tri City," p. 21.

17. Ibid., p. 24.

18. The rescued marines were Maj. James Joy, Maj. Emmett Huff, Maj. Charles Goode, Maj. Thomas Gnibus, Capt. Skip Kruger, and Capt. Skip Wells. "Statement of Maj. James Joy concerning the circumstances surrounding emergency helicopter extraction of Brigade 147 USMC Advisory Team at 0945, 2 May 1972"; Turley, *The Easter Offensive,* pp. 296–297; Melson and Arnold, *U.S. Marines in Vietnam,* p. 88.

19. Maj. Robert Sheridan, "observations and comments," 20 Mar. 90, p. 2.

20. Turley, *The Easter Offensive,* p. 298.

21. Ibid., p. 300.

22. Sheridan comments, p. 3.

23. Kroesen interview.

24. Msg, Abrams to Laird, 2 May 1972.

25. Kroesen interview.

26. "General Says Men Disobeyed Orders," *New York Times,* 4 May 1972.

27. Gen. Cao Van Vien, *Leadership,* Indochina Monograph series (Washington, D.C.: U.S. Army Center of Military History, 1981), p. 139.

28. Ibid. Lam's optimism was also reported by journalists in Hue during the early days of the offensive. "Saigon General Claims Drive from North Stopped," UPI report, 2 Apr. 1972.

29. Truong, *The Easter Offensive of 1972,* p. 50.

30. Vien, *Leadership,* p. 140; William C. Westmoreland, *A Soldier Reports* (New York: Doubleday, 1976), pp. 303, 488.

31. Truong, *The Easter Offensive of 1972,* p. 53.

32. Kroesen interview.

33. Msg, Kroesen to Abrams, 2 May 1972, subj: General Assessment: MR 1.

34. Vien, *Leadership,* p. 139.

35. Memo, Lt. Col. Craig A. Spence, Senior Adv. Ranger Command, to Director of Training and Special Assistant to COMUSMACV, 11 May 1972, subj: Activities Report of Ranger Units Operating in Northern MR 1 from 27 April to 9 May 1972.

36. 1st Armored Bde. AAR, Annex 1, Total Friendly Losses, 1 Apr.–2 May 1972; Msg, Kroesen to Abrams, 2 May 1972, subj: General Assessment: MR 1.

37. "Quang Tri's Fall Stuns South Vietnam," *Washington Post,* 3 May 1972.

38. Kroesen interview; Ltr, Kroesen to Truong, 19 Nov. 1972.

39. Ltr, Col. C. B. McCoid, Senior Adv. 3d ARVN Div, to MACV Advisory Team 155, 28 July 1972, subj: Comments of Lt. Gen. McCaffrey.

40. Emphasis in original. Ltr, Twitchell to Kroesen, undated, subj: Combat Readiness of the 3d ARVN Division as of March 1972.

41. Truong, *The Easter Offensive of 1972,* pp. 166, 62.

42. Msg, Abrams to Laird, 1 May 1972, subj: Personal Assessment of the Situation in RVN as of 1 May 1972.

43. Msg, Abrams to Laird, 26 Apr. 1972, subj: Personal Assessment of the Situation in RVN as of 26 Apr. 1972.

44. "U.S. General Says Situation in Quang Tri Is 'Tenuous,'" *New York Times,* 1 May 1972.

45. Maj. Gen. Frederick Kroesen, "Quang Tri, the Lost Province: An Identification of the Factors Which Culminated in the Loss of a Major Campaign to the Forces of North Vietnam in the Spring of 1972," Kroesen Papers, MHI, 16 Jan. 1974, pp. 19–20.

Chapter 10. The Imperial City

1. Msg, Kroesen to Abrams, 30 Apr. 1972, subj: Daily Commander's Evaluation.

2. MACV Adv. Team 3, 1st ARVN Div., Daily Staff Journal, 0600H 08 Mar.–0600H 09 Mar. 1972.

3. Senior Officer Debriefing Rpt for Period 23 May 71–21 May 72, Col. Hillman Dickinson, Senior Adv., 1st ARVN Div., p. 4.

4. 54th Regt. Adv. Team, Combat Operation After Action Report Lam Son 36/72, 15 Mar. 1972, p. 2.

5. Memo, Dickinson to FRAC, 26 Mar. 1972, subj: Analysis of TFA Sensor Data; 1st ARVN Div., Significant Activities Report, 15 Apr. 1972, p. 6.

6. MACV 1972–73 Command History, vol. I, p. 17; MACV 1972–73 Command History, vol. II, p. L-5.

7. 1st ARVN Div. Rpt, Summary Report of Operation Lam Son 45, 18 Mar. 1972.

8. Interview, author with Hillman Dickinson, SA 1st ARVN Div., 4 Feb. 1990.

9. North Vietnamese diary entries from "Diary of a Stalled Drive: Hanoi Soldier's Words Tell of Delays by VC," *Washington Post*, 25 Apr. 1972.

10. Quoted in James Walker Trullinger Jr., *Village at War: An Account of the Revolution in Vietnam* (New York: Longman, 1980), p. 178.

11. "Diary of a Stalled Drive: Hanoi Soldier's Words Tell of Delays by VC," *Washington Post*, 25 Apr. 1972.

12. "Renewal of Heavy Raids Linked to a Drive on Hue," *New York Times*, 5 May 1972.

13. "Troops Return to Hue Under Death Threat," *Washington Star*, 5 May 1972.

14. "New General Brings New Hope for Hue," *Baltimore Sun*, 16 May 1972; " 'It's Everyone for Himself' as Troops Rampage in Hue," *New York Times*, 4 May 1972.

15. Truong, *The Easter Offensive of 1972*, p. 53.

16. Lt. Col. G. H. Turley and Capt. M. R. Wells, "Easter Invasion 1972," *Marine Corps Gazette*, Mar. 1973, p. 26; Melson and Arnold, *U.S. Marines in Vietnam*, p. 92.

17. Truong, *The Easter Offensive of 1972*, p. 54.

18. MACV 1972–73 Command History, vol. II, p. L-21; "The Ground War Grinds On—South Vietnam's Prospects Now," *U.S. News & World Report*, 22 May 1972, p. 20.

19. Truong, *The Easter Offensive of 1972*, p. 61.

20. Msg, Kroesen to Abrams, 10 May 1972; Msg, Abrams to Kroesen, 11 May 1972.

21. Truong, *The Easter Offensive of 1972*, p. 62.

22. Ibid., p. 56.

23. "The Ground War Grinds On—South Vietnam's Prospects Now," p. 19.

24. Civilian quotations come from "City of Despair: In Hue, the People Talk of the War and Their Lives," *Wall Street Journal*, 18 Apr. 1972.

Chapter 11. The Slow March North

1. Melson and Arnold, *U.S. Marines in Vietnam*, p. 96.

2. MACV 1972–73 Command History, vol. II, p. L-23.

3. "Saigon Retakes Bastogne," *Baltimore Sun*, 16 May 1972.

4. Msg, Kroesen to Abrams, 18 May 1972, subj: Daily Commander's Evaluation.

5. MACV 1972–73 Command History, vol. II, p. L-23.

6. Melson and Arnold, *U.S. Marines in Vietnam*, p. 100.

7. Turley and Wells, "Easter Offensive 1972," p. 27.

8. Pham Gia Duc, The 325th Division [Su Doan 325] (Hanoi: People's Army Publishing House, 1986), p. 84.

9. FRAC/VNMC Operations, subj: Song Than 8-72, Appendix D, pp. 1–2; Msg, Cooksey to Abrams, 8 June 1972, subj: Offensive Operations in I Corps.

10. Melson and Arnold, *U.S. Marines in Vietnam*, p. 105.

11. Ibid.

12. Maj. Gen. Howard H. Cooksey, Resume of Career Service, CMH general officer records.

13. "We've Got 'Em Beaten Now," *Washington Star,* 28 May 1972.

14. Msg, Cooksey to Abrams, 17 June 1972, subj: Offensive Operations in I Corps.

15. Truong, *The Easter Offensive of 1972,* p. 66.

Chapter 12. Retaking Quang Tri

1. For more details on SOG and the deception mission, see Kenneth Conboy and Dale Andradé, *Spies and Commandos: How America Lost the Secret War in North Vietnam* (Lawrence: University Press of Kansas, 2000), pp. 261–264.

2. Unless otherwise noted, information on the South Vietnamese deception operation comes from a MACV intelligence summary entitled "Cover and Deception," 10 Sept. 1973.

3. Msg, Abrams to Kroesen, 21 May 1972, subj: Quang Tri Operations.

4. The deception plan for the Tonkin Gulf is mentioned in SPECAT Msg, Abrams to Adm. McCain, 2345Z 9 Feb. 1972; Deception operations in South Vietnam are in Msg, CINCPACFLT to CINCPAC, 0015Z 19 Apr. 1972; Msg, CINCPACFLT to COMSEVENTHFLT, 19 Apr. 1972, subj: Amphibious Operations; USMC plans to invade Vinh, Edwin W. Besch, "Blueprint for Victory," *Soldier of Fortune,* Jan. 1988, p. 92.

5. Msg, Cooksey to Abrams, 28 June 1972, subj: Commander's Daily Evaluation.

6. Msg, Brig. Gen. Hiestand, acting CG FRAC, to Abrams, 27 June 1972, subj: Commander's Daily Evaluation.

7. MACV 1972–73 Command History, vol. II, p. L-27; Senior Officer Debriefing Rpt, Maj. Gen. Howard H. Cooksey, 25 Jan. 1973, pp. 5–6. Hereafter referred to as Cooksey debrief.

8. Transcript of NBC Nightly News, 3 July 1972, p. 2.

9. MACV 1972–73 Command History, vol. II, figure L-7, p. L-26; Cooksey debrief, p. 26.

10. "Quang Tri Drive Is Still Stalled," *New York Times,* 9 July 1972; "Saigon Force Remains Bogged Down Near Quang Tri Under Heavy Shelling," *New York Times,* 19 July 1972.

11. "Vietnamese Begin to Question If War Was Worth Sacrifices," *Washington Post,* 12 Nov. 1991.

12. "South Viet Flank Pushed Back at Quang Tri City," *Chicago Tribune,* 13 July 1972.

13. "Reds Attack in North," *Baltimore Sun,* 13 July 1972.

14. Account is from "U.S. Halts Bombing of Quang Tri," *Philadelphia Inquirer,* 17 July 1972; "Battle for Quang Tri," *Newsweek,* 17 July 1972.

15. "U.S. Halts Bombing of Quang Tri," *Philadelphia Inquirer,* 17 July 1972.

16. North Vietnamese logistics were strained almost to the breaking point during July and August. According to one of Hanoi's official histories, air strikes and artillery were "continually hitting the rear of our campaign forces. We were beset with numerous difficulties in providing supplies (only 30 percent of the plan was fulfilled)." *History of the People's Army of Vietnam* [*Lich Su Quan Doi Nhan Dan Viet Nam*], p. 54.

17. "Saigon Tries to Rescue Beaten Units," *Baltimore Sun,* 18 July 1972; "Saigon Forces Inching Toward Quang Tri Center," *Baltimore Sun,* 19 July 1972.

18. "Hanoi Aiming Blow at Hue, U.S. Warns," *Washington Star,* 18 July 1972; "B-52s Hit Red Troops Moving South," *Baltimore Sun,* 17 July 1972; "Saigon Tries to Rescue Beaten Units," *Baltimore Sun,* 18 July 1972.

19. "Saigon Says Foe Fails to Thwart Drive on Quang Tri," *New York Times,* 20 July 1972.

20. "Hanoi Aiming Blows at Hue, U.S. Warns," *Washington Star,* 18 July 1972; "Saigon Reports 3—Hour Battle Northeast of Quangtri," *New York Times,* 15 July 1972.

21. Msg, Gen. Weyand to CINCPAC, 23 July 1972, subj: RVNAF Plans in Northern I Corps; Truong, *The Easter Offensive of 1972,* p. 67.

22. Melson and Arnold, *U.S. Marines in Vietnam,* p. 110.

23. Senior Officer Debriefing Report, Col. J. W. Dorsey, Senior Marine Adviser, FRAC, 23 Jan. 1973.

24. Melson and Arnold, *U.S. Marines in Vietnam,* p. 106.

25. USMC Oral History Interview, Lt. Col. Gerald Turley, undated.

26. Melson and Arnold, *U.S. Marines in Vietnam,* p. 117.

27. Ibid., p. 119.

28. Msg, Senior Marine Adviser to FRAC, 28 July 1972, subj: Operations Summary from 271800H to 281800H July 1972; Memo, Senior Marine Adviser to Senior Brigade Advisers, 25 July 1972, subj: Adviser's Planning Guidance in Preparation for the Recapture of Quang Tri City, South Vietnam.

29. Rpt, FRAC VNMC Operations, Appendix E, Bde. 258, p. 4.

30. Duc, *The 325th Division* [*Su Doan 325*], vol. 2, p. 95; *History of the People's Army* [*Lich Su Quan Doi Nhan Dan*], p. 64.

31. Artillery figures are from MACV 1972–73 Command History, vol. II, p. L-31; quotation is from Lt. Col. Richard B. Rothwell, "Leadership and Tactical Reflections on the Battle for Quang Tri," *Marine Corps Gazette,* Sept. 1979, p. 39.

32. Rothwell, "Leadership and Tactical Reflections on the Battle for Quang Tri," p. 38.

33. Duc, *The 325th Division* [*Su Doan 325*], vol. 2, pp. 95–96.

34. Turley and Wells, "Easter Invasion, 1972," p. 29; Melson and Arnold, *U.S. Marines in Vietnam,* p. 123.

35. Rothwell, "Leadership and Practical Reflections on the Battle for Quang Tri," p. 42.

36. *History of the People's Army* [*Lich Su Quan Doi Nhan Dan*], p. 64.

37. Turley and Wells, "Easter Invasion 1972," p. 29; Melson and Arnold, *U.S. Marines in Vietnam*, p. 126.

38. Melson and Arnold, *U.S. Marines in Vietnam*, p. 126.

39. "Quang Tri: An Immortal Epic," *Vietnam*, no. 172 (1972): 2–4.

40. *History of the People's Army* [*Lich Su Quan Doi Nhan Dan*], p. 65.

41. Cooksey debrief, p. 12.

42. Truong, *The Easter Offensive of 1972*, p. 75.

Chapter 13. Setting the Stage

1. "Troops at Border Outpost Unruffled by Predictions of Early Enemy Drive," *New York Times*, 2 Feb. 1972.

2. "North Viet Traffic Roars by Post at Lonely Ben Het," *Christian Science Monitor*, 3 May 1972.

3. "America's Civilian Warrior in an Era of Vietnamization," *Washington Post*, 8 June 1972.

4. Ibid.

5. Jack Anderson, "Vietnam Heroin and Lt. Gen. Dzu," *Washington Post*, 2 July 1972; Interview, author with George Wear, Deputy Senior Adv., SRAG, 14 Dec. 1989.

6. Jeffrey Clarke, *U.S. Army in Vietnam: Advice and Support, The Final Years, 1965–1973* (Washington, D.C.: U.S. Government Printing Office, 1988), p. 477.

Chapter 14. Intelligence Picture

1. Rpt, G-2 SRAG, 7–12 Jan. 1972, subj: Weekly Intelligence Estimate.

2. Msg, Vann to Abrams, 26 Jan. 1972, subj: Enemy tank sightings in western Kontum Province; MACV 1972–73 Command History, vol. II, p. K-1.

3. NVA units in western Kontum Province consisted of two regiments in the 2d NVA Division, three regiments (twelve maneuver battalions) in the 320th NVA Division, plus four regiments attached to the B-3 Front. The "Yellow Star" 3d NVA Division in Binh Dinh Province consisted of three regiments (six maneuver battalions). Army Activities Rpt, Southeast Asia, 26 Apr. 1972.

4. Msg, Vann to Abrams, 28 Mar. 1972, subj: Battlefield Situation in the Kontum Area. As fighting intensified in Quang Tri Province, the two airborne brigades were ordered north to I Corps; the 3d Airborne Brigade went first, then the 2d Airborne Brigade. They were replaced in mid-April by the 6th Ranger Group and later the 2d Ranger Command and two squadrons from an armored cavalry brigade. Army Activities Rpt, Southeast Asia, 26 Apr. 72 and 10 May 1972; Davidson, *Vietnam at War*, pp. 689–690.

5. Project CHECO Southeast Asia Rpt, "Kontum: Battle for the Central Highlands, 30 March–10 June 1972," 27 Oct. 1972, p. 2.

6. Memo, Vann to Abrams, 7 Feb. 1972, subj: Daily Commander's Evaluation.

7. MACV 1972–73 Command History, vol. II, pp. K-4–K-5.

8. Msg, Vann to Brig. Gen. Forrester, Dir OPD DA Pentagon WD.C., 23 Mar. 1972.

9. Vann's statement to the press is in "Captured North Vietnamese Soldier," *New York Times*, 17 Feb. 1972. Laird's comment is from Msg, OCJCS to DEPCO-MUSMACV, 6 Jan. 1972, subj: Comments by John Vann.

10. MACV 1972–73 Command History, vol. II, p. K-4.

11. Wear interview.

12. Army Activities Rpt, Southeast Asia, 12 and 24 Apr. 1972.

13. *History of the Central Highlands People's Armed Forces in the Anti-U.S. War of Resistance for National Salvation* [*Luc Luong Vu Trang Nhan Dan Tay Nguyen Khang Chien Chong My Cuu Nuoc*] (Hanoi: Nha Xuat Ban Quan Doi Nhan Dan, 1980), p. 152.

14. MACV 1972–73 Command History, vol. II, p. K-5; Memo, Vann to Abrams, 3 Apr. 1972, subj: Daily Commander's Evaluation; Msg, Vann to Abrams, 28 Mar. 1972, subj: Battlefield Situation in the Kontum Area.

15. Msg, Vann to Abrams, 19 Mar. 1972, subj: Daily Commander's Evaluation.

16. Msg, Vann to Abrams, 1 Apr. 1972, subj: Retention of Aviation Assistance in II Corps.

17. MACV 1972–73 Command History, vol. II, p. K-5.

18. Msg, SRAG to MACV, 9 Apr. 1972, subj: Daily Commander's Evaluation.

19. Msg, Vann to Abrams, 7 Apr. 1972, subj: Daily Commander's Evaluation.

Chapter 15. Opening Shots

1. This figure is based on Hamlet Evaluation Survey reports, which were of dubious accuracy. However, any admission by Saigon that an area was completely under the control of the communists was a significant indicator of the true situation. Staff Rpt, U.S. Senate Committee on Foreign Relations, *Vietnam: May 1972*, 92d Cong., 2d sess., 29 June 1972 (Washington, D.C.: U.S. Government Printing Office, 1972), p. 14.

2. Memo, Binh Dinh Province senior adviser to J/3 DOCSA (OJCS) et al., 4 July 1972, subj: II Corps MACCORDS Provincial Reports; *Christian Science Monitor*, 3 July 1972.

3. Dzu moved the 1st Bn., 41st ARVN Regt. from Binh Dinh to the Central Highlands. Msg, Vann to Abrams, 5 Apr. 1972, subj: Daily Commander's Evaluation; Msg, Wear to Abrams, 6 Apr. 1972, subj: Daily Commander's Evaluation.

4. Msg, Vann to Abrams, 7 Apr. 1972, subj: Daily Commander's Evaluation.

5. Neil Sheehan, *A Bright Shining Lie: John Paul Vann and America in Vietnam* (New York: Random House, 1988), p. 760; Interview, author with David Schorr, Senior Adv., 40th ARVN Regt., 7 Mar. 1990.

6. Viet Cong units were identified as the C1, C2, C3, and C4 Sapper Companies. Interview, author with Gary Hacker, DSA Hoai Nhon District; "The Fall of Hoai Nhon," 18 May 1972, U.S. Army Center of Military History Oral History Collection.

7. "The North Vietnamese Come to Hoai An," *Time*, 8 May 1972, p. 29; Douglas Pike, "Binh Dinh: The Anatomy of a Province," Oct. 1972.

8. Ibid.

9. Sheehan, *A Bright Shining Lie*, p. 760.

10. Schorr interview, 7 Mar. 1990.

11. Sheehan, *A Bright Shining Lie*, p. 761. Timing and circumstances are confirmed in Msg, Vann to Abrams, 20 Apr. 1972, subj: Daily Commander's Evaluation.

12. Msg, Vann to Abrams, 4 May 1972, subj: Daily Commander's Evaluation.

13. Binh Dinh Province Rpt, MACCORDS 31.01 R3, PSA to MACCORDS, 4 May 1972.

14. *History of the Central Highlands People's Armed Forces* [*Luc Luong Vu Trang Nhan Dan Tay Nguyen Khang Chien Chong My Cuu Nuoc*], p. 156.

Chapter 16. Closing In on the Highlands

1. Msg, Vann to Abrams, 27 Mar. 72, subj: Daily Commander's Evaluation.

2. Msg, Vann to Abrams, 4 Apr. 1972, subj: Daily Commander's Evaluation. Although the North Vietnamese claimed that Kontum was a diversion, they committed as many troops to it as they did the other two corps. "Vietnam: The Anti-U.S. Resistance War for National Salvation, 1954–1975: Military Events," FBIS Translation, 3 June 1982, pp. 146–148.

3. Sheehan, *A Bright Shining Lie*, pp. 756–757; Interview, author with Maj. Peter Kama, Airborne Div. Adv., 3 May 1990.

4. Sheehan, *A Bright Shining Lie*, pp. 757–758.

5. Memo, Vann to "My Friends," 12 Apr. 1972.

6. Truong, *The Easter Offensive of 1972*, p. 87; MACV 1972–73 Command History, vol. II, p. K-6.

7. Sheehan, *A Bright Shining Lie*, p. 766.

8. Ibid., p. 765; Ltr, Vann to Abrams, 19 Feb. 1972. Dzu was also in a quandary because Dat was the most senior colonel in the corps. Dzu's first choice, Col. Le Minh Dao, was junior to Dat, and it was feared that if Dat were only a deputy division commander, he would use his power to impede Col. Dao from doing his job.

9. Wear interview.

10. MACV 1972–73 Command History, vol. II, p. K-6; Msg, Vann to Abrams, 15 Apr. 1972, subj: Daily Commander's Evaluation; Msg, Wear to Abrams, 16 Apr. 1972, subj: Daily Commander's Evaluation; Msg, Col. Pizzi, SRAG Chief of Staff, to Abrams, 22 Apr. 1972, subj: Daily Commander's Evaluation.

11. "Settling In for the Third Indochina War," *Time*, 8 May 1972, p. 29.

12. Msg, Vann to Abrams, 20 Mar. 1972, subj: Proposed Province Chief Changes and Other Matters.

13. Msg, Vann to Abrams, 20 Apr. 1972, subj: Daily Commander's Evaluation.

14. Msg, Vann to Abrams, 11 Apr. 1972, subj: Daily Commander's Evaluation; Msg, Vann to Abrams, 21 Apr. 1972, subj: Daily Commander's Evaluation.

15. Sagger account taken from MACV 1972–73 Command History, vol. II, pp. K-6, K-7; Sheehan, *A Bright Shining Lie*, p. 767.

16. Sheehan writes that the tanks "had orders to disregard the district headquarters," but district adviser reports and the 22d DTOC After-Action Report make no mention of this. Sheehan, *A Bright Shining Lie*, p. 768.

17. Interview, author with John Hill, Deputy Senior Adv., SRAG, 1 Feb. 1990.

18. *History of the Central Highland's People's Armed Forces* [*Luc Luong Vu Trang Nhan Dan Tay Nguyen Khang Chien Chong My Cuu Nuoc*], p. 159.

19. MACV 1972–73 Command History, vol. II, p. K-8.

20. *History of the Central Highlands People's Army* [*Luc Luong Vu Trang Nhan Dan Tay Nguyen Khang Chien Chong My Cuu Nuoc*], p. 159.

21. Yonan's remains were returned to the United States in 1984 and are buried at West Point.

22. Sheehan, *A Bright Shining Lie*, p. 771; Msg, Vann to Brig. Gen. Forrester, Dir. OPD DA Pentagon, 23 Mar. 1972.

23. "5 U.S. Soldiers Tell of Jungle Survival," *New York Times*, 8 May 1972.

24. Msg, Vann to Brig. Gen. Eugene P. Forrester, 6 May 1972, subj: CPT Dolph A. Todd, IN, 548-72-2085.

25. Msg, Vann to Abrams, 26 Apr. 1972, subj: Info, Maj. Gen. William E. Potts, ACofS J-2 MACV.

26. MACV 1972–73 Command History, vol. II, p. K-6.

27. Truong, *The Easter Offensive of 1972*, p. 90.

28. Wear interview, 14 Dec. 89.

Chapter 17. Designing a Defense

1. *History of the Central Highlands People's Armed Forces* [*Luc Luong Vu Trang Nhan Dan Tay Nguyen Khang Chien Chong My Cuu Nuoc*], p. 162.

2. Msg, Vann to Abrams, 26 Apr. 1972, subj: Daily Commander's Evaluation.

3. Sheehan, *A Bright Shining Lie*, p. 781; Interview, author with John Finch, 23d ARVN Div. G-2 Adv., 20 Jan. 1990.

4. Sheehan, *A Bright Shining Lie*, p. 779.

5. MACV 1972–73 Command History, vol. II, p. K-12.

6. "Advisers: Ready To Stay, Die," *Pacific Stars & Stripes*, 2 May 1972.

7. Msg, Vann to Abrams, 4 May 1972, subj: Daily Commander's Evaluation.

8. Msg, Vann to Abrams, 29 Apr. 1972, subj: Daily Commander's Evaluation.

9. For details on the USAF role in II Corps, see *Airpower and the 1972 Spring Invasion*, USAF Southeast Asia Monograph Series, vol. 2, monograph 3 (Washington, D.C.: U.S. Government Printing Office, undated), pp. 59–76.

10. Sheehan, *A Bright Shining Lie*, p. 781.

11. Msg, Vann to Abrams, 2 May 1972, subj: Contingency Evacuation Plans.

12. Material on ROK participation in Vietnam taken from Dale Andradé, "Tigers, Blue Dragons and White Horses," *Vietnam*, Dec. 1989, pp. 47–53.

13. Lt. Gen. Stanley R. Larsen and Brig. Gen. James L. Collins Jr., *Allied Participation in Vietnam* (Washington, D.C.: Government Printing Office, 1975), p. 153.

14. Stanton, *Vietnam Order of Battle*, p. 333.

15. Msg, Vann to Abrams, 14 Apr. 1972, subj: Daily Commander's Evaluation.

16. Msg, Vann to Abrams, 15 Apr. 1972, subj: Daily Commander's Evaluation.

17. Memo, Abrams to Laird, 24 Apr. 1972, subj: Personal Assessment of the Situation in RVN as of 24 April 1972.

18. Ltr, Vann to Maj. Gen. Kang Won Chae, 16 Apr. 1972.

19. Msg, Wear to Abrams, 17 Apr. 1972, subj: Daily Commander's Evaluation.

20. Interview, author with Thomas McKenna, Senior Adv., 44th ARVN Regt., 12 Dec. 1989.

21. Msg, Vann to Abrams, 18 Apr. 1972, subj: An Khe Pass Operations and Related Matters.

22. Msg, Vann to Abrams, 20 Apr. 1972, subj: Daily Commander's Evaluation; Msg, Vann to Abrams, 26 Apr. 1972, subj: Daily Commander's Evaluation.

23. Msg, Hill to Abrams, 28 Apr. 1972, subj: Daily Commander's Evaluation.

Chapter 18. Crisis at Kontum

1. *Airpower and the 1972 Spring Invasion*, pp. 59–67; Sheehan, *A Bright Shining Lie*, pp. 781–782.

2. Sheehan, *A Bright Shining Lie*, p. 783.

3. "America's Civilian Warrior in an Era of Vietnamization," *Washington Post*, 8 June 1972.

4. Msg, Vann to Abrams, 9 Apr. 1972, subj: Daily Commander's Evaluation.

5. Gerald C. Hickey, *Free in the Forest: Ethnohistory of the Vietnamese Central Highlands, 1954–1976* (New Haven, Conn.: Yale University Press, 1982), p. 242.

6. Msg, Vann to Abrams, 12 May 1972, subj: Authority to deploy TOW Crews to Kontum Province. Although most of the document discusses TOW employment, it also details the decision to defend Kontum.

7. MACV 1972–73 Command History, vol. II, p. K-13.

8. SRAG G-3 Daily Journal, 7 May 1972.

9. Msg, Vann to Abrams, 7 May 1972, subj: Daily Commander's Evaluation.

10. MACV 1972–73 Command History, vol. II, p. K-14.

11. Msg, Vann to Abrams, 9 May 1972, subj: Daily Commander's Evaluation.

12. John Prados, "The Year of the Rat: Vietnam, 1972," *Strategy & Tactics*, Nov. 1972, p. 17.

13. Hickey, *Free in the Forest*, p. 238.

14. Msg, Vann to Abrams, 7 May 1972, subj: Daily Commander's Evaluation.

15. "Thousands Flee Kontum in Panic as Enemy Nears," *New York Times*, 1 May 1972.

16. "Kontum: They Say Get Out," *Pacific Stars & Stripes*, 9 May 1972.

17. Msg, Vann to Abrams, 3 May 1972, subj: Daily Commander's Evaluation.

Chapter 19. Tightening the Noose

1. Msg, Vann to Hollingsworth, 3 May 1972.

2. Msg, Vann to Abrams, 7 May 1972.

3. "America's Civilian Warrior in an Era of Vietnamization," *Washington Post*, 8 June 1972.

4. Msg, Vann to Abrams, 11 May 1972, subj: Daily Commander's Evaluation.

5. Truong, *The Easter Offensive of 1972*, p. 95.

6. Interview, author with John Truby, Senior Adv., 23d ARVN Div., 13 Dec. 1989.

7. *History of the Central Highlands People's Armed Forces* [*Luc Luong Vu Trang Nhan Dan Tay Nguyen Khang Chien Chong My Cuu Nuoc*], pp. 163–164.

8. MACV 1972–73 Command History, vol. II, p. K-15.

9. TOW Performance Report, Table 3-1, 13 June 1972, subj: TOW Firings (As of 1200 hrs, 12 June 72); Msg, Vann to Abrams, 7 May 1972, subj: SRAG Experience with the TOW Weapons System. TOW gunships had actually appeared on the II Corps battlefield before the attack on Kontum. They had provided support against PT-76 light tanks during the siege of Ben Het ranger camp, although they were not very effective because the TOW crews had only just arrived and were not yet up to speed. In at least one case a TOW ship got into trouble when both its gunship escorts were hit by antiaircraft fire. One Cobra went down. A search-and-rescue helicopter was unable to locate the two-man crew on the ground. TOW Performance Report, Mission Summary Form, 9 May 1972; Msg, Vann to Abrams, 12 May 1972, subj: Authority to Deploy TOW Crews to Kontum Province.

10. Truby interview.

11. MACV 1972–73 Command History, vol. II, p. K-15.

12. TOW Crew Performance, Section III, undated, subj: Summary of Results.

13. McKenna interview.

14. MACV 1972–73 Command History, vol. II, p. K-18; McKenna interview; Interview, author with Richard O. Perry, Senior Adv., 53d ARVN Regt., 20 Jan. 1990.

Chapter 20. Regrouping

1. Truong, *The Easter Offensive of 1972*, p. 99; Truby interview.

2. Monthly province rpt, Kontum Province, 31 May 1972.

3. McKenna interview.

4. Truby interview.

5. Msg, Vann to Abrams, 18 May 1972, subj: Daily Commander's Evaluation; MACV 1972–73 Command History, vol. II, p. K-19.

6. SRAG S-2, S-3 Daily Journal, 19 May 1972.

7. Truong, *The Easter Offensive of 1972*, p. 99.

8. Perry interview.

9. MACV 1972–73 Command History, vol. II, p. K-19.

10. Msg, Vann to Abrams, 18 May 1972, subj: II Corps Operation to Open Highway 14 at the Kontum Pass.

11. McKenna interview.

12. Msg, Vann to Abrams, 22 May 1972, subj: Daily Commander's Evaluation.

13. MACV 1972–73 Command History, vol. II, p. K-20.

14. Msg, Vann to Abrams, 21 May 1972, subj: Daily Commander's Evaluation.

Chapter 21. ARVN on the Offensive

1. Msg, Vann to Abrams, 20 May 1972, subj: II Corps Operation to Open Highway 14 at the Kontum Pass.

2. Msg, Vann to Abrams, 25 May 1972, subj: Daily Commander's Evaluation; SRAG G-2/G-3 Daily Journal, 23 May 1972.

3. MACV 1972–73 Command History, vol. II, p. K-22; Interview, author with John Finch, S-2 Adv, 23d ARVN Div, 23 Jan. 1990.

4. MACV 1972–73 Command History, Jan. 1972–Mar. 1973, vol. II, p. K-22.

5. McKenna interview.

6. Msg, Vann to Abrams, 26 May 1972, subj: Daily Commander's Evaluation; 23d ARVN Div G-2/G-3 Daily Journals for 25–26 May 1972.

7. McKenna interview.

8. Finch interview; Matt Franjola, "Local GI, Newsman in a Jam," UPI wire story, 9 June 1972.

9. Msg, Vann to Abrams, 27 May 1972, subj: Daily Commander's Evaluation.

10. MACV 1972–73 Command History, vol. II, p. K-23.

11. Msg, Vann to Abrams, 28 May 1972, subj: Daily Commander's Evaluation.

12. Finch interview.

13. MACV 1972–73 Command History, vol. II, p. K-24.

14. *Airpower and the 1972 Spring Offensive*, pp. 70–71.

15. Msg, Vann to Abrams, 30 May 1972, subj: Daily Commander's Evaluation.

16. MACDI Rpt, subj: PW Interrogation, 4 June 1972.

17. Msg, Vann to Abrams, 31 May 1972, subj: Daily Commander's Evaluation.

Chapter 22. Mopping Up

1. Interview, author with Donald Stovall, Senior Adv., 41st ARVN Regt., 25 Jan. 1990. The rumor that the 40th ARVN Regiment had arranged some sort of a deal with the North Vietnamese cannot be substantiated. However, the Binh Dinh Province report for May 1972 noted that the South Vietnamese did "march to the sea" from LZ English and "moved by LST to Qui Nhon." Province Rpt, Binh Dinh Province, MACCORDS 31.01 R3, report for May 1972, 2 June 1972.

2. Msg, Vann to Abrams, 2 June 1972, subj: Daily Commander's Evaluation.

3. Msg, SRAG to MACV, 7 June 1972, subj: Daily Commander's Evaluation.

4. Stovall interview, 25 Jan. 1990; "Adviser Praised in Phu My Defense," *Pacific Stars & Stripes*, 17 July 1972.

5. Msg, Vann to Abrams, 8 June 1972, subj: Daily Commander's Evaluation.

6. Msg, Brig Gen Healy to Abrams, 13 June 1972, subj: Daily Commander's Evaluation.

7. The 22d ARVN Division was split up and moved during the offensive. In early April the division consisted of the 2d Armored Brigade and the 40th, 41st, and 44th ARVN Regiments (a total of 10 infantry battalions and two cavalry squadrons) and was stationed in Ba Gi, Binh Dinh Province. During the early days of the offensive, the armor units and the 44th ARVN Regiment were separated and sent to the 23d ARVN Division, while the 47th ARVN Regiment was taken from the 23d ARVN Division and attached to the 22d ARVN Division. At the height of the fighting the 42d and 47th ARVN Regiments (seven infantry battalions) were stationed in Pleiku, while the 40th and 41st ARVN Regiments (five infantry battalions) went to English and Crystal.

8. Army Activities Rpt, Southeast Asia, 19 July 1972, p. 38; Binh Dinh Province Rpt, MACCORDS 31.01 R3, 3 Aug. 1972.

9. Msg, Vann to Abrams, 9 June 1972, subj: Daily Commander's Evaluation.

10. Technical Report of U.S. Army Aircraft Accident, witness statement of Captain Richard M. Schwartz, 12 June 1972.

11. SRAG G-3 Daily Journal, 09 0001H–09 2400H June 72; Technical Report of U.S. Army Aircraft Accident, Part IV—Narrative; Witness statement of Capt. Richard Barnes, 14 June 1972; Msg, Maj. Gen. MacKinnon, CG 1st Aviation Bde., to Abrams, 19 June 1972, subj: Aircraft Accident.

12. Msg, George D. Jacobson, Asst. DEPCORDS, to Vann, 24 Apr. 1972.

13. Msg, COMUSMACV to CG SRAG, 10 June 1972, subj: Second Regional Assistance Command.

14. *History of the Central Highlands People's Armed Forces [Luc Luong Vu Trang Nhan Dan Tay Nguyen Khang Chien Chong My Cuu Nuoc]*, p.165.

15. Truong, *The Easter Offensive of 1972*, pp. 104–105.

16. Msg, Vann to Abrams, 8 June 1972, subj: Daily Commander's Evaluation.

17. Msg, Healy to Abrams, 18 June 1972, subj: Daily Commander's Evaluation; Project CHECO Rpt, "Kontum: Battle for the Central Highlands, 30 March–10 June 1972," 27 Oct. 1972, p. 87.

18. Truong, *The Easter Offensive of 1972*, p. 105.

19. Gen. Hoang Minh Thao, "Planning a Battle," *Tap Chi Doi Nanh Dan*, no. 5, May 1983, pp. 42–51. Translated by the U.S. State Dept.

20. *Pacific Stars & Stripes*, 23 July 1972; Project CHECO Rpt, "Kontum," pp. 88–89.

Chapter 23. Hell in a Very Insignificant Place

1. Maj. Gen. James Hollingsworth, "Communist Invasion in Military Region 3: Nguyen Hue Campaign," undated draft manuscript, p. 7; Army Activities Rpt, Southeast Asia, 12 Apr. 1972, p. 42.

2. *The Nguyen Hue Offensive Campaign (1972) [Chien Dich Tien Cong Nguyen Hue (1972)]* (Hanoi: Vietnam Institute for Military History, Ministry of Defense, 1988), p. 6.

3. "Vietnam: The Anti-U.S. Resistance War for National Salvation 1954–1975: Military Events," FBIS translation JPRS 80968, 3 June 1982, pp. 143–144.

4. *History of the People's Army of Vietnam [Lich Su Quan Doi Nhan Dan Viet Nam]* (Hanoi: Nha Xuat Ban Quan Doi Nhan Dan, 1990)], vol. 2, bk. 2, ch. 4, pp. 49–50.

5. Truong believed that the intensity of the North Vietnamese offensive in III Corps would be increased if initial attacks were successful, decreased if they were not. "This flexibility was most likely what he had in mind when he attacked Loc Ninh on 2 April." Truong, *The Easter Offensive in 1972*, p. 106.

6. "An Loc Will Test the Mettle of Vietnamization," *Washington News*, 15 Apr. 1972.

7. Stanton, *Vietnam Order of Battle*, pp. 375, 380–381.

8. ARVN order of battle for III Corps in the opening days of the Easter Offen-

sive is as follows: 5th ARVN Div. consisted of the 7th, 8th, 9th, and 52d Regt. The 1st Abn. Bde. and the 3d Ranger Gp. were independent units but were opcon to the 5th ARVN Div. Army Activities Rpt, Southeast Asia, 12 Apr. 1972, p. 42.

9. The withdrawal was phased over the last half of 1971. In January 1972, Minh made the final withdrawal from the Krek area, with orders that "ARVN forces will deploy in a mobile, offensive posture in strength along the Cambodian border." Memo, Abrams to CINCPAC, 8 Jan. 1972, subj: Cambodia Situation Report—Personal Appraisal.

10. Rpt, CINCPAC to POLAD, Emb Saigon, "Command Histories and Historical Sketches of RVNAF Divisions," Part I, 6 Feb. 1973; "Debriefing Report of BG William R. Desobry, August 1965–January 1968," 1 Jan. 1968, pp. 2, 5–6.

11. "Communist Invasion in Military Region 3: Nguyen Hue Offensive, Friendly and Enemy Actions from Sept. 1971 through March 1972," undated and unsigned; Truong, *The Easter Offensive of 1972*, p. 108; Interview, author with Joseph Newman, Dep. CO, 12th Aviation Gp., 3 Feb. 1990.

12. As was generally the case with "Viet Cong" divisions at this time, the 5th and 9th VC Divs. were made up primarily of NVA troops. The 5th VC Div. consisted of the E6 and 174th Regts., both NVA units. The 9th VC Div. was made from the 95C NVA Regt. and the 271st and 272d VC Regts. Army Activities Rpt, Southeast Asia, 12 Apr. 1972, p. 43.

13. *The Nguyen Hue Offensive Campaign [Chien Dich Tien Cong Nguyen Hue]*, pp. 9–10.

14. Clarke, *Advice and Support*, p. 451; also Appendix C.

15. Journal of Maj. Peter Bentsen, TRAC G-3, 18 Apr. 1972, U.S. Army Center of Military History Oral History Collection.

16. *Christian Science Monitor*, 15 Apr. 1972; "In Furious Battle," *Newsweek*, 24 Apr. 1972, p. 32.

17. Journal of Maj. John Cash, Apr. 1972, U.S. Army Center of Military History Oral History Collection.

18. TRAC Periodical Intelligence Report (Perintrep), no. 3-72, 1 Feb. 1972, p. 12.

19. TRAC Perintrep no. 4-72, 14 Feb. 1972, p. 13.

20. AFRVN/JGS/G-2, Exploitation of VC captured documents no. 062/22, "Information related to the 272d Regt and HQ/9th Div will move from Cambodia to north of Binh Long Province," 27 Mar. 1972; DOD Intelligence Information Rpt, "The NGUYEN HUE Campaign, the 9th VC Div and the 2d Infiltration Group," PW Interrogation Report, 8 Apr. 1972.

21. Hollingsworth, "Communist Invasion in Military Region 3: The Nguyen Hue Offensive," p. 5.

22. *The 9th Division [Su Doan 9]* (Hanoi: Nha Xuat Ban Quan Doi Nhan Dan, 1990), p. 152.

23. COSVN Directive No. 43; Hollingsworth, "Communist Invasion in Military Region 3: The Nguyen Hue Offensive," p. 110.

24. "The Battle for An Loc," Hollingsworth interview transcript given to editors of *Air Force* magazine, 20 July 1972; Interview, author with James Hollingsworth, Senior Adv., TRAC, 6 Nov. 1989.

25. Hollingsworth interview transcript, p. 112; Combat After Action Report,

Binh Long Province, 1972, HQ 5th ARVN Div. Combat Assistance Team, Advisory Team 70, TRAC, 20 July 1972. Hereafter referred to as 5th ARVN Div. AAR.

26. MACV 1972–73 Command History, vol. II, p. J-2. See also *The Nguyen Hue Offensive Campaign* [*Chien Dich Tien Cong Nguyen Hue*], pp. 34–38.

27. Msg, Hollingsworth to Abrams, 13 Mar. 1972, subj: Daily Commander's Evaluation; 5th ARVN Div. AAR, Appendix 4 (Task Force 52) to Annex D (5th ARVN Div).

28. Order of battle for Task Force 52:

UNITS	AUTHORIZED STRENGTH
HQ 52d Regt. (–)	78
2-52	309
1-48	420
I&R Co., 52d Regt.	60
C Bty., 182d Arty., 18th Div.	115
155mm Plt., 5th Arty. Div.	45
Engr. Det. (D-6 Bulldozer), 18th Div.	3
Sig. Det., 18th Div.	9
TOTAL	1,039

29. Msg, Hollingsworth to Abrams, 31 Mar. 1972, subj: Daily Commander's Evaluation.

30. Truong, *The Easter Offensive of 1972*, p. 113.

31. Interview, author with William Miller, Senior Adv., 5th ARVN Div., 12 Jan. 1990.

Chapter 24. Loc Ninh

1. Miller interview; Summers, *Vietnam War Almanac*, p. 170.

2. Msg, Hollingsworth to Abrams, 12 June 1971, subj: Daily Commander's Evaluation.

3. Miller interview.

4. Ibid.

5. After-action reports recorded that the 1st ARVN Cavalry Regiment was operating in Cambodia at the time of the Easter Offensive, but advisers at Loc Ninh reported that this was a charade developed by Vinh to appease his commander.

6. *The Nguyen Hue Offensive Campaign* [*Chien Dich Tien Cong Nguyen Hue*], p. 36.

Chapter 25. Tanks in the Wire

1. Msg, Hollingsworth to Abrams, 6 Apr. 1972, subj: Daily Commander's Evaluation.

2. Maj. F. C. Collins, "The Battle of Loc Ninh: 5–7 April 1972," unpublished term paper from the Army War College, Carlisle Barracks, Penn., undated; Truong, *The Easter Offensive of 1972*, p. 115.

3. Smith makes this claim in a series of letters to the author.

4. A-37 Dragonfly material from interview, author with Skip Bennett, 8th Special Operations Sqn., 8 Jan. 1991.

5. Hollingsworth, "Nguyen Hue Campaign," p. 8; Hollingsworth interview.

6. Msg, Hollingsworth to Abrams, 6 Apr. 1972, subj: Daily Commander's Evaluation.

7. Msg, Hollingsworth to Abrams, 7 Apr. 1972, subj: Daily Commander's Evaluation.

8. The army does not believe Smith's account. According to the U.S. Army Institute of Pathology, Schott probably did not kill himself. Its conclusion is based on doctors' testimony stating that "the recoil of a .45 cal. pistol most often causes it to fly from the hand of the person committing the suicide." According to Smith's testimony, Schott still had the gun in his lap after he died. For this reason, the Army ruled that Schott's death was a result of combat, not suicide. Memo for the Record, 17 July 1973, subj: Possible Suicide of Prisoners of War. However, only Smith was present at the time, making the army's contention somewhat hollow. Also, Col. Miller and Maj. Carlson claim that Smith's version is consistent with what they surmised both during and after the battle.

9. Hollingsworth, "The Nguyen Hue Campaign," p. 9.

10. Although none of the journals from Loc Ninh appear to have survived the attack, advisers in An Loc also kept a journal. Attached to the entry for 7 April 1972 was a typed sheet entitled "Things that I remember as one of the TOC duty officers during the period 06 2300H and 07 0830H April 1972," signed Major J. Mills, 5th ARVN Div. Daily Journal.

11. Collins, "The Battle of Loc Ninh," p. 17.

12. Bennett interview.

13. "Things that I remember as one of the TOC duty officers during the period 06 2300H and 07 0830H April 1972," 5th Div. Daily Journal.

14. Hollingsworth interview.

15. Interviews with advisers as well as the 5th ARVN Division AAR agree that most ARVN troops had either fled or surrendered sometime on the morning of 7 April. 5th ARVN Div. AAR, p. D-10; Miller interview. However, one cable from Hollingsworth states, "The 9th Regiment surrendered its remaining forces in Loc Ninh to the en[emy] at 071415 Apr." Msg, Hollingsworth to Abrams, 8 Apr. 1972, subj: Commander's Daily Evaluation.

16. Schott died inside Loc Ninh, Lull made it outside the perimeter before he disappeared; Carlson, Smith, Wallingford, and Wanat were captured by the enemy and released after the cease-fire. TRAC adviser list, as of 8 Apr. 72, 5th Div. AAR; "Citizens and Dependents, Captured, Missing, Detained or Voluntarily Remained in SEA," DIA PW/MIA Branch list, 11 Oct. 1979. Davidson's escape was noted in the TRAC G-2/G-3 daily journal entry for 2012H, 12 Apr. 1972.

17. "Major Ran for His Life 4 Days—and Won," *Pacific Stars & Stripes,* 29 Apr. 1972.

18. Msg, Hollingsworth to Abrams, 7 Apr. 1972, subj: Daily Commander's Evaluation; MACV 1972–73 Command History, vol. II, p. J-5.

19. 5th ARVN Division Daily Journal, 2400H 7 Apr. 72 (summary); TRAC Operational Summary 1-30 Apr. 1972, handwritten notes from an undated staff

meeting; Msg, Hollingsworth to Abrams, 7 Apr. 1972, subj: Commander's Daily Evaluation.

20. Ltr, Col. Joseph A. Schlatter, Chief, Special Office for Prisoners of War and Missing in Action, to Lt. Col. J. G. Cole, U.S. Total Army Personnel Command, 2 Feb. 1989, subj: Release of Information in the Cases of Lt. Col. Richard S. Schott and Sgt. First Class Howard B. Lull.

21. "3 Americans Held, Photographer Says," *New York Times,* 15 July 1972.

22. "PLAF Completely Liberate Binh Long Provincial Capital," Liberation Radio broadcast, 15 Apr. 1972.

23. Douglas Pike, "When the Communists Come," U.S. Information Service pamphlet, July 1972, p. 7.

24. "Reds Execute Saigon Soldiers in Loc Ninh," *Los Angeles Times,* 24 Apr. 1972.

25. Neil Sheehan and Susan Sheehan, "A Reporter at Large in Vietnam," *New Yorker,* 18 Nov. 1991, p. 93.

26. Memo to Gen. Westmoreland, 21 Apr. 1972, subj: Cable Summary.

Chapter 26. Preparing for the Worst

1. Gen. Truong's account states that the date of Minh's conference with the JGS was 6 April: Truong, *The Easter Offensive of 1972,* p. 116; MACV Command History uses 7 April: MACV 1972–73 Command History, vol. II, p. J-7. However, Hollingsworth seems to have had a conversation with Minh about the meeting on 6 April in Bien Hoa, so 7 April seems more likely. Msg, Hollingsworth to Abrams, 8 Apr. 1972, subj: Daily Commander's Evaluation.

2. Truong, *The Easter Offensive of 1972,* p. 117.

3. 5th ARVN Div. AAR, p. D-11.

4. For the full story of the destruction of Task Force 52 see Dale Andradé, "Three Days on the Run: The Battle for Loc Ninh," *Vietnam,* Aug. 1990.

5. "N. Viet Tactics," *Washington Post,* 8 May 1972; Truong, *The Easter Offensive of 1972,* p. 118.

6. *The 9th Division* [*Su Doan 9*], p. 154; *The Nguyen Hue Offensive Campaign* [*Chien Dich Tien Cong Nguyen Hue*], p. 43.

7. Truong, *The Easter Offensive of 1972,* p. 116; 5th ARVN Div. AAR, p. D-11.

8. Hollingsworth interview.

9. Miller interview.

10. Hollingsworth interview.

11. Msg, Hollingsworth to Abrams, 14 Apr. 1972, subj: Daily Commander's Evaluation.

12. MACV 1972–73 Command History, vol. II, p. J-12.

13. Truong, *The Easter Offensive of 1972,* p. 121.

14. *The 9th Division* [*Su Doan 9*], pp. 155–156.

15. MACV 1972–73 Command History, vol. II, p. J-11.

16. MACV Rpt, "Interview with Major Larry McKay, CO 79th ARA, 3d Bde 1st Cav Div at Bien Hoa," 26 May 1972; Miller interview.

17. Rpt, Lt. Col. Richard Manus, Senior Adviser 3d Ranger Group, to Brig. Gen. McGiffert, 1 June 1972, subj: Activities Report, 3d Ranger Group, 8 April–20 May 1972, p. 2.

18. MACV 1972–73 Command History, vol. II, p. J-13.

19. Msg, Hollingsworth to Abrams, 16 Apr. 1972, subj: Daily Commander's Evaluation.

20. Unless otherwise noted, all material on Lt. Kelly and the 6th Abn. Bn. comes from interview, author with Ross Kelly, Dep. Senior Adv., 6th Airborne Bn., 5 Feb. 1992; Msg, Senior Adv., Abn. Div. Adv. Team 162 to MACV MACAG-PD, undated, subj: Recommendation for Decoration for Valor or Merit. Lt. Kelly received the Distinguished Service Cross for his actions.

21. Truong, *The Easter Offensive of 1972*, p 122.

22. *The 9th Division [Su Doan 9]*, pp. 156–158.

Chapter 27. The Shelling Game

1. 5th ARVN Div. AAR, p. D-17.

2. Msg, Miller to Hollingsworth, 17 Apr. 1972, subj: For Information.

3. 5th ARVN Div. Daily Journal, 18–19 Apr. 1972.

4. The 9th VC Div. was made up of the 95C NVA Regt., 271st NVA Regt., and 272d NVA Regt. MACV 1972–73 Command History, vol. II, p. J-14.

5. Ibid., p. J-15; Hollingsworth interview.

6. Account from Kelly interview.

7. 5th ARVN Div. Daily Journal, 20–21 Apr. 1972.

8. Hollingsworth interview, 6 Nov. 1989; Miller interview, 12 Jan. 1990.

9. 5th ARVN Div. Daily Journal, 1905H 19 Apr. 1972.

10. The official history of the 9th VC Division is completely silent on the period from 15 April to 11 May. *The 9th Division [Su Doan 9]*, pp. 150–167.

11. 5th ARVN Div. AAR, p. D-14.

12. 5th ARVN Div. Daily Journal, 1130H 23 Apr. 1972.

13. Msg, COMUSMACV to CINCPAC, 8 May 1972, subj: Trip Progress Report MR 3.

14. Msg, Hollingsworth to Gen. Vogt, CDR 7AF, and Capt. Monger, CO USS *Hancock*, 22 Apr. 1972.

15. 5th ARVN Div. AAR, Appendix 6, subj: Enemy Indirect Fire.

16. 5th ARVN Div. Daily Journal, 2245H 25 Apr. 1972.

17. Truong, *The Easter Offensive of 1972*, p. 124.

18. 5th ARVN Div. Daily Journal, 2332H 28 Apr. 1972.

Chapter 28. Air Resupply

1. Account comes from interrogation reports of NVA prisoners taken around An Loc between 15 April and 15 May 1972. TRAC intelligence report, 29 May 1972.

2. CHECO Rpt, "Airlift to Besieged Areas, 7 Apr.–31 Aug. 72," 7 Dec. 1973, p. 2.

3. The U.S. Air Force does not critically examine the VNAF, choosing instead to emphasize its own role in resupplying An Loc. *Airpower and the 1972 Spring Offensive,* p. 86.

4. 5th ARVN Div. AAR, p. D-59.

5. "Airlift to Besieged Areas," pp. 5–6.

6. Ibid., p. 8.

7. 5th Div. AAR, p. D-76.

8. Ibid., p. D-59.

9. "Combat Airdrop Report, 15 Apr.–15 July 1972," undated, Table 1, p. 2.

10. 5th ARVN Div. Daily Journal, 2230H 24 Apr. 1972.

11. "Airlift to Besieged Areas," p. 15.

12. Ibid., pp. 18–19.

13. 5th ARVN Div. Daily Journal, 2300H, 27 Apr. 1972; "Combat Airdrop Report," p. 4.

14. Msg, Hollingsworth to Abrams, 10 May 1972, subj: Daily Commander's Evaluation.

15. "Summary, Logistical Resupply to An Loc, 7 Apr.–25 June 72," 20 July 1972, p. D-57.

16. "An Loc Seen from Above: War with Unreal Quality," *New York Times,* 10 May 1972.

17. MACV 1972–73 Command History, vol. II, p. J-17.

Chapter 29. Second Round

1. Msg, Hollingsworth to Abrams, 23 Apr. 1972, subj: Daily Commander's Evaluation Report.

2. Msg, Hollingsworth to Abrams, 29 Apr. 1972, subj: Daily Commander's Evaluation.

3. Truong, *The Easter Offensive of 1972,* pp. 128–129; Miller interview.

4. Msg, Miller to TRAC, 8 May 1972, included in the 5th ARVN Div. AAR, p. D-29.

5. "An Loc Seen from Above: War with Unreal Quality," *New York Times,* 10 May 1972.

6. MACV 1972–73 Command History, vol. II, p. J-22; Hollingsworth interview.

7. "Babe, That Was Too Close for Us," *Time,* 8 May 1972.

8. TRAC Operational Summary, 2250H 9 May 72.

9. Interview with Walter Ulmer, Senior Adv., 5th ARVN Div., 26 Feb. 1991.

10. Interview, author with Joseph Newman, Dep. CO, 12th Aviation Gp., 2 Mar. 1990.

11. Ulmer interview; Msg, Hollingsworth to Abrams, 10 May 1972, subj: Daily Commander's Evaluation.

12. Advisory Team (5th ARVN Div.) Fwd, An Loc tactical logs and journals, 27 Apr.–24 May 72; Newman interview.

13. Taped interview conducted with Col. William Miller, 11 May 1972.

14. Memo, Miller to Brig. Gen. James F. Hamlet, 13 May 1972, subj: Battle of Loc Ninh–An Loc, 5 April 1972 to 10 May 1972.

15. Rpt, Lt. Col. Richard J. McManus to Brig. Gen. McGiffert, 1 June 1972, subj: Activities Report, 3d Ranger Group, 8 Apr.–20 May 1972, p. 3.

16. Quotes from "A Record of Sheer Endurance," *Time,* 26 June 1972, p. 25; "One Saigon Advance Unit Breaks Through to An Loc," *New York Times,* 10 Jun. 1972.

17. An Loc TOC Log, 11 May 72.

18. Ulmer interview.

19. TRAC Operational Summary 0600H 10 May–0600H 11 May, 0330H 11 May 1972.

20. 5th ARVN Div. Daily Journal, 0230H 11 May 1972.

21. Ulmer interview.

22. Ibid.

23. CHECO Rpt, "The Battle for An Loc, 5 Apr.–26 June 72," 31 Jan. 1973, p. 42.

24. *The 9th Division [Su Doan 9],* pp. 159–160.

25. TRAC Operational Summary, 0140H 9 May 1972.

26. *The 9th Division [Su Doan 9],* p. 160.

27. Truong, *The Easter Offensive of 1972,* p. 130.

28. MACV 1972–73 Command History, vol. II, p. J-25; Truong, *The Easter Offensive of 1972,* p. 130; *Airpower and the 1972 Spring Invasion,* pp. 98–99.

29. MACV 1972–73 Command History, vol. II, p. J-26.

30. *The 9th Division [Su Doan 9],* p. 161.

31. *The Nguyen Hue Offensive Campaign [Chien Dich Tien Cong Nguyen Hue],* pp. 52, 54; *The 9th Division [Su Doan 9],* p. 161.

Chapter 30. Relief from the South

1. Although U.S. advisers were generally critical of South Vietnamese fire and maneuver capabilities during the offensive, they were specific in their cautious praise of 21st ARVN Div. actions in late April. "Touchy Times for American Advisers," *Newsweek,* 29 May 1972, p. 41.

2. The K-6 Bn. of the 165th Regt., 7th NVA Div. reinforced the 101st NVA Regt. It is not clear whether the battalion moved into position with the regiment or reinforced later. See HQ 5th ARVN Div. Combat Assistance Advisory Team 70, Combat After-Action Report, 20 July 1972, Annex F, 21st ARVN Div. After-Action Report, p. F-2. Hereafter referred to as 21st Div. AAR.

3. "S. Viet Armor Ineffective in Fight for Road," *Los Angeles Times,* 16 Apr. 1972.

4. "On Highway 13: The Long Road to An Loc," *Time,* 24 Apr. 1972, p. 27.

5. Ibid.

6. Unedited UPI press report, 23 Apr. 1972.

7. Truong, *The Easter Offensive of 1972,* p. 132. Casualty figures during the battle are interesting. Although the South Vietnamese were attacking fixed enemy positions, they came away with a favorable kill ratio of about 8:1. Confirmed enemy dead was 157, with 21 South Vietnamese dead. 21st ARVN Div. AAR, p. F-4.

8. Msg, Hollingsworth to Abrams, 30 Apr. 1972, subj: Daily Commander's Evaluation.

9. The USAF and VNAF equally divided tactical air support missions, flying seventy-one sorties each. During the first thirteen days of May, the ARVN used 20,000 rounds of artillery on NV positions. 21st ARVN Div. AAR, p. F-6.

10. 5th ARVN Div. Daily Journal, 2345H 6 May 1972.

11. *The Nguyen Hue Offensive Campaign* [*Chien Dich Tien Cong Nguyen Hue*], p. 64.

12. Msg, Hollingsworth to Abrams, 23 May 1972, subj: Daily Commander's Evaluation.

13. Msg, Hollingsworth to Abrams, 25 May 1972, subj: Daily Commander's Evaluation.

14. The 32d ARVN Regt. had about 80 KIA and almost 200 WIA. 21st ARVN Div. AAR, pp. F-9, F-12; *Vietnam,* no. 172 (1972): 14.

Chapter 31. End Siege

1. Msg, Hollingsworth to Abrams, 26 May 1972, subj: Daily Commander's Evaluation.

2. The gas attack came on the night of 27 May, when "it was reported that the 33d Regt. received a nontoxic gas at[tac]k consisting of five rounds f[ro]m an unk[nown] type w[ea]p[o]n." Msg, Hollingsworth to Abrams, 27 May 1972, subj: Daily Commander's Evaluation; Msg, Hollingsworth to Abrams, 28 May 1972, subj: Daily Commander's Evaluation.

3. "Media Fail to Convey Good News from An Loc," *Baltimore Sun,* 16 June 1972.

4. Msg, Hollingsworth to Abrams, 16 June 1972, subj: Daily Commander's Evaluation.

5. "The Relief of An Loc," *Newsweek,* 26 June 1972, p. 34.

6. "A Record of Sheer Endurance," *Time,* 26 June 1972, pp. 25–26.

7. "Hungry Saigon Troops Hijack Rice Lorries," *The Observer,* 21 May 1972.

8. Msg, Hollingsworth to Abrams, 10 May 1972, subj: Daily Commander's Evaluation.

9. Thieu's victory speech is quoted in "Valiant Binh Long: The 1972 Failure of Communist North Vietnam" (Saigon: Nguyen Ba Tong Printing Co., undated), p. 35.

10. Truong, *The Easter Offensive of 1972,* p. 135. Thieu's gesture of promoting the fighters at An Loc was a morale booster, but it also perpetuated the old problem of advancing incompetent officers through the ranks. A good example of this was Lt. Col. Biet, commander of the 3d Ranger Group. Though he never visited the field during the battle, he managed to be present when Thieu visited An Loc and thereby was promoted to colonel. Senior Officer Debriefing Rpt, Lt. Col. Laddie B. Logan, III Corps Ranger Command Senior Adv., 13 Apr. 1973, p. 6.

11. "The Heroic Battle of An Loc," GVN government pamphlet, undated, p. 56.

12. Interview, author with Jack Dugan, CO, 12th Aviation Gp., 27 Feb. 1990; Hollingsworth interview; Interview, author with John McGiffert, Dep. Senior Adv., TRAC, 4 Jan. 1990.

13. Wilbur H. Morrison, *The Elephant and the Tiger: The Full Story of the Vietnam War* (New York: Hippocrene Books, 1990), p. 530; Truong, *The Easter Offensive of 1972,* p. 136; "A Tale of Two Broken Cities," *Time,* 15 Jan. 1973, pp. 19–20.

14. "Rating the ARVN: Lessons from An Loc," *Christian Science Monitor,* 20 May 1972.

15. Rpt, Col. Ulmer to COMUSMACV, 10 Jan. 1973, subj: Senior Officer Debriefing Report, 5th ARVN Div.

16. *History of the People's Army [Lich Su Quan Doi Nhan Dan],* p. 56.

17. *The 9th Division [Su Doan 9],* pp. 165–166.

18. *The Nguyen Hue Offensive Campaign [Chien Dich Tien Cong Nguyen Hue],* p. 76.

19. "The Heroic Battle of An Loc," p. 62.

20. "A Record of Sheer Endurance," *Time,* 26 June 1972, p. 26.

21. *The Nation,* 17 June 1972, p. 17; *Paris Match,* 5 July 1972, p. 12.

22. "A Record of Sheer Endurance," p. 26; CBS Evening News transcript for 16 June 1972.

Chapter 32. War in the Delta

1. "Combat After-Action Report of Operation SPEEDY EXPRESS," 14 June 1969.

2. For an account of SEALs in Vietnam, see T. L. Bosiljevac, *SEALs: UDT/SEAL Operations in Vietnam* (Boulder, Colo.: Paladin Press, 1990).

3. "Back to the Big Muddy," *Newsweek,* 21 Aug. 1972, p. 22.

4. Truong, *The Easter Offensive of 1972,* pp. 140–141.

5. MACV J-2 intelligence summary 104-72J for the period 12 0600 to 13 0600 Apr. 1972, dated 13 Apr. 1972.

6. MACDI Study 73-01, "The Nguyen Hue Offensive," 12 Jan. 1973, p. D-1.

7. Senior Officer Debriefing Rpt., Maj. Gen. Thomas M. Tarpley, Commander, DRAC, 15 Jan. 72–13 Jan. 73, 13 Apr. 73, pp. 9–10. Hereafter referred to as Tarpley debrief.

8. Msg, Tarpley to Abrams, 14 Apr. 1972, subj: TAOR Assessment; "The Delta War," *Time,* 19 June 1972, p. 16.

9. Truong, *The Easter Offensive of 1972,* p. 146.

10. Msg, Brig. Gen. Blazey, Asst. DRAC Senior Adv., to Abrams, 10 Apr. 1972, subj: TAOR Assessment; Msg, Tarpley to Abrams, 15 Apr. 1972, subj: TAOR Assessment.

11. Msg, Tarpley to Abrams, 17 June 1972, subj: TAOR Assessment.

12. Senior Officer Debriefing Rpt., Col. William E. Davis, Senior Adv., 7th ARVN Div., 28 Jan. 1973.

13. Senior Officer Debriefing Rpt., Col. Theodore C. Williams, Jr., Senior Adv., 9th ARVN Div., 24 Jan. 1973.

14. Tarpley debrief, p. 14.

15. Ibid., p. 15.

16 . *History of the People's Army of Vietnam [Lich Su Quan Doi Nhan Dan Viet Nam],* p. 68.

17. "The Nguyen Hue Offensive," p. D-1.

18. Tarpley debrief, p. 18; Msg, Tarpley to Abrams, 17 Apr. 1972, subj: TAOR Assessment; Msg, Tarpley to Abrams, 21 Apr. 1972, subj: TAOR Assessment.

19. Tarpley debrief, p. 17.

Chapter 33. Taking the War to Hanoi

1. Henry Kissinger, *White House Years* (Boston: Little, Brown, 1979), p. 1169.

2. Fulghum and Maitland, *South Vietnam on Trial*, p. 168.

3. John Morrocco, *The Vietnam Experience: Rain of Fire, Air War, 1969–1973* (Boston: Boston Publishing Co., 1985), p. 110.

4. Ibid.

5. Kissinger, *White House Years*, p. 1176.

6. Morrocco, *Rain of Fire*, p. 130.

7. As part of the Paris Agreement, the United States agreed to clear the mines from North Vietnamese waters. The navy always knew it would have to do so. In a letter from the chairman of the Joint Chiefs of Staff to the CINCPAC, delivered on the same day as the mining of Haiphong harbor, the navy was told: "The time may come when we must sweep the mines that have been placed in the waters adjacent to North Vietnam." Edward J. Marolda, ed., *Operation End Sweep: A History of Minesweeping Operations in North Vietnam* (Washington, D.C.: Naval Historical Center, 1993), p. 3.

8. Fulghum and Maitland, *South Vietnam on Trial*, p. 171.

9. "Lack of New Hanoi Supply Routes Indicates Blockade Is Succeeding," *Baltimore Sun*, 30 May 1972.

10. Nixon, *RN*, vol. II, pp. 85–86; Linebacker I directive quoted in Mark Clodfelter, *The Limits of Air Power: The American Bombing of North Vietnam* (New York: Free Press, 1989), p. 164.

11. John L. Frisbee, "The Air War in Vietnam," *Air Force Magazine*, Sept. 1972, p. 53; S. L. A. Marshall, "How Big Is Nixon's Biggest Gamble?" *National Observer*, 20 May 1972; "Blockade Is a Bold and Desperate Move to Warn the Soviets," *Philadelphia Inquirer*, 14 May 1972; Morrocco, *Rain of Fire*, p. 131.

12. *History of the People's Army* [Lich Su Quan Doi Nhan Dan], p. 69. See also Luu Van Loi and Nguyen Anh Vu, *Le Duc Tho–Kissinger Negotiations in Paris* (Hanoi: Gioi Publishers, 1995), pp. 291–366.

13. W. Scott Thompson and Donaldson D. Frizzell, eds., *The Lessons of Vietnam* (New York: Crane, Russak Co., 1977), pp. 104–105.

14. Joseph Kraft, "Letter from Hanoi," *New Yorker*, 12 Aug. 1972, pp. 58–65; Joseph Fromm, "Why Hanoi Came to Realize It Could Not Hope to Win," *U.S. News & World Report*, 6 Nov. 1972, p. 19; Clodfelter, *The Limits of Air Power*, p. 167.

15. Kissinger, *White House Years*, p. 1445.

16. *History of the People's Army* [Lich Su Quan Doi Nhan Dan], p. 76.

17. Ibid., p. 72.

18. Davidson, *Vietnam at War*, p. 727; Clodfelter, *The Limits of Air Power*, p. 189.

19. Clodfelter, *The Limits of Air Power*, pp. 194–195.

20. Translation of a report from the Deputy Chief of the General Staff, People's Army of Vietnam, 1 Dec. 1972, subj: On the Final Analysis of Offensive Operations in South Vietnam and Requirements for the Future Armed Struggle. This document is a Russian translation of a Vietnamese briefing presented by Gen. Tran Van Quang, Deputy Chief of Staff of the People's Army of Vietnam (North Vietnam), to Konstantin Katushev, Department Chief of the Central Committee of the Communist Party of the Soviet Union. It was translated into English in 1993.

21. "North Vietnam: Taking Pride in Punishment," *Washington Post*, 4 Feb. 1973; "Bombing Was Pinpointed," *Washington Star*, 1 Apr. 1973.

22. "Linebacker II USAF Bombing Survey," Apr. 1973, pp. 68, 129.

23. "Terror Bombing in the Name of Peace," *Washington Post*, 28 Dec. 1972; "Shame on Earth," *New York Times*, 26 Dec. 1972; *Die Zeit* quoted in "Outrage and Relief," *Time*, 8 Jan. 1973.

24. Kissinger, *White House Years*, p. 1453.

25. *History of the People's Army* [*Lich Su Quan Doi Nhan Dan*], p. 78. Despite the preparation of a detailed and largely accurate account of the air defense campaign, Hanoi continues to insist that it shot down eighty-one aircraft, including thirty-four B-52s.

26. Quoted in Davidson, *Vietnam at War*, p. 728; Kissinger, *White House Years*, pp. 1463–1464.

27. Nixon, *RN*, vol. II, pp. 257–258.

28. Nixon, *RN*, vol. II, p. 259; Kissinger, *White House Years*, p. 1461; "What Admiral Moorer Really Said About Airpower's Effectiveness in SEA," *Air Force Magazine*, Nov. 1973, p. 25; Barry Goldwater, "Airpower in Southeast Asia," *Congressional Record—Senate*, 119, part 5, 26 Feb. 1973, p. 5346.

29. Clodfelter, *The Limits of Air Power*, p. 201.

30. Fallaci, *Interview with History*, p. 56.

Chapter 34. *Winners and Losers*

1. Observations of Maj. Gen. John F. Freund, undated, p. 19.

2. Stanton, *Vietnam Order of Battle*, p. 60; Summers, *Vietnam War Almanac*, p. 236; Clarke, *Advice and Support: The Final Years*, p. 515.

3. U.S. State Dept. Research Study, "Vietnam: The July Balance Sheet on Hanoi's Offensive," 17 July 1972, p. 4.

4. MACCORDS-PSG, "Impact of Enemy Offensive on Pacification," 16 Sept. 1972, p. 2; MACCORDS-PSG, "Evaluation of the Impact of the Enemy Offensive on Pacification," 10 Oct. 1972, pp. 1–5; MACCORDS-RA, "Impact of NVA Offensive on HES Ratings," 6 June 1972, p. 1; CIA Intelligence Memo no. 0858/72, 25 Apr. 1972, subj: Pacification in South Vietnam: A Preliminary Damage Assessment, p. 2. On civilian casualties: "Bunker Says Civilian Toll Runs Higher Than at Tet," *New York Times*, 16 June 1972; MACV 1972–73 Command History, vol. I, p. D-42. On refugee figures: Washington Vietnam War Refugee Ad Hoc Committee, Final Weekly Report, 18 June 1973. State Dept. assessment: Msg, CINCPAC to POLAD,

undated (circa July 1972), subj: Assessment of the Political and Anti-pacification Efforts of the Communists During the Current Offensive; Msg, U.S. Embassy Saigon to Secretary of State, 4 Aug. 1972.

5. CBS Evening News broadcast, 19 June 1972; "A Viet Province Escapes Hanoi Offensive—and Survives," *Christian Science Monitor,* 21 June 1972.

6. End of Tour Rpt, Lt. Col. Robert E. Wagner, Province Senior Adv., Quang Tin Province, 10 June 1972, p. 4.

7. "Thunderbolt from Thieu," *Time,* 18 Sept. 1972.

8. Friendly casualty rates are for the period between 30 March and 30 July. Although many South Vietnamese soldiers died retaking Quang Tri during August and September, they are not included as part of the Easter Offensive. Army Activities Rpt, Southeast Asia, "Statistical Information on Current Enemy Offensive," 26 Aug. 1972; "Rising Hopes in South Vietnam," *U.S. News & World Report,* 24 July 1972; "Enemy Maintaining Pressure," *Washington Post,* 21 Apr. 1972. U.S. casualty figures: Rpt, U.S. Military Casualties in Southeast Asia (Except Thailand), 1 Aug. 1972; "Zero Deaths," *Newsweek,* 2 Oct. 1972.

9. Gen. Cao Van Vien and Lt. Gen. Dong Van Khuyen, *Reflections on the Vietnam War* (Washington, D.C.: U.S. Army Center of Military History, 1980), p. 110.

10. "How Good in Saigon's Army?" *Time,* 17 Apr. 1972.

11. MACV 1972–73 Command History, vol. I, p. C-26.

12. OASD Rpt: "RVNAF Appraisal," 15 Feb. 1973; MACV 1972–73 Command History, vol. I, p. C-28.

13. Clarke, *Advice and Support: The Final Years,* pp. 499–500.

14. Brian M. Jenkins, "Giap and the Seventh Son" (Santa Monica, Calif.: RAND Corp., September 1972), p. 5; Pike, *PAVN,* pp. 339–346.

15. David W. P. Elliott, "NLF-DRV Strategy and the 1972 Spring Offensive," Interim Rpt no. 4 (Ithaca, N.Y.: International Relations of East Asia Project, 1974), pp. 34–39; "A Study of Strategic Lessons Learned in Vietnam," vol. VI, book 1, "Conduct of the War: Operational Analysis" (McLean, Va.: BDM Corp., 9 May 1980), pp. 4-97, 4-98.

16. Tran Van Tra, *Vietnam: History of the Bulwark B2 Theater,* vol. 5, *Concluding the 30-Years War* (Ho Chi Minh City: Van Nghe Publishing House, 1982), p. 33. Translated as JPRS publication 8283, Feb. 1983.

17. Davidson, *Vietnam at War,* p. 710.

18. *History of the People's Army* [*Lich Su Quan Doi Nhan Dan*], pp. 58, 87.

19. Ibid., p. 61.

20. For a detailed discussion of this position, see Davidson, *Vietnam at War,* pp. 709–711.

21. OASD, "Southeast Asia Statistical Summary," table 322, 24 Oct. 1973; Robert Thompson, *Peace Is Not at Hand* (New York: David McKay, 1974), p. 110.

22. OASD, "Southeast Asia Statistical Summary," table 9, 24 Oct. 1973.

23. *History of the People's Army* [*Lich Su Quan Doi Nhan Dan*], pp. 86–87.

24. "Viet Risk Grows—for Hanoi," *Christian Science Monitor,* 8 May 1972.

Epilogue

1. "For GIs, It's a Different War—But Still Dangerous," *Newsweek,* 14 Feb. 1972.

2. The last two units were the 1st Bn., 46th Inf., and the 3d Bn., 21st Inf. (The Gimlets). Msg, Abrams to Lt. Gen. MacCaffrey, 29 May 1972, subj: Redeployment of the 196th Inf. Bde.; Stanton, *Vietnam: Order of Battle,* pp. 144, 150; F. Clifton Berry Jr., *The Illustrated History of the Vietnam War: The Chargers* (New York: Bantam Books, 1988), pp. 154–155.

3. "Reds in Caves Ambush U.S. Patrol Near Danang," *Express News,* 28 Feb. 1972.

4. "50 GIs in Vietnam Refuse Patrol Duty, Then Agree to Go," UPI dispatch, 13 Apr. 1972.

5. Account of U.S. troops around Phu Bai comes from "Combat Unit at Phu Bai: U.S. Troops Facing Threat," *Washington Star,* 14 May 1972.

6. Hugh M. Stovall Jr., "The Last Patrol," *VFW* Magazine, Aug. 1992, p. 33.

7. Ibid.

BIBLIOGRAPHIC ESSAY

Because the material for this book comes mostly from primary sources, I have chosen not to present a bibliography of secondary sources consulted during the course of my research. Most general works on the Vietnam War include at least a small section on the Easter Offensive, but few go into any detail. The best work is Phillip B. Davidson, *Vietnam at War: The History, 1946–1975* (Novato, Calif.: Presidio Press, 1988). A more recent book, Lewis Sorley's *A Better War: The Unexamined Victories and Final Tragedy of America's Last Years in Vietnam* (New York: Harcourt Brace, 1999), looks at the final years in Vietnam as a time when America turned the tide against the communists and could have won the war. Although it offers few new details on the fighting in 1972, it does make effective use of newly released messages and transcripts outlining General Creighton Abrams's thoughts and actions during the offensive. Of course, all secondary sources used are cited in the notes.

As of this writing, there are no other books focusing on the entire Easter Offensive, although a few examine parts of the battle. In I Corps, the U.S. Marine advisers were the most prolific, publishing two books on personal experiences. Lieutenant Colonel G. H. Turley's experiences in Quang Tri Province are recounted in *The Easter Offensive: The Last American Advisers, 1972* (Novato, Calif.: Presidio Press, 1985), while the exploits of Captain John Ripley around Dong Ha Bridge during the first week of the offensive are told in John G. Miller's narrowly focused book *The Bridge at Dong Ha* (Annapolis, Md.: Naval Institute Press, 1989). Another book that looks at one segment of the fighting in I Corps, the rescue of downed airmen during the battle, is Darrel D. Whitcomb's *The Rescue of Bat 21* (Annapolis, Md.: Naval Institute Press, 1998).

Only one book gives any detail regarding the Central Highlands of II Corps: Neil Sheehan's *A Bright Shining Lie: John Paul Vann and America in Vietnam* (New York: Random House, 1988).

Although the battle around An Loc in III Corps was arguably the most important of the offensive, its participants have been largely silent. James H. Willbanks, an adviser to the South Vietnamese stationed north of An Loc, wrote a monograph entitled *Thiet Giap! The Battle of An Loc, April 1972* (Fort Leavenworth, Kans.: U.S. Army Combat Studies Institute, 1993).

Of all the official histories compiled by branches of the U.S. military, only the marines have a detailed account of their role in the Easter Offensive. A volume by Major Charles D. Melson and Lieutenant Colonel Curtis G. Arnold entitled *U.S. Marines in Vietnam: The War That Would Not End, 1971–1973* (Washington, D.C.: U.S. Government Printing Office, 1991) provides a detailed look at the U.S. Marine Corps' advisory role in the early days of the offensive as well as the retaking of Quang Tri in September 1972.

Students of American military history are accustomed to studying their subject from a victor's position, which inevitably means having access to the loser's records. After the Vietnam War this was not the case. To this day we have precious little in the way of documentation explaining North Vietnamese strategy and tactics. On the other hand, the passage of time has led to the publication of literally hundreds of books by Vietnamese official historians covering all aspects of the war. Several deal with the Easter Offensive. A sizable chapter surveying the entire communist campaign is found in *Lich Su Quan Doi Nhan Dan Viet Nam* [*History of the People's Army of Vietnam*] (Hanoi: People's Army Publishing House, 1990). For those interested in knowing more about the role played by North Vietnamese artillery in the offensive, Hanoi has published *Tong Ket Tac Chien Phao Binh* [*Record of Artillery Combat Operations*] (Hanoi: Artillery Command of the People's Army of Vietnam, 1985).

Other books are more focused on specific aspects of the campaign. A unit history, the *Su Doan 325* [*The 325th Division*] (Hanoi: People's Army Publishing House, 1986), reveals details of that division's fighting in Quang Tri in the summer of 1972 as the South Vietnamese slowly recaptured the province capital.

The fighting in II Corps is detailed in *Luc Luong Vu Trang Nhan Dan Tay Nguyen Trong Khang Chien Chong My Cuu Nuoc* [*History of the Central Highlands People's Armed Forces in the Anti-U.S. War of Resistance for National Salvation*] (Hanoi: People's Armed Forces Publishing House, 1980).

For the battle in III Corps, around Saigon, two books are especially useful. *Chien Dich Tien Cong Nguyen Hue (1972)* [*The Nguyen Hue Offensive Campaign (1972)*] (Hanoi: Vietnam Institute for Military History, Ministry of Defense, 1988) is an account of the fighting on the entire III Corps front, with particular attention paid to the battles for Loc Ninh and An Loc. Another unit history, *Su Doan 9* [*The 9th Division*] (Hanoi: People's Army Publishing House, 1990), gives specific details about the fierce fighting in the streets of An Loc.

Finally, combat in the Mekong Delta was subdued compared with that in the rest of South Vietnam, but Hanoi's fighting there is outlined in *Chien Dich Tien Cong Tong Hop Quan Khu 8 (Dong Bang Song Cuu Long) 1972* [*Combined Offensive Campaign in Military Region 8 (Delta–Cuu Long River) 1972*] (Hanoi: Ministry of Defense, Vietnamese Institute for Military History, 1987).

Primary source material on the American role in the Easter Offensive is plentiful, with most of it found in three places. The National Archives in Washington, D.C., has document collections of U.S. advisory teams, including daily journals and after-action reports. The U.S. Army Center of Military History (CMH) has a more limited collection of material, much of it supporting documentation for Lieutenant General Ngo Quang Truong's monograph entitled *The Easter Offensive of 1972* (Washington, D.C.: U.S. Army Center of Military History, 1980). Also at CMH is an extensive collection of messages both to and from General Abrams, known colloquially as the Abrams Papers. These messages provide researchers with a strong sense of the immediate concerns of U.S. advisers during the battle, untainted by subsequent reflection and analysis. The U.S. Army Military History Institute (MHI) at Carlisle Barracks, Pennsylvania, holds several collections of personal papers relevant to the Easter Offensive, including an assortment of end-of-tour interviews with officers involved in the offensive.

Other collections are useful, particularly the records of U.S. Marine advisers during the Easter Offensive, which can be found at the USMC Historical Center located in the Washington Navy Yard. The collection includes after-action reports, an oral history collection, and a complete set of intelligence reports for northern I Corps during 1971 and 1972. Finally, researchers may find valuable material in an eclectic collection at Douglas Pike's Indochina Archives, now administered by Texas Tech University in Lubbock, Texas.

Some documents were obtained through the Freedom of Information Act (FOIA), though the process is cumbersome and often unproductive. Because of understaffing and budgetary problems, the National Archives has still not declassified all its records from that period. However, my FOIA requests were handled promptly, and on every occasion the documents were forthcoming. Not so with the U.S. State Department, which in some cases took more than a year to declassify documents pertaining to the impact of the Easter Offensive on pacification. In a few cases the documents were withheld for "national security reasons."

Personal interviews proved to be a valuable addition to the documents, providing insights, clarification, and "war stories" to flesh out the words on paper. Unfortunately, I found no network of Easter Offensive–era army advisers, so I had to track them down one by one. Dozens of servicemen from the army, marines, and air force—even a handful from the navy— gave freely of their time and knowledge, without which this book would not have been possible. With the exception of a very few who preferred to remain anonymous, they are cited as appropriate.

INDEX

Abrams, Creighton W.
disagreements with Gen. Hollingsworth, 341, 375, 486, 423
end of tour, 173
evaluation of I Corps situation,
147–148
fighting in II Corps, 213, 222, 266,
274, 281, 293, 297
intelligence predictions, 10–13
military background, 7–9, 100–101,
177, 215
performance of South Korean
troops, 259
recall of Gen. Lam, 141–142
Acrement, Paul, 229–230
Agency for International Development
(AID), 206
Air and Naval Gunfire Liaison
Company (ANGLICO), 53, 57,
129, 139, 189
Aircraft types
A-1 Skyraider, 69, 95, 130, 131,
312, 433, 439
A-7 Corsair, 474
A-37 Dragonfly, 363–366, 370–371
AC-47 Spooky, 295, 322, 326, 362,
370–371, 387, 396, 416, 433
AC-119 Stinger, 43, 317, 396, 403,
439
AC-130 Spectre, 224, 289, 296, 316,
411–418, 442, 496
B-52, 1, 63, 79, 88, 140, 170, 172,
178, 181, 185, 187, 193, 212,
215, 217–218, 257, 265, 266,
269, 270, 273, 279, 281, 284,
291, 296, 298, 306, 316, 336,
343, 366, 371, 383, 387, 392,
402, 422, 428, 433, 455, 466,
471, 474, 480

C-5A, 162
C-47, 176, 177, 207, 313
C-123, 289, 409
C-130, 224, 289, 296, 316,
411–418, 442, 496
EB-66, 75
F-4 Phantom, 46, 194, 225, 322,
418, 424, 439, 474, 477
MiG-21, 474
Ai Tu Combat Base, 34, 48, 54, 55,
58, 60, 62–63, 64, 72, 83, 85, 88,
92, 95, 96, 111, 115, 117, 120,
122, 124
Anderson, Jack, 226, 326
Anderson, USS, 68
Arclight, 76, 106, 170, 181, 183, 265,
270, 291, 296, 387, 392, 409,
424, 428, 498. See also Aircraft
types, B-52
Armored personnel carrier. See Armor
types, M113
Armor types
M41, 66, 123, 146, 234, 248, 268,
292, 311, 313, 357
M48A3, 66, 68, 69, 95, 113, 124,
134, 135, 146
M113, 95, 157, 225, 263
PT-76, 63, 68, 69, 108, 133, 166,
201, 271, 364
T-54, 63, 69–70, 94, 98, 104, 113,
114, 139, 188, 238, 239, 241,
248–249, 266, 271, 277, 282,
285, 287, 290, 305, 318–319,
357, 363–365, 388, 390–391,
396, 398, 431, 446, 451, 474
Armstrong, F. C., 11
Artillery types
105mm howitzer, 79, 106, 118, 123,
130, 239, 247, 272, 300, 301,

Artillery types, *continued*
    353, 360, 401, 444, 452
    122mm field gun, 109
    130mm field gun, 8, 90, 94, 109,
        113, 160, 182, 212, 291, 301
    155mm howitzer, 79, 106, 247, 250,
        257, 301, 314, 348, 353, 411
    175mm self-propelled gun, 79, 89,
        153, 161
A Shau Valley, 149–151, 161, 176, 231
AT-3 Sagger antitank rocket, 235, 440

Base areas
    Base Area 354, 345, 348
    Base Area 609, 212
    Base Area 708, 344, 345, 347
    Base Area 712, 339
Bat Lake, 9
Battreall, Raymond R., 51–52, 67–68,
    69, 70, 72, 74
BAT-21 Bravo, 75–76
Beans, James, 139–140
Benedit, William, 386
Ben Het, 201–202, 214, 271
Bennett, "Skip," 364–365, 371
Biddulph, Stephen G., 189
Blue Ridge, USS, 169
Boomer, Walter E., 39, 41–50
Borstorff, Allan, 386
Bowen, Thomas W., 89, 136–137, 148,
    158
Brodie, Donald C., 165
Brookbank, David, 76, 129, 131
Brown, Joseph, 79–81, 82, 85, 86, 88,
    89, 112
Brownlee, Robert, 248–250
Bruggman, David C., 53–58
Buchanan, USS, 54, 55, 68
Bui Thanh Van, 420
Bui Thi Lan, 160, 187, 193
Bunker, Ellsworth, 141

Cambodia, 176, 201, 203, 265, 344,
    353, 378, 421, 438, 456,
    463–464, 466, 467, 469, 476, 488
Camp Carroll, 35, 36, 62, 77–90, 100,
    101

Camper, William C., 36, 78–89, 112
Cao Van Vien, 144, 488
    evaluation of ARVN generals, 143
Carden, Charles, 248–250
Carlson, Albert E., 353, 354, 363, 369,
    376, 378–379
Carter, George, 235
Central Intelligence Agency (CIA), 5,
    486
    estimates of enemy capabilities, 11
Central Office, South Vietnam. *See*
    COSVN
Chae Kang Won, 261
Civil Operations and Rural
    Development Support. *See*
    CORDS
Cockell, Robert, 91, 95
Combat Skyspot, 75
Command and Staff School, 144
Computed Aerial Release Point
    (CARP), 411–412
Con Thien, 52
Cooksey, Howard H., 173, 175, 178,
    197
Coral Sea, USS, 475
CORDS (Civil Operations and Rural
    Development Support), 206
COSVN (Central Office, South
    Vietnam), 10, 345, 379, 388,
    400–401, 420, 434–435

Dang Van Quang, 382
Davidson, Phillip B., 491
Davidson, Richard, 237–238
Davidson, Thomas A., 353, 370,
    371–374
Defense Intelligence Agency (DIA), 6, 9
Delta Regional Assistance Command
    (DRAC), 461–471
Demilitarized Zone (DMZ), 29, 32,
    51–52, 59, 107, 325, 472
Dickinson, Hillman, 152, 153, 155
Dien Bien Phu, 18, 203, 333, 406, 407
    comparison to siege of An Loc, 451
    See also Vo Nguyen Giap
Dobbins, Raymond, 234, 239–242,
    246–247

Do Cao Tri, 336
Do Huu Tung, 93, 194, 196
Dorward, Irvin, 202–203
Dougherty, Stanley A., 136–137
Doughtie, Ronald, 235
Dugan, Jack, 425–427, 450, 451,
    452–453
Dumont, Yves-Michel, 363, 376, 379
Dunn, Gerry, 135–137
Du Quoc Dong, 182

Eaton, Thomas, 497–498
Eisenhower, Thomas, 225–226
Eisenstein, Joel, 54–58
Engineers
    at Dong Ha Bridge, 73–74
    at My Chanh Bridge, 140

Finch, John, 309–311, 314
Firebases
    Alpha, 360
    Alpha 2, 52–62
    Anzio, 152
    Arsenal, 498
    Barbara, 152
    Bastogne, 151–152, 153, 155–156,
        166, 168
    Birmingham, 498
    Bravo, 267
    Charlie, 233
    Charlie 2, 35, 52
    Checkmate, 155–156, 166
    Delta (in Kontum), 228–230, 233,
        238
    Delta (in Laos), 1
    Five, 252
    Forty-two, 272–273
    Fuller, 101
    Holcomb, 37, 62, 78, 100, 101
    Jane, 93
    Khe Gio, 37, 78, 79, 101
    King, 157, 498
    Lam Son, 267, 268
    Mai Loc, 45–48, 50, 62, 82–85, 90,
        101
    November, 279
    Nui Ba Ho, 37, 40, 42–50, 78, 100

    Pedro, 91–98, 99, 100, 108, 171
    Rakkasan, 152, 153
    Rifle, 152
    Sally, 190
    Sarge, 37, 40–50, 78, 100, 101
    Six, 252
    Veghel, 151–152
    Vida, 250
Fire Support Coordination Center, 160
First Regional Assistance Command
    (FRAC), 34, 53, 60, 62, 63, 88,
    99, 101, 106–107, 111, 128, 130,
    136, 142, 144, 149, 156, 168,
    178, 186, 192
Franjola, Matt, 309–311
Franklin, J. Ross, 436
Freund, John F., 484
Fronts
    B-2, 250, 491
    B-3, 216, 227, 233, 281, 329
    B-4, 29, 151, 192, 195
    B-5, 29
Furrow, Gail, 184

Gannon, Norbert C., 300, 312
Geneva Accords (1954), 51
Givens, James, 267–268
Gnibus, Thomas, 135–137
Golden, Glenn, 129–131
Goldwater, Barry, 482
Goode, Charles, 135–137
Ground Radar Air Delivery System
    (GRADS), 417
Group 559, 16

Hacker, Gary, 225, 226
Haig, Alexander, 3
Hai Van Pass, 151
Hambleton, Iceal, 75
Hamlet, James F., 427
Hammons, Thomas, 423
Hamner, USS, 68
Hancock, USS, 407
Healy, Michael, 327
Helicopter types
    AH-1 Cobra, 55, 56, 166, 188, 229,
        245, 292, 295–296, 319, 320,

Helicopter types, *continued*
    288, 390–391, 395, 423, 426,
    427, 450
    CH-46, 166, 188
    CH-47 Chinook, 85–86, 87, 301,
    383, 409
    CH-53, 166, 188
    HH-3 Jolly Green Giant, 131–132,
    134
    OH-6, 270, 371
    OH-58 Kiowa, 230, 243, 325
    Sky Crane, 444
    UH-1 Huey, 189, 226, 244, 245,
    282, 425, 426
High-altitude, low-opening (HALO),
    417–418
Hill, John, 255, 256, 264, 305, 325–326
Hill 169, 393–396, 399, 401, 402,
    406, 421, 447
Hoang Minh Thao, 217, 329
Hoang Xuan Lam, 31, 35, 40, 72, 97,
    100, 102–105
    command and control problems,
    105–106
    countermanding orders, 109–111,
    120, 125–126
    evaluation of, 142–143, 146
    in Operation Lam Son 719, 2
    relief from command, 141–143
Ho Chi Minh Trail
    into Central Highlands, 203, 266
    North Vietnamese infiltration, 1,
    6–10, 13–17, 24
    into III Corps, 335, 357
    through A Shau Valley, 151
Hodory, Richard W., 166
Hollingsworth, James, 276, 340–342,
    343, 453, 458
    fighting at An Loc, 392–393, 395,
    398–399, 405–408, 416–417, 418,
    420, 422, 430, 433
    fighting at Loc Ninh, 363, 365–366,
    367, 368, 374–375
    intelligence in III Corps, 348–349,
    350
    performance of ARVN helicopters,
    450

    planning for battle at An Loc,
    384–387
    relief of An Loc, 438, 440, 442, 444,
    445–446, 447, 450
Ho Xuan Tinh, 201–202
Huff, Emmett, 122, 135
Huynh Dinh Tung, 111
Huynh Van Cai, 229–230, 245
Huynh Van Luom, 70

Johnson, Lyndon B., 474
Joint General Staff, 3, 35, 36,
    143, 163, 168, 175, 193, 231,
    266–267, 333, 381, 382, 463
Joint Rescue and Coordination Center,
    130
Joseph P. Strauss, USS, 55
Joy, James, 115–116, 122, 134–136

Kama, Peter, 229
Kaplan, Phillip, 232–245
Kellar, Robert, 254
Keller, John, 244–245
Kelly, Ross, 393–396, 401–404
Kennedy, Edward, 481
Khe Sanh, 1, 176
Kingston, Robert, 325
Kissinger, Henry
    bombing North Vietnam, 474–478,
    480
    negotiations with North Vietnam,
    472, 482, 494
Kroesen, Frederick J., 51, 72, 76, 99,
    100, 111
    counteroffensive, 101–103
    evaluation of 3d ARVN Division,
    145–148
    departure, 173
    relations with Gen. Truong,
    158
    relief of Gen. Lam, 142–144
Kruger, Earl, 123

Laird, Melvin, 11, 148, 214, 231
Lanagan, William H., 76
Landing zones
    Crystal, 320–324

English, 223, 224, 226–227,
320–321, 324
Orange, 223, 224
Pony, 223, 224
Laos, 1–3, 101, 151, 168, 176, 185,
201, 216, 476, 488
Lavelle, John D., 12
Le Ba Binh, 64–66
Le Duan, 18, 20–21
Le Duc Dat, 231, 232, 234, 236–238,
242, 247–248, 250–251, 253
Le Duc Tho, 478, 479, 282
Le Nguyen Khang, 64, 127, 160
Le Van Hung
background, 351–352
fighting at An Loc, 399, 404–408,
422, 424, 427, 431, 446
fighting at Loc Ninh, 363, 374
Loc Ninh defensive preparations,
355–359
planning for defense of An Loc,
384–386, 391
promotion, 450–451
relations with American advisors,
399
Livingston, Lawrence, 96, 171, 181
Loi Phong (Thunder Hurricane),
161–162
Lovings, Wade, 283–284, 293–295,
301, 305, 306, 309
Lull, Howard B., 353, 363, 369–370,
376–377
Ly Tong Ba
background, 253–254
defensive planning, 256–258,
266–282, 286
fighting at Kontum, 287–319

MACV. *See* Military Assistance
Command, Vietnam
Mansfield, Mike, 481
Mao Zedong, guerrilla warfare theory,
3, 18, 21, 465
McCain, John S., 11, 177
McClain, Terrence, 235, 242, 244, 245
McGiffert, John R., 342, 387, 392,
425, 434

McGovern, George M., 477, 479
McKay, Larry, 390–391
McKenna, Paul, 269–270
McKenna, Thomas, 283–285, 290,
291, 293–295, 305–309
McLaren, Geddes, 269–270
McVicar, James, 500
Meese, John R., 463
Metcalf, Donald J., 34–35, 36, 54, 58,
60, 63, 88, 89, 97, 106, 116, 118,
125–126, 127
evacuation of Quang Tri, 129–132,
134
Military Assistance Command,
Vietnam (MACV), 7, 204, 210,
213, 217, 228, 261, 273, 410,
414, 423, 447
cooperation with Strategic Air
Command, 433–434
defense of Central Highlands,
218–219, 227
disbanding of, 493
evaluation of ARVN, 489–490
pre-offensive intelligence, 8–13
Miller, Richard W., 499
Miller, William, 421, 422, 423–424,
430
airdrops, 415–418
assessment of Gen. Hung, 351–352,
455
background, 343
battle of An Loc, 387–393,
398–399, 406–408
evacuation from An Loc, 424,
426–427
intelligence in III Corps, 349–350
planning for battle of An Loc, 374,
384, 386
planning for battle of Loc Ninh,
353–359, 374
relations with Gen. Hung, 399,
404–405
relief of An Loc, 441
Moffett, Larry, 416, 431
Monsoons, 5
Montagnards, 201, 203, 233, 237,
256, 273, 368

Moore, David J., 166
Moorer, Thomas, 480
Murphy, Robert L., 422

National Liberation Front, 58, 81, 89
National Security Agency, 6, 496
Negris, Rocco, 500
Neilson, Ben, 55
Newman, Joseph, 426–427
Ngo Dzu, 142, 214, 231, 489
  background, 207–209
  building defense at Kontum,
    252–264, 268, 271
  fighting in coastal II Corps,
    222–227, 233, 250
  intelligence on enemy movements,
    215–219
  relief from command, 276–277
Ngo Minh Hoang, 108
Ngo Quang Truong
  background, 142–144, 145
  defense of Hue, 158–164
  evaluation of Gen. Giai, 147
  as IV Corps commander, 463,
    464–465, 466, 467
  offensive planning, 168–175
  recapturing Quang Tri, 177–197
Ngo Van Dinh, 64
Nguyen Cao Ky, 232
Nguyen Cong Vinh, 354–355, 356,
  360, 366, 368, 378
Nguyen Dang Hoa, 188
Nguyen Dang Tong, 92
Nguyen Duy Hinh, 163
Nguyen Huu Ly, 68, 69, 71, 73
Nguyen Khoa Nam, 468
Nguyen Nang Bao, 104, 115, 117,
  121–122, 127, 134–135
Nguyen Thanh Hoang, 470
Nguyen Thoi Bung, 396–397, 401
Nguyen Trong Luat, 72, 113–115
Nguyen Van Chuc, 220
Nguyen Van Minh, 336, 338,
  348–349, 350, 370
  defense of An Loc, 381, 382, 405,
    440, 442, 445, 447
Nguyen Van Phuoc, 153–155

Nguyen Van Thieu, 2, 31, 182, 231,
  322–323, 489, 493
  demand to retake Quang Tri citadel,
    193
  Gen. Lam's recall, 141–142
  Paris Peace Talks, 482, 483,
    486–487
  planning Quang Tri counteroffen-
    sive, 175
  proclamation of victory at An Loc,
    456–457
  punishment of Gen. Giai, 146
  relief of An Loc, 442
  visit to An Loc, 450–451
  visit to Kontum, 317–318
  visit to Quang Tri Province,
    171–172
Nguyen Van Toan, 67, 292, 293, 297,
  312, 323
  appointment as II Corps commander,
    277–278, 286
Nguyen Vinh Nghi, 467, 468, 470
Nguyen Xuan Phuc, 121–122
Nixon, Richard M.
  bombing North Vietnam, 474–479,
    480
  ending U.S. combat role in South
    Vietnam, 495
  negotiations with North Vietnam,
    472, 482
  Operation Lam Son 719, 3
  relations with China and the Soviet
    Union, 22–23
North Vietnamese units
  1st NVA Division, 463–470
  1st Regiment, 247
  2d NVA Division, 212, 216, 218,
    233, 247, 252, 281, 287
  3d NVA Division, 212, 222, 260,
    269, 321, 324
  5th VC Division, 339, 344, 348,
    350, 399, 420–421, 431, 445, 468
  7th NVA Division, 339, 345, 347,
    383, 393, 399, 420–421, 445
  9th VC Division, 339, 345, 347,
    396–397, 401, 404, 405–406,
    409, 420, 421, 431, 456

10th Sapper Battalion, 300
18B Regiment, 466, 467
24th Regiment, 80, 347, 348, 349, 468
28th Regiment, 281
29th Regiment, 151, 156, 166, 168
36th Regiment, 68
48th Regiment, 281, 291, 299
52d Regiment, 467
64th Regiment, 281
66th Regiment, 156, 166, 171, 218, 304
95B Regiment, 297, 466
101st Regiment, 436, 439
101D Regiment, 466, 467
141st Regiment, 247, 281, 399–400
144th Regiment, 338
165th Regiment, 440
174th Regiment, 367
201st Tank Regiment, 102
203d Tank Regiment, 100, 212, 247, 281
204th Tank Regiment, 68, 102
207th Regiment, 467, 470
209th Regiment, 440, 441, 442
271st Regiment, 119, 191, 347, 348, 349, 432
272d Regiment, 359
275th Regiment, 399–400
303d Battalion, 222
304th NVA Division, 29, 103, 176, 182, 187
306th Battalion, 222
308th NVA Division, 29, 51, 102, 103, 182, 191
312th NVA Division, 185
320th NVA Division, 201, 212, 216, 218, 228, 252, 281, 287, 304
320B NVA Division, 190
324B NVA Division, 151–152, 153, 156, 166, 168, 171
325C NVA Division, 185, 191, 192
406th Sapper Battalion, 300
803d Regiment, 156
D-1 Regiment, 466

D-2 Regiment, 466
E-2 Regiment, 470
E-6 Regiment, 358, 359, 367

Okinawa, USS, 165, 187
Operations
  Delaware, 149
  Freedom Train, 472
  Lam Son 36/72, 152
  Lam Son 45, 152
  Lam Son 72, 177–179, 187
  Lam Son 719, 1–3, 31, 32, 39
  Linebacker I, 477–479, 481
  Linebacker II, 480–482
  Ngoc Tuyen, 177
  Quang Trung 729, 101–107
  Rolling Thunder, 474, 476, 478
  Song Than, 165–166, 169, 170–172, 187
  Speedy Express, 461

Paris Peace Talks, 174, 476, 477, 492, 493, 494
People's Army of Vietnam. *See* North Vietnamese units
Perry, Richard O., 285, 292, 300
Pham Van Chung, 93, 118
Pham Van Dinh, 78–84, 87, 88–90
Pham Van Phu, 152, 156–157
Phoenix Program, 222
Popular Forces (PF). *See* Territorial forces
Price, Donald L., 118, 120, 139

Quan Doi Nhan Dan. *See* North Vietnamese units

Redlin, Robert K., 171
Regional Forces (RF). *See* Territorial forces
Resolutions, North Vietnamese, 9–11
  COSVN Resolution 55, 18
Rhotenberry, R. M., 255, 258, 289, 292, 294, 301, 303, 309, 312
Richards, Robert, 243, 244, 245
Ripley, John W., 64–77
Robertson, John P., 325

Rocket Ridge, 212, 214, 217–218, 228, 231, 232, 234, 238, 250, 256, 257
Rules of engagement, 2, 3
Republic of Korea (South Korea), 204, 258–264

Saxbe, William, 481
Schorr, David, 224–226
Schott, Richard C., 353–354, 360–361, 363, 369–370, 376
SEAL (U.S. Navy Sea, Air, and Land Teams), 75, 461
Second Regional Assistance Command (SRAC), 209, 327
Second Regional Assistance Group (SRAG), 204, 214, 274, 276, 301, 323, 327
Sensors, 7, 12
Sheridan, Robert, 55, 138, 139
Shumway, Robert, 412–413
Smith, Mark A., 353–354, 356–363, 366–373, 376–379
Smith, Ray L., 41–50
Smock, James E., 67–77
South Vietnamese units
  1st Airborne Brigade, 256, 381–382, 383, 401, 406
  1st Armored Brigade, 71, 104, 113–115, 118, 121, 132, 140, 146, 162
  1st Armored Cavalry Squadron, 357
  1st ARVN Division, 31, 32, 144, 151–164, 175, 178
  1st Ranger Group, 31, 121, 145, 193
  1st Regiment, 156
  1st VNMC Battalion, 92, 96, 104, 105, 122–124, 135, 171, 172, 187, 188, 189, 194
  2d Airborne Brigade, 179–181, 183–187, 190, 212–213, 217, 231, 272
  2d ARVN Division, 31, 168, 179
  2d Ranger Group, 292
  2d Regiment, 32, 34, 62, 79, 89, 102, 104, 111, 116–117, 146

  3d Airborne Brigade, 213, 214
  3d Armored Brigade, 336
  3d Armored Cavalry Regiment, 297
  3d ARVN Division, 31–148, 159–163
  3d Ranger Group, 336, 344, 383, 388, 419, 453
  3d Regiment, 153
  3d VNMC Battalion, 64, 71, 102, 166, 194, 195
  4th Ranger Group, 108, 113, 116, 121, 145, 333
  4th VNMC Battalion, 40, 48, 50, 122, 123–124, 170, 187
  5th ARVN Division, 336, 342, 343, 348, 349, 352, 356, 362, 373, 382, 386, 393, 396, 398–408, 426, 428, 430, 434, 446–455
  5th Ranger Group, 102, 116, 121, 333, 344, 453
  5th VNMC Battalion, 93, 138, 140, 144, 172, 190, 192
  6th Airborne Battalion, 394–396
  6th Ranger Group, 231, 267, 269, 292, 333, 344, 453
  6th Regiment, 154
  6th VNMC Battalion, 93, 95, 170, 172, 194, 196
  7th Airborne Battalion, 181, 182
  7th ARVN Division, 204, 463, 468, 470
  7th Regiment, 347, 353, 388–389, 433, 447
  7th VNMC Battalion, 117, 194, 195
  8th Regiment, 384
  8th VNMC Battalion, 104, 105, 122–124, 135, 169, 192, 193
  9th Airborne Battalion, 249
  9th Armored Cavalry Regiment, 444
  9th ARVN Division, 32, 444, 463, 469, 470
  9th Regiment, 353, 354–356, 358–359, 369, 372, 373
  9th VNMC Battalion, 139, 166, 192
  11th Airborne Battalion, 181, 154
  14th Armored Cavalry Regiment, 235, 313

15th Regiment, 444, 445
17th Armored Cavalry Regiment, 113, 116, 123, 133, 179
18th Armored Cavalry Regiment, 111, 113, 117–118, 333
18th ARVN Division, 336, 342, 388, 447, 453
20th Tank Regiment, 66, 67–69, 95, 108, 109, 116, 117, 124
21st ARVN Division, 338, 381, 436–444, 447, 455, 463, 467
22d ARVN Division, 212, 214, 217, 219, 232–251, 253, 256, 265, 267, 300
23d ARVN Division, 212, 231, 253, 264, 298, 301
23d Ranger Battalion, 213, 257
25th ARVN Division, 336, 342, 345, 347, 349, 442, 447
40th Regiment, 224–225, 320–321
41st Regiment, 233, 320
42d Regiment, 218, 234, 236, 239, 247, 256
44th Regiment, 256, 261, 268, 269, 272, 278–279, 282–283, 285, 288, 290–291, 293–299, 301–319
45th Regiment, 268, 269, 272, 278, 288, 291, 293–319
47th Regiment, 217, 218, 233, 247, 248–249
48th Regiment, 348, 447
51st Regiment, 31
52d Regiment, 348
53d Regiment, 231, 255, 257, 278, 283, 285, 289, 291, 292–319
54th Regiment, 152
56th Regiment, 34–35, 36, 62, 78–90, 99, 146
57th Regiment, 34–35, 52, 55, 62, 72, 101, 109, 116, 118, 121, 146, 147, 162
71st Ranger Battalion, 271
72d Ranger Battalion, 201
81st Ranger Battalion, 398, 420, 434, 453–454
92d Ranger Battalion, 400
95th Ranger Battalion, 201

147th VNMC Brigade, 34, 50, 62, 101, 104, 115, 117, 121, 127, 132, 140, 145, 169, 190, 193
258th VNMC Brigade, 34, 64, 93, 95, 97, 104, 171, 191, 192
369th VNMC Brigade, 93, 117–118, 132, 134, 137, 138, 140, 165, 166, 193
Airborne Division, 2, 144, 168–169, 175, 177, 179, 187, 189, 231, 394, 437
Task Force 1-5, 360–361
Task Force 52, 348, 382
Soviet Union, 474, 477, 478, 483, 493
supplies to North Vietnam, 23–24
Special Forces, 201–203
Stewart, David, 244, 245
Stewart, Richard R., 9
Stovall, Donald, 320–323
Studies and Observations Group (SOG), 176–177, 201
Surface-to-air missile (SAM), 12, 75, 188, 431–432
in IV Corps, 468
over North Vietnam, 474, 481

Tallman, Richard, 425, 452–453
Tan My Naval Base, 169, 177
Target Acquisition Element, 160
Tarpley, Thomas M., 466–471
Task Force Alpha, 204
Territorial forces, 31, 32, 34, 108, 117, 119, 166, 177, 213, 223, 237, 278–279, 287, 300, 307, 373, 404
performance, 373, 404, 454, 471, 488, 489
Tet Offensive, 17, 210, 222, 380, 485, 486
Third Regional Assistance Command (TRAC), 333, 340, 342–344, 360, 368, 374, 386, 398, 404, 408, 421, 424, 431, 442, 452
Thompson, Lee, 498
Thompson, Sir Robert, 231, 478, 493
Thu Duc Officer Candidate School, 144
Todd, Dolph, 243, 245

Ton That Man, 89
To Ton Te, 96
TOW missile, 162–163, 166–167,
 183, 188, 282–283, 287–289,
 306, 314
Tran Ai Quoc, 438
Tran Hien Duc, 224–226
Tran Huu Minh, 233
Tran Quoc Lich, 179–180, 181, 455
Tran Tinh, 115–116, 132
Tran Van Nhut, 454
Tran Van Quang, 151
Tran Van Tra, 378, 491
Tran Xuan Quang, 40
Tripoli, USS, 187
Truby, John, 254–255, 278–279, 282,
 284–286, 287, 289
Truong Chinh, 18
Turley, Gerald
 with Advisory Team 155, 55, 60–62,
 63–64, 70, 72–73, 76–77
 as FRAC operations officer, 188,
 196

Ulmer, Walter
 into An Loc, 426–427
 background, 424–425, 428
 battle at An Loc, 446, 452–453
 comparison to Col. Miller, 430
 evaluation of Gen. Hung, 455
 relations with Gen. Hung, 430–431
U.S. units
 1st Aviation Brigade, 336
 1st Brigade, 5th Infantry Division,
 66
 1st Cavalry Division, 149, 204, 222,
 261–262, 336, 371, 384
 1st Infantry Division, 342
 4th Cavalry Regiment, 165, 188
 4th Infantry Division, 204
 8th Special Operations Squadron,
 363–364
 9th Infantry Division, 255, 461
 9th Marine Amphibious Brigade,
 169, 187
 12th Aviation Group, 425
 17th Aviation Group, 326

 17th Cavalry Regiment, 225, 226,
 336
 25th Infantry Division, 204, 336,
 343
 79th Aerial Rocket Artillery, 3d
 Brigade, 1st Cavalry Division,
 390–391
 82d Airborne Division, 288
 101st Airborne Division, 34, 204,
 424
 173d Airborne Brigade, 204
 199th Brigade, 336
 Advisory Team 155, 34, 54, 62, 72,
 76, 77
 American Division, 173

Vandergrift Combat Base, 40
Vann, John Paul
 background, 204–207
 battle at Kontum, 266–286,
 288–319
 building Kontum defense, 252–264
 at Dak To and Tan Canh, 232–251
 death of, 324–327
 fighting on the coast, 222–227,
 229–231
 intelligence predictions, 210–219
 at Landing Zone Crystal, 322–323
 South Korean performance, 260–264
Vannie, William H. J., 268
Van Tien Dung, 24, 490
Viet Cong, 154, 156, 164, 223, 259,
 485, 491
Vietnamization, 7, 39, 173, 387,
 487–488, 489, 493, 496
 North Vietnamese attitude toward,
 25, 211, 442, 491
Vinh Phoy, 81
Vo Nguyen Giap
 conventional warfare theory, 18–25
 at Dien Bien Phu, 18, 203
 evaluation of strategy, 490–491
Vu Van Giai, 34–36, 41, 54, 55,
 58–60, 62, 66, 67, 71–72, 74, 82,
 88, 89, 97–98, 101, 102
 command and control problems,
 105–107

counteroffensive, 103–104
evacuation of Quang Tri City,
128–132
evaluation of performance, 146–147
losing control of troops, 111–117,
120–121, 125–126
punishment of, 146

Waddell, USS, 68
Wagner, Louis C., 72, 74–75, 113–115,
132–134, 146
Wallingford, Kenneth, 353, 363, 369,
376, 378–379
Wanat, George, 353, 363, 379
Ward, Walter, 243, 244

Warmath, William C., 244–245
Wear, George, 209–211, 214, 215,
232, 255
Wells, Marshall N., 93
Westmoreland, William C., 8, 11–12,
144, 173, 259
operations in A Shau Valley, 150
Weyand, Frederick C., 173–174
Whitehead, John, 371
Windy Hill, 393, 396, 399, 401, 421
Wischmeyer, William, 94, 95, 96
Wise, Jon, 234, 235
Worth, James, 57–58

Yonan, Ken, 239, 242